REF. SER.   JUN 8 '92   *GW*
12-91

A11713 165302

D1009861

JUN 8 '92

Kenneth Macksey
and William Woodhouse

The Penguin Encyclopedia of

Modern Warfare

1850 to the Present Day

VIKING

VIKING

Published by the Penguin Group
27 Wrights Lane, London W8 5TZ, England
Viking Penguin Inc., a division of Penguin Books USA Inc.,
375 Hudson Street, New York, New York 10014, USA
Penguin Books Australia Ltd, Ringwood, Victoria, Australia
Penguin Books Canada Ltd, 10 Alcorn Avenue, Toronto, Ontario, Canada M4V 3B2
Penguin Books (NZ) Ltd, 182–190 Wairau Road, Auckland 10, New Zealand

Penguin Books Ltd, Registered Offices: Harmondsworth, Middlesex, England

First published 1991
10 9 8 7 6 5 4 3 2 1

Copyright © Kenneth Macksey and William Woodhouse, 1991

The authors' moral rights have been asserted

All rights reserved. Without limiting the rights under copyright reserved above,
no part of this publication may be reproduced, stored in or introduced into a
retrieval system, or transmitted, in any form or by any means (electronic,
mechanical, photocopying, recording or otherwise), without the prior written
permission of both the copyright owner and the above publisher of this book

Printed in England by Clays Ltd, St Ives plc
Typeset in 8/10 pt Lasercomp Photina

Library of Congress Catalog Card Number: 90-72128

A CIP catalogue record for this book is available from the British Library

ISBN 0–670–82698–7

Contents

List of Maps and Figures

Acknowledgements for Figures and Maps

Michael Haine
L. J. Gwyer
Gordon E. MacKay MSAI

Introduction

Since the mid nineteenth century, the art and practices of war, spurred on by the revolution in technology, have changed fundamentally at increasing speed. The pace of change has made it extremely difficult to stay abreast of events, let alone relate what has happened and maintain perspective in the present with any hope of foreseeing the future. This Encyclopedia aims to satisfy the demands of those who require a compact guide or ready reference to the principal personalities, campaigns and battles as well as developments in strategy, tactics, intelligence handling, logistics and technology which have occurred since 1850. It helps also to explain the foremost techniques, terminology and jargon in the modern military dictionary and point the way to further study in greater depth of subjects which profoundly affect human behaviour and experience.

Each main subject entry is displayed in **bold type** and explained at a length merited by its significance. Most are augmented by cross-references (also printed in bold type) to related main subject entries, in addition to subsidiary matters in the Index. Take, for example, **Air warfare**. This entry describes the evolution of air warfare and also draws the reader's attention to the subject entries dealing with: **World War I**; **Air forces, Organizations of**; **Aircraft**; **World War II**; **General Douhet**; **Chemical warfare**; **Airborne forces**; **Aircraft-carriers**; the **Torpedo**; **Anti-aircraft weapons**; **Radar**; **Radio**; **Navigation**; **Rockets and guided missiles**; the **Helicopter**; the **Falklands** War; and the **Vietnam War**. Should the reader then wish, for example, to learn more about bombers, he or she can turn to **Bomber aircraft**, where references to the following subject entries will also be found: **Italo-Turkish War**

of 1911, **World War I**, **Fighter aircraft**, **Spanish Civil War**, **Strategic bombing**, **Navigation**, **Atom bomb**, **Rockets and guided missiles**, **Vietnam War** and **Smart munitions** – besides mentions of bomber types listed in the Index. Thus one entry leads to another, guiding the reader towards further knowledge as desired.

Our selection of entries includes far more than a recitation of wars, campaigns, battles and personalities. We place emphasis on the importance of military organizations, logistics, law, military philosophers, training, weapons and technology because, since the 1850s, they have called the strategic and tactical tune. Indeed, we draw special attention to the entry **Technology, Effects of**, which highlights entries on subjects such as chemical weapons (**Chemical warfare**), **Electromagnetic effect**, **Electronics**, **Explosives** and military **Medical services**. It is essential to grasp the meaning of these controlling military techniques to begin to understand the evolution, implications and substance of modern war.

We include maps and diagrams for amplification and clarification. They are listed on pages vii and viii and appear where they are most effective, although, obviously, they may be useful elsewhere in relation to associated matters. On page 356 we provide a simplified Chronology setting out the principal wars and showing their relation to new technology as it came into use; thus assisting in connecting, at a glance, the main events of the period.

The Bibliography on page 361 is restricted to those key encyclopedias, bibliographies and reference works judged most helpful for further study. To provide an exhaustive bibliography of the innumerable works on war would be self-defeating of clarity in a compact work of this kind. The entry entitled **Bibliography of war** also may be of interest and assistance to researchers.

The sum total of knowledge acquired is in ratio to the application and quality of reading and thought. In military parlance, encyclopedias simply offer a firm base for reconnaissance and attack upon a selected objective of knowledge and indicate lines of subsequent exploitation to where further information can be found. It is hoped that the reader will benefit from wider research by the use of this encyclopedia's cross-reference system, so that, as he or she is directed from one subject to another, attention will be stimulated by natural curiosity and then drawn to focus on subjects which otherwise might not have seemed helpful or interesting. In effect, we are inviting the reader and student to become involved in a voyage of discovery, well knowing from our own experiences how rewarding that journey can be.

Kenneth Macksey
William Woodhouse

A

Abrams, General Creighton, W. (1914–74). A graduate in 1936 of the US Military Academy, Abrams won distinction as an armoured-battalion commander in 4th Armored Division during the **West Europe Campaign** 1944 and the Battle of **Germany**. Rising to Corps Commander in the 1960s he then became Commander of the US Military Assistance Command in Vietnam (**Vietnam War**) in July 1968, with the difficult task of keeping the enemy at bay while implementing his government's reduction of US forces. In 1972 he became Chief of Staff of the Army and planned the withdrawal from Vietnam as well as the conversion of the conscript US Army into an all-volunteer force.

Abyssinia. See **Ethiopia**.

Aces, Air. A system devised by the French in 1915 to idolize pilots who had shot down five or more aircraft. Taken up by the Germans (who set 10 victories as a mark) as a propaganda means of deflecting public attention from the baser aspects of a stalemated **World War I**, the system survives to the present with five victories as the standard. To begin with the British tended to reject the system, realizing how difficult it was fairly to confirm claims. Yet while the Germans insisted upon a wreck as evidence, both the French and the British were more lax and even allowed *shared* to count as *whole* victories. Top scorers in this war were Von **Richthofen** (German) 80, **Fonck** (French) 75, Mannock (British) 73 and **Bishop** (Canadian) 72.

In **World War II** some scores were, in the opinion of critics, dubiously high. The top ace was Germany's Erich Hartmann with 352 victories, mostly against the Russians. Nothing like this score has been claimed since. Charges of sensationalism have been made in some cases. Nevertheless, prolonged combat tours with high scores were a characteristic of World War II aces who made up only 1 per cent of fighter pilots but accounted for between 35 and 55 per cent of claims. In **Vietnam** American victories increased significantly as a result of so-called Top Gun courses.

Admiralty. A British government department which since the early 18th century through royal prerogative controlled and administered the Royal Navy. Governed by the Admiralty Board (usually consisting of 10 sea and civil members). In 1869 the First Sea Lord was granted overriding power at a time when the existence of an ever-spreading **Telegraph** network was centralizing control. The introduction of the **Telephone** and, above all, **Radio** gave the First Sea Lord and his staff up-to-the-minute intelligence to enable them to direct operations world-wide in some detail.

The strengths and weaknesses of this system were quite plain to see. The advantages of being able to intercept enemy forces or raiders in the exercise of **blockade** often were decisive. But inadequate handling of crucial information and signals during the Battle of **Jutland** contributed to the escape of the German High Seas Fleet. And during **World War II** radio signals to and from convoys disclosed positions to the Germans, who also benefited by deciphering vital messages.

Improving signal **communications** and the arrival of **air forces** helped the Admiralty but also posed a threat. The sheer volume of work from the complex technology of the 20th century tended to overload at a time when air-power enthusiasts sought a dominant role in sea warfare. While the Japanese and Americans gave high priority to **aircraft-carriers** European navies, including the British, tended to under-rate the need for joint control of resources and operations. The creation by the British in 1940 of a Combined Operations directorate tasked for joint service **amphibious warfare** brought closer the day when all the major powers would merge their service departments within single vast organizations. In 1964 the British Admiralty disappeared within a Ministry of Defence.

Afghanistan, Battles of. Throughout its history the tribes of this mountainous state have been in a state of turmoil which often enough has over-spilled on to its neighbours. British involve-ment was inevitable once they penetrated NW India and led to the so-called *First Afghan War* in 1839 in which a British army of 4,500 soldiers, after a series of victories, had occupied Kabul and was made to capitulate in 1842. Promised safe conduct to withdraw to India it was massacred. Thereupon a raid of reprisal was launched, Kabul recaptured and largely de-stroyed but the country then evacuated, on the sensible reasoning that it was too difficult to hold down.

Chronic British fear of Russian involvement in Afghan's tumultuous internal affairs led in 1878 to another British invasion to start the *Second Afghan War*. Defeated in frontier battles by General Sir Frederick Roberts, the Afghans were dismayed to be refused Russian assistance and forced to accept a supervisory British mis-sion in Kabul. The murder of this mission's mem-bers in 1879, however, simply caused another invasion by Roberts, who once more defeated a more numerous but less well organized oppo-nent after a 'Holy War' had been called for. In June 1880 heavy fighting took place for the control of Kandahar, in which the British were initially rebuffed at Maiwand when they ran out of artillery ammunition. At last, however, under Roberts, they won a decisive battle at Baba Wali. They then once more withdrew, this time leaving the nation in charge of a pro-British government.

The *Third Afghan War* was the result of politi-cal opportunism by the Afghans at the termina-tion of **World War I** when, by observing strict neutrality, they had refrained from embarrass-ing the British. Their request to the British in 1919 to be recognized at the Paris peace confer-ence as an 'independent' nation, followed by instant rejection, at once gave rise to frontier fighting in which the British not only used armoured cars (see **Armoured fighting vehicles**) but also sent bombers against Kabul and other targets to 'pacify' the enemy. The whole affair was brought to an end within six months when the British did recognize Afghan independence. But in the years to come the frontier remained a hotbed of discontent amidst tribal warfare.

Despite modernization and western and Com-munist influence the spirit of the Afghans was much the same as of old when the Russians, in 1979, attempted what the British had failed to do in the past. The only difference lay in the scale and nature of the Russian invasion when, in an attempt to prop up a weak pro-Russian government, it advanced to all the familiar com-munication centres. This time over 100,000 mechanized troops with tanks, jet aircraft and **helicopters** sought to subjugate the people, only to stir up an internal hornets' nest as well as aggravating world-wide feeling. Comparisons with what happened to the Americans in Viet-nam (**Vietnam War**) nevertheless are mainly symbolic. So long as the Russians managed to control the country's communications and were able to make life extremely unpleasant for the hard core of tribesmen who endured in the mountains and among the less accessible fertile valleys, they had their way at bearable cost in a war which became increasingly unpopular at home. Until weapons from friendly nations, including the USA and Britain, began to make their way via numerous frontier byways into the hands of the guerrillas (by no means a unified force) the tribesmen were at a disadvan-tage, chiefly because low-flying jet aircraft and armed **helicopters** could strike much as they pleased. But when hand-held surface-to-air missiles (SAM) reached the guerrillas the tide turned because the Russians and the dis-heartened Afghan army were no longer able to harass their victims from out of range. There-upon the guerrillas were able to move with greater safety, bring in supplies with some ease and multiply their ambushes to the extent that sometimes, for months on end, enemy garrisons were besieged. In these circumstances against a background of world-wide indignation, and with the need to recast her internal affairs, the Russians had little option but to copy an old British precedent and depart in 1989 with as good a grace as possible, leaving the Afghans to their traditional devices, since when strife has continued between factions.

Airborne forces. For all the efforts of prophets and propagandists to conjure up the vision of balloon-borne armies invading England in the 1790s, and despite the invention of the parachute in 1797, it was not until powered **aircraft** were available that the prospect could be seriously contemplated. Indeed, during **World War I**, only a handful of landings by aircraft or by parachutist agents were made behind enemy lines. But when Colonel (later General) William **Mitchell** suggested the delivery of 1st US Infantry Division by British heavy bombers behind the German lines in 1919, airborne attack looked a possibility.

Most advanced nations experimented with parachutists and **gliders**, the Italians in 1927 dropping a 'stick' of nine men with their equipment. It was the Russians who took the lead with massed drops of men and a light tank, leading to the formation of an airborne division in 1934 and the delivery of 18 men from a glider. The British had taken the operational lead with air-landed troops in the policing of Empire during the 1920s; but the Germans and, to a lesser extent, the Japanese became leaders in airborne landings during **World War II**. German transports, assisted by a few Italian machines, lifted 13,523 Fascist troops from Morocco to Spain in 1936 to help launch the **Spanish Civil War**, and in 1938 spearheaded their bloodless invasion of Austria by seizing Vienna airport with a parachute drop followed by air-landed artillery.

Henceforward nearly all German invasions included an airborne operation, though in the 1939 **Polish campaign** it was not launched. The success of the invasions of **Denmark** and **Norway** was very much assured by the seizure of strategic objectives by parachutists ahead of the main air- and sea-borne echelons; while the collapse of **Holland** in four days in May 1940 could be largely attributed to the large-scale airborne irruption at the same time as gliderborne troops were seizing vital fortresses to open the way into Belgium and **France**.

Needless to say the invasions of **Yugoslavia** and **Greece** also included airborne *coups de main*, though these mainly successful operations paled in significance by comparison with the subsequent, massed, almost entirely airborne invasion of **Crete** in May 1941. Yet so costly was this successful venture that **Hitler** drew the conclusion that airborne troops had had their day because the element of surprise was lost. In the years to come German airborne troops would be frittered away in minor raids and in conventional ground operations.

Meanwhile the British and Americans began raising substantial airborne forces in 1940, the former at first envisaging greater prospects for glider-borne troops than for parachutists. Between them they raised several divisions and employed them with varying fortunes (mainly successful) in conjunction with small amphibious raids, but chiefly as spearheads of the major invasions of **North Africa, Sicily, France, Holland** and **Germany**. Most famous of all, perhaps, was the three-division descent upon **Arnhem** in 1944 with its tragic anti-climax. But more significant were the difficulties of mounting airborne operations quickly enough to benefit from fleeting opportunities. Repeatedly in the closing, fast-moving, phases of the European war, operations had to be cancelled because ground troops had seized the airborne's intended objectives.

The Russians did not suffer from these difficulties since, despite their early lead, they failed to make mass penetrations of enemy rear areas, choosing instead to air-land troops to reinforce threatened sectors of the front and to insert parties and supplies in support of partisan forces in the enemy rear – a technique also employed extensively in all theatres of operations, including the Far East where, in 1942, the Japanese (**Japanese wars of expansion**) used parachutists during their expansion into SE Asia.

Since World War II major parachute operations have been few and far between – due partly to lack of opportunity, partly to their vulnerability and partly to the arrival of the **helicopter**. A few were used during the **Malayan War of Independence**, the **Korean War**, the **Indo-China War of Independence**, the 1956 **Suez Canal Battles**, the **Arab–Israeli Wars** and several other outbreaks of violence world-wide. But chiefly these highly trained and expensive-to-maintain forces tend to enter battle by land or from the sea. So their numbers continue to dwindle as helicopter forces flourish.

Aircraft. No sooner had François de Rozier made

a free flight in his hot-air balloon in 1783 than wise men, such as Benjamin Franklin, were prophesying **air warfare**. In 1794 a first step was made when a tethered balloon was used for reconnaissance at the Battle of Fleurus. But progress was held back because Napoleon was not interested in so immobile an instrument, and an attempt by the Austrians in 1849 to hit Venice with 30lb bombs released by a time fuse from paper balloons drifting with the wind was unsuccessful. Balloons in the **American Civil War** also found limited employment, but in the **Franco-Prussian War** made such an impact when flying dispatches, encoded messages and prominent citizens out of besieged **Paris** that the Germans began improvising anti-balloon guns – the forerunners of **anti-aircraft** weapons. Not until Gottlieb Daimler produced the first practical internal-combustion engine in 1883 was powered steerable flight made possible. And for a few years after the Wright brothers flew a heavier-than-air machine in 1903 it was steerable lighter-than-air craft which attracted most attention.

Lighter-than-air craft which could steer from one place to another began to appear in the 1880s as airships, powered first by electric motors but almost at once by Daimler engines. They were glorified non-rigid balloons until Count Ferdinand Zeppelin produced the rigid airship in 1900 and in due course sold one to the German Army in 1908 and to their Navy in 1912. Primarily these large 400ft aircraft with speeds of about 40mph and a ceiling of 10,000ft were intended for deep strategic reconnaissance over land or sea with bomb-dropping a desirable option. In these roles they were used extensively at the beginning of **World War I** until countermeasures began to take a toll. Several were damaged or shot down when they flew low to identify or bomb targets in the battle zones. One was destroyed by a bomb dropped on its hangar; in June 1915 another was destroyed by a bomb while airborne. That year the Germans began deliberate bombing of Paris and London with the intention of persuading politicians to sue for peace. They failed in that object, causing only minor damage, but by their depredations produced such panic among the population that extensive anti-aircraft resources had to be diverted from the battle fronts to the **home fronts**. Within two years the Zeppelin threat had been defeated by heavier-than-air craft armed with machine-guns firing incendiary **ammunition**.

Thereafter airships, though extensively used in the sea war for reconnaissance and **convoy** escorting, and occasional supply missions where opposition was unlikely, fell into disuse. Tethered balloons, however, were extensively employed for observation and artillery direction at the front and as deterrents against low-flying attacks on cities and important targets. The latter method was made much use of during **World War II** (not only over cities but also from ships) to guard against dive-bombers, a system which is being considered for revival in the 1990s by the use of very easily inflated balloons of exotic shape.

Heavier-than-air craft were rapidly developed for military purposes during **World War I**. Prior to its outbreak the feasibility of bomb-dropping against naval and land targets, the firing of **rifles** and **machine-guns** from them, operating from water and ships' decks, aerial **photography** and the reception and transmission of radio signals had all been demonstrated in trials.

Evidence of the value of aircraft for reconnaissance was obtained during the **Italo-Turkish War** of 1911–12 in Tripolitania, and also the inaccuracy of bombing, along with their vulnerability to small-arms fire below 3,000ft. It was with flimsy 70mph aircraft similar to those used in this campaign that **World War I** started. Machines like these, which proved capable of revealing more to the enemy than the generals liked, therefore led to a demand for **fighter aircraft** to clear the sky, in what was the first attempt to win air superiority. The specialized machines for this role that began to appear in 1915 had a machine-gun fixed to fire through the arc of the propeller. With speeds of about 100mph and a ceiling not much above 10,000ft they dominated slower, less manoeuvrable opponents, including the other specialized types of which **bombers** were the most important. As the war proceeded, bombers grew in size until, at the end, there were giants with four or even five engines and a bomb load of 6,000lb. Mostly they were single- or twin-engined with up to 2,000lb loads and were defended by two or three machine-guns against fighters by day – which were usually the only conditions in which they might find and hit their targets, particularly if the weather was bad or the range long, as in strategic missions against defended capital cities.

Specialized types were also essential in naval

warfare for the hunting of **submarines** and for **convoy** escort, as well as bombing and fleet reconnaissance. Flying boats and seaplanes were in great demand; one of the latter, lowered from a ship, was first to spot the German High Seas Fleet at **Jutland**, though its radio report did not reach Admiral **Beatty**. But the most important development by the British was the technique of deck landing and take-off which, in 1917, led to their conversion of a fast cruiser to the **aircraft-carrier** HMS *Furious*.

Alongside the specialized types flew general-purpose machines. For example, some of the earliest types were used to drop supplies to the besieged British garrison at Kut-al-Amara in Mesopotamia in 1916. And it was commonplace for fighters to carry small bombs for attacks upon troops, artillery emplacements, transport and airfields. Indeed the single-engine, two-seater British Bristol fighter was very much a multi-role combat aircraft, which saw many years of active service into the 1930s. Fighters dominated, although their margin of performance over bombers was usually a mere 20mph, while rarely could they satisfactorily claim an advantage in ceiling. By 1917 bombers could reach about 20,000ft where some German crews, at least, had the advantage of oxygen supply. Fighter pilots, who were usually without oxygen, suffered from anoxia with the result that combat above 12,000ft was infrequent.

Designers tended to lavish more care on the performance of machines than on the men who flew in them. True, they almost abandoned the monoplane owing to structural problems, concentrating instead on raising the performance of the biplane, and countering the drag created by struts and wires by installing more powerful engines. Yet the German Fokker DVII fighter of 1917 with a 185hp engine was slower than the 1916 French Spad, which went at 120mph.

At the same time, the fitting of **armour** or giving parachutes to pilots was resisted in the interests of performance until quite near the end of the war. Only the Germans issued parachutes on any scale. For about ten years after the war improvements languished, major indications of what was feasible being demonstrated by speed, height and endurance record-breakers who called upon new technology for their feats. The results of research and development in the 1920s on metallurgy – all **aluminium** or dur-alumin air frames, and engines up to 1,000hp

with improved power-to-weight ratios – enabled extremely dramatic changes to be made in the 1930s when rearmament commenced. Most vital of all was the adoption of the high-speed monoplane that existing biplane fighters were too slow to intercept. Initially stunned politicians came to the conclusion that the best deterrent (see **Deterrence**) to an enemy's bomber force was possession of a better bomber force oneself, until events in the **Spanish Civil War** and the first generation of even faster monoplane fighters suggested otherwise. For the German Messerschmitt Me109 and the British Supermarine Spitfire at more than 350mph were more than 70mph swifter than the fastest twin- or tri-motor bomber. Moreover, with cannons or batteries of machine-guns and ceilings up to 30,000ft where, with pilots supplied with oxygen, they were well above the best bomber, they had tactical freedom, even though most combat took place below 20,000ft.

Events in 1940 during the Battle of **France** and the Battle of **Britain** showed that the fighter still dominated, although without **radar** and **radio** it would have been a different matter. As it was, the ability of controllers to read the battle on displays and direct formations into the best tactical position, where the pilots could talk to each other in combat, was fundamental. For the survival of the British fighter force meant that the German bombers could not prevail in daytime and at night could not with certainty find and destroy vital targets. For the problems of **navigation** were almost as unsolved as they had been in 1918, as the British in due course realized when analysis showed their night-bomber offensive was missing its targets.

In an attempt to win the war by strategic bombing the British and Americans built great fleets of four-engine bombers of which the former's Lancaster could carry 18,000lb and the latter's Flying Fortress 8,000lb. Used, respectively, by night and day they could never achieve pin-point accuracy, even in good weather and without much opposition and with the aid of radio and radar devices. It has been argued that medium and fighter bombers might have made a greater contribution to the land battle and that dive-bombers, torpedo-bombers, fighters and flying boats were so decisive in sea warfare as to warrant priority of supply. Be that as it may, aircraft performance reached new standards of effectiveness between 1939 and

1945. The war culminated in the operational use of jet-powered fighters and fighter bombers, with speeds up to 550mph, with Boeing B29 bombers capable of lifting 20,000lb of bombs with a maximum range of up to 3,250 miles, or of dropping an **atom bomb** with the equivalent of 20,000 tonnes of TNT; and with vast fleets of transport aircraft lifting up to four tonnes of stores each, not only to solve many problems of **logistics** but also to carry large **airborne forces** into battle.

It was the invention of the jet engine which most revolutionized aircraft after 1944. It compelled a totally new wing-design philosophy to overcome compressibility as speeds reached the speed of sound. Among many other things, it put fresh demands upon metallurgists and designers to cope with the effects of speeds which increased to Mach 3 (three times the speed of sound). At the same time even greater assistance had to be given to air crew to deal with conditions beyond the body's capabilities. Since civil and military aircraft frequently flew above 10,000ft and often above 30,000ft pressurized cabins were mandatory. Only the latest **radio** and **radar** systems enabled air crew to fix their positions and co-ordinate their actions, especially in combat situations. As combat demands became more exacting significant automation linked to powered controls and **computers** had to be fitted. Since jet engines were uneconomical, particularly at lower altitudes, flight refuelling, which had been pioneered in the 1930s, became essential to extend range and reach. Military-**transport aircraft** which sometimes, but not always, were based upon civil types branched out into numerous classes for particular tasks. From the small short take-off landing (STOL) types required for restricted landing strips, through the larger, rugged assault cargo/troop transports, such as the American C130, to the enormous Lockheed Galaxy with its ability to lift a 60-tonne tank in a payload of nearly 100 tonnes, the carrying capacity of a fleet of such machines implies a significant strategic power to whoever possesses enough of them.

Likewise the advantages of vertical short take-off and landing (VSTOL) aircraft such as the **helicopter** and the British jet Harrier fighter have introduced new dimensions to both military and civil aviation. The latter demonstrated its combat capability during the **Falklands** War when it operated for an extended period from aircraft-carriers specially adapted with a ramp to assist take-off, and sometimes operated from the decks of cargo ships.

Aircraft-carrier. In 1910 the American Eugene Ely took off by plane from the deck of a US cruiser. Two months later he also made a landing. Also in 1911 the first take-offs and landings from water took place and in 1912 catapult launchings from ships. During **World War I** the British used seaplane carriers which lowered these **aircraft** into the water, but in 1917 built a deck, suitable for take-off only, on to the cruiser HMS *Furious*, which carried three seaplanes and five scouts in its hangar. In 1918 the first 'true' carrier, HMS *Argus*, with a full, unobstructed flight deck was ready but the war ended before she could be used in action.

After the war the British, Americans and Japanese experimented extensively with carriers, with particular attention paid to flight-deck arrester gear and, led by the British, the introduction of a bridge, the so-called 'island' to one side of the deck. The problem of smoke obscuration was also tackled along with the type of aircraft most desirable – fighters, dive-bombers and torpedo-bombers were all developed with varying degrees of enthusiasm (or otherwise) by each of the committed navies. In 1922 the Washington Naval Treaty which limited each nation's number of battleships, in order to prevent a building race, left a loophole permitting the construction of carriers. As a result the main signatories, with the exception of Italy, at once converted a number of uncompleted **battleship** and **battle-cruiser** hulls into large carriers of up to about 27,000 tonnes, capable of taking, in the American case, up to 72 aircraft, the Japanese 60 and the British 48. These were all, of necessity, fast ships in order to handle their aircraft, the stalling speeds of which gradually increased. Lifts were developed to the hangars below. Armament was chiefly **anti-aircraft** since it was envisaged that carriers would be prime targets for enemy air attacks. In Britain's later carriers an armoured flight deck was fitted.

Japan was first to use carriers, against the Chinese during the 1932 'incident' at Shanghai (see **Chinese–Japanese Wars**). Shore targets were bombed and aerial combat took place. At the start of **World War II** in 1937, when Japan fought an undeclared war against China, carriers were frequently employed, sometimes three at a time, in order, on occasion, to put as many as 264 aircraft into the air.

At the beginning of the war in Europe in 1939, British carriers initially were used for convoy escort and suffered their first loss to a German submarine. Subsequently they were heavily involved in the Battle of **Norway**, the Battles of the **Mediterranean Sea** (including the significant sinking by torpedo-bombers of Italian battleships at Taranto and in support of convoys to break the siege of **Malta**) and the sinking of the battleship **Bismarck**. These operations showed that the aircraft-carrier was in process of assuming the battleship's role as a fleet capital ship, as was made plain when the Japanese carrier aircraft executed their devastating blow against **Pearl Harbor** at the commencement of a series of campaigns in the Pacific and Indian Oceans which were dominated by the rival carrier squadrons.

A turning-point of the war occurred at the Battle of the **Coral Sea** and **Midway** in 1942 when carrier fought carrier through their aircraft, without coming in sight of each other, battles which cost Japan six of her original ten carriers and America four of her original eight. But whereas the Japanese lost the élite of their pre-war crews and, in the months to come, would fall behind in aircraft performance, the Americans not only went from strength to strength in numbers but also in prowess and technical capability until, in the Battles of the **Philippines** and at **Leyte Gulf**, they largely destroyed the Japanese Navy.

Meanwhile, especially to impose air power against submarines in the Battle of the **Atlantic**; but also for universal employment, light carriers had been built, some based on merchant-ship hulls, some with catapults to launch fighters against bombers in mid-Atlantic. As convoy escorts these smaller vessels were economically effective and, as was shown in the Pacific, useful in the midst even of fleet actions.

Post-1945, despite the nuclear threat, carriers were developed apace as battleships were being scrapped. British inventions such as the armoured flight deck (which had saved many a carrier), the steam-powered catapult, the angled flight deck and the mirror-landing device all contributed to greater survivability and efficiency and were incorporated in carriers which attended most of the major wars of the times. Carriers were intensively involved, for example, off Korea

(Korean Wars), Suez in 1956, **Vietnam**, and in the **Falklands** War. They tend to turn up at almost any hot spot where their aircraft can intervene or pose a threat, and their potential has been considerably increased by the arrival of British Harrier VSTOL aircraft which can operate off specially built light carriers or from the decks of merchant ships and, at a pinch, small warships.

Air forces, Organizations of. At the beginning air forces, whether naval or army, tended to copy army organizations, but with new nomenclature soon appearing. Thus the basic squadron or company was subdivided into flights; and in due course squadrons became parts of groups, battalions or wings, which were placed within brigades or groups commanded by divisions, corps, armies or, later on, air forces. Naturally, as specialist **aircraft** evolved for specific tasks, units and formations assumed titles befitting their role. By November 1914 the French had formed a Bomber Group and the Germans a so-called corps to bomb London. Fighter, reconnaissance, artillery observation, balloon, flying-boat and other units, some specializing in night operations, soon followed, along with the **communications, logistics** and administrative organizations required. In several air forces, too, **anti-aircraft** units were included.

The development of **air warfare** and, especially, strategic bombing produced demands, notably in Britain, for reprisals in kind as well as improved defence. This led to the formation in 1918 of the Royal Air Force (RAF) by the amalgamation of the Royal Naval Air Service (RNAS) with the Royal Flying Corps (RFC), a move towards centralization of the functions of air power which was copied by several other air forces prior to **World War II** – though not, significantly, by the USA until 1947. No sooner had the RAF come into being than, under public and political pressure to counter the effects of German strategic bombing of Britain, an Independent Air Force under General Sir Hugh **Trenchard** was formed to bomb German industry by day and night.

After 1918, under the impact of rationalization policies, General **Douhet**'s theory in 1921 that wars could be decided by air power almost unaided, and the belief that 'air power was indivisible', opinions among the arbiters of air power became divided. Whereas the Americans and Japanese continued to let their navies and

Operational Chain of Command in the German Air Force in 1939

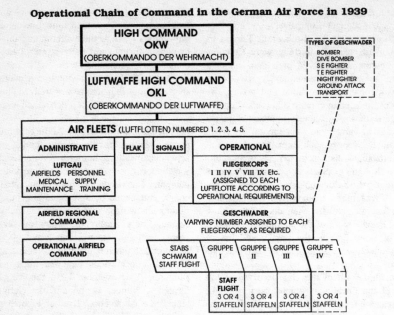

armies retain control of separate air arms (with largely beneficial results) and the Russians and Germans tended to place everything in support of land forces, with only a passing nod to their navies' requirements, the British placed everything under the RAF – to the detriment of their navy and army during **World War II**. Their belated return of the Fleet Air Arm to the Royal Navy came far too late to compensate for the inferior aircraft which the RAF had provided.

Be that as it may, the functional commands – fighter, bomber, coastal, army co-operation, balloon, training, and maintenance – had much to recommend them and over the years have been copied by other nations. They complemented the formation, as operations and the demands of land forces required, of tactical air forces, which comprised reconnaissance, fighter and medium-bomber units, whose task was to work closely with armies – formations which, like commands, exist to the present day.

Indeed, despite technological, strategic and tactical changes, the post-1945 framework remains similar to what evolved beforehand. There has been tinkering and, of course, with space warfare looming ahead, immense increases in both missile and transport commands. But as the vastly increased performance and interchangeability of modern aircraft becomes

plainer, the old divisions between commands become less distinct. At the same time as navies benefit vastly from control of their own aircraft, armies struggle persistently for possession of close-support aircraft. It was a notable event when, in 1966 during the **Vietnam War**, the US Army did a deal with the US Air Force to exchange its fixed-wing machines for possession of **helicopters**.

Air warfare. From the start of **World War I** the future development of air warfare was plain – a continuous struggle for air supremacy to enable sea, land and air operations to proceed. The struggle hinged upon the development of organizations (see **Air forces, Organizations of**) and procedures to make the best use of available **aircraft**, aircraft which, to win their battles, depended upon speed, manoeuvrability, ceiling, reach, endurance and reliability. These battles initially aimed at enabling reconnaissance aircraft to function freely over sea and land, but also sought to make possible ever deeper bombing missions into enemy territory. As the war progressed the number of aircraft engaged increased and the methods of employing them became more complex. By 1916 neither sea nor land forces could ignore the menace of the air weapon; and the size of formations engaged had greatly multiplied. Fighting, however, continued mainly at altitudes below 10,000ft between highly manoeuvrable machines armed only with machine-guns, carrying bombs rarely heavier than 25lb. By 1918 only the size of bombs had greatly increased, but many new ideas were impending.

Before **World War II** many theories were advanced of which General **Douhet's** concept of air forces winning a war practically unaided received most publicity. Douhet postulated attack upon populations with gas (see **Chemical warfare**) as the predominant area weapon. Only Britain and, to a lesser extent, the USA took him up. Everybody agreed that winning air supremacy was essential and that there were advantages in the 'indivisibility of air power' executed by independent air forces. Most major nations experimented with or formed **airborne forces**. But the Germans, French, Italians, Russians and Japanese all chose to concentrate their efforts in support of surface forces, intending to eliminate enemy aircraft industries, bases, **aircraft-carriers**, airfields and fighter forces before turning to other targets. Great attention was paid to the practice of **torpedo** dropping, and the precision attack upon small targets by dive-bombing and low-flying attacks. To counter this, balloon barrages, first used in **World War I**, were extended and **anti-aircraft weapons** multiplied and improved.

Radar and **radio** shaped the air campaigns of the 1940s and beyond. They not only assisted ground controllers to position aircraft for battle, but also contributed significantly to **navigation** and the execution of precision attacks. Nevertheless, it was only in the closing stages of the war that anything approaching precision attacks became generally feasible. Day bombers, which had the best chance of finding their targets, were highly vulnerable to fighters. Night bombers groped in the dark and also became vulnerable to radar-equipped fighters. Moreover, the dangers of low flying against ground defences and the problems of hitting targets from 20,000ft or more were extremely difficult to overcome. As a result the planning of attacks became vital to success and the avoidance of heavy losses.

The appearance of jet engines and high-flying pressurized aircraft along with the use of **rockets and guided missiles**, some with nuclear warheads, revolutionized air warfare. Since 1945 the complexity of machines and ground-support organizations has made possible highly sophisticated combat procedures with the potential for great precision of execution. But as the potential to find and hit small targets has increased, so too has the ability to thwart those weapons been improved. The engineering of highly complicated organizations and technology with vast increases in expense and long periods for the development and building of the systems required has created severe competition for resources as it becomes plain that a large number of inferior machines can be defeated by far fewer superior ones. A similar trend is noticeable with the **helicopter**, which has vastly influenced surface warfare, notably at sea (during, for example, the **Falklands** War) and on land (in **Vietnam** and in Iraq in 1991). But to survive in the surface environment it is being compelled to acquire very expensive and complicated technology.

In the final analysis, the instruments of air warfare have to be judged by their cost-effectiveness – a most difficult business in the face of political restraints and naval and army rivalries, and as greater emphasis is placed on space.

Aisne, Battles of the. In September 1914, after defeat at the **Marne**, the Germans withdrew into the steep forested slopes overlooking the valley of the River Aisne. With their backs to the Chemin des Dames, they dug shallow trenches and barricaded them with barbed wire. They thus created the first fortified (see **Fortifications**) sector, which, heavily defended by **machine-guns** and **artillery**, would soon stretch from Switzerland to the North Sea.

Here, at the *First Battle of the Aisne*, the British were stopped with heavy losses as they attempted to cross the river and continue the northwards pursuit. For the next 30 months the Germans strengthened what has been called 'the natural bastion of northern France'.

The *Second Battle*, sometimes called Chemin des Dames, was launched in 1917 on 16 April, by General Robert Nivelle as part of his offensive, linked with the British attack at **Arras**, intended to rout the Germans. Relying on artillery tactics, but also on tanks (see **Armoured fighting vehicles**) in their first use by the French, it forfeited surprise and was beaten within a few hours. This repulse, with its 120,000 losses in five days, drove the French Army to mutiny and nearly lost the war for the Allies.

The *Third Battle*, which was also the third phase of General Paul von **Hindenburg**'s 1918 offensive, achieved stunning initial success on 27 May 1918 after a surprise bombardment by 4,000 guns. It shattered a thinly held Allied front of 25 miles, hurling them back in disorder to the River Marne where the pursuit lost momentum because of **logistic** problems and stiffening enemy resistance, including the first participation in battle by a complete US Army unit.

Akaba, Capture of. The culmination on 2 July 1917 of a daring march through waterless desert by a small camel-mounted Arab group led by Captain T. E. **Lawrence**, who then persuaded the Howeitat to join him, thereby increasing his force to over 500 men. Only two Arabs were killed in a charge which overwhelmed a Turkish garrison of almost equal size. As a result the **Arab revolt**'s lines of communication were considerably shortened, creating a threat to 600 miles of exposed Turkish lines of communication to the Hejaz, at the same time enabling supply of the Arabs by the Royal Navy through the port of Akaba, thus helping them play a vital role on the right flank of General **Allenby**'s forthcoming advances into Palestine.

Alamein, Battles of El. The turning-point in the **North African** campaigns was reached in the aftermath of the fall of **Tobruk** and the pursuit of Field Marshal **Rommel**'s Axis forces of the routed British Eighth Army. His opponent, General Sir Claude Auchinleck, withdrew to the 40-mile-wide bottleneck at El Alamein between the sea and the almost impassable Qattara Depression. From hastily constructed defences he stopped Rommel in a series of hard-fought clinches in the *First Battle* (1–27 July) which exhausted both sides.

The *Second Battle*, sometimes known as Alam Halfa after the ridge of that name, which was the key to the British defensive position, began on 31 August. Rommel attempted once more to smash the Eighth Army (now under General Bernard **Montgomery**) and reach the Suez Canal. Battered by bombing and intense artillery fire, while enmeshed in minefields and difficult going, Rommel was repulsed by well-co-ordinated anti-tank fire. His withdrawal, prior to preparing deep, intricate defences of his own, was only tentatively followed up by Montgomery.

The *Third Battle* was launched, after intensive bombing of Axis lines of communications and airfields, on 23 October. By making inroads into Rommel's fixed defences, Montgomery drew the Axis armour into an attritional struggle in which his numerically superior artillery and armour did such destruction that, by 2 November, it was a case for Rommel of run or be annihilated. He ran, 700 miles non-stop for El Agheila, leaving behind over 90,000 killed, wounded and prisoners plus 500 tanks and 400 guns – against British casualties of 13,000 and 432 tanks. Taken in conjunction with the simultaneous Allied threat to **Tunisia**, and having in mind the stalemate at **Stalingrad** (soon to be resolved in Russian favour), the uplifted Allies all at once saw the beginning of the war's end.

Alanbrooke, Field Marshal Lord. See **Brooke**.

Albania, Invasions of. Long under Turkish rule and much impoverished, Albania rediscovered her sovereignty in the aftermath of the **Balkans War** of 1912–13, only to be plunged into the series of battles associated with **World War I**. The country became a battleground for the Central Powers in their conflict against Serbia and the British, French, Greek and Italian allies coming to Serbia's assistance. Not until 1920 was the country fully reconstituted, after Italian troops were persuaded by a popular uprising to withdraw. Even then independence was made short-lived when, on 17 April 1939, Benito **Mussolini** sent in 100,000 troops against what amounted to little more than scattered guerrilla resistance.

Once more Albania became a battlefield for major powers when Mussolini invaded Greece on 28 October 1940 only to be thrown back at once by the Greeks, helped by the British who bombed ports and communications targets in Albania. The German invasion of **Yugoslavia** and **Greece** in April 1941 merely prolonged Albanian agony under Axis occupation. **Guerrilla warfare** was then mainly instigated by Russian and Yugoslav Communist agents, with assistance also from Britain and the USA. As was typical in so many Axis-occupied countries, rival political parties contending for power pushed Albania into a ferocious civil war with an aftermath of massacres and terror. In Albania's case, this led to Communist domination and semi-isolation from her neighbours along with chronic poverty.

Aleutian Islands, Battles of the. As a diversion from his major attempt to seize **Midway** Island, Admiral **Yamamoto** sent a naval force to bombard Dutch Harbor on 3 and 4 June 1942 as a prelude to seizing the islands of Kiska and Attu. It failed as a diversion because the Americans, by deciphering the Japanese **codes**, were aware of the whole plan. But shock at an apparent Japanese success so close to their doorstep angered and alarmed the American and Canadian peoples.

When the Japanese attempted to run a supply convoy to Attu in March 1943, they were intercepted off the Komandorski Islands by an inferior US Navy squadron but put to flight by a gallant torpedo attack by three American destroyers. Following up, Admiral Thomas Kinkaid invaded Attu on 11 May with a well-supported infantry division. Heavy fighting amid typically fortified positions cost the Americans nearly 2,000 casualties in 18 days' fighting, the Japanese losing in killed all but 29 of their 2,500-strong garrison. Two months later a joint US/Canadian amphibious force landed on Kiska in what proved a total fiasco, since the enemy had withdrawn 17 days previously.

Alexander, Field Marshal, (Lord) (1891–1969). After distinguished service in **World War I** he came to prominence as commander of the rearguard at **Dunkirk** in 1940. Appointed too late to command in **Burma**, he arrived in the aftermath of a British defeat from which, with the forces available, no recovery was likely. As C-in-C Middle East Command in August 1942 he was in time to conduct the succession of British and Allied victories from El **Alamein** to the moment of Axis surrender in Italy (**Italian campaign, 1943–5**) in 1945, by which time he had been appointed Supreme Commander in the Mediterranean.

Algerian and Tunisian Wars of Independence. In 1847 Algeria became a French colony and in the ensuing century was heavily populated by French citizens. Tunisia, on the other hand, despite the remains of Turkish control and numerous interventions by the French, the British and the Italians in her turbulent affairs, managed to retain a measure of independence until 1883

when uprisings provoked the French to impose a Protectorate with military occupation. Colonial frictions in Morocco involving both Spain and France led to French intervention there at the start of the 20th century and the establishment of a Protectorate which, in the years to come, would frequently be disturbed by widespread **Guerrilla warfare** and some stiff fighting in the 1920s, in which the **French Foreign Legion** played a notable part.

French defeat in **World War II**, the fighting in **North Africa** which ensued in 1942 and realization of France's costly and fatal distraction in **Indo-China**, stimulated nationalist ambitions. Riots and general unrest in 1952 led to full independence for Tunisia in 1956, although a few French troops remained and became involved in overspills of violence from neighbouring Algeria. There independence was far harder to win by the Arab nationalists who had to overcome the large, almost indigenous, French population.

Tension increased, violence mounted and massacres brewed hatreds, while French promises of concessions to the nationalists between 1945 and 1954 were rarely implemented fully. The full-scale revolution launched on 31 October 1954 by the Front de la Libération Nationale (FLN) spread rapidly throughout the country and involved Tunisia and Morocco, where members of the FLN sometimes took refuge, and whence they drew some arms and supplies. French efforts to create conditions for a settlement by force of arms only led to increased guerrilla warfare in the cities and the mountains. The pattern of combat was similar to that in **Malaya**, less so than in Indo-China, with the French endeavouring by **propaganda** to pacify the Arab people and moving some 1.25 million of them into concentration camps while attempting to win their 'hearts and minds'. Raids against the FLN bands by **airborne** and **helicopter** forces were frequent and brutal. But the FLN kept on fighting, supported by the Arab nations, and successfully resisted up to 500,000 troops. Eventually there were 10,200 French casualties and 70,000 FLN in addition to numerous civilians killed and wounded.

Attempts by General de Gaulle to end the revolution in 1958 only provoked unrest among the Algerian French and the French Army. The formation of an illicit underground secret army, the OAS, which instigated riots and terrorism, hampered de Gaulle's attempts at a political solution. Uprisings, which split the French people and the Army, nevertheless were defeated when, in January 1961, the electorate indicated its approval of de Gaulle's policy. Despite a mutiny in the Army during 1961, a cease-fire was negotiated in 1962 followed by independence in July of that year.

Allenby, Field Marshal, (Lord) (1861–1936). Service in a cavalry regiment during small wars in **South Africa** in the 1880s, and later throughout the **Boer War**, taught Allenby the value of surprise and manoeuvre and the vital importance of **logistics**, lessons he never forgot during **World War I**. In 1914 he shrewdly commanded the British Expeditionary Force's Cavalry Division during the retreat from Mons to the **Marne** and in the first Battle of Ypres (see **Flanders, Battles of**). Appointed to command a corps and then Third Army, his conduct of the Battle of **Arras** in April 1917, though denied full success, demonstrated a determination to break, by innovations, the stalemate of trench warfare. Sent to command the Egyptian Expeditionary Force in the aftermath of its second defeat at **Gaza** in 1917, he soon belied, by subtle strategy and tactics, his nickname, earned by brusqueness of manner, of 'the Bull'. Victories over the Turks by deception, surprise, manoeuvre and sound logistics at Gaza, in the pursuit to Jerusalem and during the subsequent campaigns of 1918 which, at **Megiddo** and in the capture of Damascus and Aleppo, forced Turkey to sue for peace, implied more than battlefield triumphs. For his handling of **Lawrence**'s Arab irregulars and of his own **cavalry** and armoured cars (see **Armoured fighting vehicles**) hinted strongly at the shape of war to come, misinterpreted as some of the lessons later were.

Aluminium (US **aluminum**). Was first isolated by Hans Oersted in 1825 and introduced to the public as a metal rarer than gold in 1855. Not until the 1880s was this lightweight, corrosion-resistant, adaptable metal produced in large quantities by electrolytic means by Charles Hall in the USA and Paul Héroult in France. Almost at once it was used in the construction of an airship (the *Schwarz*). In 1909 the first of the many important, strong alloys – Duralumin, developed by Alfred Wilm by the addition of copper and manganese – was available and by

the 1920s was becoming the principal material for **aircraft** construction. Its casting along with hardened alloys as **armour** was also developed. Indeed, aluminium frequently supplanted **steel** as it acquired universal civil and military uses that included house construction and electric cable manufacture.

American Civil War. Although a principal reason for the war's outbreak in 1861 was failure to resolve long-standing differences over slavery, the humanitarian issue was paralleled by rivalry between the northern industrial and the southern agrarian economies. Therefore, when the militarily educated President Jefferson **Davis** severed relations between his southern Confederacy and the North and opened hostilities against the northern Federals at Fort Sumter on 12 April 1861, it was in the knowledge that his army, strong as it soon would be with 112,000 men and under some of the best-trained officers, was only marginally superior to the North's 150,000, and that it might not be self-sufficient in a prolonged struggle. Yet Davis, for political reasons, adopted a defensive strategy in the hope that the North under its lawyer President Abraham **Lincoln** would tire of war. This was Davis's greatest mistake, if only because he overlooked the danger of a naval **blockade** which, as time went by, the 90 obsolete warships initially at Federal disposal would impose in compliance with Lincoln's order of 19 April. Countervailing every future Confederate success on land had to be a strangulation which made it largely impossible to export the South's staple cotton crop to help purchase and smuggle in sufficient munitions.

Both sides were engrossed by the importance of their capital cities. Whenever, as occurred from the outset in July 1861, the untrained Federal army moved south from Washington to capture Richmond, the Confederate capital, the Confederacy would both defend stoutly and distract the Federals by threats against Washington. The essence of the many campaigns in the **Shenandoah Valley** and against the **fortifications** of the two cities were politically orientated thrusts which tied large armies to this relatively small arena while smaller forces manoeuvred in the open spaces of the West. At the root and heart of manoeuvre and co-ordination of widely separated fronts lay the extensive use of **railways** and the **telegraph**.

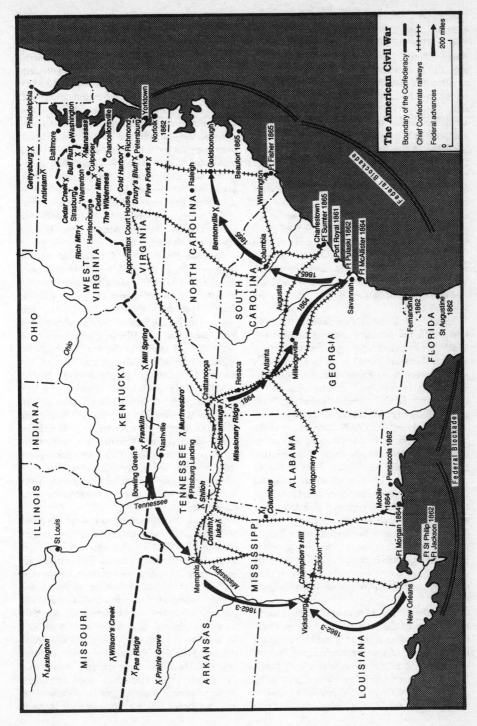

The American Civil War

Boundary of the Confederacy

Chief Confederate railways

Federal advances

0   200 miles

A pattern which was to outlast the war emerged after skirmishes in the Valley culminated in a Federal defeat at the first Battle of **Bull Run** on 21 July. At the same time the Federals began to gain a hold in the West while implementing the naval blockade. This process developed in 1862, as the armies grew in size and skill, when Federal forces under General George McClellan landed on the Yorktown Peninsula and attempted to seize Richmond from the east. His defeat by General Robert E. **Lee** in the **Seven Days Battle** was, however, no less important than the *Merrimack* versus *Monitor* fight in Hampton Roads, in March, and General Ulysses **Grant's** bloody victory at **Shiloh** in April. For the one eliminated any Confederate pretensions to sea power and the other tightened the Federal grasp in the West, a few days before Commodore David Farragut won the naval battle of New Orleans, as prelude to his advance up the Mississippi to **Vicksburg** to make junction there with Grant and effectively cut off the Confederacy from the West.

Belatedly in 1863, Davis realized the peril into which his defensive strategy had led the South. While Grant, ably supported by General William **Sherman**, closed in on Vicksburg with an improvised **amphibious** operation and General Joseph Hooker, now commanding in the East, led the Federal forces to defeat at Chancellorsville (where the best Confederate general, Thomas Jackson, was killed) Davis let Lee strike northwards into Federal territory by way of exploitation but also in the hope of preventing the Federals from reinforcing their menacing operations in the West. It all went wrong for Davis. On 4 July, as Lee admitted defeat at **Gettysburg**, Grant brilliantly captured Vicksburg after an approach march of 200 miles in 19 days, living off the country. But he judged the **logistic** problem nicely; the siege of Vicksburg, screened by Sherman's mobile troops and supported by ironclads, lasted over six weeks but was always itself sufficiently supplied despite difficult conditions.

The Federal Army now turned its attention to the capture of the vital route centre of **Chattanooga**. But after a series of battles attendant upon a siege of the outmanoeuvred Federal forces penned in the town, and which lasted from 19 September to 27 November, it took the appointment of Grant to overall command in the West to break the Confederate grip. At this point Lincoln recognized in Grant and Sherman the generals who would win the war for him and circumvent the challenge by the Democrat presidential candidate, the rejected General McClellan, whose party spoke of negotiating peace. Grant was appointed General-in-Chief in the field and moved to Washington to conduct operations in the East. Sherman took over in the West. Their opponents, meanwhile, were in distress. Cut off from the outside world apart from supplies by a few blockade runners and smuggling from Mexico via Texas, their manpower was depleted by heavy casualties; their armouries, ill-supplied by an ever-inadequate armament industry, were all but empty, and their communication systems, in particular their railways, were foundering from lack of spares and maintenance.

So when Grant attacked in the direction of Richmond in April 1864 with 105,000 men against Lee's 61,000, and initiated what evolved into the vicious **Wilderness** campaign and the Siege of **Petersburg**, there was little Davis or Lee could spare for the West when Sherman lunged from Chattanooga to **Atlanta** prior to launching his celebrated **March to the Sea**. Although by brilliant generalship and the valour of his armies, Lee managed to check Grant in the Wilderness, the Confederacy was on its last legs as Sherman ripped through its heartlands. Only scattered Confederate armies kept the field when Sherman turned northwards in 1865 in a scythe-like sweep to capture the remaining Atlantic ports and, in conjunction with Grant, close the ring upon Lee at Appomattox on 9 April – just prior to Lincoln's assassination on the 14th and the final laying down of Confederate arms on 26 May 1865.

The Civil War occurred just beyond the point of change between the first and second industrial revolutions – between the substitution of steel for iron, of railways for cart tracks, of electric for hand visual signalling, of ironclads for wooden walls, of rifled breech-loading weapons for smooth-bore muzzle-loaders – and in time to experience rapid-fire **machine-guns** for the first time. It witnessed such heavy casualties that fortifications, particularly the hastily constructed field type, became extremely popular among soldiers bent upon survival. And it was distinguished by the unusually good care taken of the wounded in campaigns logistically quite well provided for by comparison with those of the past in other parts of the world. But it would take several more campaigns before the lessons were fully digested and applied.

American Indian Wars. From the moment white settlers arrived in the Americas in the 16th century there were wars against the indigenous 'Red Indians', whose numbers steadily declined. Almost entirely they were **guerrilla**-style actions involving small raiding groups and bands against settlers and military units. They fluctuated in time with the westward thrust of settlers, moving to a culmination during the so-called Third Frontier Period which began around 1840. From 1850 there were 30 or more outbreaks of fighting (mostly in the West) prior to the **American Civil War**, when hostilities still simmered. Battles then rose to a climax in the 1870s before dying away and ending in the killing of 170 Indians (from **machine-gun** fire) along with 60 or more cavalry and civilian casualties at Wounded Knee on 20 December 1890. The whole Indian business, one of the seamiest in US history, was characterized by mutual ferocity and the bad faith of the settlers as they stole Indian land, frequently broke agreements, slaughtered the mighty bison herds upon which the plains Indians lived and, accidentally, introduced diseases which were fatal to the unimmunized Indian physical constitution.

It is recorded that 90 per cent of the US Army, prior to 1861, was engaged in Indian warfare over an area of over one million square miles and in 1857, for example, fought in 37 combat operations. Nor was there much reduction in commitment during the Civil War when one side or the other might take advantage of Indian sentiments or lax conditions. But the premeditated massacre, mainly by militia (see **Reserve forces**), at Sand Creek of 300 plains Indians, mostly women and children, on 29 November 1864 alerted the Indian tribes to their post-war peril and conditioned their reactions in the next decade or more when, 'the Civil War bloodbath had dulled the public sensibility'.

The history of anti-plains-Indian warfare is remembered chiefly by its epics and massacres. The years between 1865 and 1891 saw the slaying in combat of 82 soldiers by 2,000 Sioux near Fort Phil Kearny in 1866; the repulse in 1867 of 1,500 Sioux, circling a wagon laager, hitting little while on the move, and failing to

charge and overrun the 32 defenders; the saga of the great uprising by 4–6,000 Sioux under Chief Crazy Horse in 1876 with its highly emotive and controversial annihilation of Lieutenant-Colonel George Custer's 212 men at the Little Big Horn; and the eventual crushing of Crazy Horse at Wolf Mountain; and the magnificently skilful fighting retreat of Chief Joseph's 700 Nez Percé (400 of them women) from Idaho to Montana in 1877. But these events tend to obscure the total of 943 recorded actions fought in 12 distinct campaigns during the period.

For all their skill and bravery, the Indians never had a chance against superior weapons and inexhaustible white manpower. But they might have done better if they had known and used modern guerrilla-warfare techniques instead of engaging in so many semi-pitched battles.

Amiens, Battles of. When this vital commercial and communications centre became a main railway junction prior to 1850, its long-standing importance as a bastion of northern France was augmented. In November 1870 it was occupied by the Germans after a sharp engagement at **Villers-Bretonneux**, but was lost and then recaptured in December as the **Franco-Prussian War** drew to a close.

In 1914 it was temporarily occupied by the Germans in their sweep to the Battle of the **Marne**, but strongly held by the Allies for the rest of **World War I**. Seriously threatened as a principal objective of **Hindenburg**'s 1918 **offensive**, the line, once again, was held at Villers-Bretonneux, which became a starting-point for the surprise Allied massed tank attack on 8 August. Including reserve and supply tanks, 604 British heavy and light **tanks** and 12 armoured cars plus 90 French light tanks, attacked through mist, in conjunction with infantry and cavalry, and with massive artillery support. The poorly organized German defences were smashed over a frontage of 20 miles to a depth of six miles in the first 24 hours. A few armoured cars and light tanks cut loose in the enemy rear where panic ensued. German troops gave up in droves and some called on their comrades to cease prolonging the war. As a result General **Ludendorff** concluded that the war had to be brought to an end. The Allied attack, however, was handicapped by the inability of tanks, cavalry and infantry to co-operate, owing to communication problems and their differences of speed and protection which made them tactically incompatible. After five days the offensive had lost momentum here and was transferred elsewhere.

In 1940 Amiens again fell into German hands when overrun by General **Guderian**'s corps in its drive to the English Channel. It would remain in German hands until dawn on 31 August 1944 when British armoured forces recaptured the town, with its bridges intact.

Ammunition (see also **Artillery**). Ammunition for firearms is made up of two distinct elements: the projectile which does the damage to the target and the propellant which propels the projectile from the weapon at the required velocity. This broad definition holds good whether the weapon be rifle or naval gun, but the distinction became less obvious with the introduction in the 19th century of ammunition with the propellant contained in a casing, usually metal, and with the projectile attached to it. The resulting complete round allowed a single loading action. Even nowadays, for the larger calibre of gun the propellant is loaded separately from the projectile; this is known as separated ammunition.

The function of the propellant is to burn very quickly, the expanding gases and resulting high pressure giving the projectile high acceleration as it goes down the barrel. To initiate this burning an easily detonated cap is needed to set off a sensitive primer, which in turn ignites the slower-burning propellant. The whole is contained in a metal case or cartridge which expands on firing to seal the rear end of the gun.

Gunpowder was the first propellant to be used and it was not challenged until Austria adopted the somewhat unreliable nitrocellulose (NC) in 1860. It was not until 1888 that the real breakthrough came with Alfred **Nobel**'s development of ballistite. In 1889 Abel and Dewar in the UK independently produced the propellant in cord form, hence cordite. Cordite-type propellants have now been developed to a point where their use is very flexible, varying from small grains for small arms to large cylinders used in some rockets. Experiments with liquid propellants have not so far produced a satisfactory substitute for the solid propellant in general use in small arms and artillery.

The simplest projectile is the small-arms bullet, where the important parameter is stopping-power. This requires about 80 joules of energy and the bullet must be given sufficient weight and velocity to achieve this over the desired range. The introduction of the rifled barrel, typically in the Enfield rifle of 1853, provided a significant improvement, both in range and accuracy. Nickel is often used for the rifle bullet's outer casing, being sufficiently ductile to engage the rifling yet strong enough to withstand firing pressures. Lead and antimony is commonly used for the core, to achieve penetration combined with stability in flight. The trend nowadays is to have a lighter bullet fired at a much higher velocity so as to produce the required stopping-power.

Artillery projectiles tend to be more complex in design and can be broadly classified, whether for use on land, at sea or in the air, either as shells filled with high explosive (HE), with all their variants, or as anti-armour projectiles.

For maximum effect conventional HE shell should break up into small fragments when detonated on impact; special fusing may be fitted, for example in air defence weapons, to enable the shell to burst close to a target instead of actually having to hit it.

Anti-armour ammunition is either kinetic energy (KE), relying on the velocity of a dense core to penetrate the target, or chemical energy (CE), which relies on the explosive filling to do the work. To achieve high velocity a large base area needs to be presented to the propellant gases but for KE penetration a small dense slug is required. The complex Armour-Piercing Discarding Sabot (APDS) has been developed with the broad-based 'sabot' being discarded at the muzzle, leaving the core to fly on to the target. A further refinement is the 'long rod' penetrator which has to be fin-stabilized, resulting in the Armour-Piercing Fin-Stabilized Discarding Sabot (APFSDS) round.

The CE round most widely used is High-Explosive Anti-Tank (HEAT) which, on striking the target, penetrates by means of a semi-molten jet of explosive and armour fragments. A more effective jet is formed if the projectile does not spin, so fin stabilization is normally used and the round is well suited to the smooth-bore tank gun. An alternative is High-Explosive Squash Head (HESH), which relies on the explosive charge 'pancaking' on the outside of the target and, when detonated, sending a shock wave through the armour. This in turn detaches a large scab from the inner face, causing widespread damage within the vehicle.

Tactical developments on the modern battlefield have called for engagement of targets at ever-increasing ranges, with a consequent demand for increased accuracy, in particular the need to engage large armoured formations outside the range of tank guns. This has led to the development of Terminally Guided Munitions (TGM), giving the projectile the ability to seek out its target on arrival in the target area. Such carrier shells typically release a large number of small bomblets which provide lethal coverage of the target spread out below. It is in the development of sophisticated fusing and means of terminal guidance that the future of the gun-fired projectile lies.

Amphibious warfare. Until steam-powered vessels were available, amphibious operations were hostage to weather, water currents, wind and muscle power to deliver seaborne forces ashore. Also they were inherently hazardous and all the more so if undertaken against opposition. The **Crimean** landings succeeded because they were virtually unopposed on the beaches. Admiral Farragut's capture in 1862 of New Orleans during the **American Civil War** was unopposed after his ships' bombardment had forced the Confederates to withdraw up the Mississippi. The attempts by Generals **Grant** and **Sherman** to capture **Vicksburg** in 1863 were costly in lives and effort because many of the moves had to be made through wide and narrow waterways (including a specially dug canal) against opposition from a well-prepared enemy. Troops were moved in either rowed or towed boats, unadapted for the purpose.

During **World War I** specialized landing craft were virtually unheard of and techniques little changed since pre-1850 times. At **Gallipoli** rowing boats and towed barges were the principal assault vessels, except for the steamer *River Clyde*, which had a machine-gun battery emplaced in its bows and holes cut in its sides with catwalks for the infantry to dash for the shore after the ship had beached. While in the raid on Zeebrugge in 1918, men who were put ashore against fierce opposition came from an old cruiser placed alongside the mole.

Prior to **World War II** the Japanese and to a lesser extent the Americans, with their eyes fixed on Pacific Ocean domination based on islands, made such progress as there was with assault ships carrying mechanized **landing craft**. It took the German conquest of Western Europe (**West Europe campaigns**) in 1940 (including the largely unopposed *coup de main* amphibious landings in **Norway**) to compel the British, soon assisted by the Americans, to project amphibious warfare beyond the techniques of 1918. To launch **commando** raids in the aftermath of the evacuation from **Dunkirk** (a superb amphibious withdrawal) as preludes to the major invasions needed to defeat Germany and, in due course, Japan, new doctrines, techniques and flotillas of hastily designed and built special assault ships and craft were required. Vessels such as the 10-knot, 20-man, unarmoured Landing Craft Personnel (LCP); the slower, larger, armoured Landing Craft Assault (LCA); the bigger ocean-going Landing Craft Infantry (LCI) capable of taking 200 men; and the Landing Ship Infantry (LSI) (converted passenger ships), which carried LCPs and LCAs and their men to the assault launching areas. Also there were the ramped Landing Craft Tank (LCT) and Landing Ship Tank (LST) which, in addition to a host of small lighters, conveyed men and all manner of equipment, stores and vehicles, in addition to tanks, to the shore, where their facility to vary their draught to suit beach gradient was of inestimable value. And in due course there were amphibious tanks, of far greater power than those used by the Japanese in their **Pacific** campaign, to lead the way ashore, followed by thousands upon thousands of wading, waterproofed vehicles.

Landing techniques were developed by trial, error and battle through minor hit-and-run raids from Britain and throughout the Mediterranean. Among the most celebrated were those at **Saint-Nazaire** and **Dieppe**, each of which suffered from immediate opposition. The American landing on **Guadalcanal** in August 1942 benefited greatly from troops getting ashore against minimal opposition, though what happened when the Japanese reacted was another matter, later resolved in the American favour as much by the solution of the **logistic** problems as by combat alone.

The pay-offs for all the preliminary operations, including the dangerous tasks of pre-assault, hydrographic and beach survey under the enemy nose, came during the sporadically opposed Allied landings in French North-West

Africa in 1942; the more strongly disputed landings in **Sicily**, and the extremely tough fight at **Salerno** in 1943. Indeed, as the Allied ability to come ashore almost at will in every theatre of war became apparent to the Axis, they were forced to commit immense manpower and material resources to stop landings on the beaches in order to prevent being overrun in subsequent mobile battles inland. Yet, although the Allies got ashore almost trouble-free at **Anzio** in 1944, their failure to advance inland soon had them penned. But successive invasions of Pacific islands were usually met by fanatical resistance at the water's edge, since the Japanese could recognize, quite as well as the Americans, Australians, New Zealanders and British, which islands were strategically vital.

The invasions of **Normandy** and, on a lesser scale, of **Walcheren** in 1944 demonstrated not only how far techniques had developed but also how important was deception, to minimize opposition through surprise at the landing-place and fire-power to suppress it when unavoidable. The experience thus gained was used also against the Japanese in the **Philippines** and elsewhere in the East; and notably by United Nations forces during the **Korean War** at **Inchon** in 1950 as well as afterwards in the amphibious withdrawal, under strong enemy pressure, from **Hungnam**, which was a classic rivalling Dunkirk.

Since then the **Suez** landing, **Vietnam**, **Grenada** and the **Falklands** War have illustrated to what extent new technology, in particular the latest **communication** systems, the **helicopter**, VSTOL aircraft (see **Aircraft**), **rockets and guided missiles** have amplified, without by any means simplifying or making less hazardous, amphibious operations. That they are as important as ever is indisputable in the light of their recent repeated (indirect as well as direct) application in the exertion of political and military pressure.

Amritsar Massacre. India in 1919 was in the throes of ferment caused by the Third Afghan War (**Afghanistan, Battles of**) and Mahatma Gandhi's campaign of so-called 'non-violence' in pursuit of independence. In Amritsar, holy city of the Sikhs, on 10 April, the British arrested two nationalist leaders, whereupon rioting began and a few Europeans were killed. Public assembly was forbidden by proclamation, but several thousand people crowded the enclosed space of the Jallianwala Bagh on the 13th.

Taking 90 **Gurkha** and Indian soldiers, Brigadier-General Reginald Dyer entered the Bagh and saw the crowd being harangued by agitators. He panicked and, without warning, ordered fire to be opened. A total of 1,650 bullets were fired into the mass, killing 397 and wounding some 1,500. Dyer then withdrew without attempting medical aid. It was a turning-point in Indian, British and world history. A public outcry accelerated the pace towards the independence achieved in 1947, which was the first major step in the British retreat from Empire. As an immediate result of the massacre, rules governing the opening of fire by soldiers in aid of the civil power were tightened. Henceforward only after a request from the civil power or in self-defence was firing permitted. It then had to be as minimum force with aimed shots. The wounded had then to be properly cared for.

Analysis, Operational. It has become increasingly apparent to those involved in major military projects that quantitative methods can help them to assess the likely value of the introduction of new equipment or tactics, prior to their use in actual war. This is particularly true of a major item of equipment such as a tank or aircraft, since the sheer size of the financial burden leads the senior officers with responsibility for final acceptance to exercise considerable caution before committing themselves. The results of an operational analysis (more often referred to as operational research – OR) project is often the only means by which they can come to a properly thought-out decision. It has been defined as 'the science of planning and executing an operation to make the most economical use of the resources available'.

One of the earliest examples of military OR occurred during **World War I** and was applied to the U-boat menace. Losses of merchantmen to submarine attack mounted frighteningly as the war progressed, since the ships sailed from port individually, as they always had done, and U-boat commanders had considerable freedom of action in picking off targets as they presented themselves in the known shipping lanes. Part of the problem lay in the British reluctance to allocate sufficient escort vessels to the guarding of merchant ships, plus the Admiralty's reluctance to adopt a convoy system. Admiral **Jellicoe**, First Sea Lord, believed that about 5,000 ships were leaving and entering British ports each week and he was convinced that an effective and suitably escorted convoy system would be impossible to organize on such a scale. There was no statistical branch in the Royal Navy at that time (and indeed no naval staff college prior to 1917) and hence no correlation of facts and figures to support Jellicoe's assumption.

It was left to a Commander Henderson to prove, by studying Ministry of Transport records, that weekly sailings amounted to only 120–140. Furthermore, he was also able to show that those vessels which were escorted, such as troop transports, suffered few losses as the U-boats found it difficult to aim their torpedoes accurately when under threat. Nevertheless, it took an appeal from Henderson direct to the Prime Minister to convince Jellicoe that convoys should be tried, whereupon the accuracy of Henderson's calculations was dramatically confirmed. Within the year from May 1917, when convoys were started, monthly losses had dropped from 683,000 tonnes to about 300,000 tonnes; and this despite a significant increase in the number of U-boats at sea.

However, most of the ideas for military OR emerged during **World War II**, particularly with respect to the operations mounted by the British and American forces, who found themselves committed to large-scale sea-borne assaults many hundreds, even thousands, of miles from their home bases. The resulting **logistic** problems required radical solutions which could only be found from preliminary mathematical studies. For example, the Allied invasion of Europe in the summer of 1944, with its subsequent build-up of men and stores to enable the break-out from the bridgeheads to take place, would never have succeeded without a detailed analysis of what the armies would need on each succeeding day of the operation, carried out months before the event and largely followed as the campaign unfolded.

Not so successful was the British analysis of the likely effect of strategic bombing. Thinking had been conditioned by the limited German bombing of London during World War I, which had resulted in some 4,400 casualties. Lord **Trenchard**, Chief of the Air Staff, became convinced that air power alone could destroy the morale of a civilian population and by 1938 the air staffs were estimating that London could expect to receive 3,500 tonnes of bombs in the first 24 hours of war and that after a month there

would be over 25,000 dead; all this based on a yardstick of 50 casualties per tonne of bombs dropped. The eminent scientist Professor Haldane seriously estimated 20,000 dead from an average 500-aircraft raid. Though predicted from serious calculations, these figures were not supported by any sound statistical evidence and by 1941 the German bombing of London and elsewhere had shown that, despite the damage, morale held firm, the sinews of war remained intact and the earlier predictions were wrong. Despite this evidence, Trenchard advocated the building of a large bomber force to shatter German morale and his views were accepted (such was his reputation, even though, at age 68, he was retired). The eventual result was the systematic bombing of German cities as the war progressed, with the loss of 59,223 aircrew and with little noticeable effect on Germany's morale or her ability to wage war.

As World War II drew to a close much effort by the OR analysts went into detailed studies of particular aspects of the war. A typical example was the investigation, carried out in 1945, of a whole range of tank casualties resulting from engagements in North-West Europe. This provided detailed figures, particularly on ranges of engagement for tank guns in close country, which has proved to be of value in more modern analytical work by Nato.

One outcome of the statistical work carried out during World War II was the setting up of establishments whose specific task was to provide the advice which defence chiefs were increasingly demanding on a wide variety of problems. In Britain, for example, the wartime Army Operational Research Group developed into the Defence Operational Analysis Establishment, to provide the service that was needed. While much of the work was statistical, on occasion complex field exercises, involving the deployment of large numbers of men and equipment, were carried out, carefully monitored by scientists from the establishment, to explore practically particular problems – to establish exposure times needed for a tank to fire its main armament effectively from behind cover, for example; or to assess the effectiveness of the armed **helicopter** as an **anti-tank weapons** system.

Operational research can have its macabre side too. It was in **Vietnam** that the United States Defense Department used the number of enemy corpses found after a battle – the 'body count' – as a chilling factor in the mathematical assessment of whether or not the war was being pursued in a cost-effective manner. Indeed it could be argued that Vietnam provided an example of how not to use OR techniques. It was under Robert McNamara, the then US Defense Secretary, that the Americans tried to conduct the war on a strictly financial 'profit and loss' basis. Having had it demonstrated statistically that the employment of the latest technology must inevitably give the US forces a crushing advantage over a technically unsophisticated opponent, the American defence chiefs seemed unable to grasp that **guerrilla wars** cannot be successfully fought that way. On the few occasions that the North Vietnamese army could be brought to battle in a major engagement the statistics could be thoroughly justified by the evident American superiority. But such occasions were rare indeed and in the end the Americans were defeated.

OR attempts to model the real world, so that the performance, either of an individual piece of equipment or of military forces carrying out a tactical or strategic task, can be optimized against agreed criteria. The model may be in the form of entirely theoretical computer studies or, more elaborately, by means of 'war-gaming' where tactical situations are played out minute by minute using appropriately experienced military commanders to take the decisions at the level they would normally do, from their assessment of the situation fed to them by the exercise staff. The dispositions of troops which result would be plotted, fed into a **computer**, evaluated and a consequential new situation presented to the 'players'. Such war-gaming can be very time-consuming, with five minutes of play taking an hour or more to evaluate. Very effective assessments of new weapons systems and tactics can, however, be made by this method. Finally, as we have seen, very expensive practical exercises, carefully monitored, can be mounted using actual troops.

The techniques used in OR have been increasingly refined since World War II and it is usual to refer to that part of the real world in which the researcher has an interest as a 'system'. It is the art of mathematical modelling to identify the quantities associated with a system which, when linked mathematically with each other and to as few other variables as possible, will

together form a model describing how the system behaves. By applying the factors in the system to specific situations a picture can emerge which can in turn lead to crucial and far-reaching military decisions. One area in which this can be especially valuable is the reliability of individual components in a complex piece of equipment such as an aircraft. Establishing the component failure rate can lead to the calculation of a mean time between failures, which can in turn pin-point areas where remedial design work needs to be done or alternatively indicate the scale of spares that need to be carried in the logistic support system. And this in turn may effectively limit the tactical use of the weapon itself.

Typical of OR projects that might be set up would be one to examine the problems faced by the United States in reinforcing Europe in the event of war. The model could be required to determine deployment schedules, aircraft-lift capability and the system needed to meet the deployment requirement. Input to such a model would probably include such details as troop strengths, weights, dimensions, destinations; lift-aircraft characteristics, speed, load, load and unload times, capacity for different cargo types; and airfield restrictions, distances and attrition rates due to accidents and enemy action.

Tactical and weapon performance problems might typically be examined by means of a war game at divisional level, probably involving both land and air forces, with player-controlled units of company and battalion size. Such a model would move units, determine engagements and would include logistic aspects. It would be usual to calibrate the game with actual battle results where relevant and the aim would be to produce a realistic tactical situation as a function of time. Once the players had issued their orders to meet a given situation, previous orders would be discarded and the unit concerned would be deemed to have started on its new task. For combat simulation different weapon characteristics, artillery target priorities and similar factors could be inserted in order to evaluate particular systems; the input for such a game would also require terrain data. It would normally take perhaps two hours for about five to ten minutes of real time to be played.

Studies such as those described have become an essential part of all major powers' defence planning.

Anti-aircraft weapons. See **Artillery, Rockets and guided missiles.**

Anti-ballistic missiles. It was in the 1960s that both the Soviet Union and the United States began to study ways of destroying the other's strategic ballistic missiles just after launch – the concept of the anti-ballistic missile or ABM. The idea was fraught with technical difficulties, involving a very short reaction time, highly complex **radars** and very high velocity missiles (see **Rockets and guided missiles**) capable of reaching the target before the latter could release its warheads.

The Soviets were first in the field with their Galosh system, deployed in 1968 for the air defence of Moscow. Each site had sixteen launchers and associated with them an acquisition radar, two battle management radars and four engagement radars. The missiles themselves were high-speed three-stage rockets, each with a nuclear warhead. On the US side the Nike–Hercules system, primarily developed for use against high-flying aircraft in 1961, had a limited capability against ABM but was dropped as ineffective. It was revived in the 1980s as the **Strategic Defence Initiative (SDI)** and also in the shape of the short-range Patriot (initially anti-aircraft) missile which, over Saudi Arabia and Israel in 1991, shot down many Iraqi long-range ballistic missiles.

Anti-submarine weapons. Since the Confederate submarine *Hunley* sank the Federal ship *Housatonic* in 1864, and was dragged to the bottom by her victim, anti-submarine measures have assumed growing importance in **naval warfare.** Moored **mines**, from the outset, have been and remain among the most potent killers, particularly in shallower waters. Nets have deterred, and ramming, to begin with the only way for surface craft to score a kill, has occasionally been effective. A surfaced submarine, of course, was vulnerable like any other vessel and, in **World War I, Q-ships** were developed to lure submarines to the surface.

The depth charge, first produced by the British in 1915 and consisting of a container with 120lb of explosive dropped into the water and set off by a hydrostatic pistol, was the most effective mobile weapon. However, to be effective it had to be within 21 feet of a boat, which raised the difficult problem of how to locate the submarine precisely. Sea-bed and ship-fitted hydrophones were tried before 1914, but results were usually discouraging. Until the invention of **sonar** in 1918, visual sighting by surface craft and **aircraft** was the best method, sometimes guided by knowledge of the victim's presence through direction-finding (DF) from intercepts of submarines' **radio** transmissions used during early attempts to co-ordinate operations.

Passive defensive methods were the most potent: zigzagging to defeat the submarine commander's predictions and aim; dazzle painting of ships to give a false impression of course and speed; and, most effective of all, the **convoy** system to reduce the number of targets and economically enhance defence by escorts. Surface escorts scored the most kills; airships and seaplanes made a contribution and there were examples of successful submarine versus submarine encounters – the first on record being the torpedoing on the surface by the German U-22 of her compatriot U-7 in January 1915.

Between the World Wars remarkably little progress was made in submarine warfare. A consensus believed that the convoy system, allied to sonar's potential and to air escort, had overcome the threat. Only late in the 1930s were doubts expressed about sonar when it was discovered that asdic was not nearly so good a detector as originally thought, owing to temperature variations of water layers at different depths. Nor had the potential of centralized direction by radio of submarine packs, as developed by Germany's Commodore Karl **Dönitz**, been visualized. Depth charges were still limited to a maximum 80 feet; escorts had been given a low priority by the British and the Americans – the latter even rejected the convoy system. A highly sophisticated organization to gather and synthesize **intelligence**, to control the evasive routeing of convoys and to initiate countermeasures was only in its infancy and made all the more inadequate in June 1940 when the Germans seized most of Europe's western seaboard and launched the Battle of the **Atlantic.**

That battle and the others which raged in the Mediterranean and, later, in the Pacific and Indian Oceans would be decided by the struggle between opposing control organizations to which radio intercept and direction finding, the deciphering of codes and **radar** were central in the detection process. New weapons also played their part from faster surface escorts and aircraft of longer range equipped with the latest detection devices. Depth charges were made to burst at greater depths and thrown, instead of released, at their targets by a multiple mortar called Hedgehog. Aircraft were given rockets to fire at surfaced boats. Primitive homing torpedoes began to make it possible even for one submerged submarine to sink another, with improved sonar contributing.

After World War II, and with redoubled urgency when nuclear-armed and powered submarines with extremely long endurance and deep diving capabilities came into service, both detectors and weapons had to be much improved, with aircraft playing a prominent part. Sniffers to detect a diesel boat's fumes and magnetic-anomaly detectors which record changes in the earth's magnetic field caused by a submerged submarine complemented improved radars at the same time as static, underwater hydrophone arrays were being installed to monitor underwater movements. Helicopters proved particularly useful by their ability, at the hover, to lower sonar detectors below the temperature layers and then join in the attack as, for example, in the Falklands War. Yet these detection and defensive measures often are defeated by quieter-running submarines with equipment designed to beat the hunter. Often the submarine is ahead of its enemies who, in desperate circumstances when deeper-diving homing torpedoes fail, may well be forced to use the ultimate depth charge – the nuclear one.

Anti-tank weapons. When tanks were first deployed in 1916 they were found to be vulnerable to a direct hit from high-explosive shells fired from conventional field guns. Little thought was given at that time to the development of a specific anti-tank weapon. By 1927, however, it became clear that such a weapon was needed to defeat the increasingly well-protected tanks that were beginning to appear. A 37mm weapon developed by the Germans proved useful in Spain (Spanish Civil War), while in Britain the 40mm (two-pounder) gun, firing solid shot and highly effective out to 800m, became the standard British weapon.

Realizing the threat, all tank-producing nations began to protect their tanks to a greater degree and it was the Germans who drew ahead with the modification of their 88mm anti-aircraft gun for use in the anti-tank

role. This gun, with its 21lb solid shot fired at 810m/sec and capable of penetrating 60mm of armour at ranges greater than 1,200m, was also tried out in Spain and came to dominate the battlefields of World War II.

Gradually the Allies caught up with the British 77mm gun and, towards the end of the war (though not in action), with the 84mm (20-pounder) tank gun mounted on the Centurion. Since 1945, as armour thicknesses have increased, so has gun calibre to meet the threat, first with the widely used British 105mm and then with 120–25mm weapons which are now commonplace.

The solid shot fired by these modern weapons has developed a long way from its beginnings with the introduction of fin-stabilized penetrators, some with a depleted uranium core (see also Ammunition), being made to complex designs.

The development of the hollow-charge projectile has provided another means of attacking armour, a crucial factor in the development of the rocket-propelled Anti-Tank Guided Weapon (ATGW). The Germans had been first in this field during World War II with their planned wire-guided X-7 missile. However, the French and British took the design further with the French producing the first practicable system in the 1950s with their SS10. Operating out to about 1,000m, it was the forerunner of a whole series of Soviet systems, while the UK produced the Vickers Vigilant and later, the British Aerospace Swingfire.

It was during the Yom Kippur War in 1973 that the ATGW really showed its paces, the Egyptian infantry, equipped with Soviet 2,000m-range Saggers, being able to inflict heavy casualties on Israeli tanks, leading some ill-informed commentators to suppose, mistakenly, that the day of the tank was done. ATGW often have sophisticated guidance. Early systems such as those already mentioned used Manual Command to Line of Sight (MCLOS), which has the advantage of simplicity and accuracy, with the operator tracking both missile and target; but it relies on considerable operator training. Later systems such as Milan and TOW use Semi-Active Command to Line of Sight (SACLOS), technically more complex but simpler to operate. Maximum ranges in excess of 2,000m are usual with modern systems.

As tank protection increases with the use of

special armours, the direct-fire weapon finds it increasingly difficult to penetrate the front or side. So attention is now being paid to attacking the top armour, inevitably thinner to meet overall vehicle weight restrictions. The bomblet, containing a small hollow-charge warhead and dropped from aircraft in very large numbers to swamp an area containing a concentration of armour, is one approach. Highly complex terminally guided munitions (TGM), fired from conventional long-range artillery, are another. **Mines** too, originally expected to do little more than blow off a track, are now much more lethal to the tank, with elaborate fuzing enabling them to penetrate the vehicle's belly plate.

One thing is certain, the competition between tank protection and the weapon to defeat it will continue as the designers of each strive to counter the efforts of the other.

Anzio bridgehead. The unopposed landing by General John Lucas's VI Corps on 22 January 1944 in the German rear in Italy was intended to force the abandonment of the strong **Gustav Line**. Lucas, however, for lack of sufficient shipping did not feel strong enough to risk an immediate thrust beyond the planned bridgehead, and Field Marshal **Kesselring** was quick to take advantage of the pause to surround the lodgement area and begin counter-attacks which, throughout February, rose to a climax of ferocity in rain-soaked ground. At times the Germans were within an ace of breaking in. But once finally entrenched in stalemate on 29 February, the bridgehead remained a big thorn in the German flank until its reinforced garrison sallied forth on 23 May to make junction with Allied troops advancing from the shattered Gustav Line.

Arab–Israeli Wars. In the aftermath of the **Arab revolt** of **World War I** with its promise of Arab autonomy, the underhand Anglo-French grasping of mandates in the Middle East and approval for a Jewish national home in Palestine was a recipe for war. Incidents in the 1920s which swelled into **guerrilla warfare** in 1936, catching British troops in the middle, were first steps in the creation by the Jews of an underground army with the power to persuade the United Nations to cancel the British mandate. In May 1948 the State of Israel was declared, which acted as a signal for converging attacks upon it by Egypt, Lebanon, Syria and Jordan.

Defence of Israel, by poorly armed units, revolved around contested nodal localities. As the Arabs were worn down the fanatic Israelis acquired strength and sufficient weapons to assume local offensives. It was Israeli good fortune to be superior in mobility to the Egyptians in the south, to hold firm in the north and, after losing old Jerusalem to the **Arab Legion** in ten days of fierce fighting, nevertheless to retain modern Jerusalem. But most significant portents for the future were the events of October, when the Israeli army seized Beersheba and flung the Egyptians back into Sinai, and in March 1949 when they seized the Negev with its port of Eilat at the head of the Gulf of Akaba.

Truces, in the years to come, would be made and broken by both sides. Raids in the frontier regions, as all acquired arms from a variety of Eastern and Western bloc nations, became endemic. Tension came to a head on 29 October 1956 when, in collusion with the Anglo-French attack on Egypt at **Suez**, the Israelis struck deeply with mechanized and **airborne** troops, mainly equipped with obsolete weapons, to within 30 miles of the Canal and also to capture the remainder of **Sinai** – only to withdraw under UN diplomatic pressure in March 1957.

The next bout – the so-called Six Days War of 5–10 June 1967 – was a much more sophisticated affair in that the Arabs had, for the most part, been rearmed with Russian equipment and the Israelis had acquired modern Western **aircraft** and **tanks**. Provoked by a strong buildup of Egyptian forces in Sinai and threatening Syrian and Jordanian moves in the north and near Jerusalem, the Israelis struck pre-emptively at the Egyptians, destroying their air force in the first few hours and by overrunning Sinai, ruining their enemy in four days. At the same time, they defeated the Jordanians and captured Jerusalem, along with the entire Arab holding west of the River Jordan, also turning against the Syrians to eject them from the dominating Golan Heights.

The next six years are sometimes called the War of Attrition in which the Arabs reconstructed their forces and planned retribution, and the Israelis fortified their new frontiers and strengthened themselves. Raid and counter-raid, by sea, air and land, erupted, to almost total Israeli surprise, into an all-out Arab offensive on 6 October 1973. The Yom Kippur War, so called because the Arabs made it coincide for their advantage with a Jewish religious feast, played

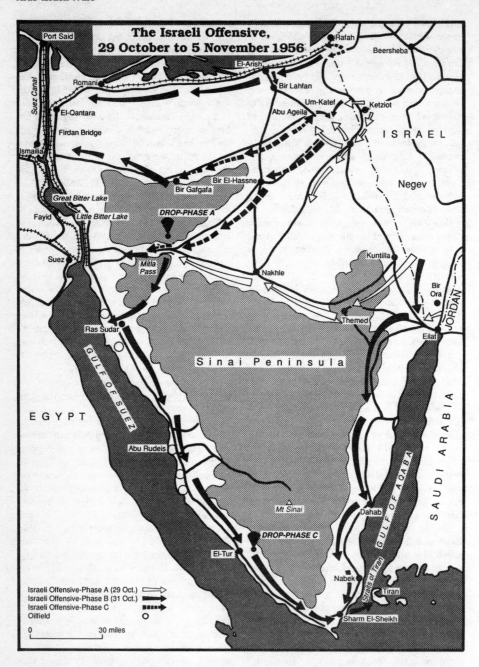

The Israeli Offensive, 29 October to 5 November 1956

Port Said
Suez Canal
Romani
El-Qantara
Firdan Bridge
Ismailia
Great Bitter Lake
Fayid
Little Bitter Lake
Suez
Ras Sudar
Abu Rudeis
El-Arish
Bir Lahfan
Abu Ageila
Um-Katef
Bir El-Hassne
Bir Gafgafa
DROP-PHASE A
Mitla Pass
Nakhle
Rafah
Beersheba
Ketziot
I S R A E L
Negev
Kuntilla
Bir Ora
Themed
Eilat
JORDAN
E G Y P T
GULF OF SUEZ
S i n a i   P e n i n s u l a
Mt Sinai
DROP-PHASE C
El-Tur
Dahab
Nabek
Tiran
Sharm El-Sheikh
GULF OF AQABA
S A U D I   A R A B I A
Straits of Tiran

Israeli Offensive-Phase A (29 Oct.)
Israeli Offensive-Phase B (31 Oct.)
Israeli Offensive-Phase C
Oilfield

0   30 miles

havoc with Israeli dispositions. A massive Egyptian crossing of the Canal smashed the Israeli defences at the same time as Israeli air attacks suffered heavy loss from Russian-type **anti-aircraft** defences. The joint Syrian/Iraqi/Jordanian thrust in the north made headway but was blunted and then thrown back with crippling losses by a desperate defence and a

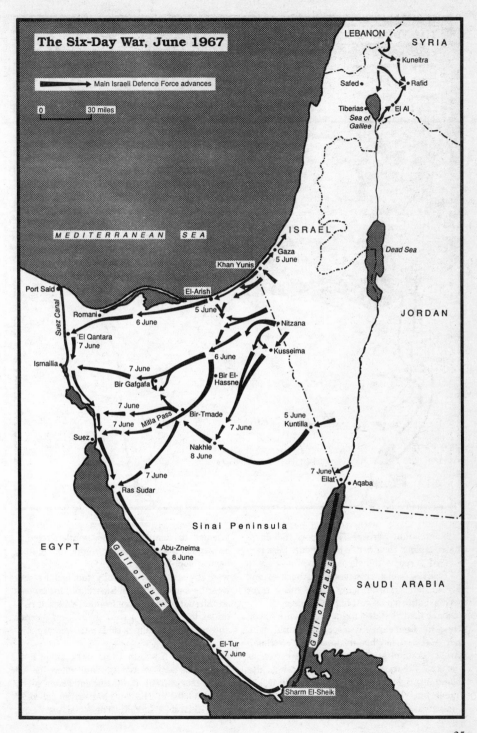

The Six-Day War, June 1967

→ Main Israeli Defence Force advances

0   30 miles

LEBANON

SYRIA

Kuneitra •

Safed •

• Rafid

Tiberias •

• El Al

Sea of Galilee

MEDITERRANEAN SEA

ISRAEL

Dead Sea

• Gaza
5 June

Khan Yunis

JORDAN

Port Said •

El-Arish •

Suez Canal

Romani •

5 June

6 June

• Nitzana

El Qantara
7 June

Ismailia •

6 June

• Kusseima

7 June

Bir Gafgafa •

• Bir El-
Hassne

7 June

7 June

Mitla Pass

Bir-Tmade •

5 June
Kuntilla •

Suez •

7 June

7 June

Nakhle
8 June

7 June
Eilat •

• Aqaba

7 June

Ras Sudar •

Sinai Peninsula

EGYPT

Gulf of Suez

• Abu-Zneima
8 June

Gulf of Aqaba

SAUDI ARABIA

• El-Tur
7 June

Sharm El-Sheik •

25

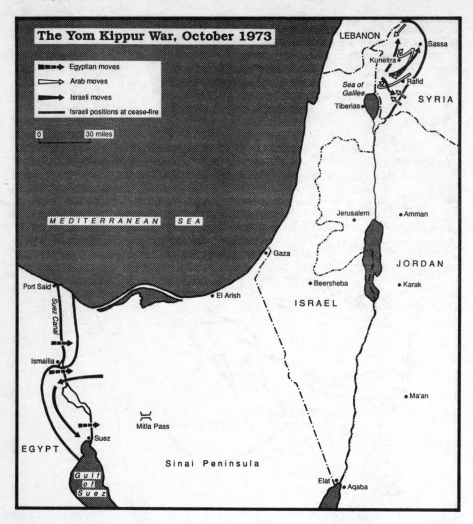

The Yom Kippur War, October 1973

- ▶▶▶ Egyptian moves
- ⇨ Arab moves
- ➤ Israeli moves
- ▬ Israeli positions at cease-fire

0   30 miles

LEBANON

Sassa

Kuneitra

Sea of Galilee

Rafid

Tiberias

SYRIA

MEDITERRANEAN SEA

Jerusalem •Amman

•Gaza

JORDAN

Port Said

Suez Canal

El Arish

•Beersheba •Karak

ISRAEL

Ismailia

•Ma'an

Mitla Pass

Suez

EGYPT

Sinai Peninsula

Gulf of Suez

Elat •Aqaba

brilliant counterstroke. Thereupon the Egyptians, against their better judgement, were persuaded to renew the offensive in Sinai, only to be defeated and themselves flung back to and across the Canal, bringing to an end a three weeks' battle which cost both sides dear.

Since then, despite a formal peace with Egypt, Israel has been engaged in sporadic conflict with her northern neighbours and the Palestinian Arabs. Confrontations emanating as often as not from **Lebanon**, where feuding Arab groups based themselves for raids into Israel, provoked Israel into large-scale action. Unfortunately their invasion of Lebanon on 6 June 1982, in an attempt to demilitarize the frontier regions, only made worse a complex imbroglio. Fighting against sophisticated Syrian forces, and others, was at times heavy. Finally touched by war weariness and a sense of frustration, the Israelis withdrew to the original frontier, which it continues to secure by a strategy of local defence and occasional punitive raids into Lebanon.

Arab Legion. It was in 1920 that Captain F. G. Peake was sent to Transjordan, where he set about reorganizing the inefficient gendarmerie he found there. The force was to be called Al Jeish Al Arabi – literally 'The Arab Army', but more usually rendered in English as 'The Arab Legion'.

The Legion expanded under Peake, and later Glubb Pasha, into a small but highly efficient army which managed to cure the Bedouin of their incessant tribal raiding; it also played its part throughout the Middle East in **World War II**. In 1948 the Legion, now expanded to divisional size, proved to be the only really effective Arab force to resist the Israeli conquest of Palestine. As the modern and well-equipped Jordanian Army it has generally held its own in the numerous **Arab–Israeli Wars** which followed.

Arab Revolts. In 1914 most of Arabia had been part of the Ottoman Empire for some 400 years. The Sultans' hold was somewhat tenuous, the tribal leaders in the remoter areas paying only lip-service to Turkish control while whole countries, such as Egypt, were virtually independent.

In an effort to preserve their independence from central control, the Arabs rose in 1916 under the leadership of Husain Ibn Ali, Sherif of Mecca. At first operations were confined to the Hejaz, where the Arabs, trying to invest Medina, made a poor showing against regular Turkish troops. Britain supplied some equipment and military advisers and gradually the emphasis shifted to disrupting the Hejaz railway, the only link the Turks in Medina had with Damascus. Constant raids on the line tied down large numbers of Turkish troops and it is this aspect of the Revolt which is familiar to most Europeans; and in particular the leadership provided by T. E. **Lawrence**, one of several British officers with the Arab army led by Emir Feisal, the Sherif's third son. Whatever else may be said of this unusual man, Lawrence it was who had the vision to see that the Revolt should be carried northwards. Now amply supplied and supported by detachments of **aircraft** and armoured cars, the Arabs provided an effective flank guard in support of the British advance through Palestine to Damascus. The Sherif's hopes for an Arab kingdom in the area, which had persuaded him to support the British, were not to be fulfilled.

After the war France became the mandatory power over Syria, much against Syrian wishes; most resistance was crushed without difficulty. In the Jebel el Druze, however, it was different. Here the Druzes rebelled against the French administration and laid siege to Suweida, the provincial capital. The relieving column was ambushed and destroyed and it eventually took 7,000 men under General Gamelin to relieve Suweida in September 1925; the province was abandoned to the rebels. A sympathetic rising then took place in Damascus, the city coming under French artillery fire. The rebellion was not finally suppressed until mid-1926.

In Iraq the British assumed the mandate in May 1920; in June the tribes rose in revolt. The rebellion was put down within a few months but soon a new threat appeared in the shape of Ibn Saud's puritanical Wahhabis, who, from 1922, carried out a series of vicious raids on the Iraqi tribes. By the use of aircraft working closely with armoured-car patrols, the country was eventually made safe. In 1932 the mandate was ended and Iraq admitted to the League of Nations.

In Palestine, the very vagueness of the wartime discussions between Sherif Husain and the British made future misunderstandings inevitable; Husain clearly understood that Palestine would remain Arab after the Turks had gone. At the same time the British had in 1917 issued the equally ambiguous Balfour Declaration, which gave the Zionist Jews (though not world Jewry as a whole) the lever they needed to claim Palestine as theirs.

By 1925 Jewish immigration had reached 33,801 and the Arabs were becoming seriously alarmed as they saw their land being taken over by the newcomers. Britain, the mandatory power, seemed to the Arabs to be actively encouraging the Jews when, by 1936, the number of Jewish immigrants had almost doubled. In April Arab resentment boiled over with attacks on vehicles and a general strike. In September an additional division had to be sent from Britain to keep order but, after pressure from neighbouring Arab countries, the disturbances ended in October.

In 1937 a Royal Commission put forward a partition plan which was rejected by most Arabs and reluctantly accepted by the Jews. Disorders quickly followed, the fighting being carried on by gangs of villagers ambushing vehicles, sabotaging the railways and cutting communications. Extra troops were brought in and by mid-April 1939 the rebellion had petered out. But the problem was far from solved. Now, however, **World War II** was looming and the **Israeli fight for independence** would soon begin.

Arakan, Battles of the. The Arakan, which was seized by the Japanese towards the end of their invasion of **Burma** in April 1942, is characterized by steep scrub-and-jungle covered hills overlooking swamps. General **Wavell** initiated the *First Battle* in his desire to restore British morale by seizing the port of Akyab with a tentative advance by the reinforced 14th Indian Division in December 1942. But the advance, hampered by inadequate **logistic** support, was too slow and the Japanese reaction so quick that, at Donbaik in February, the assault force was broken in head-on attacks among skilfully sited field **fortifications**. At which, instead of sensibly abandoning a lost battle, Wavell committed five more brigades which, in March and April, also were flung back by typical Japanese infiltrations. It was Wavell's last battle.

The *Second Battle* commenced in December 1943 when General **Slim**, also with limited forces in XV Indian Corps, advanced on Akyab with the intention of deflecting the Japanese from their impending major offensive against **Imphal** and **Kohima**. Once more deep fortifications had to be overcome in what proved to be costly operations, despite the use of tanks and strong artillery support. The key village of Buthidaung held out while the Japanese brought in a second division with which, starting on 4 February, they counter-attacked in the same old way. But this time the British did not collapse. Instead Slim supplied cut-off units – notably those in the Administrative Area (Admin Box) of 7th Indian Division – by air and poured in reinforcements. Air transport dropped 60 tonnes of supplies a day in the Box, which was under heavy attack. Light aircraft flew out the wounded. In all 3,000 tonnes were lifted to the Arakan by 900 sorties. Then the British counter-attacked the counterattackers, encircling and smashing them before resuming the offensive to such good effect that even more Japanese troops had to be subtracted from the principal thrusts into India. A breakthrough was achieved at Maungdaw as two **Commandos**, landing by sea in the enemy rear, caused further distraction. Had it not been necessary in April to reinforce the Imphal and Kohima fronts, Akyab probably would have been taken.

The *Third Battle*, commencing on 10 December 1944, was the right flank guard of the Allied broad-fronted advance on Mandalay to open the **Burma Road**. Compared with its predecessors it was a walkover, because the defeated enemy no longer had much use for its airfields now the threat to India had been extinguished. But the British did want those airfields, as well as Akyab and all the little inlets and islands down a coastline which pointed to **Rangoon**. The Japanese withdrawal under heavy pressure was masterly against the accumulation of British **amphibious** operations which developed between the evacuation of Akyab on 3 January 1945, the fall of Ramree Island and finally the landing at Taungup on 26 March as prelude to the eventual landing at Rangoon on 2 May.

Arctic convoys. With the Allied supply route to Russia via Persia difficult and those through the Black Sea and the Baltic blocked, the best way was directly to Archangel and Murmansk after the German invasion of 1941. Nature and the Germans in Norway were hostile. Long summer daylight hours aided bombers; long winter nights shielded surface and submarine attacks. The ice pack to northward and the Norwegian coast to the south canalized the approaches while the weather, rarely better than appalling especially in winter, took its toll of both sides.

To begin with the Germans were slow to react to the delivery of aircraft by **aircraft-carrier** and the first eight convoys got through without loss. Only when the land campaign stalled and the long-term potential of the convoys became apparent did opposition increase. **Hitler** not only appreciated the **logistic** implications but worried perpetually over the convoys being a cover, in the aftermath of a few **Commando** raids, for an invasion of Norway. Admiral **Raeder** saw opportunities of sinking Allied warships and merchant vessels in advantageous circumstances. And while the British wanted to tackle enemy warships, they were handicapped by fuelling problems in voyages up to 2,000 miles long.

The eighth convoy in January 1942 was opposed, as were all subsequent attempts, with mounting fury and rising losses, many from air attack. The presence of the battleship *Tirpitz* injected such dread in the British Admiralty that, in July, a misconstrued report that she was at sea prompted Admiral Sir Dudley **Pound** (against advice) to order Convoy PQ17 to scatter – with the subsequent loss to aircraft and U-boats of 23 out of 33 merchant ships. Henceforward summer convoys were avoided.

The next winter convoy was threatened on 31 December by German heavy cruisers, but

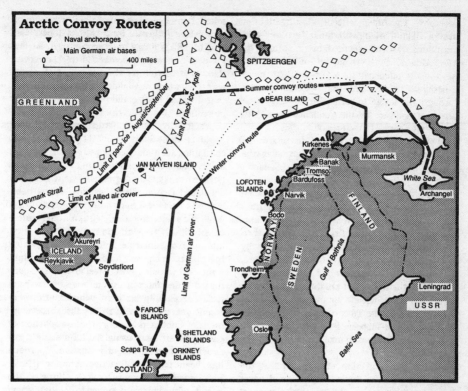

Arctic Convoy Routes

▼ Naval anchorages
✈ Main German air bases
0   400 miles

bold action by British cruisers and destroyers deterred them, making Hitler demand the scrapping of the big surface warships, to bring about the resignation of Raeder and the appointment of Admiral **Dönitz** in his place. Nevertheless, the surface vessels were reprieved and convoys continued to be run, until called off as the crisis of the Battle of the **Atlantic** was reached in March 1943 and the Russians obstructed British radio and air-support facilities.

Convoys were resumed in October with little opposition until, in December Dönitz sent out the battleship *Scharnhorst* with five destroyers. The British were forewarned and at 0840 hours on the 26th their squadron of a battleship, cruisers and destroyers screening the convoy made contact by **radar**. German radar was either not working or damaged at once by fire from a cruiser. *Scharnhorst* manoeuvred and tried again to find the convoy until brought to action by the battleship *Duke of York* whose 14in guns, at 1650 hours, scored hits with a first salvo. Her fate sealed, the battleship was eventually sunk by a combination of shell and torpedo hits.

Convoys would continue against fluctuating degrees of submarine and air opposition but with steadily decreasing losses. Between August 1944 and the end of the war more than 250 ships would carry over one million tonnes to Russia to make a vital contribution to the Soviet war effort.

Ardennes offensive. See **Bastogne, Battle of.**

Argonne, Battles of the. Lying behind the River Meuse, the slopes of the Argonne Forest barricade vital approaches to NE France. Armies manoeuvred under its cover during the **Franco-Prussian War** after Marshal **Bazaine** had retired into **Metz** and prior to the Battle of **Sedan**. In **World War I** it barred the German way prior to the Battle of the **Marne** and became part of the entrenched line.

Not until 26 September 1918 was a serious offensive launched here (by General **Pershing**'s First US Army and the Fourth French Army) to take advantage of the decline of the defeated German armies, which already had started to withdraw. The Allied concentration by night of over a million men with tanks, artillery and munitions was well executed, but the attack, by inexperienced divisions, lapsed into chaos. Renewing the offensive on 4 October with more experienced troops, Pershing battered his way through the forest towards Sedan, only to be denied its capture by the political necessity to hand that honour to the French.

In **World War II** the Argonne was once more, but only briefly, a French bastion after the German breakthrough in May 1940 at **Sedan**.

Armour. While the main offensive weapons such as the sword relied on muscle power for their effectiveness it was feasible to protect the fighting man against them, first with leather then with metal armour, culminating in the heavily protected mounted soldier of the Middle Ages. The widespread introduction of gunpowder spelt the end of the armoured knight, his ponderous protection being useless against the musket or cannon-ball. By the 18th century body armour had virtually disappeared and the soldier, on foot or mounted, had to take his chance on the battlefield.

At sea the protection of ships against the onslaught of the enemy's broadside had never been given serious thought. The thick timbers of the larger vessels were often proof against cannon shot at the longer ranges but this was coincidental, the timbers were there for structural strength. However, over the years naval gun calibres increased remorselessly and in 1859 the French recognized the threat by commissioning the world's first ironclad warship *La Gloire* (5,617 tonnes), closely followed by Britain's HMS *Warrior* (9,137 tonnes). These ships were soon outmoded as **steel** was found to be a more suitable armour material than the wrought-iron plates used in their construction, but from these beginnings it was but a step to the all-steel, heavily protected **battleships** of the 20th century.

On land armour re-emerged during **World War I** in the shape of the infantryman's steel helmet and the **tank** though the plate used on the early vehicles was woefully thin, a direct hit from a shell of any size could be disastrous. In the next two decades, however, as high-velocity **anti-tank** guns began to appear, the need for properly engineered armour plate, in ever-increasing thicknesses, became apparent. The basis for vehicle protection became, and still is,

rolled homogeneous armour, of which manganese steel (invented by the Briton Robert Hadfield in 1882) forms an essential part. At first the designers merely demanded thicker vertical slabs of it to counter the increasing threat. It was the American Walter Christie who realized that a sloped plate could provide much greater protection for a given thickness, as well as encouraging ricochets. The Russians showed what could be done with their T34 tank in 1941, combining as it did well-sloped armour plus an agility markedly superior to that of the current German tanks. The Germans, meanwhile, had developed face-hardened armour – steel heat-treated to give it a hard outer skin to shatter a projectile's piercing cap, with a softer thickness behind to absorb the projectile core as it attempted to penetrate. A form of this approach has been seen in modern Brazilian light armoured vehicles. While steel armour has continued to find most favour, **aluminium** has been used successfully on light vehicles and more recent years have seen in the British development of Chobham armour, the introduction of composite armours using special materials. An Israeli, and more recently Russian, approach has been Explosive-Reactive Armour (ERA). This consists of boxes of explosive hung on the outside of the vehicle, designed to detonate when struck by a hollow-charge projectile, thus disrupting the latter's jet before it can attack the vehicle's main armour (see also **Ammunition**).

For the man himself body armour has re-emerged as a practical proposition with the development of a specially woven lightweight bullet-proof material known as Kevlar. In the form of a sleeveless jacket Kevlar protects at least the vital organs from small-arms fire, with an equally light helmet of the same material set in resin protecting the head, and without seriously hampering the infantryman's movements.

In the air it has long been recognized that the weight penalty would rule out complete armour protection for an aircraft. Vital components, including the pilot, can perhaps be shielded, but only by using extremely expensive lightweight materials such as titanium, used effectively on ground-attack aircraft such as the American A10 and in armed helicopters such as Apache.

Thus, in their different ways, naval and land forces have come full circle. Warships have abandoned armour, relying (like aircraft) chiefly on electronic countermeasures combined with speed and agility to survive – with mixed success in the **Falklands** War of 1982. Armies, having done without armour for 200–300 years, now send almost all their soldiers into battle under armour, with dismounted infantry wearing body armour as of old.

Armoured fighting vehicles. The use of Boydell's steam tractor in the **Crimean War**, with its 'footed wheel' allowing it to cross soft ground successfully, inspired James Cowan's 1855 proposal to mount cannon behind armour on this vehicle. However, it was the appearance of the petrol-driven internal-combustion engine which really pointed the way towards powered vehicles on the battlefield. At first it was the wheeled vehicle which attracted attention – the Simms 'War Car' mounting a 1½-pounder gun and two machine-guns behind 6mm of armour and capable of 9mph was successfully demonstrated to the War Office in 1900. The British Army also carried out a successful trial in 1907 with Hornsby's petrol-driven tractor; the idea of a Major Donohue to mount a gun on it, behind armour, was instantly dismissed.

In the opening stages of **World War I** it was the armoured car, used with success by the Royal Navy in Belgium in 1914 to keep the Germans from the Channel ports, which seemed to be the way to go. Though used with success in Palestine and Russia, the armoured car soon showed its limitations as the war in France ground to a stalemate behind continuous trench lines and barbed wire. It was to break through this obstacle that a new weapon was needed and it was a Royal Engineer who proposed and pushed through to battle in September 1916 the first tracked armoured fighting vehicle (AFV). Colonel Ernest Swinton's idea was an adaptation of the Holt tractor's track (itself developed from Hornsby's original design) to carry a steel box armed with guns and machine-guns across no man's land and the enemy trenches so that the escorting infantry could reach their objectives with minimum casualties. Swinton was supported by a team of inventors of whom Walter Wilson was probably the most important, being the designer of the familiar rhomboidal shape of the early vehicles and of the entirely original track link which was far in advance of the Holt type and which superseded it after difficulties experienced with the first prototype 'Little Willie'. Slow and clumsy as the

original vehicles were, they succeeded beyond all expectations when employed in mass, first at **Cambrai** in 1917 and then even more successfully at **Amiens** in 1918.

With the return of peace in 1918, and its inevitable financial restrictions, the future of the AFV, despite its success in battle, was far from assured. However, there were thinking soldiers to take advantage of it both in Britain (J. F. C. **Fuller**, for example) and elsewhere, who saw the vital mobility conferred by the new weapon plus the need for more agile, though still well-protected, tanks. Despite the difficulties, new designs did appear and it was the British who, in 1920, created an independent armoured force to investigate the tactical potential of armour. By 1927 speeds of 20mph were beginning to be attainable by such key vehicles as the Vickers Medium tank with its barely adequate 8mm of armour, but with a rotating turret and coaxially mounted machine-gun and 47mm main armament and with a radius of action of about 150 miles.

By 1930 military opinion was suggesting that the small AFV of about six tonnes and 12mm of armour was unacceptably vulnerable; but such vehicles were built by the British partly, it was said, for colonial policing but, in reality, because they were cheap. **World War II** would see them off in short order. Nevertheless, some prototypes in the 20-tonne 70mm-armour range did emerge in Britain, France and Russia and it was these vehicles which provided the information needed in the future. America's contribution lay in the forward-looking work of J. Walter Christie with his high-speed (25mph cross-country) AFVs. Particularly impressive was his original big-wheel suspension design which made high speeds possible. His ideas were taken up by Britain and Russia and evolved into a breed of tanks which were to last in service for the next 50 years.

Many of the new German, Russian and Italian models were tried out in the **Spanish Civil War**, which reflected the current debate on the use of tanks. The Russians on the whole favoured deep penetration, supported by artillery and infantry, while General Franco used his German and Italian vehicles strictly in support of the infantry in set-piece attacks.

World War II has been described as a 'tank war' and certainly the AFV assumed a powerful role, first in the rapid German **blitzkrieg** attack on Poland (**Polish campaigns**) and **France** and subsequently in the massive armoured operations mounted by the Allies. Tanks inevitably became better armed, better protected, consequently heavier and larger, but at the same time generally faster.

The Germans, despite having the most powerful tanks deployed in World War II (Tiger and Royal Tiger with their 88mm guns and Panther with its long 75mm), emerged from that conflict convinced by the performance of Russia's T34 that agility cross-country at the expense of protection was the answer; hence the appearance in the 1950s of Leopard 1 with its powerful (British) 105mm gun, 45mph cross-country speed, but with side protection against 20mm projectiles only. The French followed a similar trend with their AMX30. To some extent the Germans have redressed the balance with their Leopard 2 which, using composite armours to provide better protection, has had to sacrifice little of its cross-country capability.

The British, on the other hand, had been deeply impressed with their own AFVs' lack of protection and of a tank gun to match the German 88mm. Their 84mm mounted on Centurion, a tank which continues to demonstrate its ability to take punishment in any number of Middle East wars, was the British answer; but agile it was not. Nor was its successor Chieftain though probably in its time better protected than most. Challenger, with the benefit of improved technology, has once again restored the balance with good protection, a highly effective gun, a computerized fire-control system, better night-fighting aids and with vastly improved mobility.

In the USA tank design went into the doldrums after 1945, US M48 and M60 tanks being adequate for the task but little more. However, the arrival of Abrams, with its 120mm smooth-bore Rheinmetall gun in the M1A1 version, has once more put America into the forefront. The first tank to have a gas-turbine as its main power source, Abrams performs outstandingly cross-country (though with a worryingly high fuel consumption). Its advanced fire-control system (based on a Canadian computer) ensures a very high performance for its armament and its composite armour, derived from the original British Chobham armour, gives it good protection.

The Soviet Union, though lagging behind technologically, has nevertheless produced a whole series of very practical AFVs since 1945, placing emphasis on armament and low silhouette rather than sheer weight of armour. Consequently its AFVs perform well cross-country and are difficult targets, but powerfully armed, typically in the T80 with a 125mm gun.

Though the Russians have concentrated on simplicity of design and have sacrificed crew comfort in their insistence on a low silhouette, they are fast catching up the West with improved fire-control systems, laser range-finders and similar aids. The auto-loader fitted to the T64, T72 and T80 is a world first into service and is a considerable achievement, bearing in mind that the ammunition on these AFVs is separated, with charge and projectile being stored separately in the fighting compartment.

While the main battle tank is the principal AFV in most armies, there has always been a need for the light, fast vehicle for reconnaissance, despite the unfortunate British experience with light tanks in World War II. In British service the armoured car was developed to its maximum potential for reconnaissance, though it came to be realized that the wheeled vehicle, while able to move at high speed on good going, could never match tracked vehicles cross-country. The answer came in the design of Scorpion and Scimitar, whose tracked suspension was able to sustain very high road speeds (up to 60mph) as well as having outstanding cross-country agility (a nominal ground pressure less than that of a man's foot). In the boggy going of the **Falkland Islands** these vehicles were able to go where even the infantry found it difficult. Such vehicles are, inevitably, but lightly protected, often with aluminium armour to save weight, and have only light armament; but they are not intended to fight for information, only to enable their crews to observe and report back safely.

Another category of light vehicle increasingly popular is the armoured personnel carrier and its more elaborate cousin the infantry fighting vehicle. The former is little more than an armoured taxi to carry the infantry safely to the point of contact, while the latter also enables the infantry section to fight from the vehicle. Such AFVs too are only lightly armoured but they are easily adapted for other roles such as command, replenishment, recovery, casualty evacuation and so on.

Since the main battle tank weighs in the

region of 45–60 tonnes, and thus poses certain logistic problems, there is now a trend towards arming light vehicles, typically the infantry carrier, with a very powerful anti-tank weapon, as a tank destroyer. Such variants have the fatal attraction in peacetime of cheapness compared to the huge cost of the modern main battle tank.

Armoured formations. It was one of war's most remarkable aberrations that for three centuries prior to 1914 armoured land forces had virtually disappeared, the development of powerful, accurate firearms and **artillery** having made it virtually impossible for man or beast to carry enough protection. Before **World War I** only some pieces of light artillery had shields, and not until fighting started were a few Belgian and British armed motor vehicles fitted with iron or steel plates. Nevertheless, by 1915 armoured cars (see **Armoured fighting vehicles**) were being built, armoured-car companies formed and investigations into **tanks** begun.

The first combat armoured groups naturally followed normal **Army organization** of sub-units and units. The British, who first used tanks in September 1916, formed companies within their Machine Gun Corps and, at first for training and administrative purposes, created battalions within a specialist Tank Corps. The French, on the other hand, adopted batteries within unit groups, but changed to companies, battalions and regiments when the close infantry support role of tanks became plain to them. Not until the Battle of **Cambrai**, however, were armoured formations first deployed, though here the paucity of **radio** communication between the British units, brigades and HQ Tank Corps, made true command and control tenuous once battle was joined. This remained the case in all later battles after the faster, light machines managed to break through enemy lines but rarely were able to co-ordinate their mobile operations.

Several British and French proposals for what, in due course, would become armoured divisions appeared during and after the war. The ideas of Captain Martel and Colonels **Fuller**, Lindsay and **Estienne** were the most prominent. But every nation (except Britain) persisted in regarding tanks as ancillary to infantry. And it was not until 1927 that the British managed to assemble the Experimental Armoured Force composed of all arms but in which neither the infantry nor the artillery travelled in armoured vehicles.

Indeed, for reasons of economy as well as policy, it would be many years before any army managed to assemble a formation whose combat elements were wholly armoured, a force which nevertheless, in the many different forms tried over the years, would comprise: reconnaissance by armoured cars and light tanks, a striking force of medium and, perhaps, a few heavy tanks, motorized field and anti-aircraft artillery, infantry and engineers, plus the necessary signals, headquarters and logistics elements.

Chiefly the intense debates of the 1930s about the role and composition of armoured divisions revolved about whether, as many British soldiers contended, it was just another cavalry division for reconnaissance, screening and counterstroke, or as the Germans, led by Colonel **Guderian**, decided, a force suitable for almost every phase of war, including direct assault, but with priority to exploiting enemy weakness by manoeuvre and infiltration. In **World War II** the Germans would demonstrate the hitting power of Panzer (armoured) divisions, which combined fire-power with protection and mobility and achieved immense speed and flexibility of operations from their excellent **communications** systems, with **radio** as the key instrument. And although, at first, the proportion of tank to infantry units in a German armoured division was between 5:3 and 4:4, in 1941 the ratio fell to about 2:5 with the original tank strength down from 560 light tanks in 1935 to fewer than 200 in 1941 – a trend copied by others. At the same time armoured brigades dedicated to infantry support were commonplace, though, as tank design progressed, these formations assumed universal roles until, by 1945, so-called infantry tank brigades had disappeared. By then, indeed, the practice of forming armoured corps, and even armoured armies, was prevalent, though actually the armoured content remained relatively low. However, the increasing use of armoured artillery and infantry carriers in larger numbers, a trend made all the more necessary by the introduction of still more powerful artillery and small arms, led inexorably to genuine all-armoured formations, an evolution made essential by the invention of **nuclear** weapons.

Since 1945 numerous powerful **anti-tank weapons**, including less effective infantry weapons, have induced doubts as to armoured formations' viability and prompted recurrent revisions of armoured doctrine and organizations to counter permutations of each new threat. Fundamentally, however, armoured formations remain shaped by long-standing all-arms principles and doctrines which have withstood strenuous tests, notably those of the **Arab–Israeli Wars**. In the meantime all the major military powers possess many armoured divisions and corps for future use.

Army, Organizations of the. In 1850 most armies consisted of the traditional **cavalry, infantry, artillery**, and engineer (see **Engineering, Military**) combat arms with **logistic** support from ordnance and commissariat services. The lowest 'sub-unit' of an arm might be a troop or platoon, of which two or more might be under the command of a squadron or company (if, respectively, cavalry or infantry) or a battery if artillery. Squadrons, companies and batteries came under the command for operational, training and administrative convenience of either a regiment (cavalry, artillery and engineers) or a battalion (infantry) or their own arm, and termed a 'unit'. Two units or more, grouped, became 'formations', called, in ascending order, a brigade (sometimes known as a regiment and usually single arm composition); a division (consisting usually of all arms); a corps; and an army (all, except the last two, being of established composition of all arms). Elements of logistic support would be found at all levels, including the individual soldier with his ammunition and emergency ration. Command, control and **communications** (in modern parlance, C^3) of units and formations would be exercised by the Commander, through his **staff**. Armies would be instructed and administered by War Departments of State which, with the introduction of the **telegraph**, began to exert direct control.

By 1918 the basic organizations had survived, but many specialized arms and services had been created to handle new technology. **Railways** needed operators and engineers; the latest signals **communications** demanded corps as did **aircraft, anti-aircraft** artillery, **tanks** and **machine-guns**. The latter mainly were founded by infantry, the rest by engineers, artillery or newly recruited civilian technicians. **Logistics** also underwent a revolution.

Although at the beginning of **World War I** each arm tended to fight independently of the others, this practice soon gave way to the necessity for all arms co-operation to be controlled by doctrine worked out by the General Staffs, the military colleges and arms' schools (see **Education, Military** and **Training**). In 1917 the Germans took a lead with the institution of ad hoc battle groups assembled as required from units or sub-units of all arms to cope with local situations. Cavalry, infantry and artillery had to co-operate among themselves and with tanks and aircraft – and so on.

Between the two World Wars the new organizations were consolidated and rationalized at the same time as army air corps began to convert to independent **air forces** and, again by German example, joint-service High Command systems were created to make combined use of available resources. Command and control systems proliferated as more special formations, such as armoured, anti-aircraft and airborne divisions, appeared. Voracious demands were made for complex signals facilities, extensive **intelligence** backing and enormous quantities of machinery, to make workable close collaboration within the army and with the other services. The requirements were easy to formulate but often very difficult to arrange without friction when change was rapid and tensions high.

Since 1945, under the pressure of the **nuclear** threat, vast progress with technology and numerous wars, the trend towards established, mixed battle and brigade groups of all arms has been consolidated, despite numerous lapses when, at their peril, arms and services have gone their own way. Joint-service defence departments and headquarters have eliminated some army establishments. But so far only the Canadian Army has found itself wearing almost the same uniform as the Navy and Air Force – an experience from which it was saved after ten long years by the strength of an irrepressible **regimental system** it never abandoned.

Arnhem, Battle of. As the pursuit from **Normandy** gathered pace in August 1944, the use of First Allied Airborne Army to maintain momentum was frequently foiled by circumstances. Early in September Field Marshal **Montgomery** obtained General **Eisenhower**'s consent to drop the entire Army ahead of Second British Army to form a corridor for a strong advance into Holland and northern Germany with a view to cutting off the Ruhr industrial complex and ending the war at a stroke. Planning for Operation Market Garden was rushed; there were too few aircraft to lift the force at once; intelligence about the German defences and, in particular, those at the vital bridges crossing the Rivers Maas at Grave, the Waal at Nijmegen, and the Neder Rijn at Arnhem was indifferent, and **logistic** support tenuous.

On 17 September the bridge at Grave was seized intact at once but failure to follow up initial successes and swift German reaction thwarted the design. The bridge at Nijmegen was not secured until late on the 20th (and could have been blown if the Germans had not been so intent upon preserving it for their own use). The bridge at Arnhem remained in German hands while they wore down the 1st British Airborne Division whose task was to capture it. By then adverse weather had delayed the fly-in of reinforcements and supplies to Arnhem and the Germans had won time to block the Anglo-American forces trying to get through from Nijmegen, and also to launch damaging strokes against the narrow corridor from the south. Inadequate radio communications with the British at Arnhem sealed their fate. Those few who survived were evacuated on the night of 25/26 September leaving behind more than 7,000 of their number. Hope of ending the war had then to be postponed until 1945.

Arras, Battles of. During the **Franco-Prussian War**, the important route centre and fortress of Arras was spared German occupation. But in 1914, prior to the Battle of the **Marne**, it was occupied only briefly, by cavalry, until evacuated on 9 September. In October, however, the Germans attempted to encircle it with a strong thrust from **Vimy Ridge** which nearly succeeded. For nearly four years the city would be pounded by artillery while beleaguered.

Twice in 1915 the French tried, with enormous losses, to drive the Germans back, but made only marginal gains without relieving the city from direct observation by the enemy. In April 1917, however, a large-scale offensive by the British and Canadians, respectively, threw the Germans back six miles to the east and captured Vimy Ridge to the north. This operation, one of the most successful founded upon **artillery** tactics, was also assisted by use of the extensive ancient tunnels under the city which were extended to the front and also to the crest of the Ridge. Once more, during the **Hindenburg**

offensive in 1918, the Germans tried to seize the city but were repulsed within hours. But when the British and Canadians began probing eastwards on 19 August, it was to find an enemy willing to give ground prior to the withdrawal of his entire front in the aftermath of defeat at **Amiens** to the south.

In 1939 GHQ of the British Expeditionary Force (BEF) was located, along with base organizations, in and around Arras. When in May 1940 the German thrust to the Channel threatened the city, in desperation an improvised garrison was assembled in time to repulse General **Rommel**'s 7th Panzer Division on the 20th. At the same time the British 50th Division, with two tank battalions, was ordered, together with French armoured forces, to attack southwards next day against the German flank. Time was short and the attack was launched in some confusion, but it made progress when it cut into Rommel's troops as they advanced round Arras to the west. The Germans suffered heavy casualties and abandoned their attack in order to counter-attack. The British attack was stopped but their garrison held out until withdrawn under pressure on the night of the 23rd/24th. In this battle the Germans suffered badly because their 37mm anti-tank guns could not penetrate the thick British and French armour; it was their dual-purpose 88mm guns which decided the tank battle. Of profounder importance were the psychological shock waves from the rebuff. These contributed to the worries of General von **Rundstedt** and **Hitler** in persuading them to call the halt which made evacuation from **Dunkirk** possible.

Artillery (see also **Anti-tank weapons**). Though rifling and breech-loading for guns were not new, the great artillery controversy of the mid 19th century revolved around those resisting change from muzzle-loaders (ML) and the progressive supporters of breech-loading (BL) guns. Some small BL guns had been tested by the British in 1853 but they were not developed. However, in 1854 W. G. Armstrong put forward his design for a 3-pounder BL rifled gun. He then developed an 18-pounder version which, when fired against a ML smoothbore of the same calibre, was more accurate at twice the range. The BL gun was also much lighter than its $2\frac{1}{2}$-tonne rival.

Though the BL gun had clearly come to stay,

technology was not yet up to the production of really large calibres and very large ML guns continued to be introduced, Armstrong building a 140-tonne weapon in 1879, though not for the Royal Navy. In 1880 a 100-tonne gun supplied to the Italian Navy blew up and this, following a similar accident in HMS *Thunderer* in 1879, finally decided the Admiralty against heavy ML guns. The stage was now set for a rapid development in BL gun design, the problem in the large calibres being largely one of barrel strength to withstand the firing pressures. To meet the requirement the 'wire wound' barrel was developed, the windings enclosing the inner, rifled tube. Later the British developed the system known as 'auto-frettage', whereby the barrel tube was subjected to controlled overstrain which, when released, leaves the outer layers in compression and the inner layers in tension. This process resulted in a much lighter barrel and has found considerable application in modern tank guns where the firing pressures are often very high indeed.

Despite the lack of good British artillery in the **Boer War**, by 1914 the only really new weapon in the British inventory was a 4·5in howitzer; the 13-, 18- and 60-pounder guns were all at least eight years old. Ranges were no more than 6,500m, except for the 60-pounder, which could reach out to 10,300m. The way ahead was indicated by the French quick-firing BL 75mm gun with its lightweight carriage and one-piece (fixed) ammunition, and using a Schneider-designed recoil system later adopted by the British for their 6in howitzer of 1915.

The 1930s saw the wide introduction of the sliding, semi-automatic breech block for field artillery, coupled with brass cartridge obturation, a system which became known as 'Quick-Firing' (QF), as distinct from BL, a term now reserved for the interrupted-screw breech block, requiring special expanding pads fitted in it to provide the essential sealing. Just in time for **World War II** emerged the ubiquitous 25-pounder, replacing both the old 18-pounder and the 4·5in howitzer; arguably the most successful field-piece of that war.

Post-1945, though the towed gun has remained in service in most armies, the ever-increasing demand for mobility and armoured protection has reinforced the trend towards self-propelled field artillery such as the British Abbot (105mm) or the US M107 (175mm).

The need for **anti-aircraft** (AA) guns became apparent in **World War I**, though the Germans had foreseen the need as early as 1871 and in 1908 with their Ehrhardt anti-balloon gun. However, it was not until 1936 that the 3·7in AA gun appeared in British service, paralleled in Germany by the slightly less powerful 88mm AA gun. The very rapid-firing 40mm Swedish Bofors gun was a formidable weapon against the ground-attack fighter and was widely used by the British. Since 1945, the very high-flying bomber has made the large AA gun obsolete, but there remains the need to engage low-flying aircraft and helicopters. Improved technology has coupled rapid-firing 35 or 40mm weapons, often mounted in pairs, with surveillance and tracking radars, the whole system mounted on the same armoured vehicle, to provide defence of the forward areas.

The arrival of the **rocket and guided missile** has meant that naval guns now have a mainly air-defence priority. To meet this threat a 20-rounds-per-minute 6in gun (also capable of shore bombardment) and a high-velocity 120-rounds-per-minute 3in AA gun were developed for the Royal Navy, both later replaced by the 4·5in Mark 8, the first naval gun to have a muzzle brake, deflecting via baffles some of the propellant gases, thus tending to carry the barrel forward and hence limiting recoil.

Guns for naval and military use have by no means become obsolescent but their modern use is perhaps more specialized and is complementary to the tactical guided missile.

Asia Minor, Battles of. Throughout the declining years of the Ottoman Empire its predatory neighbours nibbled at frontiers and coastline. On 30 November 1853, at the beginning of the **Crimean War**, six Russian battleships, armed with new shell-firing guns, set ablaze 12 Turkish ships in Sinope harbour in what was the final battle between 'wooden walls'. In that same war fighting also took place on the mountainous frontier with Armenia, notably at the Russian siege of Kars where the Turks held out until starved into surrender in 1855.

During the **Russo-Turkish War** of 1877–8 the Russians again besieged and took Kars, pressing on to Erzerum before peace was arranged. And throughout **World War I** campaigning was almost ceaseless on this front, beginning in November 1914 when the Turks endeavoured

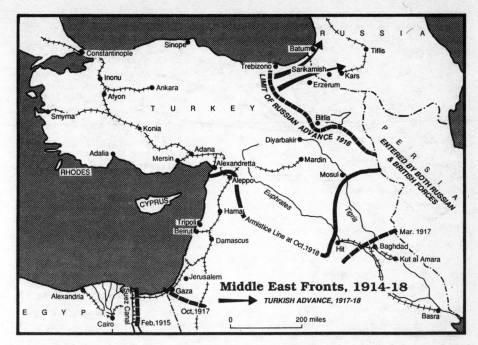

Middle East Fronts, 1914-18

TURKISH ADVANCE, 1917-18

0   200 miles

to recapture Kars and became embroiled at Sarikamish with a superior Russian force. Battle casualties, frost-bite and desertions so ate away the Turkish strength that within a few days only 18,000 of the original force of 95,000 staggered back to Erzerum. Fighting in the region of Lake Van went on in 1915, culminating in a well-conducted Russian winter offensive, the smashing of the Turkish army of 250,000 men and the capture of Erzerum and Trebizond, defeats which a subsequent Turkish counter-offensive in 1916 failed, with heavy loss, to reverse.

Russian collapse in revolution enabled the Turks to recapture all their previous territorial losses in 1918 and advance almost unopposed into the Caucasus where, with German assistance, they seized the oilfields. But within a few weeks all was forfeit when Turkey was compelled by the British victory in Palestine to seek an armistice and the remainder of their collapsed empire stood in peril of engulfment.

Now under the leadership of General **Kemal Atatürk**, the Turks fought Greeks and Armenians in the **Greek–Turkish War**. Between 1920 and 1922, Kemal fought a series of defensive battles, linked to astute diplomacy, which, by his defeat of the Greeks at Afyon in August 1922 and his

subsequent advance to Smyrna and Constantinople (Istanbul), brought the war to a victorious conclusion and earned him the Turkish presidency with the honour of being called the Father of modern Turkey.

Atatürk, Kemal. See **Kemal Atatürk.**

Atlanta, Battles for. In the aftermath of victory at **Chattanooga** in 1863, General **Sherman**'s next objective was one of the hubs of the Confederacy: Atlanta. In 1864 his army of 99,000 outnumbered the Confederates under General Joseph Johnston by 40,000 and was considerably better supplied. Sherman's advance along the railway axis, dispersing his strength to guard it as he went, was characterized by its successive low-cost turning movements and Johnston's brilliant delaying actions which, over $2\frac{1}{2}$ months, restrained Sherman to an average of one mile a day. But when manoeuvred out of the strong Kennesaw Mountain position on 2 July, and threatened on the outskirts of Atlanta, he was dismissed. General John Hood now took command, but his desperate counter-attacks merely postponed the inevitable. Yet it took Sherman a month's attacks and cavalry raids, culminating in the wheel of the mass of his army round

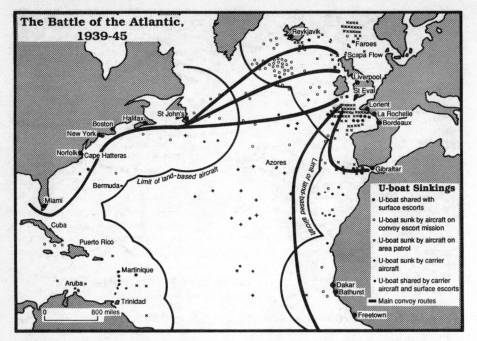

The Battle of the Atlantic, 1939-45

Reykjavik
Faroes
Scapa Flow
Liverpool
St Eval
Lorient
La Rochelle
Bordeaux
St John's
Halifax
Boston
New York
Norfolk
Cape Hatteras
Azores
Gibraltar
Bermuda
Limit of land-based aircraft
Miami
Limit of land-based aircraft
Cuba
Puerto Rico
Martinique
Aruba
Trinidad
Dakar
Bathurst
Freetown

0   800 miles

U-boat Sinkings

- U-boat shared with surface escorts
- U-boat sunk by aircraft on convoy escort mission
- U-boat sunk by aircraft on area patrol
- U-boat sunk by carrier aircraft
- U-boat shared by carrier aircraft and surface escorts
- Main convoy routes

Atlanta to cut its communications, before Hood evacuated the city on 31 August. This was a shattering blow to the Confederacy with its loss of railway and arms manufacturing and of a vital prestige communications centre. Most important of all, the way was opened for Sherman's celebrated and decisive **March to the Sea**.

Atlantic, Battle of the. With fewer than 40 operational U-boats and 15 major surface warships available in 1939, Germany could not mount decisive attacks in the Atlantic against the Anglo-French navies which controlled the Western approaches. But when France collapsed and almost the entire western European coastline fell into German possession in June 1940, the strategic balance changed. Henceforward British convoys had to run the gauntlet of enemy **aircraft**, **submarines** and surface raiders which enjoyed almost unlimited access to the Atlantic. The Germans could also lay **mines** and bomb ports with comparative ease, while the British found their **anti-submarine** resources stretched beyond the limit.

However, aircraft which at first enjoyed some successes were soon checked, though continuing to provide valuable reconnaissance. And although the German battleships, cruisers and other raiders did get loose and sink several ships

in 1940 and 1941, their depredations were cut short when the battleships *Scharnhorst* and *Gneisenau* were damaged and shut up in French ports, the *Bismarck* sunk in May 1941, and their supply ships rounded up. Admiral **Dönitz** believed that his system of U-boats hunting in 'wolf packs', which were centrally controlled by encoded **radio** signals, would provide the answer; and that the convoy escorts could be defeated by night attacks on the surface. Pack attacks began in September 1940 and in 1941 sank the great majority of 1,299 ships put down by various means for the loss of 51 submarines.

But in 1942, although the U-boats continued on top (despite losses of 128 with many experienced commanders), countermeasures were taking their toll. Direction-finding of radio signals was rendering them vulnerable to surface and air attacks as the increasing number of sea and air escorts received improved **radar** and more effective depth charges. Both sides benefited sporadically from reading their opponents' codes and each enjoyed successes due to the other's stupidity or won by their own guile. It was the obdurate unwillingness of Admiral **King**, US Chief of Naval Staff, to implement the convoy system in 1941 which gave the U-boats their happiest of 'happy times' against unescorted shipping off the American coast in 1942. And it was a well-timed change of compromised codes which enabled Allied convoys to conceal their movements in the approach to the invasion of French **North Africa** in November 1942 at a time when the U-boats still were on top.

The turning-point arrived between February and May 1943. Dönitz, with 240 U-boats, could keep 50 at sea at once supplied by so-called 'milch cow' U-boats. In February they sank 48 ships and lost 22 U-boats, in March it was 105 (72 of them in convoys) against 16 – a seemingly disastrous Allied set-back which suggested convoys might have to be abandoned, thus almost conceding defeat in the one battle which could lose the Allies the war. Suddenly in April the pendulum swung the other way; that month only 25 ships went down and 16 U-boats were missing; figures which worsened from Dönitz's point of view in May when 46 U-boats failed to return and he was forced to withdraw his packs from mid-Atlantic and tacitly admit a defeat. Worst of all, Dönitz was unaware of the reason – a combination of closer-knit Allied defences based upon the use of small escort **aircraft-carriers** to cover the so-called mid-Atlantic gap; the latest 10cm radar fitted to long-range Liberator bombers which carried searchlights to illuminate and attack surfaced U-boats; improved **Sonar** and voice radio to assist the more skilled commanders of the hunting groups. Try as the Germans would to overcome their difficulties, their losses remained high while Allied shipping increased in tonnage as the massive US building programme got into its stride. Far too late, Dönitz attempted to hasten the development and production of the snorkel, homing **torpedoes** and the faster U-boats which could outmanoeuvre escorts. Only slowly did he appreciate the 10cm radar menace and never the penetration of radio security which divulged so much that was vital to the enemy.

In the last few months of the war, amid defeat off the **Normandy** coast and after many Channel ports had been captured by the Allies, the new U-boats did prove their worth. But the convoys kept sailing and U-boats were still sunk in large numbers, bringing the total from all causes in all theatres of war to 785 out of 1,162 built.

Atom bomb. It is one of the great ironies that those intimately involved with the discoveries leading to the manufacture of the atom bomb were concerned purely with the healing and peaceful possibilities of their knowledge: the discovery of radioactivity by Becquerel in the 1890s; of radium by the Curies; of X-rays by Röntgen; and work on alpha and beta rays by Rutherford in 1900. It was Hahn and Strassman in Germany in 1938 who showed that uranium atoms could be split. From this gradually developed the realization that a chain reaction would follow from the released neutrons in turn splitting other atoms, thus releasing even more neutrons plus immense quantities of energy.

By 1939 war with Germany was imminent. Though the theory was known in Britain, scientific opinion was somewhat sceptical of the practicality of applying it to a bomb to release all this energy. However, two physicists in Birmingham – Frisch and Peierls – were able to support the theory with figures showing that a 'super bomb' was feasible and official interest was aroused. Similar work had been going on in America and in 1943 Robert Oppenheimer led a team of Europeans and Americans to produce a practical weapon. By the summer of 1945 a bomb weighing about 4,000kg, in which a few grams of uranium could, by shooting one subcritical mass into another, initiate fission, was ready. On 6 August this device (code-named 'Little Boy') was dropped on Hiroshima and three days later 'Fat Boy' followed it on to Nagasaki. Explosions resulted equivalent to igniting 20,000 tonnes of TNT, coupled with a literally blinding flash and a devastating shock wave, with radiation effects from the deadly gamma rays still being suffered by the survivors half a century later (as indeed Frisch and Peierls had predicted in their original paper). The world had entered the age of nuclear war. See also **Hydrogen bomb**.

Austria's east-front campaigns, 1914–17. One of the great miscalculations of **World War I** was Field Marshal Count Franz **Conrad von Hötzendorf**'s belief that the Austro-Hungarian Army was capable of waging war against both Serbia (**Serbo-Austrian battles, 1914–16**) and Russia. Sound though Conrad's strategy may have been of attacking Russia in the east, in order to take the strain off Germany while she attacked in the west, events in August and September showed that his forces, even with German help, were inadequate in numbers, equipment and logistics.

Thrown back at the outset in Serbia, the Austrians nevertheless persevered (against Germany's wishes) in attacking the Russians in Poland in mid-August. Groping northwards

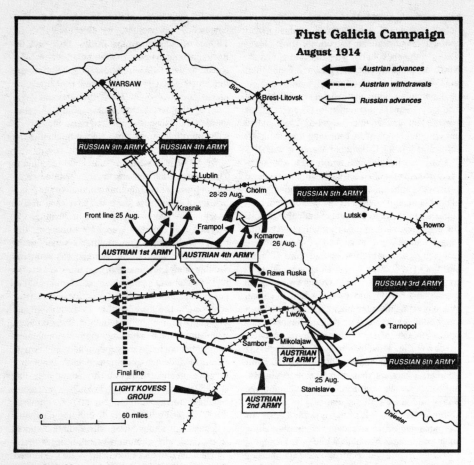

First Galicia Campaign

August 1914

Austrian advances

Austrian withdrawals

Russian advances

RUSSIAN 9th ARMY

RUSSIAN 4th ARMY

WARSAW

Brest-Litovsk

Lublin

28-29 Aug.

Cholm

RUSSIAN 5th ARMY

Krasnik

Front line 25 Aug.

Frampol

Komarow
26 Aug.

Lutsk

Rowno

AUSTRIAN 1st ARMY

AUSTRIAN 4th ARMY

Rawa Ruska

RUSSIAN 3rd ARMY

Lwów

Tarnopol

Final line

Sambor

Mikolajaw

AUSTRIAN
3rd ARMY

RUSSIAN 8th ARMY

LIGHT KOVESS
GROUP

AUSTRIAN
2nd ARMY

25 Aug.
Stanislav

0   60 miles

Dniester

towards Lublin and Chełm in search of Russian forces whose mobilization they assumed would be incomplete, they collided instead, on 26 August, with strong Russian forces at Komarow, even as it became apparent also that two Russian armies were moving to threaten Lemberg (Lvov), thus cutting into their rear. So, at the very moment the Germans, in East Prussia, were on the verge of defeating the Russians at **Tannenberg**, the Austrians were forced to retreat in disorder in Galicia after a series of intricate and costly encounter battles in the vicinity of Komarow and along the river Zlota Lipa.

This Austrian defeat at the so-called **First Battle of Warsaw**, along with the invasion of Galicia, encouraged the Russians to assemble seven armies, under Grand Duke Nicholas, in the bend of the River Vistula for an invasion of Germany. But neither side was fully beaten and

both the Germans and the Austrians were intent upon pinching out the vast Russian salient in Poland – by no means easy in bad weather in a land of extremely poor communications. Austrian attacks in Galicia made only limited progress in October. But the German offensive under Field Marshal von **Hindenburg** in mid-November, which crushed the Russians at Lodz during the **Second Battle of Warsaw**, altered the balance of power.

Henceforward Austro-Hungary's role on the East Front would be subservient to Germany's. Rout in Serbia in December 1914 (**Serbo-Austrian battles, 1914–16**), and the need to confront the Italians (**Italian–Austrian campaigns, 1915–18**) when they entered the war on the Allied side in May 1915, deprived their forces in Galicia of strength enough to engage in major independent offensives. Had not the Russians also been in a parlous logistic state and the

Germans, for their own purposes, prepared to tackle the Serbs, as well as take the offensive against the Russians in Galicia, things might have gone hard for Austro-Hungary in 1915. As it was, a series of attritional battles throughout the winter of 1915 merely confirmed that, while German troops could defeat larger Russian forces, the Russians had the edge over the Austrians, who were in steepening decline. The combined German–Austrian offensive of 2 May 1915 at **Gorlice**, which retook Galicia and caused a Russian collapse and withdrawal across the entire breadth of the Russian front, benefited only from supporting Austrian involvement. Indeed it was with some reluctance that Conrad participated at all, so pressing were the demands of the Serbian and the new Italian front.

When the last great Russian throw was made in June 1916, it was the Austrians who failed to withstand the thrusts which are known as the **Brusilov offensive**. Once more Russian troops entered Galicia – to the satisfaction of **Romania** who, bribed by the Allies, took the opportunity of declaring war on the Austrians, for whom they had no great affection. And once more it had to be the Germans to the rescue. Nevertheless, the Russian threat to Austria was almost spent. After the outbreak of the **Russian Revolution** in March 1917 there would be one last kick by the Russian Army in Galicia, on 1 July, against an Austrian army well 'corseted' by German formations. Poorly trained and largely demoralized Russian troops were massacred by an expectant enemy and then relentlessly chased back into their own country. Yet even in these favourable circumstances, Austrian combat performance was far from satisfactory, the ineptness of their commanders and staffs bringing about the collapse of an entire army before inherent Russian weakness prevented exploitation. It was a distinct relief to the Austrians when an armistice with Russia was concluded in December.

Austro-Italian War. See **Italian wars of independence.**

Austro-Piedmontese War. As an act of the **Italian wars of independence** the campaign of 1859, provoked by Napoleon III, was as much a French attempt to harm Austria as to further the Piedmontese/Italian cause. Provocative moves by Piedmont, with French connivance, engin-

eered Piedmont's mobilization, followed by Austria's, leading to war on 26 April and a rather sluggish Austrian invasion on the 29th. This gave the French time to send 54,000 troops and, after an Austrian defeat by the Piedmontese at Palestro on 30 May, to thrust into Lombardy. There followed a collision at Magenta on 4 June when a numerically superior French Piedmontese force pushed back the Austrians in an affair which was notable for costly head-on assaults. It was also the first battle in which the **railway** delivered enough men but insufficient supplies close to the battlefield.

The Austrian abandonment of Milan in an orderly retreat to Venetia came to a halt at Solferino where, reinforced, they turned to fight on 24 June. Here two large armies, each in the region of 160,000 men, made charge after charge on narrow fronts supported by intense artillery fire. Seemingly mesmerized by the **tactical** and **logistic** importance of the railway, both sides abandoned manoeuvre and, as if out of control, poured fire upon each other. At the end of the day there were 17,000 French and Piedmontese losses and 22,000 Austrian – the latter's survivors drawing off in some disorder, leaving their exhausted opponents behind.

Napoleon, for fear of loss of political advantage apropos Italy, called a halt. Piedmont had won Lombardy and brought Italy one expensive step nearer unification. Of great military importance, Solferino marked a turning-point in soldiers' approach to **logistics** and society's attitude to the humanitarian aspects of war. The breakdown in supplies when an enemy cut the railway tracks, or when incompetence, matched with inexperience, left full railway trucks unloaded, owing to lack of labour or of wagons to remove stores and munitions, demanded radical rethinking by the Staffs. The appalling plight of the wounded, who usually were left uncared-for where they fell, was dramatically brought to public attention by Henri Dunant in his book *Un souvenir de Solferino*. Coming on top of the recent Press exposures of administrative breakdowns in the **Crimean War**, this forced many democratically elected politicians to correct medieval practices which were at last unacceptable. In 1864 sixteen nations met at Geneva to form the **Red Cross** International Committee dedicated to the relief of suffering.

Austro-Prussian War. This war, sometimes known as the Seven Weeks War, was yet another phase in Otto von **Bismarck's** policy of unifying the German states, less Austria, under Prussian dominance. Goaded into political errors and a premature **mobilization** on 21 April 1866, Emperor Franz Joseph was forced into war with Prussia on 21 June, the day after Italy (see **Italian wars of independence**) also had declared war in the next phase of her struggle for independence.

This was General Helmuth von **Moltke's** opportunity to test the efficiency of the Prussian Army, which the General **Staff** had reshaped, and to demonstrate his ability to control mobilization and **railway** movements by **telegraph** from Berlin. To begin with he was to discover many defects. The planned convergence of his three armies on the intended battlefield was misdirected because **intelligence** of Austrian intentions and movements was incorrect. To make matters worse, his army commanders tended to diverge intemperately from his broadly drafted instructions. At the same time, they commandeered **logistic** transport to exacerbate troubles in an already disorganized service. Austrian movements were tentative and hampered by logistic difficulties too. Indeed, neither side made good use of the railways once mobilization was almost complete.

When, partly by chance, the collision occurred at Königgrätz (Sadowa) on 3 July, the issue was very much decided by chance. A telegram telling the Second Prussian Army to attack did not arrive, leaving the other two armies to attack unsupported and on too narrow a frontage. Well-directed Austrian **artillery** fire, followed up by infantry counter-attack, stopped the Prussians, who might have been defeated if the Austrian commander, General Ludwig von Benedek, had exploited the situation with **cavalry**. As it was he gave the rebuffed Prussians enough time to recover and for a messenger on horseback to ride 20 miles and send Second Army into an attack which hit the Austrians in the flank and rolled them back in disorder.

Superior Prussian infantry fire-power won the battle against an enemy still armed with muzzle-loading rifles; 20,000 dead and wounded Austrians and Saxons, plus 20,000 prisoners out of 215,000, have to be compared with about 15,000 Prussian casualties out of 220,000. Chaotic Prussian logistics left them stranded on the battlefield, unable to pursue the beaten enemy until transport had been sorted out. It was left to diplomacy to bring an end to the war

on 5 July, although at sea the Battle of **Lissa** was fought before peace was declared on the 27th.

AWACS. The acronym for an Airborne Warning and Control Station, an American requirement during the **Vietnam War** to provide surveillance, warning, fighter and missile control over extensive areas. AWACS aircraft flying at 15,000ft have been equipped with **radar** developed to give, for example, a horizon range of 300 miles, making it possible to identify enemy aircraft taking off and, with computer assistance, quickly arrange interception by fighters or missiles. AWACS also can direct strike aircraft to their targets, deep in hostile terrain, simultaneously bypassing detected defences – as was performed for the Indian Air Force by a Russian Moss during the **Indo-Pakistan War** in December 1981.

Axis Powers. What evolved into an anti-Communist alliance between Germany, Japan and Italy was initiated in November 1936 when the Germans and Japanese signed the Anti-Comintern Pact. They undertook 'to consult with one another on the necessary preventative measures and to carry these through in close collaboration'; and in November 1937 were joined by Italy because Benito **Mussolini** was convinced that Germany and Japan would win the forthcoming **World War II**.

In practice the Axis partners tended to consult and collaborate only when it suited them. For example, Italy shrank from declaring war on Britain and France at Germany's side in September 1939; **Hitler**, in October 1940, concealed from Mussolini his intention to occupy Romania, as a preliminary to invasion of Russia (**Russo-German wars**) in 1941; Mussolini did not tell Hitler he was going to invade **Greece**; Hitler withheld from Japan his intention to invade Russia; and the Japanese not only concluded a non-aggression pact with Russia in April 1941 but stuck to it and, at the same time, concealed from Hitler their plans to attack the Americans and British in December 1941.

Nor at any time throughout the war was there frank joint military planning between the partners. The Germans rode roughshod over the Italians; the Italians imposed a drain upon German resources; and the Japanese and Germans paid little more than lip-service to Plan Orient, the tentative scheme to co-ordinate their merging advances towards India and the Middle East.

B

Badoglio, Field Marshal Pietro (1871–1956). An Italian artillery officer with active service experience against the Ethiopians in 1896 and the Turks in 1911, Badoglio achieved distinction as a general during **World War I** and signed the armistice in Italy's behalf in 1918. Twice Chief of the General Staff in the 1920s and promoted Field Marshal, then Governor of Libya from 1928 to 1933, he became C-in-C Italian forces in Ethiopia in November 1935 with the task of revitalizing the stalled invasion of that country. Again Chief of Staff in 1940, he resigned in December in the aftermath of the poor Italian performance in Greece and North Africa. He regained prominence in July 1943 as Prime Minister, after plotting the fall of **Mussolini** and prior to declaring a divided Italy at war against Germany on the Allied side.

Baghdad Pact. Signed in 1955 by Britain, Turkey, Iraq, Iran and Pakistan to strengthen Middle East security against Russia, the principal weakness of this political/military agreement lay in Egypt's unwillingness to join. Extremely suspicious of British intentions and subsequent American involvement, while also coming increasingly under Russian influence, the Egyptians persuaded Syria and the Yemen to form a rival United Arab Republic (UAR) in February 1958. Five months later an Iraqi Army revolt, with UAR complicity, overthrew the Hashemite Iraqi monarchy (assassinating the king in the process); and in March 1959 Iraq withdrew from the Pact as she also accepted Russian arms. Thereupon the remaining members of the Pact changed its name to the Central Treaty Organization (Cento) – whose ineffectiveness became increasingly apparent as Middle East conflicts intensified.

Balaklava, Battle of. An attempt by the Russian forces to capture the British base at Balaklava, and thus break the Allied siege of **Sevastopol** and, perhaps, decide the **Crimean War**, brought on this battle for control of the vital Vorontsov ridge, commanding the Balaklava–Sevastopol road, on 25 October 1854. Russian attempts with 3,000 cavalry to exploit their initial, almost unopposed advances to the Fedyukhin heights were checked by the 93rd Highlanders, whose position (to quote a witness) was secured at a range of about 800 yards by 'a ravine deep enough to swallow up the whole lot of them had they charged'. But the Russians were thrown back by a most determined charge by 900 men of the Heavy Cavalry Brigade. It is, however, the subsequent charge of the 670-strong Light Cavalry Brigade, along with the legend of the 'thin red line' (created by the journalist William Russell for the glory of its commander, his kinsman Sir Colin Campbell), for which the battle is renowned, a futile charge which might have lost even more than the 40 per cent of those engaged had it not been for a supporting charge against the Fedyukhin heights by the French Chasseurs d'Afrique. As it was, the Vorontsov ridge remained in Russian hands.

Balkan Wars. The so-called First and Second Balkan Wars of, respectively, 1912–13 and 1913 disguise the fact that, at almost any time, turmoil gripped this part of Europe as the result of racial and religious differences and the decline of Turkish power. The *First War* was a blatant assault by the nations of the Balkan League (Bulgaria, Serbia and Greece) to eliminate Turkey's last European possessions while she

European Turkey, Bulgaria, Romania, Serbia, 1912

was involved in a war against Italy (**Italo-Turkish War**) in Libya. Some 310,000 League troops, plus 30,000 Montenegrin guerrillas, moved into Macedonia and Thrace in October 1912 against 240,000 Turks. The Turks counter-attacked and fought well, but were outgeneralled and squeezed by converging invasions from north and south. At Monastir, on 5 November, the Serbs and Greeks routed the Turks, who lost some 20,000 men; and the Greeks reached Salonika on 8 November. The Bulgarians drove the Turks back on Adrianople (which they besieged) and advanced to Constantinople. But they failed to take the city before a short-lived armistice was arranged on 3 December. When hostilities resumed in the New Year, in the aftermath of the collapse of the Turkish government, the Turkish military débâcle continued with the fall of Yannina to the Greeks, with 30,000 prisoners; of Adrianople to the Bulgars and Serbs, with 60,000 prisoners; and of Scutari to the Montenegrins.

Peace was patched up in a settlement which involved the major European powers (who took sides) and included the creation of Albania but allowed Turkey to retain a foothold in Europe at Constantinople. Yet at once the members of the League and the Romanians were at odds with each other over frontier alignments in an all-too-typical Balkan imbroglio. On 28 June, King Ferdinand of Bulgaria, in the hope of a quick victory prior to attacking the Romanians, ordered an attack upon the Serbs and Greeks. But it was too late when, on 1 July, he cancelled it. The *Second War* had started because the Army had already advanced. Without delay the Romanians and the Turks now attacked Bulgaria, with catastrophic results for the Bulgarians who had to sue for an armistice with their recent allies of the League. A year later the conflict would be reignited by **World War I**.

Bastogne, Battle of. It was of the utmost importance to the continued momentum of the German Ardennes offensive in December 1944 that the route centre of Bastogne should be captured without delay by General Hasso von Manteuffel's Fifth Panzer Army. This became all the more urgent when General Sepp Dietrich's Sixth SS Panzer Army, with the task of making the main thrust towards Antwerp, failed to break through. Somewhat reluctantly, General Eisenhower committed his two airborne divisions from reserve, sending the 101st by road to Bastogne, which, on 18 December, was closely threatened. 101st US Airborne Division's reinforcement of Bastogne raised the garrison to 18,000, an encircled force whose presence disrupted German logistics and pinned down troops who were needed for the drive to the River Meuse. On 22 December, an optimistic German call for surrender was rejected by General McAuliffe with the reply 'Nuts!' Attacks were fought off in the keen expectation of early relief by two corps from General **Patton**'s Third US Army, diverted northwards on Eisenhower's instructions.

Next day bad weather, which had prevented air activity, cleared, and, as Allied aircraft hit the Germans, essential supplies were parachuted into Bastogne. On Christmas Day, with Sixth SS Panzer Army halted in the north and Fifth Panzer Army finally checked short of the Meuse, von Manteuffel ordered a last attack upon Bastogne, appreciating that, in conjunction with Patton's approach, it placed his entire Army in jeopardy. But his columns were repulsed as supplies continued to pour in until, next day, Patton's men arrived and **Hitler** acknowledged defeat. Even so, Hitler tried to revive the offensive and, for almost a week, while the hard-pressed remnants of his armies struggled back, ordered a succession of futile attacks on battered Bastogne.

Bataan, Siege of. When disaster overcame General **MacArthur**'s plan to defend the **Philippine** Islands in December 1941, he was compelled on the 23rd to order withdrawal into the prepared bastions of the Bataan peninsula and **Corregidor** Island. But the disaster at **Pearl Harbor** had made impossible the pre-war concept of relief by the US Pacific Fleet, while an influx of 20,000 refugees and serious deficiencies in supplies, which at once put the garrisons on half-rations, precluded prolonged resistance. Moreover, the American forces had suffered badly in their retreat and were without air support.

American-Filipino withdrawal into the peninsula on 2 January 1942 was followed up by Japanese attacks on the forward defences on the 9th. Ferocious fighting, with heavy losses on both sides, accompanied the advance of the Japanese, who forced back the defenders to their rear positions, which were penetrated on the 26th. However, amphibious Japanese landings in the rear were hampered by motor **torpedo-boats** and wiped out by counter-attacks. Exhaustion was mutual. The Japanese could not renew the assault until 3 April, after MacArthur, on President **Roosevelt**'s orders, had departed, leaving General Jonathan Wainwright in command.

The Japanese, under General Masaharu Homma, began their final attack against half-starved and diseased troops (of whom about 25,000 of the original force of 130,000 were in hospital). Resistance crumbled rapidly after an immediate breakthrough. About 2,000 men escaped to Corregidor and a number retired to the jungle as a nucleus of a guerrilla force. On 9 April Wainwright surrendered.

Three years later the Americans sealed off a Japanese garrison holding the peninsula and, by bombardment and landings, neutralized attempts to prevent Manila Bay's use by shipping.

Battle-cruiser. The concept of a warship that would combine the hitting power of a **battleship** with the speed and light armour of a **cruiser** seems to have originated in the mind of Émile Bertin of France in 1896. But the first example of such a vessel was not laid down until 1906 by the British, under the influence of Admiral Sir James **Fisher**, who believed speed gave protection. HMS *Inflexible*, with its 41,000hp steam turbine engines, had a speed of 25 knots and the capability, with eight 12in. guns, of engaging battleships. But a mere six inches of side armour amidships, tapering to four inches at bow and stern, left it vulnerable even to an armoured cruiser's 8in. guns. By contrast Germany's battle-cruisers, of which *Von der Tann*, laid down in 1907, was the first, had ten inches of armour amidships and 11in. guns which were as effective as the British 12in.

Although two British battle-cruisers proved their worth, in December 1914 at the Battle of the **Falklands**, by sinking two German armoured cruisers, the vulnerability of the class was exposed at the Battle of **Jutland** when three were destroyed by magazine detonation from penetration by gunfire, as compared with only one German battle-cruiser lost from numerous hits, any one of which might have been fatal had not the German magazines been safer and British shells inferior.

Battle-cruisers went out of fashion once the necessity for thick armoured protection of high-value battleships was proven. Three were retained by the British, of which HMS *Hood* blew up after hits from the German battleship *Bismarck*, in May 1941, and HMS *Repulse* went down under Japanese air attack later that year off Malaya.

Battleship. In 1859 the French launched the steam-powered *La Gloire*, an ironclad, timber-built warship of 5,617 tonnes, armed with 36 163mm guns, designed by Stanislas Dupuy du Lôme. With its ability at 13 knots to out-manoeuvre and outshoot all wooden sailing vessels, its appearance was likened to that of 'a lion among a flock of sheep'. Within two years the British replied with *Warrior*, an all-iron warship with 18 inches of timber backing and superior armament and speed. The dominant 'capital ship' which, from the early 1870s, would be termed 'battleship' had arrived and with it a rampant naval technological race.

Although the desire to increase speed and improve mechanical reliability was strong, endeavours to augment armament to overcome the latest **armour**, and increase protection to counter better **artillery**, were prime. In 1861, John Ericsson's *Monitor* demonstrated the advantages of a rotating turret, although it had been preceded in action by Captain Cowper Coles's turreted raft, *Lady Nancy*, during the **Crimean War**. Turrets, however, were incompatible with masts and it was almost as much due to them as to improvements to engines that, in 1871, the 9,330-tonne HMS *Devastation* was launched – the first battleship without sails, with four guns in two turrets.

There were diversions from the main stream of development, such as the fitting of rams in the aftermath of the sinking by ramming of the Italian flagship at the Battle of **Lissa** in 1866. Mainly there was seen a rapid increase in size and weight of guns, up to 17·75in. calibre, mounted in turrets of improved design in steel frames, and armoured ships fitted with **torpedoes**. At the end of the century battleships such as the Americans employed in the **Spanish–American War**, and those used in the **Russo-Japanese War** of 1904, weighed anything from 8,000 to 15,000 tonnes, with 12in. guns and speeds of up to 18 knots. But combat demonstrated how vulnerable they were below the water-line from mines and torpedoes; quite as much as above when guns, after enormous ammunition expenditures even at ranges down to about 6,000 metres, managed occasionally to hit their targets.

In 1906 came a fresh revolution, the launching by the British, under the genius of Admiral **Fisher**, of HMS *Dreadnought*. This 21,250-tonne steam **turbine** ship with a speed of 21 knots, thick armour and ten 12in. guns in five turrets, made all existing battleships obsolete. Moreover, the system of main armament control from a central director, fed with data (from an optical range-finder) transmitted to the guns, promised significant improvements in the accuracy of shooting. Copied by all other nations, the dreadnought-type battleship, along with the thinner-armoured **battle-cruisers**, was steadily improved and built in large numbers, dominating naval warfare until 1940. But no amount of armour and internal watertight compartments could secure them from the underwater attacks which caused the majority of their losses during the two **World Wars**. By 1918, within two years of the battleship-dominated Battle of **Jutland**, fears of mine and torpedo, along with the threat of air attack, were having a crucial impact on design.

To thickened top armour, against bombs, had to be added batteries of **anti-aircraft weapons**, despite the reluctance of many sailors to recognize the air menace. When the great expense of a battleship-building race, instigated by the Japanese, led to the Washington Naval Treaty of 1922, with its limitation of 5:5:3, respectively in battleship tonnages, to the USA, Britain and Japan, with 1·67 each to France and Italy, it merely promoted extensive scrapping of obsolete vessels and the construction of fewer modern warships, together with **aircraft-carriers**. Moreover, despite a restriction of 35,000 tonnes for capital ships, this limit was flagrantly breached at the start of the 1930s arms race when, as articles of faith in the battleship, the Italians laid down two 41,000-tonners, the Germans two 40,000-tonners and the Japanese the mighty 65,000-tonne *Yamato* and *Musashi* with their 18·1in. guns.

Nevertheless, although Britain, France and Germany had between them in 1914 57 dreadnoughts (with 22 much improved types building, and 91 pre-dreadnoughts), in 1939, including Italy, the USA and Japan, the main combatants' totals were 56 (obsolescent and modern) battleships (with 24 building), which in many respects was an expression of the escalating cost of warships whose size and complexity, in order to improve their chances of survival and striking power, had risen beyond sensible bounds. For not only were such high-value targets expensive to man, service and protect whenever they put to sea, their combat-effectiveness also was suspect. True the initial effect of their existence as part of fleets 'in being' was considerable. But soon the air threat made its presence felt, notably over the North Sea and in November 1940 at Taranto when carrier-borne British torpedo aircraft sank or crippled three Italian battleships in port. And although Germany's three so-called pocket-battleships of 12,000 tonnes and her two 32,000-tonne battleships scored limited successes against commerce and managed to pin down disproportionately large elements of the Royal Navy, the dispatching of the *Bismarck*, after she sank the battle-cruiser *Hood* (as the first of only two examples of battleship gunfire being exclusively responsible for sinking one of its kind in this war), was a body blow to the theory of the 'unsinkable capital ship'.

Pearl Harbor, the sinking of the *Duke of York* and *Repulse* off Malaya, the Battles of the Coral Sea and Midway simply restated the battleship's decline. Even when, in the first night battle conducted with radar on 12 November 1942, the US battleship *South Dakota* crippled by gunfire the Japanese battleship *Kirishima*, the *coup de grâce* was scuttling by the latter's crew. So it was perhaps symbolic that the last battleship versus battleship action of all should have ended in a blaze of fire on 25 October 1944, during the climactic Battle of Leyte Gulf, when the guns of six US battleships pulverized and capsized the Japanese *Yamashiro* in 30 minutes at 22,000 yards. For the rest of the Japanese battleship fleet it was to be destruction by other means.

Scrapping began again after 1945, although Britain, France, Russia and the USA clung to a few battleships, the latter employing them for offshore bombardment during the Korean War. By the 1980s, however, the USA alone possessed them, and went so far as to take some out of mothballs, fit them with the latest missiles, besides their 16in. guns, and deploy their impressive presence adjacent to such trouble spots as the Lebanon, where they fired occasionally, with dubious political impact, on land targets.

Bazaine, Marshal Achille (1811–88). A French infantryman of humble birth and equivocal character who rose from the ranks to fame by virtue of his combat leadership in North Africa, Spain, the Crimean and Austro-Piedmont wars, and the Mexican War of 1861–3. Promoted for political reasons, on the back of his heroic reputation, to provisional command of the Army of the Rhine in July 1870, his incapacity for high command made him unequal to inspiring a disorganized force, whose logistics and morale stood on the brink of disaster before a shot was fired in the Franco-Prussian War. Wounded and depressed at the outset, he soon withdrew with 140,000 men into the fortress of Metz, where he lay militarily dormant while negotiating with the enemy, prior to surrendering on 28 October. Later sentenced to death as a traitor, but then exiled, he died in penury.

Bazooka. The first of a long line of infantry hand-held anti-tank weapons; so named from its likeness to a home-made trombone used by radio comedian Bob Burns, the bazooka was the brainchild of a Colonel Skinner, US Army. With no funds and a staff of one, he designed and made a tube-launched rocket using the M10 hollow-charge grenade as a warhead. Demonstrating his device at Aberdeen Proving Ground in 1942, the bazooka was so effective that it was instantly accepted for service and first used in the North African campaign of World War II. The bazooka continued in service until the Korean War of 1950, when its small warhead proved inadequate against the North Koreans' T34s. It was superseded soon afterwards by the 3·5in. rocket-launcher.

Beams. See Radio and Radar.

Beatty, Admiral Sir David (1871–1936). A dashing British naval officer who won a reputation and advanced promotion for bravery and ability in Egypt and during the Boxer Rebellion. As a protégé of Winston Churchill, he took command of the battle-cruiser squadron in 1913 and led it during the Battles of Dogger Bank and Jutland. In December 1916 he became C-in-C of the Grand Fleet and took the surrender of the German High Seas Fleet in 1918. Appointed First Sea Lord from 1919 to 1927, it fell to him to reorganize the post-war Royal Navy and, as British delegate, help formulate the crucial Washington Naval Treaty.

Beda Fomm, Battle of. As the culmination of the first phase of the North African battles of World War II, after General Richard O'Connor's Western Desert Force had triumphantly advanced from the Egyptian frontier past **Tobruk**, an opportunity arose to intercept the remnants of the routed Italian Tenth Army, as it withdrew from Benghazi into Tripolitania. Ordering the 6th Australian Division to follow the coast road from Derna to Benghazi, O'Connor sent his few remaining armoured vehicles, artillery and infantry in 7th Armoured Division across the desert from Mechili to cut the coast road at Beda Fomm. The advanced guard arrived ahead of the Italian main body on 5 February 1941. It established a road block which was reinforced a few hours later by tanks and guns that began a succession of harassing attacks against a vast jam of halted Italian vehicles.

Next day, with but 45 light and 22 medium tanks and a single artillery regiment, plus some anti-tank guns, the British (who throughout lived hand to mouth for ammunition and fuel) mixed harassment with fending off numerous Italian attempts to break through. Fortunately for them the Italians were slow to assemble and never properly co-ordinated their attacks. Nevertheless there was a moment when the delayed arrival of a few more medium tanks, along with reports of Australians approaching from the north, only just tipped the scales. Next morning a last despairing Italian thrust was thwarted at the road block before white flags announced the surrender of 25,000 prisoners and a mass of equipment including more than 100 tanks, 216 guns and 1,500 wheeled vehicles. It was a 'complete victory', as O'Connor said.

Berlin, Battles of. On the night of 25/26 August 1940, 29 out of 81 British bombers which set out to bomb the German capital caused slight damage and a few casualties in retaliation for an accidental German attack on London the previous night. Both raids had a profound psychological effect on the **Battle of Britain** by diverting the Germans away from attempting to destroy the Royal Air Force (RAF), into indecisive tit-for-tat raids against London. In the years to come Berlin would figure prominently as part of the Allies' strategic bomber offensive (see **Bombing, Strategic**).

At about 600 miles from the main RAF bases in England, Berlin was difficult to reach and, as its defences improved, a target to be avoided during the shorter summer nights. A Russian raid on 7 August 1941 was a rarity. When on 7/8 November 1941 the RAF sent 169 bombers, 21 were lost, partly owing to bad weather. But the British persevered because Air Marshals Portal and **Harris** believed it might be possible, with the combined British and American bomber forces, to knock Germany out of the war by destroying Berlin. In the autumn of 1943, despite recent expensive and none-too-rewarding visits to the city, and without positive evidence that German morale was fragile, permission to try was given on the strength of Harris's boast that 'We can wreck Berlin ... if the USAAF will come in on it. It will cost between us 400 to 500 aircraft. It will cost Germany the war.'

Between 18 November 1943 and 24 March 1944, 581 Allied bombers were lost or damaged beyond repair out of 9,111 sorties, plus 16 nuisance raids, against the city. Attacks were often ineffectual owing to the inadequacy of electronic **navigation** devices. German civil resistance was stiffened by improved shelters and harsh measures against 'traitors'. Industrial production rose instead of falling. Only the US Army Air Force's new long-range escorting fighters won a significant victory for the Allies by routing the German fighter force during the daylight operations.

Berlin was raided many more times, but its final destruction was at the hands of the eight Russian armies under Marshal **Zhukov**, which reached the outskirts on 22 April 1945 and surrounded it on the 25th. It took seven days of intense street fighting to overcome a garrison of over half a million men, which yielded 1,500 tanks and about 11,000 guns and mortars.

Bibliography of war. The number of books and documents generated by war is so immense as to give mental indigestion when listing them, which is mainly why, in addition to the tyranny of available space, this Encyclopedia's bibliography (see page 361) has been made select and concise – little more than a bibliography of bibliographies, in fact.

Modern fashion provides extensive bibliographies and notes to many learned works on war: Professor Paul Kennedy's *The Rise and Fall of the Great Powers* has, for example, 40 pages of one and 80 of the other. The problem of evaluating such a profusion of evidence remains, however, a fundamental task. Few bibliographies are analytical or critical; rarely are there guarantees of integrity or perfection. Far too many military histories are uncritical regurgitations, tending merely to perpetuate legends and myths.

Since research into documents as often as not begins among private collections or in libraries or the great national archives, the task is both laborious and expensive. Normally, even when an index of documents is provided, their contents remain obscure, with the result that much time can be lost, with consequent frustration of all but the most dedicated researchers working in ideal conditions. Ignorance of languages also bedevils. Glance at the majority of military histories in English, for example, and it will be seen that information from works in foreign languages is mainly from all-too-familiar ones picked from notably few popular translated publications. At least one honest historian of repute has admitted that his extensive bibliography is restricted to books in English.

There are people who assume that official histories, based predominantly upon public records, are repositories of truth. But official historians, like, for example, regimental historians and biographers, are subject to vested interests, national security and the laws of libel – hazards which are harder to overcome the more contemporary the events happen to be. Some overlook the fallibilities of war diaries, which are sometimes written in the aftermath of battle or under stress; under political and emotional pressures; or suffer misguided 'weeding' of 'irrelevant' material; and from genuine desires to avoid giving pain to individuals. It is unchallenged, for example, that parts of the British official history of **World War I** were deliberately equivocal for political reasons, and that nearly all Allied histories of **World War II** avoided divulgence of the breaking of the principal enemy **codes and ciphers**. And it is noteworthy that, while American official histories of that war are profusely authenticated with footnotes, the British, apart from a few unofficial, hand-annotated copies, are not – with the notable exception of the recent, extremely revealing five-volume *British Intelligence in the Second World War*. Easier freedom of access to official records will illuminate as well as complicate a labyrinth.

Biological warfare. There are records from earliest times of attempts to induce disease in the ranks of the enemy – by throwing dead animals into wells to poison the water and catapulting rotten carcasses into besieged cities in the hope that the starving inhabitants would eat them and succumb. As medical knowledge improved and the real causes of disease were identified and viruses isolated, the possibility of projecting these viruses into enemy lines to do him damage was often considered. As recently as the **Korean War** in the 1950s there was a propaganda ploy from the Communist side that the Americans were employing 'germ warfare' by dropping bombs containing a deadly virus on the North Koreans.

All this was entirely without foundation, not least because at that time no one had found satisfactory solutions to the three fundamental problems facing anyone planning to use a projectile to carry a suitable organism: (1) how to protect one's own side from contagion when filling the bomb or shell; (2) how to keep the organism alive after filling until required for use; (3) how to protect the organism from the shock of impact (plus, in the case of an artillery shell, the shock of discharge), so that it could do its deadly work. Quite apart from any moral questions which might prevent a government from pursuing the development of biological weapons, for many years these practical considerations proved to be too daunting.

Typically, biological agents are bacteria, rickettsia and viruses and they could be disseminated by spray, shell or rocket, in the form of a liquid suspension or as a powder. The effectiveness depends on the incubation period of the organism, which could be a number of days. The respirator may provide a defence if it is closely fitted, but vaccination, if practical, would be the best way. However, the real problem for the defender lies in detecting the biological cloud in sufficient time to take evasive action; since the human senses could not detect such an attack, some form of air sampling would be necessary.

By 1969 improvements in microbiology had allowed the USA to develop biological weapons (later unilaterally renounced and destroyed) and the USSR is known to carry out military and civil defence training on this subject. Furthermore, such agents could now be manufactured with comparative ease and without sophisticated technology. The threat therefore remains, though the USA, Britain and the Warsaw

Pact have all signed the UN convention banning production and use of biological weapons.

Bishop, Air Marshal William, vc (1894–1956). A Canadian who began flying as an observer in the Royal Flying Corps (RFC) but retrained as a fighter pilot in 1917. Bishop rapidly developed as an excellent shot and daring tactician, often flying seven hours a day to hunt the enemy with fanatical zeal to add rapidly to his number of kills. He won the MC, DSO and VC in quick succession, the latter for a single-handed dawn raid on a German airfield when he shot down three aircraft and damaged others on the ground. In a final operational tour he shot down 25 aircraft in 36½ hours' flying time over a period of 12 days to raise his score to 72 and win the DFC. Staying in the RCAF after the war, he was eventually made an Honorary Air Marshal.

Bismarck, Prince Otto von (1815–98). As prime minister of Prussia from 1862, Bismarck's way of unifying the German nation and pursuing an adventurous foreign policy, contrary to the instincts of his king, was founded on 'blood and iron'. In nine years, with the encouragement of the Army and its Chief of Staff, Helmuth von **Moltke**, he had, by aggressive diplomacy and war, seized Schleswig-Holstein from Denmark, won the **Austro-Prussian War** of 1866 and the **Franco-Prussian War** of 1870. By 1871 he had acquired Alsace-Lorraine from France (thus unnecessarily exacerbating ill will between the two nations), and engineered the creation of the German Empire, under the Prussian Kaiser Wilhelm I, with himself as Chancellor. Until dismissed by Wilhelm II in 1890, von Bismarck dominated Germany, developed her overseas Empire and played a leading role in European politics with the series of interlocking, and often secret, treaties which became major factors in the start and course of **World War I**. Ever flexible in his policies, trickery lay at the heart of his tactics whenever necessary for the current aim.

Bismarck Sea, Battle of the. Immediately after their withdrawal from **Guadalcanal**, the Japanese falsely believed that Allied air power had been weakened in the South-West Pacific. They therefore attempted to reinforce Lae in **New Guinea** with a convoy of eight transports escorted by eight destroyers and fighter patrols.

On 2 March, 16 US B17s sank one transport from 6,500ft and next day co-ordinated attacks by Australian and US low-level bombers, escorted by fighters, put down four destroyers and six more transports. At the same time 20 Japanese fighters were destroyed, for the loss of three US fighters and a B17. US motor **torpedoboats** torpedoed the remaining transport that night to complete the débâcle.

Bismarck, **Sinking of the.** For a raid against British shipping in May 1941, the Germans sent the cruiser *Prinz Eugen* into the North Atlantic, supported by the new battleship *Bismarck* to deal with battleship convoy escorts. They were intercepted by two battleships in the Denmark strait off Greenland on 24 May when HMS *Hood*, hit within five minutes by two salvoes of eight 15in guns, blew up. *Prinz Eugen* then parted from *Bismarck*, which shook off the surviving enemy battleship, after inflicting severe damage, but herself receiving a hit which caused a fuel leak and forced her to make for Saint-Nazaire.

Tracked by British cruisers and hit by an air-launched torpedo on the 25th, *Bismarck* temporarily shook off pursuit until found again by a flying boat on the 26th when 600 miles from Brest. Damaged by two more air torpedoes, which retarded her and enabled two British battleships to get within range, she was sunk on the 27th by a combination of heavy gunfire and two further torpedo hits from a cruiser, when her pursuers had barely enough fuel to get home.

Blitzkrieg. This German word for 'lightning war' was probably coined by Adolf **Hitler**, prior to 1939, as propaganda in support of a political bluff to conceal Germany's, as yet, military unreadiness for total war. As originally propounded by J. F. C. **Fuller** and then practised in Poland (**Polish campaigns**) and subsequent campaigns, it stood for the rapid disruption of enemy defences by a combined air and mechanized land offensive. Strokes against key targets and communication centres, deep in the enemy rear, were executed at high speed with the intention of stunning a surprised nation into submission. Linked to deception, to **propaganda**, and to **fifth column** activity, the sheer pace and violence of co-ordinated attacks by all means available was a formula commanders had long desired, but been denied by inadequate signal communications and logistic services.

Later the British shortened the word to 'Blitz', as the name for the various day and night air attacks upon their country.

Blockade. Usually regarded as the naval equivalent of a siege, the act of 'surrounding or blocking of a place by enemy to prevent entry and exit' has, since the 17th century, been governed by civil laws as well as military rules. The 'right of blockade' was established by the British, in 1650, to implement the interception of neutral shipping and seizure of cargoes – acts which have usually been disputed in prize and international courts.

Sevastopol was both blockaded and besieged, although supplies and men slipped through – as is usually the way in maritime situations.

The blockade of the Confederacy during the **American Civil War**, though decisive in the long run, by denying essential materials, could never be complete. To begin with the 90 obsolete warships at Federal disposal could not stop determined blockade runners reaching ports along such a vast coastline. But while access from the hinterland and Mexico, particularly while the River Mississippi was in Confederate hands, was easy, their initial underestimate of the blockade's potential for denying cotton to European manufacturers, in order to apply political economic pressure, was a mistake. Eventually the blockade inflicted fundamental damage on Confederate **logistics**. Yet the hazards of a 'state of blockade' such as the Federals had to declare in order to comply with the law were made plain by delicate negotiations with objecting foreign statesmen and traders, while wrestling with the military problem of a dispersed blockade net being contradictory to the principle of concentration.

Few wars of the 19th and 20th centuries have been without a blockade if one side or the other possessed a navy. Once the Spanish squadrons had been destroyed in the Philippines and Cuba at the start of the **Spanish–American War**, the Spaniards had to recognize the implications without an official 'state' being declared. Throughout the **South African War** (1899–1902), even European nations with Boer sympathies were reluctant or unable to run the British blockade – although medical supplies were allowed through. And while any Russian hope of blockading Japan evaporated at the start of the **Russo-Japanese War**, the ability of the Japanese to impose a blockade as well as a siege of **Port Arthur** only shortened its garrison's exist-

ence without embarrassing the relieving forces, who were supplied by railway from the west.

Allied attempts to blockade the Central Powers during **World War I** raised extremely complex problems exacerbated by the 1909 Declaration of London. This treaty included a list of strictly military contraband which could be seized from neutral ships, and a humanitarian 'conditional list' of supplies, for the civil populace, which were excluded if not consigned to the enemy's armed forces, or a department of state or through an enemy port. Thus Germany could legally import strategic goods through neutral countries, such as Holland and Denmark, and put Britain and France in the wrong when they interfered. But when the British, in 1914, declared the entire North Sea a 'military area', where **mines** would be laid, and the Germans said in 1915 they would destroy every merchant vessel found in British waters, the way was prepared, by stages, for unrestricted submarine warfare in 1917.

It was impossible for either side to impose an absolute blockade, although the plight of the Central Powers progressively worsened as Italy, Greece, Romania and the USA joined the Allies, and as the Allies worked out indirect blockade measures, such as placing embargoes on facilities for neutral shipping and on the movement of strategic cargoes, and by blacklisting those who broke the blockade. At the same time, vital materials, as well as food, were rationed by all the belligerents to help defeat the blockades – of which the system finally evolved by the Allies was a major factor in the defeat of the Central Powers .

Within the different circumstances of **World War II** both sides tried blockade by very similar methods to those of 1918, with the notable addition of **aircraft** to both help make and break sieges. Yet, although Britain and the **Axis powers** were embarrassed or brought close to collapse by blockades, their respective countermeasures in breaking the enemy cordon, by rationing and control of distribution, and by use of synthetic materials, including oil fuel, kept Germany going until she was all but overrun and Japan in the fight until the **atom bomb** made her prospects hopeless.

Blockades of varying intensity and effect continue to be imposed, sometimes by direct action to prevent supply to belligerents, such as during the **Korean War**, the **Vietnam War** or the

Falklands War, often by quicker-acting threats or embargoes on weapons, fuel or financial subsidy, such as by the USA against Britain and France during the **Suez** War of 1956; and by the superpowers in relation to the **Indo-Pakistani wars** and various outbreaks in Africa, the Middle East and South-East Asia. But ways round are often discovered to frustrate a way of war which rarely is decisive on its own and usually inflicts considerable misery.

Bock, Field Marshal Fedor von (1880–1945). A talented member of the German General Staff who was lucky to escape trial in 1921 for collusion with the murderous, so-called 'Black Reichswehr', and later rose to command Army Group North in the **Polish campaign**. His handling of all arms then and in the 1940 **West Europe** and 1941 Russian campaigns (when, in command of respectively, Army Groups B and Centre) was brilliant; and it was not his fault the Allied armies escaped from **Dunkirk** or that **Moscow** did not fall. Yet he was among the majority who bowed to Adolf **Hitler** and was in decline when, ostensibly for ill-health but really so he should not be blamed for Hitler's mismanagement, he was relieved of command in July 1942.

Boer War. See **South African wars**.

Bomber aircraft. Almost any **aircraft** can drop bombs, and the first to do so, in the 1911 **Italo-Turkish War** and at the beginning of **World War I**, were not designed for the purpose. The sturdy, multi-role French single-engine 'pusher' Voisin 1 of 1914, with a bomb-load of 132lb, was worthy of the title, as was Igor Sikorsky's mighty four-engine tractor biplane ordered by the Russian government in May 1914, or the twin-engine tractor British Handley Page 0/100, ordered towards the end of 1914 as 'a bloody paralyser of an aeroplane'. But with speeds below 100mph, ranges of a bare 300 miles with bomb-loads little more than 1,000lb, the majority even of purpose-built machines had but nuisance value. Moreover, from altitudes over 12,000ft, crews deprived of oxygen were as unlikely to find the target as to hit it with rudimentary sights, while smaller, single-engine machines which attacked at the lower altitudes were vulnerable to ground fire as well as **fighter aircraft**.

By 1919 it was apparent that airships had failed; ships suffered but little from bombs or from air torpedoes; industrial and civil targets had been harassed without loss of production; and only in the land battle had bombers made their presence seriously, but never decisively, felt. On the other hand, the bombers in production with ranges close to 1,000 miles, bomb-loads up to 6,500lb and adequate defensive weapons, were a strategic threat – as technical innovations in the next two decades show. By 1939 wood-and-fabric machines had been succeeded mostly by all-metal twin- or three-engined 'medium' bombers with speeds over 250mph, ranges between 1,000 and 2,000 miles, and bomb-loads up to 4,000lb. Some of these were adapted from civil airliners; for example, the tri-motor Junkers 52 transport was used for bombing during the **Spanish Civil War** to contribute to a false impression that airliners could be converted successfully into bombers with little modification.

Although **strategic bombing** was dreaded, none of the medium bombers in service in 1939 were suitable for the task or available in sufficient numbers unaided to overwhelm, except by terror, a reasonably defended nation. Bombs were of poor quality; defensive fire inadequate by day; **navigation** aids and aiming devices, despite experiments with radio beams by the Germans, unsatisfactory. But these machines could inflict much damage to targets and morale by day, provided strong fighter cover was given and the weather was good, while the latest dive-bombers, favoured by the Americans, Japanese and Germans, were demonstrably effective against ships and small targets in the battle zone. In practice, the bombers of 1939 were of great tactical value but of strategic significance only against a cowed enemy.

The British and to a lesser extent the Americans believed, however, in strategic bombing. Both developed four-engined bombers with speeds approaching 300mph, ranges in the neighbourhood of 1,500 miles, bomb-loads of between 8,000lb (the US Boeing B17F) and 18,000lb (the British Lancaster B1), operational ceilings of around 30,000ft and power-operated multi-machine-gun turrets for self-defence. But, as the British quickly discovered, even the best-armed bomber could not long survive against fighters by day. When operating beyond the range of escorting fighters, they were compelled to fly by night, with inevitable bombing inaccuracy, until electronic navigation and aiming aids and techniques were introduced in 1941. American bombers suffered similarly when attempting to fight their way through in massed formations at high altitude, until forced to curtail their operations and await long-range fighters in 1944.

The bombers in service in 1945 were a vast improvement on those of 1939, although the results of light dive-bombers (notably against ships) and medium, twin-engined machines against tactical targets from the lower altitudes had been improved more by techniques than performance. Day bombers depended on carefully planned missions, to avoid ground defences, as well as upon fighter escorts. Low-level attacks were carried out increasingly by bomb-carrying fighters. But the appearance of the medium British Mosquito, with a speed of 397 mph, a ceiling of 34,000ft and a range of 1,370 miles with a 5,000lb bomb-load, which electronic aids helped it to plant accurately, was as revolutionary as the fully pressurized American B29 heavy with its speed of 357mph, ceiling of 30,000ft, a range of 3,250 miles and with a 20,000lb bomb-load. The misemployment by the Germans, as a bomber, of their jet-engined Me 262 fighter, with its speed of 541mph, simply signposted the future.

The invention of the atom bomb assured the heavy bomber's existence into the 21st century, despite the appearance of rocket missiles (rockets and guided missiles). Huge multi-engined machines with global range, when assisted by in-flight refuelling, guarded by electronic countermeasures, could deliver not only nuclear weapons but also very large loads of high-explosive bombs, as did American B52s in the Vietnam War. They also could launch missiles from beyond the range of enemy air defences and by utilization of the latest configurations, such as with the American B1 supersonic bomber, hamper radar detection. But the atom bomb and smart munitions which could destroy a small target, without resort to area attacks, also increased the potency of supersonic multi-role aircraft. Not only can they carry weapons of immense destructive power, they have the pilot's intelligence to call upon when high-technology machinery fails.

Bombing, Strategic. Before World War I it was forecast aircraft might have an economically decisive effect on war. But German bombing of various cities, including Paris and London, caused little panic among the civil populace, and merely provoked equally ineffectual retaliatory raids by the French and British. In fact not until 1921, with General Douhet's The Command of the Air, was a coherent doctrine of strategic bombing stated in public. Douhet concurred with Generals Trenchard and Mitchell that terror attacks on cities by independent air forces, with high explosive, incendiary bombs and gas (see Chemical warfare), could destroy a nation's will to resist – opinions which, prior to 1940, created an exaggerated, world-wide dread of the bomber.

Lurid reports of the bombing of undefended populations in the Chinese–Japanese War, the Ethiopian–Italian War, Ethiopian (Abyssinian) Wars and the Spanish Civil War were exploited by Axis Powers' propagandists to bully politicians who feared the air threat into making unwarranted concessions. Yet, ironically, while none of the Axis powers created a genuinely independent strategic air force to reinforce their bluffing, the Americans and, most of all, the British intensified the atmosphere of terror by accepting that 'the bomber would always get through', using this as a pretext to create bomber forces as a deterrent (see Deterrence) against enemy strategic bombing.

This confidence trick was exposed in the course of World War II. Like Madrid, which withstood a siege of two and a half years until March 1939, Warsaw had to be taken by land assault in September 1939 with bombing used only in support. And while West Europe's resistance was undeniably weakened by Germany's tactical air force in 1940, that same force was unable, unaided, to win the Battle of Britain. Yet, despite evidence of the British people's resistance to heavy bombing, both the British and American air force commanders managed to convince their leaders that the Axis could be knocked out of the war by strategic bombing. Lacking plausible evidence, they still claimed that structural damage and casualties would be far greater than was the case, and that the populace would panic. Bomber enthusiasts also, perhaps deliberately for partisan reasons, underrated the power of the defence and overlooked how difficult it was to find and hit targets by night – as became vital once it was demonstrated that day bombing took place only by courtesy of air superiority won by **fighters**.

Between 1940 and 1945 the British Bomber Command had mainly to concentrate on dropping large tonnages of bombs on populated areas by night since its heavy bombers could barely survive by day. Meanwhile the US bomber force was in trouble by day until it acquired long-range fighters to defeat the enemy's fighters. Indeed, it was the fighters' victory over Germany in 1944 which alone made possible continuance of both night and day offensives, the British also being compelled to send night-fighter escorts with their bombers. Electronic **navigation** and aiming aids played crucial parts in getting bombs on target, to the point when area bombing became almost obsolete. Debate over which targets to attack was confused by the problems of destroying them and doubts about the effect. Not until oil and transport targets were concentrated upon in 1944 did German production collapse. Nor did their people crack, despite the dropping of half a million tonnes of bombs causing a million casualties and destroying 3·6 million homes at a price to the Allies of 15,516 heavy bombers alone against only 2,012 German fighters.

Likewise the devastation of Japan's flimsy cities by fire bombs, and of Hiroshima and Nagasaki by **atom bombs**, only hastened surrender in August 1945 by providing a face-saving excuse for military defeat.

Indeed, bombing has never done better than assist navies, armies and diplomacy in the struggle for victory. Even in **Vietnam**, where more bombs were dropped than in World War II, to force the North Vietnamese to the conference table, only a transitory settlement was arranged to help extract the Americans from a politically embarrassing situation. Armed with the atom bomb, of course, bombers, as supplements to **rockets**, have the power almost certainly to win a pyrrhic victory. Note, however, the effects of **smart munitions** in the **Persian Gulf War** in 1991 which may be significant.

Boxer Rebellion. Xenophobia by the 'Boxer' secret Society of the Righteous Harmonious Fists, encouraged by the Chinese Empress Tzu Hsi, led to military intervention in June 1900 to protect threatened British, American, Russian, French, Italian and Japanese communities. Attempts to relieve besieged legations in Peking

were defeated by larger Chinese forces. But, by 15 August, a reinforced international force of 18,700 (under no overall commander) managed, by committee, loosely to co-ordinate the taking of Tientsin, the relief of the legations in Peking and storming of the Imperial City. Self-interest governed the 'allies'. Three weeks later the Russians occupied Manchuria while the Germans carried out punitive attacks on Boxer sympathizers. At the end of the year Tzu Hsi capitulated and agreed payment of a large indemnity to the foreigners.

Bradley, General Omar N. (1893–1981). An American infantryman who, in **World War II**, commanded the Infantry School and infantry divisions before, in April 1943, taking command of II US Corps, which he led to the end of the **North Africa** campaign and in the Battle of **Sicily**. Brought to Britain to command First US Army, he was thus responsible for the right flank of Allied landings in **Normandy**. After the breakout, when given command of 12th Army Group, composed of four armies, he led the drive to the German frontier and the final advance to Czechoslovakia and towards Berlin. From 1948 to 1949 he was Chief of Army Staff and, until 1953, first chairman of the Joint Chiefs of Staff of the unified US armed forces.

Brandenburg Regiment. Fame was first won by this unit when, at **Verdun** in February 1916, a handful of its men captured the almost undefended Fort Douaumont. It was resurrected in January 1940 as an instrument of the German Abwehr (intelligence service) for special duties, akin to SAS, behind the enemy lines and as counter-**guerrillas**. It hunted partisans in Russia, Yugoslavia and elsewhere with ferocity and success, and was steadily expanded until, in 1944, it was converted into a Panzer grenadier division – with inevitable waste of many of its highly specialized skills.

Brauchitsch, Field Marshal Walther von (1881–1948). A gunner who played a leading role in the expansion of the German Army in the 1930s. Married to a rabid Nazi, he declined to oppose Adolf **Hitler**, who appointed him C-in-C in 1937. He therefore won the credit for brilliant conduct of the 1939 **Polish** and 1940 **West Europe campaigns**. But Hitler frequently bullied him into submission on such vital issues as the wisdom of attacking in the west in 1940 and strategy in Russia (**Russo-German wars**) in 1941. In December, as the offensive came to a halt in winter freeze, he had a heart attack and resigned. He died while awaiting trial for war crimes.

Braun, Werner von (1912–77). A German physicist who specialized in rocket motors and in 1934 became technical director of the Army rocket establishment at Peenemünde. Here, against his desire to develop **rockets** for peaceful purposes, he was ordered to create the series of missiles that included such surface-to-surface missiles as the V1 and V2, and numerous anti-shipping and **anti-aircraft** weapons.

In 1945 he was taken to America where he continued to work on rockets for both military and civil use. When the Russians launched their first satellite in 1957, von Braun was told in November to match it – which he managed to do within two months. In 1960 he came under the National Aeronautics and Space Administration (NASA), with the task of developing the big rockets that not only had important military roles in placing guided missiles, surveillance and **communication** satellites in **space**, but also, in 1969, carried the first men to the moon as well as mapping the surface of Mars, thus beginning to satisfy his original ambition of exploring space for peaceful purposes.

Britain, Battle of. Delayed until 12 July 1940, as was **Hitler**'s directive to invade Britain, and disputed as is its starting date, it actually began on 5 June with scattered Luftwaffe night sorties. Both sides realized invasion was impracticable without German air superiority and that the key was the **fighter** struggle. But Reichsmarschall **Göring** thought the battle might be won by **strategic bombing** alone. With 2,790 aircraft available, including 760 excellent single-engined fighters, and adequate reserves, he took a chance against Air Marshal Sir Hugh **Dowding**'s RAF Fighter Command, with 900 single-engined fighters and meagre reserves, particularly of pilots.

Attacks against English Channel ports and shipping began in earnest on 10 July. RAF defence of the convoys was costly against a slightly superior enemy and called into question the wisdom of fighting at a disadvantage in an attritional struggle. As it was, the Royal Navy was compelled, by air attacks on 29 July, to withdraw its anti-invasion destroyers from Dover. Meanwhile, Göring settled upon 10 August for Eagle Day, when the onslaught upon Fighter Command would start but, owing to bad weather, had to postpone it until the 13th. By then the attrition rate in fighters was in German favour and bombing of six **radar** stations on the 12th had knocked out one for 11 days. But, mistakenly thinking such targets were too hard to destroy, the Germans mostly left them alone thereafter.

In heavy air combat between 13 and 23 August, in which they penetrated close to London and lost aircraft disproportionately to results achieved against Fighter Command, the Germans forfeited some advantages by ignorance of where the enemy fighters were based, and how they were controlled and commanded by radio from sector airfields. As a result, their bombers often wasted effort on secondary targets, and their losses rose further when the fighters ran into trouble at their extreme range of endurance.

After 24 August the Germans placed their daylight offensive under Field Marshal **Kesselring**'s 2nd Air Fleet, and concentrated its attacks, with bombers more closely escorted by fighters, against fighter airfields. Fighter Command deteriorated as damaged airfields and the acute shortage of weary pilots impaired its combatworthiness. Shortage of **anti-aircraft** guns often compelled fighters to concentrate on defence of their own bases and factories. By 6 September the fighter contest was well in the German favour and the vital sector stations in a parlous state – though the Germans neither knew of nor suspected its significance.

Next day everything changed. Stung by an air raid against **Berlin**, and choosing to believe Fighter Command was beaten, Göring, at Hitler's command, switched the attack to London. The pressure was taken off the airfields and transferred to the German fighters, which lost their tactical advantage at extreme range and were unable adequately to protect the bombers. Though causing heavy damage to a few strategic targets, the Germans were incapable of a decisive **strategic bombing** effort. Losses of 60 aircraft during a maximum effort on 15 September, when Fighter Command intercepted in apparently massive strength (and lost only 26 fighters), convinced Hitler, as the weather got worse, that invasion was impossible. He postponed it on 17 September and cancelled it on 12 October.

Until May 1941 the night bombing of Britain, which had been stepped up on 24 August, would take over (as part of the diversion for the planned invasion of Russia) – the inconclusive, so-called Blitz of London and other major cities. Between 10 July and 31 October, Fighter Command had 449 aircrew, including Canadians, New Zealanders, Belgians, Czechoslovaks and Poles, killed. Up to 30 September it had lost 678 fighters against German losses of 1,099 machines of all types. It had won a victory which changed the course of the war.

Brooke, Field Marshal Alan (Lord Alanbrooke) (1883–1963). A talented gunner who, in the 1930s, played a leading part in the development of **artillery**, **anti-aircraft** fire and **training** of the British Army. His leadership of II Corps in the retreat to **Dunkirk** and withdrawal from France in June 1940 was brilliant, but were his last actions in the field. Appointed to command Home Forces in July 1940, with the tasks of defence against imminent invasion and of re-forming and training a defeated Army, he had made impressive progress before Winston Churchill made him Chief of the Imperial General Staff in December 1941. Thereafter, as Chairman of the Chiefs of Staff Committee and a powerful member of the Allied Combined Chiefs of Staff, he would play a dominating role in shaping Allied **strategy**. By reaching a working agreement with the American Chief of Army Staff, General **Marshall**, he was able to persuade the Americans to invade North Africa, instead of a very risky invasion of Europe in 1942; and to curb Churchill's often dangerous impetuosities while he skilfully steered a course towards a victory of which he was very much a master architect.

Brusilov, General Alexei A. (1853–1926). A cavalryman whose tactical genius became apparent during the 1877–88 **Russo-Turkish War**, a reputation confirmed by his leadership of the Eighth Army in Galicia in 1914. Appointed to command the South-West Front in 1916, his professional organization and execution of the offensive (see next entry), by which he is remembered, was one of the few illustrious pieces of Russian generalship in **World War I**. Lacking favour at Court and in the High Command,

Brusilov was among the generals who, upon the Revolution's outbreak (see **Russian revolutionary wars**), pressed for the Tsar's abdication. Disillusioned by the Tsar, he served the Bolsheviks and, in 1920, was made chairman of the commission commanding the Russian armed forces.

Brusilov Offensive. When General **Brusilov** became C-in-C of the South-West Front in the spring of 1916, opposing **Conrad's** Austro-Hungarian front in Galicia, the Italians were asking Russia to try, by an offensive, to divert Austrian pressure from the Italian front. But although Russia complied by preparing a general offensive, the Chief of Army Staff, General M. V. Alexeyev, chose to regard the southern front as subsidiary yet failed to press hard enough with preparations elsewhere. Moreover, he mistrusted Brusilov's doctrine of attacking with all available forces on a wide front in order to pin down enemy reserves.

With an unusually meticulously prepared attack on 4 June, the Russians, for once well organized and supported by artillery, and better trained than before, achieved Brusilov's aim by breaking in on a wide front and attracting the Austrian reserves. Next day, close to the Pripet Marshes where an over-confident, under-strength defence was overrun, Austrian resistance collapsed. Within a few days their entire army was in rout, giving the Russians a victory beyond their dreams. This was the moment for their Central Army Group to attack to prevent the Germans going to Austria's aid. But Alexeyev and General Evert, the army group commander, equivocated by trying to reinforce Brusilov without abandoning the central front offensive.

In the event Brusilov was denied vital support from an army on his right flank while, inevitably, Russian communications proved incapable of reinforcing his armies as they began to roll westwards. And although an advance of 40 miles was managed in less than a week, the momentum could not be sustained because the Germans, unengaged in the north, could spare eight divisions to prop up the Austrians. But the Austrian débâcle continued, to the accompaniment of sharp disagreements between Conrad (who was loath to take away troops from Italy) and the German Chief of Staff, General von Falkenhayn (who was averse to removing forces from **Verdun**). Brusilov's armies advanced along

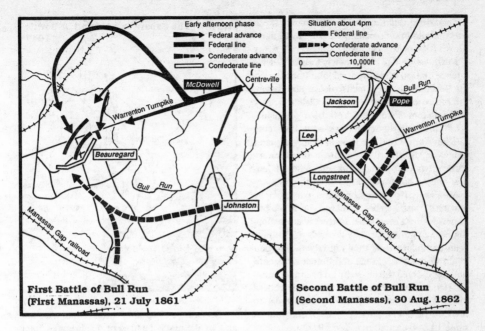

**First Battle of Bull Run
(First Manassas), 21 July 1861**

Early afternoon phase
- ➤ Federal advance
- ▬ Federal line
- ◼▬▶ Confederate advance
- ▭ Confederate line

McDowell
Centreville
Warrenton Turnpike
Beauregard
Bull Run
Manassas Gap railroad
Johnston

**Second Battle of Bull Run
(Second Manassas), 30 Aug. 1862**

Situation about 4pm
- ▬ Federal line
- ◼▬▶ Confederate advance
- ▭ Confederate line

0   10,000ft

Bull Run
Jackson
Pope
Lee
Warrenton Turnpike
Longstreet
Manassas Gap railroad

his entire front, even though the breakthrough on his northern flank was checked as much by logistic failure as by enemy resistance and counter-attack.

Deprived of reinforcements and supplies, Brusilov went on attacking until 20 September – without reaching a single strategic objective, but constantly helping the Allied cause by relieving the Italians, French and British of strain. This also strongly influenced the **Romanians** in joining the Allied side in August, an event which, ironically, persuaded the Russian High Command to persist with Brusilov's exhausted offensive. For about one million casualties, which pushed Russia towards revolution in 1917, and over half a million Austrian casualties, which placed a fatal strain on the Austro-Hungarian Empire, Brusilov had scored his country's finest victory.

Buller, General Sir Redvers, vc (1839–1908). An officer of wide experience and outstanding bravery in colonial wars who, as Quartermaster-General and Adjutant-General successively, implemented many much-needed British Army reforms in the 1890s, including the **logistics** system. Too late in life he was made C-in-C in **South Africa** in 1899 against the Boers. Lacking sufficient troops and adequate logistic support,

his dispersed forces suffered a quick succession of humiliating defeats. Replaced by Field Marshal Lord **Roberts**, he remained in field command and, after much travail, conquered the east Transvaal. Upon return to a command in England, he was forced to retire by strength of public indignation at his re-employment.

Bull Run, Battles of. The first major battle of the **American Civil War** took place on 21 July 1861 because a Federal army of 28,500 under General Irvin McDowell invaded the Confederacy with a view to capturing Richmond. It was met on the line of the Bull Run stream by 22,000 men under General Pierre Beauregard whose army, unbeknown to McDowell, was being reinforced by General Joseph Johnston's 12,000 men from the **Shenandoah Valley**. Covered by General J. E. B. Stuart's cavalry, they were being sent by railway to the nearby Manassas junction. Rushed into an outflanking movement, the inexperienced Federal troops were checked by an unyielding brigade under General Thomas Jackson, and then thrown into rout as Johnston's units arrived to take the Federals in their own flank. Neither side was fit for further battle or pursuit after this exhausting *First Bull Run* – where, incidentally, Jackson won the nickname 'Stonewall'.

The *Second Bull Run*, on 29/30 August 1862, was the culmination of manoeuvring by General Robert E. **Lee's** 50,000 strong Confederate Army of North Virginia to trap a newly formed Federal force of 56,000 under General John Pope, covering Washington. Lee aimed to defeat Pope before the return of General George McClellan's army of the Potomac from the Yorktown peninsula, after its defeat at the **Seven Days Battle.** By having Jackson's army raid the Federal supply depot at Manassas, Lee lured Pope into a diversionary battle intended to obscure the emergence of General James Longstreet's army from the **Shenandoah Valley.** Unaware Longstreet was near by and in the mistaken belief Jackson was in retreat, Pope advanced even as Longstreet was enveloping his flank and rear. The Federals might have been annihilated had they not recognized their plight in the nick of time and if their rearguard had not delayed the chase by an obstinate stand on Henry House Hill. As it was, they retired upon Washington in sufficiently good order to hold off Jackson's pursuit, yet suffering in all some 14,500 casualties to Lee's 9,000.

Burma, Battles of. The Japanese occupation of Thailand prior to hostilities in **South East Asia** in December 1941, enabled their Fifteenth Army, helped by Burmese dissidents, to invade Burma in mid-January 1942, in the wake of their heavily defeated air attacks on **Rangoon.** At Moulmein, however, two unfit British divisions were thrown back to the River **Sittang** where there was another British disaster in mid-February. Reinforcements from India and the Middle East, plus the arrival from Yunnan province of a Chinese army, were insufficient for General **Alexander** (who took command on 5 March) to stop the rot. The outmanoeuvred British fell back on Mandalay and yet again, along with the Chinese on their left, were defeated with serious losses of men and equipment. Mandalay fell on 1 May, forcing Alexander to retreat to the Indian frontier and the Chinese to retire in disorder into Yunnan. Japanese losses were about 7,000: those of their enemies at least 60,000.

The long-term aim of the British was to recapture Burma while that of the Americans was to reopen the **Burma Road** in order to supply China. In the short-term the Americans flew supplies to China and the British attempted two minor offensives as a means of restoring confidence.

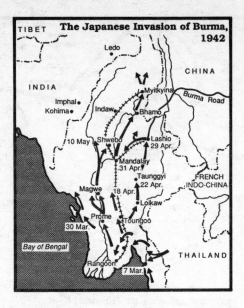

The Japanese Invasion of Burma, 1942

In December 1942 they attacked in **Arakan** and in February 1943 sent 77 Brigade (later known as the **Chindits**), under Brigadier Orde Wingate, to cut enemy communications from Mandalay. Both operations were failures but useful lessons were learned. Then in October the Chinese under command of General Stilwell, and with American assistance, tried to reopen the land route to China, but this too met fierce resistance and made only marginal progress.

The arrival of Admiral Lord **Mountbatten** in October 1943 as Supreme Allied Commander produced better joint planning. It involved the British in the second **Arakan** campaign in January 1944 and in the second, much more ambitious, insertion of Chindits to tackle the Mandalay–Myitkyina route in March. Both operations enjoyed some success, as did the more important advance by Stilwell's army on Myitkyina, which he besieged in May but which held out until August. Meanwhile the Japanese launched their great invasion of India against which the Fourteenth British Army under General William **Slim** had to concentrate all its resources.

The Japanese Fifteenth Army under General Renya Mutaguchi crossed the River Chindwin on 6 March and headed for **Kohima** and **Imphal** at great speed despite the rugged, jungle country. By 5 April both places were under siege, outnumbered and on air supply. Only

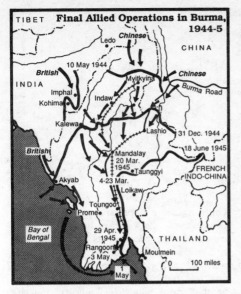

Final Allied Operations in Burma, 1944-5

TIBET

CHINA

Ledo

Chinese

British

10 May 1944

INDIA

Myitkyina

Chinese

Imphal

Burma Road

Kohima

Indaw

Kalewa

Lashio

31 Dec. 1944

British

18 June 1945

Mandalay
20 Mar.
1945 Taunggyi

FRENCH
INDO-CHINA

Akyab

4-23 Mar.

Loikaw

Toungoo

Prome

Bay of
Bengal

29 Apr.
1945
Rangoon
3 May

THAILAND

Moulmein

0   100 miles

1
May

Imphal could be reinforced by air, so Kohima had to be relieved by a land advance. But the Japanese, although several times close to capturing Kohima, themselves were in dire **logistic** trouble because they had not reckoned on the British standing fast, supplied by air, and themselves had expected to live off captured supplies. On 20 April a British column broke through to Kohima and, on 22 June, Imphal was relieved, though never in great danger. As the monsoon broke the enemy, starved of everything and riddled with disease, collapsed as a British pursuit commenced.

The Japanese withdrawal was conducted with skill. Not until 19 November was Slim able to cross the Chindwin and head for Mandalay, where the Japanese intended to fight a decisive battle. But the sheer breadth of what now became an Allied offensive converging from Yunnan, from Myitkyina, from Imphal and also in the Arakan, was overwhelming. In January 1945 the Chinese and Americans reopened the Burma Road as the enemy slipped away. Lashio fell on 7 March, but by then the Japanese bastion at Mandalay was being eroded by Slim's adroit manoeuvres. By crossing the River Irrawaddy on a broad front in January and February, he was able to fall swiftly with tanks upon a thinly defended Meiktila and thus envelop the entire Japanese army. A long fierce battle was fought

by the Japanese to throw the British out of Meiktila and save the situation. But at the end of March the Fourteenth Army had won. Mandalay and Meiktila had fallen and the enemy was in headlong retreat by a poor secondary route. The way was then open for a race to Rangoon where Slim's troops arrived on 2 May to find the enemy gone and elements of an amphibious force, which had landed near by on the 1st, in possession.

At the same moment the monsoon broke and the only task remaining for the British was rounding up the thousands of Japanese infesting the countryside while also coming to terms with Burmese dissidents who now conducted **guerrilla warfare** against their erstwhile allies.

Burma Road. When the Japanese cut off China from the sea in 1939, the Chinese began to use a narrow, 681-mile winding road from Kunming to Lashio. But in July 1940 the Japanese politically coerced the British into closing it. It was a matter of priority for the Allies in 1942, after **Burma** had been seized by the Japanese, to reopen the road. But not until January 1945, after hard campaigns, was this accomplished. In the meantime work on a 478-mile spur from Ledo was put in hand, but of far greater immediate use was the air lift over the 21,000ft so-called Hump. General Stilwell initiated it in June 1942 to provide fuel for American aircraft operating in China. Mostly civil aircraft were used. Sometimes over 6,000 tonnes a month were carried in all sorts of weather.

Burmese Wars. Long-standing friction between the British East India Company and the Burmese came to a head in 1852 when 8,100 men, under General Sir Henry Godwin, seized Rangoon as a prelude to annexing the whole of South Burma, including Mandalay, in what is known as the *Second Burma War*. The *Third Burma War* in 1885 was the result of a breakdown of internal order in North Burma, interference with British trade and an invasion by 12,000 British under General H. N. D. Prendergast. Carried in 55 Royal Navy steamers, a rapid advance was made up the River Irrawaddy to the capital, Ava, where King Thibaw surrendered. Guerrilla warfare persisted for another decade and, to this day, is practised somewhere or other in this mountainous, jungle country.

C

C³. Modern jargon abbreviation standing for the joint functions of Command, Control and Communications, and therefore a subject of increasing and vital importance as the sheer volume of information generated and fed into military communication networks by surveillance and other sources of information threatens to overwhelm commanders and staffs. Considerable attention is being paid to rationalizing the presentation of essential information, through ADP (Automatic Data Processing) and visual displays, and how to separate essentials from non-essentials. Necessarily, electronic and mechanical aids are required. But since these often need a stable environment in which to operate, their use in forward combat zones, where machinery must be extremely simple and rugged, has to be limited. Over-dependence upon mechanical means in unstable situations, when human judgement is so often at a premium, can be very risky for the commander, who also has to take into account such variables as human performance, mechanical reliability and unperceived enemy intentions and moves.

C³I is simply the inclusion of the vital **intelligence** factor as a very important adjunct of C³. It is easy to forget the number of times in which the lack of close and discerning integration of Intelligence with Command and Control has led to military disasters, and how often it has been failures in human as well as signal Communications which have caused this.

Caen, Battle of. On 6 June 1944, the communication centre of Caen was General **Montgomery**'s main objective on the first day of the Battle of **Normandy**, an ambitious target for I British Corps. Against a surprised enemy, whose reactions to the landings were by no means positive enough for the occasion, its attainment was, however, an extremely close-run thing. Troops who had suffered from a rough landing in surf and had been delayed breaking free of the beaches, came within two miles of the city at last light. By then, however, a German armoured counter-attack had forced the leading British and Canadian elements to pause, giving time for a reinforced perimeter defence.

Hitler and Field Marshal **Rommel** were as anxious to hold Caen as was Montgomery to capture it, each realizing that possession was the key to Allied exploitation of the more open terrain to the south and deep into France. But although I Corps tried next day to reach the city, it was also distracted by fierce German attacks and the need to help link up with XXX Corps on its right. While directing that Caen must be taken, Montgomery regarded the city not only as a vital pivot but also, as planned from the outset, a strategic bait. A threat there would distract the Germans from First US Army as it consolidated on the right, tackled Cherbourg and prepared for the decisive breakout. Every effort by I Corps to work round Caen's flanks, with thrusts towards Troarn and against Carpiquet airfield, lured the German armoured forces into an attritional struggle which was very expensive for both sides.

Between 25 and 29 June, VIII British Corps advanced to Hill 112, simultaneously beating off Rommel's major counterstroke. The Germans now knew Caen was untenable, but Hitler would not permit withdrawal. On 4 July the Canadians stormed Carpiquet airfield in a desperate fight, but still without persuading the Germans to evacuate the city. So, on the evening of 7 July, as a prelude to assault next day, heavy bombers dropped 2,560 tonnes of bombs which hit the city much harder than its defended perimeter and largely blocked access. When three divisions advanced next day it was against stiff resistance from fanatical Germans in the centre, but yielding troops on the flanks. Mainly it was craters and ruins blocking the roads which made it easier for the Germans to slip away on the 8th/9th, blowing the river bridges as they departed.

Calais, Battles of. This English Channel port was a German objective during the first Battle of Ypres (see **Flanders, Battles of**) in 1914, but remained in Allied hands as an important British naval and supply base throughout **World War I**.

Calais became a German objective again in **World War II** on 21 May 1940 when General **Guderian**'s XIX Corps advanced on **Dunkirk** to envelop the Allied armies in Belgium. General Lord **Gort** put Boulogne, Calais and Dunkirk in a state of defence simply to supply the cut-off, retreating Allied armies. The garrisons were brought over from England to join whatever Allied troops happened to be present. Boulogne's meagre, immobile defenders held out until 25 May. The Calais garrison, which included a motorized infantry brigade and an armoured regiment, took abortive offensive action on 23 May against German spearheads advancing on Dunkirk. Thereafter it concentrated on perimeter defence when a Panzer division began its assault on 24 May. Largely the defence was based on the 17th-century Vauban **fortifications**, which stood up well to bombing and shelling. But at 1500hrs the British War Office ordered withdrawal, an order which was rescinded at 2323hrs after Winston **Churchill** had decided that a stand must be made for the sake of 'Allied solidarity'. Fierce attacks drove the defenders back into the town on the 25th, when repeated German calls for surrender were, on War Office instructions, rejected. Resistance continued until 1600hrs on the 26th, with very few defenders managing to escape by sea or by road to Dunkirk. The defence, however, was among several factors enabling evacuation from Dunkirk.

Until October 1944, Calais stood in the front line as a base for invasion of Britain, as a target for British air and amphibious raids and as one of the strongest bastions of the German West Wall. Early in September, however, along with Boulogne, it was once more besieged, this time under **Hitler**'s orders to resist Canadian and British troops to the bitter end. Boulogne was attacked on the 17th, the last of its 10,000-strong, well-fortified garrison holding out until the 21st. Calais, plus the long-range artillery positions which still bombarded England from Cap Gris Nez, was tackled on the 25th in a series of carefully prepared siege-warfare-type operations headed by British specialized **armoured fighting vehicles**. Deep minefields and the numerous thick concrete fortifications were overcome, one by one, at remarkably low cost to the assailants. But by the time the last Germans had been 'winkled out' on 1 October, both ports had been made unusable by demolitions and mines. It would be several weeks before they could help ease serious Allied **logistic** shortages.

Cambodia, Battles of. The ancient civilization of Cambodia fell under French suzerainty in 1862 and later became part of French Indo-China. When the Japanese moved in during 1941 they reallocated some provinces to Thailand, but these were restored in 1946 on the eve of the **Indo-China War of Independence**. The guerrilla combat of that war overspilled into Cambodia prior to the French withdrawal in 1954 and as Communism took hold, leading to friction with Thailand and South Vietnam. As American involvement in the war grew, North Vietnam, with permission, established a military base in Cambodia, with large quantities of supplies entering through the port of Sihanoukville. Nevertheless in 1969, the ruler, Prince Sihanouk, permitted 'secret' American bombing of the base installations – with marginal military success but major political ructions when made public.

Appreciating the menacing scale of **logistic** support from within Cambodia, the Americans and South Vietnamese raided the bases in 1970. They found elaborate and well-stocked depots which yielded, it was estimated, sufficient to feed 25,000 troops for a year and enough weapons to equip 55 divisions. They also killed 11,362 soldiers. In conjunction with several subsidiary raids, it was a shattering blow to the North Vietnamese whose supply line down the River Mekong to Saigon almost dried up, thus taking pressure off the South. But in due course, the damage, from lack of repeats by the South Vietnamese, was repaired.

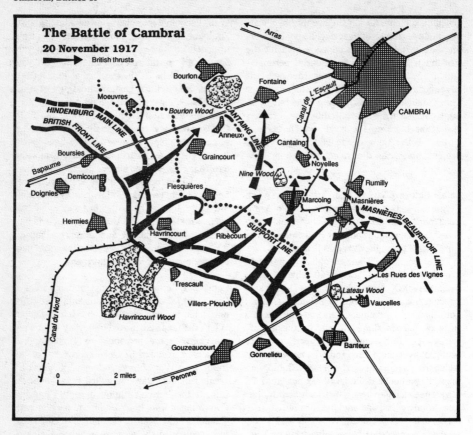

The Battle of Cambrai

20 November 1917

➤ British thrusts

Arras

Bourlon

Fontaine

Moeuvres

HINDENBURG MAIN LINE

BRITISH FRONT LINE

Bourlon Wood

CANTAING LINE

Canal de L'Escault

CAMBRAI

Anneux

Cantaing

Boursies

Graincourt

Noyelles

Bapaume

Demicourt

Nine Wood

Rumilly

Doignies

Flesquières

Marcoing

Masnières

MASNIÈRES/BEAUREVOIR LINE

Hermies

Havrincourt

Ribècourt

SUPPORT LINE

Les Rues des Vignes

Trescault

Lateau Wood

Villers-Plouich

Vaucelles

Canal du Nord

Havrincourt Wood

Gouzeaucourt

Gonnelieu

Banteux

0   2 miles

Peronne

The collapse of South Vietnam in 1975 and the withdrawal of all American assistance gave the Communist Khmer (Cambodia) Rouge guerrillas their opportunity to seize power by force. Under Saloth Sar (known as Pol Pot) they became estranged from North Vietnam and embarked on a pseudo-intellectual agrarian programme which led to the genocide of more than one million Cambodians. Invasion in 1978 by Vietnam almost put a stop to this by reducing the Khmer Rouge to a jungle guerrilla force. Henceforward the country under Vietnamese tutelage, and now known as Kampuchea, endured a guerrilla war against the Khmer Rouge, based in part on hide-outs in Thailand. Vietnamese troops withdrew in 1989. Fighting continues.

Cambrai, Battles of. The important route centre of Cambrai fell to German cavalry in August 1914 and, as trench warfare began, became a main base for the German armies in Northern France. When construction of the **Siegfried Line** began in 1916, one of its strongest sectors shielded Cambrai, a quiet front to which German divisions were sent to recuperate, earning it the name 'Sanatorium from Flanders'.

In June 1917 Lieutenant-Colonel J. F. C. **Fuller**, senior staff officer of the British Tank Corps, submitted a plan for tank raids on favourable ground, such as at Cambrai. Then, and again in August, it was turned down by the British Expeditionary Force's C-in-C General **Haig**. But in October, when the Third Battle of Ypres was plainly a disastrous failure, Haig, yearning for a whiff of success, revived the idea but augmented it to a full-scale offensive at Cambrai of two days' duration. Third Army was to attack at dawn on 20 November with six divisions in the assault, supported by the entire Tank Corps with 476 tanks, 1,003 artillery pieces, massed machine-guns and air bombing.

When the Siegfried Line had been breached, the Cavalry Corps was to pass through and seize the Bourlon Ridge and Cambrai, thus isolating the Germans' Arras front. The greatest secrecy was observed in assembling the troops by night; and, to obtain surprise, the **artillery**, for the first time, adopted fire by silent registration, off the map, in order not to disclose the intention.

Fuller dictated the tactics. A wave of tanks headed the attack, subduing enemy machine-guns, crushing the deep wire entanglements and filling the deepest trench with the wood fascines carried on top of each tank. A second wave, with infantry in close attendance, then occupied the trenches, whereupon tanks drove to the final objective.

Almost total surprise was achieved. The British tactics worked well. Nearly all the days' objectives were reached. British losses were remarkably few in men and tanks while those of the enemy were over 10,000 and included 123 guns. But the Germans, by staunch defence of Flesquières, managed to prevent the British reaching the Bourlon feature; and although the cavalry was poised to overrun a broken enemy, it failed to seize the opportunity. In consequence, the Germans, although on the point of a wholesale withdrawal from the Arras front, held on and, in the ensuing seven days, checked desperate British attempts to seize the Bourlon Ridge.

On 3 December the Germans counter-attacked. Using their latest infiltration tactics behind a surprise bombardment, they drove the British back to Flesquières and seized ground on the southern flank which had been in British possession before 20 November. On balance of losses and prestige, honours were even. But tank dominance and surprise tactics marked a turning-point in the history of war.

Cambrai would be the scene of renewed heavy fighting in March 1918 at the commencement of the **Hindenburg offensive** when the British were pushed back towards Bapaume. And yet again when, on 8 October, a British attack on an 18-mile front, which included 82 tanks (all that could be made fit after an exhausting pursuit), broke through, brushed with German tanks, and entered the badly damaged city on the 9th.

Battle came to the city once more on 18 May 1940 when a German Panzer division, taking advantage of the total French collapse, stormed in with scarcely any resistance. Four days later, however, French tanks broke back into the city

as spearheads of a small French counter-attack which savaged a German infantry division. The Germans countered with bombing, strafing and anti-tank fire from 150 yards which finally drove the French off.

Early in September 1944, the Germans, badly routed, would not pause to defend Cambrai as they fled for the frontier.

Caporetto, Battle of. After the eleventh Battle of the **Isonzo**, in September 1917, both the Italian and Austrian armies in Italy were war-weary, the latter near collapse. General **Hindenburg** decided to back a sound Austrian plan for a counter-offensive on the Isonzo with 14 divisions in a newly formed Fourteenth Army under General Otto von Below. It began in vile weather on 24 October on a frontage of 25 miles employing General von Hutier's new infiltration tactics. In difficult terrain behind a surprise bombardment, General Luigi Cadorna's armies were routed and rolled back to the River Tagliamento. The insubordination and indolence of Italian commanders, with a breakdown of communications, compounded the disaster. The Austro-Germans, to their surprise, advanced more than 25 miles in a week, eventually capturing 275,000 prisoners, 2,500 guns and masses of equipment.

Responding to desperate pleas by the Italians, who showed signs of total disintegration, the British and French sent 11 divisions to the River Piave front where Cadorna made a stand. But although their enemies pursued with vigour, **logistic** problems soon intervened and the pace slackened. Cadorna was replaced on 8 November by General Armando Diaz, who confirmed existing arrangements and garnered the credit for Cadorna's leadership in the final days of retreat. For on the Piave the Italians, without direct Anglo-French support, held off an enemy who had outstripped his supplies. A renewal of the offensive by von Below on the 23rd was soon brought to a halt; but already the Germans were withdrawing their best troops to Germany.

Meanwhile, as a direct result of the Caporetto experience, a Supreme War Council was formed to improve the Allies' co-ordination. (See map page 64.)

Cassino, Battles of. A name often generally given to the struggle for the mountainous German **Gustav Line**, of which the Benedictine monastery-topped Monte Cassino was one of the

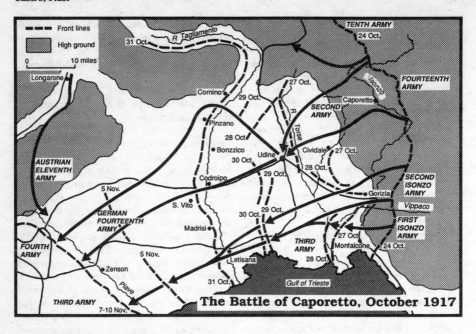

The Battle of Caporetto, October 1917

- - - Front lines

High ground

0   10 miles

R Tagliamento

31 Oct

TENTH ARMY
24 Oct.

Longarone

Cornino

27 Oct.

29 Oct.

Caporetto

FOURTEENTH ARMY

Pinzano

SECOND ARMY

28 Oct

R Torse

Bonzzico

Udine

Cividale

27 Oct.

AUSTRIAN ELEVENTH ARMY

30 Oct.

29 Oct

28 Oct.

5 Nov.

Codroipo

Gorizia

SECOND ISONZO ARMY

S. Vito

30 Oct.

29 Oct.

Vippaco

GERMAN FOURTEENTH ARMY

Madrisi

FIRST ISONZO ARMY

27 Oct

Monfalcone

24 Oct.

FOURTH ARMY

5 Nov.

THIRD ARMY

28 Oct.

Letisana

Zenson

Plave

31 Oct.

Gulf of Trieste

THIRD ARMY

7-10 Nov.

---

key positions. Field Marshal **Kesselring** established the line along the rivers Garigliano, Rapido and Sangro to stop the Allied advance on Rome. The Fifth US Army under General Mark Clark did not get within striking distance of the monastery until 26 January 1944, when the Rapido was crossed by a US infantry division, but attempts to scale the mountain were frustrated. In the weeks to come several fresh, expensive and abortive assaults were made. The Americans tried between 5 and 11 February and were fought to a standstill. The New Zealand Corps tried next on the 15th, after heavy air bombing had devastated the monastery, and did no better. Whereupon the Germans, who had stayed out of the building, occupied the ruins with élite parachute troops. Another attempt behind the heaviest bombardment yet was attempted by an Indian division on 15/16 March and the fighting, which included a New Zealand tank attack (which was annihilated), raged until the 22nd when at last both sides called a breather.

On 15 May, Fifth Army started again, but this time the monastery was to be left to the last. The main thrust to **Anzio** on the road to Rome was into the Aurunci mountains and along the Liri valley to outflank Cassino. Indeed, the Allied breakthrough was 25 miles beyond Cassino on

17 May before the Polish Corps moved up for the kill. For ten hours a fierce struggle raged amid the ruins of Cassino town and on the slopes above. But not until then, when the monastery had lost its tactical significance, did Kesselring order withdrawal. Only wounded Germans were captured.

Castro, Fidel (b.1927). A Cuban Marxist political agitator whose first attempt at armed revolt in 1953 to unseat his country's ruler, Fulgencio Batista, ended in fiasco. His second attempt in 1956 with 82 men, which also led to disaster, enabled him nevertheless to establish the cadre of a guerrilla party. From his dynamism sprang the powerful organization that in three years, enabled him to overthrow Batista. Since then, at the Bay of Pigs in 1961, he has defeated Cuban exiles who, with US support, tried to unseat him; and with Russian support has acted as the power behind many revolutionary movements throughout the Americas. Besides being a threat to the USA he also became involved in Africa by sending up to 50,000 troops to Angola from 1975 onwards to fight on the side of the Marxist government against Unita guerrillas; and also to **Ethiopia**, to fight on the government side.

Cavalry. Rooted in history as a military force on

horseback, the term since the 1920s has come also to embrace soldiers in **armoured fighting vehicles** (AFVs) and **helicopters**. In the 1850s, owing to significant improvements in firepower, horsemen were finding it increasingly difficult to carry out their traditional mobile roles of reconnaissance and shock action. It was often preferable to dismount for scouting and the discharge of weapons, and usually suicidal to charge with lance or sword. The **Crimean War** is better known for cavalry disasters than successes. The last successful massed, close-order charges took place, with 45 per cent losses, at Vionville in 1870, during the **Franco-Prussian War**, when General von Bredow's brigade carried out its celebrated 'Death Ride' against emplaced artillery, only to be run down by French cavalry.

An interim way ahead appeared in the **American Civil War** when cavalry found room to manoeuvre in vast undefended spaces where they could live fairly easily off the country. Nevertheless, great cavalry commanders, such as Generals J. E. B. Stuart, Philip Sheridan and Nathan Forrest, found no real profit in the charge. They preferred reconnaissance, the screening of infantry formations, deceptive manoeuvres and swift raids against enemy lines of communication (mainly **railways**). Carbine and pistol superseded lance and sword as the armament of what became mounted riflemen. And though these lessons were largely ignored by the apostles of shock action in Europe, British troops in colonial wars and, notably in the **South African Wars**, used the same tactics in the veldt's vastness when hunting **Boer** guerrillas whose raiding depended upon the horse.

The application of the internal combustion engine to land warfare sounded the knell of horsed cavalry and transport. By 1914 it was apparent to the enlightened how much more reliable and easy to fuel, handle and maintain was the motor vehicle than the temperamental horse, which consumed so much bulky fodder and whose endurance and range of action was extremely limited by comparison. Throughout the opening, mobile phases of **World War I**, when 10 German cavalry divisions faced 10 French and one British; and when the Russians had 24 cavalry divisions to 10 Austrian, horsemen achieved but little. No sooner did artillery or machine-guns open fire than they checked. The only occasion a German cavalry formation

had an opportunity to ride through a gap during the advance to the **Marne**, the horses needed their shoes replacing. French massed cavalry achieved nothing and the British division did its best work with dismounted rifle fire. In the East, at **Tannenberg**, cavalry's best service was by a single German division holding off one Russian army while the other was defeated.

Yet cavalry divisions, despite repeated demonstrations of their inability to survive under fire and the appalling wastage of horses' lives in the hardships of a war environment, remained in being – the Russians raising 54 in all. But not once on the Western Front did cavalry manage to find the G in Gap (as was the term) after infantry, artillery and tanks had made progress – not even at **Arras** and **Cambrai** in 1917, nor **Amiens** in 1918 when wide gaps were opened. Even in the Middle East, where cavalry found freedom for manoeuvre in the desert, they relied largely upon artillery, aircraft and AFVs to prepare the way.

Between the two **World Wars**, despite illogical opposition by cavalrymen but hastened by significant reductions in the horse population following mechanization of civil transport, most cavalry units were either disbanded or mechanized. By 1942 only a few horsed divisions were to be found on the Russian front where space was available. In 1939 Britain's cavalry units became part of a Royal Armoured Corps, along with the Royal Tank Regiment; in 1940 the US Army's Armored Branch superseded the Cavalry Branch. Traditional horsed operational functions, of necessity, were taken over by AFVs in all armies. Only the old traditions remained to cavalry regiments which survived in name.

Indeed, the concept of Air Cavalry, now sponsored so strongly within the US Army and demonstrated in **Vietnam** and elsewhere, is possibly closer in affinity to latter-day horsed than present-day armoured cavalry doctrine, whereby lightly protected, moderately hard-hitting helicopters and light aircraft, with their inherent speed and mobility, can carry out the reconnaissance, screening, raiding and mounted-weapon roles, but become involved at their peril in a face-to-face fire-fight in the manner of tanks.

Censorship, Military. Censorship of military information has increased in relation to the growth and pace of signal communications. Before the **telegraph**, **telephone** and **radio**, secrets long in transit usually lost value. But as soon as it was possible, towards the end of the 19th century, for mass-circulation newspapers to publish vital information which might be of immediate use to the enemy, censorship became essential for military security. Press reports, for example, assisted the Japanese to monitor the approach of the Russian Fleet to **Tsushima**. Any enemy who read in good time even speculative reports by correspondents might benefit – or be deluded. Not only did the danger of war with Germany prompt the British, for example, to introduce in 1911 an Official Secrets Act to prevent the passage of secrets by old-fashioned espionage, its drafters also had in mind Press censorship.

Military men dread newspaper correspondents who, like William Russell during the **Crimean War**, expose incompetence. In 1914, the British Army forbade their presence with the British Expeditionary Force on security grounds and fed information of its choice to the Press from an officer called 'Eyewitness'. But several published speculative rumours as often as not originated in government and social circles. Even if, in 1916, the prolonged preliminary bombardment on the **Somme** had not announced the battle's imminence, any self-respecting spy in London or Paris would have known. Censoring sailors' and soldiers' mail, and hampering war correspondents in their duties, stopped some leaks, but diplomatic channels through neutral powers could not be censored any more than 'careless talk' could be suppressed. And intelligent reading even of innocent reports in German newspapers, for example, disclosed much about the **blockade**'s effect.

The lessons learnt in **World War I** were largely applied in **World War II**. Before it began Germany, like all dictatorships (including Russia), had created a Ministry of Propaganda which not only told the people and the world what the leadership wanted them to know, but also imposed a rigorous censorship on newspapers and radio broadcasts. The British were more flexible when setting up a Ministry of Information, which endeavoured to maintain censorship by persuasion, though swift to guard security by coercion. But slow-moving bureaucratic censors often forfeited opportunities to benefit by timely **propaganda**. Enlightened commanders, such as Admiral Lord **Mountbatten** and General **Montgomery**, took war correspondents into their confidence in order to guard their plans and also win favourable reports about their men – and themselves.

The minutiae of censorship, such as the prohibition of merchant shipping sailing-time advertisements and of weather reports, were vital to security, particularly during the Battle of the **Atlantic**. A supreme act of censorship was General **Marshall**'s action, during the US presidential election of 1944, to dissuade Governor Thomas Dewey from disclosing, for political advantage, the Allied capability to read high-grade enemy **codes and ciphers**.

Censorship is politically controversial in democracies, whose ethos demands freedom to communicate. It is as important to maintain military security as it is to maintain the right to know and to debate in public. The US Freedom of Information Act may well goad military leaders into most devious excesses of secrecy. In Britain the 'Spycatcher' case has shown how provocative to all concerned can be publications by past intelligence agents who break the rules of secrecy, and to what extent censorship can be evaded internationally. The struggle continues.

Central America Wars. The tropical rain forests which mainly cover this part of the world are hardly suitable for large-scale warfare. Such hostilities that occurred in the 19th century were of a local complexion within or between the politically unstable provinces. In 1885 an attempt by Justio Barrios of Guatemala to unify the provinces by force led to war – Guatemala and Honduras against Costa Rica, Nicaragua and El Salvador – in which the former invaded El Salvador and were defeated at Chalchuapa where Barrios was killed.

Mexican Wars affected the region but of far greater strategic consequence was the construction by the USA of the Panama Canal (completed 1914) and the increasing involvement of US forces in Panamanian affairs after a local revolution in 1903, an involvement which grew as the result of Nicaragua's defeat of Honduras in 1907 and of US troops being sent in 1912 to protect US interests during the civil wars which had broken out in both countries. The ferocious Nicaraguan civil war of 1925 induced a US military presence until the situation was stabilized in 1933. But the entire region remained a hotbed of intrigue and revolution with one strong man after another coming to power and being deposed as often as not by violence.

The political stability of the region was increasingly undermined after World War II by Communist-orientated activities, among which the coming to power of Fidel **Castro** in **Cuba** was crucial. Frequent border clashes, military coups between factions and assassinations were often linked to anti-US activities. In 1969 El Salvador bombed and invaded Honduras in the aftermath of violence associated with disputed World Cup soccer matches. Fighting went on into the 1970s and, by stages, escalated into a war which continues sporadically to the present day between Communist and anti-Communist forces – the former with Russian and Cuban support, the latter with US help.

Political destabilization became endemic prior to 1980 as **guerrilla warfare** flourished, with Honduran and Costa Rican involvement, in El Salvador, Guatemala and Nicaragua, in a series of encounters in which Communist forces progressively won both political and military advantages, to the frequent embarrassment of the USA. A notable occasion in 1987 was the so-called 'Iran–Contra affair' when members of the US Executive diverted funds to Nicaraguan rebels from the illicit sales of arms to Iran, but without managing to bring a continuing struggle to a conclusion.

In 1990, however, the Contras abandoned the fight and surrendered their arms to a newly elected democratic government.

In Panamá there was a brief outbreak of fighting in December 1989 when President Manuel Noriega, who was sought by the USA for drug trafficking, declared war on it. US Task Forces flown in to support the garrison rapidly overwhelmed troops loyal to Noriega, who was captured and taken to the USA for trial.

Chaffee, Brigadier-General Adna (1884–1941). A US cavalryman who served with distinction in France in 1918 and in the 1930s became the leading American advocate of armoured forces. Though opposed by vested interests in the Cavalry Branch in particular, he managed to generate such strong interest in experiments with mechanized cavalry that in May 1940 he persuaded the US Army to create an entirely new Armored Branch, the foundation of a mechanized force which expanded to 16 armoured divisions and 139 armoured battalions during World War II.

Champagne, Battles of. The first of five major offensives in this province was an attempt by the French Army to break through the German trenches between 20 and 30 December 1914. As was to become the norm, infantry made only limited gains behind inadequate artillery fire and the Germans counter-attacked with similar ineffectiveness. They tried again in January 1915 but collapsed in exhaustion; as they were to do again and again during further assaults throughout February until 30 March – by which time French losses alone amounted to over 240,000. Renewed French attacks in September on a frontage of 15 miles behind a three-day bombardment by 1,600 guns cost 140,000 casualties for the capture of 25,000 prisoners and 150 guns, but without strategic value.

In February 1916 the Germans attacked at **Verdun**, in what was to become the archetype of attritional warfare when, for the better part of that year, both sides came close to complete exhaustion. And although General Nivelle boasted that his April 1917 offensive on the Chemin des Dames was new in concept, in practice this French effort was of the familiar artillery-dominated pattern without hope of success, a failure which drove the French Army to mutiny.

It was also in Champagne that the great **Hindenburg offensive** of 1918 finally foundered and from there in September that French and American troops launched attacks that exploited the German weakness which had been caused as much as anything else by excessive attrition in trench warfare.

Charts and maps. In any military operation there are few hazards more alarming than 'running off the edge of the map' and not having the adjoining sheet immediately available. A commander without maps, even with modern reconnaissance techniques, is at a serious disadvantage. It is not surprising therefore that both armies and navies, and more recently air forces too, have always had a considerable influence on their country's mapping and survey effort. By the mid 19th century, under the impetus originally of years of European war, the Ordnance Survey in Britain was well established under firm military control; similarly the Institut Géographique National of France (Napoleon's 1:100,000 survey of Europe was well under way at the time of his downfall) and the

Landestopographie of Switzerland are other examples. Gradually the civilian element took over in these organizations (the British Ministry of Defence no longer has control of the Ordnance Survey) and in the USA, where military considerations were less paramount, the US Geological Survey had the responsibility. Only during **World War II** did the US military become closely involved in mapping with the Oceanographic Office (navy), the Aeronautical Chart Service (air force) and the US Army Topographical Command.

World War I, and more especially World War II, brought great progress in mapping, with vast areas of the world, previously unmapped, being covered, much of it by aerial survey. Post-1945, continuing tension between East and West has maintained an interest in and continuous improvement of maps and charts. Though mostly generated for military purposes, much of the work has played its part in opening up more remote areas of the world, most of which is now covered by terrain data at least; but many areas remain sketchy and Antarctica, for instance, will not be completely mapped for some years to come.

While the more detailed maps are used by land forces, equally important are the charts used by navies. Surprisingly perhaps, nautical chart coverage of the world as a whole leaves much to be desired, though the areas bordering continents and islands are reasonably well covered. For general navigation, ships are increasingly reliant on satellite fixes and on radar coverage, but the chart on which positions are plotted remains an essential ingredient.

Aeronautical charts are in effect small-scale topographic maps on which navigation aids have been superimposed. Principal features of the land that would be visible in flight are shown, to the exclusion of much other detail. World wide coverage is now extensive.

For military purposes specialized maps are often needed and one example developed during World War II was the normal topographic map with, printed on the reverse, a photomosaic of the same area showing much more detail than could be included on the standard map. Similarly, three-dimensional or relief maps, often crudely made on the ground (the 'sand-table' model) have long formed a useful aid to military tactical planning. An accurate relief map was costly and time consuming to build; nowadays such maps can be constructed much more easily by the pantograph-router, which cuts a model, typically from plaster, as the contours are followed by the operator on a topographical map.

While computerization and electronic measuring have revolutionized the accuracy and speed of survey, the problem for an army in the field remains its ability to produce the enormous number of map sheets needed to meet, at short notice, the requirement for a particular operation. Modern printing and photocopying techniques have speeded up the process, but nevertheless the map reproduction element of any major headquarters is a crucial part of its successful prosecution of its tasks.

Chattanooga, Battles of. The series of battles fought for this vital route centre between 7 September and 25 November 1863 were among the most decisive of the **American Civil War**. After the Federal army under General William Rosecrans had manoeuvred General Braxton Bragg out of the city, the Confederates were sufficiently reinforced to make a costly counterstroke at Chickamauga Creek on 19 September which nevertheless came close to routing Rosecrans. But instead of following up, Bragg only laid siege to Chattanooga until it was resupplied by boats down the Tennessee River on 27 October. In the meantime, Bragg had detached 20,000 men to besiege the Federal garrison of Knoxville and General **Grant** had taken command of the Federal forces.

Substantially reinforced by troops under Generals Joseph Hooker and William **Sherman**, Grant, with 61,000 men, sought to expel Bragg's 40,000 from their extremely strong position on the steep-sided Lookout Mountain and Missionary Ridge, which dominated Chattanooga. In fog and mist on 24 November, Hooker's men fought their way to the top of Lookout Mountain in what came to be known as 'the battle above the clouds'. But Sherman's attempt to storm the eastern end of Missionary Ridge was repulsed on the 24th and made only slow and costly headway when attempted again next day. Indeed, the stalemate was broken by two divisions of General Thomas Hood's army which, contrary to orders, converted their diversionary attack into a gallant scaling of the ridge's steepest sector (whose surprised defenders could not depress their guns enough to fire down the slope) to seize the crest. Losses were about equal: 5,824 Federal; 6,667 Confederate. But it was a mere formality when Knoxville was relieved on 6 December as Bragg retired, opening the way to **Atlanta** and the **March to the Sea** in 1864.

Chemical warfare. The Germans achieved a first in modern warfare by their ineffective use of irritant tear gas against the French at Neuve Chapelle in October 1914, and against the Russians at Bolimov in February 1915. But their use of 150 tonnes of poisonous chlorine in support of an attack in the Ypres salient on 22 April 1915 panicked two French divisions, although causing remarkably few casualties among totally unprotected troops.

The possibility of using toxic gases had its origins in ancient times but it was not until the 19th century that serious studies into the subject were pursued. There was, too, considerable repugnance at the idea of chemical warfare, exemplified by the 1899 Hague Convention renouncing 'the ... diffusion of asphyxiating or harmful gases'. Britain and the USA were not originally signatories of this Convention, though the former did sign in 1907.

Despite the Convention, experiments were made before 1914 by the Germans, French and British and the stalemate on the Western Front led both sides to look again at the possibilities. The German General Staff, presented with a working system, were reluctant to embark upon the use of gas; they were persuaded that the Allies had no means of retaliation and so gave it a try. The gas was carried to the battle zone by rail in liquid form, filled into cylinders at the railhead and then discharged as a cloud at the front line. The inconclusive results of the first attack led the Germans to redeploy the special unit formed to operate the cylinders to the Eastern Front, where more success was achieved during the attack on **Warsaw**. Nevertheless, intermittent gas attacks were launched by the Germans on the Western Front throughout 1915.

The German assessment of Allied capability proved to be very wrong and by July 1915 the British had formed several special companies for gas operations and the French had three. It was at first thought that a cloud expelled from cylinders would be the best method of dissemination, but the British found that gas-filled shell and special projectors firing gas bombs were more

effective. Success of the operation depended entirely on the wind direction being both steady and favourable; there were a number of disasters on both sides, resulting from the gas cloud being blown back on to friendly forces.

Both sides at first used chlorine but new developments were quickly in hand. The British favoured phosgene, which could be inhaled without immediate effect and was thus less easily detected; the Germans used this gas also.

As the Allies developed more effective respirators, so the Germans sought for more effective agents. Two scientists – Lommel and Steinkopf – suggested the use of dichlordiethyl sulphide, given the code-name LOST from their two names, and this was developed into an effective gas known as 'mustard' to the Allies from its smell and the yellow cross used to identify its canister. Difficult to detect, it had the additional and unpleasant characteristic of causing blistering on exposed skin and with its low vapour pressure and solubility in water could lie for days on the surface of the ground. Mustard gas was used by the Germans up to the end of **World War I**, while the Allies had supplies of it available from early 1918.

The Italians had some successes with poisonous gases, including mustard, against the unprotected people during the Italo-Abyssinia War (see **Ethiopian (Abyssinian) Wars**) in 1935–6. This, between the world wars, contributed to a terror of gas in the minds of the populace and politicians, with impact on strategic considerations and **deterrence**. Undoubtedly it was fear of retaliation which deterred the use of gas in **World War II**, despite the availability in Germany of deadly new 'nerve' gases – Tabun, Sarin and Soman which are lethal within fifteen minutes of skin contact or inhalation.

The first recorded use of nerve gases on a large scale was in the Gulf War (**Iran–Iraq War**) in 1984 when Iraq, exhausted and bankrupt, appeared to be losing the struggle against fanatical but unprotected hordes of Iranians. Along with mustard gas, these agents caused heavy casualties to soldiers and civilians, bringing several offensives to a halt and, no doubt, influencing a cessation of hostilities in 1988 – by which time improved protective clothing was mitigating the effect of the gases.

Chiang Kai-shek (1887–1975). A Chinese soldier who served from 1907 to 1911 in the

Japanese Army, he was involved in the **Chinese civil wars** and a prominent supporter of Sun Yat-sen. In 1927 he turned against the Communists and, in 1928, became an able Commander-in-Chief and Head of State, soon to be embroiled in the **Chinese–Japanese Wars**. Almost unaided, he managed to hang on until America came into the war in 1941 to provide military support and a place on the Allied War Council. After **World War II**, however, he was beaten by the Communist forces under **Mao Tse-tung** and ejected from the mainland to Taiwan where, with American support, he continued to rule a puppet Nationalist government.

Chindits. A force of 3,000 men, named after a mythical Burmese lion, formed from 77 Indian Brigade in 1942 by Brigadier Orde Wingate to raid Japanese lines of communication in **Burma**. Its marching columns, supplied by air drop, crossed the River Chindwin in February 1943 and a month later cut the Mandalay–Myitkyina railway. Strong Japanese reaction prevented further attacks and forced a withdrawal in April of the emaciated columns, whose losses were 1,000. The only successes Wingate could justly claim were the feasibility of air-drop supply and the ability of British troops to compete against the Japanese in jungle.

The second Chindit expedition in March 1944 was a far more elaborate affair by five brigades, mainly inserted by glider and transport aircraft after landing grounds had been constructed adjacent to the same railway attacked as before. Although damage was done and the Japanese seriously distracted while mounting their invasion of India, the outcome was not worth the effort and the heavy losses incurred. Impetus declined after Wingate was killed in an air crash on 25 March. The spent force was withdrawn in July.

Chinese civil wars. In 1851 the Manchu empire was shaken by the T'ai P'ing Rebellion, a complicated uprising (with foreign involvement) by political, religious and criminal elements which, until it collapsed in 1865 after the fall of Nanking in 1864, had ravaged 17 provinces and cost an estimated 20 million people's lives. The struggle went on to the accompaniment of the second **Opium War** and was followed by continuous, nation-wide revolts by tribal chieftains

and, from 1883 to 1885, a small, victorious, undeclared war against France which further weakened Manchu naval power.

In the aftermath of the **Boxer Rebellion**, the rise of Nationalism led to revolution in 1911, a period of turmoil which began with an army mutiny, spread rapidly through the country and led to the replacement of the Manchus by a republic in 1912 as the nation broke into fragments. Fighting between powerful war lords became endemic in the 1920s as the Nationalist Kuomintang under Sun Yat-sen came to power in 1924, assisted by **Chiang Kai-shek**. The latter, in 1926, struck at the war lords and wore them down by a combination of **propaganda** and military action. Xenophobia became rampant, as the Japanese began staging 'incidents' and as the Kuomintang came into conflict with the newly formed Communist Party. Fighting between Nationalists and Communists became widespread in 1928, with large areas falling into the latter's hands while the struggle to quell war lords continued to Nationalist benefit.

In 1930 the Communists revolted and the fight against them merged with the struggle against the war lords as Chiang also tried to prepare the country for war against Japan. Chiang's ruthless anti-Communist 'extermination campaigns' between 1930 and 1934 were interrupted by **Chinese–Japanese** 'incidents'. Nevertheless, in 1934 he managed to bring such pressure on the First and Second Front Armies (in which **Mao Tse-tung** was a political commissar) that the Communists were forced to make the celebrated Long March to northern China. Covering 6,000 miles in 13 months, fighting some of the way, losing perhaps 100,000 out of the 200,000 with whom they started, they spread Communist cells wherever they went. Yet they left Chiang temporary master of China, in a position to attack war lords until the Japanese invaded in mass in 1937.

Throughout the struggle against Japan civil war was waged, to break out in full flood in August 1945 when both sides competed to take possession of Japanese arms. Offensive followed offensive as the Communists, supported by Russia, held off the Nationalists, supported by America. But after American aid was halted in 1946, the initiative passed permanently to the Communists who, throughout 1948 and notably at **Mukden**, won the series of victories under General Chu Teh which swept them from

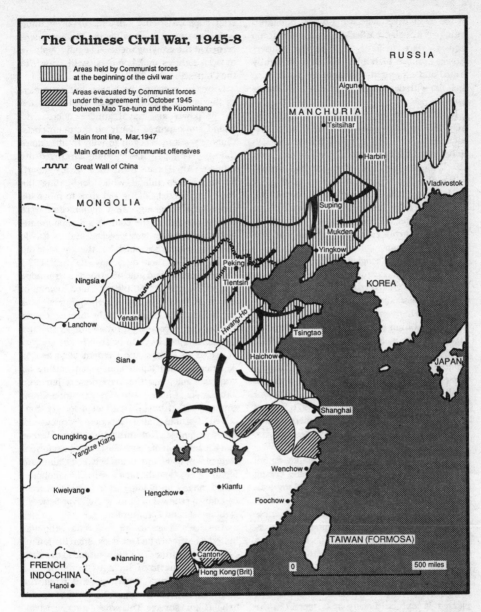

The Chinese Civil War, 1945-8

Areas held by Communist forces
at the beginning of the civil war

Areas evacuated by Communist forces
under the agreement in October 1945
between Mao Tse-tung and the Kuomintang

Main front line, Mar. 1947

Main direction of Communist offensives

Great Wall of China

RUSSIA

MANCHURIA

Aigun

Tsitsihar

Harbin

Vladivostok

MONGOLIA

Suping

Mukden

Yingkow

KOREA

Ningsia

Peking

Tientsin

Lanchow

Yenan

Hwang-Ho

Tsingtao

Sian

Haichow

JAPAN

Shanghai

Chungking

Yangtze Kiang

Changsha

Wenchow

Kweiyang

Hengchow

Kianfu

Foochow

TAIWAN (FORMOSA)

Nanning

Canton

0   500 miles

FRENCH
INDO-CHINA

Hong Kong (Brit)

Hanoi

one end of the country to another until the
Nationalist government was compelled to retire
to Taiwan in 1949, leaving Mao Tse-tung to
govern a unified China.

Chinese–Japanese Wars. *War of 1894–5.* The
modernization of Japan in the late 19th century
was an overture to aggression and war in 1894

over Chinese influence in Korea. In July, without
declaration of war, the Japanese sent troops to
Korea, defeated a small Chinese army at Songh-
wan and attacked a Chinese convoy at sea. War
was declared on 1 August as both sides reinforced their armies in Korea. At Pyongyang, on
15 September, 20,000 Japanese overwhelmed
14,000 Chinese and chased them northwards

to the **Yalu River** where a Chinese squadron with two ironclad **battleships** guarded a troop convoy. Here a force of Japanese cruisers attacked on the 17th and, though more lightly armed and armoured, managed to concentrate their fire with deadly effect and sink five Chinese ships.

Freed from Chinese naval threat, the Japanese were able to enter Manchuria in October and advance to **Port Arthur**, which fell on 19 November with little resistance after a surprise dawn attack. Meanwhile the Chinese fleet had escaped to **Wei-Hai-Wei**, which was put under siege by the Japanese Army and Navy in January 1895, and captured by the end of the month. Nine days later, after another defeat at Tapingshan, the Chinese Army collapsed and the war was brought to an end.

The Mukden and Shanghai incidents and invasion of Jehol. Blatant Japanese aggression against China came to a head when they manufactured a pretext to seize the Chinese arsenal in **Mukden** as a prelude to overrunning Manchuria. A trade boycott by China provoked Japan into landing 70,000 troops at Shanghai in January 1932, an invasion which was fiercely resisted by the Chinese who for over a month prevented the Japanese getting far inland. Air fighting, though on a small scale, introduced the world to the power of the Japanese naval air force flying 76 fighters and bombers from two **aircraft carriers** against Chinese airfields and in support of the landings. Fighting came to an end in March. But a year later the Japanese were on the march again, invading Jehol province and threatening Peking before extracting concessions from **Chiang Kai-shek** and the weakened Chinese.

The War of 1937 to 1945. Increased Japanese pressure aimed at subjugating China, and exacerbated by typical border incidents, instigated a full-scale undeclared war on 7 July 1937; in effect the beginning of **World War II**. Vastly superior in weapons technology and training, the Japanese Army was able to do much as it pleased. It captured Peking and Tientsin in the first onrush, while the Navy mounted an amphibious attack against Shanghai. But once more Shanghai proved a tough nut to crack, the Chinese holding out for nearly two months while the Japanese refined their **amphibious** forces and naval air forces in fierce combat. For the first time the Japanese carrier-borne aircraft met strong resistance from modern American air-

craft supplied to the Chinese, in air fighting which was to intensify when the Russians, concerned at the growing menace, began supplying modern fighters and bombers, with crews, to the Chinese.

Losses mounted on both sides but gradually, as the Japanese ground forces, well supported by air power and naval gunfire, encroached inland and captured nearly all the main ports, Chinese resistance began to wilt. In little more than a year Japan had virtually destroyed the Chinese Air Force, torn their Army apart, advanced deep inland while dominating the coast, and forced Chiang Kai-shek to move his capital to Chungking. Many major cities were heavily bombed as the country's limited manufacturing capacity was wrecked and its fragile communications smashed. Yet the Japanese did not have it all their own way. In April 1938 Chinese regular and guerrilla troops surrounded a Japanese army of 60,000 at Taierchwang, of whom 20,000 men and much equipment was lost before the remainder fought their way out.

Japanese successes throughout 1939 and December 1941 have to be seen in the context of events in Europe and German victories. As America warned Japan and began cutting off vital war materials, the movement of Japanese forces, via China, into French Indo-China emerged as an integral part of a loosely conceived German–Italian–Japanese strategy of world conquest. Not until after **Pearl Harbor** and the invasion of **South-East Asia** did a formal state of war come into being between China and Japan. But by then the Japanese in China concentrated mainly on holding their gains, a process eased by a renewal of **Chinese civil war** between Nationalists and Communists.

America's desire to supply China with war material received a bad set-back when the Japanese overran **Burma**. The Allies intended to establish an air link from India to Kunming and reopen the Burma Road by reinforcing the Chinese forces and seizing North Burma in order to help China survive. This proved a very frustrating process. Not until late 1943 did the Chinese have much effect in Burma while minor Japanese offensives designed to deprive the Chinese of food – the so-called 'rice offensives' – neutralized Chiang's Nationalists who remained at loggerheads with Mao's Communists. Such successes as there were came from American aircraft under General Claire Chennault, which raided

China in the Second World War, 1944

as far afield as Formosa (Taiwan). In 1944 these raids prompted the Japanese, coincident with an invasion of India in 1944, to attempt the conquest of South-East China. Although the Japanese in a series of fierce battles pushed the Chinese back and captured 12 airfields, they were unable against improved Chinese troops, supported by Chennault's aircraft, to reach the key logistics centre at Kunming.

The Allied victory in Burma, which reopened the Burma Road early in 1945, ensured China's survival. Nevertheless, the Japanese persisted with offensives along the Chinese coast and in the central region until checked and forced, in May, to make limited withdrawals in order to

conserve strength. The end came in August when the Russians conquered Manchuria in seven days, smashing a Japanese force of about 60,000 which had been drained of its best units. Afterwards civil war flourished again.

Chinese–Vietnamese incidents. Throughout history there has been friction between the Chinese and Vietnamese people, kept in check during the French occupation of Indo-China and set aside in 1950 when the Chinese Communist government gave aid to the Vietminh. Friction reappeared, however, at the conclusion of the **Vietnam War.** A series of border clashes flared up in 1979 when the Vietnamese army

73

demonstrated its superiority by inflicting a number of disastrous rebuffs on the Chinese, who lacked the recent combat practice of their opponents.

Churchill, Winston Spencer (1874–1965). Commissioned into the Hussars in 1895, Churchill's apprenticeship in war began as a correspondent during the **Cuban War** of 1895; as a soldier in the Malakand in India, 1897; as a correspondent in the **Sudan** in 1898 (when he charged with the cavalry at Omdurman); and in the Boer War (**South African Wars**) as a correspondent, when he was captured but escaped.

It was when he became First Lord of the Admiralty in 1911 that his military talent was given rein; when **World War I** broke out he could claim credit for having the Royal Navy at a high pitch of readiness. And during the initial battles he played a personal part in the defence of Antwerp and the founding of Britain's air defences, while also setting in motion the development of **armoured fighting vehicles**. Churchill's sponsorship of the disastrous **Gallipoli** venture in 1915 put a temporary end to his higher direction of the war. For a few months in 1916 he served in the trenches and in 1917 became Minister for Munitions, in which capacity he had a voice in strategy before becoming Minister for War in 1919, charged with demobilization of the Army, British involvement in the **Russian Revolution**, and military assistance in the policing of the Empire, notably in India.

After 1921 Churchill was either in civil ministries or out of office. But he kept in touch and, with the emergence of aggressive Japanese, Italian and German designs in the 1930s, became a lonely and largely ignored voice of warning. Once more appointed First Lord of the Admiralty at the outbreak of **World War II**, he immediately took the lead in proposing aggressive strategies and, through radio broadcasts, reacquired a strong following inside Britain and abroad. When the Chamberlain government fell in May 1940, on the eve of Allied defeat in the West by the Axis, and Churchill became Prime Minister and Minister of Defence, it was his determination and inspiration which kept Britain in the war.

His dominating, all-embracing conduct of the war was often controversial, owing to a personal belief in his military genius and wide experience. A pronounced tendency to interfere in detail and to propose unsound schemes frequently dismayed military leaders. But for the most part his conduct of grand strategy was sound and vital to victory, notably by his shrewd wooing of President **Roosevelt** to bring the USA into the war; his immediate acceptance, against the political grain, of Joseph **Stalin**'s Russia as an ally; and his adherence, once convinced after prolonged debate, to the strategies and plans of his professional advisers. Above all, his projection of character kept the people steadfast in the darkest hours and held the Alliance together when the stresses were overbearing, through a personality which he impressed upon all by indefatigably travelling the world and the battle fronts to see things for himself and keep in touch with the leaders and the fighting men.

It was a sad irony that, having seen Britain to victory in Europe in May 1945, the electorate denied him the opportunity of remaining Prime Minister when Japan sued for peace, and to help lay the foundations of the post-war world.

CIA (Central Intelligence Agency). The USA's principal intelligence organization, under the National Security Council (NSC), formed by the National Security Act of Congress in 1947. As a distant successor to the Office of Strategic Services (OSS), with many members of that wartime organization involved, its tasks include: security; co-ordination of intelligence departments; gathering, evaluation and distribution of intelligence; and performance of special tasks as directed by the NSC.

In practice the CIA delves in every form of covert state activity, sometimes stormily crossing the path of the Federal Bureau of Investigation (FBI). It wages guerrilla and anti-guerrilla warfare, and not only against the Communists, who are its principal targets. Little escapes its agents' attention. Many are the crises it has either caused or stepped into, including undermining the Iranian government in 1954 and overthrowing the Chilean one in 1973, quite apart from its interminable contest with Russian and Chinese Communist agents throughout the world and in such hot spots as **Cuba, Afghanistan, Central** and **South America**. Assassination and abduction are among its trades, along with dissemination of propaganda of all shades.

Frequently portrayed by its enemies as a thoroughly corrupt and destabilizing influence, one capable of acting independently without presidential approval, it has only occasionally been challenged by Congress during such dramas as the Watergate affair in the 1970s and the 'Iran–Contra' scandal of 1987. In a traditionally dirty trade, in which all secret services play shady roles, the CIA has a vital role in defence of the West.

Civil defence. There has always been a demand for passive defence of the civil populace in wartime, notably during sieges. Its modern form, however, dates from the dropping of aerial bombs by German aircraft in 1914 and, in particular, from the bombing of London and Paris by Zeppelins and long-range bombers throughout **World War I**. To begin with people were warned of approaching danger and the need to take cover in cellars and beneath stairs by the sounding of sirens. These manifestations of governmental care usually averted panic and sustained morale against light and sporadic raids.

The threat prior to **World War II** of intensified **air warfare** as postulated by the apostles of **strategic bombing** of cities, such as Giulio **Douhet** and others, compelled governments to give high priority to civil defence, or 'Air Raid Precautions' as, for example, they were first called in Britain. Badly scared by the protagonists of bombing, who produced spurious evidence (much culled from the **Spanish Civil War** and the **Chinese–Japanese Wars**) of the devastating effects of high explosives, gas and incendiary bombs, authorities spent vast sums on building public shelters, issuing respirators and forming organizations to evacuate city populations to safer areas. Also they formed rescue, fire-fighting and medical services to deal with damage and casualties on a huge scale to maintain the nation, industry and law and order.

Although the effects of short, sharp attacks on Warsaw in 1939 and Rotterdam in May 1940 tended to endorse the Cassandras, the prolonged air attacks on Britain – the so-called Blitz between August 1940 and May 1941 – brought matters into perspective. Gas was not used and damage from high explosives and fire, though often extensive as the result of concentrated attacks, was neither so crippling as forecast, nor so expensive in lives or erosive of morale. As the civil defence services improved with practice (in particular in post-raid welfare, repair and rehousing), and as people learned to take shelter and 'live with the Blitz', the dangers of a collapse in morale and serious loss of production receded. The experience of Germany and Japan as their cities were razed under the most intensive bombing of the war, was on a far worse scale. Provision of very strong shelters helped in Germany and draconian measures by the police and military stamped out such signs of relapses of steadfastness as became evident among pre-eminently apathetic people.

The dropping of the **atom bomb** on Hiroshima and Nagasaki in 1945 and the subsequent development of the **hydrogen bomb** and extremely deadly **chemical** weapons stimulated greater interest than ever in civil defence, even though the prospects of survival against weapons of mass destruction seemed problematical, to say the least. The reinforced organization and measures of nations who saw themselves as possible targets were mainly scaling up of what previously existed, with greater emphasis on post-attack survival than anything else. While some nations, such as Britain in the 1960s, virtually abandoned efforts to control the effects of nuclear attack by disbanding their major civil defence services, the Russians seemed to reinforce theirs. It was suggested that, in the event of a nuclear holocaust, surviving Russians, sustained by efficient civil defence, would have a decisive advantage over unprotected opponents, a contention which declined in credibility in the aftermath of the Armenian earthquake of 1988 when Russian rescue and welfare services failed badly. In effect, civil defence plans provide little more than guide-lines for action in a major catastrophe.

Clark, General Mark Wayne (1896–1984). A US army officer who came to notice in 1942 in a clandestine meeting with French officers prior to the invasion of French North-West Africa. He commanded Fifth US Army at **Salerno** and, after hard fighting for **Anzio**, Rome and North Italy, took command of 15th Army Group in December 1944 until the end of the war in Italy (**Italian Campaign 1943–5**) and Austria. After further Army commands in the USA, he took over the United Nations forces in Korea (**Korean Wars**) from May 1952 until the war's end in 1953.

Clemenceau, Georges (1841–1929). A French statesman who struggled throughout **World**

War I to improve the supply of munitions and who in November 1917, at the nadir of French fortunes, became Prime Minister. By demanding nothing less than absolute victory and ruthlessly sacking defeatists, he restored French self-confidence. At the same time, without indulging too much in strategy, he negotiated joint command for the Allied armies, and, against popular disapproval, he placed General **Foch** at their head in the rank of Marshal to break the **Hindenburg offensive** and, unexpectedly, lead the Allies to victory in 1918.

Clocks and watches. Reasonably accurate mechanical timepieces had been developed by the British for navigation at sea by the end of the 18th century. However, the need for military operations on land was not so readily apparent, since all elements of armies engaged in battle tended to be within sight of one another. Correct timing of when to open fire or to deliver an assault could usually be co-ordinated by visual or audible signals. Split-second timing rarely entered into a commander's calculations and would have been difficult (if not impossible) to achieve if it had. (Nevertheless, the French co-ordinated their attacks on **Sevastopol** in the **Crimea** with synchronized watches.)

The operations of **World War I**, however, introduced a new dimension with its immense fire programmes from hundreds of guns, all out of sight from the infantry they were supporting, all of which had to be carefully co-ordinated with the forward movement of attacking troops. Accurate timing became vital and a good watch became an essential part of an officer's equipment.

Even so, up until 1925 the *pendulum clock*, first constructed in 1625, remained the most exact timepiece available, with rates constant to about 0.001sec per day; hardly appropriate for use in military operations on land, sea or in the air. No longer used for precise timekeeping the *pendulum clock*, and indeed the ordinary *mechanical watch*, has been supplanted by the *quartz-crystal clock* and *watch*, operating either a conventional hands-and-dial counter, or with a digital read-out. A difference in electrical potential applied across the face of a quartz crystal will deform the crystal – the piezo-electric effect. This enables the crystal to control the frequency of an electrical circuit; since frequency is measured in cycles per second (or Hertz) the

property can be related to a visible time-scale in a timepiece. The best such devices have very low accelerations of the order of one part in 10^{11} per day.

An even later development has been the *atomic clock*, which uses energy changes within atoms to produce coherent, regular, electromagnetic radiation waves. These can be counted to give a measure of time. Small versions weighing about 30kg have been made, accurate to about two parts in 10^{12}.

With military operations in the 1990s ranging far and wide over land, sea and in the air, and with missiles aimed at targets on the other side of the world, such accuracy of timing becomes an essential feature of military planning and of the execution of those plans.

Clothing, Military. The soldiers of the Roman Empire must be one of the earliest examples of an army uniformly dressed and bearing indications of rank and status. Their leaders understood well not only the fundamental importance of ensuring that their men could easily recognize their comrades in the heat of battle, but also the aid to morale that a smart and practical uniform could be.

Following the decline of Roman power uniform for national armies virtually disappeared, not least because, during the Dark Ages, few standing armies existed. However, by the 17th century military uniforms were in general use throughout Europe, though little or no thought was given to their suitability for wear in battle. Rather, uniforms in the British Army at least reflected the taste, or lack of it, of individual commanding officers. Dress regulations specifying official patterns for clothing were well established by the mid-19th century, but even as late as the **Crimean War** wealthy commanding officers not infrequently paid for distinctive embellishments to their men's uniforms out of their own pockets. A typical example was the flamboyant Lord Cardigan, of whose 11th Hussars *The Times* said in 1854: 'The splendour of these magnificent light horsemen, the shortness of their jackets, the tightness of their cherry-coloured pants made them 'utterly unfit for war service . . .'

The **American Civil War** saw the Federal forces clad in sober blue, while the Confederates wore a generally grey uniform, which often degenerated into a locally dyed 'butternut' colour as the war went against them. The extent to which Southern grey was a stylistic choice rather than a conscious effort at camouflage is not clear, but gradually it was beginning to dawn on soldiers that smart parade uniforms were neither comfortable nor safe to wear on the battlefield.

Nevertheless, the British Army clung to their eye-catching red coats, as colourful as they were impractical for war, to the end of the 19th century, suffering accordingly at the hands of the **Boers**, an enemy clothed in a way which allowed for easy concealment. But change was on the way and it stemmed from the Indian Army, where the Corps of Guides had been raised in 1846. Their first commanding officer, Lumsden, decided that his Corps should be clothed in brown – to some extent, it seems, to be different from Coke's Rifles who wore green. He ordered the cloth expensively from Britain, but before it could arrive the Guides were in action dressed in locally dyed material, which subsequently they continued to use. Sir Charles Napier, Commander-in-Chief India, commented after the Kohaut Pass campaign: 'The Guides are the only properly dressed Riflemen in India.'

Gradually, khaki, as it came to be known, was adopted in the Indian Army and, during the Boer War, by the British Army also. An Army Order of 1902 laid down regulations for the new form of dress, described as 'service' dress, i.e. for use in the field, the old forms being retained for use in peacetime conditions. This was the first time in the British Army that a specific 'combat' dress was ordered; it is an ironic development that, in the late 20th century, service dress is kept for smart and semi-formal wear.

However, khaki service dress clothed the British Expeditionary Force that went to France in 1914 and photographs of that period show how almost equally unsuitable it was for fighting in (apart from the colour) as previous styles had been: tight-fitting; choker collar (for non-commissioned ranks); cumbersome puttees; peaked caps. The Germans, for their part, had gone into a field grey uniform, broadly similar in style to the British; only the French were clinging to their unchanged blue coat with red facings. **World War I** produced only one major change in military clothing, the introduction of the steel helmet: the German 'coal scuttle' (probably the most effective); the British 'tin

hat' (clearly derived from the minimal armour worn by British infantry in the Middle Ages); and the distinctive French helmet.

The next major change came about through mechanization in the British Army, when it was realized that service dress was ill-suited to men fighting in armoured vehicles. The Royal Tank Corps, the Royal Artillery and other mechanized units thereupon put their men into one-piece 'combination overalls', shapeless garments such as garage mechanics wore. From this evolved the battledress adopted throughout the British Army in 1938 – the first really practical combat clothing to be designed (though the doctors were concerned about the lack of climatic protection to the lower abdomen given by the blouse top). The Germans put their tank crews into black overalls similar to those of the Tank Corps, but they, and most other armies, retained for most of their troops the service-dress-type jacket which by this time was in almost universal use.

In the latter half of the 20th century it has been belatedly realized that, if the soldier is to maintain his efficiency on the battlefield, he must have properly designed clothing for the purpose. Formal wear remains broadly unchanged, but almost all armies now have special tough, lightweight, water-repellent, windproof, camouflaged combat clothing, worn in action with a helmet and, often, some form of body armour. Especially difficult has been the search for a satisfactory boot, one combining hard wear, waterproof, comfortable and easy to put on and remove. The Soviet soldier retains his high boots – an unsatisfactory design for long distance marching – while in the West calf-length lace-up boots have found most favour. Headgear, apart from the combat helmet and full-dress caps in various forms, is almost universally the beret, in the style first adopted by the British Tank Corps and worn now even by the Royal Air Force (whose uniform has generally followed Army patterns) and by the Royal Navy.

Underlying all this is the need to distinguish the soldier from the civilian during active operations. It has been tacitly recognized since the 18th century, when warfare became more formalized in Europe, that the uniformed soldier was a legitimate target while the civilian should be spared, even when found on the battlefield. At the same time it also became usual for the soldier fighting in uniform, and subsequently captured, to be treated humanely as a prisoner of war; but if fighting out of uniform, be he soldier or civilian, he became liable to execution as a guerrilla or spy. In the 20th century, and especially with the development of the Resistance movement in occupied Europe during World War II, the definition of what constituted a uniform, or indeed a soldier, became less clear; an armband, such as worn by the British Local Defence Volunteers (later the Home Guard) was generally considered an acceptable minimum. The distinction between soldier and civilian was formally defined for the first time by the Geneva Convention of 1949, the soldier being required to wear clothing indicating he was 'of the military', to be under formal command and to carry his arms openly.

As for naval uniform, sailors have traditionally worn more casual and practical dress than soldiers and it was not until the 19th century that members of the lower deck had a formal uniform of any kind. Blue has not surprisingly been the predominant colour and while full dress for officers has, like that of the Army, generally reflected national styles, embellished with their own particular trimmings, working dress has always been and remains much less formal. In the modern Royal Navy sailors carrying out operational tasks ashore have sensibly adopted the soldiers' standard combat clothing.

Coast defence. Any country with a coastline to defend knows very well that it would be impossible to guard every conceivable landing-place. Even such a comparatively small area as the British Isles has a coast which is several thousands of miles in length. The first line of defence, for Britain at least, has always been the Royal Navy and, in modern times, the Royal Air Force, in the hope that any sea-borne attack can be intercepted before it reaches the shore.

In Britain the south coast ports have always been fortified from ancient times, facing as they do the obvious threat from across the English Channel. The works protecting Plymouth provide a good example of the elaborate defences put in hand during the mid 19th century to contain the threat which Britain perceived from the expansionist policies of France under Napoleon III; that the threat came to nothing is irrelevant. The defence of Plymouth Sound and the dockyard against bombardment were deemed paramount. This called for a ring of forts both seaward and landward, running from

Tregantle on the Cornish coast round to Staddon Heights to the east. The aim was not only to frustrate enemy gunfire from ships, but also to prevent any force getting ashore within bombardment range (set at 6,000 yards) of the **dockyard**. There were, with the existing much-neglected defences, to be 10 forts on the inner line and 14 on the outer, each ring with a continuous rampart to allow reinforcement of any part of the line from under cover. The cost was to be some £11,850,000 – an astronomical sum for those days. The defences would be manned by volunteer reserves, as they traditionally had been, with the Regular Army held in reserve inland for counter-attack.

By 1865 Tregantle Fort (87 guns) had been completed; 12 guns, with an inadequate arc of fire, faced seawards. By 1885 the work was still incomplete and as late as 1903 the question of arming the Plymouth defences was still in issue and was never brought to a conclusion. This example underlines the enormous problems facing the defender, made worse as gun range increased. An interesting development employed in the defence of the River Thames in 1885 was the Brennan torpedo, wire-guided and launched down slipways from a number of Thames forts. The torpedo was steered by varying the unwinding speed of two spools, each geared to separate propellers. The device, which had a range of two miles, soon became obsolete as gun accuracy and range improved.

By 1940, when Britain's coastline was once again under threat, the Army, lacking in mobility, anti-tank guns and field artillery, stood guard at selected points protected by primitive defences: barbed wire, some concrete emplacements and such devices as drums of petrol to set light to the landing beaches. Opinions varied as to which the likely landing-places were and the principal defence had therefore to be the Royal Navy and Royal Air Force.

When it came to Germany's turn in defending Europe's coastline from Allied attack in 1944 she had had time to erect complex concrete gun positions coupled with elaborate waterline obstacles set into beaches between low- and high-water marks. This was all to no avail when the attack came and it is now generally accepted that if an invading force cannot be intercepted offshore, it will be extremely difficult to prevent it from landing, as the **Falklands War** so clearly showed. Once the enemy is ashore, defence must be based on the traditional concept of direct defence of key points, with a mobile force available for reinforcement and counter-attack.

Codes and ciphers. Since writing began, codes (systems of words, letters or symbols to represent others) and ciphers (disguised writing) have been in demand for secrecy and brevity in communication. They have been developed not only for military use but also in diplomacy, commerce, crime and day-to-day reporting of events. Simultaneously, great ingenuity has been applied to the interception and decoding of messages, a process which called for vastly greater effort with the introduction of 'open' electronic communication by **telegraph**, **telephone** and **radio**.

Although ways of concealing writing (*steganography*), such as use of invisible ink, have been used with some success, the most secure, rapid and efficient methods have been by *transposition* of letters by jumbling them or by *substitution* by other letters, numbers or symbols. Samuel Morse invented his code of dashes and dots in the 1830s for standard non-secret simplicity in transmitting telegraphic pulses. At once hundreds of different ways of encoding messages in Morse code were invented; at the same time, people skilled in decoding concentrated upon breaking each system. To begin with code systems either were written, recorded in documents and books, or were mechanical, such as the compact-wheel cipher invented by Thomas Jefferson at the end of the 18th century. Usually these systems were bulky, complex and vulnerable to decoding if they or their key fell into enemy hands, or if they could be rapidly broken. A code's value is in proportion to its degree of resistance to attack.

Codes were extensively used during the **American Civil War**. The Stager transposition cipher employed by the Federals could be carried on a man's back and was both easy to use and reliable. The very secure Vigenère cipher in Confederate use was complicated, prone to corruption and easy to break once the keys were detected by Federal decoders. Most codes were vulnerable but interception of messages was dependent on wire-tapping (mainly in cavalry raids) and capturing messengers – methods which produced only sporadic results. Indeed, not until radio came into adequate operational use during the **Russo-Japanese War** was the prospect of continuous intercept possible.

Needless to say codes were employed from the start to disguise radio messages, although to begin with most systems and many operators were slipshod. The Russian Fleet's signals en route to **Tsushima** were monitored and understood by the Japanese. At the beginning of **World War I** messages were as often decoded as not. The Russian defeat at **Tannenberg** was largely due to extremely lax security discipline which precisely disclosed to the Germans their deployment because messages were faultily encoded or even sent 'in clear'. On the Western Front the French, who had established an elaborate monitoring system, obtained remarkably correct intelligence of German organization, deployment and intentions as they advanced to defeat at the **Marne**. While at sea, the British, having obtained a copy of German naval codes from a wrecked cruiser (and, later, other vessels), read much German naval traffic for the rest of the war, to enormous advantage in the Battles of **Dogger Bank** and **Jutland** as well as in **Blockade** operations.

Between the **World Wars** a number of sophisticated electromechanical encoding machines were developed, of which the German *Enigma* was the most famous. Assumed to be unbreakable by the Germans, the combined work of the Poles and the British had, by 1940, produced an electromechanical **computer** which could rapidly break the majority of German Enigma keys as well as those used by the Italians and Japanese on similar machines. As a result the Germans, who made only limited penetrations of enemy high-grade codes, were at a war-losing disadvantage to the Allies, who for most of the war read a vast quantity of high-grade, top-level messages by opponents who used radio with abandon. At the same time widespread use of simplified codes was employed for operations at lower levels and by agents and partisans operating behind enemy lines. Of these the only ones which were both compact, reliable and unbreakable were the one-time-use kind – sometimes, in simplest form, known as OTP (One-Time Pad).

In **Cold War**, espionage and outbreaks of violence, the struggle between code makers and code breakers has intensified. To baffle more sophisticated computers and methods, immensely complex and more secure encoding systems have been developed, such as manpack radio sets with an inbuilt computer capable of informing a receiver of its automatically selected random key at start of transmission. Such systems are difficult to break. They place enormous demands on technology and code breakers, besides employing enormous numbers of people and machines to handle the ever-growing volume of traffic sent by hand and electronic means. Codes will be broken but by saturation a vast amount of intelligence will get through unread or unreadable.

With so vast a subject only an outline can be given here. Since David Kahn's *The Codebreakers* was published in 1966 a subject previously little known has become popular, yet remains deep in the secrecy upon which it thrives.

Cold War. A term describing the state of mistrust and hostility which existed between Russia and her principal Western **World War II** allies. Sometimes considered to have started at the time of friction during the **Warsaw** Uprising in 1944, its name was coined by a journalist, Herbert Swope, and first used politically in 1947. Since then it has collectively described frigid diplomacy, political manoeuvring, economic pressures, subversion and almost any conflict, usually fuelled by propaganda, which falls short of outright war. Although during brief periods of detente in the mid-1960s and the late 1980s there were periods of thaw, the state of Cold War remains.

Cold War was created by mutual suspicion between Britain and America, on the one hand, and Russia on the other. To Joseph **Stalin**, America's possession of the **atom bomb** posed a threat to security. To President Harry **Truman**, Russia's occupation of Eastern Europe by large military forces was no less menacing. A host of unresolved difficulties which could not be settled by negotiations (which, as often as not, were themselves integral with the Cold War) contributed to a series of major confrontations fomented by escalating disenchantment.

Some battle grounds were located at United Nations meetings and peace-treaty conferences. Elsewhere overt and covert campaigns were conducted on the slightest pretext with the Russians encouraging Communist activists to stir up dissent and strikes wherever blossoming nationalism or anti-colonialism were taking root. For example, as part of the **Greek Civil War**, the siege of **Berlin**, and in the subversion of Czechoslovakia in 1948. Or in Korea (**Korean Wars**), where Russian and Chinese support of the North Korean ambitions in South Korea got out of control and led to **limited war** in 1950. On the other side, American and colonial powers' initiatives to defeat or pre-empt further Russian and Chinese-sponsored take-overs were quoted as blatant examples of acquisitive Western motives and exploited to aggravate the situation (notably in the case of ineffectual American attempts to frustrate Communist domination of **Cuba** in the 1960s).

An early major turning-point was the immense success of the American Marshall Plan, with its revitalization by 1952 of the European economy, and the simultaneous setting up of **Nato** and **Seato** as military bulwarks of joint defence by threatened nations. Thereafter the Communists lost the initiative and, in turn, were brought under pressure by Western, often CIA-inspired, uprisings such as in **Berlin** in 1952, Hungary in 1956 and Czechoslovakia in 1968. At the same time the possession of the **hydrogen bomb** by both sides in the mid-1950s made it far less likely that global war would occur, and thus more possible for limited and cold wars to be preferred as ways of continuing diplomacy by other means.

Cold War strains can be detected in virtually all the major as well as minor confrontations of the post-World War II period, penetrating almost every aspect of evolving high technology in the struggle for weapons superiority as part of the balancing act of **deterrence**, infected by espionage and corruption on a vast scale, and often becoming an integral way of life in international relationships when attempts by one party or another to lessen tension tend to be interpreted as just another round in the continuing contest. Thus, for example, **disarmament** and arms limitation treaties were frequently regarded as means to an end in the struggle for military advantage.

Even in the political revolutions of 1989–90 Cold War survives mildly.

Colt, Samuel (1814–62). An American inventor who was one among many, after the invention of the percussion cap in the early 19th century, to produce a practical, multi-chamber, rotating-breech firearm. Fame came from the revolver he patented in 1835 and manufactured in large numbers for the **Mexican War** of 1846. He also built electrically fired submarine **mines**, was involved with **telegraphs** and laid the first underwater cable.

Combat Drill. Armed forces depend upon thoroughly considered and practised drills and procedures in the approach to battle and in combat. Success often goes to the best indoctrinated side which manages to inspire a disciplined self-confidence in simple and effective tactics through the co-ordinated use of weapons in the heat of battle. Prior to 1850 the shortcomings of signal communications and the limitations of weapons imposed close order for adequate control of basic fire and movement on formations at sea and on land. Initiative at lower levels was not expected. Electronic communications and far more deadly weapons imposed dispersal, initially on formations and subsequently on units and sub-units. Whereas at the start of World War I, fleets fought in large groups and armies in dense masses, by 1918 individual warships, notably submarines, were hunting alone and control of dispersed combat troops often depended upon the initiative of junior officers.

By 1940 radio had made possible a high degree of centralized control of sea, land and air operations by headquarters whose battle procedures were governed by established drills. Standard combat drills were also devised and rehearsed, over and over again, to make fighting men, particularly on land and in the air, react positively to every imaginable minor tactical situation. Fundamentally this implied the issue of outline instructions in preference to precise and rigid orders, a method which flourishes today as educational standards are raised.

Combat Fatigue. A psychiatric disorder which, under the title 'shellshock', came to notice in World War I as the result of men enduring prolonged periods of stress in warships, the trenches and aircraft. Its manifestations include 'jumpiness' from hypersensitivity to noise; loss of appetite and sleep; irritability; and ailments such as ulcers and headaches in conjunction with nervous collapse, all of which can be accumulative and reduce efficiency. Little sympathy was shown to numerous sufferers, who usually were regarded as malingerers or cowards, and quite frequently court-martialled and shot.

As a result of publicity between the World Wars, public concern and a better enlightened understanding of nervous disorders induced a more sympathetic and constructive approach to the recognition and treatment of what, in World War II, came to be known as 'battle exhaustion'. On medical advice, attempts were made to limit men's exposure to stress, chiefly by reducing time spent in combat (for example, by restricting the number of operations undertaken by air crew) and providing periods of rest and recuperation in comfortable accommodation at a distance from the front. Treatment of bad cases included prolonged periods under sedation and electric-shock therapy to both cure and return the patient to duty, a practice which, in its modern form, has been improved upon in some forces by the establishment of stress management centres close to the front line where minor cases are dealt with at the earliest moment, often returning a high proportion of cases to the front within 72 hours.

Command, Control and Communications. See C³.

Command, Control, Communications and Intelligence. See C³I.

Commando. A Portuguese word adapted by the South African Boers as the title of militia units, based on electoral districts. In the Boer War they won a great reputation, despite a certain indiscipline, for their outstanding marksmanship, horsemanship and endurance in prolonged combat and, subsequently, guerrilla warfare against the British.

In 1940 the British used the word to describe élite Army infantry units earmarked for amphibious raiding against Axis forces in Europe. All-volunteer and of high standard, they were well disciplined and specially trained in rigorous conditions (often under live fire and to the point of exhaustion) to use their initiative. Their 'battle drills' became models for all infantry. But valid objections were raised by those who feared that ordinary combat units would suffer from the loss of so many potential leaders. Had it not been for the efforts of Winston Churchill and Admiral Sir Roger Keyes the Commandos would have been disbanded.

As it was they produced a cadre for many specialized British 'private armies', such as the airborne forces, the Special Boat Squadron (SBS) and Special Air Service (SAS) and were copied by other nations, notably the USA who raised Marine Corps 'Raiders' and Army 'Rangers'. Also, in Britain, the Royal Marines who, by tradition, were the exponents of amphibious warfare, began forming their own Commandos in 1942. After the war, when the Army Commandos were disbanded, they continued to perform this role.

Commandos, most inadequately equipped and trained, and carried in inferior **landing craft**, started raiding the French coast on 23 June 1940. Thereafter the number and magnitude of their forays only slowly increased as they also were sent to work in the Mediterranean. Indeed, although in 1941 only a few small raids were launched from Britain, it was in the Mediterranean and Middle East where, sometimes as ordinary infantry, they were most active – with patchy results at a high price. As techniques and training improved and more special craft and equipment became available in 1942, the scale of raiding increased, rising to a peak with the **Dieppe raid** in August and culminating in the invasion of North-West Africa in November when SBS and Commandos spearheaded the sea-borne assaults.

In all the forthcoming major landings in **Madagascar**, **Sicily**, Italy (**Italian Campaign**), **France**, and **Holland**, Commandos were in the lead and usually fought on as ordinary infantry until exhausted or required for another task. Likewise in the **Pacific Ocean War**, Marine Raiders, who raided Makin, led the way in 1942 at Tulagi and on **Guadalcanal**, while Army Rangers were to the forefront in the **Philippines** in 1944. Simultaneously, however, small-scale raiding was restricted, the majority of Commando operations being concentrated upon pre-invasion beach reconnaissance and the pilotage of main assault flotillas to landing-places. There was a tug of war between those who wanted to raid and those who feared that larger plans would be disclosed or that 'stirring up' coastlines would endanger the movement of intelligence agents and guerrillas into and out of occupied territory. By the war's end, in Europe and **Burma**, Commandos were chiefly employed as shock troops in conventional land operations.

Since 1945 amphibious warfare has, in the main, been performed by Marines. British Royal Marines have been in the thick of the **Malayan War of Independence**, Korea (**Korean Wars**), **Suez**, **Irish Reunification** and the **Falklands** War of 1982. The US Marines played a leading part in Korea and in **Vietnam**, besides involvement in lesser operations such as **Lebanon** and **Grenada**. They now are lifted in more sophis-

ticated craft than originally and, since Suez, have adopted the **helicopter** as a prime means of mobility and **logistic** support between ship and shore.

Communications, Signal. Until the advent of a practical electrical **telegraph** in the 1840s, strategic and tactical military communications depended upon personal contact, couriers, homing pigeons and such visible signalling instruments as mechanical semaphore, flag, light and smoke. Most of these were hampered by inherent limitations of speed and capacity in transmission. Time of day and the weather, quite apart from obscuration in battle by dust and smoke, also degraded performance.

The primitive **telegraph** system first used in war by the British and French during the **Crimean War** provided a poor service, but it did, nevertheless, introduce close government interference with operations. Really it was the fast steamship service across the English Channel, linking with the railway to Marseilles and the longer steamship voyage to Scutari and the Crimea, which carried the bulk of messages at revolutionary speed. Courier dispatch and visual signals would still be needed, as they are today, but less so as land and submarine cable networks carrying multiplex Morse code messages and, in the 1880s, speech by **telephone** had come into general use. These changes were revolutionized by electronics with the introduction of **radio** transmissions early in the 20th century.

Navies and armies were quick to exploit the importance of these inventions, taking their cues from the alacrity of merchant shipping firms and the railways, for example, to enhance their control of business and traffic. Operational uses, including the security problem posed by the adoption of suitable **codes and ciphers**, were slower to develop. It was 1885 before the Germans used the telephone for the direction by forward observers of **artillery** fire. And, despite unsuccessful British attempts to use radio during the **Boer War**, not until the end of the **Russo-Japanese War** was it seen how effective in naval war this method was. Thus it was all the more remarkable that, although the Germans pinned great hopes on control by radio of the armies advancing into France at the start of **World War I**, they failed utterly to devise workable operating procedures, a lapse which certainly contributed to their defeat at the **Marne**.

No doubt it was the ramification of rapid signals growth which baffled military leaders, few of whom were technically educated. If there were many officers who delegated speaking on the telephone because they thought it beneath their dignity, it was hardly surprising that so many problems remained unnoticed prior to 1914. Take, for example, the unwillingness of the German General Staff to discuss their plans with the Signal Corps, thus denying forward planning of cable routes to replace those destroyed by the retreating enemy; and the tardiness of the Royal Navy to take full advantage of their insight into German codes, a reluctance which probably cost them victory at **Jutland**.

During World War I there was such a vast expansion of signals services that those armies like the British which had not already (as had the Germans and Americans) formed a Signals Corps felt compelled to do so afterwards. The corps could not only improve the handling of signals traffic but also give advice on and lead development of the flood of new technology. As knowledge of the ionosphere increased, worldwide communication networks improved, leading to 'beam' transmissions. In the 1920s the next generation of smaller, more robust, quenched radio sets, some with crystal tuning, working at ever higher frequencies of 40 megahertz (MHz), enormously improved reception. In conjunction, voice radio sets became commonplace for **aircraft** and land vehicles, and were complemented by high-speed teleprinter transmissions carried on cable which could be laid mechanically at 100 miles per day.

Military signalling in **World War II** benefited immeasurably from pre-war integration with civil systems. In Germany the armed forces dominated. But so keen was awareness of signals potential that problems of generating sufficient capacity often arose at the same time as vulnerability to intercept increased. For example, the dependence of German U-Boat operations upon radio was a weakness not only in providing a plethora of *Enigma*-encoded messages for the Allies to attack, but also frequently disclosing the location of boats from Direction Finding (DF). When secure cable routes were either destroyed or overloaded, additional use was made of less secure multi-channel radio. Net radio, however, was vital to the tactical control of ships, aircraft and of armies (particularly fast mechanized forces and artillery), in addition to

being crucial to the control and logistic support of clandestine and **guerrilla** forces behind the enemy lines. Only strictly enforced operating procedures and traffic limitation could mitigate the risks.

Since 1945 utilization of immensely improved and sophisticated signals systems has gone on apace, a revolution to which space satellites have contributed more than anything else. Vastly quicker methods of transmission with higher capacity working are allied to the sending of documents by facsimile and the capability of reducing the threat of DF by high-intensity radio 'burst' transmissions. When integrated with **television** displays and **computers**, modern signal communications provide commanders and administrators with a tool of immense power. Not only is it possible to solve and disseminate the most complex operational and **logistic** problems at immense speed, but greater opportunities to assert minute-by-minute combat control from the highest level are provided, a practice frequently indulged in by **Hitler** (often with disastrous results) and during the **Falklands** battles when, had she wished, the British Prime Minister could have spoken direct to commanders at sea.

Computers. The use of computers is now a commonplace part of every child's education; the computer is no longer a rarity in private households and electronic computing is an almost essential tool in every aspect of life from the running of small businesses to the control of major public services. The art of war has not been left behind in this advance and indeed it could be said that it was the stimulus of war which helped to provide the incentive for the development of computer technology.

The need arose during **World War II** for a machine which could decipher encoded teleprinter messages transmitted by the German *Geheimschreiber* device. After promising experiments with a semi-electronic machine known as Robinson, a far more powerful computer called Colossus was designed by T. H. Flowers of the British General Post Office research station. This very large machine had no less than 1,500 valves and could decipher the German transmissions within hours, compared to the days the Robinson machine took to do the same task. Encouraged by this success, an even more ambitious Colossus II was built. This had 2,400 valves and, with its limited memory, binary adders and decade counters, was the first programmable electronic digital computer. Colossus II came into service most opportunely, on 1 June 1944, just before the Allied invasion of Europe and was able instantly to decrypt the vital information passing along the *Geheimschreiber* link between Paris and Berlin.

The next breakthrough came with the transistor, which began to replace the electronic valve in the 1950s. This development heralded the rapidly increasing miniaturization and reliability of **electronic** components, making the general application of electronics to military uses even more attractive. The initial impetus for miniaturization had been the **space** programme, but the incorporation of on-board computers as part of the guidance system for long-range missiles quickly followed. While inertial **navigation** equipment had been available in 1954, the new developments enabled much more accurate and less bulky systems to be developed both for **submarines** and surface vessels.

For land forces developments took rather longer to reach fruition but obvious requirements were soon identified: logistics systems; control of predicted fire from field artillery; fire control for tank guns; improved communications. It was for control of resources that, in the British Army at least, computers were first introduced and it is hard to imagine, for example, how the British in 1982 could have assembled and launched, at under a week's notice, the task force to recover the **Falkland** Islands without the aid of a computerized logistics system to control the correct provision and loading of all the men and stores needed.

The arrival of the microprocessor – a complete computer on a single tiny chip – has done much to enhance weapon performance. FACE (Field Artillery Computing Equipment) has been in service with the Royal Artillery for some twenty years and provides an effective analysis of such aspects as target acquisition, ballistic data, fire planning and logistics to enable the battery to make the best use of its limited resources. However, FACE is not fully automated and is being replaced by an improved version, taking advantage of the latest technology, known as BATES (Battlefield Artillery Target Engagement System) in which more battery functions will be automated. In tank **gunnery** too the computer is now a well-established component, analysing such variables as ambient temperature, ammuni-

tion characteristics, wind speed and range; all in an effort not only to reduce human error but also, so vital in a tank engagement, to reduce the interval between seeing the target and obtaining a hit.

It is, perhaps, in the field of communications that the computer has allowed the most significant improvements to be made. Military communications need secure means of transportation from many mobile stations. The staff need to process the information flowing along the communication links: reconnaissance data from all surveillance sources, to be compared with the operational plan; decisions to be made from that comparison; consequential orders to be passed to the forward troops for action. Improvements in ADP (automatic data processing) mean that, not only can much more data be handled, but also that it can be handled much more swiftly. In the British Army the WAVELL system has been developed for this purpose, the world's first automated battlefield command and control system to enter service at corps level and below, providing secure data links between formation headquarters.

Such developments point the way for the future when a commander can almost take for granted that he will be able to pass information and orders, by voice or other means, directly and securely to his subordinates, with reports and returns continuously updated and available to all staff levels. Similarly it is certain that weapon performance will continue to be enhanced by electronic means.

Concentration camps, Military. Places of confinement for citizens, usually during a state of **guerrilla warfare**, as a means to prevent them helping the enemy or as a terror measure. First used in modern times by the Spanish in 1896 to put down a **Cuban** rebellion, the system acquired notoriety when the British, between 1901 and 1902, incarcerated some 200,000 **Boers** in temporary camps. The measure was illegal and the camps, grossly overcrowded and poorly administered, became riddled with diseases, such as cholera, with high death rates.

During the **Malayan War of Independence**, the British again built concentration camps, to prevent the Chinese Communists from exploiting rural settlers and to deny food to the guerrillas. On this occasion, however, care was taken over the administrative and humanitarian aspects.

As a result the military aim was achieved without much political harm. Indeed, a clear distinction has to be made between camps established only for the duration of a crisis and those maintained, for example by Nazi Germany and Soviet Russia, solely for the purpose of isolating political dissidents in the long term.

Condor Legion. This air formation was formed in November 1936 to command the units of the German Air Force already involved in the **Spanish Civil War** in support of Fascist Nationalist forces. Led initially by Hugo Sperrle, it comprised Ju52 **transport aircraft** (also used as bombers), fighters, seaplanes, communications and ground support units, including **anti-aircraft** artillery, the 88mm version of which was used also for **anti-tank** work. Employed in support of sea and land operations, its anti-shipping role was in a minor key and **strategic bombing** tasks very few, even when the latest medium bombers were supplied and tried out. In the main the Legion was utilized as a proving unit for the latest machines and techniques, besides giving invaluable training to the future leaders and instructors of the Air Force. It played a vital part in establishing the role of the dive-bomber as heavy artillery in support of ground forces – thus tilting the Air Force's strategy in the direction of tactical as opposed to strategic policy. It was withdrawn in 1939.

Coningham, Air Marshal Sir Arthur (1895–1948). A British pilot with a fine record in **World War I** and between the wars who, in 1941, took command of air forces in support of the British Army in **North Africa.** Progressively he developed the organization and techniques of tactical air forces in support of the land battle, successively commanding them in the Mediterranean theatre of war, the **Normandy** battles and the closing battles of **Germany.**

Conrad von Hötzendorf, General Count Franz (1853–1925). A warmonger who became Austro-Hungarian Army Chief of Staff in 1906, having set himself the task of modernizing a force in decline. In 1912 he was temporarily removed from office for advocating a 'preventive war' against Italy. He was reinstated as the **Balkan Wars** intensified, and was only too ready in 1914 to take advantage of political deterioration to make war on Serbia and Russia, thus partly instigating **World War I**, only to find that

the quick victory he hoped to achieve in alliance with Germany was beyond grasp. Until dismissed in 1917, his conduct of strategy on the Eastern Front, in Serbia, Italy and Romania, though sound, failed in its aims because the Central Powers were overstretched and his own army's morale and condition were in steady decline. He finished the war in 1918 as an army group commander in Italy.

Conscription. Throughout history there has been an element of compulsion in military service, either to maintain tribal, feudal, private or national forces or on the principle that every citizen has a responsibility to bear arms in defence of the state. For although genuine volunteers, inspired by cause, patriotism or the desire for wealth or glory, tend to be more professional, **recruiting** of their like cannot always be relied upon to meet demand. Hardship deters and of old compelled the Royal Navy, for example, to resort to impressment to man its ships in wartime. Modern conscription, however, is considered to be modelled upon the *levée en masse* enacted by the French government in 1798 to protect the Revolution. Their system of registration of men by age groups which were called up for training and service for specified periods of time and then transferred to the **reserve**, with the obligation of recall in emergency or for retraining, was copied in peace and war by the majority of military nations.

It was conscripted armies which, for the most part, faced each other in the major European wars after 1850. Each nation, of course, had its own special variations. The French balloted for those called up and placed themselves at a disadvantage in the **Franco-Prussian War** of 1870 against an enemy who conscripted in mass. The British eschewed conscription in peacetime until 1939, although they had been forced to introduce it during **World War I.** The USA also managed to resist what was called 'the draft' until World War I; but having revived it during **World War II**, with a ballot provision, kept it in force until the early 1970s, with serious political repercussions during the **Vietnam War.** Russia tended, even after freeing the serfs in 1861, to practise a sort of random impressment, with men snatched off the streets for lifetime service. Gradually, after the Revolution, this practise was modified but conscription remains universal to this day, as it does in China, which also maintains massed forces.

Russia, China and their Communist allies shrink from exemptions on conscientious as well as on medical grounds. More liberal nations, such as the USA, Britain, France and Germany, have usually been far more sympathetic with proven conscientious objectors and flexible on medical grounds.

The ethics and sense of conscription in the age of discernment and high technology are open to question. Undoubtedly, large numbers of trained reserves will be needed in time of exacting emergency, and judicious military **training** benefits the individual's education. Yet states which insist on periods of less than two years service by unwilling people all too easily produce inadequately trained personnel to operate very complex weapon systems. Arguably a well-equipped, volunteer force with high morale will defeat a much larger conscript one. But it must be backed by adequate reserves.

Convoy, Naval. One of many convoy battles to occur took place between Carthaginian and Roman squadrons off the Sicilian shore in 256 BC. Since command of the sea is as often as not essential for **amphibious warfare** or protection of commerce, it stands to reason that such engagements are likely to be of fundamental strategic importance. As they were, for example, at the Battles of Lissa, between Austria and Italy (see **Austro-Prussian War**), in 1866 and the Yalu River, between China and Japan (**Chinese–Japanese wars**), in 1894. Needless to say, the convoying by warships of merchant ships, particularly neutral vessels, has given rise to legal wrangles over 'search' and so-called 'rights of convoy' under conditions of **blockade**. In the final analysis, might was usually right whatever agreements were in force.

It was thus all the more surprising that when, in **World War I**, the Germans posed a major threat to the Allies (Britain in particular) by unrestricted **submarine** warfare, the British Admiralty was most reluctant to institute convoys. In part this was because **destroyers**, the most effective hunter and escort vessels, were literally tied up in case of need to support the Grand Fleet. But also because Admiral Sir John **Jellicoe**, Chief of Naval Staff, reasoned that not only was the method dubious in the circumstances but technically impossible. Only after statistical **analysis** of operations and a trial had proved him wrong in all respects was the system fully adopted.

Not only did the presence of warships deter attack by surface as well as submarine vessels, the act of concentrating hundreds of merchantmen, which normally sailed individually as they chose, into a few compact groups also made the enemy's task of detection far harder and prevented him attacking with unopposed gunfire when surfaced, thus forcing him to attack with expensive **torpedoes** when submerged. Prior to effective use of convoys in June 1917, monthly shipping losses averaged 750,000 tonnes. Subsequently they declined to below 300,000 tonnes per month at the same time as U-boat losses rose from about three a month, mid-1917, to double figures in May 1918.

Between the **World Wars** improvements in anti-submarine techniques and technology (meaning detection by **sonar** and attack by depth charge) persuaded some sailors that the submarine threat was neutralized. Therefore interest in convoys declined with only low priority given to the construction of escort vessels. Britain, for example, did not hold a single convoy-protection exercise in this period. Nevertheless, at the start of **World War II**, convoys were formed and proved reasonably protective against enemy surface raiders and submarines (which mostly hunted singly) and aircraft, whose crews' techniques were raw. Not until the Germans built more U-boats, seized control of the European seaboard and began to control packs by **radio**, in conjunction with **aircraft**, did the convoys come under intense pressure. But by then techniques had been rationalized, security raised and the system of fast and slow convoys introduced to improve average transit times and thus reduce waste of shipping.

Come April 1943, the Battle of the **Atlantic** was the one campaign which could have lost the Allies the war. As it was the pendulum of success swung their way through a combination of technical and operational innovations which prevented the fatal abandonment of the convoy system which, because losses seemed out of control, was mooted in March 1943. The keys to victory were more escort vessels with improved sonar and weapons working in concert; voice radio to facilitate hunting in groups; Direction Finding (DF) of submarine radio signals to provide information enabling diversion of convoys round lurking packs; breaking of **codes** for insight into enemy intentions; introduction of longer-range aircraft and light **aircraft-carriers**

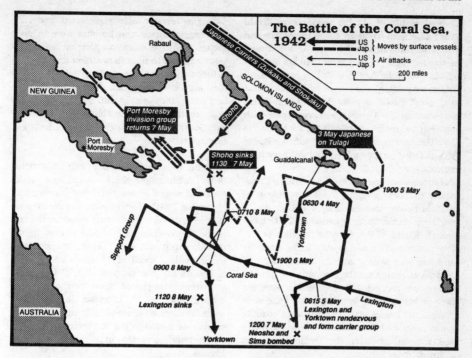

The Battle of the Coral Sea, 1942

Rabaul

Japanese Carriers (Zuikaku and Shokaku)

NEW GUINEA

SOLOMON ISLANDS

Port Moresby invasion group returns 7 May

Shoho

3 May Japanese on Tulagi

Port Moresby

Shoho sinks 1130 7 May

Guadalcanal

1900 5 May

0630 4 May

0710 8 May

Yorktown

Support Group

1900 6 May

0900 8 May

Coral Sea

1120 8 May Lexington sinks

0615 5 May Lexington and Yorktown rendezvous and form carrier group

Lexington

AUSTRALIA

1200 7 May Neosho and Sims bombed

Yorktown

US } Moves by surface vessels
Jap
US } Air attacks
Jap
0   200 miles

to provide cover in mid-ocean; development of centimetric **radar** to detect surfaced submarines (and even their periscopes), thus enabling illumination and attack by night.

Even though the crucial battles ended in victory for the convoy system in the Atlantic and in the Mediterranean (where the principal menace to both sides was aircraft based at relatively short ranges), it had become apparent by 1945 that faster German submarines, fitted with improved sonar and weapons, posed a serious threat to convoys whose speed, after all, was restricted by that of the slowest vessel. In the Pacific, moreover, US Navy submarines did much as they chose in a slaughter of Japanese convoys whose weapons, detectors and techniques were poor.

With the arrival since 1945 of vastly improved nuclear submarines and torpedoes, the future safety of convoys hangs in the balance. For their position is easily established by reconnaissance satellites (see **Space vehicles**); their merchant ships are not that much faster than their predecessors; and their escorts are stretched to the limit to find, track and kill hunters who move fast, dive very deep and can detect foes at extreme range.

Coral Sea, Battle of the. The Japanese intention to consolidate their conquests in the South-West Pacific prompted the planned capture of Port Moresby in May 1942. Their invasion **convoy** was covered by three **aircraft-carriers** in two task forces which entered the Coral Sea on 5 May. Awaiting them were two American carriers, which were well forewarned by **radio** intercept of their enemy's intentions. In a battle during which surface vessels never came to blows, **aircraft** did all the damage. After successful air attacks on a small Japanese invasion convoy at Tulagi on 4 May, the American carriers headed west, hunting the Port Moresby amphibious force. On 7 May, when aircraft from the *Yorktown* sank the *Shoho*, the Japanese crippled an American tanker in the belief it was a carrier. Next day, after the Japanese accurately located the American carriers, there were concentrated exchanges of attacks from 69 American and 51 Japanese dive- and torpedo-bombers. They caused the loss of the uss *Lexington* and damage to *Yorktown*, and severe damage to *Shokaku*. But in what may be judged a drawn tactical battle, the Japanese had to concede strategic defeat by calling off the invasion of Port Moresby and domination of the Coral Sea.

Coronel, Battle of. At the outbreak of **World War I** a German naval squadron under Admiral Count Maximilian von Spee, consisting of two armoured **cruisers**, two light cruisers (one of which, *Emden*, he detached for highly successful commerce raiding) and a number of colliers was at large off the China coast. When Japan joined the Allies on 21 August 1914, von Spee, with the eventual intention of making for home via Cape Horn, steamed across the Pacific for Easter Island. There he was joined by two more light cruisers.

Hunting von Spee was Rear-Admiral Sir Christopher Cradock with an inferior squadron of two old heavy cruisers, a light cruiser and a merchant cruiser, a force joined on 22 October at its Falkland Islands base by the slow battleship *Canopus*. The British Admiralty correctly surmised von Spee's intentions and had told Cradock to search for the Germans and protect trade – an order barely compatible with the force at his disposal. Leaving behind the slow *Canopus*, he began searching the west coast of South America for an enemy whose radio signals sounded stronger the farther north he steamed.

In a rough sea, with three hours daylight remaining on 1 November, the opposing light cruisers sighted each other off Coronel, prompting both Admirals to race for the point of contact. When Cradock eventually saw he was up against von Spee's entire squadron, it would have been prudent and feasible to retire upon *Canopus*. Instead, no doubt in the knowledge of the recent court martial of Rear-Admiral Trowbridge for unwillingness to attack a superior force, Cradock closed. Perhaps he hoped to inflict critical damage before meeting his own inevitable doom – but meet it he did within the hour after von Spee had skilfully manoeuvred for the best light conditions to enable his superbly trained gunners to make deadly practice. Both British heavy cruisers were sunk in flames with all 1,440 hands. The Germans had two men wounded and only minor damage. Thus von Spee was free to carry out the next phase of his plan: to enter the Atlantic – and meet *his* destiny at the **Falkland Islands** Battle.

Corregidor, Siege of. The fortified island of Corregidor defending the entrance to **Manila Bay** held out against the Japanese until 6 May 1942 after **Bataan** had fallen on 9 April. Only one 14in gun turret was fully protected, and only the command post and hospital were in deep shelter. Thus the American garrison was hopelessly exposed to intense bombing and shelling without adequate means of reply. So it was to their immense credit that, short of ammunition and water, they managed to inflict some 4,000 losses on the enemy amphibious landing before, with 2,000 losses of their own, being forced to surrender.

Corvette. The most famous and easily constructed British ocean escort vessel, named after single-deck sail sloops of war, and first launched in November 1940. Of a whale-catcher design with excellent, if lively, sea-keeping qualities, the first of the *Flower* class were of 925 tonnes, lightly armed, equipped with **depth charges** and **sonar**, with a speed of 16 knots and a crew of 85. As the war progressed, 150 were built and steadily improved upon by the addition, among other things, of **radar**. In effect they were far more economical, efficient and deadly **submarine** hunters than **destroyers** – especially when later increased in size and renamed **frigates**.

Crete, Battle of. The German invasion of Crete on 20 May 1941 was conceived as an exploitation of the conquest of **Greece** to acquire dominance of the eastern Mediterranean and the Middle East, and also to enhance the prestige of Hermann **Göring**'s German Air Force. The Air Force, under General Alexander Löhr, had available 430 bombers, 180 fighters, 500 Ju52 transports and 100 **gliders**. They supported and lifted XI Airborne Corps of one parachute and one air-landed division, under General Kurt Student – its heavy equipment to be convoyed by sea.

The island's garrison, under Major-General Bernard Freyberg, consisted of 27,500 inadequately equipped troops (of whom 15,500 had recently been evacuated from Greece), 14,000 Greek soldiers, a small fighter force (which was withdrawn on the 19th under overwhelming German air attack) and strong naval units without air cover. Well supplied with intelligence from **radio** intercept, Freyberg was able to concentrate his troops at known enemy landing-places.

As a result, although the Germans had complete air dominance to pound the defences as they chose, and to drop parachutists at small

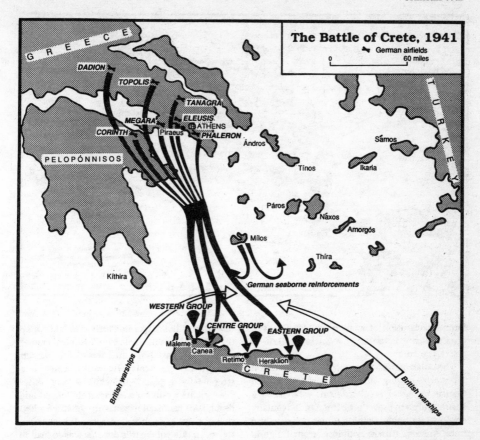

The Battle of Crete, 1941

German airfields
0 _____ 60 miles

GREECE

DADION
TOPOLIS
TANAGRA
MEGARA
ELEUSIS
CORINTH
Piraeus
ATHENS
PHALERON
Ándros

PELOPÓNNISOS

Tínos
Ikaria

Sámos

TURKEY

Páros
Náxos
Amorgós

Mílos

Thíra

Kíthira

German seaborne reinforcements

WESTERN GROUP

Maleme
Canea
CENTRE GROUP
Retimo
Heraklion
EASTERN GROUP

CRETE

British warships

British warships

cost in Ju52s, they had it far from their own way on the ground against alert garrisons. By nightfall landing grounds had not been secured. In consequence, when Student persisted in dropping more parachutists and flying in the air-landing division next day, their losses in men and machines were extremely heavy. Moreover, the sea convoy was intercepted on the night of the 21st/22nd and turned back with loss. Indeed, there was a period when it only required a determined (and feasible) counter-attack by the British to remove a German toe-hold at Maleme, thus making further reinforcement impossible and sealing the fate of the invaders.

But Freyberg vacillated, despite clear intelligence of the situation, and the German crisis passed when large air reinforcements were landed, forcing the garrisons back. Evacuation to Egypt began on the 28th under deadly air attacks. By attempting to operate in broad daylight, the Royal Navy exposed its ships to constant bombing which eventually sank four cruisers and nine destroyers, besides damaging many more, including two battleships. The evacuation ended on 31 May. British losses were over 18,000; those of the Germans numbered about 13,000. So heavy, indeed, was the loss of parachutists that **Hitler** ruled out all such future use of them.

Crimean War. This limited war, fought chiefly in the Black Sea and on the Crimean peninsula, came about in October 1853 when Turkey declared war on Russia, whose political threats she could no longer tolerate. On 30 November a Russian naval squadron of nine vessels, armed with the latest shell-firing cannon, overwhelmed in Sinope harbour, in six hours, a Turkish squadron of 10 wooden-hulled warships. As an expression of concern at this destabilizing event, a combined Anglo-French fleet entered the Black Sea in January 1854, an act which led to a

The Crimean War, 1854-6

formal declaration of war on 28 March, seven days after a Russian army invaded Bulgaria to attack the Turks.

The Allies aimed to support Turkey and, on 29 April, having already severely damaged Odessa by naval bombardment, established a base at Varna to prevent the Russians advancing on Constantinople. Coming under pressure also from Austria, Russia withdrew from Bulgaria and sought a diplomatic solution. But France and Britain now decided to punish Russia by destroying her power in the Black Sea through destruction of the naval base at Sevastopol. On 13 September their armies, already suffering from cholera and with the British component in **logistic** chaos, landed unopposed in the Crimea.

There now ensued a sequence of costly battles, fought by weakened troops at the end of tenuous lines of communication, for possession of Sevastopol. The Russian army, under the command of Prince Alexander Menshikov and by no means strong, first tried to halt the Allies, under General Lord Raglan and Marshal Armand-Saint-Armand, at the Alma River on 20 September. They were pushed back with heavy losses. The Siege of **Sevastopol** began on 8 October. But it was rarely complete; a naval bombardment by the Allies on 17 October was a costly fiasco; while attempts by the Russians to drive the British back to their base were only just thwarted at the desperate Battle of **Balaklava** on the 20th, and at **Inkerman** on 5 November.

What followed that winter represented a nadir for the British Army. Its ranks were catastrophically depleted by cholera and other diseases, its wounded were scarcely tended and its logistic organization virtually collapsed when supply ships in open waters were wrecked by a storm. In due course this disaster was to lead to a radical overhaul of its supply services and, under Florence **Nightingale's** urging, the administrative reform of the Medical Branch. The scandal, well publicized in *The Times*, brought down the government of the day. Indeed, it was a Turkish force which defeated the next attempt by the Russians (now under Prince Gorchakov) to attack Balaklava, and the better-serviced French, who carried the main burden of the bombardment of Sevastopol's defences, which might have fallen in April had not governments in Paris and London set a precedent by interfering by **telegraph**.

As it was, the capture of Kerch on 24 May at last cut Sevastopol's communications, although it was not until 9 September, after the exhausting Battle of the Traktir on 16 August, that the city fell. Thereafter fighting continued in a desultory fashion in the Baltic and the Caucasus, as well as off the Black Sea coast (when ironclad French warships were used for the first time to bombard forts at Kinburn), until peace was restored in February 1856. By this time estimated Russian losses amounted to 256,000 and those of the Allies to 253,000 – of whom a high proportion died from disease and deprivation.

Crimes, War. Mainly in the 20th century and chiefly as a result of **World War II**, war crime has been controversially codified under the headings of *jus contra bellum* – acts provoking war – and *jus in bello* – violation of the customs and **laws of war** and of humanity. In this entry only violations of law by military personnel connected with acts of war will be considered.

The identity and definition of a war crime began to emerge in the 1860s in conjunction with the accelerating evolution of the **laws of war**. That process, starting with the trial and execution of the Confederate officer Henry Wirz, who was charged with ill-treating and murdering prisoners of war during the **American Civil War**, is incomplete. In the present day the inhumane administration of **concentration camps** by the British during the **Boer War** might be classified as a war crime. After **World War I** consideration was given by the victorious Allies to setting up international tribunals to deal with alleged German atrocities at sea and in occupied territories. Although these efforts came to nothing, customary international rules making aggressive war and its initiation by individuals illegal were established, along with the understanding that many crimes committed in war, such as murder, rape, ill-treatment of prisoners and pillage, were punishable under ordinary criminal law.

The trials of war criminals after **World War II**, though criticized as *ex post facto*, because they dealt with acts not rated illegal before trial and for being unfair, because the vanquished were being tried by victors, nevertheless established crimes now internationally accepted. They may not have prevented numerous and flagrant breaches of law in the many wars since waged, but undeniably the extensive amendments to existing manuals of **military law**, made imperative by the War Crimes trials, have acted as a deterrent by inducing a clearer understanding among the military of what they may or may not do even in the heat of battle. As several American soldiers discovered, for example, in the aftermath of massacres in **Vietnam**.

Significant precedents were established (by controversial and occasionally dubious methods) to establish the views of the victors that war crimes were: (1) crimes against peace, including the planning, preparation for and execution of aggression contrary to international treaties; (2) violations of the laws and customs of war such as murder, ill-treatment of prisoners, killing of hostages, looting and the unjustified destruction of property; (3) crimes against humanity such as extermination, enslavement, persecution and deportation of civilians.

It is wishful thinking to imagine that the mere establishment of a code of war crimes will ever apply compelling deterrence to the conduct of war, that most violently unstable human activity. And it is worth registering that, although the hunt for German Nazi war criminals continues with some vigour, the zest for prosecution lost public favour in the 1950s. Also that in the numerous outbreaks of war since 1945 the commissions of crimes are countless and rarely brought to court, although useful publicity concerning their alleged perpetration has frequently been employed to political and propaganda purpose and advantage.

Cruise Missiles. The precursor of the modern cruise missile was the German low-flying, comparatively slow V1 'flying bomb' developed during the later stages of **World War II**. Powered by a ram-jet engine, V1 was a crude weapon of limited accuracy and with no on-board guidance to correct any in-flight drift from its pre-set course. However, V1 was capable of hitting an area target such as a city and its large high-explosive warhead could inflict considerable, if indiscriminate, damage.

The low-altitude flight path of the cruise missile means that it has a good chance of escaping observation by the enemy's air defence **radars**, which are usually designed to detect high-flying aircraft or incoming ballistic missiles with their high trajectory. When this characteristic is coupled with comparatively small size and a sophisticated guidance system such weapons, air, ground or sea-launched, can pose a real threat in both the tactical and strategic spheres. Post-1945 the Soviet Union were first in the field, with several examples such as their air-launched Kitchen, with a range of 720km. Better known is the more advanced United States Tomahawk with a range of about 2,400km.

The problem with the low-flying cruise missile

is to provide a guidance system capable of steering the missile clear of intervening obstacles to allow it to hit the target with sufficient accuracy to allow its warhead (which may be nuclear) to do the required damage. The development of terrain-following radar (originally a requirement for low-flying fighter aircraft) pointed the way. Also incorporated in the US Tomahawk is an inertial guidance system (TERCOM) linked to a pre-recorded radar map to enable the missile to find its own way to the target. For such a device to work properly an accurately surveyed start point is essential, not so easy to achieve for air and sea launches. Furthermore, the radar map is less effective if much of the flight takes place over the open sea.

Development problems were immense, particularly with the naval version, but in the **Persian Gulf War** of 1991, US Tomahawks, launched from **battleships** and **submarines**, found their way over sea and desert to strike pin-point targets in cities at long range with remarkable accuracy, thus adding a new dimension to strategic bombing (**Bombing, Strategic**).

Cruiser. The cruiser is probably the most amorphously named class of warship, ranging from **frigates** in the days of sail, to 21,000-tonne heavy cruisers armed with guns, **torpedoes**, and **missiles** in the mid 20th century. By definition fast with medium armament, cruisers were (as first designed by the British – HMS *Shah* for example – in 1868, with steam power and sail and a speed of 16 knots) built of iron or mild steel, with a displacement of about 6,000 tonnes. The inevitable demand for better protection, however, soon produced vessels with armoured decks and armoured belts intended to shield magazines and machinery, raising displacements considerably. Likewise, armament could be anything between the two 10in guns and torpedo tubes in HMS *Shah* and the 14,200-tonne HMS *Powerful* of 1895 with its two 9·2in, sixteen 6in and sixteen 3in guns, its 6in armoured deck and speed of 22 knots.

Protected cruisers were followed by 'armoured' cruisers, such as the German *Scharnhorst* and *Gneisenau* of 11,240 tonnes which won at **Coronel** but were sunk by **battle-cruisers** at the **Falkland Islands** in 1914. With eight 8·2in and six 5·9in guns they were best suited for commerce raiding, but with a speed of only 21 knots useless for scouting. Indeed it was in the scouting role, as well as commerce raiding and protection, that 'light' cruisers – the 3–4,000 tonne, thinly protected, very fast kind with speeds of about 30 knots, armed with six or more 6in guns, plus torpedoes – which would prove most effective in **World War I**. In major battles such as Coronel and the Falkland Islands, they located the enemy and hunted his light cruisers; at **Jutland** they were the eyes of the battleship squadrons and potent in the anti-torpedo-boat role. While in numerous actions, when battleship squadrons were absent, they were often decisive by their presence.

In 1922 the Washington Naval Treaties stipulated that no British, American, French, Japanese or Italian warship (other than capital ships) should displace more than 10,000 tonnes or mount a gun with a calibre greater than 8·1in In fact, many cruisers of only 6–7,000 tonnes with guns of less than 8in calibre were built between the wars and, in **World War II**, were successful, with their speeds in excess of 30 knots, in the commerce protection and **anti-aircraft** roles. Nevertheless, Washington Treaty violations were common enough, notably by the Japanese. The Germans, too, managed to conceal their breach of a 10,000 tonnes upper limit on warship construction, imposed by the Versailles Treaty, to build three fast, welded-hull 'armoured' cruisers (nicknamed 'pocket battleships') which, with six 11in, eight 5·9in and six 4·1in guns, plus eight torpedo-tubes, eventually displaced 12,000 tonnes.

Cruisers in the nuclear and missile age seem in decline, displaced, for the most part, by more ubiquitous, almost equally deadly and considerably less expensive **destroyers**. Nevertheless, both the US and the Russian navies keep numbers in service, their role as headquarters and missile ships of undeniable service in support of **amphibious** forces engaged in such operations as fire-support off **Vietnam** and convoy escort in 1988 during the **Persian Gulf War**.

Cuban Wars. Mounting objections by the Cuban population to Spanish rule came to a head in bloody civil war in 1868 with a demand from Carlo Borja del Castillo for emancipation of slaves and universal suffrage. The Ten Years War brought devastation, mainly in the eastern provinces, and an estimated 200,000 deaths. But when Spain declined to implement promises of reform, made by agreement at the war's end in 1878, and insisted on reparations for damage caused, ferocious fighting started again in 1895. Some of the latest weapons and barbed-wire entanglements were used, and **concentration camps** for rebels were introduced by the Spaniards. These produced such an outcry that henceforward nothing short of independence would satisfy the Cubans. When, within a few months of the USA's offer to mediate, the US battleship *Maine* blew up in Havana harbour, triggering the **Spanish–American War** of 1898, everything went into the melting pot.

The handing over of the island by the Treaty of Paris to US trusteeship was exploited by the USA to obtain concessions, including the leasing of naval stations and US right of intervention to preserve Cuba's independence. In 1906, however, a local insurrection brought American military intervention until 1909. Further outbreaks of violence occurred in 1912 and 1917. In this land, with its fluctuating economy, corruption was rife, politically motivated sabotage endemic and a US presence ever pronounced. Shortly after one-time sergeant Fulgencio Batista became unopposed President in 1954, Fidel **Castro** took the field as leader of a growing, reforming Marxist force. His three years' civil war against the Batista regime and Cuban Army was waged on classic **guerrilla warfare** lines, with Russian assistance.

War was followed in 1959 by ruthless extermination of opponents and the seizure of American assets. On 17 April 1961 a force of 1,400 exiled Cubans, led by José Cardona, inspired by the CIA and equipped with US arms, made a landing in the Bay of Pigs. The armed attempt to rally effective anti-Castro support and start a counter-revolution was bungled and collapsed at once. Since then Castro has strengthened his grip. He came close, in 1962, to starting a major war during the so-called 'Missile Crisis', when the Russians blatantly began installing rockets on the island; and, with Russian encouragement, has spread Communism in the Americas and sent troops to join Marxist forces fighting in Angola and **Ethiopia**.

Cunningham, Admiral Lord (1883–1963). Andrew Browne Cunningham joined the Royal Navy in 1898 and served with distinction in **World War I**. Between the wars he helped develop naval gunnery and night-fighting capability. As C-in-C Mediterranean Fleet from 1939 until 1942, he at once won moral superiority over the Italians at such battles as Calabria and Taranto in 1940 and **Matapan** in 1941. But the heavy losses off **Crete** and towards the end of 1941 in the Eastern Mediterranean were the nadir of his fortunes. They were compensated for when, as Allied Naval Commander in November 1942, he led the invasions of French North-West Africa and, in 1943, **Sicily** and Italy (**Italian campaign 1943–5**), prior to becoming First Sea Lord and Chief of Naval Staff in 1943 until 1946, thus steering the Royal Navy through its final struggle against Germany and Japan and into its peacetime reorganization.

Currie, Lieutenant-General Sir Arthur (1875– 1933). A Canadian militia artillery officer who, at the beginning of **World War I**, came to Europe as a battalion commander and was appointed to command a brigade in 1915. Made Commander 1st Canadian Division in 1916, he was soon given command of the Canadian Corps, an appointment he held until the end of the war when he became Inspector Canadian Militia. Currie not only commanded Canadians with great skill in all their major actions on the Western Front, he also managed significantly to stimulate Canadian nationalism. The brilliantly executed capture of **Vimy Ridge** in April 1917, his insistence thereafter that the Canadian Corps must be used only as an entity, and the part the Corps played at the Battle of **Amiens** and in the final advance to victory in 1918, all strengthened Canada's post-war claims to nationhood.

Cyprus imbroglios. Cyprus was ruled by Turkish sovereignty from 1573 until Britain, with Turkish agreement at a time of political crisis with Russia, took over the administration in 1878. At once the 80 per cent Greek populace asked for *Enosis*, union with Greece, but without much hope until after the British annexed the island in November 1914 as a result of Turkey joining the Central Powers in **World War I**.

In 1931 agitation for *Enosis* intensified and reached a high pitch in the 1950s under the leadership of Archbishop Makarios III. Greek guerrilla troops of EOKA (National Organization of Cypriot Struggle), led by Colonel Georgios Grivas, began attacks upon the Turkish minority and the British in 1952. These became more widespread and savage as the British refused Makarios's demands for self-determination and as the British garrison was reinforced. The violence grew far worse when, in 1956, Makarios was deported to the Seychelles. But EOKA fought all the harder until Makarios was released in 1957, though still excluded from Cyprus. A lull in the fighting accompanied tortuous negotiations in which the Turkish community steadfastly objected to *Enosis*. Fighting began again in 1958 as Makarios raised his demands for Cyprus to become an independent state. A settlement was reached in 1959, enabling the British to retain important bases and Makarios to become President – though still without *Enosis*.

Greek agitation persisted along with worsening relations and fighting with the Turks in 1963, in which the British inevitably were involved. In March 1964 the United Nations intervened and sent a peacekeeping force. Meanwhile Makarios bought arms from Eastern Europe and, with Greek complicity, strengthened his forces. The Turks threatened war against Greece and their aircraft bombed Cypriot Greek villages in August. Yet the UN presence, together with negotiations, managed to contain a consistently tense situation for another decade. In 1974 affairs deteriorated to the point at which Turkish troops invaded from the mainland to establish by force of arms a separate Turkish sector in the north of the island. Since then UN forces have patrolled the border with the Greek sector and the British garrison has maintained its bases in an island that is perpetually uneasy.

Dakar, Battle of. After the fall of France in June 1940, the French West African port of Dakar threatened Britain's vital sea communications in the Battle of the **Atlantic** and to the east via the Cape of Good Hope. Its Vichy French garrison, strengthened by the incomplete battleship *Richelieu* and other units of the French Fleet, was very hostile since the attack on **Oran** in July. A proposal by General Charles **de Gaulle** to seize the port with Free French Forces was welcomed by the British as of great strategic value. An Anglo-Free French **amphibious** force of 7,000 men, poorly equipped but supported by a strong British fleet, left Britain on 31 August, but was beaten to Dakar by French naval reinforcements, sent with German and Italian approval.

Confused political and naval manoeuvring preceded the arrival of the invaders in mist on 21 September. As *Richelieu* and shore batteries hit and drove off British warships, the garrison refused de Gaulle's request for its surrender and resisted Free French troops put ashore on the 22nd. Exchanges between warships and shore batteries on the 24th and 25th inflicted far more damage on the British than the French. The only consolation for the British was denial of the port to subsequent German occupation, prevention of the French reinforcing their other West African colonies and sufficient damage inflicted on *Richelieu* to keep her in port until the end of 1942, when Dakar rejoined the Allies.

Darlan, Admiral Jean-Louis (1881–1942). As Chief of Staff, 1936–1939, and then C-in-C, he made a great contribution to the efficiency of the French Fleet prior to **World War II**. In the aftermath of the fall of France in 1940, he had the difficult duty of keeping his ships out of German and British hands, a political task he fulfilled with what was left of the Fleet under Vichy government control between July 1940 and November 1942. As a minister in the Vichy government, his activities earned him much abuse, even after he became commander of all French forces in 1942. Undeniably his presence in Algiers, when the Allies landed in November 1942, was crucial in preventing prolonged French resistance and in ensuring the French ships at Toulon were scuttled before the Germans arrived. Yet, politically, his assassination on Christmas Eve was a relief for the Allies.

Davis, Jefferson (1808–89). A graduate of West Point Military Academy who became the reluctant President of the Confederate States in 1861. With limited resources, his defensively orientated strategy in the **American Civil War** rested on the hope of so exhausting the Federals that they would abandon the struggle. In this he was supported by General Robert E. **Lee**. Yet, because he feared what might happen to the South, he continued the struggle even after defeats at **Gettysburg** (his main attempt to carry the war into the North) and **Vicksburg** had secured President **Lincoln**'s political position for continuance of the struggle.

Dayan, Moshe (1915–81). A member of the Israeli 'night squads' fighting the Arabs in the 1930s and a pupil of Orde Wingate in **guerrilla warfare**, Dayan was a founder of Haganah, the underground force which became the Israeli Army. He served on active service with the British Army in **World War II** and was commander of the Jerusalem sector during the **Israeli Fight for Independence** in 1948. As Army Chief of Staff, 1953–8, he planned and led the advance into Sinai in 1956: a campaign in which his infantryman's outlook was sometimes at odds with that of tank soldiers. But as Minister of Defence he also had a dominant effect on the pre-emptive 1966 campaign, while in the Yom Kippur War of 1973 he was responsible to some extent for Israel being caught unprepared.

Defence, Ministries and departments of. Before the arrival of **air forces**, navies and armies were controlled and administered by bureaucratic departments respectively, of **Admiralty** and of War responsible to central government. Usually they had a political and a military head who worked in council and were served by permanent civil and military staffs who gathered intelligence, planned, arranged finance, manning and procurement, and transmitted requirements to subordinate formations at home and in the field. Rarely until the **telegraph** did they have a direct operational function; but with the arrival of **radio** this opportunity to interfere was often irresistible to ministers and commanders-in-chief – and all the more so should the latter, as in the USA for example, also be President and head of state with a pronounced political orientation.

When a requirement arose for joint or combined operations involving both services, it was customary, whether or not the head of state was also C-in-C, to form committees which would settle who should make the plan, appoint the commander, issue the orders and allocate resources. In 1902 the British formed a Committee of Imperial Defence which evolved gradually into a sophisticated joint staffs committee system. Nations with limited or no access to the sea at all had fewer problems; the army dominated. But for the Americans, for example, in the **American Civil War** and the **Spanish–American War**, intricate problems of allocation and command and control had to be solved. These were matters which readily produced clashes and rivalries and which could only by resolved at the pinnacle of power, often by a person in ignorance of the subject who lacked unbiased professional advice.

As weapons and communications technology became more widespread, and as **aircraft** were added to navies and armies, the traditional systems bent under a weight of complexity beyond their organization and flexibility to sustain. The **Gallipoli** battles in **World War** I were chaotic examples of the existing departmental and command machinery's inability to mount operations in which naval and land forces, with new technology available, had complementary parts to play. As air power not only demonstrated its impact upon sea and land warfare, but also (and of fundamental political importance) attacked homelands, the need for separate departments of aviation controlling a third, independent service became evident. The British creation in 1918 of an Air Ministry running the Royal Air Force (RAF), which combined the Royal Navy's air service (RNAS) and the Army's flying corps (RFC), inaugurated a revolution – but without making any easier combined or joint operations between all three Services. Indeed it complicated matters and exacerbated rivalries.

Between the **World Wars** attempts to create ministries of defence to co-ordinate the three Services were usually either blocked or accepted, in diluted form, as secretariats without power. Only in Germany was the subject grasped with any determination when the Wehrmacht (Armed Forces) was created in the mid-1930s under OKW (Armed Forces Command). But with **Hitler** in charge as head of state, supreme commander, minister of war and, after 1941, Army C-in-C, it caused as many problems as it solved. For one thing the Army, Navy and Air Force retained their autonomy in almost every respect, including the vital area of weapon procurement, ensuring that interdepartmental rivalries and waste from duplication flourished as always. Only later, during **World War II**, was a central Ministry of Armaments given the authority to rationalize the allocation of materials and production facilities. Operational command to begin with was orthodox, although the Air Force intruded wherever it could (as in **Crete**). But soon the practice of creating so-called OKW Theatres of War, such as **Norway**, reflected Hitler's internal, divisive, political whims and determination to subjugate the Army.

The principal Allied nations, with the exception of Russia where the Red Army was predominant under Josef **Stalin**, moved cautiously and empirically towards centralized systems based on small, co-ordinating ministries of defence and joint staff committees. In Britain joint staffs were highly developed, but the divorce of design and supply of weapons from the defence departments proved as much a disaster as did the pre-war unwillingness of the RAF to provide the Royal Navy with suitable **aircraft**. In the USA, on the other hand, where the Navy, the Marines and the Army retained their own air forces and right of direct access to the President, waste in the acquisition of supply continued.

Since World War II all the major nations have created separate air forces and merged them within departments or ministries of defence which have control over design, development and procurement of equipment. The USA took the plunge by Act of Congress in 1947, when they also formed a separate air force. The British moved reluctantly to a fully merged Ministry of Defence in 1964. But although each Service, at first, largely retained its old structure and influence within the new agglomerations, remorseless rationalization, notably in **logistics** and procurement of weapons, whittled away ancient privileges and traditions. As an example of extreme rationalization, the Canadian decision in the 1960s to unify their three Services, dressing them in one uniform, and centralizing finance, weapons procurement and administration in a National Defence HQ, was not a success. The imposition of an all-embracing, amorphous bureaucracy eroded the basic loyalties which are so vital to combat efficiency, making reconsideration essential in the 1980s. Yet there is much to be said for standard logistic services, wherever possible, for sea, ground and air forces – provided a doctrinal approach does not stifle initiative in the extraordinary and exacting circumstances of war.

De Gaulle, General Charles (1890–1970). An infantryman who was taken prisoner at **Verdun** in 1916. In the 1930s he emerged as a leader of French military thought with advocacy of mobile defence by **armoured** forces in his book *Vers l'armée de métier*. Taken note of by the Germans, he was given command of the incomplete 4th Armoured Division in 1940 in time to lead it against the Germans in May. In battle it made some impression, but on 6 June he was made Under-Secretary of War as France entered her death throes. In Britain on 18 June he raised the Free French movement of his countrymen who wished to continue the fight.

Four years later, after struggling to build up his forces and acquire political status, he returned to France determined to revitalize his country. Rejected in 1946, he returned to power in June 1958 when France stood on the verge of civil war. After winning adoption of a new Constitution, he became President in December, a post he held until December 1969, having extracted France from the **Algerian War of Independence** and improved her self-confidence significantly.

Denikin, General Anton (1872–1947). The son of a former serf, Denikin fought in the **Russo-Japanese War** and rose to be a successful corps commander in **World War I**. Although at first he supported the **Russian Revolution**, he soon changed sides and in March 1918 took command of the anti-Communist White forces in the south. Choosing to advance on Moscow in 1919, he was within 250 miles of his objective before **guerrilla warfare** and **logistic** collapse in his rear pronounced defeat. When the army fell apart he joined its remnants in evacuation from the Crimea in 1920.

Denmark, Invasions of. This small country has been involved in many wars, but since 1850 has been overborne by its stronger neighbours. Coming into dispute with Prussia and Austria over possession of Schleswig-Holstein, she bravely resisted invasion in March 1864 and blockaded the Elbe and Weser rivers. But in July the fall, with heavy casualties, of the fortress of Dybbol and loss of Als island quickly brought an end to a very unequal struggle.

Cowed by Germany in **World War I**, she retained her neutrality. But on 9 April 1940, when Germany swept in without warning, in conjunction with her invasion of **Norway**, only a few shots were fired in defence. For the rest of **World War II** she lay under the German heel, putting up only sporadic internal resistance until liberated by the British in May 1945.

Desertion, Military. This military crime is best defined as a prolonged absence without leave when a soldier has no intention of returning to duty. Clear evidence of intention to be absent, such as concealment, disguise or deliberate evasion of important duty, all contribute to this crime. It is viewed far more seriously in wartime and when, technically, the deserter is on active service. In many armies it is still punishable by death though, in these more enlightened days, and with a better understanding of **combat fatigue**, a more lenient view is sometimes taken.

As often as not, desertion, particularly *en masse*, is an indication of low **morale**. A high rate of desertion or absence without leave is often an index of poor man-management. Few are the defeats which are unattended by numerous desertions in the face of the enemy, a set of circumstances whose remedies are to be found in outstanding leadership (sometimes backed by instant, draconian measures) rather than ponderous process of law according to the book.

Desert warfare. Campaigning in country which aptly has been described as the tactician's paradise and the quartermaster's hell is among the most exacting of military arts, in which **logistics** and, above all, the supply of water are always vital. Prior to **mechanization**, therefore, large armies shied away from a military theatre of such arid terrain, depending on small-scale forces, as often as not supplied by or mounted on camels. But when Major-General Sir Horatio **Kitchener** reconquered the **Sudan** in 1898 with over 25,000 men, his lines of communication depended on river steamers and the **railway** he built as he advanced.

World War I was distinguished by the pioneering of large-scale desert operations in the Middle East employing motor vehicles and **aircraft**. The Turkish attempt in 1915 to cut the **Suez Canal** would have benefited from greater mechanization as it crossed the Sinai desert. The British invasion of **Mesopotamia** would have been impossible without the great rivers and the building of a railway, while the use there in 1917 of armoured cars and light lorries conferred hitherto unattainable tactical mobility on long-range forces. But already in 1916, armoured cars had soon put paid to a Turkish-inspired insurrection in Cyrenaica. Supported by aircraft, they would greatly enhance the striking power of the camel forces of the **Arab Revolt** and the British advance into Palestine across Sinai, which also benefited hugely from the rapid laying of a pumped-water-supply pipeline.

Experiments between the World Wars in the desert with rough-terrain transport, principally by the British, French and Italians, demonstrated not only the importance of track laying vehicles (especially French half-tracks), but such things as improved air filters to minimize engine wear, sealed cooling systems to save water and the sun compass for accurate navigation in the wastes at a distance from the coast where most

traffic moved. Mastery of these techniques, many of which were associated with unusual **medical** and psychological problems, made survival possible in **North Africa** during **World War II** for the men of entirely mechanized forces when operating, in strength, deep in the interior and under extremely testing conditions.

Tactically, too, mechanized vehicles, above all the **armoured fighting vehicles**, were the key to success in terrain with few 'tank proof' places for **infantry** to shelter, and in which major natural obstacles were few and far between. Mobility was all-important to bypass and encircle strong points which fell as soon as their water ran out. Aircraft played a crucial role because they could so easily detect and attack targets in wide open terrain. **Photography** was all-revealing. The side without air cover was only safe by night. Concentrations and convoys of supply vehicles were especially vulnerable unless widely dispersed, placing demands on highly disciplined **combat drills** and C^3.

It goes without saying that the lessons learnt prior to 1946 were fundamental to the subsequent **Arab–Israeli** and **Persian Gulf wars**.

Destroyers. The invention of the **torpedo**, and the call for special warships to carry it into action, led in 1878 to the first fast **torpedo-boat** (HMS *Lightning*, speed 19 knots) and, later, to stealthy **submarines**. Countermeasures were at once imperative and included increases in secondary armament on **battleships** and **cruisers** and in 1893 the first unarmoured torpedo-boat destroyer (HMS *Havoc*, speed 27 knots, armament four quick firing guns), soon to be known as 'destroyers' and made even faster with the installation of steam-turbine engines.

In the normal course of development, to satisfy demands for more seaworthy boats with improved armament and protection, displacement weights increased from the initial 300 tonnes. By 1912, for example, the French had built a 700-tonne boat with a speed of 34 knots and two 3·9in and four 9-pounder guns, plus four torpedo-tubes. After the **Russo-Japanese War**, boats such as these were built in large numbers to escort the battle fleets. No sooner had the submarine threat been recognized at the start of **World War I** than the requirement for destroyers became insatiable for use as escorts for commerce and, in due course, **convoys**. Come 1918 destroyers had sunk battleships and cruisers, fought one against the other, helped curb, none too efficiently with ram and depth charge, the submarine menace, and shot down **aircraft**. As maids of all work they had acquired light armour and come close to the equivalent of pre-war light cruisers with displacements of 1,500 tonnes, four 4·7in guns and secondary weapons, plus six torpedo-tubes and depth charges.

This enlargement, at ever increased expense, continued in the inter-war period. The need for **anti-aircraft** escort ships called for high-angle guns and multiple cannon and machine-guns, all of which, along with ammunition, required extra space. Speeds remained around the 30-knot plus mark but displacements rose to over 2,000 tonnes. Indeed, so complex were these ships that no longer were they best suited as convoy escorts. In **World War II** sloops, **corvettes** and **frigates** assumed the principal anti-submarine role.

The so-called destroyers of 3,700 tonnes or more built in the 1950s, for example, by Britain and the USA, had, with their extensive **radar**, numerous guns and **rocket missiles**, sophisticated **Sonar** and anti-submarine weapons, grown into light-cruisers. Indeed, the name 'destroyer' lost its original meaning as battleships and cruisers became outmoded, and as the submarine began to assume an important anti-submarine and **deterrence** role. So as economics, as well as the tactical requirements of the nuclear age, indicated that smaller and yet more effective surface vessels, backed up by aircraft, were necessary, the nomenclature frigate and corvette came back into vogue.

Deterrence. Armed forces have always had a deterrent role against predators related to the political concept of *Balance of Power*. Until the 1850s it was mainly by demonstration of the number, size and efficiency of units and forces. But the appearance in 1859 of the French ironclad, steam-and-sail *La Gloire*, with its potential to outmatch all existing warships, compelled navies to build still better weapon systems to counter this menace to their power. Since then the technological race at sea, on land and in the air has escalated without interruption. As one nation has gained a decisive military (and therefore political) advantage, the others have tried to discourage aggression by demonstrating equal retaliatory capability.

The pre-**World War I** naval races between Germany and Britain; among the major powers before **World War II**; and since the 1950s between Russia and Nato, all contained strong overtones of national deterrence. The threat to homelands by **bomber aircraft**, which some assumed in the 1930s to be unstoppable, prompted Britain, in particular, to build better bombers as a deterrent – even though the bomber's effectiveness was overrated and the **fighter**'s underrated. Likewise, controversy over the offensive and defensive merits of the **tank** enabled the Germans to create **armoured** forces against which, in 1939, there was no credible deterrent.

It was not, however, until the arrival of nuclear weapons (**Atom bomb**) that the concept of deterrence assumed more than a passing effectiveness. Demonstration of the **hydrogen bomb**'s total destructiveness made governments far more careful to control such weapons and to defuse potentially menacing situations which, in years gone by, would have led to major clashes of global dimensions. They concentrated more on achieving their aims by diplomacy, by **cold** and **limited wars** – though at the same time the Americans, British, Russians, Chinese and French, who possessed nuclear weapons, paraded their willingness to use them.

The intellectual and strategic debates at the heart of an enormous accumulation of nuclear weapons by the major powers have tended to focus excessive attention on their means of delivery and the defence against them. Jargon and clichés litter this battleground in which the contenders, on the whole, attempt to maintain stability through mutual deterrence to prevent inflicting unacceptable damage on each other. Fresh concepts or emerging technology, such as the theory of **nuclear winter** or the anti-missile **Strategic Defence Initiative**, can either destabilize or enhance deterrence. But integral with the quite ludicrously excessive accumulation of nuclear weapons, intended to ensure no power can out-obliterate the other, is the equally dangerous buildup of forces whose highly accurate, non-nuclear weapons pose a far more realistic threat of destabilization if one rival or another feels able to win a war by conventional means alone. Effective deterrence always demands unambiguous willingness to meet force with force.

Dewey, Admiral George (1837-1917). Served during the **American Civil War** with the Federal naval forces on the Mississippi until 1863 and then with the Atlantic squadron. He won fame by wiping out the Spanish squadron at the Battle of **Manila Bay** during the **Spanish–American War**.

Dieppe Raid. Despite instructions to execute large-scale hit-and-run **amphibious** raids across the English Channel in 1942, to take the strain off Russia and bring the German Air Force to battle, the British had failed to do so by mid-July. At that time Admiral Lord **Mountbatten** won acceptance for revival of a very recent, last-minute cancellation of a raid against strong defences at Dieppe. The plan called for three **Commandos**, the better part of the 2nd Canadian Division (with tanks), heavily supported by naval and air bombardment, to capture the port by a landing at dawn on 19 August, and withdraw that day.

Surprise was achieved, but by a series of accidents the enemy was partially prepared. Intelligence about the beaches and defences was faulty. Only one Commando reached its objective, the rest of the landing force being slaughtered either at sea or on the beaches. In addition to sailors from 38 sunken vessels, 3,403 Canadians, 247 Commando soldiers, 13 US Rangers, and 153 airmen were lost, along with their equipment. In aircraft the score was 48 to 88 in the German favour. But the lessons learnt by the Allies of the need for avoidance of very strong defences, complete beach intelligence, heavy, carefully planned naval and air bombardment, greatly improved signal communications between all three Services and each echelon of attack, and exact navigation, along with beach-traffic control, handsomely justified an important aim of an operation which was regarded as an essential experiment. The lessons were to be applied in numerous future landings.

Disarmament. Amidst an interminable series of mainly ineffectual negotiations which, for more than a century, have endeavoured to control armaments, it is easy to forget the many occasions when very considerable reductions have been made. That is, at the end of wars, by what may be termed *unilateral* measures, when the vanquished have been relieved of their weapons, or forbidden to possess them; and the victors, for

reasons of economy or because there is no further requirement, scrapped or disposed of theirs to others. The aftermath of nearly every major war since the **Crimean** has witnessed this process; indeed it is simpler to quote occasions when it has not happened – such as after the **Russo-Japanese War** of 1904–5, when neither side had won a clear-cut victory; and **World War II**, when Josef **Stalin**'s paranoia, allied to traditional suspicion, secretiveness and fear of the **atom bomb** in American possession, persuaded the Russians to raise rather than greatly reduce their forces in the manner of their erstwhile allies.

The urge by people, sickened of excessive violence, to disarm is of ancient standing. As is the desire to protect vested interests – as, for instance, a ban of the long bow by the knights of chivalry when it threatened their warlike occupations. Not until the Hague Conferences of 1899 and 1907 were international attempts made to limit armaments – and with scant hope of success at a time when popular glorification of war, along with a burgeoning arms race in Europe, was in progress. Called by Tsar Nicholas II, who was aware of Russia's military inferiority, they were hardly likely to appeal to nations, particularly Germany, France and Britain, with forces that were growing increasingly strong. Hague declarations in 1899 to prohibit poison gas (see **Chemical warfare**) and expanding bullets were not renewed in 1907. A ban on the dropping of missiles from balloons looked absurd after the advent of aeroplanes.

After **World War I** the 1922 Washington Naval Treaty achieved a measure of *multilateral* limitation – after the League of Nations had begun in 1920 to seek large-scale disarmament. But by 1932 when an international Disarmament Conference at last was arranged, rearmament in Japan and Europe was under way, the Washington Naval Treaty had already been broken and an atmosphere of heightening tension precluded agreement between the 59 nations – who tended to propose reductions of their rivals' most cherished weapons while resisting attempts to dispose of their own. Germany's flouting of the Versailles Peace Treaty which, among other penalties, limited her Army to 100,000 men and denied her heavy **artillery**, **tanks**, gas, an **air force**, **submarines** and warships in excess of 10,000 tonnes, put the Disarmament Conference in suspense.

At the core of resistance to disarmament were nationalist fears for security, mutual distrust and inability effectively to monitor agreements. After **World War II** the United Nations became the forum for international efforts to limit and reduce armaments. **Deterrence**, the advent of nuclear and **rocket** weapons and the outward movement into **space**, were productive of inevitable deadlock among frightened politicians and peoples. The testing of atomic devices continues under tenuous control by agreement, and explosions in space are outlawed, largely because of disruption of vital signals communications. **Cold** and **limited wars** bred weapons of unheard-of power, making armament control all the more difficult. Not only did the Great Powers, Russia to the fore, vastly increase their armouries, they armed the smaller nations whose nationalist aspirations drew them into a continuing world-wide struggle, despite three major Limitation Treaties signed since 1969.

Of the two **Strategic Arms Limitation Treaties** (SALT 1 and 2) negotiated between 1969 and 1979, SALT 2 has not been ratified by the USA. Meanwhile the 1971 Seabed Treaty, which made illegal the emplacement of nuclear weapons on the sea-bed, outside the 12-mile limit, had only limited application and no guaranteed method of enforcement. But the key to what little, though much publicized, unilateral and multilateral disarmament as has taken place in the 1980s would appear to be Russia's need to put her overstretched economy to rights as to any real change of heart. The major portion of the military formations and their weapons which have been designated, unilaterally, by Russia for abolition are obsolete. Only a very small proportion of modern weapons have been disposed of. Meanwhile, however, the admission to the international inspection of military installations, although restricted, at least improves safeguards against subterfuge.

Discipline. See **Law, Military**.

Dockyards and naval bases. In the 1850s these vital shore establishments were in course of a revolution as steam-powered, ironclad warships began to supplant the old sailing 'wooden walls'. Not only had wharves, slipways and dry docks to be greatly enlarged to accept bigger ships, and the engineering facilities completely changed to deal with machinery and iron instead of

sailcloth and wood, the labour force had to be retrained in totally different skills and the warehouses stocked by an immense variety of stores and spare parts.

The **artillery** revolution also had a radical effect, one which went beyond the need to cope with the more complex rifled, breech-loading pieces which replaced the old muzzle-loaders, but to withstand what the British envisaged as a new threat to security. No longer was a harbour kept safe by batteries guarding its entrance. Henceforward it might be possible for an enemy (the French) to put ashore shell-firing guns and deny main base facilities to the Fleet, which then would be unable to repel an invasion. At Portsmouth, and elsewhere, rings of expensive **fortifications**, nicknamed 'Palmerston's follies', were constructed to keep enemy forces at a distance from the docks.

The technological revolution and added complexity of ships enforced increased reliance on sophisticated dockyards where ships tended to spend longer times for maintenance. Since steamships could no longer remain at sea for long periods, more dockyards with coal (and later oil) bunkering facilities were required at strategic locations to satisfy need. Bases, along with suitable commercial ports, became targets for **blockade** and attack by the enemy from sea, land and, in due course, the air – calling for **anti-aircraft** defences to supplement the forts.

Just how vulnerable navies were becoming from threats to their dockyards was demonstrated in the **Crimean War**, the **American Civil War**, the **Spanish–American War** and the **Russo-Japanese War**, when ships were penned in and destroyed at anchor, occasions when rings of forts merely delayed the inevitable crushing of squadrons which would have done better manoeuvring at sea than sitting as targets in harbour. Nevertheless, it was appreciated prior to **World War I** that ports themselves were becoming additionally vulnerable to moored **mines** and **torpedoes** – the former laid secretly by sea (in due course by air) in the approaches, the latter fired by submarines infiltrating the netted and mined seaward defences. Henceforward defence had to be all-round and umbrella-like. Ships had to be at short notice to escape to sea.

In **World War I** it had been realized that flotilla craft, such as **torpedo-boats**, **submarines** and **landing-craft**, required base and repair ships to provide mobile accommodation and technical facilities. These auxiliary support vessels were the forerunners of the huge fleet trains, including floating docks, which accompanied fleets and **amphibious** forces during **World War II** when they operated for weeks on end at long distance from shore bases. By their mobility the trains provided a security not always absolute in heavily defended ports, where major warships were several times sunk – by **aircraft** at Taranto and **Pearl Harbor**, **submarines** at Scapa Flow, Diego Suarez and **Singapore**, and raiders at **Saint-Nazaire**.

The need for well-defended shore bases as well as fleet trains is greater than ever to serve warships whose requirements are increasingly complicated. How important the latter are has been demonstrated on innumerable occasions since 1945, notably, for example, off **Vietnam**, in the **Persian Gulf** and off the **Falkland Islands**.

Dogger Bank, Battle of. Faced by the immense strength of the British Grand Fleet in **World War I**, the German High Seas Fleet's only hope of scoring successes was by hit-and-run attacks designed to lure enemy ships to destruction on minefields (see **Mines, Sea**). On 3 November 1914, under the command of Rear-Admiral Franz **Hipper**, four German **battle-cruisers** and four light **cruisers**, covering minelayers, ineffectually bombarded Great Yarmouth. Mines sank one British submarine and one German cruiser. Despite intelligence of German intentions by decryption of intercepted radio messages, the British failed to bring Hipper to action; and bungled again on 16 December when he successfully bombarded Hartlepool (a defended port), Whitby and Scarborough.

On 24 January, supported by the High Seas Fleet, Hipper, with three battle-cruisers and the armoured cruiser *Blücher* went hunting British ships and was intercepted near the Dogger Bank by five British battle-cruisers and a light-cruiser squadron under Admiral Sir David **Beatty**. As Hipper ran for home, *Blücher* was fatally hit. But a few minutes later Beatty's flagship also was slowed by three hits, whereupon his orders to the remaining four battle-cruisers, to 'attack the enemy rear', were misinterpreted by his second-in-command, who allowed Hipper's battle-cruisers to escape while concentrating on *Blücher*.

Dönitz, Admiral Karl (1891–1980). A U-boat officer in **World War I** who specialized in the technical and tactical development of German **submarines** and, in September 1935, was given command of the first U-boat flotilla. Dönitz was convinced that Germany's main weapon against merchant shipping was U-boats which, controlled by radio, should operate in so-called 'wolf packs' and concentrate on hunting by night.

Throughout **World War II** he developed these tactics, first as Commander, Submarines, later, after January 1943, as C-in-C of the Navy. From beginning to end he was deprived of sufficient resources to win the Battle of the **Atlantic**. But he came close to doing so in 1943 – and might indeed have succeeded if he had sooner appreciated and taken measures against the deadly enemy **radar**, and had given much higher priority to the development of the snorkel and much faster U-boats, all of which could have been in service in 1943 instead of, respectively, 1944 and 1945. As one of the few military leaders who could handle **Hitler**, he became Head of State after his Führer committed suicide in Berlin.

Douhet, General Giulio (1869–1930). An artillerist who commanded Italy's first aviation unit from 1912 to 1915, but whose criticism of his country's conduct of **World War I** brought about a court martial and imprisonment in 1917. Exonerated by the débâcle at **Caporetto**, he was brought back to command the Italian Air Force. In 1921 he published *The Command of the Air*, which postulated a doctrine (already strongly voiced in Britain) of strategic **bombing** against enemy cities by independent air forces. The book won international fame but did more to terrorize politicians and populaces than influence **air force** leaders.

Dowding, Air Chief Marshal Sir Hugh (later Lord) (1882–1970). An artillerist who, serving with the Royal Flying Corps in France throughout **World War I** and, between the wars, in senior staff appointments, was to have a profound influence on the development of RAF doctrine, training and, as director of research and development from 1930 to 1936, equipment policy. In that post and the next as Air Officer Commanding Fighter Command, he was responsible, among many vital innovations, for adopting the eight-gun Hurricane and Spitfire fighters, radar and the air defence system he was to command during the Battle of Britain. It was he who dissuaded Winston Churchill from dissipating RAF fighters during the Battle of France; who was quick to jam enemy radio beams; and who, although misled by faulty intelligence concerning German air strength, adhered, under intense pressure, to the strategy and tactics which saved Britain.

Drill, Military. By definition military drill is the inculcation in personnel, often by repetition, of methods thought most likely to produce efficient combat forces. Although there are those who regard 'drill' only as the manoeuvring of men and machines in ceremonial, close-order formations, it in fact encompasses nearly all functions concerned with war and, by no means infrequently, civil practice. Close-formation drill by mounted and dismounted men was, in fact, combat drill, designed to enable leaders to manoeuvre their commands with the least trouble in order to bring maximum fire-power rapidly and effectively to bear. Until the introduction of rapid-fire weapons in the 1850s, the shoulder-to-shoulder packing of men bearing small arms was indeed the best, sometimes the only, way to create sufficient weight of fire and to provide a solid enough front against the charge of a similarly massed enemy.

In the 20th century many leaders have reasoned that private soldiers would yield under fire if not crowded together under the immediate supervision of their officers. With greater prescience, they believed close contact between officers and men in combat was synonymous with drilling, a foundation of morale. It took the experiences of the Boer War, the Russo-Japanese War and World War I to show not only that close-order tactics were exorbitant in lives, as well as tactically outmoded, but also that educated soldiers, properly trained, motivated and led, would fight well without close supervision. It was hard for many traditionalists to abandon the rigidity of tactical formations, although in essence nearly all successful operations in the later stages of World War I depended, in the final analysis, on personal initiatives by lowly individuals operating in loosely knit groups.

Enlightened leaders who survived World War I and recognized the value of flexibility in the control of mechanized operations as well as tac-

tics, devised procedures which applied efficient drills to almost every function at sea, on land, in the air, in headquarters, on the lines of communications and airfields and at bases. Repeatedly it was shown how intelligently directed junior commanders in command of individual ships, small army detachments and single aircraft could be persuaded to fight without coercion. Nevertheless, it is undeniable that usually a commander has to be heard clearly even if not seen. Voice radio made this possible, enabling the leaders of, for example, submarine-hunting groups, armoured units and aircraft formations, to command and inspire their subordinates as if by remote control. Hence the subtler disciplined drills of officers using signals communications were often substituted for raised parade-ground-type voices. This system makes it increasingly feasible, as radios become smaller and more reliable, for leaders to command any soldier at the touch of a switch.

Dung, General Van Tien (b. 1917). An enthusiastic member of the Vietminh guerrillas who, from 1936, unrelentingly fought the French and Japanese in French Indo-China (Indo-Chinese War of Independence). As Chief of Staff of the North Vietnamese Army in 1953, he played a prominent role in the French defeat at Dien Bien Phu and later in preparations for the campaign of the 1960s to conquer South Vietnam (Vietnam War). North Vietnam's costly failures led in 1974 to Dung replacing General Vo Giap as C-in-C, whereupon he began limited attacks in December which evolved into the offensive which overran the South by April 1975. In 1980 he took over as Minister of Defence and became a member of the Politburo.

Dunkirk, Battles of. Throughout history this strategic French port has been battered by many wars. During the whole of World War I it was within artillery range of the Germans, garrisoned by the French and British. The latter used it as a forward base for light coastal forces and aircraft engaged mainly in defence of Britain and the Straits of Dover and in attacks on the ports of Ostend and Zeebrugge.

In World War II, when the Germans broke through in Holland and the Ardennes in May 1940 and headed for the Channel ports, it became plain that the Allied forces in Belgium would soon be cut off from their bases in France.

Dunkirk, Battles of

The British nominated Boulogne, **Calais**, Dunkirk and Ostend as alternative, temporary supply ports at the same time as plans were made to evacuate the armies through Dunkirk – if possible. In the event, Ostend was never used, and Boulogne and Calais were surrounded on the 23rd and captured by the 26th. On the 24th, with the Allied armies still well to the east in Belgium and only a small, ill-organized garrison holding Dunkirk, General von Kleist's overwhelmingly strong Panzer Group had only to advance a few miles to cut off the Allies from the sea.

He was prevented from doing so by General Gerd von **Rundstedt**, who called a halt because he feared for his left flank. He was supported by **Hitler**, who agreed with Marshal Hermann **Göring** that the German Air Force should complete the job for the Wehrmacht. But the task proved beyond the Air Force, which was overextended and incapable of operating at night when the bulk of Allied troops were being evacuated by sea. On the 26th, when Hitler rescinded the halt order, it was too late. By then the Allies had rushed strong forces back to Dunkirk and had let in the sea, making the task of immediately seizing the port beyond the German Army, thus giving time for the British to retreat within the perimeter and carry out a famous naval operation which, by 4 June, had evacuated 338,000 Allied soldiers – with hardly any equipment.

For the rest of the war, Dunkirk was regarded by the Germans as a base for naval operations against Britain, a staging post for coastal convoys and a bastion of their Atlantic Wall. In that capacity it was frequently bombed by the British. When the Allied armies advanced from Normandy in August 1944, the task of clearing the Channel ports fell to First Canadian Army. But the exacting business of capturing Le Havre, Boulogne and Calais, and clearing the approaches to Antwerp, induced the decision to leave the port encircled for the rest of the war. On 10 May 1945 it was the last French town to be liberated.

E

East Africa, Wars of. Increasing Portuguese, German and British influence throughout East Africa in the latter half of the 19th century produced, in addition to frictions between the colonial powers, sporadic clashes with Arab slavers and involvement in local tribal and religious wars. In 1885, Germany established a Protectorate over Tanganyika and in 1887, 1890 and 1893, respectively, the British followed suit in Kenya, Zanzibar and Uganda.

At the outbreak of **World War I** the British aimed to deprive the Germans of bases from which sea raiders could operate and, in October 1914, were successful in blockading and later destroying the cruiser *Königsberg* in the Rufiji delta. At the same time, the offensive operations by the outnumbered German forces under General Paul von Lettow Vorbeck progressively attracted considerable British, Indian, South African, Belgian, Portuguese and eventually, with reluctance, locally raised native forces. Damage to the vital Uganda railway and losses of vital equipment and stores to highly mobile German columns (which proved the value of native troops), provoked British counter-offensives in 1915 which fared badly. It took a year to eliminate German gunboats which preyed on British and Belgian shipping on Lake Tanganyika. **Logistics** and, in particular, health care in such primitive country were crucial. Largely forsaking costly pitched battles, the Germans concentrated on conserving their resources while indulging in the hit-and-run raids and sabotage of classic, mobile **guerrilla warfare**.

Not until 1916, after the appointment to command of the experienced ex-Boer Commando leader, General Jan **Smuts**, was Allied progress made against the Germans. Even so, his initial ponderous attempts to envelop his opponent rarely enjoyed success against a will-o'-the-wisp enemy whose aim, as time went by, was reduced to remaining intact and pinning down disproportionately large Allied forces. Smuts, meanwhile, tried to develop his **intelligence** of the enemy, build up logistic services and lines of communication with road-building for use of mechanized transport, while depriving the enemy of supplies and bringing the survivors to battle. In effect, he managed only to weaken and drive von Lettow Vorbeck from one sanctuary to another. Converging columns, which in 1916 drove the Germans southward, failed to make the kill. Still intact in 1917, but desperately short of supplies, medicines and weapons, the Germans invaded Portuguese East Africa and carried on the struggle from there, an attempt at long-range resupply by Zeppelin having been aborted. In November 1918 these were the last German troops remaining in action at the war's end.

In **World War II**, Kenya became the base for the Allied invasion in January 1941 of Abyssinia. In the war's aftermath, as almost everywhere else in the continent, East African nations strove for independence. In Kenya the secret Mau Mau organization began a campaign of massacre and sabotage which, in 1952, compelled the British to declare an emergency. It took three years of guerilla warfare to eliminate the menace by the killing of 10,000 dissidents and the capture of 25,000 others. Soon after Kenya achieved independence, as did Uganda. But whereas the former has remained politically stable, her neighbours, Ethiopia (**Ethiopian (Abyssinian) Wars**) and Uganda, have been rent by devastating internal conflicts, involved

The East Africa Campaign in the First World War

with and armed by the principals of the world-wide Communist struggle.

Edged weapons. It might be thought that with the advent of firearms, universally available long before 1850, the edged weapon would soon have become obsolete. However, the straight-bladed cutting and thrusting sword was worn by infantry officers throughout the 19th century, used in the **Crimean War** and even, in a few cases, carried into action in **World War I**; the development of trench warfare on the Western Front from 1914 quickly rendered the infantry sword unnecessary and it never appeared again except for ceremonial wear.

For horsed cavalry the sabre remained in service until **World War II** when, in the early stages, it saw action in the hands of Soviet cavalry. The sabre was derived from the Eastern scimitar, its curved blade allowing the initial cut, followed by drawing the blade to provide friction, to be performed in one single motion. Developed in turn from the sabre was the naval cutlass, a heavy weapon with a similar, but shorter, curved blade, designed for close-quarter fighting in the cramped confines of a sailing ship. In service on British naval vessels until 1918, the cutlass was gradually phased out thereafter and is now no longer used.

The other cavalry weapon, the lance, was introduced into Europe by the Poles in 1840 and that, too, saw action in both World Wars, with the German Uhlans in 1914 and with the Polish cavalry, bravely but ineffectively deployed against German tanks in 1939.

For the infantry soldier it is the bayonet which

has remained in service since it was first introduced in the 17th century, when it was found that the long musket made a tolerable short pike with a blade attached to the muzzle. Plug bayonets came first, with the haft inserted in the muzzle of the firearm, thus making it impossible to fire with the bayonet attached. The ring and socket bayonet, which fitted over the muzzle, was invented by Vauban in 1688 and variations of that have been used ever since. The length of blade has varied over the years – the British long sword bayonet of 1914, for example, being followed in the 1940s by a short 8-in spike having neither cutting edge nor haft, hence useless for anything other than stabbing when attached to the rifle. In recent years the British have reverted to the broad-bladed knife bayonet, similar to those of most other countries. A bayonet is included in the design of the British Army's new SA80 rifle, more versatile than its predecessors in that it can be used also as a knife, a tin opener and, with its scabbard, as a wire cutter.

Of similar size to the short bayonet, though quite distinct from it, the dagger, in the modern form of a broad-bladed knife, is retained in service with special forces such as the SAS. The edged weapon thus remains an essential element of the soldier's equipment.

Education, Military. It was the appearance of standing armies in the 17th century which vitally stimulated formal military education. Until then **strategy, tactics, drills** and **training** were in the hands of a few experts and mainly disseminated by example and word of mouth. Textbooks were scarce, colleges and instructional institutions few. The first modern military academy, founded in Russia by Peter I in 1698, mainly educated officers of the nobility, a privileged tendency followed by many other nations. The advance of **technology** along with increases of population, **conscription** and, as a result, the urgent requirements for improved systems of supply and control of large, massed forces, imposed demands for better organization and training of General Staff officers (**Staffs, Military**).

The employment by Napoleon Bonaparte of a Chief of Staff to regulate his armies, and the establishment of the École Spéciale Militaire in 1802 (the same year in which West Point Military Academy was formed in the USA) to train officers, pointed the way to the creation of professional General Staff Corps – like that of Prussia, formed in 1801, which required specialized Staff Colleges to train an élite. Throughout the 19th century, naval and army academies and colleges for commissioned officers proliferated, yet hardly at all for other ranks who continued to learn their trades within their own units.

Scholarly analysis and the publication of such books as Karl von Clausewitz's *On War* in 1832 and Antoine Jomini's *Précis de l'art de la guerre* in 1836, significantly advanced the study of military philosophy, strategy, tactics and organization. Simultaneously, science, new technology, weapons and equipment imposed considerable demands upon technicians – of whom navies and armies possessed few. In an age when classically educated people predominated and gentlemen who were officers rarely were involved with industry or commerce, it was mainly civilians and non-commissioned military men who grappled with engines, mechanized vehicles, the latest weapons, signalling systems and suchlike.

Paradoxically, the Royal Navy which, in 1917, was almost the last to form a Staff College, was among the first, in 1830, to form a Gunnery School – a mere 50 years after the first use of cannon! Its task was not only to teach the handling of the latest complicated pieces and gunnery techniques, but also to establish uniform doctrine and training in a vital subject which, until then, was taught at the whim of individual captains. In armies it was the principal technical branches, the Artillery, Engineers and Transportation Corps, which were ordered to study, operate and teach about the majority of new weapons and devices. Since the 14th century, gunners and sappers had been treated as specialists and paid extra. In the 17th century, the French military engineer, Sébastien Vauban, educated his officers in fortification, though without greatly raising the status of technically qualified people or overcoming a snobbery which exists to the present day in many armed forces.

Nevertheless, schools and specialized organizations for each new weapon system had to be formed. Normally it was artillerists who dealt with **rockets**, missiles, some **mortars** and **anti-aircraft weapons**, and engineers who took on signalling, chemical warfare and, in conjunction with transportation experts, helped develop **armoured fighting vehicles**, as well as, through work on balloons, providing the nucleus of **air forces**, leaving **machine-guns** and also some mortars to the **infantry**.

Self-evidence of the need for improved military educational standards and instructional methods created pressures for well-educated recruits. To begin with, illiteracy could no longer be tolerated. Where parents or civil schools had failed, the military had to put matters right before progressively educating its members in all subjects. Throughout the 20th century, the extent to which any nation's armed forces have raised their standards of education has become a bench-mark of progress. By sponsoring students at universities and technical colleges, for example, the armed forces have done more than stimulate their own **recruiting** and complement the work of their own colleges and schools. They have reinforced national standards of education. Indeed, in many ways they have pioneered personnel selection, enlightened discipline, syllabus planning and instructional methods which have been copied in civil schools and industry.

It is no exaggeration to say that the considerable advances in military education have fundamentally altered the relationship between officers and lower ranks. The old-fashioned 'do as I say, not as I do' discipline is outmoded in well-educated forces. Authority becomes based on knowledge and reasoning as much as on rank. The educated officer who realizes he cannot 'know it all', listens carefully to the advice of subordinate experts – who, when ordered, are expected to carry out tasks in a skilful way. In this environment criticism and insights which at one time would have been rated as insubordination simply become part of the decision-making process.

Egypt, Battles of. The historic, strategic importance of Egypt as a communication centre at the crossroads of the Middle East was vastly enhanced in 1869 by the opening of the Suez Canal and later by the importance of oil in transit. Expansionist Egyptian plans to control the waters of the Upper River Nile during the reign of King Ismail brought war with Abyssinia (**Ethiopian wars**) in 1875 and the rout of Egyptian forces at Gundet in 1875 and Gura in 1876. The revolt in 1881 by Ahmet Arabi, against Turkish, British and French control, led to far stronger British than French counter-

action, culminating on 13 September 1882 when 25,000 British troops, under General Sir Garnet Wolseley, launched a surprise night attack (very unusual in those days) against 38,000 Egyptian troops at Tel-el-Kebir. Routed with the loss of about 3,000, Egypt capitulated.

In **World War I** the Allies used Egypt as a main base for their campaigns against the Turks at **Gallipoli** and throughout the Middle East. A Turkish invasion via Sinai was repulsed on the **Suez Canal** on 2 February 1915 with the loss of over 2,000 men.

When Italy entered **World War II** in June 1940, she entertained hopes of acquiring Egypt in the aftermath of British withdrawal from the war. Instead the **North Africa** battles went badly for her. Checked short of Mersa Matruh in September, the Tenth Army was finally annihilated by the British Western Desert Force at the Battle of **Beda Fomm** in February 1941. From the culmination of the German–Italian counter-stroke, which rolled the British back to the frontier in April, until the final ejection of the Axis forces in November 1942 after the Battle of El **Alamein**, Egypt was in the front line, enduring air raids against the Canal and attacks on the naval base (**Dockyards and naval bases**) at Alexandria.

Anti-British sentiment after World War II came to the boil with the minor hostilities of 1951. Strife continued until the British withdrew in June 1956, having negotiated arrangements for care and maintenance of the base with the Egyptian Republic, under Colonel Gamal Abdel Nasser. Meanwhile Egypt had been to the forefront in the **Arab–Israeli War**, which had started in 1948, and on 29 October 1956, when under threat of attack by Franco-British forces to win control of the Canal, she was invaded by the Israelis. Complete defeat by the Israelis in Sinai and ejection from **Port Said** by Franco-British forces on 5 November brought the country to the verge of a collapse from which international intervention alone saved it.

Since then the Israeli victories on June 1967 and October 1973 have forced Egypt to negotiate an uneasy peace with Israel.

Eisenhower, General Dwight David (1890–1969). The son of a Texan railroad worker who graduated from West Point Military Academy in 1911, but who never saw action in **World War I** and spent the major portion of his career, until

1942, at important staff duty, without commanding troops. Then, while helping to prepare plans for an Anglo-American invasion of Europe, he was sent to Britain and given command of the European theatre of operations. Thereafter, he commanded the Allied invasions of North West Africa, Sicily, Italy (**Italian campaign 1943–5**) and **Normandy** through to **Germany**.

In 1950 he was appointed Commander of the newly established Supreme Headquarters, Allied Powers, Europe (SHAPE) within **Nato**, before becoming a candidate for President of the USA and winning the election in 1952. Gifted with a talent for welding diverse personalities into a strong team, it has been said he was a better chairman than commander. Nevertheless he not only successfully waged war by an alliance but managed, by diplomacy, to arrange an armistice for the **Korean War** in 1953.

Electromagnetic effect. Electromagnetic radiation is the propagation of energy through space by means of electrical and magnetic fields that vary in time. An electromagnetic wave travels through space or the atmosphere at 300,000 metres/second and the number of such waves passing a given point per second gives a measure of the frequency in hertz (cycles/second).

The discovery and evaluation of these effects during the 19th and 20th centuries has had the profoundest influence on the development of warfare, especially in the field of communications. Because electromagnetic waves travel in straight lines, Marconi's pioneering work on wireless telegraphy was derided by some of his contemporaries until his success proved them wrong; indeed, radio ground waves are normally limited to a range of about 160 kilometres by the Earth's curvature. However, the discovery of the ionosphere and its ability to refract electromagnetic waves and return them to Earth (skywaves) meant that radio signals could have almost unlimited range.

The electromagnetic spectrum runs from one hertz, covering at the lower end radio, then radar and infra-red, through ultra-violet, X-rays and to gamma rays at about 10^{11} gigahertz (1 gigahertz = 10^9 hertz). Radio waves, occupying a fairly wide part of the lower end of the spectrum, illustrate well the problem the electronic engineer has in harnessing the electromagnetic effect to military needs. Radio bands range from low frequency at 30–300kHz up to extra high frequency at 30–300gHz. The various bandwidths between these two extremes are becoming increasingly crowded with demands for space from different military requirements; typical channel bandwidths are: teleprinters, 150 Hz; facsimile, 1·5kHz; computer data, not less than 2·4kHz; high-frequency radio, 3–6kHz; very high to extra-high-frequency radio, 12·5–25 kHz; television, 5·5MHz. Thus a television channel, which needs a wide bandwidth, would take up the space required for about 250 voice channels – which is why television is rarely used for military communications purposes.

While the electromagnetic effect has encouraged the development of sophisticated **radio**, **radar** and **computer** equipment for military use, there are dangers from it too. Since electromagnetic radiation depends, broadly, on the excitation of electrons, it follows that there can be significant effects from a nuclear explosion (**Atom bomb**). Though often ignored by the layman, to whom the blast and radioactive effects on humans and objects gainsay all else, in the context of military operations the electromagnetic effect can be of dramatic importance. An airburst at over a 100 kilometres above the ground can produce an electromagnetic pulse covering an enormous area, perhaps a whole continent. As well as damaging equipment the pulse can make changes in the electrical conductivity of the ionosphere. This could make high-frequency communications completely unworkable and would reduce radar effectiveness; very-high and extra-high-frequency links should not be affected. The damage to electronic components following a nuclear explosion, from electromagnetic radiation, could be equally catastrophic since it would affect computers as well as radios and radars. The phenomenon is known as Transient Radiation Effects on Electronic Equipments (TREE). Typically, computer magnetic stores would be corrupted, relays tripped and there could be insulation failures and burn-outs in signals equipment.

The overall effect of a nuclear explosion could be to disrupt communications in the widest sense over a whole theatre of operations, if not world-wide. So dependent on sophisticated electronic equipment is modern warfare that it is hard to see how coherent operations could be continued under such circumstances, perhaps one of the most cogent military reasons for not crossing the nuclear threshold.

Electronics. The electronics age may be said to have been ushered in with the invention of the vacuum diode valve in 1902 by the Briton John Fleming (himself coining the word 'electronics'), the immediate application being in the field of **radio**. It was the invention of the transistor in 1948, however, which saw the emergence of electronics as a particular branch of electrical engineering, now showing every indication of becoming the biggest single industry in the world, permeating as it does every aspect of daily life. The effect of electronic developments on the art of war have been similarly dramatic. Not only has miniaturization reduced the sheer bulk of radio and other equipment, but the introduction of the transducer as a means of changing energy from one form to another and the development of solid-state circuitry has meant a dramatic improvement in reliability – always a high priority for military equipment.

Perhaps one of the most significant electronic developments from the military point of view was the invention of the cathode-ray tube, patented in 1923 by the Russian-American Vladimir Zworykin as the iconoscope cathode-ray camera. This made feasible the development of **television**; for the military it was radar that beckoned.

The cathode ray tube fires electrons on to a photoelectric luminescent screen to produce an image, not necessarily a picture but perhaps a displayed radio pulse or other electrical phenomenon. The impact of this essentially simple device on the location of objects, range-finding (see **Range-finders**) and navigation, for example, was immense.

Electronic engineering lies at the heart of the weapons system that is the modern naval vessel, with its automatically controlled rapid-firing guns and its various missile systems (**Rockets and guided missiles**) and electronic anti-submarine equipment. The modern naval battle could hardly be fought without such aids, which form a major part of the equipment on both surface vessels and submarines. Military aircraft too would fare ill without an impressive array of electronics; the speed of modern fighter aircraft is such that a pilot who could not rely on, for example, on-board computers to determine the best moment for an attack, coupled with a head-up (i.e. at eye level) display to present the information he needs without the distraction of studying his instrument panel, would be at a serious disadvantage.

Such dependence on electronics means that the enemy will always be looking for countermeasures to enable him to dodge the (electronically) guided missile that seeks to destroy him, or to disrupt his opponent's **radars, communications** and **computers** so as to render him ineffective. The *electronic battlefield* is now a reality and it means that a whole new aspect of war has emerged – *electronic warfare*; a powerful weapon indeed. All electromagnetic emissions may be intercepted and can be of value to an enemy: formations may be identified, locations revealed and intentions discovered. Certain specialist electronic equipment, such as air defence radars, if detected, could identify particular units and help to disclose the order of battle.

The importance of electronic warfare began to emerge during **World War II** with the rapid development of radar, with improvements in radio communications, and with the Allied successes in intercepting and decoding German encrypted transmissions. Post-1945 electronic warfare has become an accepted part of Nato's naval and air operations, not only for intercept but also as a means of jamming guidance systems and similar electronic emissions; the ground forces have tended to lag behind in this field, but are fast developing the necessary techniques. **The Warsaw Pact** armies, on the other hand, have developed electronic warfare into an important intelligence gathering operation, so as to improve their offensive capability.

Electronic warfare may be divided into three main elements:

– *Electronic support measures* are mainly concerned with producing operational intelligence and with providing advice for countermeasures, warning of the need for higher-level surveillance and the deployment of target acquisition systems when it seems necessary.

– *Electronic countermeasures*, as the name implies, aim to disrupt the enemy's transmissions by jamming of radios, radars or missile-guidance systems, or to mislead him by deception.

– *Electronic counter countermeasures* are designed to foil the enemy's countermeasures deployed against one's own forces. Encryption of transmissions is one obvious, though expensive, means. Frequency-hopping techniques, where transmission frequencies are changed automatically and frequently, help to confuse the enemy by forcing him to search a wide spectrum. A similar system for radar allows transmissions over a sweep of frequencies. Free-channel search involves the selection of one unoccupied frequency from a set of frequencies and using it for one transmission only; this helps to disguise the structure of a radio net since adjacent nets may share the same frequency allocation.

Computers come into a category of their own, though they are equally vulnerable to electronic attack if countermeasures are not taken. An unprotected computer terminal is vulnerable to interception at quite long range, while material is being displayed and worked on by the user, unless the terminal is kept inside a specially screened area. The cost and complexity of such screening means that only terminals and computers handling sensitive material are likely to enjoy such protection. For most defence computers security is maintained by forbidding the input of material above the appropriate classification. Nevertheless, the problem is severe, since developments in electronics technology in the second half of the 20th century mean that most staff officers in a military headquarters will have a computer terminal on their desks and can expect to be using it constantly.

Empty battlefield theory. The widespread dispersal of men in combat, brought about by increased fire-power (see **Drill, Military**), is said by proponents of this theory to have produced 'a void of the battlefield'. They point out that in the **American Civil War** the ratio of men to space was 1:257 square metres and at the end of **World War II** 1:27,500: while at **Gettysburg** in 1863 Federal casualties were 17 per cent and at **Kursk** in 1943 3 per cent per day. It is argued that the increased lethality of weapons compels soldiers not only to disperse but also to take cover behind armour or below ground as they cling to the desire to live. Hence, the vast majority of fire is aimed indirectly at the void with minimal chances of killing an invisible enemy who also rarely aims directly to kill.

Engineering, Military. Traditionally the engineer was always the technologist in the military world, practising a black art which the 'real' soldier could not aspire to, but without which the war could not be fought: bridges to be built, defences constructed, fortifications mined. These activities all required special skills and indeed, in a more modern context, still do. At the same time, the field engineer was always a fighting man, as he still is, ready to take an active part in the battle when the need arises.

Thus the military engineer has from the first needed to combine general engineering knowledge with a sound military education. France had specialist engineer officers as early as 1690, for example, though her sappers and miners at that time belonged to the artillery. By 1715 all engineering was combined in a single corps; in 1868 they acquired responsibility for the electric telegraph; in 1876 military railways came under their wing; and in 1904, aeronauts. It is interesting to see how closely this parallels the British Army experience – the Royal Engineers can fairly claim to have had a hand in the beginnings of most British military technological developments.

In the United States the Engineer Corps has traditionally had a civil function as well and many major civil engineering projects have been pushed forward under military leadership – the Panama Canal is a typical example.

In most modern armies nowadays, where separate technical corps exist to deal with specific aspects such as communications or vehicle repair, the field engineer has reverted to the many and varied tasks of his traditional role. In the battle zone a prime engineer function in support of mobility is the overcoming of obstacles. Of these, perhaps the most important is gap crossing, which can be undertaken in many ways, from fascines carried on the front of a tank and dropped into a ditch to provide a quick way forward, to more permanent bridge structures. Pioneered by the Frenchman Colonel Gillois, the amphibious floating bridge has become essential engineer equipment for use in the forward area. Individual units can be driven independently to the bridge site, straight into the water, then linked together to form a raft capable of carrying a main battle tank, or to form a continuous floating bridge from bank to bank. Not only is bridging time reduced but the bridge can be broken up and dispersed equally quickly when the tactical situation demands it. The German M2 bridge, developed from Gillois' idea, is in wide use in Nato, and the US Army has its own system, as does the USSR. Shorter combat bridges, developed from ideas pioneered by the British in **World War II**, carried on tank hulls and laid and recovered from under armour, are a vital element in mobile operations. More elaborate fixed-girder bridges are built to improve lines of communication.

Other counter-obstacle work involves clearing lanes through enemy minefields and the techniques involved range from sappers searching for mines with electronic detectors and digging them up manually, to various forms of mechanical mine-clearing equipment. Until World War II, mine-clearing was entirely a manual operation, though there were one or two experiments carried out using World War I tanks. The first practical mechanical mine-clearer, a rotating drum carrying lengths of chain which flailed the ground, exploding the mines in its path, mounted on the front of a Matilda tank and known as Scorpion, was used at the Battle of El Alamein in 1942. Successful, but very slow and cumbersome, the idea was developed into the much more efficient Sherman Crab, widely deployed in the later stages of World War II. Other devices, such as rollers pushed in front of a tank and ploughs to dig the mines up, have also been used; the British have evaluated a new flail system, developed as a result of the Falklands War, which can be mounted on various vehicles. Yet another solution tried is the explosive hose, projected over a minefield and then detonated, in turn detonating the mines by overpressure, again pioneered by the British and known in its modern version as Giant Viper. A combination of flail, mine plough and Giant Viper appears to offer the most promise; but no system is foolproof.

The engineers have an equally important task in supporting military operations by route improvement and road and airfield building; an increasingly important aspect of the latter is the rapid repair of existing runways, particularly in North-West Europe where the threat to Nato's permanent airfields from cratering munitions is very real. In contrast, engineer effort also has to go into counter-mobility tasks, where the requirement is to deny routes and key points to the enemy, mainly achieved by demolitions at bottlenecks such as bridges, road junctions, etc.

Not so glamorous perhaps, but equally vital are the provision of adequate and safe water-supply points in military operational areas, and a general engineering requirement to provide military works of all kinds wherever they may be needed.

Finally, in British service, the Royal Engineers take on the task of bomb disposal (though not generally the dismantling of terrorist devices), a relic of their World War II involvement and also, by a curious anachronism which demonstrates their versatility, the provision of postal facilities for all three Services.

English Channel, Battles of the. Since Roman times the narrow but hazardous waters of the Channel have been a preferred crossing place for invaders of one shore or the other, the wider North Sea being yet more perilous. Britain and France persisted until the 20th century in their fears of each other, and fortified coastlines accordingly. But in World Wars I and II these defences were turned to good account against Germany.

From the outbreak of war in August 1914, the Anglo-French Allies determined to prevent the Germans interfering with cross-Channel routes and with using these waters for access to the Atlantic. The German seizure of Antwerp, Zeebrugge and Ostend, and their failure to capture the other French ports as the prize for the Battle of Ypres in 1914, set the scene for the next four years' action. While Britain based fighters near Dunkirk to intercept German Zeppelins and aircraft heading for England, German U-boats entered the Channel and, on 22 September 1914, sank three British cruisers with the loss of nearly 1,400 men. Throughout the war the Royal Navy regularly bombarded Ostend and Zeebrugge docks, hoping to prevent their use, and convoyed ships to Holland through waters infested with mines and submarines.

As the German submarine campaign got into its stride, a mine and net barrage was laid to shield the Straits of Dover in April 1916 and patrolled day and night by armed drifters and aircraft, supported by destroyers. The Germans took to raiding the barrage. For example, on the night of 26/27 October 12 of their destroyers, without loss, sank a destroyer, a transport and six drifters, damaged other vessels and bombarded Folkestone. Destroyer sought destroyer in combat, sometimes by ramming. Gradually the German threat was curbed – notably after the amphibious hit-and-run raids against Zeebrugge and Ostend in 1918.

Throughout World War II the struggle for the Channel was intense, commencing with anti-submarine measures in 1939 plus attempts to prevent the laying of mines from the air, but

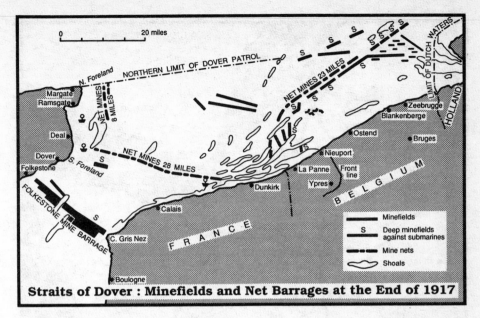

Straits of Dover : Minefields and Net Barrages at the End of 1917

escalating to endless action after May 1940 as the Germans seized the entire coastline. During the **Dunkirk** evacuation and throughout the Battle of **Britain** a pattern emerged. Both sides' convoys would be attacked by aircraft by day and night and, off Dover, by **artillery**. At night, too, **torpedo-boats** would stalk each other and the convoys they guarded. Overhead the struggle for air superiority was ceaseless and the bombing of ports a regular feature of amphibious raiding and invasion countermeasures. In fact, although the British made their first of many amphibious hit-and-run raids in June 1940, the Germans never copied them. Nor was there a real German threat of invasion after September 1940, disbelieve it as the British did.

Occasionally, prior to the **Normandy** invasion in 1944, there would be unusually sensational events – such as the passage up-Channel from Brest on 11–13 February 1942 of the **battle-cruisers** *Scharnhorst* and *Gneisenau* and the **cruiser** *Prinz Eugen*. They had been out of action in French ports since March 1941, kept under close surveillance and repeatedly bombed. Yet, despite ample warning of what was intended, thick weather and a series of accidents and cumulative human errors enabled the Germans to steam half-way up the Channel in broad daylight on the 12th before the British were alerted. They were tackled by a few torpedo-

bombers, at great cost, and torpedo-boats after passing Calais. To great public indignation, they escaped without damage until both battle-cruisers struck mines laid in their path from the air off the Dutch coast.

Other events were the costly **Dieppe** raid on 19 August, against which German naval forces played only an accidental role in repulsing the attackers; and the attack, kept secret until long after the war, by torpedo-boats against an American invasion rehearsal off the Devon coast in May 1944 when several **landing-craft** were sunk with heavy loss of life.

These sensations apart, it was the British and their Allies whose small ships and aircraft fixed an unbreakable grasp on the narrow seas from 1941 onwards. This enabled them to sail convoys almost as they chose while, at the same time, deterring the enemy from venturing out by day. Because of this unremitting effort, at no small cost, it was possible to raid and invade almost with impunity.

Estienne, General Jean-Baptiste (1860–1936). A French artillerist who, in 1909, experimented with air support of armies and, in December 1915 at the third attempt, managed to persuade his C-in-C, Marshall **Joffre**, to permit an experiment with a gun mounted in an armoured Holt tractor – the first French **tank** (really an assault

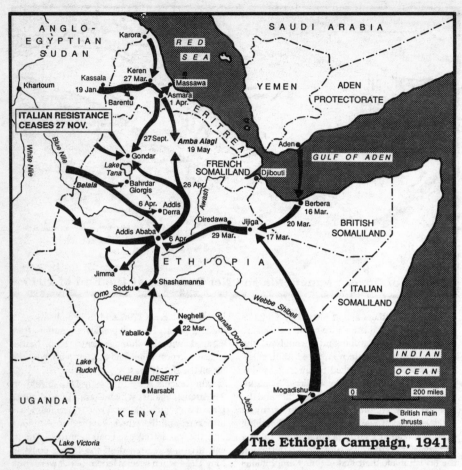

The Ethiopia Campaign, 1941

gun) which saw action in April 1917. By then Estienne had managed to initiate work on what, in due course, would be a 70-tonne tank and, of practical application in 1918, a two-man, turreted Renault FT light tank, of which about 3,200 were built. After World War I, Estienne persuaded the Army to experiment in 1922 with a mixed division of all arms, including tanks and aircraft. Although a success, this model for an armoured division was not pursued.

Ethiopian (Abyssinian) Wars. After 1856, when Theodore II crowned himself emperor of the tribes he had amalgamated by force as one nation, internal or external wars continued to be commonplace. In 1868, after British people had been murdered, his army was defeated by the British at Arogee and Magdala and he committed suicide. From then until 1872 civil war raged, followed in 1875 by a victorious war against Egypt. Starting in 1869, Britain, France and Italy began colonizing the coastal regions, leading in 1887 to armed resistance against the more aggressive Italian presence and the defeat of a small force by Emperor John IV at Dogali. Two years later, John also defeated a large Sudanese Mahdist army at Metemma, but was himself killed.

Menelik II then seized the throne and at once was plunged into a sporadic civil war which, nevertheless, did not prevent him in 1896 from concentrating an army of 90,000 to resist invasion by a partly native Italian army of 20,000 under General Oreste Baratieri. At Adowa on 1 March, Baratieri let his formations attack out of

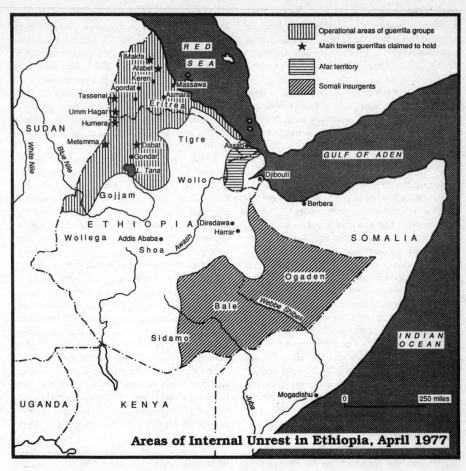

Areas of Internal Unrest in Ethiopia, April 1977

Legend:
- Operational areas of guerrilla groups
- ★ Main towns guerrillas claimed to hold
- Afar territory
- Somali insurgents

control, enabling Menelik to throw overwhelming force against each of his four isolated brigades in turn, with the loss of nearly half their number. Thereafter Menelik managed to maintain peace with independence through treaties with the surrounding colonial powers. Moreover his pro-German successor was deposed with minimum violence at the start of **World War I**.

In October 1935, after a period of tension and Italian provocation, Benito **Mussolini** sent his forces against Emperor Haile Selassie's hopelessly ill-equipped army. But although Adowa was soon captured, neither in their operations from Eritrea nor Somaliland did the Italians make much progress. Unfortunately for the Abyssinians, however, diplomacy by the League of Nations to prevent reinforcements and oil reaching the Italians failed. Nevertheless, not until Field Marshal Pietro **Badoglio** took command in 1936, beginning a campaign of terror by bombing and the use of poison gas (see **Chemical warfare**), did the Abyssinians give way. Addis Ababa fell in May and Haile Selassie fled.

Italy's entry into **World War II** in June 1940 gave Haile Selassie the opportunity, with strong British and South African help, to recover his country after initial Italian offensives had been checked. **Guerrilla warfare** started and in January 1941 the British, who had earlier evacuated British Somaliland, invaded Eritrea and Italian Somaliland. The Italians and their native troops, under the Duke of Aosta, had little heart for the fight and gave way everywhere against superior forces. The capture of the port of Mogadishu and of mountainous Keren, after

115

fierce fighting in March, was decisive. The British met little resistance when they returned by sea to Somaliland, and the fall of Addis Ababa made the subsequent reduction of the mountain strongholds of Amba Alagi and Gondar inevitable.

Since the 1960s the country has again been in turmoil. In the immediate aftermath of British and Italian Somaliland achieving independence in 1960 there was an outbreak of frontier hostilities which, in 1964, spread into the Ogaden, where dissident tribesmen fought the Ethiopian Army. Haile Selassie, meanwhile, had tried to modernize Ethiopia, but his deposition in 1974 by an Armed Forces Committee – a classic example of revolt by militarists against an autocratic, corrupt regime – was to put back Ethiopia by decades. For not only did Somali rebels intensify their guerrilla warfare in the Ogaden, but the Eritreans demanded independence and also started a guerrilla campaign. Haile Selassie was assassinated in 1975 and civil war raged, creating a destabilized political situation in which Russia and her allies took the Ethiopian side, giving both arms and military advice; China and the USA supported the rebels. In 1978, hundreds of **tanks** and **aircraft** were used against the Somalis, who gave as good as they got. At the same time the Eritreans managed to seize control of much of their mountainous regions and spread guerrilla warfare into Ethiopia, where Cuban troops have been used on the government side.

Both struggles have inflicted the most appalling famine and slaughter, in conflicts which have also carried violence and deprivation into neighbouring **Sudan** and, to a lesser extent, Kenya.

Explosives. Ever since the introduction of the first crude firearms, efforts to improve the explosives which discharge the projectile from the weapon and, from guns, detonate the explosive shell at the target have concentrated on two, sometimes contradictory, aspects: the efficiency of the explosive in performing its function; and the safety of the firer.

The first effective challenger to gunpowder as a propellant was created by C. F. Schönbein in 1846 when he added nitric acid to cotton, producing gun-cotton (nitrocellulose). It was adopted by Austria in 1860, though unpopular elsewhere after a serious explosion in an Aus-

trian factory. Nevertheless, interest continued as gun-cotton was much more powerful than normal gunpowder, and a version known as Poudre B, developed by Paul Vieille, was adopted by the French Army in 1885. Meanwhile, in 1875 the Swede Alfred Nobel successfully used nitroglycerine as a gelatinizing agent with gun-cotton and produced ballistite, which was smokeless. Abel and Drewer from Britain were working on the same lines but extruded their propellant in the form of cord – hence cordite.

These smokeless propellants not only increased the effective range of artillery and small arms, but also opened a new era in shooting techniques since guns would no longer be shrouded in smoke, giving away their position, and gunners would the more easily be able to observe the fall of shot and hence correct their aim.

The cordite taken into British service, though efficient, caused serious barrel wear owing to the very high temperatures developed on firing. Because of this the Admiralty had demanded better propellant as early as 1900, but it was not until flashless propellant was demanded during **World War I**, to avoid blinding the gunners and giving away gun positions, that serious efforts and improvements were made; success was not finally achieved until after **World War II**. This success largely met the Admiralty's earlier complaints about barrel wear, since flashless propellants tend to have a lower flame temperature.

The requirement for shell fillings was quite different, a detonation some 100,000 times the burning rate of propellant being needed to burst the shell casing and generate sufficient blast at the target. Picric acid (known as lyddite in British service from the ranges at Lydd where it was first fired) was originally demonstrated in France in 1885. Though used for many years it had serious disadvantages: a high melting-point which made filling difficult; a tendency to form dangerous compounds with heavy metals; over-sensitivity for use in armour-piercing shell.

Germany meanwhile found a safer alternative in Trinitrotoluene (TNT), which was adopted in 1902. In the USA a less sensitive replacement for picric acid (known as 'Explosive D') was taken into service.

By 1907 the British too had adopted TNT in place of lyddite. However, though safer it was also less powerful and work between the wars and subsequently has led to the development of RDX (Research Department Explosive) for use in British shells and to the development of various plastic explosives, mostly developed by Imperial Chemical Industries for demolition and similar tasks – much favoured by terrorists in the form of the Czech-made Semtex, safer to handle until primed, easily moulded to fit any container and hard to detect.

The explosive properties of liquid fuels mixed with air have been well understood ever since the invention of the internal combustion engine but its possible value as a military explosive has only been appreciated in recent years. World War II saw the extensive use of minefields in land warfare and it has been the continuing need to find some means of clearing mines, other than by sappers digging them up with their bare hands, that has inspired both British and American research into the development of what has become known as fuel-air explosive.

A projectile is filled with a mixture of liquid fuel and solid flammable particles. Over the target area a bursting charge scatters the contents of the projectile as a fine mist which, mixed with the surrounding air, becomes a highly efficient explosive when subsequently detonated. This induces an overpressure covering the minefield that detonates the mines. The problem lies in a form of delivery that will ensure coverage of the target with a fine enough fuel mist to form the necessary explosive mixture, but not so dense that it merely burns. The use of slow, low-flying aircraft to spread the fuel has shown that, while anti-personnel mines and single-impulse anti-tank mines can be detonated by this means, the double-impulse mine may well survive the attack (see also **Mine, Land**). Fuel-air explosive can also be particularly damaging to exposed personnel in the target area.

F

Falkenhayn, General Erich von (1861–1922). An unusual Prussian infantryman who instructed the Chinese Army and served as a General Staff officer in the **Boxer** War. As a favourite of the Kaiser, he became Minister of War in 1913. His disagreements with General Helmuth Johannes von Moltke, the Chief of the General Staff, led to his replacing von Moltke on 14 September, as the Army retreated from the **Marne**. Successes against Russia in 1915 were to his credit, but his disastrous decision to attempt to defeat France by attrition at **Verdun** in 1916 brought his transfer in August brilliantly to command the German invasion of **Romania**. Sent to command Turkish forces at **Gaza** in October 1917, he was too late to prevent defeat and was replaced in January 1918.

Falkland Islands, Battles of. *World War I.* Following his victory at **Coronel**, Admiral von Spee dallied until 26 November 1914 before, after instructions from Germany, making for home via Cape Horn. Meantime the British had sent two **battle-cruisers**, under the command of Vice-Admiral Doveton Sturdee, to the Falkland Islands to join the old **battleship** *Canopus* and five **cruisers** to catch von Spee's squadron of two armoured and three light cruisers. Von Spee closed to attack Port Stanley early on 8 December, 24 hours after Sturdee's arrival for coaling. When *Canopus* opened fire at extreme range, von Spee withdrew. Not until Sturdee left harbour in pursuit did he recognize the presence of battle-cruisers which were both faster and better armed than his ships. Von Spee manoeuvred to get within range, but inflicted only minor damage. Sturdee aimed to engage from long range and, using the latest **gunnery** director

techniques, overwhelmed his enemy. All the German ships, except one cruiser, were sunk with the loss of 1,540 lives.

War of 1982. During **World War II** the island base was extensively used. Afterwards it was of declining importance to Britain while Argentina increasingly pressed claims to what she calls 'the Malvinas'. On 2 April 1982 substantial Argentine forces under General M. Menéndez landed near Port Stanley, as well as a small group on the island of South Georgia. After overcoming brief resistance, they assumed control of all the islands and began to prepare a defence many, mistakenly, thought might not be called upon.

Immediately, Britain began dispatching ships and **submarines** as the advance guard of an **amphibious** task force, under Rear-Admiral John Woodward, which moved via Ascension Island (that became a half-way main staging base 4,000 miles from the Falklands) to recapture South Georgia. On 25 April, after **helicopters** had crippled a submarine and after a brisk fight ashore, South Georgia was retaken to become an advanced base for the approaching main task force. The establishment of a **blockade** and the buildup of British forces off the Falklands were conditioned by **logistic** restrictions: the time it took to prepare, sail and assemble the 31 warships (including two **aircraft-carriers** and six submarines) and 80 support vessels involved; and the weather, which in the South Atlantic was appalling.

It was a considerable feat that the naval blockade was in place by nuclear submarine on 12 April and complete on 1 May when the main force arrived in what was known as the (200-mile) Exclusion Zone. On the 1st, Port Stanley

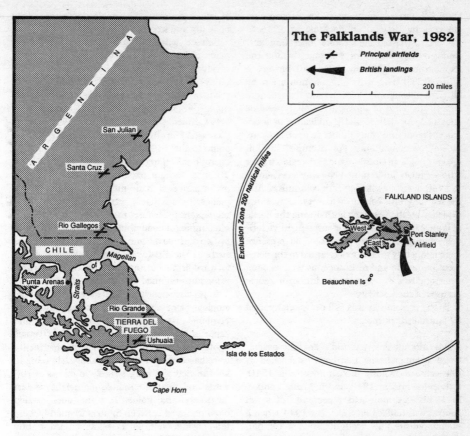

The Falklands War, 1982

✈ Principal airfields

◀ British landings

0   200 miles

airfield was bombed by Harrier fighter-bombers from the aircraft-carriers and a Vulcan bomber, which was seven times refuelled in flight, from Ascension. Thereafter, until the last night of the war, only supply by air from Argentina for the garrison of about 11,000 was possible. Furthermore after 2 May, when the cruiser *Belgrano* was sunk by a British submarine on the 2nd and Argentine naval forces (including an aircraft-carrier) withdrew to port, their best strike aircraft were compelled to operate at their extreme range of endurance. Thus, after the failure of the Argentines to sink the British carriers, the struggle for air superiority went the British way, helped by a successful hit-and-run amphibious raid by SAS against aircraft on Pebble Island on 15 May.

On 21 May, under the command of Major-General Jeremy Moore, British troops landed at San Carlos Water, unopposed except for suicidal attacks by Argentine fighter-bombers which sank warships, but without harm to the assault ships, including the cruise ship *Canberra*. Nevertheless loss to a **missile** of the container ship *Atlantic Conveyor*, with three out of four heavy-lift helicopters, placed a strain on logistic support as the land forces marched on Goose Green and over 60 miles of marshy, roadless terrain to attack the hilltop perimeter strongholds of Port Stanley.

The British had ascendancy over the poorly led Argentines from the outset, but were always operating on a logistic shoestring. It was of great assistance when, on 6 June, Bluff Cove was captured unopposed. Thereafter, although two logistics ships were hard hit on the 8th, this advanced base greatly boosted the buildup to the assault on Port Stanley. Phase 1, the taking of the outer defences, was complete by 12 June. Phase 2, the seizing of the inner ring dominating the town, was carried out against demoralized opposition by the 14th and compelled General Menéndez to agree to a cease-fire.

Fifth Column. A term used for **propaganda** purposes by General Emilio Mola in 1936 to describe Fascist collaborators operating disruptively, by rumour or sabotage, behind the Republican lines (initially in **Madrid**) during the **Spanish Civil War**. It was in common usage by all sides throughout **World War II** to denote almost any form of subversive activity, real or imagined. As such it had significance as a demoralizing or unsettling influence upon civilians as well as combatants. For example, the followers of Vidkun Quisling, the Norwegian traitor who seriously undermined **Norway's** resistance in 1940, were classified as fifth columnists. And the fear of a fifth column was very successfully exploited by the Germans both during the Battle of **France** in 1940, and their subsequent victorious campaigns, when reports of its presence were frequently grossly exaggerated to the detriment of morale and resistance, as well as often causing dire consequences for innocent people accused of such activity.

To the present day it is still occasionally used for journalistic purposes.

Fighter aircraft. Before **World Ward I** the feasibility of arming **aircraft** had been established. A **rifle** was successfully fired from one in 1910, a **machine-gun** in 1912 and a 37mm cannon in 1913. The long-held expectation of aerial combat was fulfilled on 5 October 1914 when a French Voisin V89 brought down a German Aviatik with its machine-gun, an event which coincided with an acknowledgement that special fighting aircraft had to be developed to counter hostile reconnaissance and bombing.

It was also clear that the best way of shooting was by pointing an aircraft with a forward-firing weapon at the target. To begin with only rear-engined, pusher types were suitable. But on 1 April 1915 Roland Garros, flying a tractor Morane monoplane with a machine-gun firing through the propeller (which was armoured to deflect bullets), shot down an unsuspecting German aeroplane in flames. Within a few days of the Morane itself falling into German hands, a Dutchman, Anthony Fokker, had invented an interrupter allowing the gun to fire without hitting the propeller and had sold it, mounted in his monoplane, to the Germans who scored their first victory with it on 15 July. Henceforward, the struggle between so-called fighters to dominate **air warfare** was the key to the winning

of air superiority to enable reconnaissance, bombing and so on to be carried out.

Since it was quickly realized by the fighter pilots, above all the **aces**, that their success and survival depended upon machines which could outfly the enemy's, competition flourished to produce fighters which were faster, more manoeuvrable, higher climbers, sturdier and better armed. Between 1914 and 1918, speeds increased from the 87mph of the Fokker monoplane to the 138mph of the French Spad XIII; operational ceilings rose from 12,000ft to over 20,000ft (where oxygen deprivation reduced performance of both man and machine); biplanes (twin-winged) were much preferred to monoplanes because they were sturdier and often more manoeuvrable; and armament could be two or three machine-guns. Indeed, machines such as the Bristol Fighter F2B had a single forward-firing gun and one or two rearward-firing guns manned by a gunner/observer.

In practice nearly all fighters were multi-role, employed for reconnaissance, ground attack and bombing (usually low level), and bomber and Zeppelin interception, as well as fighter versus fighter combat. Fundamentally, fighter tactics were based upon a dive from above, shooting to kill the victim at ranges rarely in excess of 100 yards and then a scramble for height or dart for safety and home. But the duels which often occurred between fighters frequently were tail-chasing contests as pilots circled tightly and attempted to turn within the turning circle of the enemy plane to bring guns to bear. Manoeuvrability was crucial.

In the 1930s, as engine performance improved and all-metal construction began to supersede wood and fabric, the biplane fighter, which was no longer able to catch faster monoplane **bombers**, was replaced by sturdier, faster and better-armed monoplanes whose poorer manoeuvrability proved no great handicap. The very sturdy and reasonably agile German Messerschmitt Me109, which was improved upon throughout **World War II**, in 1939 had a top speed of 357mph, a ceiling above 30,000ft and one 20mm cannon (firing through the propeller boss) plus two wing-mounted machine-guns, making the fitting of armour for vulnerable places essential. They and their reciprocating-engined opponents would carry out all the traditional roles and, at war's end with long-range fuel tanks, operate freely, like the 437mph North

American Mustang, at combat ranges in excess of 500 miles to Berlin and back. At the same time, fighters were built not only larger, but also, like the Bristol Beaufighter, for long-range and night fighting, with two engines and a second crewman to navigate and work the air-to-air **radar**.

The appearance of the jet engine, which almost coincided with the reciprocating engine reaching its peak of performance, brought about a new breed of fighter. The German Messerschmitt Me262 was the first combat-worthy type. With a speed of 541mph, a ceiling of nearly 35,000ft and four cannon, it would have won Germany outright air supremacy in 1944 had not **Hitler** insisted on it being developed primarily as a bomber. Yet it was aerodynamically unable to make full use of its twin-engine power to overcome compressibility and fly above the speed of sound (Mach 1) – as could the next generation of swept-winged machines, such as the Russian Mig15 with its speed of 683mph in level flight and a ceiling around 50,000ft.

Nearly all jet fighters, with their variety of wing configurations (some variable), are multicombat. Most have speeds in excess of Mach 2, are fitted with sophisticated **electronic** equipment (including **computers**), are greedy for fuel and benefit from in-flight refuelling, and are capable of carrying a variety of cannon, bombs, **rockets** and **missiles**, mostly externally. They place extreme physical and cerebral loads on their crews and call for sophisticated direction from ground controllers, plus support by complex technology based on **aircraft-carriers** or airfields with high-grade runways. Indeed, it was the desire to escape from such vulnerable airfields which prompted the invention of the British subsonic Vertical Short Take-Off and Landing (VSTOL) Harrier, which can operate efficiently from very small spaces and from ordinary ships' decks.

The technology which enables aircraft to engage targets with fire-and-forget missiles well beyond visual distance has revolutionized combat tactics. On-board electronics engineers, supplied with intelligence of the enemy from a variety of ground and airborne sources, now spend as much time arranging defensive electronic countermeasures (ECM) as striking at the enemy. Stand-off engagements in which neither pilot sees the other are as likely as visual, shorter-range shots with heat-seeking homing missiles. Cannon fire is virtually a last resort.

Finland campaigns. With German sponsorship, Finland benefited from the **Russian Revolution** by achieving independence on 6 December 1917. It took hard fighting by the Finns, led by Marshal Baron Gustav von Mannerheim with German assistance in what amounted to a civil war, to expel some 40,000 Russians and their Finnish Communist sympathizers in 1918. In October 1939, however, on the grounds that Finland was in their political sphere, the Russians demanded frontier concessions the Finns were unwilling to concede. On 30 November Russia bombed Helsinki and invaded, but the Finns fought back to expose serious defects in the Red Army's prowess and bring its advances to a halt, successes which encouraged France and Britain to offer help. In February 1940, more carefully organized but extremely costly Russian attacks against the Mannerheim Line defending the Karelian Isthmus, plus an invasion to the north, at last broke the Finns, who conceded Russian demands in March.

Finland sided with Germany at the start of the **Russo-German War** on 22 June 1941, although her participation was never wholehearted, being chiefly aimed at recovering the territorial losses of 1940, which she did while supporting, somewhat ineffectually, the German Siege of **Leningrad**. Hostilities simmered as the Finns put out peace feelers to the Russians, who, having recovered from earlier setbacks, defeated both Germans and Finns between 10 July and 19 September 1944, to recover (approximately) the frontier of March 1940, yet permit independence.

Fisher, Admiral John Arbuthnot (later **Lord**) (1841–1920) saw active service in the **Crimean War**, in China in 1858–60 and **Egypt** in 1882. Although he commanded many ships, it is his tenure at the Gunnery School, his strong influence on naval **gunnery** and his welcome to new technology in a conservative age for which he is most celebrated. 'Jackie' Fisher thrust the Royal Navy into the 20th century ahead of its rivals when the German navy was challenging for supremacy. As First Sea Lord, from 1904 to 1910, he is credited with pushing through reorganization of **dockyards** to cope with the latest vessels (including the revolutionary Dreadnought **battleships**), the Director Fire Control System, **submarines** and the conversion from coal fuel to oil. He regarded submarines as a deadly weapon and ruthlessly scrapped obsolete vessels. On retirement in 1910 he had created a modern fleet ready for war.

Called back by Churchill as First Sea Lord in October 1914, it was he who ensured victory at the **Falklands** and who resigned in May 1915 because he disapproved of the **Gallipoli** campaign.

Flame warfare. The use of fire in support of military operations has been an option available to commanders since ancient times. However, the problem has always been how to project the flame at a sufficient range to inflict damage on the enemy while at the same time protecting the firer; at too long a range the flame would tend to break up and thus be less effective; at too short a range the firer would himself be vulnerable to enemy counteraction.

Flame warfare as such did not emerge as a serious consideration until the 20th century, when it was one of several weapons introduced by the Germans to try to break the deadlock on the Western Front during **World War I**. The *Flammenwerfer* – literally 'flame-thrower' – was first used in 1915 against the French. The apparatus was crude, consisting of steel tubing bolted to a base-plate. An oil jet, ignited automatically, was propelled towards the target by compressed air.

The Allies were soon busy preparing their own version. The first British system was devised by Captain Vincent of the Royal Engineers but, being dependent on heavy oil containers, was cumbersome, and dangerous to operate because the compressed air used still had oxygen in it. The projectors were usually fired from a fixed position in a forward trench or sometimes from underground; in the latter case the tubes were pushed up through the earth immediately before firing. An improved version designed by Captain Livens had a range of about 70 metres and was safer as he used deoxygenated air. He also produced a semi-portable version with a range of about 30 metres.

Both sides continued to use flame-throwers but with only modest success. Certainly the smoke, flame and heat were terrifying and men caught in bunkers could be terribly burned; yet the short range of the projectors, with positions given away as soon as they were fired, exposed the operators to immediate retaliation.

Despite the dubious value of these early weapons the idea emerged again in **World War II**. Short range was again a problem but the projec-

tors themselves had been made more reliable and easier to operate; the Germans, especially, had an effective manpack set in use during the Battle of **France** in 1940. The United States, too, found flame-throwers, both manpack and mounted in amphibious tractors, particularly effective in dealing with the Japanese, deeply dug-in on the Pacific islands they so tenaciously defended.

British attention turned to larger equipments. Crocodile, a system based on the Churchill tank, towed an armoured trailer full of jellied petrol (napalm). The fuel was fed through pipes running under the vehicle's hull to the flame gun in the hull gunner's compartment at the front. Pressurized by nitrogen, the fuel was ignited by a petrol jet and an electric spark as it left the projector. The gunner could fire 100 shots to a range of about 80 metres without replenishment, a system used with considerable effect against the concrete defences of the Atlantic Wall and throughout the campaign in North-Western Europe in 1944/5.

The British have now abandoned the flame-thrower but a system mounted in the American M60A2 tank was used in **Vietnam** and the Soviet Army has a system in service mounted on T55. The latter displaces only the coaxial machine-gun, so that the main armament can still be used; in both systems the fuel is carried on the vehicle so the gunners have only a limited number of flame rounds available before replenishment is needed.

The **Korean War** saw the use of air-dropped napalm as a flame weapon, also used extensively in Vietnam, and this is now the more usual application of the concept.

Flanders, Battles of. When the Germans wheeled through Belgium in August 1914, they covered their right flank in Flanders (the word is said to mean 'flooded land') with **cavalry** which made no real attempt to reach the coast. They were checked by the Belgian Army and light British forces, whose improvised **armoured** cars played an important role in tasks which included denying bases to German **aircraft** bent on attacking Britain and retaining possession of the vital Channel ports.

First Battle of Ypres. The last lap of the so-called **Race to the Sea**, in the aftermath of the Battle of the **Marne**, began on 12 October when General von **Falkenhayn** committed eight (mainly reserve) infantry and three cavalry corps to a blow intended to overrun Flanders and capture Calais. Facing him, to begin with, was the depleted Belgian Army, one French infantry corps, four regular British infantry corps and the Indian infantry corps, plus one British and one French cavalry division; the three nations' armies co-ordinated by General Foch. The first objective in terrain dominated by numerous copses and villages was the route centre of Ypres, pounded with the rest by intense artillery fire as the offensive developed. Yet strong bastions upon which the Allies, who had little time to dig in, founded their unyielding defence. Until the battle's end on 11 November, the brunt was borne by the British Expeditionary Force (BEF) whose high-standard marksmanship played havoc with the German masses. Both sides suffered crippling losses, but, although on 1 November the Germans seized the vital Messines Ridge to threaten the encirclement of Ypres, they failed in their aim. For four years more the entrenched lines of the salient would move but little, even after three major offensives and numerous skirmishes.

The *Second Battle of Ypres* was a limited attempt by the Germans on 22 April to win ground and divert Allied attention and strength. It included the first use of poison gas (**Chemical warfare**), which panicked two French divisions whose troops, like the nearby British and Canadians, were without respirators. Finding, to their surprise, they had advanced to within 2,500 yards of Ypres, the Germans with inadequate reserves, went on attacking the Allies who, for the next five weeks, struggled to restore their lines. At great cost nobody was any better off at the end.

Messines Ridge was a classic siege-warfare operation on 7 June 1917 to capture ground which would threaten the forthcoming British offensive in the Ypres salient. The assault, prepared over 18 months by General Sir Herbert Plumer, took the Germans completely by surprise. Within the day, as 500 tonnes of ammonal were detonated in 19 mines, and as gas containers and a huge quantity of shells were hurled at the enemy, immediately followed up by tanks and infantry, the Ridge was seized. Yet British casualties were 17,000 to 25,000 Germans, who lost 67 guns too.

The *Third Battle of Ypres* was perhaps the most dolorous in British Army history, when General Sir Douglas Haig, ostensibly with the aim of seizing the Flanders ports at the request of the Royal Navy, undertook a campaign of attrition to maintain an Allied offensive strategy while the French Army recovered in the aftermath of its May mutiny. By assaulting wetlands whose drainage system had been wrecked by shellfire, Haig made it impossible to use tanks to pave the way for infantry against a well-forewarned enemy who effectively used the new mustard gas. Starting in rain on 31 July 1917, the attackers were mired in a morass of the artillery's making. Sheltering in concrete pillboxes and shattered villages commanding the vital Passchendaele Ridge, the Germans held the whip hand with their system of 'elastic defence' (rebounding with counter-attacks after giving ground under pressure). Yet their casualties piled up to some 260,000 against about 300,000 British and 8,500 French, before it was called off on 10 November with the capture of the ruined village of Passchendaele – a mere five miles advance during a battle synonymous with misery.

The Germans abandoned Flanders in October 1918 only because the Allied eastwards advance in the south no longer made its possession tenable. But they were back as **World War II's West Europe campaign** approached a climax in May 1940.

The 1940 Battle. The wide-fronted German invasion of the west, which started on 10 May, rapidly overran **Holland** and penetrated deeply through the Ardennes to the Channel coast at Abbeville, was slower reaching Flanders because Army Group B, under General von **Bock**, was not only under orders to hold back in Belgium but was also meeting stiffer resistance from the best of the Allied armies. The German Army High Command wanted the Allied armies to remain to the east while their own troops moved up the Channel coast, towards Ostend, to complete a grand envelopment. By 25 May the bulk of the British and French armies were in a sack to the south-east of Ypres, and the Belgian Army was backing towards the Flanders coast. Then **Hitler**'s famous 'halt order' forestalled the envelopment and gave time for the BEF, and those Belgian and French troops who wished it, to retire on **Dunkirk**. Thus, once the Belgian Army surrendered on the 28th, what little of Flanders remained in Allied hands comprised a rapidly contracting bridgehead barring the way to evacuation beaches. Ypres fell that same day.

The Allies, spearheaded by First Canadian Army, would not return until September 1944, against a broken German Army.

Fletcher, Vice-Admiral Frank Jack (1885–1973). One of the US Navy's most experienced airmen, who in 1942 won the most exacting **aircraft-carrier** battles against the best Japanese carrier forces, but who was underrated and denied due credit. In February 1942 he led aircraft-carriers in raids on Japanese bases in the Pacific Ocean. As commander Task Force 17, with two carriers, he succeeded in May, despite misleading intelligence and errors, in defeating the Japanese strategic plan in the drawn Battle of the **Coral Sea**. A month later, when in command of carrier Task Forces 16 and 17 at the decisive Battle of **Midway**, his dive-bombers massacred the Japanese carriers, though his own *Yorktown* was also sunk and he was wounded. But when commanding Task Force 61, with three carriers in support of the Battle for **Guadalcanal**, he was faulted for abandoning the amphibious-force transports to the mercy of the Japanese. He lapsed again in the initial Battles for the **Solomon** Islands between 22 and 25 August, when poor intelligence and misjudgements again appeared to let opportunities slip. On 18 October, an exhausted man, he was replaced, but later given a command in the **Okinawa** battles.

Flexible response, Strategy of. A philosophy of **deterrence** regarded as a means to match threats with graduated measures. Although conceived in the 1950s with nuclear deterrence in mind, it has been widened in scope by the desire to maintain forces strong enough to resist non-nuclear aggression. Therefore it contributes to expansions of military might.

Foch, Marshal Ferdinand (1851–1929). An artillerist and controversial military thinker who came to fame at the start of **World War I** by his command of a corps which defeated the German invasion of Lorraine. At the **Marne** and in the pursuit to the **Aisne** he again distinguished himself as much by sheer determination as skill. He was then appointed by General **Joffre** to co-ordinate the Allied armies in **Flanders** – a difficult task he performed with brilliance at the first Battle of Ypres. Given command of the Northern Army Group, he had to cope with the gas attack

at Ypres and control the unsuccessful 1915 offensives in the vicinity of **Vimy Ridge**. When Joffre was replaced in 1916 he was relegated to the shadows, but recalled to prominence as Chief of the General Staff in May 1917 to help revive the French Army in the aftermath of the disastrous battle for the Chemin des Dames. He was responsible for the masterly Allied propping up of the Italians after **Caporetto** and in March 1918, when the **Hindenburg offensive** seemed on the verge of overwhelming the Allies, was appointed Supreme Allied Commander. It was his tact and firmness in winning the trust of politicians and senior commanders that held together the Allies when they threatened to break apart. The Germans were stopped, making possible the counter-offensive at **Amiens** in August which was the beginning of the war's end.

Fonck, Captain René (1894–1953). France's greatest air **ace**, a brilliant tactician and shot who, following service as a sapper in the trenches, learnt to fly in 1915. On one of several perilous reconnaissance missions, he claimed on 1 March 1916 to have destroyed a Fokker E3 fighter – the first of many unconfirmed victories. In April 1917 he joined a fighter squadron and at once revealed his talent. Several times he shot down two aircraft in a day; on a day when he destroyed six (a feat he was to repeat), three fell to his guns in 45 seconds. Finally credited in November 1918 with 75 victories, his own estimate was 127. Remarkable to relate, he died peacefully in bed.

Food, Military. Until scientists developed the technology of food preservation beyond the salted, spiced, dried or smoked-meat stage, armies, like many civil communities, were at the mercy of **logistics**. Tenuous sources of supply and transport usually made it impossible for armies to maintain large forces without causing famine by a scavenging which denuded the countryside. Likewise, on long sea voyages, ships' companies were dependent on what livestock they could carry to supplement an otherwise unappetizing diet. In effect, navies and armies had need to keep on the move in search of fresh food to survive.

The development of modern food technology may be dated to the discovery in the 18th century that scurvy was caused by an unbalanced diet lacking fresh fruit and vegetables. Warships' crews were among the first to benefit. Research begun in France in 1795 inspired Nicolas Appert's bottling of heat-sterilized preserved foods, which the Royal Navy used on a polar expedition in 1825. Then, in 1839, an Englishman, Peter Durand, used lighter, stronger, tin-plated canisters, but without ensuring prevention of contamination during the canning process. Indeed, not until Louis Pasteur's research into fermentation showed scientifically in 1864 how control of preservation could be achieved, were food manufacturers able to supply the military with food which could be stockpiled safely for long periods.

Foods which were 'pasteurized', dehydrated or refrigerated became commonplace in the 1860s. To their immense relief logisticians henceforward could base their calculations upon reliable sources of food; the medical authorities were less concerned about food poisoning; the transport services economized by moving concentrated foods on wheels instead of on the hoof; and all this was approved by those whose diet was assured and improved as well as made more attractive. In fact, the standard of military food was never better nor worse than the logisticians and cooks who supplied, prepared and served it. It usually reflected a nation's eating standards; the more so whenever cooking was carried out by sailors and soldiers in their own messes, instead of by better-trained cooks working in well-equipped kitchens.

As always, siege conditions, when large bodies of men lodged for long periods in trenches, made feeding difficult. Starvation causes obsession with feeding. During the Siege of **Port Arthur**, the Japanese suffered badly from beriberi, caused by eating little but polished rice, and the Russians had scurvy from the lack of vitamin C (as yet undiscovered) from fresh vegetables. The morale and health of those who dwelt for days on end in damp, cold trenches during **World War I** suffered because it was difficult to provide regular hot meals. Eating out of tins was not always appetizing, and the variety of tinned food was limited and monotonous. Fresh hot food in insulated containers helped.

In **World War II** national standards of diet varied greatly. Gradually strangled by **blockade**, the Axis powers' diets declined as substitute (*ersatz*) food became commoner. On the other hand, the Western Allies made strenuous and by no means unsuccessful efforts to feed their troops with a high-calorie, varied diet. More-

over, in a war when small groups often had to cook for themselves, improvements were often achieved by an exchange of rations between allies. The standards reached since then, as the latest additives and freeze-drying have been introduced, have improved in quality as technologists have found better ways to compress and pack combat rations.

Formosa, Battles of. The large island of T'ai-wan, as the Chinese called it, was partly and temporarily occupied by the French in 1885 during the **Franco-Chinese War.** Japan was also interested and in 1874 had sent an expedition to punish islanders for murdering fishermen. Then in 1895, by treaty after the **Chinese–Japanese War**, she took possession.

Apart from exploiting Formosa's natural resources, Japan developed it as a strategic base – once called Japan's 'largest aircraft-carrier' – for her **World War II** invasions of mainland China and of the Pacific. Heavy American air attacks by Boeing B29 long-range bombers, and also by carrier aircraft against airfields on Formosa, began in October 1944 in support of the Battles of the **Philippine Islands**. In a week's intensive fighting, the Japanese lost some 650 aircraft and the Americans about 150. As a result of this defeat and their inability to bomb or torpedo enemy warships, the Japanese launched the very successful, so-called **kamikaze** suicide attacks against warships by fanatical pilots, many of whom were based on Formosa.

In 1945 Formosa was returned to China and renamed Taiwan. With the collapse of the Nationalist armies on the mainland during the **Chinese Civil War**, it became General **Chiang Kai-shek**'s base for continued resistance against the Communist regime. Air combat occasionally occurred in the 1950s over the Straits, but in face of American guarantees, the Communists refrained from attempting to take possession.

Fortifications. Military positions strengthened against attack, usually built of masonry or concrete and usually erected in peacetime against the threat of war. *Field fortifications* are usually much more temporary, consisting of entrenchments, emplacements for crew-served weapons and often protected by barbed wire, **mines** and such natural obstacles as rivers, canals or deep ravines.

Before firearms were introduced, the medieval

castle was able to hold out under siege for long periods, often for years. The situation did not change dramatically as guns began to appear, since they were neither sufficiently accurate nor powerful enough to pierce the walls. However, as guns became more efficient the traditional moated castle became an anachronism, though the need for permanent fortifications to protect cities and vital centres remained. Designers gradually introduced more complex structures with as little as possible rising above ground level. The influence of the Frenchman Marshal Sébastien de Vauban in the 17th century is probably the most significant, his ideas governing fortress design until the late 19th century. Vauban retained the traditional plan of inner enclosure, rampart, moat and outer rampart – already refined to counter the effects of gunfire; however, he extended the outer works so as to compel the enemy to start his siege operations much farther away. Every face of a Vauban fort was supported by other works to flank and rear and his fortresses became vast polygons featuring great bastions interspersed with smaller ones, all capable not only of providing mutual support but also of surviving independently, supplied by underground magazines and covered walkways.

Most European countries followed Vauban's lead and his fortresses may still be seen today. However, across the Atlantic another form of fortification began to appear as the United States was drawn into civil war in the 1860s. Few permanent masonry forts had been built in the New World, though the familiar wooden frontier post provided a basis for the defence of troops and settlers during the **American Indian Wars** in the far West. It was the **American Civil War** which provided a portent for the future with its extensive use of entrenchments in the defence of vital areas.

In the late 19th and early 20th centuries the age of the permanent fortification was by no means dead and the Belgian Henri Brialmont emerged as a worthy successor to Vauban with the fortress complexes he designed to protect major cities such as Liège (surrounded by no less than twelve) and Antwerp. Similar massive defences were erected at Verdun and Belfort. These forts were built of concrete, with much of the construction underground and the armament mounted in steel rotating turrets, many of Brialmont's 'disappearing cupola' design, only emerging above ground to fire. These complexes

were so vast they were described as 'land battle-ships' – a real misnomer since, unlike their maritime namesakes, they were immobile, a basic weakness in a world of increasing mobility. There was invariably a way round, even if the forts themselves were impregnable – which few actually were. Such defences are never, in the end, impervious to modern weapons. Nevertheless the heroic defence of **Verdun** by the French during **World War I** is a classic of its kind.

Though permanent fortifications played their part in World War I it was field fortifications which were such a significant feature of that conflict. Elaborate entrenchments stretched from the Swiss border to the North Sea, consisting of lines of fire trenches in depth to several miles, with communication trenches running forward to link them together. Numerous dugouts – often very deep – provided shelter for frontline and supporting troops, for stores and for the treatment of casualties. All of this created a world of its own below ground level which left an indelible impression on those who experienced it; a defensive system when supported by artillery and protected by belts of barbed wire and the quagmire that was no man's land which the infantry of neither side could breach. The war in **France** and **Flanders** could be described as a perpetual siege.

Despite the arrival of the **tank** and general **mechanization** of armies during the 30s, the European powers still saw the need for permanent defences. The best known is probably the Maginot Line (named after the French Minister of Defence of the period) which consisted of an elaborate network of large fortresses, connected by tunnels and with its own railway system and electrical supply, the whole provisioned for several months. Starting at the Swiss border the Maginot Line ended on the Belgian border at Montmédy; a fact the Germans were quick to grasp in 1940, turning the French flank with ease as they poured through Belgium, making the Line useless.

The Belgians themselves had built a line of forts along the Albert Canal, the most famous and supposedly impregnable of which was Eben Emael; it fell in a few hours to a combined **glider** and parachutist attack which landed on top of it.

There were others, but none so elaborate as the Maginot Line and none in the end were any more effective, though the Stalin Line facing Poland did manage to delay the German

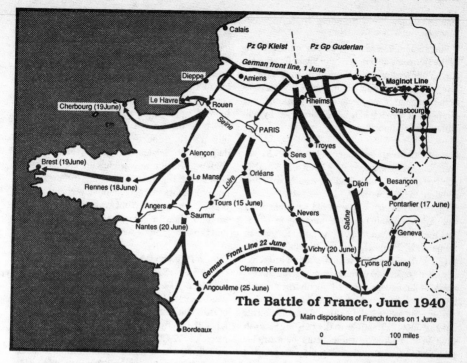

The Battle of France, June 1940

Main dispositions of French forces on 1 June

0   100 miles

invasion of Russia in 1941 for about two days. Others worthy of mention are the Mannerheim Line in Finland; the Czech Little Maginot Line; the Greek Metaxas Line facing Bulgaria; Germany's own Siegfried Line opposite the Maginot Line and the Atlantic Wall to oppose Allied landings in Europe; and **Corregidor**, America's fortress in the Philippines, which fell to the Japanese in a month. Since 1945 the only comparable system has been the Bar Lev Line, held by the Israelis along the eastern bank of the Suez Canal. The false sense of security which this gave them allowed the Egyptians to breach it with remarkable ease when the opportunity arose.

The defender behind fixed fortifications has invariably put himself at a disadvantage by surrendering the initiative to his opponent and has often, as a result, lost the war.

France, 1940, Battle of. The aim of **Hitler's** invasion of the West in 1940 was the elimination of France and Britain from contention in **World War II** to enable him to tackle Russia without fear of a second front in his rear. The opening attack on 10 May into Holland, Belgium and through Luxembourg was also directed into

Northern France, with its left flank extending along the line of the River Somme to Abbeville. But it is the final offensive, starting on 5 June, which is generally known as the Battle of France. Preparations, of course, started before the **Dunkirk** evacuation was complete. The Germans were quick to refurbish their mechanized forces and extensively redeploy, while the French, shorn of their best divisions and with only three understrength armoured formations, worked hard to turn villages and copses into a network of unyielding defences.

Army Group B's break-out from the Somme bridgeheads, with its armoured groups leading, headed for the Channel and Biscay ports. Army Group A made the main thrust four days later, followed on the 14th and 15th by subsidiary attacks by Army Group C through the Maginot Line (**Fortifications**). Unrevealed is the self-sacrifice of French Army resistance which, at this nadir in its fortunes, was more resolute than before. German losses in tanks and men were heavy, progress slow at first. But with neither air support nor mobile reserve, the French, with minor help from the British Expeditionary Force (little more than a corps in strength), had not the remotest hope of withstanding the armoured onrush.

Paris was declared an open city on the 13th as the Germans also neared the Swiss frontier to cut off the entire French eastern army group. The government resigned on the 17th. Marshal **Pétain** came to power, seeking capitulation. Once more, what was left of a British army left by sea without its equipment.

Franco, General Francisco (1892–1975). A founding senior officer in 1920 of the Spanish Foreign Legion, Franco had previously won distinction in Morocco by his gallantry against bandits and insurgents; and did so again with the Legion, notably at Alhucemas Bay in 1925. As Chief of the General Staff, he failed to come to terms with the newly created Republic and, in July 1936 when faced with a state of anarchy, assumed leadership of the anti-government, Nationalist forces who rebelled openly throughout Spain. With material and men from Nazi Germany and Fascist Italy, he used Morocco for his base against the Republic in the ensuing **Spanish Civil War**. Following three years of fratricide and destruction, he concentrated on restoring his country, shrewdly resisting **Hitler**'s urgings to join the Axis against Britain in 1940, but in

1941 sending a 'volunteer' force to fight alongside the Germans in the **Russo-German War**.

Franco-Chinese War. The expansion of French interests in **Indo-China** and China brought fighting to Tongking when the Chinese tried unsuccessfully to drive them out in 1883. Further heavier fighting on land and sea broke out in 1884 as the French strengthened their grip, although in June a small French force was defeated at Bac-le. In reprisal, French warships sank Chinese warships at Foochow and bombarded the forts of Chi-lung in **Formosa** to enforce a blockade. Defeat, however, at a second battle at Langson in Tongking, in March 1885, brought about a complete French withdrawal and the fall of their government at home.

Franco-Prussian War. The outbreak of hostilities on 15 July 1870 may be deemed the result of Napoleon III's delusion that the French Army was superior to Prussia's, and his underrating of **Otto von Bismarck**'s diplomatic ability in unifying the German states. As a result a French force of 224,000 men, in a state of utter **mobilization** and **logistic** confusion, was faced by 475,000 well-organized Germans, admirably directed by General Helmuth Karl von **Moltke**.

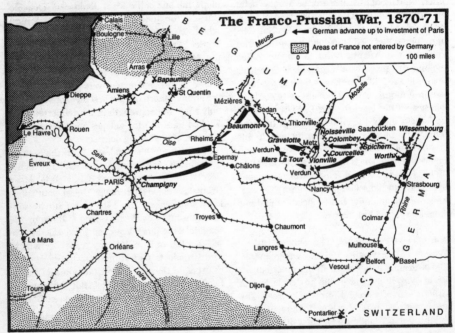

The Franco-Prussian War, 1870-71

Whereas the assembly of German formations and stores at the frontier proceeded with smooth precision, Frenchmen wasted immense time and effort wandering from place to place trying to find units which, as often as not, were concentrating in the wrong place with only a minimum of stores and equipment.

Lacking a plan and intelligence of the enemy, Napoleon ordered an advance on Berlin. But the Prussians advanced too, colliding with the French near Saarbrücken on 2 August in the first of several frontier battles. Casualties were heavy, but marginally in the German favour. German tactical handling was not all it might have been, but it was more than a match for the French, whose **artillery** was outmatched, and who were forced remorselessly backwards as their morale faded. At Fröschwiller and Spichern on the 6th and Mars-la-Tour on the 16th, the two sides blundered into each other, making charge after countercharge – but leaving the Germans in possession of the field.

On the 12th, Napoleon, a sick man, handed command of the Army of the Rhine to Marshal **Bazaine** (who was retreating under constant pressure on the fortress of **Metz**) and to Marshal **MacMahon** with an army at Châlons he was trying to reorganize. At Gravelotte on 18 August von Moltke, with 200,000 men, brought Bazaine's 100,000 to battle – and suffered appalling losses storming the village of Saint-Privat, at the same time seeing his right wing collapse in a panic which he personally helped check by leading up reinforcements. Bazaine, who was on the verge of a significant success, failed to follow up his temporary advantage and withdrew supinely into Metz, where he and 173,000 men remained almost impassive in the hope of relief by MacMahon's army.

Accompanied by Napoleon and with 100,000 men, MacMahon moved to the rescue by an indirect route, close by the Belgian frontier, whence von Moltke skilfully manoeuvred him into the trap at **Sedan** where on 1 September he was crushed and Napoleon taken prisoner.

Belatedly, as the Germans surrounded the frontier fortresses of Strasbourg, Belfort and **Verdun** and began to march on Paris, the French proclaimed the Third Republic and began a last-ditch resistance by **guerrilla warfare** as they tried to rebuild their armies in the field. **Paris** was surrounded on 19 September, but held out despite dire shortages of food and munitions and the mutinous behaviour of garrison elements. At the same time the Germans had great difficulty restoring the railway to supply their troops and bring up the siege train with which to batter the defences and city, starting on 5 January 1871.

Meanwhile Bazaine surrendered Metz on 27 October and desultory engagements were fought in the vicinity of **Amiens**, Coulmiers, Orléans and Le Mans, battles which offered no greater benefit to the French than a salving of pride, and simply tried German patience while peace negotiations dragged on. Paris sued for an armistice on 26 January, but Belfort's garrison fought on until ordered to capitulate on 15 February, marching out with full military honours two weeks before the German Army entered Paris in triumph.

Fraser, Admiral (Lord) Bruce Austin (1888–1981). A specialist in **gunnery** who served in **World War I** and in 1933 became Director, Naval Ordnance prior to being made Controller. To a large extent he managed the Royal Navy's expansion at the start of **World War II**, but it is as C-in-C Home Fleet, from May 1943 to 1944, and his conduct of **Arctic convoys**, including the sinking of the battle-cruiser *Scharnhorst* in a night action by **radar**, for which he is most famous. In 1944 he took command of the Pacific Fleet and thus was engaged in the final stages of the **Pacific War**. From 1948 to 1951 he was First Sea Lord, involved with the **Korean War**.

French, Field Marshal (Lord) John (1852–1925). A cavalryman with extensive experience of small colonial wars who distinguished himself in the **Boer War** and was made Inspector-General of the British Army in 1908. Appointed C-in-C British Expeditionary Force (BEF) at the start of **World War I**, his handling of his own officers and of those of allies left much to be desired. In the retreat to the **Marne** and during the battle he was unenterprising and hardly in control. At First Ypres and then the major offensives in 1915 in **Flanders** and the vicinity of **Vimy Ridge**, he was out of touch with situations beyond his experience and competence. An unwell, peppery officer, largely in the hands of his staff and senior commanders, he was blamed for failure at the Battle of Loos and relieved by General **Haig** in December 1915.

French Foreign Legion. Formed in 1831 in

Algiers to assist with the policing of French North African possessions. Composed of mercenaries from many countries who swear allegiance to the Legion, not France, it is officered by Frenchmen. Its severe discipline is as celebrated as its reputation for self-sacrifice. In the Carlist War (1834–9) in Spain it lost 50 per cent of its strength. Since then it has fought in the majority of France's colonial campaigns, including the **Mexican War** of 1863 and the **Indo-China War of Independence** (and the Siege of Dien Bien Phu). During both **World Wars** it fought in Europe, some of its units joining the Free French under General **De Gaulle** in 1940 and fighting alongside the British. In 1961 one of its regiments was disbanded in disgrace for joining the rebels in Algeria. A year later its depot was moved to France for the first time.

Frigates. The nomenclature of popular, fast, sailing warships dating from the 16th century and used, from the 18th century onwards, for scouting and as maids of all work. With the arrival of steam the name went out of use towards the end of the 19th century as **cruisers** and **destroyers** took over the frigate's function; but it was revived during **World War II** to denote an enlarged **corvette** with a displacement of a little over 1,000 tonnes and a speed of 20 knots. In 1943 the US Navy also readopted the name, but to describe vessels of similar speed but 2,400 tonnes displacement – a sort of slow **destroyer**. Mostly these vessels were employed on escort and anti-submarine tasks, fitted with **Sonar**, **radar** and suitable weapons.

Following World War II the name has become almost meaningless since it has been used to describe vessels with displacements between 1,000 and 3,500 tonnes and speeds well over 30 knots. Once more, however, they are maids of all work, fitted with sophisticated weapons and equipment for anti-submarine and anti-aircraft roles, escort and scouting duties, plus all manner of other tasks deemed unsuitable for smaller craft and less expendable destroyers.

Frogmen. A name given in **World War II** to specially trained free divers wearing thin waterproof clothing, flippers (dating from the 16th century) and self-contained breathing apparatus to enable them to operate at shallow depths for protracted periods of time. Reliable breathing apparatus and techniques were developed between the World Wars, notably in Britain by Sir Robert Davis and in France by Jacques Cousteau. The Italians too were very active and used such equipment in 1941 for men riding torpedoes against shipping in harbour. Frogmen carried out many vital roles in **amphibious warfare** such as beach reconnaissance (usually coming and going in **landing-craft**, canoe, or **submarine**), pilotage for approaching assault craft, and demolition of underwater obstacles. They were used extensively for the **Normandy** invasion in 1944 by so-called Combined Operations Pilotage Parties (COPP) and for all the US Navy's **Pacific War** landings by Underwater Demolition Teams (UDT) after heavy casualties to the assault parties at Makin in November 1943 caused by reefs and obstructions. Sabotage is carried out by frogmen against shipping and bridges, usually by laying limpet **mines** against their targets or placing charges beneath vessels in shallow water. They also take part in clandestine operations to examine, for example, ships' underwater, anti-submarine equipment; and are in common use for inspection and maintenance of marine equipment of all sorts.

Fuller, Major-General John Frederick Charles (1878–1966). A British light infantryman and arguably the most important and prescient military philosopher of the 20th century. He led an anti-**guerrilla** force in the **Boer War** and in **World War I** developed instruction techniques for senior commanders before, in December 1916, becoming chief staff officer of the Tank Corps. To his brilliantly analytical and far-seeing mind may be traced the genius of the Battles of **Cambrai** and **Amiens** and the basic concepts of today's **armoured** forces. After World War I he was instrumental in creating the climate for experiments with **tanks** and armoured forces. Owing to his acerbic temperament and forthright speech and writings, he made many enemies and, after 1927, was diverted from the main military stream of promotion. Nevertheless his books, notably *Lectures of FSR III*, which was about modern war, had a profound influence on German and Russian armoured and guerrilla warfare doctrine, while in journalism he was a gadfly whose pronounced Fascist sympathies ensured that, in **World War II** he was not offered further employment. However, he provided to his own country useful intelligence of German preparations.

G

Galland, Lieutenant-General Adolf (b. 1911). The best-known German **ace** of **World War II**. Among the first to join the secret German Air Force, he commanded a squadron of biplane He51 fighters in the **Condor Legion** in Spain. His first victory (flying an Me109) was not scored, however, until May 1940 over France. In the Battle of **Britain** and over France in 1941, as commander of a fighter group, he rapidly added to his score, developing all the time as a leader and innovative tactician. In November 1941 he was promoted major-general and made head of the fighters. Thereafter he fought with Reichsmarschall **Göring** and Field Marshal Milch for better machines, while sometimes flying in combat to keep in touch. His efforts to obtain the jet Me262 as a fighter were thwarted by **Hitler** until 1944. Promotion to lieutenant-general did not appease him. Early in 1945 he protested so hard about misuse of resources he was relegated to command of a squadron of Me262s. His final score, all in the West, was 104.

Gallipoli, Battles of. It was a Russian request for aid to Britain and France in 1914 which initiated the misconceived attempt, after Turkey's entry into the war (**Turkish wars**) on 29 October on the side of the Central Powers, to strike at Constantinople. It was doubtful if the presence of an Allied fleet in the Bosporus would knock Turkey out of the war, as intended by Winston **Churchill**, and in addition the feasibility of forcing the Dardanelles Narrows was uncertain. Uncertainty was augmented when, as an experiment without Cabinet approval, the Royal Navy advertised intentions by bombarding the other Dardanelles forts on 23 November.

Thus the subsequent drift into a full-scale operation in 1915 to force the Narrows by ships alone forfeited surprise, the one factor which might have bought success. Even with surprise, in this grossly mismanaged campaign, the chances of forcing and then keeping the Narrows open without occupying the Gallipoli peninsula – as attempted with the loss to **mines** of three battleships and damage to other ships between 19 February and 18 March 1915 – were dubious in the extreme.

The landings by the Army, then inevitably called for, were delayed until 25 April because there had been no prior consultation between the two Services. When it came to launching **amphibious** attacks on the Asian shore, and at the neck as well as the tip of Gallipoli, the Turks, under the supreme command of the German General Liman von Sanders, were ready with strengthened defences on both shores. The result was that General Sir Ian Hamilton's troops, who came ashore for the most part in rowing boats and without preliminary naval bombardment, either landed unopposed in wrong and inhospitable places (as at Anzac Cove, where the skill of General Mustafa **Kemal** prevented expansion), or elsewhere, against emplaced opposition, to be massacred. Instead of on the first day cutting the peninsula at the neck and forming a four-miles-deep beach-head at the tip, only four toeholds were obtained, lodgements which, in the weeks to come, were never fully linked up.

Conditions ashore were appalling, supply precarious and health undermined by sickness which sapped the troops' morale. Though the French had secured temporary possession of the Asian shore at Kum Kale, passage of the Narrows remained closed to surface vessels. British

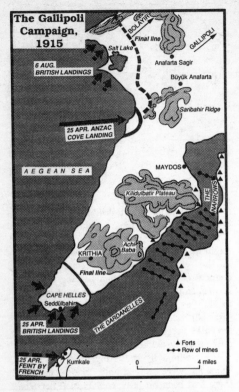

The Gallipoli Campaign, 1915

BOLAYIR
Final line
GALLIPOLI
Salt Lake
6 AUG.
BRITISH LANDINGS
Anafarta Sagir
Büyük Anafarta
Saribahir Ridge
25 APR. ANZAC
COVE LANDING
AEGEAN SEA
MAYDOS
Kilidulbatir Plateau
THE NARROWS
Achi Baba
KRITHIA
Final line
CAPE HELLES
Seddülbahir
THE DARDANELLES
25 APR.
BRITISH LANDINGS
Kumkale
25 APR.
FEINT BY
FRENCH
▲ Forts
●━● Row of mines
0   4 miles

Garibaldi, Giuseppe (1807–82). A seaman in the Sardinian Navy, and then a pirate, who became a founder of the Italian 'Redshirts' in 1843, committed to **Italian independence**. Henceforward he waged **guerrilla warfare** against the Austrians, the French, the Spaniards and their Italian collaborators. His courage, charisma, integrity and combat skill won him an international reputation as the living symbol of Italian patriotism. He was a fighting man first and last, but best employed leading only smaller, independent forces.

The campaigns of the 1850s, which culminated in his leading the Sicilian revolt to victory in 1860, set him on the road to the capture of the Kingdom of Naples, all on behalf of King Victor Emmanuel II. The defeat at Aspromonte in August 1862, when he was wounded leading his guerrillas against Italian troops, made him pause until 1866 when again he successfully led guerrillas against Austrians during the **Austro-Prussian War**. But in 1867 he unwisely engaged well-armed regular French and Papal States troops at Mentana and was routed. Nevertheless, three years later, once the French had been forced to withdraw from Rome, following their defeat in the **Franco-Prussian War**, he fought for the French against the Prussians, judging this a way of ensuring acceptance of Italy's complete unification.

submarines penetrated into the Sea of Marmara but could not stop Turkish supplies. However, the depredations of German submarines, which sank three battleships among other vessels, caused severe curtailment of naval support at Gallipoli.

In a renewed effort to outflank the unyielding defences of the neck and seize the Narrows, a surprise, unopposed landing at Suvla Bay, in conjunction with a night attack at Anzac Cove, was made on 6 August. At first it made excellent progress. But once more an over-optimistic plan, difficult terrain, supply and water shortage, indecisive British command and stubborn Turkish resistance stopped the advance, this time in sight of its final objectives.

In November a political decision to withdraw was made on military advice. Heavy losses were expected. Yet, as the only brilliantly executed plan of the entire campaign, it was carried out with secrecy and surprise in two phases with vast loss of stores but few men. In total each side had lost about 251,000 men since the start.

Gaza, Battles of. When the Turks withdrew into the Sinai desert after their rebuff at the **Suez Canal** in February 1915, and later suffered a heavy defeat when they attacked the British at Romani on 4 August 1916, they fell back to a line before Gaza, between Beersheba and the strong Ali Montar ridge. The British, following up under General Sir Archibald Murray, constructed elaborate lines of supply to support the invasion of Palestine, in conjunction with the **Arab revolt**, with a view to knocking Turkey out of the war. However, with a force that was little larger than the 16,000 men with 74 guns deployed by the Turks under General Kress von Kressenstein, Murray's chances of breaking through were doubtful. At the *First Battle* on 26 March 1917, victory was in his grasp when the Anzac cavalry almost encircled the Turkish position, only to be withdrawn for shortage of water when, mistakenly, it appeared the infantry had not captured Ali Montar. A direct assault at the *Second Battle* from 17 to 19 April failed also

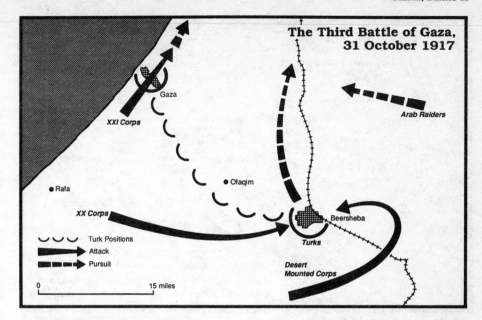

**The Third Battle of Gaza,
31 October 1917**

Gaza

XXI Corps

Arab Raiders

• Rafa

• Ofaqim

XX Corps

Beersheba

∪ ∪ ∪ Turk Positions

➡ Attack

▪▪▪➡ Pursuit

Turks

0   15 miles

Desert
Mounted Corps

when, with 6,500 casualties, it too did not take Ali Montar.

In June General Sir Edmund **Allenby** took command of a reinforced army which won the *Third Battle* on 31 October in a masterly stroke. For this time the infantry merely demonstrated in front of Gaza while mounted troops, just adequately supplied by water, made a surprise right hook through the desert to seize Beersheba and its wells in an all-day battle with little margin for error. At this, Turkish instinct was for withdrawal, but von Kressenstein tried to cling on at Gaza, and would not budge until directly assaulted by three divisions with massed artillery and a few tanks on 1/2 November. Turkish casualties were many thousands and those of the British approaching 3,000. But pressure from the desert flank, as Allenby struck northwards on the 6th, at last persuaded the enemy to withdraw to avoid complete envelopment.

In the **Arab–Israeli Wars**, Gaza and its Arab population has often been fought over and become synonymous with their resistance. In May 1948 the Egyptian Army passed through on its way to defeat before Tel Aviv and then withdrew to establish the enclave known as the Gaza Strip – which was repeatedly entered by Israeli raiders later in the year. During the 1956 campaign, on 2 November, Ali Montar and the

strip were overrun by the Israelis. And in the Six Days War of 1967, as the Israelis invaded Sinai on 5 June, their paratroops and infantry entered the strip from the desert systematically to clear resistance in the Arab camps, yet again capturing the Ali Montar ridge before taking Gaza.

The town and its vicinity remain a centre of Arab resistance.

Gazala, Battles of. Gazala was an insignificant coastal hamlet between Tobruk and Derna which witnessed the comings and goings of Turks and Italians as the latter wrested control from the former in the **Italo-Turkish War** of 1911–12; it saw Senussi tribesmen resisting the British in a pro-Turk uprising in 1915; and was further witness to Italian colonization between the **World Wars** and the return of the British in January 1941 as they pursued the Italians to destruction at **Beda Fomm**. On 4 February 1942, however, in the aftermath of the swings of British and Axis fortunes during the **North Africa** battles following the German arrival in February 1941, the British settled on Gazala as the coastal end of a line protecting **Tobruk** against renewed siege.

The Gazala Line, running south to Bir Hakeim, was constructed of thickly wired and **mined** infantry localities (known as 'boxes')

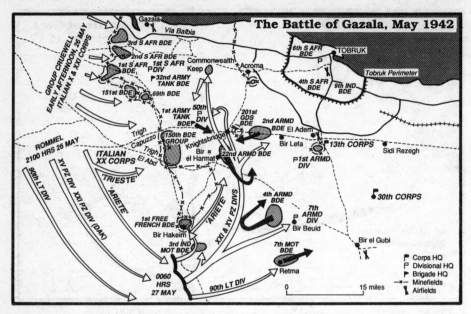

The Battle of Gazala, May 1942

supported by artillery and armour. General Sir Claude Auchinleck, the British commander, intended it as the start line for another offensive. But General **Rommel** pre-empted the British by swinging wide of Bir Hakeim on the night of 26/27 May with a view to enveloping the Line and capturing Tobruk. In spite of heavy tank losses, the British stopped Rommel and pushed his mobile forces back against the minefields into a disputed area which became known as the Cauldron.

Cut off from supply via Bir Hakeim (which was held by a Free French unit of the **Foreign Legion** with many Germans in its ranks), Rommel succeeded in forcing a hole in the minefield in time to bring through enough supplies and munitions to hold off a tardily mounted British assault on the Cauldron. Then he broke out, attacked Bir Hakeim on 10 June, made the French withdraw next day, and swung against the British whose badly handled, mechanically unreliable armoured forces he destroyed to the south of Tobruk, leaving British and South African infantry formations trapped in the boxes either to await their doom or break out and escape into Tobruk or Egypt – whence Rommel pursued them. Each side lost about 40,000 men, but the British lost nearly all their 740 tanks and a great many guns too – with worse to come.

Geneva Conventions. In the shadow of the excesses of **World War II**, an effort was made to draw up international agreements regulating the conduct of nations at war. In 1949 the Holy See and 58 governments signed four Conventions dealing with: (1) the amelioration of wounded and sick in the field; (2) armed forces at sea; (3) prisoners of war; and (4) protection of civilians in time of war. In many instances the conventions confirmed what was already generally practised by many countries, such as registration of and recognition of military dress (see **Clothing, Military**) and respect for prisoners' rights. But they also reflected the findings of international courts dealing with **war crimes** and thus established more precisely the human rights of civilians as well as the military.

The Conventions have been only partially effective, and often virtually unrecognized in many **guerrilla**-type conflicts. Prisoners, hostages and the wounded continue to be maltreated by fanatics who probably neither know nor care about humanitarianism or the Conventions. Nevertheless, the existence of rules which threaten penalties through international law, or the observance of which offer material or psychological and political advantages to those who comply, have made the exercise worth while, as many repatriated people discovered, for example in **Korea**, **Vietnam**, the Middle East and the **Falklands**. Compliance with the Conventions is at least civilizing.

Germany, Battles of. As a result of her aggressiveness and good fortune, Germany, post-1813, was largely spared combat on her own soil until well into **World War II**. In **World War I** the Battle of **Tannenberg** in August 1914 quickly rid East Prussia of Russian invaders; and

lightweight bombing of targets in the west did only slight damage. The post-war ferocious and socially harmful encounters between Communist and Freikorps factions were sporadic and of short duration.

World War II was a very different matter owing to **air warfare**. At the start enemy machines overflew the Fatherland, mostly dropping **propaganda** leaflets but, occasionally,

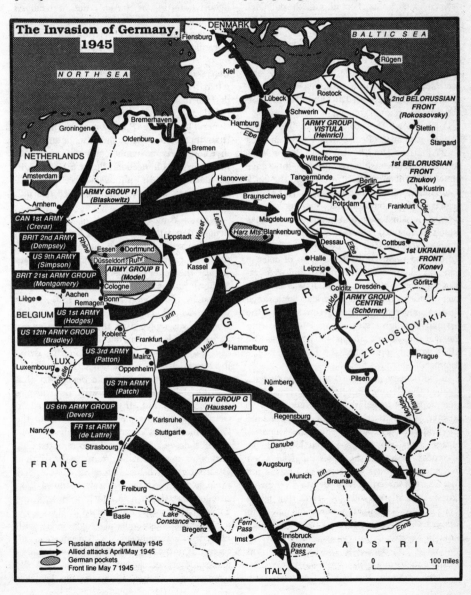

The Invasion of Germany, 1945

Russian attacks April/May 1945
Allied attacks April/May 1945
German pockets
Front line May 7 1945

bombs on naval and coastal targets. But no sooner had her armies invaded the west on 10 May 1940 than the Allies began the **strategic bombing** campaign against transport and industrial targets, a campaign which, although notable at first for the inability of bombers to find and hit their targets, or the defences to shoot down many bombers, compelled the Wehrmacht to divert very large resources to home defence (**Home fronts**). For although the populace soon got used to raids and were encouraged by the gradual improvement of the defences and relatively minor damage inflicted, the government feared political repercussions. The menace assumed terrible dimensions as the scale and accuracy of British attacks increased dramatically in June 1942 with 1,000-bomber raids on Cologne, Essen and Bremen.

Furthermore, the occasional low-level daylight attacks by the British, when supplemented on 27 January 1943 by American Boeing B17s bombing Wilhelmshaven in daylight, gave notice of forthcoming accurate, round-the-clock bombing. In consequence, **fighters** had to be withdrawn from the battle fronts to strengthen the defences against day and night area attacks which devastated cities and vital industrial targets. Nevertheless, by December 1943 the fighter and **radar**-controlled system of defence had curbed the daylight bombers and was getting the upper hand at night. It was a short-lived victory only, once American long-range fighters appeared, even over **Berlin**, to defeat the German day fighters in spring 1944, clearing the way for almost unopposed attacks as the Allied armies approached the frontiers in the summer.

In both west and east the Allied armies reached the German frontier in September but were stopped by **logistic** deficiencies and a revived German army. In the west the **Siegfried Line** provided the shield behind which the Ardennes counterstroke was prepared and launched in December. However, the losses incurred when that ill-judged attack was repulsed deprived the East Front of forces badly needed to defend East Prussia and Silesia, with the result that when the Russians launched massive offensives in January 1945 the Front soon gave way, despite fanatical resistance by young and old. By 31 January it had backed to the River Oder and southwards through Silesia into Austria.

At that moment the British, Canadians and Americans were engaged in clearing territory to the west of the Rhine (**Rhineland, Battle of the**) in operations which destroyed the best of what remained of the German Army. On 7 March, at Remagen, the Americans made the first of several subsequent Allied crossings of the Rhine, presaging the overrunning of the country as far as the River Elbe, leaving the eastern half, including Berlin, to fall to the Russians in their last offensive starting on 16 April. All that remained on 7 May were a few recalcitrant pockets in a ruined country which proved incapable of the **guerrilla warfare** that **Hitler** had called for.

Gettysburg, Battle of. In the American Civil War when the Confederate President **Davis** at last decided to abandon his defensive strategy and invade the North in 1863, he was advised by General **Lee** that the South's morale was higher than that of the North and that a successful invasion of Pennsylvania, coming so soon after his victory at Chancellorsville on 6 May, might persuade European nations to recognize the Confederacy, and even panic the Federals into making peace.

With a three-corps army of 75,000, Lee headed down the **Shenandoah Valley** early in June, crossed the Potomac (having on the 9th seen his cavalry, under General Stuart, get slightly the better of Federal cavalry at Brandy Station) and advanced on Chambersburg – trailed by the Federal Army of 115,000 men whose fearful commander, General Joseph Hooker, was replaced on the 28th by General George Meade. Meanwhile Lee had permitted Stuart to raid towards Washington, thus denying himself intelligence of Meade, who made for Gettysburg in knowledge from his cavalry that Lee might be heading that way. Both armies were scattered, but on the 30th converged on Gettysburg, arriving piecemeal throughout the fight which began in earnest on 1 July.

Still short of information, Lee committed only part of his force to seizing ground to the south of Gettysburg, which Meade and his commanders rated as vital. As the Federals occupied it in strength, Lee declined to attack in force on the 1st, when he might have seized it. He delayed again on the 2nd because of disagreements with his corps commanders. In consequence, although Confederate attacks against Meade's flanks almost succeeded, they most probably would not have been decisive since Lee was

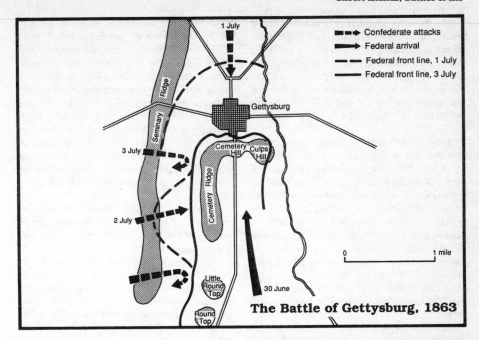

1 July

■ ■ ▶ Confederate attacks
▶ Federal arrival
▬ ▬ Federal front line, 1 July
▬▬ Federal front line, 3 July

Gettysburg

Seminary Ridge

3 July

Cemetery Hill   Culps Hill

2 July

Cemetery Ridge

0 ———————— 1 mile

Little Round Top

30 June

Round Top

The Battle of Gettysburg, 1863

unready to exploit. Indeed, Lee might have done well to manoeuvre on the 3rd instead of attempting a deliberate assault under General George Pickett, heavily supported by artillery, to break through Meade's centre at its strongest part – Cemetery Ridge. This so-called charge proved a disaster. It cost Lee about 7,000 casualties, lost him the battle, and the South the war.   .

Giap, General Vo Nguyen (b. 1912). A North Vietnamese history teacher who joined the Communists in the 1930s to resist the French in Indo-China. In 1944 he organized a propaganda unit for the Vietminh and thereafter played a leading role as guerrilla leader in the **Indo-China War of Independence**. He achieved fame with his brilliant handling of **logistics** and the Battle of Dien Bien Phu in 1954, when his crushing defeat of the French forced them to withdraw from **Vietnam**.

As Minister of Defence and C-in-C of the North Vietnamese Army (NVA), Giap prepared the military action against the South which began in January 1959. But his initial strategy of infiltration by the Viet Cong guerrillas was too slow-acting and gave time for the Americans effectively to reinforce the South, compelling Giap to attempt to entice a major enemy force to

destruction, as at Dien Bien Phu. This led to the commitment in 1964 of NVA units to reinforce the Vietcong guerrillas as a prelude to the series of disastrous offensives which culminated in the utter failure of the 1968 **Tet offensive**. Giap nevertheless pursued the same strategy again in 1972 when the Americans withdrew ground units, only to be defeated once more by the much improved South Vietnamese Army. He was then replaced by General **Dung**.

Gilbert Islands, Battles of the. In January 1942 the Japanese took unopposed possession of the islands with a small garrison. On 17 August, as a distraction from the **Guadalcanal** landing, 222 US Marine Raiders, carried 2,500 miles by **submarine**, landed on Makin. Though the island was eventually taken, the raid was a fiasco with unnecessary loss of life.

The Japanese now fortified Makin and Tarawa, which the Americans, under Admiral Kelly Turner, assaulted on 20 November 1943 with heavy loss. For although Makin was easily overwhelmed by army infantry, beach obstacles caused difficulty and an escort **aircraft-carrier** was sunk by **submarine**. At Tarawa, which was very strongly held, crossing the reef seriously held up the **landing-craft** and Amtracs. As a result casualties to the 4,700 **Marines** finally amounted to 985 killed and 2,193 wounded. On the other hand, only 17 Japanese out of the garrison's 5,000 survived. Turner admitted the failures to reconnoitre thoroughly, to 'gap' obstacles and to provide sufficient supporting fire, lessons already learned and passed on by the British after the **Dieppe raid**.

Gliders. Before suitable power plants were invented, heavier-than-air craft were of necessity gliders. Their first indirect military use was by the Germans in the 1920s to train pilots for the day when they would again be permitted an air force. It was the Russians who, in the 1930s, built an assault glider (to carry 18 men), without making much use of it since they preferred **parachutists**. As did the Germans who, nevertheless, formed a secret glider-borne unit and built a few 10-man DFS230 gliders (fitted with three braking rockets and a tail parachute to arrest landing), supported by fewer, still larger, cargo DFS242s.

On 10 May 1940 the Germans committed 11 DFS230s, towed by Junkers Ju52s, to land on the Belgian fort of Eben Emael. Two went adrift when towing cables broke, but the rest swiftly seized the fort from its thoroughly surprised garrison. Meanwhile nearby bridges over the Albert Canal had also been taken by glider-borne troops. At various times throughout **World War II** the Germans again would use gliders for small operations, such as the *coup-de-main* Corinth Canal crossing in April 1941, anti-**guerrilla** raids and the rescue of Benito **Mussolini** in 1943. But never again after **Crete** in May 1941 (where about 80 gliders were landed) would they use them on a large scale.

In the summer of 1940 the British (still unaware of German gliders in Belgium) preferred glider-borne troops to parachutists for large-scale landings. They built two main operational types; many 29-man, side-loading Horsas (which could also carry **jeeps** and small artillery pieces); and a few enormous nose-loading Hamilcars which could carry a light tank. Similarly enthused, the Americans built the 13-man, nose-loading Waco Hadrian. The first British glider operation, in Norway on 19 November 1942, failed when two gliders crashed attempting to land **Commandos** on a glacier to attack the heavy-water plant at Vermork.

Large-scale Anglo-American employment

began with the invasion of **Sicily** on 11 July 1943 when several gliders, out of 144, cast off in the wrong place. Some landed in the sea, with the loss of 250 men; the rest were scattered. In **Normandy** on 6 June 1944, however, they played vital roles by capturing strategic bridges and gun-sites at night and in daylight, bringing in large numbers of infantry to reinforce parachute formations dropped ahead of them. In **Holland**, in September, and the Rhine crossings, in March 1945, they landed to plan in daylight in well-concentrated mass – although too far from the bridge at **Arnhem** to help the parachutists.

Meanwhile, in **Burma**, Waco gliders had played a vital role by landing the first wave of General Wingate's **Chindits** behind the Japanese lines in March 1944.

After World War II gliders fell out of favour, partly because parachutists were regarded as operationally more flexible and economic but very largely because the **helicopter** offered a far better means of transport which could get in *and out of* much smaller landing-places.

Göring, Reichsmarschall Hermann (1839–1946). A larger-than-life Bavarian politician and colleague of **Hitler** who won fame in **World War** I as an air **ace** and as later leader of the Richthofen squadron. Although responsible for organizing the training of pilots and the supply of aircraft for the secret air force, and becoming Air Minister and C-in-C of the German Air Force in 1935, his military talents were regarded as little better than those of a battalion commander. As Hitler's right-hand man, he ably and ruthlessly eliminated political opposition, yet his claim that the Air Force could single-handed prevent the evacuation from **Dunkirk** and win the Battle of **Britain** were fundamental errors in letting Britain survive in 1940. The wasteful assault on **Crete** in 1941 was another mistake, which deprived the Army in Russia of vital resources; and claiming ability to supply **Stalingrad** by air in 1942 was as irresponsible a boast as saying Germany could not be bombed. Worst of all was his permitting the Air Force to fall behind in the technological race. He very much contributed to Germany's defeat and was condemned to death for **war crimes** at the Nürnberg Trials.

Gorlice Offensive. In April 1915 the town of Gorlice was chosen by the Austrians and Germans as the focal point for an offensive to clear the Russians from Galicia and Austro-Hungary. Eight German divisions were transferred from the west, placed under the command of General August von Mackensen (whose Chief of Staff was General Hans von **Seeckt**) and launched on 2 May at the centre of a combined Austro-German attack. The Russians were outnumbered as well as outclassed by their enemy's **artillery**. Within 24 hours the Germans had taken Gorlice and torn a 12-mile gap in the Russian front. A week later the breakthrough was nearly 50 miles deep and the entire Galician front was being withdrawn with enormous losses in men and material, nudged along by flank leverage from the Germans, who skilfully declined to become involved in head-on assaults. Rapidly the retreat spread the length of the East Front (see map page 140). Though not a complete victory, it was a disaster for the Russians (costing some two million casualties, mostly prisoners) from which they never recovered, and which enabled General von **Falkenhayn** to concentrate German forces against France at **Verdun** in 1916.

Gort, Field Marshal Viscount, vc (1886–1946). A Grenadier Guards officer with a legendary reputation for bravery and personal leadership in **World War I**, who also distinguished himself in Shanghai in 1927 during the **Chinese Civil War**. In December 1937, following a series of staff and command appointments, he was made (over the heads of many senior to him) Chief of the Imperial General Staff, a post he filled without distinction until (having never commanded anything larger than a brigade) appointed C-in-C British Expeditionary Force (BEF) on the outbreak of **World War II**. During the **West Europe Campaign** in May 1940 he made some crucial and brave decisions to bring the British Expeditionary Force to **Dunkirk**, intact for evacuation. Although lacking some vital qualities of a high commander in the field, he proved a source of great strength when made **Malta's** Governor and C-in-C at the height of the siege in May 1942.

Grant, General Ulysses (1822–85). An American infantryman with experience of war against Mexico in 1845–7, who resigned from the Army in 1854 but rejoined on the Federal side on the outbreak of the **American Civil War**. Soon given command of a brigade, his first action, at Bel-

mont on 7 November, was a defeat. But thereafter he improved to win the first Federal victory (with the capture of 15,000 Confederates) at Fort Donelson in February 1862 and was promoted major-general. He was severely criticized for the high casualty list at the Battle of **Shiloh**, though his progress to the top was barely delayed. His inspired conduct of the campaign in the West, with the capture of **Vicksburg** and of **Chattanooga** in 1863, were achievements which won him President **Lincoln's** unshakable confidence. Soon after he was transferred to command of the Army of the Potomac in 1864. There followed the very costly **Wilderness** battles which failed to produce an immediate victory. Yet, although General **Sherman's** Atlanta campaign looked the more impressive and was the less expensive in lives, it might have been very different had not Grant maintained his aim and pinned the Confederate army to Richmond.

From 1869 to 1877 Grant was President of the USA, a two-term period of office which, like those of other soldiers in that job, lacked lustre.

Graziani, Marshal Rodolfo (1882–1955). An Italian soldier with wide experience of war in Abyssinia, Libya and during **World War I**, who put down insurrection in Libya between 1930 and 1934 with great brutality. Likewise, when sent to finish off the Abyssinians in 1935, he showed no mercy. But in 1940 the better generalled and equipped British in Cyrenaica proved more than a match for him, and he was replaced. After Benito **Mussolini** was deposed in July 1943 and Italy joined the Allies in September as co-belligerents, Graziani stayed loyal to the Duce and the Germans. In 1950 he was tried and given 19 years' imprisonment, almost at once commuted.

Greece, Invasions of. Owing to her Balkans position, Greece has been in turmoil for much of the past 150 years. In 1850 she was **blockaded** by Britain in a botched attempt to enforce a loan repayment. Four years later the British and French occupied the Piraeus to deter her activities against Turkey in the **Crimean War**. In 1878, nursing her perennial hatred of Turkey, she again was coerced by the other European nations to prevent her joining in the latest **Russo-Turkish War** in 1877–8. Once more, in 1886, Britain blockaded, this time to defuse a pending attack upon Turkey. As a matter of

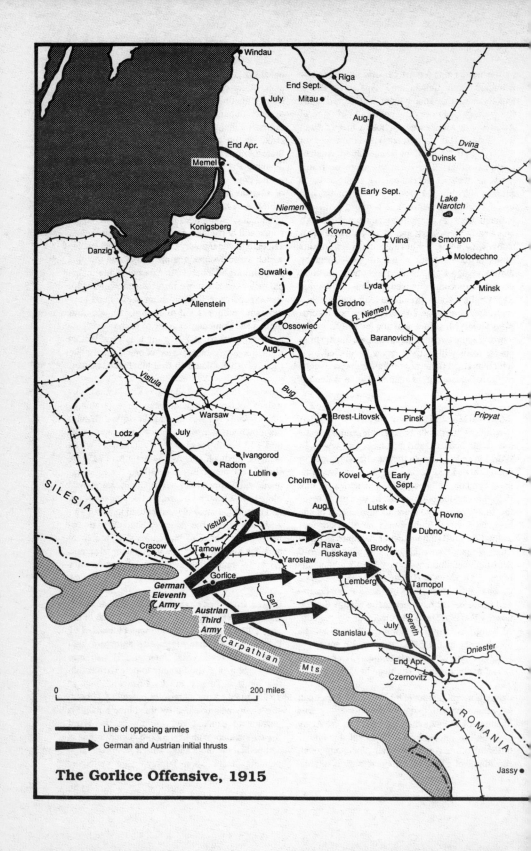

The Gorlice Offensive, 1915

course, Greece was involved in all **Balkan Wars**, although her delight at the ejection of the Turks from the Balkans in 1913 was at once tarnished by rancour with Bulgaria, a rivalry which blossomed into full-scale warfare during **World War I** as Greece opted, in 1914, to help Serbia and asked for British and French troops in aid. For the Allies this 'sideshow' assumed importance as Turkey and then Bulgaria joined the Central Powers in, respectively, 1914 and 1915. Troops sent to **Salonika** as a base for the defence of Greece and future counter-attack into the Balkans spent the rest of the war most unproductively. In 1916 they repelled and then counter-attacked, with heavy losses, a Bulgarian thrust which reached the Struma river. A festering stalemate then persisted until September 1918, when an Allied force commanded by General Franchet d'Esperey routed the Bulgarians and drove them up the Vardar valley – and out of the war.

Border clashes with Bulgaria continued after World War I, but it was the Italians who next invaded from **Albania** on 28 October 1940, only to be stopped by a brilliant defence among the mountains by General Alexander Papagos, who then, with minimal British naval and air assistance, threw the demoralized Italians back into Albania. This Italian failure to conquer Greece compelled **Hitler** to occupy **Yugoslavia** and Greece in 1941. He feared British access to airfields within striking distance of Romanian oilfields; and also for the security of Germany's flank and rear while attacking Russia. The onslaught on 6 April hit Greek troops already exhausted by fighting the Italians; and a British army which was short of **tanks** and air support. The Greeks were enveloped and destroyed close by the frontiers, the British hurled back into the Peloponnesus whence, less equipment, they were evacuated to **Crete** by 28 April.

For the remainder of **World War II**, occupied Greece was a battleground for politically factional **guerrilla** groups who spent as much time skirmishing among themselves as striking at the Italians and Germans. The arrival of British troops on the heels of the withdrawing German army in October 1944, and their suppression of Communist groups in 1945 in a ferocious campaign on the side of the legal government, was but the first phase of the civil war (see next entry) which erupted in May 1946.

Greek civil wars. Greek independence had been firmly established between 1830 and 1849, though not until 1913, after the **Balkan Wars**, was she in possession of **Crete**, Samos and other islands and the bulk of Macedonia. During these expansive years she also struggled internally with outbreaks of fighting, often in the anti-Turk context – for example over Turk-occupied Crete in 1896 and in the **Greek–Turkish War** of 1897. There was strife between monarchists and republicans which lasted well into the 20th century, with repeated comings and goings of kings accompanied by factional violence and military intervention. The rise of a Communist party and the Italian invasion in 1940 set the scene, however, for an outright struggle between rival political groups and their **guerrilla** bands which had been established for their own ends by the main contestants of **World War II**.

In 1943 the Communist National Liberation Front and National Popular Liberation Army (EAM and ELAS, respectively) were pitted in combat against the Greek National Army (EDES) and had set up a provisional government which was eventually broken by EDES and the British in 1945 when the monarchy was restored. In May 1946, however, the Communists, under General Markos Vafiades, established a militarized zone in the northern provinces with Albanian, Yugoslav and Bulgarian support, using this as the base for guerrillas to try to seize total control in the classic manner throughout the country. Assisted by the British, the Greek Army fought losing skirmishes in the mountains while the rest of the security forces struggled to destroy the urban guerrillas. Early in 1947 the British, overstretched elsewhere, handed over responsibility to the Americans, who then supplied and trained the Greek Army.

A turning-point was reached at the end of the year when the urban guerrillas began to flag and the Albanians, besieging the town of Konitsa, were driven back across their frontier and were unable to make a come-back. Thus Vafiades's recent proclamation of a Communist government was made hollow – all the more so when his northern bastion began to crumble under heavy military pressure in 1948. The end came into sight after Yugoslavia withdrew from the Cominform and reduced help to Vafiades. He was replaced in 1949 shortly before the last formed body of his army was destroyed in August at Mount Grammos. Two months later the war was over as Bulgaria also lost interest.

Greek–Turkish wars. Throughout the 19th and 20th centuries, Greece has attacked Turkey at every opportunity and the Turks have never given way without a real struggle. Reference to the **Balkan Wars**, **Crimean War**, **Cyprus**, **Greece** and **Russo-Turkish wars** will show how the long-standing vendetta was pursued – as it is to the present day regardless that the two countries are allies in **Nato**. In so far as this entry is concerned, therefore, only two specific wars will be recorded:

The War of 1897. This was the culmination of many years' discontent over the condition of Greek rebels in **Crete**. In February, Greek troops arrived on the island in support, an act which provoked fighting on the mainland between an incompetently led Greek army against Turks, under Edhem Pasha, who had been trained and advised by the German General Colmar von der Goltz. A Greek invasion of Macedonia in April was soundly beaten off and an armistice soon concluded.

The War of 1921–2 started as the result of the Allies awarding Turkish territory (with large Greek communities) in Asia Minor and Gallipoli to Greece; the refusal of Turkey, led by General **Kemal Atatürk**, to agree; and the arrival of Greek forces on the coast of the Sea of Marmara in June 1920. The Greek Army's attempt, under General Papoulos, to seize western Anatolia was checked at the Battle of İnönü in January 1921, and again decisively beaten, after furious combat at the same place, in March. Then King Constantine, an experienced soldier, took command of the Greeks, outmanoeuvred the Turks at Afyon and rolled them back. But at Sakkaria in August, where Kemal was in personal command, it was he who outmanoeuvred Constantine, who fell back in September to winter quarters. Not until August 1922, after nearly a year's diplomacy in which Kemal vastly strengthened Turkish morale and strength, did he strike again, breaking the Greek Army at Afyon on the 18th and hurling it back. The pursuit was remorseless, stained by the massacre of Greek civilians, as well as their army, and culminating in the old-fashioned sack of Smyrna. Seizing his opportunity, Kemal next threatened the small Allied garrison at Constantinople and brought such political pressure to bear that he was able to obtain restoration of forfeited territory.

Grenada, Invasion of. When a Communist-inspired faction, with Cuban support, seized control of this West Indies island in 1983 and began to put it into a state of defence, the USA felt unable to stand aside (as Britain did) from a strategic threat to the political stability of the region. On 25 October 1983 an American **amphibious** force, spearheaded by **helicopters**, landed at strategic points. After a brisk fight, in which several helicopters were lost, the Americans, helped by other Caribbean countries, took charge and ousted the dissident minority.

Grenades. Small bombs capable of being thrown by hand or fired from a rifle or projector. Grenades have been used regularly in war since the 17th century and had been revived for modern warfare by 1914, when they were a standard issue in the German Army. As trench warfare developed, with often quite short distances between the opposing armies, the grenade became an essential weapon. The few that the British had, known as 'jam pots' and 'hairbrushes' from their shape, were crude devices lit by an ordinary match. Early in 1915 a Belgian company developed a new type containing a striker, detonating cap and fuse. A lever retained the striker against a spring which, when released, struck the detonating cap. The explosive filling was ammonal.

William Mills, a British foundry owner, saw how the Belgian grenade fusing could be improved and produced a successful version which became known as the No. 36. Some 75 million were produced in the UK during **World War I** and the pattern remains in service, essentially unchanged in concept, to this day.

The limitations of a hand-thrown grenade led to demands for a longer-range projector. The first idea was to fit a cup over a rifle muzzle, from which the grenade was discharged by the firing of a special ballistite cartridge; normal ammunition could not be used while the cup was fitted. A typical refinement is that of the Belgian FN Company's Telgren telescopic rifle grenade which can be fired with any type of rifle ammunition. The grenade fits directly on to the rifle muzzle and the tail telescopes into the head for stowage so that the infantryman can carry several on him. The Soviets in their turn have produced a number of magazine-fed grenade-throwers giving a rapid-fire capability.

In addition to their original high-explosive

filling, grenades have now been developed specifically for **anti-tank** use, with smoke fillings and with irritant gas fillings for riot control.

Ground-effect machines. Also known as aircushion vehicles or hovercraft, capable of travelling across water and reasonably obstacle-free terrain. It was Sir John Thorneycroft who, in the 1870s, first proposed the theory that if the hull of a ship was shaped to form a plenum chamber and then filled with pressurized air, the ship would rise out of the water and hence create less drag, allowing greater speeds with fuel economy. He was unable to suggest a system to prevent the air escaping round the sides of his design and it was Christopher Cockerell in the 1950s who produced the first practical hovercraft. He included a slot round the circumference of his vehicle which jetted the pressurized air inwards towards the centre, thus saving most of it to provide the necessary lift. Subsequent development showed the advantage of using a flexible skirt to enhance this effect if high loadings were to be achieved and this is the configuration to be seen on most modern vehicles.

The layer of pressurized air on which the hovercraft rides has two functions: to reduce surface friction, thus requiring less power for forward motion, and to provide a suspension system for the vehicle. The effect is comparable to a saucer sliding on ice and is equally difficult to control without aircraft techniques; the result is a seagoing vehicle using aircraft-construction methods and tending to be very expensive in consequence.

With only about 30 per cent of the world coastlines able to accept the beaching of a conventional landing ship, while it has been estimated that about 70 per cent would accept a hovercraft, the concept has an obvious attraction for military **amphibious operations**. One study suggested that a large hovercraft capable of carrying four main battle tanks would theoretically be able to embark its vehicles in Malta and land them in the vicinity of Baghdad without meeting any serious obstacles in its way.

Though Britain led the way in hovercraft design and construction, it abandoned the military application chiefly because of cost, though it has in service some large cross-Channel ferries carrying upwards of 400 passengers and 60

vehicles at about 60 knots. She did, however supply the Imperial Iranian Navy with BH7 hovercraft, though little has been heard of them since the revolution there. The United States made very successful use of the SRN5 (US designator SK5) during the **Vietnam War**, operating in the marshy area known as the Plain of Reeds. The US Marine Corps are now operating large seagoing LCAC – Landing Craft Air Cushion – built by Bell Aerosystems and capable of carrying some 70 tonnes of cargo across open beaches and as far inland as the terrain will allow. The Soviets too operate their large AIST220 in a similar way and the French are building a 200-tonne NES2002.

Guadalcanal, Battles of. The Japanese arrived, unopposed, on Guadalcanal Island early in May 1942. It was not until after the Battle of **Midway** that they decided to develop it and nearby Tulagi Island to dominate the Solomons on the periphery of their conquests, and not until 6 July that they began construction of an airfield – which was instantly notified to the Americans by a coast watcher. The urgent need to wrest the initiative from the Japanese and Chief of Naval Staff Admiral Ernest **King**'s determination to obtain maximum resources for the US Navy in the Pacific, spurred his attempt to capture Guadalcanal and Tulagi, despite logistic resources that hung on a shoestring and the presence nearby of strong Japanese forces.

On 7 August the Amphibious Force, under Rear Admiral Kelly Turner, landed US **Marines**, under Major-General Alexander Vandegrift, on the north shore of Guadalcanal and adjacent islands, including Tulagi. Marine Raiders made an almost unopposed landing on the latter but then lost 20 per cent in discovering that the Japanese never flinched, counter-attacked suicidally and would hold out for 24 hours to the last man. On Guadalcanal, however, there was no fighting until next day against the light resistance they met taking possession of the airfield (named Henderson) – only seven days before Japanese fighters were due to fly in. Japanese air attacks on shipping from the 7th onwards, however, were daunting, testing the fighters of Vice-Admiral **Fletcher**'s three aircraft-carriers to the limit. Meanwhile, Admiral Shige-yoshi Inouye also dispatched a naval task force to hit the invaders, thus setting the pattern for

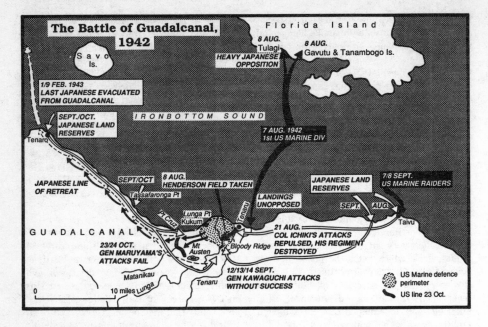

The Battle of Guadalcanal, 1942

Florida Island

8 AUG.
Tulagi

8 AUG.
Gavutu & Tanambogo Is.

HEAVY JAPANESE OPPOSITION

Savo Is.

1/9 FEB. 1943
LAST JAPANESE EVACUATED FROM GUADALCANAL

IRONBOTTOM SOUND

SEPT./OCT.
JAPANESE LAND RESERVES

Tenaro

7 AUG. 1942
1st US MARINE DIV

JAPANESE LINE OF RETREAT

SEPT/OCT
Tassafaronga Pt

8 AUG.
HENDERSON FIELD TAKEN

LANDINGS UNOPPOSED

JAPANESE LAND RESERVES

7/8 SEPT.
US MARINE RAIDERS

SEPT
AUG.

Taivu

Cruz
Lunga Pt
Kukum

Tenaru

GUADALCANAL

23/24 OCT.
GEN MARUYAMA'S ATTACKS FAIL

Mt Austen

Bloody Ridge

21 AUG.
COL ICHIKI'S ATTACKS REPULSED, HIS REGIMENT DESTROYED

Matanikau

Lunga

Tenaru

12/13/14 SEPT.
GEN KAWAGUCHI ATTACKS WITHOUT SUCCESS

US Marine defence perimeter

US line 23 Oct.

0   10 miles

six months' naval and air attrition in which the battles of the **Solomon Sea** were the factor conditioning events on Guadalcanal.

On the island the struggle centred upon possession and use of Henderson Field. Vandegrift's first task was to complete construction of the airfield, using Japanese equipment because Turner's ships carrying plant and stores had been withdrawn under the enemy threat. He managed to do so and receive the first fighters on the 20th – two days after the first Japanese reinforcements arrived and one before the enemy attacked the perimeter defences. On the 21st it was the Japanese who learnt a lesson. They were wiped out when impulsively attacking the airfield. So too was the next wave of reinforcements, brought in during September and thrown into the assault against, by now, well-constructed defences – although they fought their way to within a mere 1,000 yards of the airfield.

Indeed, despite their heavy losses at sea, the Americans managed to keep ahead in the reinforcement race on land by bringing in another Marine division and an Army regiment through September into October, outmatching the single division brought in by the Japanese over the same period, a formation which was also slaughtered as, once more, ill-supported and uncoordin-

ated, it entered the perimeter but broke against defenders who now had their enemy's measure. Both sides were now exhausted and suffering from disease, but loss of a division (less a mere 2,000 men) at sea in November at last compelled the Japanese to admit defeat. Grudgingly they withdrew the last of 11,000 survivors on 9 February 1943.

Guderian, General Heinz (1888–1954). A light infantry man who, prior to **World War I**, specialized in **radio**. Between 1914 and 1918 he served mainly with the **Staff** on the Western Front. In 1922 his task was to help develop the mechanization of the German Army: by 1929 he had become convinced that **tanks** in all-arms, armoured (Panzer) divisions would in future dominate land warfare. With **Hitler's** support, but obstructed by traditionalists, he promoted the creation of the German **armoured** forces which spearheaded the invasion of **Poland** in 1939. As an armoured corps commander then and at the head of a corps and a group in the invasion of **France** in May 1940, he proved his theories right by brilliant leadership. Likewise in Russia in 1941 (**Russo-German wars**) he led the drives towards **Moscow** and Kiev, but was sacked when he disobeyed Hitler in the winter defeat.

In the aftermath of **Stalingrad**, in February 1943, Hitler recalled him as Inspector to restore the armoured force from ruination. He laboured effectively but only to see the armour repeatedly squandered by Hitler. On 21 July, after the attempt on Hitler's life (of which he was aware), he was made Chief of the General Staff, principally directing operations on the Eastern front, a task made impossible by Hitler's follies – to which Guderian repeatedly and tempestuously objected until sacked once more in March 1945.

Guerrilla warfare. From the earliest times until the appearance in more general use of uniformed troops in the 18th century, a great many small armed groups, living off the countryside and merging with the populace, fitted today's notion of the guerrilla band. The name was coined from the Spanish *guerrilleros* waging a small war against the French from 1809 to 1813, meaning lightly armed irregulars operating behind the enemy lines in the sort of underground struggle which then, as now, gave rise to terrible excesses among participants and to civilians caught up in what usually amounted to civil war.

Since 1850 most formal wars have been accompanied by some kind of behind-the-lines combat, including sabotage, while insurrections have often been of the essence of guerrilla warfare. For example, Giuseppe **Garibaldi's** 'unorthodox' independent forces in Italy (**Italian wars of independence**), which were at the heart of Italian nationalism, were guerrillas who suffered their worst setbacks when attempting to stand and fight unshaken regular troops. The Frenchmen in plain clothes who cut lines of communication during the **Franco-Prussian War** in 1870, though called *francs-tireurs* by the Germans and shot out of hand, were guerrillas. Many were the bands at large during the **American Civil War** – some in uniform, some not. The situation was the same in most of China's struggles (including the **Boxer Rebellion**), as well as in the South African **Boer War**. Generally it was the wearing of a recognized military uniform (**Clothing, Military**) which, as often as not, distinguished regulars from irregulars bearing arms – although recognition of an arm-band as a uniform sometimes stretched imagination.

World War I was fought, for the most part, by uniformed armies. Even the so-called German guerrillas under General Lettow von Vorbeck in **East Africa** were in uniform, as were British soldiers fighting in the **Arab revolt** against the Turks. On the other hand, the Irish patriots who rose against the British in 1916 wore plain clothes, and some were shot after trial. During the **Russian revolutionary wars**, when guerrilla warfare was rife and identification usually uncertain, injustices and excesses in the name of freedom and liberty often were quite barbaric. Indeed, what happened then opened a new chapter in guerrilla warfare through development of systematic, large-scale support and supply by outsiders (for example of the Whites by the Americans and British).

In the **Chinese Civil War** it was the defeat of the Communist revolt by the Nationalists in the 1930s (their so-called 'bandit suppressions' were really counter-guerrilla operations), that compelled the famous Long March – in effect a large-scale, evasive migration by irregulars and their camp followers. China, in fact, was infested by guerrillas of all kinds. So too was Spain during the **Spanish Civil War** with the so-called **Fifth Column** behind Republican lines and prevalent use of **aircraft** and **radio** for supply and control. These, indeed, were rehearsals for **World War II**'s guerrilla groups (sometimes called resistance fighters and sometimes partisans) which sprang up among the invading Germans and Japanese.

Guerrilla operations evolved to a pattern. Bands of various sizes were recruited from the local populace, initially organized by agents sent in by air or sea from bases such as Britain, Russia, North Africa and India, and then supplied by air with arms, ammunition and other warlike stores. Usually the bands assumed local political affiliations – some pro-government, others not, many Communist – and fought (like the Greeks and Yugoslavs) as much among themselves as against the Axis. Amid Russian forests and swamps, large bands hid prior to striking at the Germans in support of major offensives. Only in Yugoslavia, parts of France and Italy did bands in the West engage in overt resistance long before the arrival of approaching Allied troops, and usually with disastrous consequences, as in northern Italy and the Vercors in 1944, when bravery did not compensate for lack of heavy weapons and inadequate training against German regulars. Prudence dictated that guerrillas limited their attacks to sabotage, as ordered by radio messages from the so-called **Special Operations Executive (SOE)**; made full use of well-trained Allied troops sent in to support them; and did not come out in force until the moment was ripe – when the enemy was departing.

After World War II many guerrilla organizations remained in being and hid their arms for future use in political struggle. Notably in China, the **Philippines**, **Vietnam**, **Malaya** and Indonesia (**Indonesian wars of independence**) in the Far East and in Palestine (**Israeli fight for independence**), Greece (**Greek civil wars**) and elsewhere, cadres remained for the prolonged struggles to come. In addition to these hot spots there were countries that had not been major battlefields but whose nationalist aspirations or internal conflicts prompted resort to arms and guerrilla warfare. Their belligerents, like the majority throughout Africa, in **Cuba**, **Central** and **South America**, used political affiliations with the Great Powers, or such oil-rich ones as revolutionary Libya, to advise, train and supply their bands in readiness for the day of action.

Modern guerrilla warfare, ranging from coercive terror bombing as in **Ireland**) to overt resistance by large bands, is more commonplace than ever before. Although guerrillas have won total successes (as in Algeria and Cuba), the vast majority have either been defeated (as in Malaya) or contained in struggles which continue for years, without decision, to the desolation of peoples and places – notably in **East Africa** and **Afghanistan**. Technique becomes more sophisticated as **communications**, weapons and explosive technologies improve. Struggles now take place in urban surroundings as well as rural areas. Counter-guerrilla precautions and operations demand an immense outlay in **intelligence** networks, skill in execution and precautionary measures. It is an unending struggle which, materially and socially, consumes almost as much as full-scale war.

Guided missiles. See Rockets and guided missiles.

Gunnery. The art of gunnery is concerned with the operation of equipment and the control of fire (for guns themselves see **Artillery**). Even in the mid 19th century guns, both on land and at sea, had no effective fire-control system and the method of pointing the gun at the target ('laying') was crude in the extreme. As there was no recoil system guns had to be relaid after every round. However, effective ranges were so short that such simple techniques mattered little.

At sea. By the beginning of the 20th century the need for significant changes in shooting methods was revealed by the design of the new **battleships** and fast **battle-cruisers**. It was becoming increasingly difficult to estimate the speed and bearing of a target which, with the guns then coming into service, could be engaged at ranges of 12,000m or more. In 1905 Captain Percy Scott proposed that control of a ship's guns should be from a fire director placed high up on the foremast. The director contained an observer officer, a gun-layer and a gun trainer, the latter two equipped with instruments indicating elevation and azimuth respectively, transmitted electrically to the gun turrets below. This system was full of errors but it did significantly improve gun control and was adopted by the Royal Navy by 1913.

Fire control, the bringing of fire to bear and subsequent correction of the fall of shot, was another matter. Changes of range and bearing had to be integrated, together with the effect of the ship's motion, and passed continuously to the gun sights. The Dreyer fire-control table, adopted prior to 1914, met the basic requirement, despite many shortcomings. The German system, designed by the electrical firm of Siemens & Halske, incorporated a mechanism for automatically adjusting the sight so that all the layer had to do was align his sight with the target and fire. Neither side, nor the French who adopted a system similar to the Dreyer table, had at this stage looked at gyroscopic control, though the Germans were about to do so when the outbreak of war in 1914 brought trials to an end.

World War II saw an increase in naval air power which tended to make direct engagements between surface ships something of a rarity. It is probably true to say that the larger ships generally practised their gunnery against land targets in support of **amphibious** operations during this war. The requirement for accuracy was just as urgent but at least the targets were stationary.

Since World War II the surface-to-surface **rocket** missile has largely superseded the gun for ship-to-ship engagements, though most warships of any size will have at least one gun of up to 105mm calibre, rapid-firing and automatically controlled by computer. Such weapons were used effectively against shore targets during the **Falklands** War.

On Land. Until the late 19th century land service guns were used in the direct fire mode, i.e. the layer could see the target at which he was required to shoot. As gun ranges and accuracy improved it became feasible to withdraw the guns from the main battle line and to conceal them behind natural features. This in turn required the guns to fire indirectly, where the layer could not see his target and hence fire had to be corrected by a forward observer. The simultaneous improvement in battlefield communications, the introduction of Morse code transmitted by flags or **heliograph**, provided the vital link between observer and guns and made indirect fire a practical proposition – to some effect during the **American Civil War**, especially where tethered balloons were used to lift the observer aloft.

The big change came in **World War I** as a combined result of positional warfare and the widespread use of the field **telephone**. Now the forward observer could talk direct to the guns and precise and detailed corrections could be given. However, because it was difficult to determine accurate ranges, the artillery still found it necessary to register the target by firing a number of ranging rounds before bringing the full weight of fire to bear. This inevitably alerted the enemy but the only alternative, predicted fire (i.e., firing for effect on a target whose location had been worked out from the map), was much less certain, although it was in extensive use at the Battle of **Cambrai** in 1917.

Nevertheless, techniques improved and by **World War II** communications and survey methods had become so accurate that the artillery of an entire corps, firing without registration, could be at the disposal of a single forward observer communicating simultaneously by **radio** with all gun positions, either observing from the forward infantry or from a spotter aircraft. Post-1945 indirect fire techniques have been even further refined with the use of **radar** and **computers**; many of the variables previously limiting accurate fire have been eliminated or much reduced.

Two tasks still remain for the direct-fire weapon: air defence and **anti-tank** fire. The need for anti-aircraft guns, which had arisen during the **Franco-Prussian War** of 1870, was met by the Ehrhardt anti-balloon gun. By 1910 high-angle 75mm guns were available. The problem of achieving hits on fast-moving aerial targets was not easily solved, even with the introduction of fire-control radars, which improved the kill rate from 20,000 shots per aircraft in 1940 to 4,000 per aircraft in 1941. Modern high-flying jet bombers are beyond the reach of any gun system and surface-to-air missiles have now taken over against high-altitude targets. However, most countries have retained low-level air-defence gun systems of 35–40mm calibre. Usually vehicle-mounted, computer-controlled and incorporating surveillance and tracking radars, these are sophisticated and expensive equipments which, like the German Gepard, can claim a chance of a hit of about 80 per cent against a transonic crossing target – the worst case.

The tank gunner is concerned with visible targets at 3,000m or less, small targets which he must hit first time or perish himself from retaliatory fire. Modern technology has now largely overcome the range-finding problem but that in turn has revealed other variables which need to be corrected: wind speed, ambient conditions, muzzle velocity, barrel bend and wear. A modern tank fire-control system integrating all these problems is computer-controlled with electronically stabilized guns and sights, leaving the gunner with the simple task of aligning his sight on the target and firing when the time is ripe. With such a system, an 80–90 per cent chance of a first-round hit is to be expected.

In the Air. During World War I the **machine-gun** quickly became the **fighter aircraft**'s weapon and on the single-seater biplane it was mounted pointing forwards above the upper wing or, later, firing between the propeller blades by means of an interrupter gear. The pilot pointed the aircraft at the target and manoeuvred to obtain a hit. Results were not impressive, though it was not before 1916 that much was done to improve matters, when the Frenchman Yves Le Prieur demonstrated a wind-vane corrector. It was very complex and Major Geoffrey Norman designed a simpler system which altered the setting of the machine-gun foresight to allow an aim-off related to aircraft and bullet velocities. This sight was adopted by the Royal Flying Corps in 1917.

The introduction of multi-gun fighters in the 1930s did not materially alter the means of fire control. As late as 1937 it was felt that air combat would be at such short range that special sighting equipment would be unnecessary. However, increased aircraft speeds and the need to engage attacking fighters accurately from the power-operated gun turrets being fitted to bombers soon called for improvements; gyro-stabilized gun sights were in service with the Royal Air Force by 1943.

The air attack of ground targets became an important feature of air warfare during World War II and this called for the fitting of larger guns (though Westlands had fitted a 37mm gun to a fighter as early as 1927). The use of armour on fighters and bombers also had its effect and 20mm cannons were specified for German fighters before 1939, with Hawker's 40mm anti-tank gun being on trial in 1941; by 1943 a six-pounder anti-tank gun had been successfully mounted in a Mosquito. However, in the later stages of World War II rockets gradually replaced guns for ground attack, paving the way for their introduction for air-to-air combat in the jet era. Nevertheless, the US A10, specifically designed for ground attack, carries a six-barrelled 30mm Gatling gun as part of its weapon fit and it is in this role that air gunnery chiefly survives, now controlled by computer and with head-up displays allowing the pilot to aim his weapons without being distracted from control of his aircraft.

Gurkha soldier. In the midst of the war between the British East India Company and Nepal in 1814–15, three battalions of Nepalese troops, known as Gurkhas (or Goorkas) were formed by the British. In East India Company service they took part in several campaigns in India, culminating in their loyal and crucial service to the British in the **Indian Mutiny**. Indeed, loyalty is among the strongest virtues of these soldiers of small stature who have won a legendary reputation for their courage and steadfastness in battle, as well as for their sense of humour. After the Mutiny their units became part of the British Indian Army and, virtually as mercenaries in

British pay by agreement with the Nepal government, played an important stabilizing role in the policing of India. As light infantry they saw much combat during **World War I** in France, Italy and the Middle East; and in **World War II** (when some became paratroops) in the Middle East, Italy and **Burma**.

At the partition of India in 1946, six battalions joined the Indian Army and four the British. Both later expanded – the Indian battalions considerably, the British less so. Both increased the percentage of native Gurkha officers. Some trained as engineers and signallers. Indian Army Gurkhas have fought in their various frontier wars. Those with the British were a mainstay in the **Malayan War of Independence** and **Indonesian confrontations**. They were also engaged in the **Falklands** War. Nepal herself maintains a small army and depends quite extensively upon the pay and pensions of her 'exported' soldiers for foreign currency.

Gustav Line, Battles of the. In the autumn of 1943, in the aftermath of the Allied landings at **Salerno**, Field Marshal **Kesselring** managed to change **Hitler**'s mind and gained his agreement to the defence of Italy (**Italian campaign, 1943–5**) along the line of the Garigliano, Rapido and Sangro rivers. This 10-mile-deep position, founded on mountain bastions (of which **Cassino** was the most celebrated) was first known as the Winter, then as the Gustav Line. The Allied armies under General **Alexander** came up against its outposts along the Volturno in October and henceforward made only slow progress until finally checked at the end of the year. Once the **Anzio** landing in January 1945 had failed to turn Kesselring's flank, Alexander concentrated on limited attacks on the Rapido sector to pin down the Germans and prepare for the main offensive which opened on 11 May.

American, British, Canadian, French, Indian and Polish troops were flung into the attack on 11 May on a 20-mile front between the sea and Cassino. Attacks at first failed on the coast and before Cassino, but bore fruit in the Aurunci mountains where General Alphonse Juin's French Expeditionary Corps made spectacular gains which broke the Gustav Line's spine and forced German withdrawal on the 15th to the lay-back Adolf Hitler Line. Cassino was evacu-

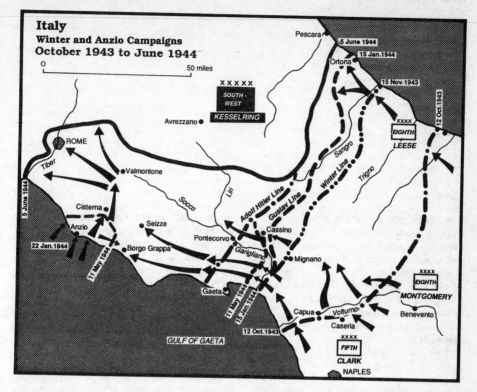

Italy
Winter and Anzio Campaigns
October 1943 to June 1944

0   50 miles

Pescara

5 June 1944

15 Jan.1944

Ortona

15 Nov. 1943

12 Oct.1943

XXXXX
SOUTH -
WEST
KESSELRING

Avrezzano

XXXX
EIGHTH
LEESE

ROME

Tiber

Valmontone

Sangro

Winter Line

Trigno

Liri

Socco

Adolf Hitler Line

Gustav Line

5 June 1944

Cisterna

Seizze

Pontecorvo

Cassino

Anzio

22 Jan.1944

11 May 1944

Borgo Grappa

Garigliano

Mignano

XXXX
EIGHTH
MONTGOMERY

Gaeta

11 May 1944

13 Jan.1944

Capua

Volturno

Benevento

Caseria

12 Oct.1943

GULF OF GAETA

XXXX
FIFTH
CLARK

NAPLES

ated on the 17th to the Polish Corps. The Hitler Line was overrun by I (Canadian) Corps on the 22nd, as the Anzio garrison broke out, impelling Kesselring into full retreat with heavy losses and bringing the abandonment of Rome on 4 June to VI (US) Corps.

H

Haig, Field Marshal (Earl) Douglas (1861–1928). A cavalryman who served in the **Sudan campaign** and the **Boer War** with distinction and, as a firm believer in the tactical soundness of the knee-to-knee charge, was Inspector of Cavalry in India (1903–6) before rising through key staff and command appointments to command I Corps in France in 1914.

Throughout the Battle of Mons and of the **Marne**, he retained firm control of his formation and was most steadfast at the first Battle of Ypres. In February 1915 he took command the First Army and led it during the Battles of Neuve-Chapelle, Festubert and Loos at which the full difficulties of trench warfare were made plain. In December 1915 he took command of the rapidly expanding British Expeditionary Force (BEF) and remained in that post for the rest of **World War I**. He was conscious of the need for the BEF to collaborate fully with the French and remained on good terms with Marshal **Joffre**, in trying to relieve the strain on the French army at **Verdun** with his own strategically controversial offensive on the **Somme** in 1916; but sceptical of General Nivelle in 1917. At **Arras** in April and May the BEF played its part and, for the rest of the year in **Flanders** and at **Cambrai**, took at dreadful cost the full strain in the aftermath of the French Army's mutiny. In March 1918, he placed the BEF under Marshal **Foch** to see them through the crises of the **Hindenburg offensive**, and, at **Amiens** in August, he opened the way to the war's end in 1918. Often maligned as anti-tank in outlook, in fact he was ready to use any tools made available to achieve victory.

Halder, General Franz (1884–1972). A Bavarian artillerist and one of the best brains in the General Staff, he specialized in operational and training matters. As Army Chief of Staff from August 1938, he willingly carried out the planning and execution of **Hitler**'s campaigns in Poland (**Polish campaigns**), West Europe, North Africa, the Balkans and Russia (**Russo-German wars**). But when things began to go seriously wrong in the Caucasus in September 1942, he was removed after a final disagreement with Hitler. Yet, indignant as Halder sometimes was at Hitler's interference in military matters, and flirt as he did with the notion of deposing him, he was no political resister, simply a soldier who stuck to the military last and took pride in winning victories – until awakening too late to a hopeless situation.

Halsey, Admiral William (1882–1959). A naval officer's son of charismatic dimensions, Halsey was in command of US **aircraft-carriers** at **Pearl Harbor** in December 1941, though he had not become an aviator until 1935. Highly rated for his aggression by Admiral **Nimitz**, Halsey's carriers raided Japanese shipping in 1942 and launched the air attack on Tokyo in April. As a result he missed the Battle of the **Coral Sea** and was relieved of command with a skin complaint prior to **Midway**. In October 1942 he relieved the weak Admiral Ghormley, Commander South Pacific, and immediately inflicted heavy losses on the Japanese in the attritional Battles of the **Solomon Islands**. In June 1944 he took command of 3rd Fleet, an immensely powerful force of battleships and carriers, and smashed Japanese air power in the battles preceding **Leyte Gulf**. At Leyte Gulf, however, Halsey's obsession with the sinking of Japanese aircraft-carriers led him, to Nimitz's disgust, to uncover the amphibious force in order to chase Japanese carriers, whose role was known from intelligence to be diversionary. But his fame remained undimmed.

Hanoi, Battles of. As the capital of French Indo-China from 1887 until 1945, the city grew into a vital industrial and communications centre linked by rail to the port of Haiphong and to the hinterland. Occupied by the Japanese in 1943, it was often bombed by the Americans from 1943 until 1945 during **World War II**. Immediately after that war, the Vietminh made it their main objective at the start of the war for **Vietnam**'s independence from the French. Vietcong guerrillas fought within its urban sprawl. When the French were defeated in 1954 it became the capital of North Vietnam.

Throughout the struggles of the 1960s and 1970s, the city's outlying communications, along with Haiphong port, became targets for US bombing. Transport, plus airfields and anti-aircraft batteries, were the principal targets, the city itself receiving relatively slight damage at first. In 1966 oil-fuel targets, power stations and railways in the so-called Iron Triangle of Hanoi, Haiphong and Thanh Hoa were hard-hit – forcing the building of pipelines and delivery of oil in drums instead of bulk. Targets in urban areas were attacked accurately by **smart missiles**. In 1967 the Americans attacked bridges and railways to seal off Hanoi and Haiphong from the rest of the country, causing a major evacuation of both cities and the dumping of stores in urban areas which pilots were forbidden to attack. Not until December 1972, in an attempt to bring the procrastinating North to the conference table subsequent to the collapse of their offensive in the south, did President Nixon at last permit attacks on all targets regardless of location. Hanoi city was bombed heavily and 1,318 people reported killed. When American anti-war activists asked the mayor of Hanoi to condemn the 'Christmas Offensive' and claim 10,000 had been killed, he refused in order to protect the North's political credibility. A month later the Paris Accords (which the North never intended to keep) were signed, bringing the war to a close.

Harris, Air Marshal Sir Arthur (1892–1984). Took part as a British Home Defence fighter pilot and then artillery observation pilot in **World War I**, developing an enthusiasm for Gen-

eral **Douhet**'s theories in the 1920s. In key command and staff appointments in the 1930s, he pressed the development of heavy RAF **bomber** forces as an independent war-winning instrument, by advocacy that lacked absolute scrupulousness. In **World War II**, when made Commander Bomber Command in 1942, the bombers at his disposal were incapable of fulfilling his task of 'knocking Germany out of the war'. Unable to hit small, military targets, he was compelled to adopt 'area bombing', in which urban areas were devastated without achieving the main aim. Bomber Command contributed mightily to final victory, but Harris's reputation was tarnished by his seeming insensitivity and unwillingness to abandon area bombing in favour of more accurate and economic methods.

Health services, Military. In 1850 the awakening of scientific and public concern to the need for vastly improved hygiene and health, demanded above all by overcrowding in urban areas, had hardly begun. Water and insect-borne diseases (such as, respectively, cholera and typhus) flourished out of ignorance of their causes and the difficulty of educating the **medical services**, let alone people, in basic preventive cleanliness, diet and general physical fitness. Publicity about the suffering of sailors and soldiers in the **Crimean War**, when, as in so many wars gone by, deaths from disease were greater than from shot and shell, instilled a turning-point in the development of health care (see **Nightingale, Florence**). Henceforward far greater attention was paid to **logistic** services, which provided more nutritious **food**, sensible **clothing** and shelter, not only to economize in lives and improve combat fitness, but also to enhance **morale**. But it would be many years before there was adequate awareness of what was implied or required, and many campaigns, such as the **Spanish–American War**, the **Boer War**, the **Russo-Japanese War** and **World War I**, before the main causes of ill-health and the worst of its problems, abuses and defects had been discovered and eradicated by research, technical developments and organization.

Yet it was in the latter half of the 19th century that the medical authorities began to pay stricter attention to prevention than to cure. The implementation of legislation in civilized countries raised standards and concentrated the minds of surgeons and doctors on the need to care for sailors and soldiers by supervising their living conditions, feeding arrangements and physical well-being. The public's consciousness of the need for proper sanitation was imposed upon the military, who were compelled to study and enforce sanitation and hygiene in the field by specialists, particularly when operating in underdeveloped countries, waterless deserts and frozen wastes where standards and facilities were primitive.

Education and health-discipline measures went hand in hand with advances in medical science; and although it was realized before 1900 what caused most water-borne disease, it was not until the 20th century that insects and parasites, such as flies, lice and mosquitoes, were discovered to be bearers of many intestinal complaints as well as such mass killers as malaria and yellow fever. From the identification of cause to the discovery of vaccines to immunize people against such scourges as smallpox, cholera, typhus and tetanus, was a relatively short step, one which contributed significantly to reduced sickness and mortality rates in **World War I** and almost total extinction of some afflictions in **World War II**. Likewise, as the reduction in insect population was tackled in campaigns to eliminate the static water in which they bred, so new drugs emerged to suppress or prevent malaria and yellow fever in World War II, even more effectively when insecticides, such as DDT, rid humans of lice and typhus. Indeed, one decisive advantage of the Allies over the Japanese was their possession of the latest health technology and techniques, enabling them to operate in environments which were fatal to the unprotected.

The present day's efficient sophisticated fighting men are as dependent as ever upon physical and mental fitness, complemented by comprehensively enforced health regulations and procedures, as well as by balanced diets and clothing that is compatible with good health as well as combat function. They can make the difference between victory and defeat.

Helicopters. Interest in Vertical Take-Off and Landing (VTOL) **aircraft** reached back to the 15th century and a powered man-carrying machine made a hop in 1907. But it was not until 1923 that Juan de la Cierva's Autogiro (with unpowered rotor blades) came close to vertical take-off and 1936 before the first practical, powered rotor machine, the Focke Wulf 61, flew, and 1946 before the small American Bell 47 met a military requirement.

Thereafter military usage and development was rapid starting with slightly larger machines during the **Malayan War of Independence** and burgeoning during the **Korean War**. To begin with they carried men, stores and wounded in and out of small jungle clearings and to and from the front line. They undoubtedly saved many lives by speedy evacuation of casualties to the **medical services**. Used by the French for counter-**guerrilla warfare** during the **Algerian War of Independence** and by the British for **amphibious** assault at **Suez** in 1956, they reached a level of maturity during the **Vietnam War**. Helicopter units were, in 1961, the first US air units to serve in Vietnam. To begin with mostly single-rotor types with payloads of between 600lb and 5,000lb and speeds in the region of 100mph were employed. But soon they were joined by twin-rotor cargo machines, such as the Chinook, which could lift 33 troops or about 20,000lb of cargo. Machines of these types were principally under development in Britain, France and Russia but it was in both technology and strategic and tactical techniques and concepts that the USA thrust itself into the lead in Vietnam.

To begin with great progress was made with support and maintenance services for machines which required a great deal of each through normal wear and tear and frequent battle damage. Cost-effectiveness was always under scrutiny by the critics, but to begin with were well on the helicopter's side. In undeveloped terrain it introduced vital mobility by its ability to move large numbers of troops, with their **logistic** support, into normally inaccessible places. As a result existing **airborne forces** of parachute and glider-borne troops became outmoded. But as the helicopter engaged more closely in the combat zone and counter-fire increased, it had also to be armed, initially as a defensive measure. **Machine-guns, rockets and guided missiles** were successively fitted and used for suppressive fire against landing zones and, in due course, offensively against **armoured fighting vehicles** (AFVs). Alongside these developments emerged the revolutionary concept of *airmobility* (sometimes designated *air cavalry*) and the suggestion that the armed helicopter might be a substitute for AFVs, instead of just a complement. The vulnerability of helicopters to ground fire, above all guided weapons, has nevertheless been frequently demonstrated, especially in **Afghanistan** (where Russian-armed Hind machines lost heavily), the **Arab–Israeli wars** and the **Falklands** campaign.

It is in **naval warfare** however, that the helicopter is most comfortable, since it is not so easily ambushed as on land and can play a major role in most operations. As **submarine** and **mine** hunter it is supreme, as well as being a vital tool for **amphibious** operations and **logistic** support. Numerous operations, such as those in the Persian Gulf (**Iran–Iraq War**) and, most of all, the Falklands have demonstrated this.

Currently the helicopter (particularly when designated for land warfare) is becoming like most sophisticated weapon systems, highly expensive in the effort to extend its versatility and improve its protection. It is arguable that when a single battlefield helicopter such as the USA's Apache costs many million dollars the time for reappraisal has arrived.

Heligoland Bight, Battles of. On the first day of World War I the German Navy began laying **mines** in British waters while the Royal Navy made sweeps of the North Sea. On 5 August a minelayer was sunk against the loss of one British **destroyer.** Minor contacts and a few losses occurred until the 28th when two British light cruisers, with destroyers, supported by Admiral Beatty's five **battle-cruisers**, with scouting cruisers, steamed towards the Heligoland Bight and encountered two German light cruisers, with destroyers, off the naval base of Heligoland. As the British cruisers withdrew westwards through heavy mist towards Beatty's approaching ships, they were chased by four scattered but gathering German light cruisers – which ran straight into Beatty. Beatty had been well informed of the enemy presence, but the Germans were in ignorance of their peril and they were either overwhelmed by gunfire at short range or pursued to the death, with the loss of 1,000 sailors.

As a result of this battle the Germans became more cautious and began to lay minefields in the Bight while the British tightened their block-**ade**. Not until November did the Germans emerge again to bombard the British east coast in the sort of raid which, in due course, led to the Battle of **Dogger Bank**.

Heliograph. A signalling system invented by Sir Henry Mance (1840–1926), consisting of two mirrors reflecting sunlight in any required direction, the beam being interrupted by a key-operated shutter. Thus messages could be sent to a distant observer using Morse code. Mance's design was first used in 1878 during the Second Afghan War (**Afghanistan, Battles of**) and was soon generally adopted throughout the British Army, though a version known as the heliotrope had also been used during the **American Civil War** of 1861. Since the idea required bright sunlight it was of limited value in Europe, though very successfully used for many years by the Indian Army and during the **Boer War**.

Hindenburg, Field Marshal Paul von (1847–1934). A Prussian infantryman who distinguished himself in both the **Austro-Prussian War** of 1866 and the **Franco-Prussian War** of 1870. He retired in 1911 as a general but was recalled in August 1914 to command the retreating Eighth Army in East Prussia. Teamed most happily with General **Ludendorff** as his Chief of Staff, they won the Battle of **Tannenberg**, defeated all enemy offensives in 1914 and threw the Russians back in Galicia and Poland in 1915 (**Russo-German wars**).

On 29 August 1916 he became Chief of the General Staff, authorized to exercise the Kaiser's powers as Supreme Commander. With Ludendorff as his chief executive (First Quartermaster-General) he went on the defensive in the West and successfully knocked Russia out of the war in 1917. At the same time he approved unrestricted **submarine** warfare and rigorously tightened up the war economy. Following failure of the Hindenburg offensive (see next entry) of 1918, it was Hindenburg who instructed the Kaiser to abdicate and who brought the defeated troops home. Even his great prestige, for which he owed much to Ludendorff's dynamic ability, was insufficient to stave off revolution. Nevertheless, as President from 1925, he managed, in tumultuous times, to retain a measure of control until appointing **Hitler** as Chancellor in 1933.

Hindenburg offensives of 1918. When Russia withdrew from **World War I** in 1917, it released the mass of the Germany Army for offensive action in the West. Generals Hindenburg (see above entry) and **Ludendorff** had little option but to throw their full weight into an attempt to knock out Britain and France before the trickle of American strength became a deluge. Having a mere 40 tanks (mainly captured British) the

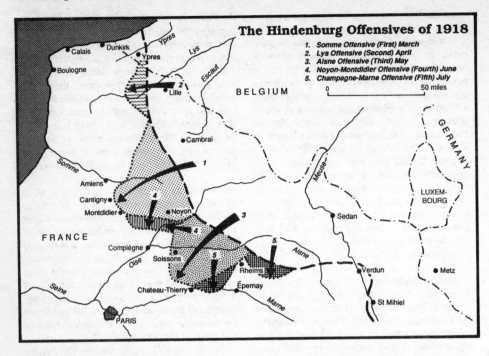

The Hindenburg Offensives of 1918

1. Somme Offensive (First) March
2. Lys Offensive (Second) April
3. Aisne Offensive (Third) May
4. Noyon-Montdidier Offensive (Fourth) June
5. Champagne-Marne Offensive (Fifth) July

series of attacks depended upon tactical surprise produced by the latest **artillery** techniques of silent registration and from **infantry** infiltration tried out at **Riga, Caporetto** and **Cambrai** during 1917. But they ran on a shoestring because the **blockade** had created serious material shortages.

The first offensive on 21 March on a 60-mile front to the west of Cambrai caused semi-collapse of the British Armies and widespread retreat with heavy losses of men and material. At one moment it looked as if the French Army under General **Pétain** would withdraw to protect Paris and leave the British Army under General **Haig** to its fate. But the appointment of General **Foch** as Supreme Allied Commander put a stop to that and gradually the German attacks, suffering from **logistic** defects, were slowed down and stunned when the attempt at **Arras** on 28 March to widen the flanks of the offensive was halted in its tracks. It ended on 5 April just short of the vital route centre of **Amiens**.

The second offensive, in Flanders on a 30-mile front on 9 April and also against the British, caused serious shock waves, but no surrender of vital ground. Haig's famous 'backs to the wall' exhortation steadied his troops as Foch moved

in an Allied reserve to stabilize the front by the 29th. Losses on each side were about 100,000, but already the Germans were faltering.

The third offensive struck the British and French on 27 May on a 40-mile front from the line of the River **Aisne** and thrust towards Paris. Again Foch responded by positioning Allied reserves, including American divisions for their first major engagement. Once more the initial German onrush was slowed down by enemy resistance as well as their own fading morale and logistic strength, until brought to a halt on 5 June. This time, indeed, the French counter-attacked with such vigour that the Germans lost their farthest gains.

The fourth offensive was a much smaller effort, indicating the erosion of German resources. On 9 June, on an enemy-anticipated 25-mile front, the assault between Noyon and Montdidier was enmeshed in French defences in depth, disrupted on the 13th by a Franco-American counter-stroke, and killed off on the 15th.

The fifth offensive on 15 July, which reached and crossed the River **Marne** after a ten-mile advance, received equally brusque treatment on either side of Reims from French and American divisions. The attack to the east of that city was stopped on the first day. To the west it lasted only four days.

With the collapse of the fifth offensive, Hindenburg and Ludendorff conceded failure and began contemplating local withdrawals to economize in troops holding the salients they had seized. But their disappointment turned to dismay when, on 18 July, Foch launched a powerful counteroffensive on the Marne which surprised and overran an enemy whose morale was at low ebb and whose defences were unformed. Hastily evacuating the Marne salient and pulling back to a shortened line on the River Vesle, the Germans left behind 30,000 prisoners, 600 guns, 200 **mortars** and 3,000 **machine-guns**. The mass Allied counter-attack at **Amiens** on 8 August was the beginning of the end.

Hipper, Admiral Franz von (1863–1932). A torpedo specialist in the German Navy, who at the outbreak of **World War I** commanded the **battle-cruisers** and other ships of the High Seas Fleet's scouting force. He led the North Sea raids which culminated in the Battle of **Dogger Bank**, and was in the van at the Battle of **Jutland**. There his skilful enticing of the British battle-cruisers towards the High Seas Fleet, and his bold, almost sacrificial, handling of his own ships in the middle and closing stages (when he was forced to leave his sinking flagship), won nothing but praise. As C-in-C High Seas Fleet at the war's close, he was preparing a valedictory sortie with his main force, but was denied the honour as the sailors mutinied and the Armistice was declared.

Hitler, Adolf (1889–1945). An Austrian who served as a corporal in the Bavarian Army throughout **World War I**, was several times decorated and wounded – and who loved war. He formed a hatred of Communism (among other things, which included Jews), was lucky to survive the Revolution and in July 1921 took over the Nazi Party. The failure in 1923 of his first attempt, in league with General **Ludendorff**, to seize power also alienated his trust of high-ranking officers. Nevertheless, when made Germany's Chancellor, in 1933, it was at the call of Field Marshal von **Hindenburg** (the President) and with Army support.

From the outset Hitler was bent on war against Russia. Rearmament and repossession of territory lost through the Versailles Treaty

were steps in that direction. Yet, although naval and army expansion and re-equipment, along with creation of an air force (the Luftwaffe), were central to his aims as Supreme Commander, he seems to have been confused in mind as to how they should be employed – except, initially, as a card in a political, bluffing hand in a game in which he won all the tricks he contracted for. Nevertheless, by March 1939 when virtually all lost German territories had been reassimilated without war, he gambled. The occupation of Poland (**Polish campaigns**), which might well have been achieved without resort to arms, was an outright expression of Hitler's megalomanic desire for war.

As a charismatic bully, who divided to conquer and who often tried to be all things to all men, Hitler's handling of his commanders and his conduct of war was that of a gifted amateur. Mentally wedded to his experience of the trenches, he had a capacious memory that could absorb every detail of the military art which fascinated him, but his lack of a sound military education prevented him putting it to skilled use. None of this mattered while he followed the directions of the expert staffs who, sometimes, were too content to admit the soundness of his appreciations. Unfortunately for Germany, Hitler not only increasingly imposed unsound decisions upon the General Staff, but also indulged in systematically undermining their authority, converting them to lackeys. At the same time he failed to give the Navy adequate support and also permitted his favourite, Hermann **Göring**, to ruin the Luftwaffe.

Hitler reached his peak of power at the start of **World War II**. The story of his decline and destruction is reflected in many entries here.

Hobart, Major-General Sir Percy (1885–1957). A tempestuous Sapper of great ability and courage who won distinction in **World War I** and became a leader of **armoured** forces prior to **World War II**. In 1939 his career was sidetracked by enemies and he was forced out of the Army. But he was recalled by Winston **Churchill** and given command of armour. As Commander 79th Armoured Division, he was given the task of developing and training the specialized armoured forces which would lead the **amphibious** assault on **Normandy**. To a considerable extent he ensured success with economy of lives both on 6 June 1944 and in many subsequent operations, including landings in **Holland** and the River Rhine crossing in 1945.

Ho Chi Minh Trail (see map on page 336). A strategic supply route which North Vietnam began constructing through Laos in 1959 to carry the **logistic** burden of their projected invasion of South Vietnam. Built by 30,000 troops under General Vo Bam to follow mountainous jungle tracks and connect with routes eastwards towards the coastal centres, it was developed during the **Vietnam War** to become a main artery with roads up to 9 yards wide in stretches. It was 625 miles long, and had more than 10,000 miles of subsidiary trails and a 3,125-mile pipeline. In due course trucks were used but in the early days most stores were man-packed or pushed on bicycles of French manufacture.

The existence and significance of the Trail was soon realized by the South, but it was not until 1965 that the Americans tried cutting it by air attack. Over the years they expended enormous efforts on this, compelling the North to divert great resources to repairs and reducing capacity and flow, but never shutting it down. Indeed, only physical occupation could have done that with an invasion of Laos, which America rejected for political reasons.

Holland, Invasions of. Holland spent **World War I** fearing invasion by Germany but avoided it until **World War II** when attacked on the orders of **Hitler**. On 10 May 1940 German ground forces crossed the frontier as **airborne** troops landed at such key places as the Moerdijk bridge, Rotterdam and The Hague. The Dutch opened the sluices, but although their Air Force gave a good account of itself, the surprised and outmatched Army was inevitably overrun before it could be reinforced by French troops. An armistice was arranged on the 14th shortly after Rotterdam had been inadvertently devastated by bombing.

Under German occupation the Dutch were among the first to express outright resistance to the Germans, its effectiveness undermined by enemy penetration of its organization and the loss of many agents. British troops advancing through Belgium in 1944 reached the frontier in pursuit of the Germans in mid-September. On the 17th the Allies launched their combined land and airborne thrust towards Arnhem, via Eindhoven and Nijmegan. When this was brought to a halt, the Allies had to concentrate

on clearing the approaches to Antwerp, in order to solve their logistic problems. Pushing westwards from the Arnhem corridor and northwards from Antwerp, they gradually cleared southern Holland in heavy fighting up to the line of the River Maas. But the Germans also held on grimly either side of the West Scheldt estuary, demanding heavy fighting by Canadians for the so-called Breskens Pocket, on the south shore, and for the extensively inundated islands of North and South Beveland and **Walcheren**. Eventually major amphibious landings by British troops were needed to clear South Beveland and Walcheren before minesweeping of the river could commence on 4 November.

Holland had to wait until 22 March 1945 for the crossing of the Rhine. First Canadian Army had the task of side-stepping leftwards from Emmerich, taking Arnhem (which was done by 2 April) and thrusting northwards to the coast near Groningen and Leeuwarden. They largely completed this task by the 18th but were unwilling to inflict unnecessary casualties and suffering on the rest of the country, whose inhabitants were starving. On 28 April, however, negotiations with the Germans were held and next day the air forces began dropping food to the people as fighting ceased.

Home fronts. Naturally there have always been those at home who have supported the men at the fighting front, yet not until the 18th century, with the spread of **conscription** and the Industrial Revolution, was the emerging 'totality' of war recognized. **Blockades** and sieges had always affected civilians but in the 19th century imposed an increasingly heavier strain upon them in company with significant social changes. Maintenance of the **American Civil War** and the **Franco-Prussian War**, for example, demanded close government controls on **communications** and **railways** – which irked the public. Governments, therefore, felt the need to explain and issue **propaganda**, besides taking measures to ease the civil lot.

It was **World War I** and the start of **air warfare**, with its direct attacks upon cities and, therefore, civil **morale**, which concentrated minds upon what gradually became known as home fronts. While such measures as the Prussian Law of Siege and the British Defence of the Realm Act gave powers to make regulations for 'public safety', they did not impose discipline in the military sense. **Censorship**, which stifled the flow of 'bad' news (and consequently encouraged rumours), encouraged exhortations and cheerful news which were not always truthful and all too frequently indoctrinated people with hatred for the enemy. Indeed, although the so-called Campaigns of Hate may have stiffened the morale of many citizens, they also created divisions with fighting soldiers who regarded the enemy differently.

Air raids, however, could not be so easily concealed as news of lost battles and sunken ships far away. The populace needed proof of government concern through demonstrations of protective measures, such as early warning of enemy approach and loud, if inaccurate, gunfire. The commitment of political parties and trade unions was found essential to involve every man and woman (**Women's military forces**) in support of the war effort. This had to be paid for financially and by concessions. Voluntary service to the community was preferred but compulsion was not excluded. Thus systems evolved which immeasurably sharpened social consciences and not only promoted fairer legislation in the administration of, for example, rationing, but also demonstrated women's abilities in all manner of work and won them political emancipation.

Among the defeated nations, Germany spuriously concluded (for military and political reasons) that her armed forces collapsed in 1918 because of defeatism at home. Victors and vanquished alike learnt much about the manipulation of civil morale, but drew inaccurate, alarmist conclusions from dread of **strategic bombing**, as postulated by General **Douhet** in the 1920s. The result was that many nations approached **World War II** without the enthusiasm of 1914, in trepidation over the strength of their home fronts. Correctly it was assumed the bomber would get through; incorrectly that gas (**Chemical warfare**) and **explosives** would have catastrophic material and morale effects. German propaganda claimed her air defences were impenetrable. Britain assumed the worst and concentrated **civil defence** resources on inferior shelters and the disposal of wounded and dead, while almost overlooking post-attack care of the homeless. But defence of the home front, no matter how ill-considered or poorly administered, was rarely ignored and usually consumed manpower and resources which, in wars gone by, would have been committed elsewhere.

As the Battle of **Britain** demonstrated, people under aerial attack, even when as ineptly cared for as some were by uncoordinated local government officers, were not easily broken. Despite misguided leadership, people 'carried on' in order to earn a living and survive personally – though not invariably out of patriotism and fear of the enemy. Nearly everywhere it was doubting politicans and military, not the people, who tended to break under pressure. Devastated by bombing, the Germans kept going in apathy and under ruthless repression by their own authorities. Dramatically they raised production until actually invaded. Similarly devastated in the last year of war, Japan surrendered as much because of her ruined war effort as out of consideration of the **atom bomb**, whose initial impact was mainly restricted to Hiroshima and Nagasaki. Almost universally, internal law and order were maintained as people worked for themselves and the common good.

Under nuclear threat an inability to ensure adequate shelter has generally been assumed. Present-day defence of home fronts therefore either plays ostrich or concentrates planning on survival measures. But the **Vietnam War** experience, among others, has shown that communities still can establish law and order amidst chaos. None of the post-1945 wars has demonstrated any decay of the individual's spirit in resisting threats to existence and autonomy.

Hong Kong, Siege of. This British colony was doomed the moment the Japanese opened hostilies against the British, Americans and Dutch on 7 December 1941. Cut off from nearby friends, its garrison of 12,000 (including two British and two Indian battalions, plus two newly arrived Canadian battalions, but meagrely supported by artillery and defenceless from the air) was attacked on 8 December by a well-supported Japanese division. Twin thrusts into the New Territories rapidly dislodged frontier positions, forcing the survivors to withdraw to the island by the 13th. A Japanese surrender demand was refused that day, as was another on the 17th as a bombardment was reaching its climax.

The mountainous island was fortified but by no means well supplied. Once the principal forts commanding the narrow Lei U Mun Strait had been knocked out by dive-bombing, the Japanese were able to ferry men across with impunity on the 18th. Intense pressure pushed the British back as they gradually became disorganized. By Christmas Day they were out of water and penned in the island's east end and two small peninsulas. Surrender was negotiated, but not before wounded had been bayoneted in hospital by the Japanese – whose total losses were about 3,000.

Hungnam, Battle of. In the **Korean War**, after the **Inchon** battle and defeat of the North's invasion of the South, permission was given to General **MacArthur** to destroy the North's army. This required a thrust up the east coast towards the ports of Wonsan, Hungnam and the Russian frontier at Unggi. X (US) Corps (consisting of 1st (US) Marine Division and a British Commando, two US and two South Korean infantry divisions) was transferred by sea to Wonsan on 26 October 1950 and by 24 November had captured the Chosin reservoir and Hyesanjin, at which point the Chinese attacked with 120,000 troops in the vicinity of the reservoir, threw back the infantry divisions and cut off the Marines as they headed for Hungnam and Wonsan. Facing similar pressures on the western front, MacArthur decided to evacuate North Korea. While the Marines, in appalling cold and bleak country, struggled to escape envelopment, the South Korean divisions were brought back at full speed to Hungnam and Wonsan where evacuation of the base was at once put in hand.

The ten days' fighting retreat of the **Marines** became an epic. It might have been a disaster had not Chinese **logistic** services, pummelled by air attacks, starved their spearheads of fuel and ammunition, making it impossible to follow up with strength at speed. As a result, not only did X Corps's rearguard survive, it held the ports until 15 December, It was long enough to evacuate, mainly by sea, 105,000 troops, 98,000 civilians, 17,500 vehicles and 350,000 tonnes of stores, leaving little but smoking debris for the enemy.

Hydrogen bomb. The idea for a thermonuclear bomb, based on the fusion of deuterium, was first mooted in 1942 but, though work was done to show the idea was feasible (the US Super Project), there was no further development till 1950, when President **Truman** authorized work to proceed. It was decided to use tritium, an isotope of hydrogen, mixed with deuterium to keep down the otherwise very high ignition temperature; the name 'hydrogen' bomb stems from this 'burning' of the hydrogen isotope. On 1 November 1952 the first test device of between four and eight megatonnes was exploded in the Pacific, obliterating a small island and leaving a mile-wide crater. The device relied on an atom-bomb trigger, releasing neutrons to bombard a lithium liner which in turn started the fusion process generated by the reaction of the tritium/deuterium. The device had a uranium jacket and it was the fission of this, from the neutrons emitted by the reaction, that produced the radioactive fission materials.

Practical warheads and bombs soon followed the early tests and hydrogen bombs now form a significant proportion of the major powers' nuclear armoury.

I

Imphal, Siege of. In a long-delayed attempt to complete the conquest of **Burma**, the Japanese Fifteenth Army under General Renya Mutaguchi launched a two-pronged thrust on 6 March 1944 against the **Kohima** and Imphal forward maintenance areas, intent upon capturing their contents. Surprised as General **Slim**'s Fourteenth Army was by the speed of enemy advance, he nevertheless managed to place IV Corps (three divisions with some 50,000 men in addition to 40,000 civilians) around Imphal before it was besieged on 5 April. Both Kohima and Imphal were placed on air supply as Slim tasked XXXIII Corps to advance from the railhead at Dimapur, first to relieve Kohima and then Imphal, the latter's garrison steadily reinforced by air to 100,000. With a single division, which was short of supplies, Mutaguchi had no hope of seizing Imphal. Really it was the Japanese who were under siege as they struggled to prevent XXXIII and IV Corps from relieving Kohima and thus deny Slim freedom to concentrate on the mountainous battlefield. When that happened on 22 June, after fierce fighting to clear Japanese road blocks between Kohima and Imphal, Fifteenth Army was at Slim's mercy. In semi-collapse the Japanese retreated, to the Chindwin.

Inchon, Battles of. At the start of the **Korean War** in June 1950, the port of Inchon was bypassed by the North Korean Army as it advanced towards **Pusan**. As, in mid-August, the Pusan bridgehead held out, General **MacArthur** planned a major **amphibious** counterstroke by X Corps against the enemy rear at Inchon. It meant risking the withdrawal from the bridgehead of 1st (US) Marine Division, landing amid difficult approaches to the port and possible loss of surprise from the decision to begin air attacks two days ahead of the landing. But even if the enemy had guessed right, he was in no state to reinforce the threatened areas, such was his run-down condition. Resistance to the **airborne** and seaborne landings on 15 September was negligible. The **Marines** occupied the vital Kimpo airport on the 17th as 7th Infantry Division came ashore and moved to surround **Seoul**, cutting communications to Pusan. On 26 September a link up with advancing troops from the south was made as Seoul fell.

Indian Mutiny. The so-called mutiny, which broke out on 10 May 1857 amongst Bengal units of the East India Company's Army in India, had long been coming with many different causes: inefficient administration by the Company's officers; racial and caste differences between Hindu and Muslim soldiers, who were denied promotion to commissioned rank since all officers were British; and low **morale**, due to recent disasters in **Afghanistan** and lax discipline, all contributed. Outrage at having to bite the new Minié bullet, which was smeared with animal fat and thus prohibited on religious grounds to both Hindus and Muslims, merely put spark to tinder which was fanned into flame by official denials (soon disproved) and severity in disciplining men who refused the new bullet.

When Indian soldiers began massacring British officers, officials and traders, along with their families, the Indian Army was 233,000 strong against a mere 36,000 British troops, scattered throughout the subcontinent. The reaction of the British was delayed when the C-in-C died of cholera but they were strengthened at once by

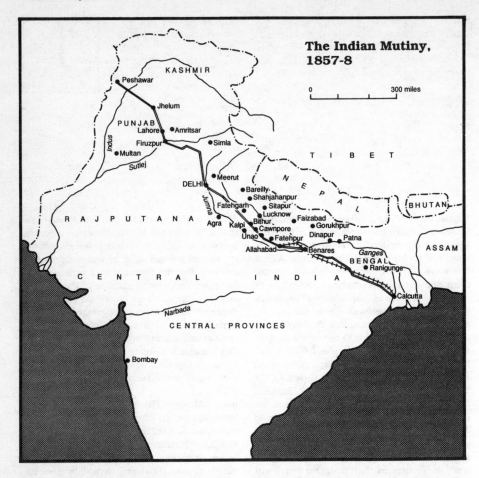

The Indian Mutiny, 1857-8

0   300 miles

Punjabi, Sikh and **Gurkha** troops who remained loyal. Indeed, although the north of the country was seething, the spontaneity of the outbreak and lack of a unifying command constantly mitigated against co-ordination of the mutineers' efforts. It was thus no planned war of independence.

All the British could do at first, led by such as Sir John and Sir Henry Lawrence and Sir Henry Havelock, was contain the outbreak by disarming mutineers and securing key centres; move to the relief of besieged Lucknow; and save lives where possible. Meanwhile the rebels, who declared Bahadur Shah their ruler, massacred the surrendered British at Cawnpore and weakened their mobile forces in order to prosecute sieges. Indeed, although the rebels fought well given the opportunity, they lacked sound leader-

ship, except that provided by the highly competent Rani of Jhansi and by Kunwar Singh. But the British, whose anger was aroused by evidence of massacred women and children, and who cheerfully bit the new bullet, fought with terrible fury and were well led as they approached Lucknow and Delhi. Havelock's 2,500 men, marching 126 miles in nine days in temperatures over 100 degrees Fahrenheit from Allahabad, successively defeated Nana Sahib's much larger army by superior fire-power at Fatehpur, Aong, and Cawnpore in mid-July, and at Bithur in mid-August, whereupon exhaustion made them retire to await reinforcements.

Meanwhile a small British force under General Sir Henry Barnard, which had neared Delhi on 7 June after twice defeating larger enemy forces, was also by then exhausted. The enemy, four times its strength, should have thrown it back. Instead the two months defence by the so-called besiegers of Delhi against Indian attacks was every bit as epic as Lucknow's. Not until 14 September were the British, Punjabis, Sikhs and Gurkhas sufficiently reinforced to assail the city's strong defences. Three days' bombardment of the city was a prelude to an assault by 4,000 men and a street battle lasting six days, at a price of 1,574 attackers, before the place fell. Five days before, Havelock's force reached Lucknow, a mere 2,000 strong against 60,000 Indians, only itself to join the besieged.

At this turning-point reinforcements from Britain, called by **telegraph**, were arriving at Calcutta and travelling by **railway**, still under construction, towards Cawnpore, whence the second relief of Lucknow was mounted and finally completed on 16 November, prior to the rout of the local mutineers on 6 December. In spite of this, strong mutineer forces were still at large – some dormant, others (such as those who had to be hunted down between Cawnpore and Lucknow) active until well into 1858. Indeed, not until the Rani of Jhansi was killed at the major Battle of Gwalior on 19 June was the mutiny considered crushed. Even then **guerrilla warfare** continued for some time. Meanwhile rule by the defective East India Company was transferred to the British government, who reorganized the Indian Army.

Indian Ocean, Battles of the. After the Japanese Navy had smashed the Americans at **Pearl Harbor** and the British and Dutch in the **Java Sea** in December 1941, it sent a force of three **battleships** and five **aircraft-carriers**, commanded by Admiral Chuichi Nagumo, into the Indian Ocean as cover for movements of vital shipping to Rangoon. The target was Admiral Sir James Somerville's fleet of two modern aircraft-carriers and one old one, plus five old battleships – meaning 27 obsolete British fighters and 58 torpedo-bombers against 117 modern Japanese fighters and 260 bombers. Somerville aimed to conserve his force by partial dispersal at sea and withdrawal out of reach to Addu Atoll. Nagumo managed only to sink the small carrier and eight other warships, shoot down 43 aircraft and damage shore installations on Ceylon. Far more devastating was a raid into the Bay of Bengal by Admiral Jisaburo Ozawa with a car-

rier and seven cruisers. In ten days, virtually unopposed, he sank nearly 150,000 tonnes of shipping, totally disrupting vital traffic to Calcutta and Burma, and causing a reappraisal of Allied **logistics** in that theatre of war, including the need to seize **Madagascar** as denial of a base to the enemy.

Indo-China War of Independence. From the moment the French imposed their rule upon Cambodia, Laos and Vietnam in the 1880s, nationalist resentment was born. There was a minor uprising in 1908 and growing agitation and action in Vietnam during the 1930s by Ho Chi Minh's Indochinese Communist Party. At the end of the Japanese occupation after **World War II**, Ho Chi Minh proclaimed a Vietnamese Republic but his 10,000 man Vietminh **guerrilla** force in the north, under Vo **Giap**, was kept in order by British, Indian, French and Japanese troops, and then tackled head-on by the French in 1946.

The guerrilla war which ensued was conducted most skilfully on Chinese Communist lines by Giap against French forces whose equipment, like the Vietminh's, was a mixture obtained from the last war's contestants. Forty thousand Frenchmen under General Henri Leclerc were unable to stamp out 30,000 guerrillas who infested the countryside and the towns, including **Hanoi**. Vietminh **logistics** were tenuous and dependent upon the goodwill of the populace, who were cared for with tact. But things changed decisively after China had fallen to the Communists in 1950. A regular supply route to the north was opened and Russia too recognized the Vietminh and sent aid. Attacks upon French communications and bases took place in unison with the taking of control of hinterland communities by the Vietminh. From 1951 onwards, thousands of French-made bicycles, each carrying 450lb, were being pushed through jungle trails to the guerrillas. Such successes as the French sometimes enjoyed in capturing concealed stockpiles were only transitory because replacement was swift.

The crunch came in November 1953 when the French announced they were seeking an 'honourable' settlement and, almost simultaneously, flew 15,000 men with 28 field guns and a few light tanks to Dien Bien Phu, which they developed as a jungle base for decisive operations deep into the enemy rear. Giap accepted the challenge by surrounding Dien Bien Phu with numerous anti-aircraft guns (to shoot down transport aircraft) and 200 field guns, all well supplied with ammunition via the jungle trails. It took nearly four months to assemble these pieces along with the 60,000 infantry (80 per cent of Giap's army) needed for the assault – a concentration neither French troops nor air strikes could check. By 13 March 1954 the French were penned, with air supply strangled by anti-aircraft fire in the approaches to the fortress. Then, strong point by strong point, the Vietminh eliminated their prey who were doomed on the 27th when the airstrip was seized. Thereafter survival depended upon air drops alone without hope of relief. By holding out until 7 May, however, the French merely delayed the inevitable: the negotiated agreements which put an end to French Indo-China and granted sovereignty to Cambodia, Laos and Communist North and non-Communist South Vietnam, thus composing the prelude to the **Vietnam War**.

Indo-Chinese War. On 20 October 1962, after laying claim to various strategic territories between Bhutan, in the north-east, and Jammu, in the north-west, the Chinese Army launched massive attacks to hurl back the weak Indian Army – giving the impression of an overture to major invasion. Yet, a month later, the Chinese as abruptly announced a cease-fire and withdrew behind the new frontier of its own choosing. The aftermath of this humiliation for India, however, has witnessed (with American, Russian and British assistance) a significant modernization of her armed forces.

Indonesian confrontations. President Achmed Sukarno's insecurity in power, owing to the disruptive struggles between Communists, the military and racial groups (some backed by the USA, the Dutch or the Chinese, with British and Malaysian involvement), persuaded him to try external, nationalist ventures to strengthen his internal position. In 1957 he began harassing the Dutch in West New Guinea on the pretext it was Indonesian territory. Following five years of naval and guerrilla skirmishing, the Dutch eventually gave way and handed over to the Indonesians in August 1962. Four months later the Indonesians engineered a violent uprising in the Sultanate of Brunei, in North Borneo, which

the British instantly put down. But Sukarno was determined to destroy the newly formed Federation of Malaysia (consisting of Malaya, Sarawak and North Borneo) and in September 1963 began the campaign of economic and military skirmishing which was termed 'confrontation'.

Confrontation included attempts, with Chinese Communist participation, to undermine British, Singaporean and Malaysian trade in concert with hit-and-run raids across the straits into Malaya and across the border with North Borneo. Malaysian forces, substantially supported by the British, managed easily to contain these irritations. Only minor damage was done and the raiders were frequently rounded up or chased away, until 1965, when an Indonesian/Chinese Communist-led coup against the military (including the killing of six generals) provoked a furious internal Indonesian backlash. The Communists were outlawed and massacred in tens of thousands; Sukarno's powers were severely curtailed; and confrontation was brought to an end.

Indonesian wars of independence. Between the demise of the Dutch East India Company's interests in Indonesia in 1870 and a Communist-inspired rebellion against the Dutch colonial power in 1926, Indonesian nationalism lay fairly dormant. But in the years prior to **World War II** and the Japanese invasion in 1942 there were numerous brushes between Dutch security forces and Indonesian nationalist guerrillas who, under Achmed Sukarno, collaborated with the Japanese. At the war's end the Japanese vacillated, one moment encouraging the Indonesians to resist the Dutch return, the next refusing to hand their arms to anybody but the British. The British found themselves caught in cross-fire with the Indonesian People's Army (IPA) attempting to seize arms from the Japanese, by their commitment to help the Dutch regain their colony.

Sukarno's self-proclaimed Indonesian Republic declared war in October 1945 against Holland and Britain, but the capture of the Indonesian capital, Surabaya, by the British after a tough fight on 29 November placed the Dutch in control. A year later negotiations and sporadic guerrilla warfare were still in progress as the Dutch, weakened by World War II, temporized. Reinforced in 1947, they began very determined efforts in the next two years to stamp out the IPA, despite UN recognition of Indonesian independence and attempts at reconciliation. The Dutch were encouraged, since almost invariably they overcame the poorly armed IPA whenever it emerged from cover, and also because an all-out offensive launched in July 1947 and a surprise airborne operation in December 1948 not only captured Sukarno's capital at Jogjakarta but largely gained control of Java.

In January 1949, however, the UN Security Council ordered Holland to hand over power, though it took four months for them to withdraw. A drawn-out civil war then erupted between political and military factions (some 170) seeking control of the new republic. It dragged on until 1961, by which time the government of President Sukarno was also involved in confrontation (see previous entry) with Indonesia's neighbours.

Indo-Pakistani wars. Within two months of the partition of India in 1947 and the appalling massacres of Hindus and Muslims, India moved troops into Kashmir to quell Muslim rioters. At once Pakistan responded with forces sent in support of their brethren. Thus began the series of spasmodic hostilities which have continued ever since. For, though the cease-fire of 1 January 1949 put an end to large-scale fighting until 1965, border incidents were frequent.

In April/May 1965, however, a dispute over territory in the Rann of Kutch sparked a two-week frontier war which, in August, reignited **guerrilla warfare** in Kashmir and provoked a raid across the cease-fire line by strong Indian forces on the 24th. UN observers tried to stop the action which drifted politically and then flared into a 22-day **limited war** on 1 September. Neither side had clear strategic aims but both committed major armoured formations, backed by intense air support and scattered use of **airborne** troops, to battles in Punjab and Kashmir which tended to be head-on and unimaginative. In an attritional struggle the Pakistanis got the better in the air and the Indians the better on land, without either side winning vital advantages. In the end a threat by China against India, and an embargo on arms and fuel supply by the major powers, brought the affair to a UN-negotiated end. Of immense interest to the major powers, however, were the contests be-

tween American equipment on Pakistan's side against British on India's.

Guerrilla war broke out again in August 1971 over the deteriorating situation of East Pakistan, this time dominated by India's politico/strategic object of detaching that country from the Karachi government. Air clashes in November rapidly escalated into full-scale war on 3 December when Indian troops, supporting dissident Pakistanis, invaded. The result was inevitable. Unable to come to the direct or indirect rescue of its appendage, Pakistan was forced to accept its conversion to self-governing, Muslim Bangladesh on 16 December. The hostility between both countries continues.

Infantry. The introduction into service in the 1850s of breech-loading **rifles**, soon to be augmented by magazine-charged types, imposed a complete change on the appearance and handling of infantry in battle. No longer was it necessary for men to stand in close-packed formations to generate adequate fire-power; nor could they afford to do so and provide easy targets for improved weapons of all kinds. Instead, the need to disperse, to fire from behind cover and to abandon bright uniforms and wear drab **clothing** (which had been slowly adopted over at least the past 100 years) rapidly became obligatory and was virtually universally complete by the end of the century. The role of infantry, however, remained largely unchanged: to hold and seize ground, particularly terrain (such as woods, swamps and built-up areas) which was unsuitable for the mobile arms, that is, horsed **cavalry**, until the advent of motorized **armoured** forces.

The **Crimean War** marked the beginning of the end of the period when infantry were taught to receive cavalry in square formation. But the trenches infantry dug encircling **Sevastopol** were like those in many sieges past and in countless wars to come – the best shelter possible against weather as well as shellfire and bullets. This was the period in which the **empty battlefield theory** emerged. Henceforth the need to give the individual infantryman better protection was vital, if not immediately recognized. If the suffering of men in every siege argued for warmer, waterproofed clothing and boots, the appalling losses from torrents of shot and shell in combat demanded the tactics of dispersal and evasion as well as armoured protection.

The **American Civil War** and the **Boer War** indicated not only the wane of cavalry as the arm of shock action, but also the feasibility of mounted infantry. Vital as it was (and is) for infantry to be fit and capable of marching long distances, they always rode when they could – in river craft, farm carts, railway wagons and on elephants during the **Indian Mutiny**, for example. In the American Civil War they were to be found in armoured railway trains, so it was logical for **armoured fighting vehicles** to appear within a few years of the invention of the petrol engine. And equally logical that, when infantry were massacred and bogged down in **World War I**, the suggestion they should travel inside **tanks** was acted upon. Infantry transport has been developed ever since, in the shape of the specialized armoured personnel carrier, lorries and **helicopters**, besides motor cycles.

Since the invention of the **machine-gun** and the trench **mortar**, infantry have been forced to adopt the first for close combat and both to give longer-range, heavy-fire support for movement and in static defence. Likewise, the appearance of the tank at once made infantry call for their own **anti-tank weapons**; while the latest signals **communication** systems, particularly **radio**, were adopted once weight and reliability had been got right. This accumulation of technology has turned some infantry into all-arms units with sophisticated **tactics**, besides calling for skills far beyond those of the simple marching rifleman and grenadier. By the beginning of **World War II** the average infantry unit was packed with specialists whose average intelligence ratings had to be much higher than their predecessors', a trend which made it necessary for units, basic rifle companies each of three or four platoons, to acquire an additional special support company, as well as a logistics company which cared for transport, supply and administration.

World War II also brought forth any number of élite infantry units, such as **airborne** and the **Commando**, which were often criticized for swallowing the best men to the detriment of leadership in ordinary units. Be that as it might, wise commanders have learnt to conserve their infantry in the knowledge that they are indispensable in most circumstances and terrain, and all too easily squandered through their vulnerability, no matter how good their fieldcraft, their accurate fire in support of fluent movement or their endurance in exacting conditions. With-out infantry it is almost impossible to operate efficiently in tank-proof terrain, such as mountains, swamps, woods and built-up areas. On the other hand, infantry depend greatly upon artillery, tanks and engineers to operate almost anywhere and are at a distinct disadvantage in wide open desert or steppe which lack natural barriers.

Finally, it should be remembered that **guerrillas** and armed civilians, as well as any sailors, soldiers in general or airmen if so redirected, are potential infantrymen.

Inkerman, Battle of. In the opening stages of the fighting in the **Crimea**, Prince Menshikov's aim was to destroy the Anglo-French forces besieging **Sevastopol**. His first major offensive failed at **Balaklava** on 25 October. His second was an attempt by 42,000 men under General Dannenberg on 5 November to envelop the British holding a ridge overlooking the Chernaya River. In heavy early morning mist, which persisted throughout the battle, the British were surprised but stood their ground. Unaware of what was taking place, Dannenberg continued to feed in troops piecemeal against an opponent who also was in ignorance but who steadily reinforced his infantry to about 8,500. Properly controlled the Russians should have overwhelmed their opponent. But as their losses mounted amid terrible confusion, and as French troops began to arrive around midday, Dannenberg lost heart and withdrew, having suffered some 10,000 casualties against 3,000 Anglo-French.

Intelligence services. Prior to and during all military operations, intelligence of the theatre of war, the geography, local economy and political situation and the state of one's own forces, not merely about the enemy and his intentions, are fundamental. Therefore counter-intelligence is equally important in maintaining security. It follows that successful intelligence operations depend upon adequate advanced provision of finance to create the sources and the processing and disseminating organizations required. It is one important lesson of history that laxity in establishing an intelligence service in peacetime (as did Britain between the World Wars) has caused the downfall of nations and loss of many a campaign.

The types of intelligence are many and various: political, economic, strategic, tactical, technical, industrial, **logistic** and so on. Their variety and complexity have increased in pace with the advance of **technology**, particularly of **electronics**. Covert sources include spies (agents of variable trustworthiness who are not nearly so romantic as often portrayed), patrols, decrypted **codes and ciphers**, intercepted mail and telephone messages and the pattern and volume of traffic using **communication** networks. Overt sources include reports in journals, ground and aerial (including **space**) photographic reconnaissance missions, plain-language messages, industrial catalogues, transport timetables, overheard careless conversations and disclosures during routine diplomatic exchanges. The establishment of reliable sources and the collection of data are time-consuming and complex, involving much subterfuge. So too is the transmission of information, which is liable to interception by hostile counter-intelligence organizations. Double agents, deception from the planting of spurious material and the inadvertent disclosure of sources are among the perils involved when setting up channels of communication. Many a thriving network has been shut down or destroyed because of organizational or technical defects, an astute enemy, carelessness or sheer bad luck.

The synthesis of information received is, of course, vital and dependent upon expert recognition of the evidence's truth and falsehood (duly corroborated), the rejection or filing of dubious clues, and the presentation of clear, concise reports and summaries sufficient for assured planning of operations. **Computers** help accelerate the analysis of vast volumes of material and avoidance of overlooking relevant material. Today, as in the past, the most disconcerting errors can be made in the transmission of crucial information, as for example, when a vital report about German night dispositions was not sent to Admiral **Jellicoe** at **Jutland** in 1916 and made all the difference to his chances of victory; or the inadequate exploitation and interpretation of available political intelligence, which deluded the Germans as to Russian vulnerability in **World War II**; or the misinterpretation of information about the movements of the battleship *Tirpitz*, which led to disaster for **Convoy PQ 17** in 1942. Errors such as these were mainly due to typical human and organizational breakdowns, which delayed reports, induced incompetent synthesis, allowed poor presentation or

highlighted commanders' unwillingness or inability to credit the evidence and the conclusions drawn from what, to the uninitiated, could appear as a black art. Indeed, the secretiveness which is central to the functioning of **secret services** and associated, numerous intelligence agencies, is itself an enemy of credibility. As a major example, the vital security need strictly to limit the access of Allied commanders in World War II to awareness of the deep penetration of high-grade enemy codes and ciphers prevented those in the know emphasizing to subordinates, who were not in the secret, the authenticity of startling news, a dilemma which led to misunderstandings over **Pearl Harbor** in 1941 and many another incident.

Intelligence of quality is vital to economy of effort and national survival. It is dearly bought or obtained, potential political dynamite (particularly during **cold wars**) and vulnerable to misinterpretation. It can be abused and misused, but ignored at peril. Well organized and run, it pays dividends beyond price. There is a vast **bibliography**, much of which, owing to inherent secrecies and deceptions, contains faults and misconceptions of the sort common to intelligence matters. Instances of intelligence effect will be found among many entries in this Encyclopedia.

Iran–Iraq War. Disputes between Iran (Persia) and her Muslim neighbours reach far back in history. Border incidents in the 1960s owing to Iraq taking action against dissident Kurds in the north were only stifled by agreements in Iranian favour in 1975. The chaos in the aftermath of the Shah of Iran's deposition in 1979 gave Iraq under President Saddam Hussein an opportunity to reassert her authority and also gain possession of the important waters of the Shatt al Arab at the head of the **Persian Gulf**. With armed forces roughly equal in number in September 1980, Iraq (mainly equipped by Russia) invaded Iran (mainly equipped by the USA and the UK), whose forces had lost some 60 per cent effectiveness with the Revolution.

Initial thrusts towards strategic and economically vital Abadan and Khorramshahr misfired in bad weather against unexpected resistance. Iranians, inspired by the religious zeal of Ayatollah Khomeini's followers, mounted suicidal counter-attacks which gradually produced stalemate along the length of the 750-mile frontier.

The Iran-Iraq War, 1980-8

Land battle zone

x Areas of chemical attacks by the
Iraqi army against civilian & military targets

0   100 miles

Iran continued to attack, despite a debilitating equipment poverty following arms embargoes by America and Britain. She traded men's lives in vast quantity to wear down the numerically smaller Iraqi population. Besieged Khorramshahr was relieved in May 1982 as the Iraqis, facing exhaustion, were forced back across their own border and as Basra came under threat. When Iraq, in effect, sued for peace, Iran demanded the overthrow of the Iraq government as a condition. Iraq reverted to a sullen defensive posture.

Iran went to great lengths to obtain arms in order to prosecute a war of attrition which cost an immense number of lives (precise figures have not been substantiated). Between September 1981 and January 1984, thirteen offensives, of which five were at corps and four at divisional strength, had been counted, with claims of over

half a million Iranian and 250,000 Iraqi casualties. By then gas, supplied by Russia and dispensed by Russian weapon systems, had been used for the first time since 1936 in **Ethiopia**. The collapse in February 1984 of a promising attack by 100,000 Iranians to capture Basra, was put down largely to the use of **chemical weapons** – mustard and nerve gases – which contributed to loss of **morale** and 40,000 casualties to virtually unprotected troops. Immediately Iran was compelled to purchase protective clothing and attack in the knowledge that the slightest success on their part was liable to provoke chemical attack. In 1985 further disastrous repulses occurred as Iran's recruiting fell off from lack of enthusiasm. Even the zealots could only raise 12 per cent volunteers for the slaughter. In 1986, however, there was an improvement, once protective clothing was widely issued, and attacks made ground. Again Iraqis had their backs to the wall as Iranian morale improved.

Yet stalemate on land followed in 1987 and 1988. Iraq opened air attacks on oil installations as Iran began pin-prick attacks against and mining (**Mine, Sea**) of international shipping in the Gulf. Iran, realizing she could not break the enemy, went in for limited ground attacks, rocket bombardment of cities and guerrilla warfare, with armed Kurdish collaboration, threatening Iraq's oilfields. Iraq responded in kind and killed thousands of unprotected Kurds caught down wind of a gas attack. All at once in 1988, it seems, Iran's military morale momentarily collapsed. Her forces withdrew with heavy losses when Iraqi troops advanced on a wide front across the frontier, taking vengeance on the Kurds with massacre by gas attacks which drove the survivors into Turkey, where they were disarmed. In May 1988 Iran took advantage of UN mediation to accept an armistice and a UN supervisory presence.

Ireland's wars of independence. The founding of the Fenian movement in 1858, in reaction to seemingly heartless British treatment of the Irish people in the famines of the 1840s, led in 1873 to formation of the Irish Republican Brotherhood (IRB) and demands for Home Rule (self-government). Among numerous factions involved in three abortive attempts to push Home Rule bills through Parliament prior to **World War I**, the Ulster Protestants of Scottish descent, who were in a majority in the six northern counties of Ulster, made plain their determination to resist by force of arms any attempt to impose rule by the Catholic Irish majority from the south. As Ulstermen began secretly to arm in 1914 (helped by Germany) and a mutiny by British officers indicated the Army might not take action against Ulster Volunteer fighters. Sinn Féin ('Ourselves Alone', founded in 1907) created its own force of Irish Volunteers and began to arm. There were minor clashes between Volunteer bands, but World War I's outbreak postponed civil war.

In frustration a few hard-core members of the militant IRB planned an insurrection. Without telling Sinn Féin they took up arms on Easter Day, 23 April 1916, but without an essential arms cargo from Germany that had been inter-

cepted on the 21st, and an attempt to cancel the uprising was only partially effective. The 1,200 active rebels in Dublin at once were isolated and killed or captured by 1 May. Moreover they drew upon themselves the wrath of the people for making such a futile attempt, causing so much damage to Dublin. Had not the British ruthlessly executed 15 surviving leaders of the attempt, organized Irish Republicanism might have wilted away. As it was, news of the secret executions aroused intense revulsion and zeal, stronger-yet expressions of American support, and the forming in 1919 of an Irish Republican Army (IRA) from the IRB and Irish Volunteers, committed to **guerrilla warfare**.

In January 1919 Sinn Féin declared independence from Britain as a prelude to an outright rebellion in November. When the Irish police refused duty, the British formed an auxiliary counter-guerrilla force of veteran soldiers, known as 'the Black and Tans', who fought alongside the Army. While efforts were made to resolve the problem politically and strong pro-Irish American pressure was brought to bear, civil war raged. The IRA intimidated waverers. Both sides committed atrocities. Damage to property was widespread in punitive raids and hit-and-run ambushes. Ancient feuds re-emerged as racial and religious differences between North and South widened. The British public, no longer kept in the dark by wartime **censorship**, wanted a solution. In December 1921 a Treaty forming an independent Irish Free State, which excluded Ulster, was agreed. Then, in 1922 after the British withdrew, it was the Irish Free State's misfortune to suffer from its own bitter civil war generated by factional disputes about the legality of the Treaty. Underlying all was resentment at the existence of independent Ulster and hostility on the part of the Republic of Ireland (renamed Eire) government, Sinn Féin and the IRA (in due course made illegal on both sides of the border) aimed at reunifying Ireland.

Irish reunification. Eire stayed neutral throughout **World War II** and German attempts to stir up trouble were total failures since the outlawed IRA was in a state of disarray; but the country was a haven for spies based on the German Embassy in Dublin and there were Irishmen only too pleased to help anybody against the British.

An attempt by the IRA to renew hostilities

in Ulster between 1956 and 1962 failed from lack of Catholic support after a few minor incidents and raids on military armouries. The IRA were more subtle in 1967, taking advantage of social and sectarian injustices in Ulster to exploit civil-rights demonstrations and a successfully orchestrated series of marches. Indeed, by 1969 the violence fomented had produced a breakdown in law and order, with rioting, fire-raising and the blowing up by the IRA of public installations. The British Army had to intervene in support of the police against rioters in August, and used non-toxic CS gas, whereupon the IRA used firearms. Casualties and anger rapidly mounted. A classic guerrilla war developed in which the IRA, supplied with arms smuggled from the South and elsewhere, sought to compel a British withdrawal. This struggle reached a peak in August 1971 when the Ulster government ordered internment of dissidents, and yet another early in 1972 when pitched street battles were fought in Belfast, Londonderry and along the borders. By then the IRA had split into the so-called Official, Communist-infected faction and the more traditionally militant Provisional IRA (PIRA).

The use of 30,000 troops (9,000 of them members of the part-time Ulster Defence Regiment) did have the effect, in conjunction with internment, of suppressing PIRA and driving it and Sinn Féin into a terrorism which persists to this day. This has been carried occasionally into Britain and mainland Europe and has been supported by arms from Libya and money from abroad, notably the USA, but without hope of forcing the British out of Ulster. For the terrorist campaign of ambushes, murder, bombings and political intrigue (designed to generate politically useful **propaganda** coups, but also uncomfortably associated with ordinary crime) has only hardened attitudes and stiffened Ulstermen's resistance to reason. Bigotry and vengeance continue hand in hand, without an end to it in sight among people who are unable to let bygones be bygones.

Iron Curtain. A term employed by the German **propaganda** machine during **World War II** to describe the political barriers created by Soviet Russia. It was taken up by Winston **Churchill** and first used by him in a significant speech at Fulton, USA, to encapsulate the significance of the physical, as well as political, obstructions

surrounding Russia. It thus became a popularized symbol of **cold war**, one often used as a convenient index of the state of relations between the major powers. Thus in periods of détente, such as that current in the 1980s, Russia's stop to jamming the West's **radio** news and propaganda, and her relaxation of cross-frontier movements, are meant to be interpreted as a dismantling of the Iron Curtain to improve relationships.

Isandhlwana, Battle of. This first major encounter of the **Zulu War** on 22 January 1879 occurred as a surprise to a well-armed British force of 1,800 under General Lord Chelmsford. He had pushed forward into Zululand without careful reconnaissance and was caught by surprise in the open by 10,000 charging Zulus. In a prepared position with an ample ammunition supply the British might have beaten off the attack. In the event a simple **logistic** misunderstanding, when quartermasters refused to issue ammunition to units other than their own ('Go get it from your own people' was one fatal rebuff to hard-pressed clients), reduced riflemen to searching dead comrades for bullets. Few escaped.

Isonzo, Battles of. Upon Italy's declaration of war against Austria in May 1915 the only front which, by the less mountainous nature of the terrain, offered possibilities of a blow to shatter the Austrians was along the Isonzo valley beyond the frontier with Gorizia. The Italian Army under General Luigi Cadorna was ordered to advance from the frontier, cross the valley and seize the commanding ground and Gorizia in what was hoped might lead to a triumphant advance to Vienna. Well aware of the threat, the Austrians held the 40-mile sector in strength. In terrain well suited to defence, the Italians, who were short of artillery and ammunition, had only the slimmest chances of making much headway. Yet they went on trying with scarcely any encouragement in a costly attritional struggle. Up to October 1917 there were eleven separate battles in the valley:

The First Battle, from 23 June to 7 July, involved 200,000 Italians and a seven-day preliminary bombardment by 200 guns prior to an assault which gained less than a mile at a price of 15,000 Italian and 10,300 Austrian casualties. Outgunned as they were, however, the

Austrians' confidence was boosted – with long-term effects.

The Second Battle, from 18 July to 3 August, was a more expensive repeat of the first with 42,000 Italian and 47,000 Austrian casualties in exchange for the capture of a few unimportant hilltops.

The Third Battle, from 18 October to 4 November, also got nowhere despite employment of 1,200 Italian guns. Far more carefully prepared than its predecessors, it did temporarily scare the Austrians; but this time too, with losses of 42,000 against 67,000 Italians, they clung on, only to be attacked once more on 10 November on the same ground in what is called the *Fourth Battle*, with the same negative results and casualty lists of 25,000 Austrians and 50,000 Italians.

Both sides were disenchanted. Yet Cadorna returned to the charge again between 11 and 29 March 1916 in the *Fifth Battle*, which again got nowhere as evidence began to accumulate of an impending Austrian offensive near Trentino. No sooner had that offensive broken down in mid-June than Cadorna took the opportunity to strike again on the Isonzo, starting the *Sixth Battle* on 6 August against an opponent weakened by sending troops to Trentino and the Russian front to meet the **Brusilov Offensive**. This time recognizable progress was made along a 25-mile front in a series of battles culminating in the *Ninth Battle*, the advances penetrating to a depth of eight miles at one point to include the capture of Gorizia. It was exhaustion and winter which called another halt to the doleful, unimaginative business on 4 November.

When in 1917 the dire events in Russia and mutiny of the French Army called for Allied diversionary measures, all Cadorna could manage was the *Tenth Battle* from 12 May to 8 June, at a cost of 117,000 Italians and 75,000 Austrians and the *Eleventh* from 18 August to 15 September – which surprisingly produced a most significant result. For this time when Cadorna threw in 52 divisions of disillusioned troops, supported by 5,000 guns, a breakthrough of six miles to the vital Bainsizza Plateau, spearheaded by infiltrating shock troops, was achieved. It cost 150,000 casualties, but for a time the Austrians were on the run – and might have been kept retreating if broken-down ammunition supply and weariness had not overtaken the Italians. As it was, the Austrians were shaken

and called for German help – which led to the Battle of **Caporetto**, sometimes known as *Twelfth Isonzo*.

Israeli fight for independence. In 1922, when the League of Nations granted a Mandate to the British Government to rule Palestine and implement the Balfour Declaration of 1917 (thereby supporting the establishment of a Jewish homeland), there were only 85,000 Jews in the country, living among about 600,000 Arabs and other minority nationalities. Immigration of Jews, from among the millions scattered throughout the world and often under repression, was on economic grounds limited to a strict quota. The plan was renounced by the Arabs who correctly surmised the Jews had political dominance in mind, taking away the fruits of independence so recently won in the **Arab revolt** against the Turks. There were anti-Jewish disturbances in 1922 and 1929 stirred up by the Mufti of Jerusalem in objection to the threat of a 'future overlord'. In August 1929, 133 Jews were killed and 339 wounded by Arabs in an incident at the Wailing Wall in which 116 Arabs were killed and 232 wounded by the British. In 1936 a prolonged **guerrilla war** started in which, chiefly, the British had the task of defending Jews against Arabs who disliked living among a growing Jewish population and saw no future, as did the British, in ethnic partition.

From the outset, with or without British approval and assistance, armed Jewish units had been formed to protect their settlements. These comprised the part-time Haganah (Defence Organization) which, by 1939, was 2,000 strong, lightly armed, British officered and tasked to counter Arab guerrillas. A few very militant Jews also formed a dissident group called Irgun Zvai Leumi, which preyed on Arabs. In May 1941, when the Axis threat to the British Middle East position became acute, Haganah created a full-time force called Palmach which fought alongside the British in the **Syrian battles** that year and acted as a cadre for a Jewish Brigade of the British Army, forces many Jews visualized as essential for their survival after **World War II** when a flood of refugees from Europe were expected to meet Arab opposition.

Irgun and another even more extremist gang, the Stern (Lehi) Group, attacked the British in 1944 with sabotage and assassinations, including that of the British Minister of State in Cairo.

Simultaneously the Jews, powerfully supported by money and a strong political lobby in the USA, began secretly stockpiling numerous weapons and ammunition from all manner of sources, as well as from their own underground industry. The struggle for power began in earnest in 1946 when an Anglo-American commission recommended continuation of the Mandate and the admission of 100,000 Jews, mainly refugees from Europe.

At once Irgun and the Stern gang, contrary to official Jewish policy, intensified terrorism against British and Arabs. On 22 June 1946 they blew up the British HQ in the King David Hotel, Jerusalem, with the loss of 91 lives including many hotel guests. They also attacked Arabs. Both sides retaliated: the British by hanging a few Jewish terrorists, the Arabs by attacking Jewish settlements. At the same time Haganah prepared for war against the Arab League countries which pledged support for the Palestinians. Sporadic Irgun/Stern terrorism continued as the British referred the problem to the United Nations, which on 29 November 1947 voted for partition of the country, a solution the Arabs rejected. The British were scheduled to complete withdrawal in May 1948 and were witnesses, meantime, with more sympathy for Arabs than Jews, to the mobilization of the two sides. The Palestinians were badly led, poorly armed, demoralized and largely dependent on their neighbours for arms and, above all, intervention once the British departed. In fact, when the Jews declared the independent State of Israel on 14 May, they already had taken possession of the strategically important ports of Haifa and Jaffa and had secured strong positions against Syria and Egypt, as well as commanding the approaches to Jerusalem from Jordan. With the two sides already locked in a confused civil war, the first of the **Arab–Israeli Wars** commenced.

Italian–Austrian campaigns, 1915–18. Upon the outbreak of war between Italy and Austria on 23 May 1915, terrain confined operations to land. Italy attacked, with Gorizia as the primary objective and Vienna the dream destination. There ensued two and a half years of twelve doleful **Isonzo** battles, fought in one area because, almost everywhere else, mountains (**Mountain warfare**) precluded large-scale offensive operations. Naval operations in the Adriatic Sea were likewise confined, largely, to frequent engagements involving Austrian **cruisers** and **destroyers** that bombarded coastal targets and raided Adriatic convoys, as well as (more significantly from 1916) Austrian and German **submarines** that passed through the Straits of Otranto to attack Allied shipping in the Mediterranean.

Austrian strategy was defensive, mostly owing to overall weakness and her commitments in Russia. General **Conrad von Hötzendorf**, however, was determined in 1916 to impress the Germans with Austria's vigour and also punish Italy for originally deserting the Central Powers. He planned an attack southwards from Trentino down the Adige valley into the plains, with two armies achieving a useful superiority over First Italian Army. The Italians were well informed of the Austrian plan, however, which was long postponed and subject to fierce controversy within the Austrian higher command. Yet when it opened on 15 May the bombardment inflicted such heavy damage on the inadequately prepared Italian positions that First Italian Army broke as the Austrians poured down the Adige valley. General Luigi Cadorna began assembling a fresh army to prevent a breakthrough into the plains. Fortunately for him the Austrian Command vacillated and carried out an unnecessary regrouping which caused loss of momentum. Frantically the Italians built up their defences to bar the predictable Austrian axes of advance. On 17 June the Austrians stalled 15 miles from the start line, partly owing to resistance but also because the **Brusilov Offensive** had routed the Austrians in Russia. Conrad called off the offensive and withdrew to a secure position. The Italians had suffered 147,000 casualties (including 40,000 prisoners), the Austrians 81,000 (including 26,000 prisoners).

Twice more the Austrians attacked in Italy, first at **Caporetto** in October 1917, once again to be frustrated, this time along the line of the Piave after a remarkable Italian recovery from rout. Next, also on the Piave on 15 June, with a double-pronged offensive designed to support the **Hindenburg Offensive** in France. This met fierce resistance, which blunted the right prong, while flooding of the Piave, which swept away bridges, stifled initial progress as air attacks on ravaged overstrained Austrian supply lines smashed the left prong.

By 23 October, with the Germans reeling back in France and the Austrian government seeking peace, an offensive, led by Italian troops, with British, French and American formations intermingled, soon overcame initially strong resistance in what is known as the Battle of Vittorio Veneto. As the Austrians disintegrated, the Allies poured forward, capturing some 300,000 prisoners before an Armistice on 3 November.

Italian campaign, 1943–5. When at the Casablanca Conference in January 1943 the British persuaded the Americans that an invasion of France was impossible that year, the decision was taken to invade **Sicily** soon after **North Africa** had been cleared of the Axis. The decision to invade mainland Italy followed once success was assured in Sicily. Within 24 hours of **Mussolini's** fall on 25 July, General **Eisenhower** ordered General **Clark** (Fifth (US) Army) to prepare for a landing on 7 September to take Naples – the place chosen being **Salerno**. Already a landing on the toe of Italy by General **Montgomery's** Eighth (British) Army had been projected and this was now confirmed, and eventually carried out on 3 September. By then, however, secret negotiations between the Allies and the Italian government under Marshal **Badoglio** had arranged an armistice which became effective on 8 September and which, in June 1944, allowed Italy to become a 'co-belligerent' of the Allies.

Guessing what the Allies might do was but one of Field Marshal **Kesselring's** tasks as German C-in-C South. He had also to cope with the subterfuges of his Italian allies in Rome, the fulminating irrationality of **Hitler**, the conniving of Field Marshal **Rommel** (who was after his job) as well as preparing for both disarming the Italians and meeting an **amphibious** invasion. In due course the Italians and Allies outsmarted him with an armistice, but he largely had his way with Hitler and, in October, would be preferred by Hitler to Rommel. When the armistice was announced the Germans brilliantly disarmed most of the Italian Army and Air Force, but let slip several warships, although sinking the battleship *Roma* by guided missile (**Rockets and guided missiles**). They also correctly foresaw the landings on the toe (and withdrew to plan), and the Salerno landing, which they resisted fiercely. But having lost at Salerno, Kesselring was compelled to begin the superbly conducted, slow withdrawal into the **Gustav Line** for the prolonged defence of Rome. At the same time he

applauded the successful German ripostes in the Italian Dodecanese Islands where several British lodgements in September had been eliminated by 16 November.

To the Allies the Italian campaign was an important diversionary operation to sap German strength prior to the **Normandy** landing in June 1944. To the Germans it was politically necessary to hang on, as well as militarily desirable to prevent the Allies establishing air bases within easy striking distance of Germany. But they did expend immense resources in a process which was seriously hampered by Allied air superiority and made even more tiresome and damaging by the need for ferocious counter-**guerrilla** operations against the bands which infested the countryside. Kesselring's withdrawal in the summer of 1944, through successive delaying positions until the Germans backed into the Gothic Line amid the Apennine Mountains on 3 September, was helped immensely by the defensive strength of the mountainous country. Only the coasts offered an open flank – which constantly worried Kesselring – of which (except at **Anzio**) the Allies under General **Alexander** took little advantage.

The higher priority in shipping and manpower allocated to Normandy and, in August, the landings in Southern France, reduced Alexander to bare essentials in the overcoming of successive German stop lines, which were prepared with extraordinary **engineering** skill. Progress slowed to a crawl through the outer works of the Gothic Line in steadily deteriorating weather with troops who were nearing exhaustion – and whose reinforcement was made almost impossible by the draining off of troops to **Greece** and **Yugoslavia**, where German withdrawals were releasing their troops to reinforce the Italian front. The end came on 22 October when a final last despairing push by Clark's Fifth Army failed to take the key city of Bologna, whereupon a winter's stalemate set in.

Not until 9 April 1945 were the Allies, by now comprising British, American, Commonwealth, Polish, Brazilian, Jewish and Italian troops, plus other Allied detachments, ready to complete the destruction of the Gothic Line and the enemy forces now under General Heinrich von Vietinghoff. An assault, initiated by Eighth Army across Lake Comacchio on the right, threatened the rear of the central Bologna sector which was broken into by Fifth Army on the

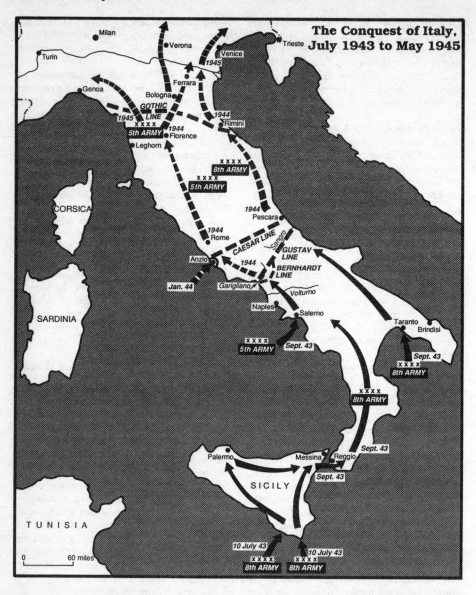

The Conquest of Italy, July 1943 to May 1945

14th. By the 20th the Germans were in full retreat everywhere to the River Po. Bologna fell to the Poles and Americans on the 22nd as Americans reached the Po at Ostiglia, and an Indian division entered Ferrara on the 23rd. There was then virtually nothing to prevent a crossing, followed by a full-blooded pursuit as a general uprising of Italians struck the Germans and their supporters. On the 26th Genoa fell

and Mussolini was murdered by partisans. The Piave was crossed on the 29th as von Vietinghoff negotiated an armistice. This came into force on 2 May when nearly one million Germans in Italy and Austria laid down their arms.

Italian wars of independence. The resurgence of Italian nationalism which followed the exclusion of France from Italian soil after the Napoleonic

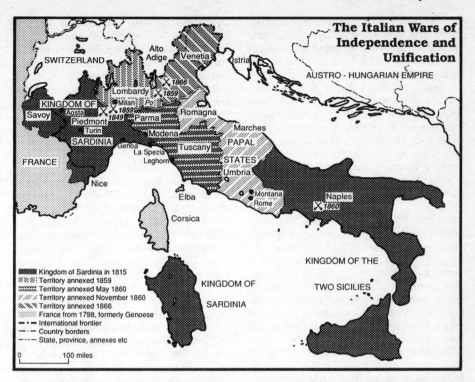

The Italian Wars of Independence and Unification

AUSTRO - HUNGARIAN EMPIRE

SWITZERLAND

Alto Adige

Venetia

Istria

Lombardy ✕ 1866
✕ 1859
Milan Po
KINGDOM OF
Savoy Aosta ✕ 1859
Piedmont ✕ 1849 Parma
Turin
SARDINIA Genoa
La Spezia
Leghorn
Modena
Tuscany
Romagna

Marches

PAPAL STATES

Umbria

FRANCE

Nice

Elba

Montana
Rome

Naples ✕ 1860

KINGDOM OF THE

Corsica

KINGDOM OF

SARDINIA

TWO SICILIES

▓▓ Kingdom of Sardinia in 1815
▨▨ Territory annexed 1859
▒▒ Territory annexed May 1860
▨▨ Territory annexed November 1860
▨▨ Territory annexed 1866
░░ France from 1798, formerly Genoese
━ ∙ ━ International frontier
━ ∙ ━ Country borders
━ ━ ━ State, province, annexes etc

0   100 miles

wars, focused chiefly upon the ejection of Austria from her occupation of Lombardy and Venetia. The siting of a French garrison in Ancona in 1832 created Austrian–French rivalry in Italy, underlying the events which came to a head in 1848, a turbulent, revolutionary year of disturbances throughout Europe and, notably, in Austria in March. When Austria displayed signs of military feebleness in Italy, Piedmont took the plunge and, with a weak army, attempted to seize Lombardy and Venetia. The nationalists were defeated at the first Battle of Custozza on 24 July by an Austrian army under Marshal Josef Radetzky. But, guided by Count Camillo Cavour, the Italian cause continued to flourish.

In the **Austro-Piedmontese War** of 1859, with French participation on Piedmont's side, Austria lost Lombardy to Piedmont and might have lost Venetia as well if the French had not, without telling Cavour, concluded a separate peace with Austria. In April 1860, however, a populist uprising in Naples (savagely suppressed) was revived in the aftermath of Giuseppe **Garibaldi**'s invasion of Sicily in May with his Redshirts (secretly sponsored by Cavour). His defeat of a Neapolitan force at Calatafini and Milazzo and his crossing, with British assistance, to the mainland, followed by the capture of Naples on 7 September, enabled Garibaldi to present Naples to King Victor Emmanuel of Piedmont. Piedmont thereupon, taking advantage of simmering revolts, took over the rest of what is modern Italy, except for Rome (which remained the Pope's with French support) and Austrian Venetia, permitting the proclamation of the Kingdom of Italy in 1861 under Victor Emmanuel.

Nevertheless a year later, Garibaldi's attempt (encouraged by Cavour with local patriots) to wrest Rome from the Pope and France was thwarted at the Battle of Aspromonte on 29 August – by the Italian Army! For suddenly Cavour had awoken to the danger of a collision with France, and also the menace of Garibaldi's popularity. Italy's independence was, indeed, won by devious means as well as much fighting – no small part of the latter incompetently managed. The treaty with Prussia in 1866, which was integrated with Otto von **Bismarck**'s contrived **Austro-Prussian War** to help secure Venetia, would have failed but for Prussia's defeat of Austria. For the Italian Army, 120,000 strong and ineptly led by Victor Emmanuel, suffered a second crushing defeat at Custozza by 80,000 Austrians. The Navy, too, was worsted at the Battle of Lissa; and another attempt by Garibaldi's 4,000 guerrillas to seize Rome was routed because they unwisely charged 3,000 Papal and 2,000 well-trained French troops at Mentana on 3 November.

When in 1870 Rome was incorporated into Italy it was again due to Prussia's efforts – her defeat of France in the Franco-Prussian War having deprived the Pope of French military and political support.

Italo-Greek War, 1940–43. Benito Mussolini's greed, plus his anxiety to demonstrate independence from Hitler, prompted him to launch an invasion of Greece (see Greece, Invasions of) from Albania on 28 October 1940. Lacking surprise and with only 162,000 none too well-equipped or led troops against 150,000 Greeks, expertly deployed in the mountains by General Alexandros Papagos, the Italians never had much hope of overrunning the country. Indeed, as Britain came to Greece's aid with naval and air forces, the Greek Army quickly checked the Italians and then unleashed a counter-offensive on 22 November. This chased the disillusioned Italians back into Albania with the loss of much equipment and many soldiers. A struggle in the mountains for possession of the port of Valona continued to mutual exhaustion throughout the winter. Meanwhile the political crisis and likelihood of German intervention in the Balkans increased. The British Army arrived in March, just in time to meet the German invasion which struck the Metaxas Line defending Salonika on 6 April, and then swung westwards to envelop the Greek Army as it withdrew before the Italians from Albania. By the 20th Papagos was on the verge of encirclement and urging the British, from whom he was isolated, to evacuate. On the 23rd Papagos's army surrendered to the Germans and Italians: the prelude to British evacuation from Greece, to Axis occupation and resistance by sporadic guerrilla warfare.

Italian occupation forces on the mainland and throughout the islands of Greece were never at ease with the population and perpetually involved in the political imbroglio of the nascent Greek Civil War simmering among rival Greek resistance movements. Local arms deals were arranged to play Greek against Greek. Germans and Italians often were at cross-purposes. Greek partisans regarded all and sundry as suppliers of arms by any means. When Italy left the Axis in September 1943 and the Allies instructed the Italian Army to resist German attempts at disarmament, it was the Germans who prevailed. They scooped most of the arms and prevented the Greeks from exacting a significant, last contribution from the now neutralized invaders of 1940.

Italo-Turkish War, 1911–12. The expansionist policies of Italian governments in the aftermath of independence, checked by the disastrous events in Ethiopia in 1896, began to revive after 1910 when Nationalist politicians favoured war as a means of asserting power. They believed that taking Libya by force from the fading Turkish Ottoman Empire would counterbalance France's presence in North Africa (in Morocco, Algeria and Tunisia) and also distract attention in 1911 from the government's difficulties at home. Without due consideration, Prime Minister Giovanni Giolitti used provocative incidents with the Turks as a pretext for declaration of war on 29 September. Simultaneously a naval bombardment of Preveza, on the Epirus coast, and the sinking of Turkish torpedo-boats removed any threat to Italy's sea lines of communication.

On 3 October the Italian Fleet bombarded Tripoli and on the 5th sailors occupied the capital with little resistance. The previous day a similar coup had seized Tobruk and soon all ports – Homs, Derna and Benghazi – had been secured. It was six days, however, before the Italian Army arrived, by which time the Turks, whose resistance had been desultory, were beginning to concentrate and, furthermore, stir up their Arab Muslim army to sterner resistance. Use by the Italians of nine aircraft and two airships for reconnaissance and bomb-dropping, the first example of air warfare, caused more alarm than despondency to the Turks. For the Italians were quite unready for desert war at such short notice, as soon became apparent, enabling the Turks to operate freely inland, inflicting heavy losses, while pinning the Italians to the coast.

Not until July 1912 were the Italians ready to bring the outnumbered Turks to battle and win decisively at Derna and Sidi Bilal. These victories coincided with the threat of the **Balkan Wars** and Turkey's urgent need for peace with Italy, a peace she bought by surrendering Libya, Rhodes and the Dodecanese Islands by treaty on 15 October.

Iwojima, Battle of. This volcanic island of eight square miles, located 700 miles from Saipan and Tokyo, was strategically vital to the Battle of **Japan** since its two airfields, with a third under construction, were crucial for Japan's air defence as well as an essential staging base for American bombers and fighters. It could not, like so many other islands, be bypassed, and was always a prime American objective, though heavily fortified by the Japanese with a garrison of 23,000. The US Navy began sporadic bombardments in November 1944 and these built up to a non-stop, three-day pounding between 16 and 19 February 1945.

Two **Marine** divisions landed on 19 March and were heavily engaged by all arms fired from bunkers. But by the end of the first day 30,000 men and nearly all their heavy equipment, including tanks, were ashore. From then on it was a grim business of locating and, position by position, killing every Japanese on the island except the 1,083 who surrendered. On the 23rd the key Mount Suribachi was taken; on the 25th a third Marine division came ashore; and by 1 March both airfields were in Marine hands, able to receive two B29 bombers on the 4th. Not until 26 March was the last pocket of resistance cleaned up, by which time American casualties amounted to 6,281 dead and 18,000 wounded.

On 7 April 108 **fighters** flew the first escorted mission of bombers to Japan. By the war's end 2,251 B29s made emergency landings there, possibly saving nearly 25,000 airmen's lives.

J

Japan, Battle of. The first direct attack on Japan took place on 18 April 1942 when 16 B25 Mitchell medium bombers, launched from the US **aircraft-carrier** *Hornet*, bombed Tokyo. Material damage was slight, but the impact on Japanese and American morale considerable.

From the outset the Americans determined to wreck Japan with a campaign of **strategic bombing**, using their chosen instrument, the B29 **bomber** with its 30,000ft ceiling, 3,250 miles range and 20,000lb maximum bomb-load. It was intended to base the aircraft at Chengtu, in China, and on Saipan Island in the **Marianas** (once it had been secured) which, respectively, were 1,550 and 1,400 miles from Japan. The Chengtu B29s opened their attacks on Japan with a night raid on 15 June 1944, but in the months to come would also hit targets in Manchuria, Formosa and Hanchow. Overall they were not a success, bedevilled as they were by target-finding difficulties, frequent engine failure and **logistic** difficulties which reduced the number of missions. Losses also were heavy – about 18 per cent, including a few from deliberate ramming.

Operations from Saipan began on 24 November, aimed at the Japanese aircraft industry. They were only moderately succesful even though the Japanese air defences, lacking **radar**, made only a patchy impression. But so effective were seven Japanese air attacks from **Iwojima** on Saipan's airfields that occsionally the B29s were diverted to attack that target as a defensive measure. Gradually the Americans improved their techniques, but the most damaging raid prior to 9 March 1945 was by Naval **aircraft-carrier** bombers against the Tokyo area on 16 and 17 February, which destroyed 200 Japanese

aircraft against the loss of 60 machines to much improved Japanese air defences. On 9 March, however, the B29s began night area attacks with incendiary bombs on Tokyo and other major cities and with devastating results. Several B29s were lost to gunfire but the Japanese night fighters made no interceptions. A month later, once Iwojima began operating fighters, the offensive was pressed home also by day, supplemented by carrier-borne aircraft and, towards the end, by medium bombers from **Okinawa**. They laid waste to Japan as her defences, deprived of sufficient fuel for outclassed fighters, crumbled. The dropping of **atom bombs** on Hiroshima and Nagasaki in August merely underlined the hopelessness of Japan's condition and made it easier for her to sue for peace.

Japanese wars of expansion. Having resisted repeated efforts by foreigners to form trade and diplomatic relations with her, Japan bowed to pressure by the American Commodore Matthew Perry in 1853 and signed treaties of collaboration with the USA (and other powers too), thus prompting a modernization and industrialization which steadily gained momentum despite much internal unrest during the 1860s. The assumption of power by Emperor Mutsuhito in 1869 and the rescinding of self-isolation imposed since the 17th century were reflected in 1874 by punitive raids against **Formosa** and in 1875–6 by the imposition by force of a trade relationship with Korea. An outward-looking adventurousness grew into a habit as Japan studied Western ways and flexed her muscles, equipping her Navy and Army with the latest weapons. Between 1882 and 1885 she entered

Korea and came into diplomatic collision with the Chinese. Tension mounted until 1894, when the Japanese provoked the **Chinese–Japanese War** which ended very satisfactorily for Japan with the acquisition of Formosa, the Pescadore islands and the Liaotung Peninsula with **Port Arthur**. Of far greater significance, Japan's rulers awoke to a destiny of expansion – one stimulated by antagonism when Russia grabbed Port Arthur for her own purposes.

The **Russo-Japanese War** in 1904 was an act of Japanese vengeance and shrewd military realism reflecting the need to strike before the Trans-Siberian Railway was completed to Russia's immense strategic and logistic advantage. Victory won more than territorial advantages: Port Arthur, the southern half of the island of Sakhalin and a free hand in Korea, which they annexed in 1909, imposing military rule. It inflated their predatory ego and won them immense prestige, along with time to study the lessons of their wars, and also to develop their own military doctrine and weapons technology instead of slavishly copying Western ideas. Still the Japanese played a small part on the Allied side in **World War I**, emerging in possession of several strategic North Pacific islands previously in German possession, plus vital spheres of influence in Manchuria, Shantung and Fukien. Thus, with only a few shots, they obtained footholds on the mainland (to the alarm of China) and control over their own seaward approaches – setting them on a collision course with the USA as it too expanded.

Japan acquired an overpoweringly obsessive ambition to dominate the Far East by force of arms – yet lacked certain fundamental material resources. For no matter how sacrificial her fighting men, how technically wonderful the naval and air fleets she built after World War I, and how modern the techniques she learned so avidly, fundamental deficiencies in **electronics** and, most serious of all, indigenous supplies of base metals and oil fuel were potentially crippling. For, when developing the naval and air forces deemed necessary to expand in Asia and hold the Americans and British at arm's length, even if Japan could acquire parity in **battleships** in the 1920s and did achieve an advantage with **aircraft-carriers**, the situation was likely to arise when her opponents could impose a complete check by cutting off oil supplies.

That situation grew closer with every move in the **Chinese–Japanese War** from 1937 onwards, and could no longer be ignored when, in 1940, German victories in Europe presented a unique opportunity to strike southwards to seize the oil of the East Indies. For with America on the eve of vast rearmament and already in 1940 threatening Japan with an oil embargo to curb her ambitions, it was then or never. Yet, as Admiral **Yamamoto** knew when plans to destroy the American, British and Dutch fleets were under consideration, it was a gamble. For 18 months he might give the Allies hell. But unless oil stocks were seized at once serious consequences would ensue. With that philosophy Japan struck on 7 December 1941 at **Pearl Harbor**, at **Malaya** and through the **Java Sea** to the Solomon Islands; westwards into **Burma**, the **Indian Ocean** and towards **Madagascar**, and north-eastwards to the **Aleutians**. A colossal expansion which cost rather more in fuel stocks and shipping than expected and failed utterly to cripple the enemy, but which did place Japan in possession of enormous oil stocks and other vital materials.

Thereafter, it was contraction all the way for Japan. The squeeze began in the **Coral Sea** and at **Midway** and gradually increased in pressure after the American landing at **Guadalcanal** in August 1942, followed by the eventual American victory of the **Solomon Islands**. The destruction in these battles of the cream of Japanese naval and air forces made inevitable the ensuing débâcle as massive Allied forces closed in upon Japan itself. The converging of Allied forces on the **Philippines** in October 1944 from Australia and **New Guinea** in the south, and island-hopping across the **Pacific Ocean** from Hawaii, together with victories in Burma and a check in China, all spelt doom for Japan, a doom ensured by the **blockade** imposed by air power and **submarines**, which denied industry the raw materials won by conquest; and guaranteed by American heavy bombers based in China, Saipan and **Iwojima** as they began the Battle of **Japan** in 1944 with a devastating campaign of **strategic bombing**.

The supreme irony is that since **World War II** the Japanese recovery, so powerfully stimulated by American aid, has brought about a peaceful, world-wide expansion such as the originators of her military expansion could never have dreamed of: an economic aggrandizement achieved by unchanged ruthlessness. Yet Japan still lacks her own basic materials, the import of which can so easily be blockaded.

Java Sea, Battle of the. After the fall of **Malaya** and **Singapore** in 1942, the Japanese Navy hunted American, British and Dutch **cruisers** and **destroyers** at the same time as they escorted the **amphibious** forces tasked to seize the Dutch East Indies. Backed up by **aircraft-carriers**, Japanese cruisers and destroyers failed to prevent the loss of four transports off Balikpapan on 23 January but on 4 February in the Madoera Strait, the 13th and 14th off Palembang and on the 19th and 20th in Bandoeng Strait, managed to whittle away enemy ships while safeguarding their convoys, soon to complete the conquest of **Sumatra and Java.** On the 27th a climax was reached when four Japanese cruisers and 13 destroyers, firing the excellent Long Lance **torpedoes** for the first time, fought and won a seven-hour battle against five Allied cruisers and 10 destroyers, which resulted in the loss of all bar two Allied cruisers and five destroyers. The disaster was compounded next day when both cruisers and another destroyer were put down when making a do-or-die attack upon a heavily escorted convoy off Banten Bay. Nine days later organized resistance in the East Indies came to an end.

Jeep. Supposedly originating from 'GP' (General Purpose), the word has passed into the language as describing any small four-wheel-drive vehicle. The Jeep emerged as the result of a US Army requirement in 1940 for a small vehicle seating three passengers and with room for a 0·30in machine-gun mount. Willys-Overland won the contract, producing a four-seat vehicle which saw service in all theatres of **World War II**, being used for reconnaissance, raiding, casualty evacuation, signals and many other tasks. Some 600,000 were built by 1945 and no subsequent equivalent has quite matched the simple ruggedness of this unique vehicle.

Jellicoe, Admiral Sir (Earl) John (1859–1935). A Royal Navy **gunnery** specialist who played an important role in developing long-range shooting at sea. Shortly after the outbreak of **World War I** he assumed command of the Grand Fleet, which he led at the Battle of **Jutland**. It was his misfortune that, having brilliantly lured the German High Seas Fleet into a deadly trap, he

was denied the fruits of victory by inadequate transmission of vital **intelligence** and the shortcomings of his fleet in relaying signals and in night fighting. Made First Sea Lord at the end of 1916, he obdurately refused, against the evidence of **operational analysis**, to institute the **convoy** system to combat the **submarine** threat. He had to be overruled by the Prime Minister, who removed him from office at the end of 1917.

Jet engines. See **Turbines**.

Jodl, General Alfred (1890–1946). A German artillerist who became Chief of the Wehrmacht Operations Staff in 1939 and thus principal military adviser to **Hitler**, a position he held throughout **World War II**. A most able staff officer with probably the best military brain in Hitler's entourage, he early on fell under the spell of the dictator, whose will he always declined to resist; as a result he frequently signed orders contrary to international law. He was tried, found guilty of **war crimes** at Nürnberg and hanged.

Joffre, Marshal Joseph (1852–1931). A Sapper who took part in the Siege of **Paris** prior to serving in many parts of the French Empire. In 1911 he was made Chief of Staff over the heads of others because he was rated a safe Republican. He was responsible therefore for the faulty Plan XVII adopted at the outset of **World War I**, and when that was defeated magnificently rallied the Allied Armies to win the Battle of the **Marne**. When the stalemate of siege and trench warfare set in along the Western Front in October 1914, he was tasked to clear France of the Germans, but the job proved beyond him with the resources at his disposal. Only his high prestige kept him in place. He was none too receptive to such new ideas as **tanks**, preferring the traditional use of fire-power and sapping to achieve a breakthrough – and exhausting the French Army in the process. As the enormous casualty list increased throughout 1915 and 1916 his authority waned, and he was replaced in December 1916.

Jungle warfare. The techniques of fighting among dense forests are as old as mankind, but have only received special attention since the **Spanish–American War** of 1898. In the past numerous small colonial campaigns against jungle tribes had nevertheless invariably emphasized: the tactical problems of fighting at extremely close ranges against a completely concealed enemy; the menace to **health** in regions where disease was rampant; and the **logistic** and **engineering** difficulties, which could be crippling. Indeed, the main differences between the enervating jungle wars of the 20th century and those of the past was the increase in scale and, as a result of the latest demands of humanitarianism associated with higher valuations of life, the need to take greater care of soldiers. The American soldiers sent in haste to fight in Cuba were ill-clad for the conditions and unprotected against the ravages of malaria and yellow fever. But, as experience was gained in their successive involvements in **Central America**, they were better prepared to cope with the fundamental problems.

World War I provided only one major example of jungle warfare, in **East Africa**, where for four years the Germans waged a **guerrilla** war in which the jungle provided a vast hiding-place. The campaign absorbed some 160,000 British troops at a cost of about 18,000 casualties, plus some 50,000 dead black Africans at a price to the Germans of 18,000 soldiers and 7,000 labourers. In the struggle disease accounted for many more deaths than did wounds.

World War II was abundant in jungle warfare, once the Japanese expanded into South-East Asia and the Pacific islands. For an urban nation, too, they demonstrated remarkable adaptability to the conditions and tactically outmanoeuvred their opponents by outflanking movements, closely supported by engineering effort, through deep jungle. Their conquests of **Malaya**, the Dutch East Indies and **Burma** in 1942 were largely the result of these psychologically unsettling methods against opponents who were mentally unprepared for the circumstances. These threats were only thoroughly overcome when, in 1943, Allied troops had been taught how to move and live in the claustrophobic jungle; and when reliable supply by air drop into clearings did away with the need to react to outflanking – a logistic answer to a tactical problem, one that exploited a campaign of long duration in hostile terrain for which the Japanese were less well prepared medically than their enemies.

The lessons of World War II were carried forward into the **cold** and **limited wars** to come.

All the contestants who survived prolonged periods of combat in **Indonesia, Malaya, Vietnam**, the **Philippines, East Africa** and **Central America** drew on well-recorded past experience for survival. There are few other military activities which require more careful and thorough **training** and acclimatization.

Jutland, Battle of. The Germans' realization at the start of **World War I** that they were outmatched at sea, plus the failure of their limited **submarine** campaign in 1915, pushed their naval command to the conclusion that only by a strategy of attrition might they wear down the Royal Navy and perhaps loosen the Allied **blockade**. A new C-in-C, Vice-Admiral Reinhard Scheer, planned in February 1916 to lure a portion of the British Grand Fleet into a trap against the High Seas Fleet. At the same moment Admiral **Jellicoe** was prepared to seek battle, provided the conditions were not dangerously adverse. In taking risks, Jellicoe had the advantage of superior **communications** and **intelligence**, with the capability of reading the German intentions through possession of their **codes**. Thus when German light forces, and later the High Seas Fleet, began sweeps across the North Sea, Jellicoe was always able to have overwhelming, undisclosed forces at sea to meet them – though several times missing contact.

Despite **radio** deception measures, overall British Intelligence told them the Germans were preparing for sea on 30 May, with the result that their ships left port two hours ahead of the Germans. Both sides led with their **battle-cruiser** squadrons (nine British ships against five German). When making contact in mid-afternoon 31 May, Admiral **Beatty** was not aware that the High Seas Fleet was at sea and Scheer was unaware that the British were near, since his Zeppelins had not spotted them and he had discounted submarine sighting reports. Admiral **Hipper** ran before Beatty to lure him on to the High Seas Fleet and, by superior **gunnery** with better **ammunition**, caused two battle-cruisers to blow up. At 1630hrs Beatty's scouting **cruisers** found the High Seas Fleet, causing Beatty to reverse course and speed northwards, pursued by the Germans – straight into Jellicoe's 28 **battleships**. By 1735hrs, when the Grand Fleet was almost in sight, Beatty had inflicted considerable damage on all but one of Hipper's battle-cruisers (including a **torpedo** hit from a **destroyer**).

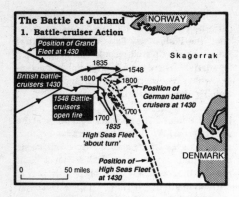

The Battle of Jutland
1. Battle-cruiser Action

NORWAY

Position of Grand Fleet at 1430

Skagerrak

1835

1548

British battle-cruisers 1430

1800

1800

Position of German battle-cruisers at 1430

1548 Battle-cruisers open fire

1700

1700

1835

High Seas Fleet 'about turn'

Position of High Seas Fleet at 1430

DENMARK

0 — 50 miles

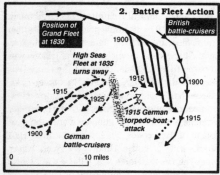

2. Battle Fleet Action

Position of Grand Fleet at 1830

British battle-cruisers

1900

High Seas Fleet at 1835 turns away

1915

1915

1925

1900

1915 German torpedo-boat attack

1900

German battle-cruisers

1915

0 — 10 miles

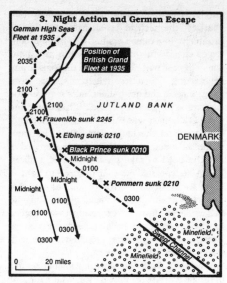

3. Night Action and German Escape

German High Seas Fleet at 1935

2035

2100

2100

2100

Position of British Grand Fleet at 1935

JUTLAND BANK

× Frauenlöb sunk 2245

× Elbing sunk 0210

DENMARK

× Black Prince sunk 0010

Midnight

0100

Midnight

Midnight

0100

0100

0300

0300

× Pommern sunk 0210

0300

Minefield

Swept Channel

Minefield

0 — 20 miles

But his reporting to Jellicoe was lax and it was only at 1800hrs that Jellicoe received accurate information of the enemy, enabling him to form line and steam across the approaching High Seas Fleet (crossing the T) to deluge it with shells. Scheer turned away to avoid annihilation of his 22 battleships, permitting Jellicoe to manoeuvre between the Germans and their ports as darkness drew near. When Scheer turned intuitively back against Jellicoe, to inflict further losses (including another battle-cruiser) and damage, it was only once more to run into a storm of fire from a better-placed Grand Fleet, which now had superior light conditions for gunnery. Again he was forced to turn away westwards, his retreat most valiantly covered by a charge from the four remaining battle-cruisers and by 17 destroyers. Only twice in this phase of the battle did the Germans score hits, whereas the British scored 19 as the Germans retreated into the gloom.

Jellicoe (who had not trained the Grand Fleet for night action) adopted a defensive formation, confident that the Germans had been cut off and could be overwhelmed the next day. During the night, despite numerous indications by sight and sound of engagements that the Germans were working their way past the rear of the Grand Fleet towards the safety of their minefield's swept channel, Jellicoe continued on a course which allowed Scheer to escape. In the dark only light British forces engaged. Lacking rehearsed and sound night-fighting techniques, they were fooled by the Germans (who were aware of the British signal challenges) and failed adequately to report what was happening around them. Furthermore, radio intercepts by the British Admiralty confirming Scheer's course were not passed on to Jellicoe. The result was that the Germans escaped with trivial losses.

Germany, whose losses in ratio to the British were in capital ships two to three, in cruisers four to three and destroyers five to eight, claimed a victory, though their battle-cruisers, with one exception, were in a very poor way. It would be August before they were ready again, whereas the British had merely to refuel and rearm to be at sea to continue the unrelenting blockade. When Scheer did make further break-out attempts on 18 August and 3 November 1916, and again in April 1918, it was to no real avail, and two battle-cruisers were torpedoed by British submarines on 19 August 1916. Inactivity therefore doomed the German navy to that steady decline in morale which ended in mutiny in November 1918, after one more foray had been mooted.

Kaffir Wars. Between 1779 and 1846 there were seven so-called wars between the white Dutch and British settlers in **South Africa** and the Xhosa branch of the indigenous black Bantu people – despised and called Kaffirs by the Boers. Really they were incidents in a continual struggle over seizures by the white settlers of land from the Xhosa, whose reactions usually took the form of extremely damaging **guerrilla** raids which the Boers, in particular, ruthlessly put down by superior firepower against tribesmen with spears.

The *Eighth War* (1850–53) was the most serious yet because the Xhosa massacred settlers and fought with the desperation of those fearing to lose everything: in fact they did lose most of their possessions and were penned into slums. Worse was to follow in 1857 when the Xhosa were persuaded by a priestess that, if they destroyed their own cattle and crops, their ancestors would return to help drive out the whites. Inevitably such deeply held religious convictions in the *Ninth War* created a desperate struggle in which disastrous Xhosa losses were caused far more by their self-induced famine than by the whites – and led to the creation of even worse slums as more Europeans poured in. The *Tenth War* in 1877 was a final uprising in which the Xhosa, with a lot more firearms, inflicted a great many casualties before the British overcame it. This time the Xhosa lost such independence as they possessed in 'Kaffraria' and were completely disarmed at a time of tension when a **Zulu War** loomed and Anglo-Boer frictions were worsening.

Kamikaze operations. The Japanese word 'kamikaze' means 'heavenly wind' (after a typhoon in 1570 which wrecked a Chinese invasion fleet). In June 1944 it described Japanese pilots recruited by Captain Jyo Eiichio to crash-dive on to enemy ships, particularly **aircraft-carriers**, as the most likely way of destroying the vastly superior Allied navies. Although the method complied with the martial spirit of *bushido*, it was not adopted by the Japanese until the aftermath of the Battle of **Leyte Gulf** – thus forfeiting a golden opportunity to inflict possibly decisive damage on the American Fleet during that crucial encounter. For when the kamikaze pilots struck at carriers on 25 October, they sank one and seriously damaged four more within four hours – a higher success rate than achieved throughout the foregoing, massed air attacks on the Seventh Fleet. In the months to come they caused immense damage to material and **morale**. By 12 December seven heavy carriers and 16 other ships were damaged and seven others sunk. On 9 January 1945 34 hits from 100 kamikaze aircraft put down one carrier and damaged four more; there were similar results off **Okinawa** when 355 suicide sorties launched on 6 April alone scored 28 hits and sank six ships, despite intense, improved defensive measures. To these can be added a few B29s brought down by ramming during the Battle of **Japan**. In effect, kamikazes were relatively economic human **guided missiles**, impervious to electronic jamming.

Kasserine Pass, Battle of. As a final fling to delay the Allied conquest of **North Africa**, the Axis launched a series of spoiling offensives in Tunisia. On 18 January 1943, General Jurgen von Arnim raided south from Pont du Fahs and routed French troops before being checked by the British and Americans. A month later he

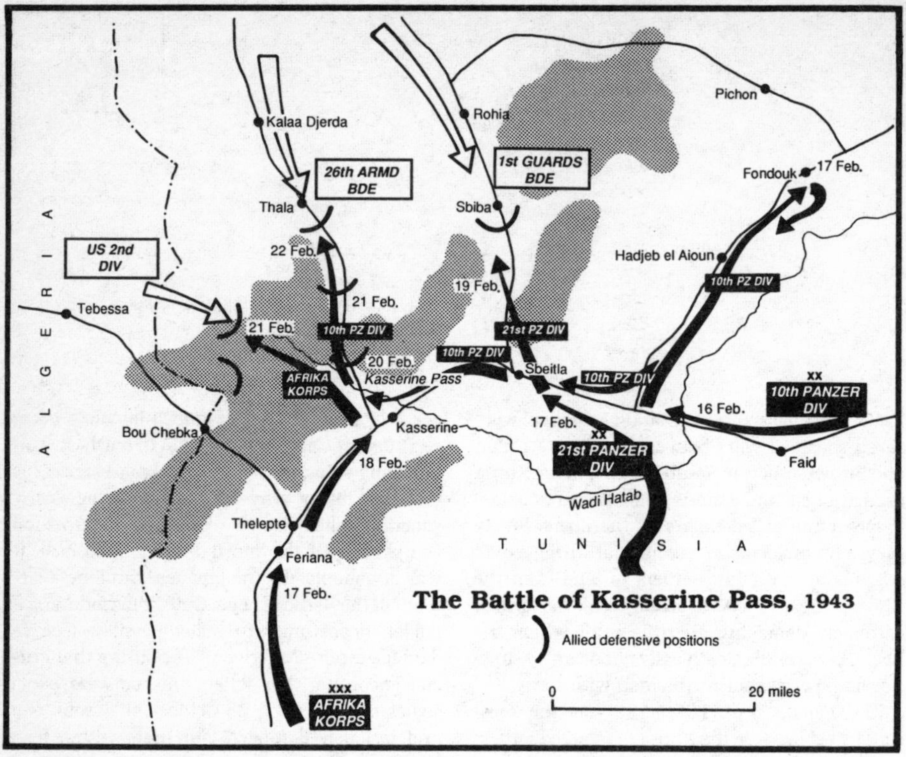
Pichon
Rohia
Kalaa Djerda
26th ARMD BDE
1st GUARDS BDE
Fondouk
17 Feb.
Thala
Sbiba
22 Feb.
Hadjeb el Aioun
US 2nd DIV
19 Feb.
21 Feb.
10th PZ DIV
Tebessa
21 Feb.
10th PZ DIV
21st PZ DIV
10th PZ DIV
20 Feb.
AFRIKA KORPS
Kasserine Pass
Sbeitla
10th PZ DIV
XX
10th PANZER DIV
16 Feb.
Kasserine
17 Feb.
XX
21st PANZER DIV
Bou Chebka
18 Feb.
Faid
Wadi Hatab
Thelepte
ALGERIA
TUNISIA
Feriana
17 Feb.
Allied defensive positions
0
20 miles
XXX
AFRIKA KORPS
The Battle of Kasserine Pass, 1943

threw two Panzer divisions against 1st (US) Armored Division at Sidi Bou Zid, overran it by sheer violence of attack and drove what was left eastwards towards Sbeitla and Kasserine. Meanwhile the German Afrika Korps, commanded by Field Marshal **Rommel**, also advanced towards Kasserine from the south, brushing aside scattered resistance. He then proposed to Field Marshal **Kesselring** a deep penetration into the enemy rear, via Kasserine Pass and Thala, to envelop the Allied armies in Tunisia. Von Arnim was loath to collaborate with Rommel's risky scheme. He doubted Axis (in practice, German) strength to carry it out; and preferred his own plan for another spoiling attack in the north. The Axis chain of command was weak. Kesselring was unable to compel von Arnim to give full support, but he encouraged Rommel to make the attempt with a mere two, understrength Panzer divisions, from which von Arnim withheld some tanks.

Meanwhile General **Eisenhower** had been sending strong reinforcements to block the anticipated thrust. They were too late to prevent Rommel overrunning the demoralized American defenders of the Pass and from rushing northwards on 19 February, but on the 21st he was stopped by British tanks and infantry, supported by American artillery, at Thala and also by US troops near the Djebel El Hanra. At once a disheartened Rommel admitted defeat and withdrew to prepare an attack elsewhere, while von Arnim pursued his own designs.

Keitel, Field Marshal Wilhelm (1882–1946). An artillerist who, because of his habitual compliance, was chosen by **Hitler** in 1938 as Chief of Staff of the Wehrmacht (German Armed Forces). A third-rate staff officer, he held this key position throughout **World War II** by toadying to Hitler's slightest whim and by gross flattery. Never did Keitel oppose Hitler's errors and misjudgements, even when he recognized their enormity. He signed many orders for the execution of hostages, contrary to international law, and sat on the 'Court of Honour' examining officers involved in the attempted assassination of Hitler in July 1944. At the Nürnberg Trial he was found guilty of planning a war of aggression, of war crimes and crimes against humanity, sentenced to death and hanged.

Kemal Atatürk, General Mustafa (1881–1938). A brilliant mathematician and staff officer who became the Father of modern Turkey after **World War I**. He served in Libya during the **Italo-Turkish War** of 1911 and in the **Balkan War** of 1912. At **Gallipoli** in 1915 it was his leadership of 19th Division which largely frustrated the initial British landings. In 1916, having fallen out with the Turkish War Minister, Enver Pasha, he was sent to command in Anatolia where he defeated the Russians at Lake Van. In 1918 he extricated what was left of Seventh Army from defeat in Palestine. Henceforward he was deeply involved in Turkish politics, demanding independence from foreign influence. On 23 April 1920 he became President of Turkey and in the **Greek–Turkish War** of 1921–2 was also C-in-C of the forces which routed the Greeks. Until his death he worked frenetically, not only to rid Turkey of the corrupt Ottoman influence and to modernize the new Republic he had created, but also successfully to establish friendly relations with Turkey's enemies of World War I.

Kesselring, Field Marshal Albert (1885–1960). A brilliant artillerist and staff officer who won a reputation for colossal energy and powers of command and organization in **World War I** and afterwards was selected as a member of the élite Truppenamt. He played an important role in reorganizing the Reichswehr and laying the foundations of an Air Force (Luftwaffe) once Germany again was permitted one. When the secret Luftwaffe was formed it was Kesselring who, in 1933, was its Chief of Administration and who built it up until June 1936 when the Chief of Staff designate was killed in a crash. Kesselring took his place in August – fifteen days after the Luftwaffe's existence was announced. It was he, therefore, who shaped the new force for its wartime role as a tactical air force, shorn by him of **Douhet**'s theories and a **strategic bombing** role. He, too, steered it through the early days of combat involvement in the **Spanish Civil War**, before asking Hermann **Göring** for command of First Air Fleet in June 1937.

In this appointment he was responsible for the principal air effort in the **Polish campaign** of 1939, frequently debating matters with **Hitler**. Given command of Second Air Fleet in January 1940, he led it in the invasions of **Holland** and **France**, the Battle of **Britain** and in the first five months of the invasion of Russia (**Russo-German wars**) – operations in which it always was the predominant air element. But on 28 November 1941 Hitler made him C-in-C South, tasked to control German interests in the Mediterranean theatre where the war was not progressing in the Axis' favour. Henceforward his difficult task was to supply the **North Africa** battles and attempt by diplomacy to resolve German–Italian wrangles. In 1943 he increasingly took control in the withdrawal from Africa and the defence of **Sicily** and of Italy (**Italian campaign, 1943–5**), until given overall command in Italy in October, where he was to stay until appointed Commander Army Group West in March 1945 as the war drew to a close. He was made titular head of state in the south when Hitler was cornered in Berlin.

Tried for ordering the execution of partisans in Italy in 1944, the sentence of death was commuted to imprisonment. He was released in 1952.

Khalkin River, Battle of the. Long-running bellicosity, which flared in 1938, broke out into a four months' undeclared **Russo-Japanese War** in Outer Mongolia in May 1939. Contrary to orders, the Japanese Kanto Army in **Manchuria** attacked the Russians by air and seized a slice of Russian territory between the frontier and the Khalkin River. The Russians, under General Georgi **Zhukov**, were reinforced strongly and counter-attacked in June. By mid-August the Japanese, who had the better of heavy air fighting, had assembled three infantry divisions, 180 tanks, 500 guns and 450 aircraft against 100,000 Russians with 498 tanks (in five armoured brigades), strong artillery and 580 outclassed aircraft. The Japanese planned another attack for 24 August, but Zhukov struck on the 19th along the length of the front behind heavy bombing. An infantry grapple pinned the Japanese down as a prelude to the launching of Russian armoured forces round the Japanese flanks in a pincer movement which cut off the Japanese lining the river. Attack and counter-attack ensued at the pincer meeting-point. But ten days later the Russians, with losses of about 10,000, had won. The shaken Japanese lost about 18,000 men.

Kharkov, Battles of. As Russia's fifth largest industrial city, a vital route centre with a population of 352,000 in 1917, Kharkov was a strategic target in the **Russian Revolutionary War**. As capital of Ukraine it was both a rallying-point and capital for those wishing for an independent state; and for the Bolshevik, Red revolutionaries a base also against White counter-revolutionaries. This struggle was temporarily resolved in December 1917 when the Reds overcame the Ukrainians in the city and drove them westwards. But by June 1919, White armies (including such strong **guerrilla** forces as Nestor Makhno's) had routed the Reds and driven them from the city, which remained a hive of underground warfare until the Whites collapsed in 1920–21.

Kharkov ceased to be capital of the Ukraine in 1934. In October 1941, during **World War II**, it was defended temporarily by demoralized Russian troops while its industrial contents were evacuated. German occupation began at the end of October and lasted until 1943, despite major Russian offensives to retake it in January and May 1942, both of which started well but failed due to tardy exploitation. On the second occasion the recovering Germans were given a crowning opportunity to encircle a defeated enemy, whose weakening here contributed substantially to initial German success in the forthcoming advance towards **Stalingrad**.

Not until February 1943, following the German débâcle at Stalingrad, did the Russians re-enter the city, for a temporary stay. For Field Marshal von **Manstein**'s abandonment of it simply lured weakened Russian armies towards the River Dnieper, as prey to his brilliant counterstroke. This nipped off the Russian spearheads and bundled them out of the city on 14 March towards Belgorod and **Kursk**.

Defeat of the German offensive at **Kursk** in July was the prologue to the Russian counter-offensive, whose southern thrusts on 3 August headed straight for Kharkov. **Hitler** ordered that the strongly fortified city must be held, to bar the way further into Ukraine. Fighting on the outskirts began on 11 August as the Russians cut the main railway line to the west, and mounted in fury when the German SS Corps tried to recover the railway, while the city's garrison contracted under heavy pressure. From the 11th to the 20th the German counter-attacks continued to exhaustion against a numerically superior enemy. By the 22nd Kharkov was being bypassed on the grand scale and thus forfeiting its importance. That day the withdrawal order came, only hours before the Russians launched a furious night assault. Fighting went on at point-blank range by the light of burning ruins. By midday the 23rd the city was cleared, leaving a mass of prisoners and equipment in Russian hands.

Kiev, Battles of. Like **Kharkov**, Kiev suffered from the struggles of the **Russian Revolution**, but also was caught up in the **Russo-Polish War** of 1920. General **Piłsudski**'s Polish/Ukrainian forces occupied the city on 8 May 1920 and gave a boost to anti-Bolshevik sentiment. But the powerful Red counter-offensive on 15 May, which began to envelop the city from both flanks, forced the Poles to withdraw on 16 June, leaving the natives to the mercy of the Reds.

In **World War II**, Kiev, as Ukraine's capital since 1934, in 1941 was a prime objective of Field Marshal von **Rundstedt**'s Army Group South, its approach welcomed by many Ukrainians. The weaker of the three German Army Groups, it met some of the sturdiest resistance by Marshal Semen Budenny's strong South-West Army Group. Decisive, however, was **Hitler**'s change of plan in August when he diverted General **Guderian**'s Panzer Group from the advance against **Moscow** to have it converge on Kiev in combination with von Rundstedt's troops. Kiev fell on 21 September. Five days later over 600,000 surrounded Russians were netted, laying the rich eastern Ukraine open to conquest. But the war would continue.

Once the **Kursk** front had been broken open in July 1943 and Kharkov had fallen in August, the Russians were able to flood towards and across the River Dnieper no matter how well Field Marshal von **Manstein**'s defeated Army Group South fought. Kiev became the prime Russian objective once the river had been crossed lower down on 24 September. They considered its possession vital, as did the Germans. Regrouping and resupply delayed the Russian attack while the Germans reinforced the city and the river line. On 3 November the main assault, in overwhelming numbers, went across to the north of the city, in company with distractions to the flanks. Sheer weight of fire-power and numbers, along with scant regard for losses, ensured success. A devastated and looted city

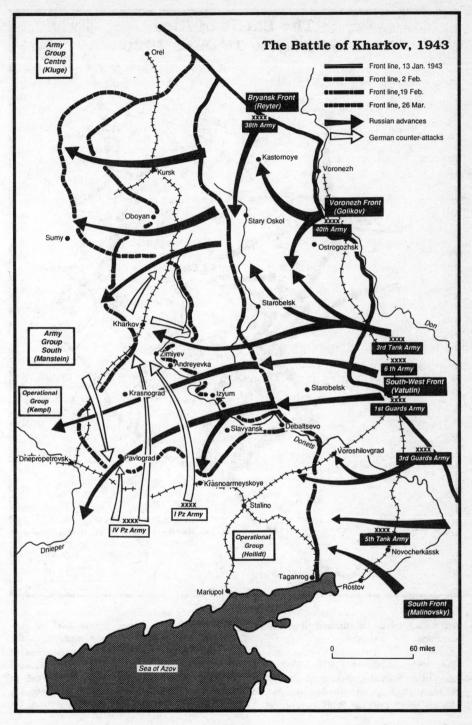

The Battle of Kharkov, 1943

Front line, 13 Jan. 1943
Front line, 2 Feb.
Front line, 19 Feb.
Front line, 26 Mar.
Russian advances
German counter-attacks

Army Group Centre (Kluge)

Orel

Bryansk Front (Reyter)
XXXX
38th Army

Kastornoye

Voronezh

Kursk

Voronezh Front (Golikov)
XXXX
40th Army

Oboyan

Stary Oskol

Ostrogozhsk

Sumy

Starobelsk

Don

Army Group South (Manstein)

Kharkov

XXXX
3rd Tank Army

Zimiyev
Andreyevka

XXXX
6th Army

Operational Group (Kempf)

Krasnograd

Izyum

Starobelsk

South-West Front (Vatutin)
XXXX
1st Guards Army

Slavyansk

Debaltsevo

Dnepropetrovsk

Pavlograd

Donets

Voroshilovgrad

XXXX
3rd Guards Army

Krasnoarmeyskoye

XXXX
I Pz Army

Stalino

Dnieper

XXXX
IV Pz Army

Operational Group (Hollidt)

XXXX
5th Tank Army

Novocherkassk

Taganrog

Rostov

Mariupol

South Front (Malinovsky)

0   60 miles

Sea of Azov

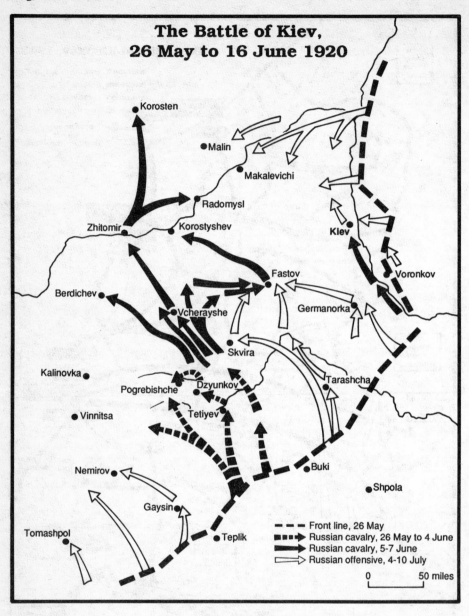

The Battle of Kiev,
26 May to 16 June 1920

Korosten

Malin

Makalevichi

Radomysl

Zhitomir

Korostyshev

Kiev

Voronkov

Berdichev

Fastov

Vcherayshe

Germanorka

Skvira

Kalinovka

Tarashcha

Pogrebishche

Dzyunkov

Vinnitsa

Tetiyev

Buki

Nemirov

Shpola

Gaysin

Tomashpol

Teplik

- - - Front line, 26 May
Russian cavalry, 26 May to 4 June
Russian cavalry, 5-7 June
Russian offensive, 4-10 July

0   50 miles

fell on the 6th with the elimination of numerous Germans.

King, Admiral Ernest (1878–1956). A US Navy officer who was rather more distinguished for his Anglophobia than his intellect. As C-in-C Atlantic Fleet prior to **Pearl Harbor**, he was responsible for defence against German **submarines** when the USA was involved in the Battle of the **Atlantic**. His unwillingness to adopt the **convoy** system, a refusal he persisted in after becoming Chief of Naval Staff in December 1941, had disastrous consequences for Allied shipping in the West Atlantic. A bully whom President **Roosevelt** treated with kid gloves, King fought tooth and nail against the US Army and the British to obtain priority for Navy operations in the **Pacific Ocean** campaign. To his credit goes the decision to invade **Guadalcanal** 'on a shoestring' in August 1942.

Kitchener, Field Marshal (Lord) Horatio (1850–1916). A Sapper who won praise for his performance during the **Sudan Campaigns** of 1884–5 and fame as C-in-C the Egyptian Army in the eventual crushing of the Mahdi's forces at Omdurman in 1898. As Chief of Staff and, subsequently, C-in-C British Army in South Africa during the Boer War (see **South African wars**), he won notoriety for an obdurate ruthlessness, as demonstrated by his ill-considered and disastrous overturning of the **logistics** organization, and the construction of badly administered **concentration camps** as a counter-guerrilla measure which so antagonized public and Boer opinion. His dictatorial behaviour nevertheless found favour in Britain (but not with the Viceroy of India) during his tenure as C-in-C India (1903–9). It was to popular acclaim that he was made Minister for War in 1914 on the outbreak of **World War I**.

Characteristically he upset current War Office planning by insisting the war would not be short but of at least three years' duration; and refusing to make use of the existing reserve force Territorial Army organization as the foundation of the great citizens' army he demanded – without careful study. Indeed he assumed dictatorial, over-centralized powers not only to direct military **strategy**, but also for the mobilization of the nation's industrial resources. The results were states of administrative, equipment and training chaos which were long in being overcome. Nevertheless, such was the people's adulation for this politically naïve man, but whose leadership of recruitment and national purpose was dynamic, that it was politically impossible to remove him. Instead the government sent him on a fact-finding journey to **Gallipoli** in May 1915 to advise on continuance of a campaign he disapproved of. It took the opportunity in his absence to strip him of many functions and much power, stopping short of sacking him. On 5 June 1916 he was drowned in a mined cruiser on a mission designed to help Russia out of her difficulties.

Kohima, Battle of. While the siege of **Imphal** was under way in April 1944 to halt the Japanese advance into India, an equally important siege to prevent the Japanese 31st Division (General Kotoku Sato) reaching the vital railhead at Dimapur was in progress at Kohima. Here the garrison consisted of a mere 1,500 men (including a single British infantry battalion), commanded by Colonel Hugh Richards. The Japanese began arriving piecemeal on 5 April, to be repulsed prior to carrying out their usual drill of encircling the close, hilltop perimeter and pressing on towards Dimapur. From the outset the fighting at Kohima was at close range with hand-to-hand combat and meagre but effective British artillery support from the village of Jotsoma. Throughout, the Japanese were denied sufficient forces by the need to divert troops to Imphal and towards Dimapur, where the British relief force was assembling. Supplied by air, the battered garrison was within a few hours of collapse on 18 April when, supported by a division's artillery, the leading relief battalion put in its final, successful assault. Kohima was now allowed to fall into Japanese hands, but their troops were exhausted and got no further. Indeed, they were soon almost besieged themselves when on 4 May, British and Indian outflanking attacks gradually made the place untenable, compelling the Japanese to withdraw on the 13th and opening the way for the relief of Imphal.

Korean Wars. It was Korea's misfortune to be caught in the cross-fire of Japanese and Chinese rivalry and thus to become, after occupation by Japan in 1894, a battleground in the **Chinese–Japanese War** of 1894–5. Likewise she was marched over during the **Russo-Japanese War** of 1904–5 and finished up under the Japanese heel until the close of **World War II**.

After she was overrun in 1945 (up to the 38th Parallel) by victorious Russian troops from Manchuria, she was partitioned into two zones. To the south US forces took the surrender of the Japanese; to the north the Russians, who converted their zone into a Communist state with Pyongyang as capital. On 15 August 1947 the South declared itself a republic, with Seoul as capital. No sooner had the US Army withdrawn in 1949 than the North exerted political, **propaganda** and **guerrilla** pressure upon the South, a campaign which culminated in a full-scale, Russian-equipped invasion with seven

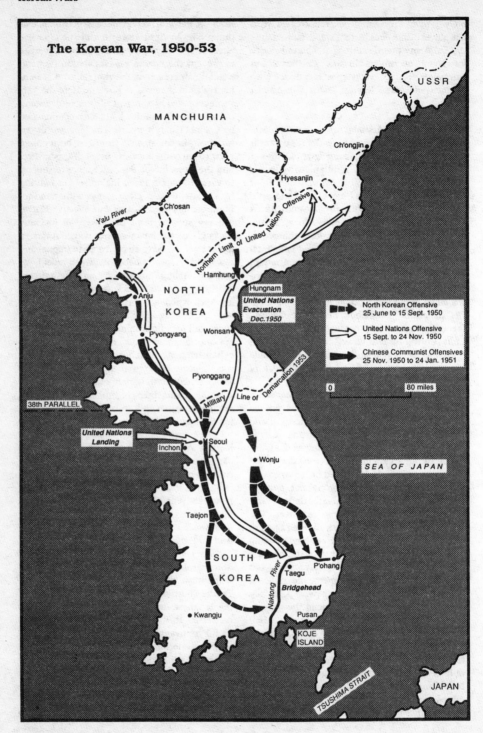

The Korean War, 1950-53

USSR

MANCHURIA

Ch'ongjin

Hyesanjin

Yalu River

Ch'osan

Northern Limit of United Nations Offensive

NORTH

Anju

KOREA

Hamhung

Hungnam

United Nations Evacuation Dec. 1950

P'yongyang

Wonsan

	North Korean Offensive 25 June to 15 Sept. 1950
	United Nations Offensive 15 Sept. to 24 Nov. 1950
	Chinese Communist Offensives 25 Nov. 1950 to 24 Jan. 1951

P'yonggang

Line of Demarcation 1953

0   80 miles

38th PARALLEL

Military

United Nations Landing

Inchon

Seoul

Wonju

SEA OF JAPAN

Taejon

SOUTH

KOREA

Naktong River

Taegu

P'ohang

Bridgehead

Kwangju

Pusan

KOJE ISLAND

TSUSHIMA STRAIT

JAPAN

infantry divisions and one armoured brigade of the North Korea Army (NKA) on 25 June 1950.

The Republic of Korea's (RoK) Army was newly formed, under-equipped and inadequately trained. The US troops who, under a United Nations resolution, began arriving piecemeal by air and sea on 30 June were unready for immediate combat. Seoul had fallen on the 28th when the RoK army withdrew in confusion. US troops came into action on 5 July near Osan and were almost annihilated when RoK troops gave way. There followed a none-too-orderly retreat towards the port of Pusan. On 7 July General MacArthur was appointed C-in-C United Nations Command and Eighth Army, consisting of American and RoK troops, plus a British brigade, was formed under General Walton Walker. The farther North Korean forces advanced the stronger the resistance they met from air attacks and the continually reinforced UN armies, until stalemate occurred around the Pusan perimeter.

Then came the Inchon battle in September, the UN advance to the Yalu River, the entry of China in the war in November and the UN retreat to the 38th Parallel, along with the epic Battle of Hungnam and the evacuation from Wonsan in December. In this period the UN forces again plumbed depths of demoralization, but in January 1951, when they bent once more under the weight of a renewed Chinese offensive and again lost Seoul, they reasserted themselves. Under General Matthew Ridgway (who took over when Walton was killed in an accident) they checked and threw back, almost to the 38th Parallel, a very brave opponent, who lacked sophisticated weapons and techniques.

Once more on 22 April the Chinese tried to break through on the west flank, but this time the UN forces had their enemy's measure and, except where an RoK division broke and the British 29 Brigade narrowly was saved from engulfment as it stolidly filled the gap, yielded ground grudgingly. Fighting continued across the front. On the east flank on 15 May, an RoK corps cracked but American troops restored the position by the 22nd and the UN launched a general counterstroke next day to roll the Chinese back to their start lines where both sides entrenched. The War's mobile phase was over. Until an armistice was arranged on 27 July 1953 the two sides glared at each other from deep emplacements, occasionally indulging in outbreaks of aggression which frequently were timed to coincide with critical stages of the peace negotiations, accompanied by endless propaganda, including unproven North Korean accusations of biological warfare by the UN.

Meanwhile sporadic naval warfare accompanied the UN blockade of North Korea and North Korean mining (Mine, Sea) operations (under Russian direction and often by sampan). Carrier-borne aircraft regularly struck the North, and helicopters were used to detect mines. Indeed, it was now that the helicopter demonstrated its versatility in rescue missions of airmen shot down behind the enemy lines; for command and control; and, above all, resupply and the evacuation of wounded. The principal air activity, however, was over the North where attacks on logistic and tactical targets during the mobile phases of the war were continuous. After 1950 the North Korean Air Force was wholly on the defensive and dog-fighting between Russian jet fighters (mostly piloted by Russians, Chinese and East Europeans) and US jets escorting bombers was confined to the region of the Yalu River. In these engagements the superiority of US Air Force and Allied training was repeatedly shown with a claimed ratio of ten to one in their favour. But the UN's losses of ground-attack aircraft were much heavier. From all causes UN losses were 1,213 aircraft between June 1950 and July 1953.

Kursk, Battles of. This important Russian route centre on the main railway line from Moscow to Kharkov and the Crimea fell into German hands without much resistance in October 1942 at a time the Russians were hard pressed to stay in World War II. It was retaken early in February 1943 as the Germans fell back precipitately after defeat at Stalingrad, but held as the centre of a salient formed in the aftermath of Field Marshal von Manstein's counterstroke in March, after the wet season put a stop to movement.

Von Manstein's aim was to pinch out the Kursk salient as soon as possible, before the Russians could fortify so obvious an objective. But when Hitler decided to augment this relatively limited operation to a major offensive with political overtones – and employ the latest, untried Tiger and Panther tanks in mass – delay was inevitable and surprise forfeited. Not until 5

189

July was a start made. By then the Russians, under General **Zhukov**, were forewarned and had assembled 1,330,000 men, 3,600 tanks, and nearly 20,000 guns behind deep defences to meet 900,000 Germans with 10,000 guns and 3,700 tanks. Each side also had about 2,500 aircraft. Predictably the Germans attacked the flanks of the salient to pinch it out. Always in control, the Russians snuffed out the northern pincer within hours and by 16 July had absorbed the southern thrust after an intense armoured struggle. On 10 July the Americans and British had landed in **Sicily** and on the 12th the Russians had begun their summer offensive at Bryansk. Hitler's decision to adopt defence was therefore inevitable as evidence of a massive Russian counterstroke at Kursk accumulated. From the very heavy losses in this, the last German offensive in the East, the German Army never recovered.

L

Landing-craft and ships. Until **World War II** very few specialized landing vessels for **amphibious warfare** had been developed. Before then, notably at **Gallipoli**, ships' rowing-boats were used – though in the initial landing a converted tramp steamer (*River Clyde*) was modified for an assault landing under fire after beaching. At the Zeebrugge raid in April 1918 troops were disembarked under fire on the mole from an adapted **cruiser**. Adaptation of craft such as barges and fishing-boats for beach landing was the Germans' chosen improvisation when preparing to invade Britain in 1940; but when Britain and the USA were faced with no alternative other than large-scale amphibious operations to defeat the Germans, Italians and Japanese, they were compelled to develop a considerable fleet of specialized vessels.

As a model, only faintly recognized, they had the Japanese, who had used special landing ships carrying mechanized, shallow-draught craft during their landings in China in the 1930s. Both the Americans and the British adopted such ships, mostly by conversion of seagoing ferries with strengthened davits, known as LSI (Landing Ship Infantry). Fast motor-launches were initially used by the British in 1940 for hit-and-run coastal raiding, and ramped, mechanized lighters to carry vehicles and stores ashore (LCM, Landing Craft Mechanized) – such as intended at **Dakar**. But it was 20-man, wooden, 5-tonne Higgins LCP (Landing Craft Personnel), speed 10 knots; and steel, partially armoured, 13-tonne LCA (Landing Craft Assault), speed 6–10 knots, which were used in very large numbers for raiding and by assault infantry. They were followed by 384-tonne, seagoing LCI (Landing Craft Infantry), speed 14 knots, which could embark about 200 men.

To get **tanks** and other vehicles ashore, LST (Landing Ship Tank) and LCT (Landing Craft Tank) were built. The first LSTs were converted cargo ships, but these could not function on sloping beaches in tidal conditions. The British developed a special ship whose draught could be adjusted by the flooding of ballast tanks – a method since employed by modern roll-on-roll-off ferries, which is what LSTs (with a displacement of anything between 1,600 and 5,000 tonnes) were. LCTs displacing some 500 to 600 tonnes were intended for use well forward in an assault, carrying five 40-tonne or eleven 30-tonne tanks, or ten 3-tonne lorries. Only partially armoured, it was often desirable for LCTs to launch amphibious tanks when well off shore. The Japanese used British-designed 3-tonne swimming tanks, but the British produced 30-tonne Sherman tanks (called DDs, from Duplex Drive), kept afloat by a collapsible screen and powered by twin screws driven by the tank's engine (via the rear idler).

Numerous variations of these basic landing vessels were produced to perform all manner of roles: beach survey and obstacle clearance; close fire support by guns and rockets; assistance with navigation; and a host of **logistic** tasks once a foothold had been secured ashore. Highly adaptable was the American amphibious wheeled DUKW, which carried a useful load and could drive on land without adjustment after swimming ashore, as too could the American Amtrac assault vehicles which were propelled through the water by their tracks and served as light tanks or armoured personnel carriers once ashore.

Since World War II landing vessels have been improved upon for both military and civil purposes, although to some extent the **helicopter** has supplanted them. To their number has been added **ground-effect machines** (often known as hovercraft), which can skim over almost any flat surface without changing mode and have many military uses.

Laser (*l*ight *a*mplification by *s*timulated *e*mission of *r*adiation). When atoms are stimulated to a higher level of activity than normal they emit light as they revert to their usual level. In ordinary light sources the atoms are randomly stimulated and consequently emit light independently. However, if all the atoms emit radiation in step with the stimulating wave, and if this effect can be sufficiently multiplied, the resulting beam of coherent light (i.e. at a single frequency) can be extremely powerful. This is the laser effect and the phenomenon was recognized by Einstein in 1917, though it was not until 1960 that the first practical laser was built by the American T. H. Maiman.

It was quickly recognized that the laser beam was able to burn through many materials and could cause serious injury to human tissue. There was much talk of its use as a 'death ray', but this was not a seriously pursued option; the first practical military application was as an extremely accurate **range-finder**. In the field of tank gunnery this made a dramatic impact since the problem of judging distance correctly had always far outweighed all other system difficulties. Lasers have likewise been used as markers to indicate the target for homing missiles.

The laser has also found a ready military application as a training aid. The British Simfire system uses a low-power ruby laser to trigger sensors mounted on vehicles, and even on infantrymen's helmets, when an 'enemy' weapon was correctly aligned on a target and the trigger pressed, the sensor in turn activating a smoke generator to indicate a hit. Simfire produced a realism in training previously unimagined and such systems are now widely used.

Law, Military. Most modern states have developed laws governing the discipline of their armed forces. Usually they are enacted by their national legislatures and are subordinate to the state's common law. Sailors, soldiers and airmen have more often than not been subject to separate disciplinary Acts, earlier known as the Articles of War, a term which largely went out of use by the mid 20th century. Current practice tends, as in the USA, towards a uniform code of military justice to enforce both civil and military law under military jurisdiction, with the proviso that a member of the armed services may be dealt with if required by a civil court. For example, a person found innocent by a British military court on a civil charge may be retried by the civil power – but not the other way about.

Military disciplinary Acts are designed to enforce the exacting conditions of armed forces service with its demands upon obedience and sacrifice of personal life and liberty. The Acts give powers to deal, in addition to civil offences, with military misdemeanours, such as desertion, dereliction of duty, disobedience, negligence, misuse or loss of equipment, and trivial untidiness. Besides authorizing the issue and implementation of regulations governing the Services, the Acts lay down procedures for the investigation of offences and their trial by military authorities. Usually minor offences are dealt with summarily by authorized officers granted limited powers of punishment by detention, extra duty, fines or admonishment. More serious cases are referred for trial by courts martial of varying status, depending upon the circumstances. Court procedures reflect civil practice. Finding and sentence (which can include the death penalty) usually are subject to confirmation by a superior authority and, if demanded, by appeal to a higher civil court.

Military law reflects both the nation making it and international law, both of which are in constant evolution. Since **World War I** and, to an even greater degree, **World War II**, extensive amendments of a humanitarian nature have been made to this necessarily harsh form of justice, particularly among the more sensitive, democratic nations. Elsewhere and under duress in combat, the chances of rough justice are never impossible.

Lawrence, Thomas Edward (1888–1935). Born in North Wales, Lawrence spent most of his youth in Oxford, where he was educated. As a young archaeologist before **World War I** he worked in North Syria. When war started Lawrence was first employed in military intelligence in Cairo, subsequently being sent to the Hejaz to work with Sherif Feisal, leading the main Arab forces fighting against Turkish rule. Here Lawrence soon took a prominent part in the **Arab revolt**, leading raids against the Turks and advising Feisal in his support of the British drive through Palestine to Damascus.

After the war Lawrence took part in the discussions about the future of the former Ottoman Empire, at the Versailles Conference. He then sought obscurity in the ranks of both the RAF and the Tank Corps. He died in a motor-cycle accident in Dorset.

Laws of war. The medieval Rules of Chivalry were laws of war by a privileged minority characterized by the self-interest of feudal societies world-wide, and continued into the 20th century. Not until the upsurge of humanitarianism, accelerated by the horrors of the **Crimean** and **Austro-Italian wars** in the 1850s, were strenuous attempts made to codify and enforce international laws. The Declaration of Paris in 1856, which clarified the rules of **blockade**, and the **Geneva Conventions** of the 1860s, which created the **Red Cross Society** and gave better treatment to prisoners of war and the wounded, were milestones on the way to The Hague Conferences of 1899 and 1907, which in turn established rudimentary but almost unenforceable rules of war. After **World War I**, improvements were made to the Hague rules regarding **submarine** warfare, the outlawing of **chemical warfare**, the rights of neutrals and attacks on open cities – most of which were broken at some time or other during **World War II**. However, the flagrant atrocities of the latter war, well publicized and, to some extent, codified during the post-war **war crimes** trials, did produce significant changes of approach to the conduct of war by individuals. The acknowledgement, *ex post facto* though it might be, of crimes connected with starting an aggressive war and against humanity found their way on to the statute books of many nations and into **military law**, with a deterrent and educational effect not to be underrated.

A fairly comprehensive set of laws now exists. Unfortunately the means of enforcement are not always available, particularly since 'might', with the threat of force, has a tendency to be 'right'. But the mobilization of public and international opinion against those in breach of the laws has been effective many times, even if not immediately; against the superpowers in **Vietnam** and **Afghanistan**, for example.

Lebanon, Wars of. The Arab State of Lebanon came into existence under French mandate in 1920 and was declared a republic in 1927 amidst the turmoil of the Druse rebellion against the French. It was transferred to Free French control in July 1941 after the Vichy French forces were defeated by the British in **Syria**. In 1957 the French withdrew, but already the **Arab–Israeli Wars** were having an impact in cross-border **guerrilla** activity connected, after 1956, with the United Arab Republic (UAR) and Syria in particular. An insurrection inspired by the UAR in April 1958 was temporarily quelled by 14,300 US, British and French troops invited in at United Nations suggestion. But a nation factionalized by several Arab tribes (including stateless Palestinians) and sects, besides a large Christian community, and located alongside Israel had no hope of peace. On top of political instability was added sporadic cross-border raiding by Israelis, Syrians and the Palestinian Liberation Organization (PLO). The influx of Palestinian Arabs increased and a PLO state within the state sprang up.

Complex civil war between the factions broke out in 1975. Israel and Syria (which has grudgingly recognized Lebanon) supported the Christians. The PLO fought for survival. In July 1981 intense PLO artillery and rocket fire fell upon Israeli settlements and industry. At once the Israelis retaliated with attacks on PLO bases. Violence intensified. Mediation by Arab states and others failed until, on 6 June 1982, the Israeli Army entered Lebanon and advanced on Beirut and the Beqa'a Valley, where 30,000 Syrians with 19 surface-to-air (SAM) **guided missile** batteries were in residence. Fighting was extremely heavy against 15,000 PLO men with about 100 obsolete T34 **tanks**. Soon the Syrians were involved, using the latest Russian tanks against the Israelis and Christian militia. Fighting between armoured forces took place in the approaches to the Beqa'a Valley, where the SAM batteries were practically annihilated by Israeli air attacks. In fierce air combat the Israelis had by far the better of it against Russian-built aircraft.

Although the Israelis won the land and air battles, destroying about 150 Russian-built tanks, the cease-fires negotiated on 12 and 26 June failed to end hostilities. In occupation of a considerable area, including parts of Beirut, the Israelis found themselves intractably entwined with the chronic civil war, in which the divided PLO was ousted and a multi-national force was moved in to restore peace. When the Israelis eventually withdrew under internal and external political pressures in 1985, the imbroglio was no closer to solution in a country which has become inured to the struggle for causes which to most people are almost incomprehensible. There is even a possibility that Lebanon's sacrifice in combat is a safety-valve for Arab and Israeli pressures.

Lee, General Robert E. (1807– 70). A Virginian and West Point Military Academy graduate who saw active service in Mexico (**Mexican wars**) in 1847 and 1848 and willingly took command of Virginia's forces in the **American Civil War**. He was less enthusiastic when made military adviser to Confederate President Jefferson **Davis** in 1861, responsible for the direction of military operations. Initially his generalship was diffident. Yet Davis retained him and, after 1862 when his masterly conduct of the **Seven Days Battle** saved Richmond and the Confederacy, made him (in modern terms) Chief of Staff as well as Commander of the Northern Army.

An exponent of manoeuvre, Lee realized that Davis's politically orientated defensive strategy was likely to lose the war for the South. Yet on both occasions when he invaded the North to threaten Washington, defeat was the outcome: at Antietam in September 1862 and **Gettysburg** in July 1863. The latter exposed flaws in his method of command – and also indicated that the South's chances of survival were remote against a powerful opponent who always outnumbered him. Nevertheless it was Lee's thrifty utilization of ever weakening armies which prolonged the war until 9 April 1865, when he surrendered in person to General **Grant**.

Leningrad, Siege of. Leningrad, or St Petersburg as it was from 1703 to 1914, and Petrograd until 1927, was capital of Russia until 1918, and thus at the heart of the Russian Revolutions (see **Russian revolutionary wars**) of 1905 and 1917. The civil war and collapse of administration in 1917 brought conditions almost amounting to siege, with starvation that reduced the population from 2,100,000 in 1914 to 770,000 in 1920.

In **World War II**, when Germany invaded Russia, Leningrad was a prime objective, al-

though Army Group North did not reach the eastern outskirts until 8 September 1941. When the Finnish Karelian Army arrived at the city's northern fortifications next day, the siege can be said to have begun, even though access remained possible across Lake Ladoga. Had the Finns, led by Field Marshal Baron Gustaf von Mannerheim, been prepared to assault at once there is little doubt the city would have been completely cut off and its fate sealed, but the Finns, without a political desire for the city, held back; and the Germans lacked the strength ever afterwards to complete the job.

The siege lasted 900 days, during which the defenders and citizens suffered appalling hardships as the place was reduced to ruins. In winter they were supplied across the frozen Lake Ladoga, and also by pipeline and electricity cables laid along the bottom. The first winter was the worst. That of 1942/3 was easier since people were acclimatized, and in January 1943 chinks had been opened in the enemy lines. None the less, not until the Germans withdrew troops in December 1943 was the Red Army, supported by the Baltic Fleet, able to mount the major offensive which, in January 1944, threatened envelopment and drove the besiegers away.

Leyte Gulf, Battles of. After defeat in the **aircraft-carrier** battle of the **Philippine Sea** in June 1944 and ahead of the correctly anticipated invasion of the Philippines in October, Admiral Soemu Toyoda concluded that Japan's last hope lay in a surprise naval victory aimed at destruction of the enemy's **amphibious** fleet. He devised a complex plan conditioned by lack of strong carrier air forces and the inescapable **logistic** imbalance which made him concentrate his Fleet at Brunei, where oil was plentiful, instead of Japan where, owing to **blockade**, it was not. Admiral **Nimitz** was fully informed of the plan through access to Japanese **codes**. He therefore knew that the battleships and carriers (under Vice-Admiral Jisaburo Ozawa) sailing from Japan, with few aircraft, were intended as a decoy from the main battleship force which, under Vice-Admiral Takeo Kurita and supported by two subsidiary fleets and land-based air attacks, were tasked to destroy the invaders disembarking in Leyte Gulf.

The landings began on 20 October, but already the Japanese were (incorrectly) satisfied they had won a great victory off **Formosa** on

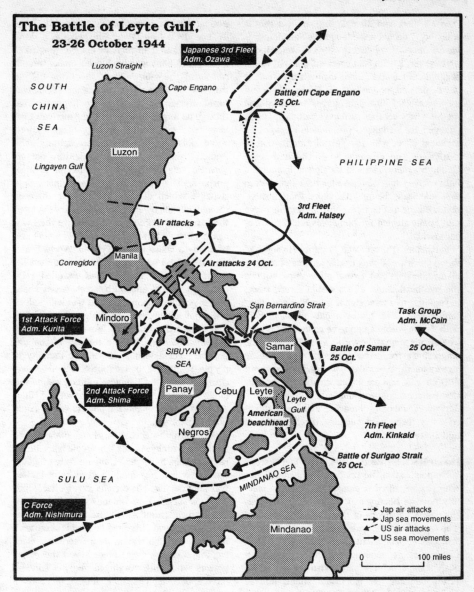

The Battle of Leyte Gulf,
23-26 October 1944

Japanese 3rd Fleet
Adm. Ozawa

Luzon Straight

Cape Engano

Battle off Cape Engano
25 Oct.

SOUTH

CHINA

SEA

Luzon

PHILIPPINE SEA

Lingayen Gulf

3rd Fleet
Adm. Halsey

Air attacks

Corregidor   Manila   Air attacks 24 Oct.

San Bernardino Strait

Task Group
Adm. McCain

1st Attack Force
Adm. Kurita

Mindoro

SIBUYAN
SEA

Samar   Battle off Samar   25 Oct.
25 Oct.

2nd Attack Force
Adm. Shima

Panay   Cebu   Leyte

Leyte
Gulf

American
beachhead

7th Fleet
Adm. Kinkaid

Negros

Battle of Surigao Strait
25 Oct.

SULU SEA

MINDANAO SEA

C Force
Adm. Nishimura

Mindanao

- - ➤ Jap air attacks
- - ➤ Jap sea movements
◄- -   US air attacks
──➤   US sea movements

0   100 miles

13–16 October against Admiral Halsey's carriers. They were thus unaware, as they approached San Bernardino Strait and Surigao Strait, that Halsey's Third Fleet was guarding the former and Admiral Thomas Kinkaid's Seventh Fleet the latter. At the same time as Ozawa's Fleet had been allowed, through American error, to slip through unreported, Kurita's Fleet was detected on the 23rd, hammered in the Sibuyan Sea by submarines and Halsey's aircraft (with the loss of the super-battleship *Musashi* and two heavy cruisers, plus other ships) and forced to turn back on the 24th at the same time as Japanese aircraft were annihilated. Meanwhile the two subsidiary Japanese forces converging on Surigao Strait were running into a hot reception from Kinkaid's **torpedo-boats** and battleships. Halsey, hearing belatedly of the approach of

195

Ozawa's Fleet and disregarding the fact that it was only a decoy, abandoned the San Bernardino Straits to charge northwards to attack it.

However, Kurita had reversed at night to his original course and passed through the strait at dawn, headed for Leyte Gulf. There only a few escort carriers and light forces protected the invasion fleet because Kinkaid's battleships were engaged in Surigao Strait, albeit engaged to excellent effect with the virtual annihilation of battleships and cruisers. So Kurita had Leyte Gulf at his mercy, attacks by aircraft from a few light carriers manoeuvring for their lives before Japanese guns being little more than harassment. But he lost tactical control, then his nerve and finally turned for home, his mission unaccomplished.

Farther north, off Cape Engano, Halsey had found Ozawa and was in the process of sinking all four carriers and several other ships, but not the two battleships. These would escape since, in response to a terse signal from Nimitz. Halsey tardily sent back his own battleships to deal with Kurita – only again to be robbed of his prey by Kurita's premature withdrawal. Despite some staggering errors on both sides, it was a crushing victory for the Americans, who destroyed about 500 aircraft and sank four carriers, three battleships, six heavy and four light cruisers, eleven destroyers and one submarine, at a loss to themselves of three light carriers, three destroyers and 200 aircraft.

Liddell Hart, Sir Basil (1895–1970). A defence correspondent of the London *Times* newspaper who philosophized copiously on war and cleverly rewrote history in support of his theories. His nebulous theory of the 'indirect approach' was an effort to dissuade Britain from land warfare on the Continent linked to a reversal of earlier support for armoured forces on grounds of the tank's vulnerability. With the ear of the Prime Minister (Neville Chamberlain) and as adviser to the War Minister (Leslie Hore-Belisha) he carried great weight. World War II utterly discredited him. The manner of his corrupt, post-war recovery of credibility is documented in Professor John Mearsheimer's *Liddell Hart and the Weight of History* (1989).

Limited war. A term in popular use from the 1950s to describe wars with limited aims conducted in well-defined areas; also to the exclusion of nuclear weapons and, until the 1980s in the Iran–Iraq War, the chemical kind too. Throughout history, of course, pragmatic attempts to limit war have been made, though not until the aftermath of the Crimean and the Austro-Piedmontese wars of the 1850s was humanitarianism a prime motivation. Vast though its dimensions were, the American Civil War remained limited because other nations could not influence the actual fighting. The Franco-Prussian War stayed within bounds because neighbouring states saw no political purpose to be achieved by involvement in a struggle which did not immediately threaten the balance of power in Europe. Nations sympathetic to the Boers did not intervene in their war against Britain in 1899 because they were in no position to do so effectively. But World War I spread far and wide and became unlimited because so many nations had founded relationships upon treaties with secret clauses, based on the popular assumption that war was a glorious, unavoidable, even desirable natural activity – provided the initiators felt they could win quickly and cheaply. The tragedy of the unpopular World War II lay in the inability of people to dispose of irresponsible and greedy demagogues – the Japanese military clique (including Emperor Hirohito), Mussolini and Hitler – who acquired dictatorial powers which could not be restrained.

Although the threat of global nuclear war has been contained since 1945, cold war's many ramifications have perpetuated a state of global tension which has made outbreaks of limited war unavoidable. The various wars for independence (for example in Indonesia, Malaya, Indo-China, throughout Africa and the Middle East) have all generated limited conflicts, often with outbreaks of civil war in their aftermath. Controlling such wars has preoccupied the major powers who, with varying degrees of success, have applied diplomatic, economic or coercive measures to stop them or restrict their spread – the Arab–Israeli and Indo-Pakistani wars are prime examples of relative success. Limiting the wars in which the major powers are directly involved, notably the ones in Vietnam and Afghanistan, was much more difficult, though achieved in the long run.

The 20th century has seen more fighting than any other in history. Two global wars and ceaseless cold and limited wars are nothing to be proud of. Nor can there be much confidence in preventing nuclear war in the future if **atom bombs** and the most sophisticated chemical weapons fall into the hands of megalomaniacs as irresponsible as those who started World War II.

Lincoln, Abraham (1808–65). A lawyer with experience as a soldier (without seeing action) who, because he was President of the USA throughout the **American Civil War**, was C-in-C the Federal forces. His strength in this role lay in understanding that only by a strategy of offensive action by superior forces could the North win the war. Hence his adoption of **blockade** and insistence upon invasions of the South. But the key to the North's victory was his willingness to give commanders wide powers of initiative within the broad strategic plan; and to dismiss those who failed his expectations, despite the political consequences.

Lissa, Battle of. On 20 July 1866 when the **Austro-Prussian War** was almost over an Italian fleet, under Count Persano, covering a convoy invading the island of Lissa (off the Yugoslav coast) was intercepted by an Austrian fleet under Count Tegetthof. A few ships were armoured but only the Italian *Affondatore* had a ram and a turret. The Italians interposed as the Austrians charged with the intention of ramming. Some managed to do so (though not *Affondatore*), resulting in one seriously damaged ship and the Italian flagship sunk with 381 hands. The Austrians sank the biggest Italian ships and claimed a victory which led tacticians to false conclusions concerning the ram's potency, though to correct ones about the need to fire straight ahead.

Lithuania, Battles for. For centuries Lithuania has been a jousting ground for rival Russians, Swedes, Poles, Prussians and other warlike peoples passing through. From 1864 it was 'russified', but granted freedom of speech and its own congress in 1905. The Germans arrived in September 1915 in pursuit of Russians withdrawing in the aftermath of the **Gorlice offensive**, and held it as a buffer against the Russian Bolsheviks until the end of **World War I**. In January 1919 the Russians were back, though contested in the west until December by German Freikorps troops; and 'liberated' in April by the Poles as an overture to the **Russo-Polish War**, a liberation which was reversed when the Poles withdrew under pressure in July 1920 and the Russians returned, only to hand over to a Lithuanian government in August after the Polish victory at **Warsaw**. The victory left disputes over Lithuania's frontiers unsettled, temporarily to be arbitrarily resolved in October 1939 when the Russians again moved in, this time by agreement with Germany.

World War II once more involved Lithuania in battle as the German Army Group North rapidly overran the country in June 1941 on the way to **Leningrad**, starting a heartless occupation which lasted until July 1944, when three Russian Baltic Front armies and a Byelorussian Front army began a concerted series of attacks. They pushed the broken German Army Group Centre back into East Prussia and fought their way through Lithuania and Latvia to pen Army Group North in Courland (Latvia) and Memel. With their backs to the Baltic Sea, **Hitler** insisted upon the maintenance of these wasted bastions and the launching of unavailing, extremely expensive counter-attacks in support. Dreadful damage was inflicted such as Lithuania never before knew, with heavy losses to its population, some caused by fighting among its own pro- and anti-German factions – of whom the former were in the minority. But Memel fell in January as the country reverted from one repressive regime to another which restored russification with unprecedented savagery.

Lloyd George, (Earl) David (1863–1945). A radical, reforming politician of outstanding eloquence who became Britain's Prime Minister in December 1915. His reorganization of government through a Cabinet of only five, in permanent session, served by a strong secretariat; his unrelenting and by no means irrational pressure on admirals and generals, linked to strong dissatisfaction with their strategies and ways of waging war; his management of industrial production and manpower shortages through **conscription** and reorganization; and his handling of Britain's allies, producing in March 1918 an effective unified Allied Command, were major performances during a war-winning period in office.

Logistics. It seems that the first use of the word

logistics to describe the 'practical art of moving armies', in every respect except strategy and tactics, appeared in Antoine Jomini's *Précis de l'art de la guerre* in 1836. It appears to have been rescued from obscurity by Captain Alfred **Mahan**'s influence on the US Navy in the 1880s, helping it assume modern usage in what is now defined as ways and means of financing and procuring war resources, in conjunction with the supply and transport of men and materials to and from the battle zones.

The introduction of steam-powered **railways** and of the **telegraph** in the 1840s were more revolutionary to logistics than any other military activity, especially when associated with advances in the long-term storage of **food** by bottling, canning and pasteurization, which released navies and armies from constraints on deployment imposed by slow, unreliable, animal-powered transportation and the need to scavenge food. Such constraints on the one hand handicapped movement and on the other, owing to the need to move to fresh pastures after a neighbourhood had been stripped, compelled armies to shift, or, at sea, denied sailors a satisfactory diet.

Not only was the **Crimean War** almost the last British campaign attended by disastrous logistic consequences, it also demonstrated (partly because its mismanagement brought down the government) that the public were not entirely indifferent to the welfare of the armed forces. For although the transport of men and stores to the theatre of war by rail and steamship had worked well, the provision and handling of supplies and their delivery to the combat zone had been almost medieval because the Commissariat had fallen into decay since 1815. The soldiers' **food** and **medical** care provided were a scandal brought quickly to public attention by the more rapid signals **communications** of the day – which also expedited identification and implementation of the remedial measures required, as in the sending of nurses under Miss Florence **Nightingale**. At the same time it was discovered that the **engineering** services required to support the handling of equipment and provisions themselves created a more complex logistic load that could best be dealt with by **mechanization**. The unloading of ships and docks clearance work at Balaklava, for example, were in due course partly carried out by steam cranes, a light railway and tractors.

The accelerating development of mechanization and signal communications fundamentally conditioned logistics to the point at which, provided adequate forethought was given to the matter (based on sound **intelligence** and administrative practice), armed forces need never want. Pasteurization, refrigeration and dried foods (all of which were available by the 1870s) solved the problem of the long-term storage of food. The invention of practical, liquid-fuelled internal combustion and turbine engines in the 1880s led to much faster and more reliable means of propulsion and created a demand for a network of greatly superior roads as well as enormously simplifying the bunkering of ships and, in due course, railway locomotives. The conquest of flight by heavier-than-air machines in 1903 opened the way to the greatest transport revolution of all. Discoveries of the cause of such diseases as malaria and yellow fever, which ravaged armies in the **Spanish–American War**, led to prevention and cure, at the same time as disciplined hygiene and the latest medical practice marginally reduced human wastage.

World War I stimulated demand of all the above, including the first air delivery of supplies to besieged land forces at Kut al Amara in 1916. By 1918 a major switch from animal to mechanized transport on land had taken place; a significant reduction in fatalities to the wounded; a considerable increase in the size and scope of logistic services, with consolidation of the best basic organizations and methods required; and development of the vital communications networks without which response to rapidly changing conditions and circumstances was impossible.

World War II not only benefited from the lessons of World War I, but also introduced numerous sophisticated improvements, of which the most important were the conquest of sickness in disease-ridden places (such as **Burma**, South-East Asia and parts of the **Pacific**) and air transport (**Airborne forces**) on so large a scale that, given the resources, mobility was vastly enhanced, **blockade** made more difficult and seige surmountable. Indeed, it was the calls of war which created the infrastructure (such as airfields in the most inaccessible places) and the latest means of transport (such as the **landing-craft** which were forerunners of roll-on–roll-off ferries) which made far easier the supply of wars to come, besides enhancing everyday life and the mobility of peoples world-wide. In the electronic epoch, the diversity of communications made possible extremely swift, flexible and well-calculated reactions to the most surprising circumstances. No better example is that of the improvised, overnight British response in the mounting of the **Falkland Islands** campaign in 1982, done without previous planning at a range of 8,000 miles from Britain and with the nearest base 4,000 miles distant.

Ludendorff, General Erich (1865–1937). A brilliant member of the German General Staff with a large share of the credit for rapid capture of the Liège **fortifications** in August 1914. Later that month, as Chief of Staff to General **Hindenburg**, he helped win the Battle of **Tannenberg**. From then onwards, he dominated the partnership controlling the Eastern Front until appointed to supreme command of Germany's war effort in August 1916. As Quartermaster-General, he executed the defensive strategy in the West and the undermining of Russia in 1917, followed by the **Hindenburg offensives** in 1918. Arguably, his loss of nerve after the Battle of **Amiens** shortened a war already lost. He was sacked on 26 October. In 1923 he was at **Hitler**'s side in the abortive Munich *Putsch*.

M

MacArthur, General Douglas (1880–1964). An infantryman who took part in the **Mexican War** in 1914 and was a divisional commander in **World War I**, followed by command of American forces in Germany. He was Chief of Staff of the Army, 1930–35, at its nadir and military adviser to the Philippines Army 1935 to 1937, when he retired. Called back to command the US and Philippine forces in July 1941, he was defeated by the Japanese and forced back to **Bataan**. From there, on President **Roosevelt's** order, he was evacuated to Australia to take command of the Allied forces, tasked to advance through **New Guinea**. MacArthur's relations with the Navy and Allies were not always easy. He managed to have overruled the Navy's intention to bypass the **Philippines** in order to satisfy his ego by conquering the islands in 1944–5. The Japanese surrendered to him on 2 September 1945. He remained in Japan as Supreme Commander to democratize the nation and restore its economy.

Upon the outbreak of the **Korean War** in 1950 he was made Supreme Commander of UN forces. While Eighth Army withdrew into the **Pusan perimeter**, MacArthur planned and, in September, launched the **Inchon** landing and then invaded North Korea. In November the Chinese stopped Eighth Army short of the **Yalu River** and forced it back to the 38th Parallel, where the position was secured. On 11 April 1951 MacArthur was sacked by **President Harry Truman** after a disagreement over his insistence upon bombing enemy bases in Manchuria.

McClellan, General George (1826–85). A West Point graduate and Sapper who, in 1846, took part in the **Mexican War** and later observed the **Crimean War**. In July 1861 he secured West Virginia for the North and was appointed General-in-Chief of the Federal Army, which he reorganized. Pressed by President **Lincoln**, he tried in March 1862 to capture Richmond via the Yorktown peninsula, but was outgeneralled by General **Lee** and forced to evacuate. On 12 September, with Lee's army at a disadvantage near Sharpsburg, he advanced only tentatively and later was checked at the bloody Battle of Antietam by Lee's numerically inferior force. Lincoln sacked him when, again, he was indecisive in following up the retreating Confederates.

Machine-guns. The American (Sir) Hiram Maxim gave his name to the first successful automatic machine-gun (MG) (the earlier Gatling with its seven rotating barrels was manually operated), in which operation was based on recoil energy; that is, the force opening and closing the breech, feeding rounds into the chamber, extracting and ejecting the empty cartridge cases, came from the firing of the cartridge itself. The Maxim was a water-cooled 7·69mm (0·303in) calibre weapon capable of sustained rates of fire of up to 500 rounds per minute (rpm) and was first used in action by the British in 1895. The Maxim's reliability immediately attracted attention; it was said of it, and of the Vickers version which became the British Army's standard medium machine-gun (MMG), that there were over 50 possible stoppages detailed in the manual – but none of them ever actually occurred.

The Maxim was widely used during the **Russo-Japanese War** of 1904 and rapidly became a valued weapon in most European armies; it was used, in various versions, by all the combatants in **World War I** and the immense casualties that could be inflicted by a MG probably did more than anything else to bring about the positional warfare that so characterized that conflict.

The Vickers MMG, originally designed in 1891 and used successfully by the British in both world wars, was, however, comparatively heavy and cumbersome with its tripod, ammunition, water supply and the water-jacketed gun itself. The British, perhaps partly for this reason, originally concentrated their MGs into a special Machine-Gun Corps; only later was the MG seen as an essential infantry support weapon and integrated into the battalion organization.

The Maxim design was not universally adopted. The French at about the same time introduced a gas-operated Hotchkiss which used some of the propellant gases, diverted via a barrel port, to operate a piston connected to an extractor and ejector which disposed of the empty cartridge cases, while at the same time a spring was compressed which, on reasserting itself, allowed a new round to be fed into the chamber on the breech mechanism's forward stroke. The Hotchkiss was air-cooled, but with a very heavy finned barrel to dissipate the heat generated by firing.

A third type of MG, which emerged from Austria in the early part of the 20th century, was a version operating on the blow-back principle, in which barrel and breech block were not locked together, there was no piston, the action taking place purely on recoil energy. The **World War II** Sten sub-machine-gun was a similar idea and was equally unsafe and unreliable, depending as it did on consistency of cartridge-filling techniques that was not always achieved.

These earlier cumbersome weapons, all weighing around 70kg, soon generated a need for a lighter MG which one man could carry and fire. The best known in World War I were probably the British (though American-invented) 7·69mm Lewis gun and the US 7·62mm (0·30in) Browning automatic rifle; both weapons, gas-operated, magazine-fed and weighing about 7kg, survived to be used during World War II. They could be fired like a rifle or, using a bipod, as a MG and in this mode were almost as effective as the heavier Vickers, though without the long-range accuracy.

Developments in the 1930s to meet the needs of the infantry section and of tank second-

ary armament produced some very successful designs. On the British side the 7·69mm Czech-designed Bren became the universally used infantry light machine-gun (LMG), a typical feature being the ease with which a hot, and hence inaccurate, barrel could be removed during action and replaced by a new one carried by the crew. The Germans introduced two highly effective LMGs: the 7·92mm MG34 (800–900rpm) and the later MG42 (1,200–1,300rpm). Both could be fired from a tripod, giving them a MMG capability. For armoured vehicles the British had developed another Czech-designed MG: the 7·92mm Besa, while the Americans relied on the World War I 7·62mm Browning.

All these weapons fired rifle ammunition but there was also a need for a larger-calibre MG for longer-range and more substantial targets such as light armoured vehicles. Both Vickers and Browning produced a 12·7mm (0·50in) MG and the British also developed a 15mm Besa mounted in some armoured cars.

The trend in recent years has been to reduce the infantryman's burden and this is reflected in the design of MGs. The British have introduced a 7·62mm General Purpose Machine-Gun (GPMG) to replace both the Bren and the Vickers MMG. It can be magazine- or belt-fed, fired from bipod or tripod and, with an easily fitted heavy barrel, is capable of sustained fire; the US M60 MG has a similar versatility. The larger-calibre (12·7mm) US M85 provides two rates of fire: 450rpm for ground targets and 1,000rpm for air defence – an interesting reflection of Maxim's original design, which offered the same facility.

MacMahon, Marshal (Duke) Marie Edmé Patrice Maurice de (1808–93). A French soldier with distinguished service in North Africa, who commanded the division which stormed the Malakov fort and brought about the fall of **Sevastopol** in 1855. As commander of the French forces in the **Austro-Piedmontese War** of 1859, he blundered to victory at the costly battles of Magenta and Solferino. In the **Franco-Prussian War**, he was outmanoeuvred in Alsace, defeated and wounded at Froschwiller and then given command of the Army of Châlons with the role of relieving the siege of **Metz**. With characteristic misjudgement he led that army to its doom at **Sedan** and spent the rest of that war as a prisoner. As President of France from 1873 to 1879 he was almost as much a failure as when in high command.

Madagascar, Battle of. After the Japanese Navy's victories in 1941 and early 1942, which opened the way for Japanese penetration of the **Indian Ocean** in March, it became strategically essential for the Allies to take control of the port of Diégo-Suarez in Vichy-held Madagascar to stop its use by both Japanese and German naval forces, including **submarines**. British **Commandos** led a divisional **amphibious** operation ashore on 5 May and fairly easily seized the objective. But on 29 May a Japanese seaplane, launched from a submarine, was spotted, and next day a battleship was damaged and a tanker sunk in harbour by a mini-submarine. Imagining that the enemy was based somewhere on land, the British decided to occupy the entire island. The operation provoked stiff French resistance in the **jungle** and took two more landings in a campaign spread over five months. The island was transferred to the Free French.

Madrid, Siege of. General **Franco**'s first objective at the start of the **Spanish Civil War** was the capital city of the Republican Government. He might have succeeded had he not diverted forces to relieve a Fascist garrison at Toledo. Be that as it may, the city's garrison, under General José Miaja, reinforced by the International Brigade, was strong enough on 6 November 1936 to repulse the first assault. For the next four months persistent Fascist attempts, supported by artillery and bombing, failed to break in. Fighting also went on in the surrounding countryside to complete the city's isolation. But the Italian troops involved were routed; indeed, Madrid was never completely cut off, men and materials got through. It was even possible in July 1937 for the garrison to launch a sustained counter-offensive – which was thwarted by the besiegers after nearly three weeks' grapple.

Not until February 1939, when the Republican cause was collapsing, was the battered city – by now on the verge of starvation – in peril again. As the Fascists closed in, a weeklong factional struggle among the defenders finally brought the garrison to its knees. On 28 March the enemy walked in unopposed. Madrid had been a symbol of government determination. But through the cloud of **propaganda** gener-

ated about its resistance, commentators failed to note that General **Douhet**'s theories of air power were suspect. **Bombers** had failed to destroy the defence.

Mahan, Admiral Alfred (1840–1914). A US Navy officer who fought in the **American Civil War**, but won his great reputation as a military philosopher when a lecturer at the Naval War College, of which he became President in 1886. From the study of history he formulated celebrated theories concerning the influence of sea power on history, published in three classic volumes prior to 1897. When not at ordinary naval duty (he commanded a **cruiser** from 1893 to 1895), involved with the **Spanish–American War** or engaged in international affairs, he was studying **strategy**. He concluded that commerce and **logistics** were key issues and that sea power was decisive. He believed that, as a deterrent (**Deterrence**), Anglo-American sea power should guarantee peace.

Malaya, Battles of. As a vital act in the **Japanese War of Expansion**, simultaneously with attacks on **Hong Kong**, the **Philippines** and **Pearl Harbor**, the Twenty-fifth Army under General Tomoyuki Yamashita landed in southern Thailand and at Kota Bharu on 8 December 1942. Within hours British air power was smashed by bombing of airfields, leaving an abortive attempt by the Royal Navy to destroy the invasion shipping without air cover, so that, on the 10th, the **battleship** and **battle-cruiser** involved were caught at sea, without air escort, and quickly sunk by bombs and **torpedoes**.

Their bases and **logistics** secure, the Japanese force of 100,000 well trained and strongly supported men could advance through **jungle** and rubber plantations much as they chose. For the British had deployed in strength far to the south, shielding **Singapore**, without counting on a major attack so far north. In consequence the Indian brigade defending Kota Bharu had to be withdrawn, beginning the long retreat down the west coast of the peninsula. Everywhere the British, unprepared for jungle warfare, gave way before the Japanese, whose tactics of infiltration were far superior. Successive, hastily prepared river-line defences collapsed when the Japanese found weak spots, crossed and unexpectedly appeared in strength far to the rear.

Penang was captured on 16 December, Port

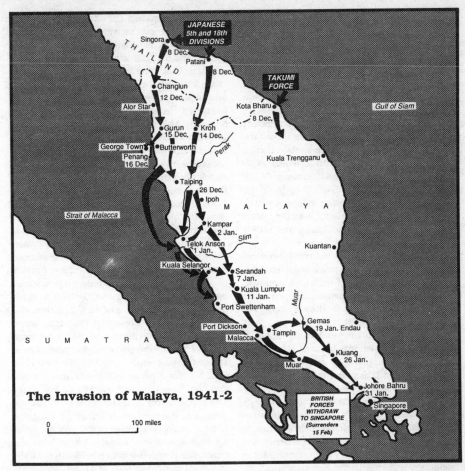

The Invasion of Malaya, 1941-2

0   100 miles

Swettenham on 9 January after the Slim River line was broken by tanks on the 7th in a débâcle. The withdrawal was virtually unchecked since the original Johore Line on the River Muar was only briefly defended by Indians and newly arrived Australian troops, who acquitted themselves well. By the 15th it had been penetrated and by the 31st those of Malaya's shattered defenders who were left had retreated across the causeway into Singapore.

For the rest of **World War II** the peninsula lay dormant except for trivial **guerrilla** raids by the British and parties of the Chinese-run Anti-Japanese Army (AJA), a force which was ready to help with the unopposed British reoccupation in September 1945 – and preparing its role in the **Malayan War of Independence** to come.

Malayan War of Independence. It was the intention of the minority Chinese-dominated Malayan Communist Party (MCP) to employ the Malayan Races Liberation Army (MRLA, previously the Anti-Japanese Army), to seize power from the British after **World War II**. Finding that political pressure against their economically embarrassed opponent was ineffective, they gradually escalated a campaign of strikes, sabotage and murder by the clandestine Min Yuen, which also was responsible for **propaganda** and **logistic** support. When the MCP was declared illegal in July 1948, it retired, along with the MRLA and Min Yuen, into the **jungle** with the aim of expanding a **guerrilla** war from there.

Lightly armed, between 7,000 and 10,000 strong (90 per cent Chinese in content) and lacking an external source of supply, the MCP was extremely optimistic in imagining it could prevail. For not only were its **logistics** on a shoestring, it drew on the support of only a very small proportion of the populace, and was unpopular for its bullying tactics. The fact that it managed until 1952 to hold the initiative was as much due to British unreadiness as its own prowess. Yet in those years the British, under General Sir Harold Briggs, laid the foundations of an efficient **intelligence** organization. They strengthened the security forces and developed an effective counter-guerrilla doctrine, with emphasis on offensive action, to seek and kill the enemy. Of still greater importance, they worked to solve the political problem by promising independence to Malaya, thus isolating the MCP from the majority of the people while also hitting the MCP's **communications** and logistic systems.

The Min Yuen preyed on the rural populace, particularly Chinese so-called squatters, for supplies and information. Briggs built well-run, protected **concentration camps** and populated them with the squatters, thus forcing the MRLA, short of food, to come out and fight – with mounting casualties and reduced returns, turning the Min Yuen into farmers. When General Sir Gerald Templer took over as High Commissioner in 1952, he raised the security forces to 45,000 and strengthened aggressive military methods in harmony with a sustained political initiative (linked with subtle **psychological warfare**) which won the people's confidence ('hearts and minds'). This ensured independence for Malaya with an elected government, under a monarchy, in 1957. In the meantime the Min Yuen had fallen into decline, the MCP's communications were in disarray and the squeezed MRLA, short of money and food, was reduced to excesses of violence which further reduced its **recruiting** appeal. In 1954 its leaders decamped to Indonesia, while others were driven towards Thailand. By 1957, only a hard core remained. With some 7,000 guerrillas dead by 1960, the Emergency was declared over.

Malta, Siege of. When the Italians declared war on Britain and France on 10 June 1940, they immediately launched air raids from Sicily on Malta, which at that moment had only three biplane **fighters** and a few guns and men to defend it. However, although far distant from the nearest friendly bases, in Egypt and Gibraltar (after France capitulated on 21 June), the island was never completely cut off. Indeed, throughout 1940 the Italians were unable to prevent the passage of **convoys** through the Mediterranean and the reinforcement and supply of the garrison. Hurricane fighters arrived in August, along with more guns. Offensive action by surface warships, **submarines** and **bombers** so hampered the movements of Italian convoys to **North Africa** that the Germans were compelled to intervene. On 10 January 1941 they launched the first of many furious and extremely damaging attacks on ships, the dockyards and airfields. British bombing was curtailed and surface warships withdrawn. Yet, to complete a pattern repeated throughout, no sooner were Axis air attacks diminished than British offensive operations increased.

The populace lived in caves and shelters when under attack. Casualties were not excessive, but damage considerable and food and fuel supplies short, desperately so when only cargo submarines could get through. But the will to resist never faltered. The scale of air attack coincided with the intensity of operations in North Africa, rising to crescendos during the spring campaign of 1941 and in the period of the November to January 1942 offensives; it reached a peak when Field Marshal **Kesselring** opened a massive pre-invasion air offensive from March until May 1942, and again in mid-August 1942 during passage of the last convoy before the siege was lifted. The invasion never came, because **Hitler** feared the outcome. Convoy battles were decisive. The garrison was in trouble when all the merchant ships were sunk in a February convoy and when, in April, 30 out of 47 Spitfires flown in from **aircraft-carriers** were destroyed in two days. It felt better when 64 more, flown in during May, produced a daylight air victory over a convoy which, nevertheless, got only two out of six ships through. It drew courage when, as in mid-August, a tanker and four other ships out of fourteen arrived, even though the escorts had suffered terribly, losing a carrier, two **cruisers** and three **destroyers**.

Once French North-West Africa had been invaded in November 1942, the passage of convoys became much easier and Malta reverted entirely to the offensive against southern Europe. By 30 June 1943 1,436 Maltese civilians had been killed and 3,415 wounded.

Manchurian battles. See **Russo-Japanese wars.**

Manila Bay, Battle of. Within six days of the start of the **Spanish–American War** in April 1898 a US Navy squadron, under Commodore George Dewey, had arrived in Manila Bay from Hong Kong. With six cruisers armed with 8in and 6in guns, he outclassed the 10 run-down, largely unarmoured wooden warships (including four cruisers), under Rear-Admiral Patricio Montojo, he found at anchor in the bay. In two phases, totalling three hours of none-too-accurate **gunnery** (14 hits out of 157 8in shells fired), the Americans (with eight wounded) destroyed the Spanish squadron (with 381 dead and wounded). Dewey then bombarded the shore forts and sent for the Army, which took possession of Manila in August.

In **World War II** the bay was to witness the arrival of the Japanese on 2 January 1942 and the ensuing sieges of **Bataan** and **Corregidor**, followed in 1944 by numerous attacks on shipping in the harbour and the eventual fall of the badly damaged city to US troops in February 1945 as a culmination of the **Philippines** battle.

Manstein, Field Marshal Erich von (1887–1973). An infantryman with wide experience on most fronts in **World War I**, who was rated by some Germans as their best strategic brain in **World War II**. As Chief of Staff Army Group A he took part in the **Polish campaign** and is credited with the idea of invading **France** via the Ardennes in 1940 – a campaign in which he commanded an infantry corps. In Russia in 1941 (**Russo-German wars**) he commanded a Panzer corps in the advance on **Leningrad**. In September he took command of Eleventh Army and led it in the rout of the Russians in the **Crimea** and the siege of **Sevastopol** in the summer of 1942. As a field marshal he returned to Leningrad where he defeated a Russian offensive at Lake Ladoga, only to be sent south again to command Army Group Don (later South) in the attempted relief of **Stalingrad** and the subsequent retreat to the Ukraine. There (despite interference from **Hitler**, with whom he was never at ease) he executed the brilliant **Kharkov** counterstroke in March 1943, but was thwarted in the defective **Kursk** battle in July. He continued in command until March 1943, during the withdrawals into Poland, when he finally lost patience with Hitler and was dismissed.

Mao Tse-tung (1893–1976). A mostly self-educated peasant who was a co-founder of the Chinese Communist Party in 1921. In 1927 he began staging unsuccessful peasant revolts against the Kuomintang in the latest round of **Chinese civil wars**, but by 1931, as Party chairman, had established a reputation and a foothold, with Russian help, in the south-east. By 1934 he had demonstrated that, for the time being, **guerrilla warfare** alone offered long-term success and that short-term survival demanded the Long March to the north-west to win respite from Kuomintang pressure. By 1937, at the start of the **Chinese–Japanese War** and **World War II**, he had won control of the party and created a military doctrine which dovetailed his own style of Marxist dogma. Until 1946, Mao collaborated with General **Chiang Kai-shek** in resisting the Japanese, but was careful not to exhaust his followers in the process.

Resumption of the civil war was not long delayed, followed in three years by the complete overthrow, with Russian help and numerous captured weapons, of the Kuomintang. In this period his doctrine of guerrilla warfare as the way to create a secure base for ultimate seizure of absolute political power was fully vindicated, to become the model for most other Chinese-motivated struggles for independence, e.g. in **Malaya** and **Vietnam**. Thereafter Mao concentrated more on consolidating Chinese power, only resorting to force of arms in **Korea** and India (**Indo-Chinese War**) when it seemed China's frontiers were directly threatened.

March to the Sea. After General **Sherman** had advanced from **Chattanooga** to capture **Atlanta** on 31 August 1864, he conceived a deep penetration aimed at the coast and Savannah to tear the heart out of the Confederacy and perhaps end the **American Civil War**. Sending the Army of the Cumberland back to Chattanooga eventually to defeat a Confederate army at Nashville on 16 December (and also reduce his **logistic** load), Sherman struck out on 15 November in three self-contained columns amounting to 68,000 men. With a view to economizing in manpower guarding lines of communication, he destroyed the railway behind him. Taking only 600 ambulances and 2,500 ammunition wagons with him, he lived off and laid waste the country as he went. With barely 15,000 troops, the Confederates fell back to hold Savannah, but Sherman seized Fort McAllister at the mouth of the Ogeechee River on 13 December, made a junction with the Navy and occupied the city on the 21st when the enemy withdrew. Then he turned northwards to seize Columbia and Wilmington, won the Battle of Bentonville on 20 March 1865 and entered Goldsboro on the 23rd, thus poised to join General **Grant** at **Petersburg** for the war's last act.

Mariana Islands, Battles of the. Transferred to Japanese mandate after **World War I**, these strategic islands were a strongly held corner-stone of her defence and a prime US objective in 1944. The American invasion of Saipan Island on 15 June by Admiral Kelly Turner was preceded by heavy air attacks and an air battle which cost the Japanese some 200 aircraft and several ships. Supported by **battleships**, US **marines** had a tough fight gaining a foothold and made slower progress after the 19th, when naval support was withdrawn to fight the Battle of the **Philippine Sea.** Nevertheless they had taken the airfield on the 18th and thereafter, reinforced by an Army division, had to capture every acre to eliminate the 32,000 enemy, fewer than 2,000 of whom survived after a last charge on 9 July. Neighbouring Tinian was then assaulted on 24 July, its 9,000-strong garrison holding out until 1 August when its survivors were wiped out in a traditional valedictory charge. The total cost to the Americans for both islands was 3,515 dead, to which should be added another 1,400 dead in the capture of Guam (where about 11,000 Japanese died) between 25 July and 10 August. Possession of these islands, however, brought Japan within range of US heavy **bombers** and opened a gap in her inner defences.

Marines. Navies always have needed specially trained soldiers to help man guns, to act as marksmen in combat, to help maintain, if necessary, the sailors' discipline and to lead the way in **amphibious warfare**. The British formed the first modern corps in 1664. They were copied in 1665 by the Dutch, who used them during the Anglo-Dutch War to raid the Medway **dockyards** in 1667. A US Marine Corps, modelled on the British, was formed in 1775 and saw action against the British in 1776.

The variety of tasks on ship and shore performed by Marines developed in line with technology and its impact on tactics. When ships' companies disappeared under armour in steam-

ships, and there no longer was a role on deck to snipe enemy marksmen or take part in boarding operations. Marines were often allocated to man at least one gun turret per ship. The latter role led in 1862 to the formation in the Royal Marines of the Royal Marine Artillery, to differentiate them from the ordinary Royal Marine Light Infantry, which had been formed in 1855. Whatever the branch they belonged to, Marines were used ashore as an arm of sea power: seizing or defending forts and dockyards, as the vanguard of invasions and carrying out hit-and-run raids.

Both the British and the Americans in **World War I** formed Marines into units as parts of field-force formations in France, but their most significant fight was as assault landing parties in the Zeebrugge raid on 23 April 1918. Between the wars, while all countries (not Japan) neglected amphibious warfare the US Marines began developing the technology and techniques they foresaw might be necessary in a **Pacific War** against Japan. This process led to the creation of a self-contained organization that included armoured vehicles and aircraft as well as special **landing-craft**. Like the British, they did little more than formulate ideas and make a few prototypes of craft – just enough to have something in mind when, suddenly in 1940, the German victories in Europe and mounting Japanese aggression in the East made it plain that large-scale amphibious warfare was unavoidable. When the British were compelled to take the lead in 1940, however, the Royal Marines were unready, owing to other commitments, to adopt the **Commando** role at once. That would wait until 1942, in time for the **Dieppe raid**.

Since then, Marines the world over have spearheaded nearly all the major amphibious operations, besides helping develop the latest assault techniques with surface vehicles and **helicopters**. As a result they have augmented their élite status by reaching such high professional standards, in most phases and natures of war, that they are automatically considered for immediate employment in dealing with so-called 'brushfire' outbreaks in the **Cold War** and in the opening stages of unexpected small wars such as that of the **Falkland Islands** in 1982. At the same time they also pioneer or keep alive raiding techniques and the special skills needed in arctic, **jungle**, **mountain** and **desert warfare.**

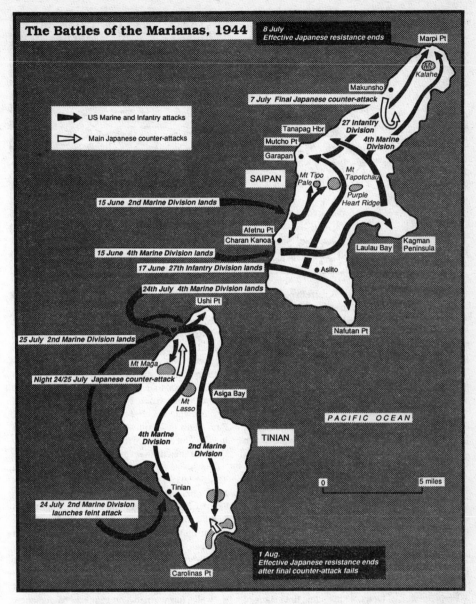

The Battles of the Marianas, 1944

8 July
Effective Japanese resistance ends

Marpi Pt

Mt Kalahe

Makunsho

7 July Final Japanese counter-attack

27 Infantry Division

4th Marine Division

Tanapag Hbr

Mutcho Pt

Garapan

US Marine and Infantry attacks

Main Japanese counter-attacks

SAIPAN

Mt Tipo Pale

Mt Tapotchau

Purple Heart Ridge

15 June 2nd Marine Division lands

Afetnu Pt

Charan Kanoa

Laulau Bay

Kagman Peninsula

15 June 4th Marine Division lands

17 June 27th Infantry Division lands

Aslito

24th July 4th Marine Division lands

Ushi Pt

Nafutan Pt

25 July 2nd Marine Division lands

Mt Maga

Night 24/25 July Japanese counter-attack

Mt Lasso

Asiga Bay

PACIFIC OCEAN

4th Marine Division

2nd Marine Division

TINIAN

0   5 miles

24 July 2nd Marine Division launches feint attack

Tinian

1 Aug.
Effective Japanese resistance ends after final counter-attack fails

Carolinas Pt

Marne, Battles of the. The German plan devised by General Count Alfred von **Schlieffen** before **World War I** was dominated by the concept of a wide swing through Belgium, west of Paris, with a strongly reinforced right wing aiming to envelop the French army between the capital city and the eastern frontier forts. By August 1914, however, the Chief of Staff, General Helmuth Johannes von Moltke, had not only reduced the number of formations in the right wing but launched them with an inadequate system of signal **communications** as well as a defective **logistic** plan.

The First Battle. On 3 August the Germans stormed into Belgium, pushing the Belgian Army back into Antwerp and falling upon the

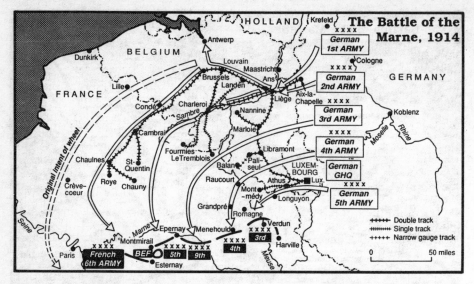

The Battle of the Marne, 1914

French Fifth Army and the British Expeditionary Force (BEF) between Namur and Mons. Obligingly the French assisted by launching strong attacks with their reinforced right wing in Alsace and Lorraine on the 4th, thus denying resources to their threatened left in Belgium. This offensive was checked by the 18th with heavy loss and thrown back by a violent German counter-offensive which, nevertheless, diverted further strength from their own right wing. Heavy attacks at the Battles of the Sambre and Mons on 22 and 23 August at last warned the Allies under General Joffre of their peril. They began a long retreat towards Paris, pivoting on Verdun and gradually reinforcing their left wing while the French defeated the German offensive on the eastern frontier.

By 30 August the Germans were in some difficulty because, owing to inadequate planning of telephone communications and much reliance on a defective radio system, their C³I was beginning to fail. Their First Army therefore made several erratic movements and swung east of Paris (instead of west). At the same time signs of exhaustion appeared among men and horses when the railway system failed to keep pace and supply dwindled. Seeing an opportunity to strike the German right flank while also protecting Paris, Joffre created a Sixth Army north-east of the city, a presence which compelled First German Army to stop advancing in order to form a strong flank guard, a diversion which

opened a large gap between the First Army and the Second on its left, into which the BEF and Fifth French Army entered, largely unopposed and only belatedly noticed by the Germans. Indeed, at this very moment on 8 September a worried German staff officer with plenipotentiary powers arrived at HQ Second Army to find it about to retreat. Appreciating that the troops were exhausted he ordered a general withdrawal, which saved Paris and, perhaps, First German Army – a retirement which ended in an entrenched river-line position for the Battle of the Aisne on 15 September.

The Second Battle was fought between 15 and 19 July 1918 as part of the Fifth and last Hindenburg offensive. It was intended to exploit the Third Offensive, which had been brought to a halt by the French and Americans at the Battles of Cantigny and Château-Thierry in May and June respectively. On this occasion the German left wing, attacking to the east of Reims in an effort to reach Epernay in conjunction with the right wing attacking from Château-Thierry, met a well forewarned and prepared defence. Directed by General Foch, it gave but little ground. To the west of Reims, however, where the defences were weaker, a large penetration was made to allow a strong crossing of the Marne, a success soon obliterated when heavy air and artillery bombardments were directed against the bridges and their approaches, while reinforcements blocked further advances by

German troops, who at last saw the hopelessness of their situation.

General **Ludendorff** ordered a withdrawal of the Soissons–Reims salient, but was pre-empted on the 18th when French and American troops launched Foch's long-prepared counterstroke aimed at its elimination. Caught on the wrong foot, the dispirited Germans were hurled back by well-co-ordinated **tank** and **artillery** attacks, which inflicted heavy casualties and indicated to Ludendorff that the Hindenburg offensive was over. He cancelled the next offensive in Flanders, evacuated what was left of the Soissons–Reims salient and reverted to the defensive on the eve of the Battle of **Amiens**, which broke his resolve.

Marshall, General George (1880–1959). A brilliant infantryman who was First US Army's Chief of Staff in France in **World War I** and went on to become Chief of Staff of the Army on 1 September 1939. It was his task therefore to lift the Army from a low point in its history to readiness for a war he never doubted was coming, a task he carried out with enormous success. Yet it is for his great influence on President **Roosevelt**, Winston **Churchill** and many another top Allied leader during **World War II** that he is most renowned. The way in which he shaped American policy to obtain priority for tackling Germany before Japan (and thus securing preference for the Army over the Navy) and his dogged resolve to invade Europe at the earliest moment had immense impact, for better or worse, on the post-war world. He helped shape this world when, as Secretary of State from November 1945 to January 1949, he put through the European Recovery Programme (the famous Marshall Plan) to save Europe from economic chaos and Communism. In this period he helped obtain recognition for Israel and the founding of Nato. Later, as Secretary of Defense from September 1950 until September 1951, he implemented the Nato agreements and strengthened the armed forces during the **Korean War**. In 1953 he was awarded the Nobel Peace Prize.

Matapan, Battle of. In an endeavour to interfere with British reinforcement of **Greece** in March 1942, the Italian Fleet, with a **battleship** and eight **cruisers** commanded by Admiral Angelo Iachino, attempted to intercept convoys off **Crete**. Aware of the move, Admiral **Cunningham's** cruisers made contact on the 27th and lured the Italians towards his three battleships and an **aircraft-carrier**. An abortive **torpedo** attack on the Italians persuaded Iachino to turn for home. A second attack scored one hit on the battleship and a third attack stopped a cruiser. The delay inflicted led to a night action aided by **radar** and searchlights, resulting in the sinking of three Italian cruisers, but British signalling errors let the battleship escape.

Mechanization, Military. The term has been defined as the application of the internal combustion engine to land warfare in the transportation: (a) of men and weapons to and on the battlefield; and (b) of supplies.

The scene had been set as early as the **Crimean War** of 1854, which saw the use of early steam-traction engines, but it was the petrol engine, developed during the later part of the 19th century, which made the motor vehicle a practical proposition; by 1900 the automobile was in general use and armoured cars were beginning to appear. In 1911 the need for military motor transport had been foreseen by the British War Office, which introduced a scheme whereby manufacturers were encouraged to build their vehicles to strict military standards. These were so rigidly enforced that even in the dark a driver could expect to put his hand on the controls without difficulty, whoever the manufacturer of the vehicle might have been. The drawback to the civilian owner was that, on the outbreak of war, the vehicle would be immediately requisitioned. Thus, when war did come in 1914 the British Army had an effective transport fleet immediately to hand. This was, however, a far cry from complete mechanization with purpose-built vehicles; the British Army, like its European counterparts, was still a largely marching and horse-drawn force.

The successful deployment of the **tank** in the later stages of **World War I** changed the picture completely, with the British becoming the pioneers in mechanization during the 1920s. Despite all the obstacles the motor vehicle began to play an increasingly prominent part in military thinking. With the tank reluctantly given a permanent place in the order of battle, the need for cross-country vehicles to support the new weapon in the field became apparent, successfully demonstrated in trials in 1925 where the French Kegresse half-track vehicle perfomed particularly well. However, by 1927 six-wheelers had won the day for the British Army at least, and a whole series of sturdy wheeled vehicles began to appear, though mostly, it must be said, with only two-wheel drive. These vehicles formed an essential element in the 1927 and 1928 Experimental Mechanized Force exercises on Salisbury Plain; also to be seen there were small tracked infantry carriers – forerunners of the modern armoured personnel carrier (see **Armoured fighting vehicles**) – and the 18-pounder Birch gun, pointing the way for the self-propelled **artillery** of the future. The Salisbury Plain exercises showed the possibilities for mobile warfare, but the British were slow to learn their own lessons, partly because of conservatism amongst senior officers, the economic depression and a reluctance to commit a British Army to a future European war; garrisoning the Empire was the primary task and the value of mobile warfare in that context seemed dubious at the time.

However, even the most conservative saw the need for mechanization in the supporting services and the need to introduce motor transport into traditional arms. So mechanization of the British Army continued with the result that, when war came again in 1939, the British were possessed of a fleet of some 90,000 transport vehicles, which were in general far superior to those of the French and German armies.

In France it was General **de Gaulle** who had taken to heart the lessons of the British experiments, though he was unsuccessful in effecting a major change in French Army doctrine. In Germany the Panzer divisions which swept through Poland and France, and later Russia, also owed much to British ideas; in Russia too the tank was early recognized as a crucial weapon. However, in none of these countries was mechanization taken to its logical conclusion. The German Army, for example, relied on horse-drawn transport for much of its **logistic** support throughout **World War II**. Even in the United States, where the motor vehicle might be thought to reign supreme, mechanization was slow to penetrate throughout the Army. The British Expeditionary Force which went to France in 1939 can fairly be said to have been the only fully mechanized army in Europe at that time.

World War II soon saw the domination imposed by the motor vehicle: wheeled and tracked; armoured and 'soft-skinned'; as a fighting vehicle and in numerous supporting roles. Nowadays all arms and services are fully mechanized, with many of them, including logistic support, being under armour and a high proportion using tracked or four-wheel-drive vehicles. No recognized army in the world today, however humble, would consider itself other than a mechanized force. At the other extreme it has been estimated that a Soviet mechanized division has so many vehicles that, advancing along two parallel routes, it would extend for some 150km; the numbers of vehicles on the modern battlefield thus impose their own restrictions on mobility.

Medical services, Military. Although the scandals about care of the wounded during the **Crimean** and **Austro-Italian wars** of the 1850s marked turning-points in a change of attitude to and treatment of sailors and soldiers, a trend in that direction had long been apparent. How to prevent scurvy among sailors had been demonstrated (why it did was not known) in the 1770s, and helped spur the **Admiralty** to appreciate the merits of preserving life and raising efficiency. But the much publicized breakdown of medical care caused by totally inadequate services in the Crimea and at Scutari, which brought down the British government and inspired the dispatch of Florence **Nightingale** and her nurses to help put matters right, was to induce reforms which were copied by many other civilized nations. An Army Hospital Corps (later to become the Royal Army Medical Corps) was formed and Miss Nightingale's *Notes on Matters Affecting the Health, Efficiency and Hospital Administration of the British Army* and her *Notes on Nursing* became bibles for all reformers, including administrators on both sides during the **American Civil War**.

Medical technology advanced at the same time. Anaesthetics, often objected to by doctors on religious grounds, were used for the first time for surgical operations. In parallel with a drive to cleanse and adequately ventilate hospital wards went campaigns to improve public, as well as military, sanitation and raise health standards with water-borne sewage systems everywhere. At the same time improvements to **food**, plus Joseph Lister's discovery of antiseptics in 1865 leading to sterilization of medical instruments and wounds, were revolutionary. Mortality rates were reduced dramatically. Populations rose enormously, producing vast pools of manpower to expand industry and fill the ranks of enlarged armed forces, a process improved upon after the **Spanish–American War** in 1898 when the causes of malaria and yellow fever, along with means of their suppression and prevention, were discovered.

Nevertheless, mortality rates in **World War I**, though lower than before, remained high, notably from disease in undeveloped countries, such as those of **East Africa**. Even though it was discovered that Lister's carbolic acid had serious defects as an antiseptic, the latest generation of surgeons (against the objections of their seniors) were able to show in practice that it was thorough cleansing of a wound, with the removal of infected tissue, which best controlled the deadly gangrene. In addition, medical organizations which evacuated casualties rapidly and treated them early saved the most lives.

Mechanization and the use of motor ambulances, which had hastened evacuation of casualties in World War I, were put to even better use in **World War II**. Evacuation by lighter-than-air craft had first been tried in the **Franco-Prussian War** and sporadically, with France setting the example, in World War I. It was much more widely used in World War II, principally in such underdeveloped theatres of war as **Burma** and the **Pacific**. The greatest revolution, however, was through increased use of vaccines against disease and tetanus, together with blood transfusion and use of plasma. Most dramatic of all was Alexander Fleming's antibiotic penicillin to control infection and strikingly improve the wounded's chances of survival. Such chances were further enhanced by the introduction of DDT insecticides to control the carriers of disease (particularly malaria), in addition to suppressive drugs such as mepacrine. Armed forces lacking these benefits (as did the Japanese in particular and the Germans to some extent) risked the loss of battles and significant decline in **Morale**.

Commanders, above all those with men in action, have a duty to care for their men's health: in the latter half of the 19th century it became normal for medical practitioners to act as their advisers on such matters, giving advice which was ignored at one's peril, with the risk of serious consequences. Naturally the medical authorities had no difficulty in obtaining priority for **helicopters** to evacuate the wounded with unprecedented speed to medical units; they helped raise survival rates, in the **Korean War** for example, to 98 per cent of those who arrived alive at a surgical station. More controversial was the employment of psychiatrists to deal with cases of **combat fatigue** once a more enlightened view of this phenomena was taken after World War I. Improvements continue as knowledge increases and prejudices are overcome.

Mediterranean Sea, Battles of the. This large inland sea serving so many nations has frequently been the scene of naval actions, its strategic importance increasing significantly with the opening of the **Suez Canal** in 1869 and the subsequent discovery of Middle East oil. Yet between 1850 and 1914, when armed forces frequently traversed its length and breadth, no major actions occurred in its four principal basins, though the Battle of **Lissa** in the Adriatic was near by. At the start of **World War I**, however, there was a brisk and unsuccessful hunt by the Royal Navy for a German **battle·cruiser**, *Goeben*, and a **cruiser**, *Breslau*, which managed to escape to Turkey. Thereafter, there was persistent **submarine** warfare as Austrian and German boats tried to enter the Sea from the Adriatic and the Bosporus to attack Allied shipping – with no little success, but also no decisive results.

Italy's entry into **World War II** on 10 June 1940 immediately caused action as she attacked **Malta** and attempted to prevent the passage of British **convoys** from Gibraltar to the Middle East and, at the same time, reinforce her forces in **North Africa** to invade Egypt. On 3/4 July, however, the British Fleet (under Admiral **Cunningham**) attacked French warships in **Oran** and seized others in Alexandria. It then appeared off Messina to damage and drive into port the Italian Fleet at the Battle of Calabria on 9 July. There the Italians mostly remained until 11 November when British **aircraft-carrier**-borne torpedo-bombers in a celebrated night attack at Taranto severely damaged three **battleships** and two cruisers for the loss of two machines, a blow from which the Italians never recovered.

Before the Germans attacked Malta in January 1941, Britain managed to fight through a few convoys with relative ease. But from then on convoys were sent mainly to sustain Malta and its interceptions by air, surface vessels and submarines of Axis shipping to North Africa. Every

The Battles of the Mediterranean Sea

convoy provoked a battle in which Axis aircraft and submarines played the leading roles. Occasionally the Italian Fleet put to sea, usually to be driven off, as at **Matapan** in March 1941. Off Greece, Crete and North Africa, however, the Royal Navy suffered heavy losses in 1941, mainly from submarines and aircraft. In December 1941 it was almost crippled by Italian two-man midget submarines which entered Alexandria harbour and severely damaged two battleships, in addition to suffering the sinking at sea of another battleship by German submarine, and the loss in a minefield (**Mine, Sea**) of three cruisers and a destroyer, thus making it easy for the Axis armies to be reinforced for the major offensive in May 1942.

This was the nadir of British fortunes, even though, with American assistance, Malta was kept in action. Soon the boot was on the other foot when the British, amply supplied by aircraft, strongly reinforced and invariably well posted by **intelligence**, were able to play havoc with the Axis supply lines. This was the overture to victory at El **Alamein** and the Allied landing in North-West Africa (see **North Africa, Battles of**). As a prelude to the relief of Malta, it guaranteed the clearing of the North African shore, thus reopening the Sea to convoys, with enormous benefits to Allied **logistics**.

For the remainder of the war the Allies had free use of the Mediterranean to strike where they chose against the enemy in **Sicily**, Italy (**Italian campaign, 1943–5**), the Adriatic and Aegean Seas and France. Such freedom was largely denied the Italians (until they surrendered in September 1943) and Germans who were hunted relentlessly whenever their submarines, small craft and aircraft ventured forth – the surviving major elements of the Italian Fleet having either surrendered or been destroyed.

Since 1945 sporadic naval actions by light forces have taken place in the Eastern basin in connection with **Arab–Israeli wars**, plus the major **amphibious** invasion of **Suez** in 1956. The Sea remains of vital strategic importance in connection with the defence of Southern Europe and containment of the volatile Middle East situation (notably **Lebanon**) and the occasional depredations of Libya.

Megiddo, Battle of. A communications centre in Palestine, Megiddo was the scene of many battles in ancient times, and adjacent to the concluding Allied offensive against the Turks in **World War I**. After defeat at **Gaza** in 1917, the Turks withdrew to a naturally strong position between Jaffa and the Jordan. They fortified it with three armies, numbering 36,000 men, under General Liman von Sanders. General **Allenby** had 57,000 men, 12,000 **cavalry**, plus

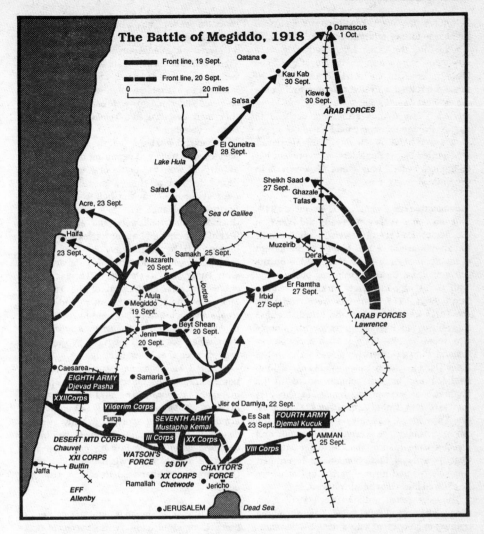

The Battle of Megiddo, 1918

Front line, 19 Sept.
Front line, 20 Sept.

0   20 miles

Damascus
1 Oct.

Qatana

Kau Kab
30 Sept.

Kiswe
30 Sept.

Sa'sa

ARAB FORCES

El Quneitra
28 Sept.

Lake Hula

Safad

Sheikh Saad
27 Sept.

Ghazale

Tafas

Acre, 23 Sept.

Sea of Galilee

Haifa

23 Sept.

Muzeirib

Der'a

Samakh   25 Sept.

Nazareth
20 Sept.

Er Ramtha
27 Sept.

Afula

Irbid
27 Sept.

Megiddo
19 Sept.

ARAB FORCES
Lawrence

Jordan

Beyt Shean
20 Sept.

Jenin
20 Sept.

Caesarea

EIGHTH ARMY
Djevad Pasha

Samaria

XXIICorps

Jisr ed Darniya, 22 Sept.

Yilderim Corps

Es Salt
23 Sept

FOURTH ARMY
Djemal Kucuk

Furqa

SEVENTH ARMY
Mustapha Kemal

DESERT MTD CORPS
Chauvel

III Corps

XX Corps

VIII Corps

AMMAN
25 Sept.

XXI CORPS
Bulfin

**WATSON'S
FORCE**

Jaffa

53 DIV

**CHAYTOR'S
FORCE**

EFF
Allenby

XX CORPS
Chetwode

Ramallah

Jericho

JERUSALEM

Dead Sea

armoured cars, (**Armoured fighting vehicles**), and the Arab **guerrilla** force operating in the desert on his right flank. By elaborate deception he deluded von Sanders into believing the attack would fall on the Turkish inland flank. Instead he attacked near the coast, where only 8,000 Turks with 130 guns stood against 35,000 British with 400 guns. The attack started on 19 September, overran the Turks on the coastal sector and pivoted inland. Those Turks not enveloped were thrown into rout, harried by **aircraft**, mobile forces and Arabs. Damascus fell on 1 October, Aleppo on the 25th. Five days later Turkey signed an armistice.

***Merrimack* versus *Monitor*.** In the **American Civil War**, *Merrimack* was a wooden, screw steamship which the Confederates converted into an ironclad, fitted with a ram, armed with six 9in, two 7in and two 6in guns firing broadside. *Monitor* was a Federal low-freeboard, steam raft mounting a rotating turret with two 11in guns. *Merrimack* raided Federal shipping blockading the James River on 8 March 1862, sank a sloop by ramming and a **frigate** by gunfire and forced another frigate ashore. But when next day she appeared again, *Monitor* was waiting. *Merrimack* tried to ram but was evaded by the more manoeuvrable *Monitor*. For three and a half hours they bombarded each other at close range, the former firing more rounds and scoring 23 hits, the latter firing 53 rounds at a much slower rate, because the turret had to be hand-traversed inboard to reload, and scoring 20 hits. Each retired with slight damage and weary crews. Next day *Merrimack* was back, but *Monitor*, on orders from Washington, declined to engage in case damage would leave her opponent a free hand. A few days later *Merrimack* was burned by the Confederates, to prevent her falling into Federal hands, and *Monitor* sank in rough water.

Mesopotamia campaigns. On 6 November 1914, nine days after Turkey entered **World War I** on the side of the Central Powers, a small British Indian military force was landed at the mouth of the Shatt-al-Arab to capture Abadan on the 8th and Basra on the 23rd after overcoming, with naval support, fierce Turkish resistance. Throughout 1915 both sides were reinforced, the Turks less easily than the British because the **railway** to Baghdad from Constantinople was unfinished. In May a division under Major-General Charles Townshend was sent up the River Tigris to explore the possibility of reaching Baghdad, and another column moved up the Euphrates. After winning battles at Qrna on the 31st and Kut-al-Amara on 28 September, Townshend was ordered to continue the advance, though he warned his strength and **logistics** were inadequate. He met a superior Turkish army at Ctesiphon on 22 November, was defeated and thrown back into Kut where he allowed himself to be surrounded.

The siege lasted until 29 April 1916. Successive attempts at relief failed. Townshend did nothing to co-operate with a sortie. Maladministration and the collapse of British logistics created sufferings of **Crimean** magnitude for the troops, 8,000 of whom surrendered in Kut while the relief force suffered 21,000 casualties.

In August 1916 the British put General Sir Frederick Maude in command and raised his force to 166,000 (two-thirds Indian) in what was, after all, a subsidiary theatre of war. He began an offensive up the Tigris in December 1916, and in a most skilful and well-administered advance outmanoeuvred the Turks in a series of battles below Kut on 23 February 1917. The Turks were outnumbered, outfought and strongly pursued as they

retreated on Baghdad, which they defended on the Diyala River until overrun. Baghdad fell on 11 March and Maude pursued the Turks up the Tigris, Euphrates and Diyala to secure the city, which was his terminal objective. Turkish attempts to assemble a counterstroke with the so-called Yilderim Army were cancelled owing to their more urgent need to reinforce the front at **Gaza** in Palestine.

In September Maude advanced up the Euphrates with a view to capturing the oilfields of Mosul and won the Battle of Ramadi on the 28th. He died of cholera in November but General Sir William Marshall continued the northward advance with a force of 500,000 (including camp followers) and an enormous fleet of river craft and motor lorries. Rarely was he opposed by more than 20,000 Turkish combat troops. Yet not until after the armistice with Turkey on 30 October 1918 was Mosul entered, after a final defeat of the Turks at Sharqat on the 29th. On the other hand, British troops advancing from Baghdad to capture the oilfields of Baku on 5 August by a crossing of the Caspian Sea were thrown out by the Turks in September after heavy fighting.

In 1918 Mesopotamia assumed its modern name of Iraq, as an Arab state but with a British-mandated responsibility until 1932 which involved its forces – mainly aircraft and armoured cars – in sporadic fighting against dissident tribesmen until 1920. It would be occupied again by the British from India and Palestine in May 1941 when the Iraqis, with German incitement and aid, threatened vital oil-fields.

Metz, Battles of. Owing to its vital strategic position as a communications centre, the city of Metz was heavily fortified through the ages to guard one of the traditional routes into France. Moreover, until the **Franco-Prussian War** it had never fallen to the enemy. Because the **railway** from Saarbrücken to Reims, Châlons and Paris ran through the city, it was a prime German objective in 1870. Marshal **Bazaine**'s retreat from the frontier, attended by a series of setbacks, was finally brought to an end by the defeats at Mars-la-Tour, Vionville and Gravelotte-Saint-Privat which forced his army back into Metz on 18 August. The Germans, commanded by Prince Frederick Charles, encircled the city and decided to starve it out. From Châlons, Marshal Mac-

Mahon set forth on the 21st to its relief as Bazaine planned a sortie to join hands. But the ineptly executed sortie was repulsed as Mac-Mahon crashed to defeat at **Sedan**. Inadequately provisioned as the city was, Bazaine was judged to have surrendered supinely on 28 October and was made a scapegoat for France's failings in the war.

In **World War** I. Metz was the pivot of the great German wheel into France in August 1914. In **World War II** it was barely defended against the Germans in 1940. But the Americans in General **Patton**'s Third Army met tough resistance in mid-September 1944 and were unable to capture the city. They tried again on 9 November in snow and rain, but were held in mud and minefields, not encircling the city until 18 November, and not capturing it until 13 December after enormous expenditure of ammunition caused much damage.

Mexican wars. The expansionist policies of the USA which led to the Mexican War of 1846–8 continued to nettle the Mexicans. Border frictions continued into the 20th century. More destabilizing were the internal struggles: the civil war from 1857 to 1860 between conservative and liberal factions, and a further prolonged outbreak from 1863 to 1867 in the aftermath of British, French and Spanish intervention in 1861 to protect their interests. This adventure was pursued only by the French in 1862, in strength, without reaching a conclusion against Mexicans who resisted well in conventional and **guerrilla** actions. After the **American Civil War** in 1865, US pressure upon the French to withdraw was backed up by threat of force. The French left in 1867, whereupon internal chaos persisted until 1877 when the reformist Porfirio Díaz fought his way to power and governed with some moderation until ousted in 1911.

Again factional civil war disrupted the country and continued on and off until 1923, interspersed with American interventions, first at Veracruz after the arrest of unarmed American sailors on 9 April 1914; next in March 1916 after the revolutionary Pancho Villa (who challenged for control of the country) raided Columbus in protest against American policy in favour of the Carranza government in power. The punitive expedition of 10,000, under General **Pershing**, crossed the border to catch Villa, but failed in its aim and simply stirred up increased anti-American feeling when Pershing's men sometimes fought government troops also hunting Villa. Pershing was withdrawn in February 1915 as his country stood on the verge of entering **World War I**.

Midway, Battle of. Midway Island, which the US Navy began developing as a naval and air base in 1940, was the main objective of the Japanese in June 1942 to consolidate their perimeter defences by extending their earlier conquests and at last destroying the American **aircraft-carriers**. Having in May failed at the Battle of the **Coral Sea** to seize Port Moresby, Admiral **Yamamoto** still attacked the Aleutian Islands, as a diversionary operation. Against Midway he sent the carrier fleet as advanced guard to the **battleship** fleet and the **amphibious** invasion force. Amply forewarned of the Japanese plans, Admiral **Nimitz** assembled three carriers with 250 aircraft (under Vice-Admiral **Fletcher**), plus 109 machines on Midway, against Admiral Chaike Nagumo's four carriers with their 275 aircraft.

A complicated plan, over-confidence and sloppy staff work attended the Japanese approach to Midway on 4 June. They were unaware of Fletcher's presence, whom their reconnaissance failed to locate. The initial air strike against the island was complete and a second being prepared when Nagumo received news of the American carriers. A **bomber** attack by the Americans went astray and the **torpedo** aircraft, attacking unsupported, were annihilated. A moment later, however, the dive-bombers arrived, caught the Japanese in the midst of rearming their machines and set three carriers ablaze. The fourth carrier, however, escaped and it was her aircraft which crippled the US carrier *Yorktown* (finally sunk by **submarine**) before herself being found and sunk by the Americans. Realizing there was no hope of taking Midway, Yamamoto withdrew, having lost the cream of his naval airmen and Japan's hope of victory (see map page 216).

Militia. See **Reserve forces.**

Mine, Land. In the military context the term 'mine' derives from the work of those sappers toiling away in tunnels beneath ancient fortifications to undermine the walls and cause a breach. With the appearance of guns able to batter down the defender's walls mining fell into disuse until

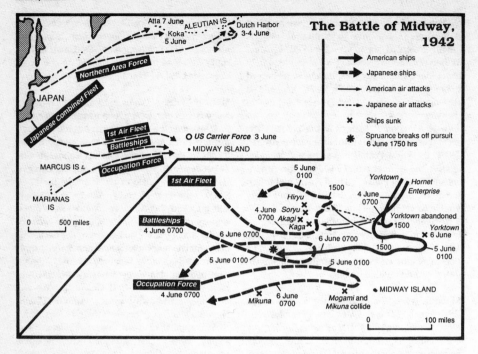

The Battle of Midway, 1942

Atta 7 June
Koka 5 June
ALEUTIAN IS
Dutch Harbor 3-4 June

Northern Area Force

JAPAN

Japanese Combined Fleet

1st Air Fleet
Battleships

MARCUS IS

Occupation Force

MARIANAS IS

0   500 miles

O *US Carrier Force* 3 June
• MIDWAY ISLAND

1st Air Fleet

Battleships
4 June 0700

→ American ships
⇢ Japanese ships
→ American air attacks
⇠⇢ Japanese air attacks
✗ Ships sunk
✳ Spruance breaks off pursuit 6 June 1750 hrs

5 June 0100

1500

Yorktown   Hornet
             Enterprise

4 June 0700

Hiryu

4 June 0700   *Soryu* ✗
               Akagi ✗
               Kaga ✗

6 June 0700

Yorktown abandoned
1500   Yorktown
        ✗ 6 June

6 June 0700

1500   5 June 0100

5 June 0100

5 June 0100

Occupation Force
4 June 0700

✗ 6 June 0700
Mikuna

✗ *Mogami* and *Mikuna* collide

• MIDWAY ISLAND

0   100 miles

the **American Civil War**, when the widespread use of entrenchments led to the development of the explosive land-mine. During **World War I** although the Germans did experiment with buried shells in an effort to stop British and French tanks, it was once again the subterranean mine exploded beneath the enemy's trenches which was widely used. One of the more spectacular efforts was at Messines Ridge in 1917, where 500 tonnes of ammonal were fired under the German front line.

However, it was in **World War II** that the buried mine came into its own. By 1939 the need for two basic types had emerged: the small anti-personnel mine designed to wound; and the larger anti-tank mine designed to break the track of a **tank**. Both categories were cheap to produce and easy to handle, but much more difficult to detect and remove once buried in the ground. Extensive minefields were laid in every theatre of war, usually sited to channel the enemy into a defile where he could be suitably attacked.

Both anti-tank and anti-personnel mines were detonated by pressure fuses and usually encased in metal boxes. One of the first improvements was to replace the container with a wooden one, to defeat the metal detectors then in use.

The anti-tank mine was comparatively insensitive to handling and, since the only certain way to clear a minefield was to dig up the mines by hand, it was not long before explosive anti-handling devices were fitted. Anti-personnel mines designed to jump up and spray pellets at body height, when triggered remotely, also began to appear.

Minefields became such a hazard, and could be laid so much more quickly than they could be cleared, that mechanical clearing devices were soon being developed, particularly by the British. Probably the most successful idea was the flail tank: a set of chains mounted on a rotating boom extended from the front of the vehicle; the chains beat the ground as the tank moved forward, exploding the mines as it went. Other ideas included heavy rollers and ploughs.

Since 1945 mines have become even more complex. In the anti-tank field they have been designed to attack the more vulnerable belly, or even the side, as well as breaking the track. This has led to much more sophisticated fusing, such as by fuses actuated on contact with the tank hull, or influence fuses actuated by heat, noise, vibration or magnetic effects. It is now common to encase mines in plastic to outwit the metal detector.

Modern anti-personnel mines are made in innocent shapes to look like small stones or other casually discarded objects and then scattered widely and rapidly from **helicopters** or vehicle-mounted projectors. Deployed over large areas by the Argentines during the **Falklands War**, they have continued to be a major hazard long after the war has ended. In Afghanistan similar mines, distributed far and wide by Soviet helicopters have caused innumerable casualties among the civilian population.

Modern mine clearing has not really advanced a great deal from World War II; the British-designed Aardvark flail is merely an updated and more efficient version of the successful Sherman Crab. Similarly, Giant Viper – an explosive hose carried across a minefield by rocket and then fired, exploding the mines by sympathetic detonation – is the modern development of a wartime device (see also **Explosives**). The unseen mine will continue to be a major hazard in all land-warfare operations.

Mine, Sea. The first controlled sea-mine was constructed in 1843 by **Samuel Colt**. He succeeded in blowing up a ship at a range of five miles with an underwater mine detonated by an electric current passed through underwater cables. A similar device was used by the Prussians against the Danish Fleet in 1848. The real need, however, was for a mine which could be detonated independently when a passing ship struck it. The Herz horn made this possible and the device, in various forms, was in use for many years. Inert until struck, and with unlimited life, the horn consisted of a glass vial containing acid. When the horn was broken the acid formed the electolyte for a primary cell which produced enough current for an electric detonator to explode the main charge.

During **World War I**, though the Herz contact mine was widely used, various influence-detonated mines also began to appear, actuated by magnetic, pressure or acoustic means. The magnetic mine is triggered by the approaching ship's own magnetic field; the pressure mine relies on the reduction of pressure beneath a ship in shallow water to deflect a diaphragm which triggers the detonator; the acoustic mine originally used hydrophones to detect a passing ship – a somewhat unreliable device which, in

its modern form using micro-electronics, is once again popular.

Modern technology has improved all these types of mine in current service with the world's navies and has also introduced the atomic mine (whether or not such a device has been deployed is unknown).

Extensive minefields were laid by surface ships and submarines during both world wars, especially in the confined waters of the English Channel, where they had some success as an anti-submarine weapon. Buoyant mines attached to anchors on the sea-bed, floating just below the surface, were also, of course, a considerable hazard to surface ships. Techniques have changed over the years and during World War II the availability of larger aircraft meant that mines could be laid from the air. This was used to best effect by the Americans during the **Vietnam War** when much of the coastline was denied to Vietcong supplies by this means; in particular, Haiphong harbour was quickly and effectively closed from the air in 1972 by the dropping of thousands of magnetic, acoustic and pressure mines, thus denying to North Vietnam its major port and causing her a major supply crisis. However, it must be said that mine warfare is perhaps more effective in the threat it poses than in the actual damage done. In World War II the Axis lost 1,316 ships to mines and the Allies 1,118; comparatively small numbers in proportion to the total shipping losses of that war.

Nevertheless, minesweepers have become an important element in the naval armoury, though their methods may originally have seemed somewhat crude. By streaming a para-vane attached to a long cable from the side of the ship, the aim was to snag the mine's anchor chain, which would then slide along the cable into the jaws of a cutter, allowing the mine to bob free to the surface. The ship's crew would then engage it with rifle fire until one of the horns was struck and the mine exploded. Though modern technology has improved on this, sailors were still to be seen firing at floating mines during the **Iraq-Iran War** of the 1980s.

Magnetic mines posed a different problem when the Germans launched them on the British early in World War II. However, a solution was quickly found and ships were degaussed by passing an electric cable round the hull to neutralize the ship's own magnetic field. Some modern minesweepers are constructed of glass-reinforced plastic to overcome the magnetic mine threat.

Missiles. See **Artillery** and **Rockets and guided missiles**.

Mitchell, General William (1879–1936). An officer in the US Army Signal Corps who learnt to fly in 1916, flew as an observer in **World War I**, but by September 1918 was commander of a Franco-American air force of 1,500 machines. He used the force in mass (sometimes with formations of 200 aircraft) in the Saint-Mihiel battle and the Meuse Argonne offensive. By then he was a fervent champion of air power, proposing the parachuting of **airborne** infantry behind the German lines in 1919, and of **strategic bombing** by independent air forces on the British model.

In the early 1920s, as Assistant Chief of Air Services in the Army Air Corps, he tried to prove, by a somewhat spurious demonstration against an anchored **battleship**, that warships were outmoded by aircraft. His vigorous campaign on behalf of the Air Corps made many enemies. It led to his conviction by court martial and suspension from duty in 1925 for accusing the Army and Navy Departments, in the aftermath of the *Shenandoah* airship crash, of 'incompetency, criminal negligence and almost treasonable administration'. He resigned from the Army in 1926 and devoted the rest of his life fighting for air power.

Mobilization. The assembly of military manpower plus the resources to support them in combat has underlain preparations of war since the earliest times. Only very strong national economies are able to support large standing forces or afford vast stockpiles of weapons and material. Planning for aggression or defence almost invariably calls for the largest possible permanent force for the envisaged situation, supported by adequate **reserve forces** and an industrial plan to satisfy their future **logistic** requirements. However, the rapidly expanding **technology** from the 1850s onwards, particularly in **communication** systems, **Mechanization** and **conscription**, plus the impact of humanitarianism, has vastly complicated planning and procedures besides creating highly significant political issues.

Permanent staff (**Staffs, Military**) corps were formed to cope with the military problems of the 19th century. The Prussian General Staff was to the forefront with organization and method of mobilization for the **Austro-Prussian** and **Franco-Prussian wars** of 1866 and 1870 respectively. In these struggles the relatively smooth movement of the Prussian permanent and reserve forces to their pre-invasion assembly points was sometimes undone by inefficient control beyond railhead – but it was undeniably superior to that of their enemies. The mobilization of the French armies in 1870 was a monument to poor planning and inefficient control and execution. Recalled reservists roamed in search of their units which, as often as not, lacked equipment and supplies and were not located where required. **Morale** sank. Defeat and revolution ensued.

Orders to mobilize are expensive expressions of national policy, usually actuated by proclamation. They can be selective or general in scale of application. Either way they have political meaning since they demonstrate militant intent. The European nations' mobilizations in advance of **World War I** were not only managed with commendable efficiency, their implementation also fell little short of declarations of war. There were instances of the military authority informing politicians that cancellation was impossible and war inevitable. The long-prepared mobilization schemes of 1914 were closely dovetailed with strategic plans and economic policies, knowledge of which by an enemy could forfeit surprise. It assisted the Germans to be aware of France's Plan XVII and its intention to invade Germany via the Thionville–Metz area; and that the French were unaware of the Schlieffen Plan.

All these plans were based on the concept of a short war which would be 'over by Christmas'. Britain was among the few nations to plan for a long war, though she had made no preparations for such an event. After Christmas, therefore, the major participants suffered from shortages, principally of **explosives** and **ammunition** which, in cases, took over two years to rectify. Likewise the unexpected development of a war of material made demands on weapons and equipment, such as motor vehicles, **aircraft** and **tanks**, which had hardly been envisaged; which required the creation of brand-new production facilities; and which placed such immense demands upon manpower that the armed forces began to suffer and women had to be mobilized to a far greater extent than ever before, thus inducing states of total war.

Mobilization for **World War II** reflected the lessons of its recent predecessor. Control of manpower and resources was applied beforehand. Allowances, often excessive, were made for the disruptive effects of **air warfare**. China had long been in a state of civil war (**Chinese civil wars**) before Japan, with large permanent forces, struck in 1937. Most European nations had begun a partial mobilization before 1 September 1939. Several of Poland's (**Polish campaigns**) combat troubles occurred because she delayed mobilization for political reasons – though air attack caused disruption too. It was a defect of German policy that, for political popularity as well as economic reasons, **Hitler** restricted industrial production until far too late; and resisted the **recruiting** of **women** to the end. Instead, Germany lived off her victims and employed unreliable slave labour.

Since 1945, in an almost universal environment of **cold** and **limited war**, many nations have retained large forces, supplied by **conscription**, and large reserves. The overshadowing **nuclear** threat suggested the need for large pools of manpower and resources for **civil defence** and to replace the wholesale destruction of global war. The massed Communist forces, which are bankrupting their nations, are faced by anti-Communist nations which, to defend their economies, depend on sufficient warning to mobilize their cheaper reservists and move them long distances to threatened places. It has become an element of **deterrence** to demonstrate an ability effectively to mobilize at speed to match any variety of threats: how, for example, to reinforce Germany from the USA and Britain before an invasion from Russia makes deep penetrations. But the urgency of such moves, with the implication of running the gauntlet to seaport or airport of disembarkation and the immediate taking up of pre-positioned equipment, is not cheap and has raised doubts as to feasibility. The fact remains that the slightest indication of a hostile mobilization from **intelligence** sources acts as a warning for counter-mobilization and for diplomatic activity to defuse the political situation.

Moltke, Field Marshal Count Helmuth Karl von (1800–91). A member of the Prussian **General Staff** with a bent for history who eagerly embraced the **railway** as a revolutionary factor in war. He envisaged the Prussian Army playing a leading role in the unification of Germany and, with royal backing, was appointed Chief of the General Staff in 1857. He then joined Chancellor Otto von **Bismarck** and Minister of War, General Albert von Roon, in the foundation of the German Empire through the war with **Denmark** in 1864, the **Austro-Prussian War** of 1866 and the **Franco-Prussian War** of 1871. These conflicts were quickly won within economic bounds through von Moltke's brilliant modernization of the Army and his own firm, if not faultless, handling of combat operations.

The key to modernization was his strengthening of the General Staff corps by the inculcation of intensive professionalism together with a broad outlook that encouraged this élite to take decisions within a framework of general directives (as opposed to precise orders). The sense of initiative evolved created expert planners and commanders who were given advanced promotion to the highest appointments. He envisaged prolonged battles by armies moving on broad fronts, poised to concentrate at decisive battlefields to overwhelm the enemy by heavy firepower with the latest weapons. His Staff officers and the **telegraph** controlled carefully devised movements in which the railway was the vital instrument. The effectiveness of his ideas was expressed in victory, though he never entirely managed to co-ordinate operations in the combat arena and was often embarrassed by **logistic** shortcomings.

Monitor. See *Merrimack* versus *Monitor.*

Montgomery, Field Marshal (Lord) Bernard (1887–1976). An infantryman who won a reputation as a Staff officer in **World War I** and who, in 1940, commanded a division with flair in the retreat to **Dunkirk**. By 1942 he had been an Army commander in Britain, but it was when given command of Eighth Army in Egypt in August that he came to public attention. His conduct of the second and third Battles of El **Alamein** restored that formation's **morale** and won Montgomery a reputation for care, without taking risks, in his conduct of war. He was to lead Eighth Army in pursuit of the Axis armies to **Tunisia**, to Sicily and into Italy (**Italian campaign, 1943–5**) – a period in which he managed to sow mistrust of his methods with American allies. Yet he commanded the Allied armies brilliantly in the **Normandy** battles in 1944 and, if he had been allowed his way by General **Eisenhower**, might have finished **World War II** that autumn with a narrow-front advance through **Arnhem** into Germany. He had to be content with commanding 21st Army Group on the Allied left flank in the final Battle of **Germany**, the culmination of which was his acceptance of the German surrender on 4 May 1945.

As Chief of the British Imperial General Staff after the war he was not a success, but as Chairman Western Europe's C-in-C's Committee from 1948 until becoming Deputy Supreme Allied Commander in Europe in 1951 until 1958, he played an important role in establishing Nato's forces.

Morale. There is sometimes confusion about what morale is, not just how it is created and maintained. The *Oxford English Dictionary* refers to it as 'conduct, behaviour, especially with regard to confidence, hope, zeal, submission to discipline'; and records its appearance in this context in 1842 in relation to military affairs. Recognizing morale is difficult. For example, it is not high, as some British government ministers seemed to think in **World War II**, only if people are 'cheerful' or in 'high spirits'; it can also be detected in silent, dour resolution.

The military usually place maintenance of morale next to top among the principles of war (**War, Principles of**) and go to immense trouble enhancing it. Chiefly the aim is to provide strong senses of purpose and motivation, clear, sensible leadership, excellent weapons and equipment, sound **logistic** services, adequate pay and sustained successes in all activities, including the ultimate one of battle.

Every skirmish, battle, campaign and war provides examples of the effects of morale. At all levels individuals have demonstrated varying spiritual qualities which accounted for only part of a group's overall morale. A leader of high morale may very well compensate for several followers with low morale. In moments of extreme duress or euphoria there can be wild swings of morale – often only passing reactions if a corrective is sensibly applied by leaders, who need not necessarily be appointed officers. But (as will be seen below) in total war the maintenance of civil morale has also to be assured.

History contains many examples of morale breaking down in units and sub-units. When a few men or small groups abandon the battlefield it is as likely as not due to collapse of morale – perhaps only temporarily, for any of a number of reasons, and some quite insignificant. In such instances, loss of or failure of a leader was often the cause. It is the far fewer, battle-losing collapses that start a rot which catch greatest attention, sometimes blotting out the numerous occasions when, in appalling conditions, men have persevered and triumphed.

The reasons for the rise and decline of morale are many, variable and difficult to understand. Morale was at a low ebb in the British Army during the first winter of the **Crimean War**. Yet, although weakened by sickness, inferior medical care and inadequate shelter, treated with scant regard by their leaders, and subject to harsh discipline, British soldiers held firm and won battles. In the **Austro-Prussian War** of 1866 it was more than a decline in the Austrian soldiers' morale, after defeat at Königgrätz, which brought the war to an abrupt end: the military and political leadership was lacking in determination and purpose, amounting to poor morale at the top. Conversely, once incompetent preparations and inept leadership allowed the rout of the French Army in the **Franco-Prussian War** of 1870, the collapse of the nation's morale followed (though even during the sieges of **Paris** and Belfort, and battles in some provinces, flashes of higher morale appeared which the Germans could not ignore). The **Boer War** provides a significant example of how a populace whose army has been defeated and main centres occupied can fight on as **guerrillas**, with virtually no assistance at all from outsiders. Outstanding leadership and belief in the cause helped keep the Commandos going, but there also existed a grim racial and religious fervour in all ranks.

World War I was a turning-point for reasons other than its sheer scale. **Air warfare** denied the bulk of populations the luxury of psychological detachment from danger. A few bombs on Paris, Warsaw, Antwerp and London in 1914 and 1915 caused a profound, if passing, shock to civilian morale. Although casualties were few, the public outcry scared governments into taking noticeable aggressive and passive measures, demonstrating that, however ineffectual the effort, morale was steadied by a sense of something being done. Later the **Russian**

revolutionary wars and the German revolution showed how volatile morale could be when the demoralized mutineer of one day became the uplifted revolutionary fighter on the next – a phenomenon frequently observed in most struggles of that nature.

World War II, on the other hand, was remarkable for the manner in which military and civil communities maintained their morale, notably when exposed to intensive bombing on the home fronts, where apathy was often the reaction of people whose only option was to 'carry on'. Only France among the great powers was brought down, in 1940, by military demoralization. Of the Axis powers whose civil morale did not break, Italy's change of sides in 1943 split the nation and did not stop them fighting, Germany fought to the last breath and Japan only stopped when defeat was imminent. People simply adapted to the conditions.

As for events in Vietnam, be it noted that the North withstood the most intensive bombing of all time, yet only accepted a temporary halt in 1972 after defeat in the field. Meanwhile, the South collapsed as soon as its army, never assailed from the air, lost confidence and fell to pieces once US support was denied. Finally, let it be remembered that in the 1930s it was assumed air warfare would destroy morale – and did not – and that similar forecasts about nuclear war have been made with rather less assurance. Like life, morale is difficult to maintain but easy to extinguish.

Mortars. Short-barrelled smoothbore high-angled weapons for dropping shot behind the enemy's defences had been used throughout the 19th century, but it was the static warfare of World War I which brought the mortar to the fore as an infantry support weapon. The Germans had anticipated the need with a large 305mm (12in) mortar already in service. Initially the British (and French) had none, but, by 1915 the British had developed weapons, operated by infantrymen and simple to use, with a range of about 300–400m and intended to reach targets dug-in within the trench system.

However, the British weapons were cumbersome and it was the development of the Stokes mortar that provided the infantry with what they really needed; a simple 102mm (4in) tube mounted on adjustable legs and resting on a base-plate weighing 32kg. It threw its bombs to about 350m at a rate of 30 rounds a minute. Firing was a simple matter of dropping the bomb down the tube on to a fixed striker which detonated the percussion cap. This remains the broad principle upon which most modern mortars operate.

In the 1930s German development continued and by 1939 two extremely effective weapons were available: an 80mm with a range of 2,000m and an 81mm reaching out to over 4,000m. The devastating effect of the German mortars exposed the inadequacy of the British equipment, rectified in time by improvements to the 76mm and by the introduction of the heavy 107mm (4·2in) mortar with a range of about 4,000m.

The need for mortars in mobile operations was fully appreciated by the end of World War II and, though basic designs remain generally unaltered, much effort has gone into improving bomb ballistics and sighting equipment. Larger mortars, with calibres up to 240mm, have been produced, notably by the Russians, some breech-loading, some rifled, some automatic, like the 82mm Vasilyek, and some vehicle-borne. However, most armies have found the 81mm calibre satisfactory for close infantry support, backed up by the 107mm weapon and with a light section mortar such as the British 51mm, hand-held and firing a 2kg bomb out to about 750m.

Moscow, Battles of. Moscow became the capital of Soviet Russia in March 1918 and suffered from the Revolution like most other cities. In June 1941 it was the objective of the German Army Group Centre, under Field Marshal von Bock, with 55 divisions including two Panzer groups, against Marshal Semen Timoshenko's Western Front Army Group. On 27 June von Bock encircled a group of Russians at Minsk, and on 16 July another mass at Smolensk, though numerous Russians escaped and it was not until 5 August that 600,000 men with over 5,000 tanks were bagged. At that Hitler vacillated, preferring to give priority to the capture of Leningrad and Ukraine. Not until 23 August was General Guderian diverted from Army Group Centre to attack Kiev, thus delaying a general advance on Moscow until 30 September.

The Russians always assumed Moscow was the enemy's main objective. Air raids had begun

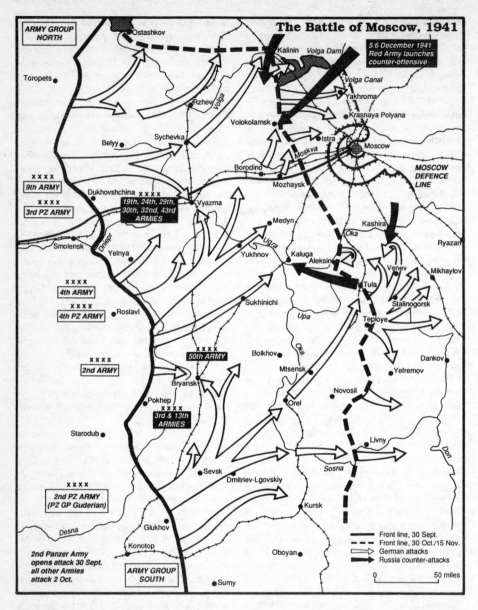

The Battle of Moscow, 1941

5/6 December 1941 Red Army launches counter-offensive

ARMY GROUP NORTH

ARMY GROUP SOUTH

2nd Panzer Army opens attack 30 Sept. all other Armies attack 2 Oct.

MOSCOW DEFENCE LINE

xxxx 9th ARMY

xxxx 3rd PZ ARMY

xxxx 19th, 24th, 29th, 30th, 32nd, 43rd ARMIES

xxxx 4th ARMY

xxxx 4th PZ ARMY

xxxx 2nd ARMY

xxxx 50th ARMY

xxxx 3rd & 13th ARMIES

xxxx 2nd PZ ARMY (PZ GP Guderian)

Ostashkov · Toropets · Kalinin · Volga Dam · Volga Canal · Yakhroma · Krasnaya Polyana · Rzhev · Volga · Belyy · Sychevka · Volokolamsk · Istra · Moskva · Moscow · Borodino · Mozhaysk · Dukhovshchina · Vyazma · Medyn · Kashira · Oka · Ryazan · Smolensk · Dnepr · Yelnya · Ugra · Yukhnov · Kaluga · Aleksin · Venev · Mikhaylov · Roslavl · Sukhinichi · Upa · Tula · Stalinogorsk · Bolkhov · Oka · Teploye · Dankov · Bryansk · Mtsensk · Novosil · Yefremov · Pokhep · Orel · Starodub · Livny · Don · Sevsk · Dmitriev-Lgovskiy · Sosna · Glukhov · Kursk · Desna · Konotop · Oboyan · Sumy

Front line, 30 Sept.
Front line, 30 Oct./15 Nov.
German attacks
Russia counter-attacks

0   50 miles

on 22 July. Ground defences were being prepared with woefully inadequate forces which, on 6 October, were placed by Josef **Stalin** under the command of General **Zhukov**. Von Bock began well with a rapid encirclement of enemy groups at Vyasma and Bryansk, as Guderian advanced on Tula from Kiev. But on 6 October Guderian suffered a check at Mtsensk, snow began to fall and autumn rain clogged the Vyasma front. For the next two months, Zhukov stood on the brink of despair with crumbling forces. A state of siege was declared on 20 October, but the Germans also despaired when the advance suffered from stop and go in alternating conditions of mud, freeze and thaw. With neither men nor equipment suitably prepared for these conditions, momentum was lost and the Russians won time for recuperation. Yet Guderian reached Tula and Army Group Centre broke Zhukov's defence line and came within 25 miles of Moscow in temperatures below $-40°C$, though by then the logistic services were in chaos and the men fought to a standstill.

With by no means well-supported infantry, Zhukov launched a counterstroke on 6 December and rolled the Germans back, in the sort of blow which, in September, would have been stopped in its tracks, but to which the Germans now bowed as they withdrew; Hitler sacking many senior commanders as morale declined. Moscow was saved, never to be directly threatened again.

Mountain warfare. Since commanding heights are the embodiment of vital ground, mountains create extreme conditions for warfare. Not only do they dominate terrain by providing naturally strong fortifications to reinforce defensive operations, they make logistics and endurance more difficult than in any other kind of terrain. Every route has to be cleared of enemy observation, which as often as not means struggling to every peak in sight, peaks which, if much over 10,000ft, cause anoxia to men or animals which have to carry equipment and supplies, in cloud and cold, where every ridge can hide an ambush. Mobility is at a premium in warfare which is inherently slow-moving – calling for the infantry specialist and much patience. It demands climbing equipment and techniques and is usually unsuitable, to a large extent, for mechanized forces – though, as in jungle warfare, the presence of a single tank, dragged to commanding ground by ingenuity and engineering toil, can be worth a squadron in an open plain.

Mountains, particularly forested ones, make ideal hide-outs for guerrilla forces. That is why such campaigns have been prolonged and effective in, for example, Afghanistan, northern India and Pakistan, Italy, parts of France and Spain, Greece, (Greek civil wars), Yugoslavia and parts of China (Chinese civil wars) and Burma. It does not follow that hill people make the best mountain soldiers, but their feel for the uplands is an obvious advantage. It was no fluke, for example, that Gurkha and French North African troops did so well in the Italian mountains before Rome in 1944, or that battles among the Himalayas have taught so many

tactical lessons, such as the need to picket and fortify all heights overlooking a line of march – and the need to retire quickly, with fire support, when abandoning them in face of anticipated enemy reoccupation.

Fire and movement is as much the essence of mountain warfare as anywhere else. It simply calls for: more exacting aiming techniques in ranging on targets at varying heights above or below gun positions; the most skilful siting of forward observers; and the use of pieces, including mortars, which provide plunging fire from the upper register. For a shrewd enemy rarely deploys on a forward slope to face direct fire, but sites behind crest-lines where shots in the lower register cannot easily reach and are difficult to observe. On the other hand, construction of positions, which also provide essential shelter against weather, can be difficult in rock. The effect of the defensive is thus emphasized and has rarely been better demonstrated than by the Germans in Italy, from 1943 to 1945, when their systematic route denial by demolition and booby trap placed an even heavier work-load than usual on Allied engineering resources.

Aircraft, needless to say, have changed the conduct of mountain warfare, even though flying among peaks and steep-sided valleys in unstable weather and against enemy anti-aircraft artillery can be daunting and where accurate delivery of bombs is difficult. They still provide intelligence and can be of immense assistance delivering ammunition and supplies to isolated positions, as well as evacuating wounded, thus saving them prolonged and painful journeys by stretcher down rough tracks and precipices, tasks which, since the Korean War, have been made immensely easier with the arrival of the helicopter.

Mountbatten, Admiral Lord Louis (1900–79). A Royal Navy signalling specialist whose royal connections made him a social celebrity prior to World War II, in which he displayed his great talents as a leader. After commanding a destroyer flotilla from 1939 until the Battle of Crete in May 1941, when his ship was sunk, he was appointed Chief of Combined Operations in October. This post made him responsible for development of amphibious warfare and hit-and-run raiding and, in 1942, obtained for him a seat with the Chiefs of Staff and the ranks, in addition to Admiral, of General and Air Marshal. The **Dieppe raid** was his responsibility and the lessons learnt disseminated by him to the immense benefit of commanders in all theatres of war. In October 1943 he became Supreme Commander South-East Asia Command (SEAC), charged with the reconquest of **Burma** and **Malaya**, tasks accomplished by September 1945 with the collaboration of Generals **Slim**, Stilwell and others, though throughout with only the minimum of resources.

In 1947 he was sent to India as the last Viceroy, to transfer British power to what would be India and Pakistan. From 1955 to 1959 he was First Sea Lord, involved with the **Suez** operations in 1956. As Chief of Defence Staff from 1959 to 1965, he brought the three armed services under the control of a single Ministry of Defence. He was assassinated by the Irish Republican Army while on holiday in Eire.

Movement control. The control of movement by military forces throughout the world is fundamental to operations by sea, land and air. It is a major General **Staff** responsibility starting at ministries and working through formation HQs to sub-unit level. It aims to make efficient and economic use of available facilities to move men and material to their right destination in good order, on time. It depends upon foresight, the availability and use of full information about resources and conditions, and the execution of control through clear instructions at every phase of an operation.

The introduction of fairly reliable steamships and **railways** in the 1840s made it possible to schedule movements with a higher degree of certainty than when dependence was upon wind conditions and animal power. Once it became possible to calculate quite accurately the rate and volume of delivery at any of a number of destinations on the world's surface – a reliability which improved with the development of **mechanization** and **aircraft** – chance was reduced in **strategic** and **tactical** planning. From the **Crimean War** onwards the integration of civil handling and transport agencies under military control was increasingly formalized. At the heart of most **mobilization** schemes were to be found detailed movement plans, allied to defensive measures against enemy interdiction or disruption. The German military, indeed, were insistent upon having a say in the development of their railway

and **communications** system in peacetime. Later the British began subsidizing shipping companies to provide, for example, adequate lifting gear for heavy equipment to enable handling at ports lacking adequate shore facilities.

As control became more necessary and complex in line with new **technology** in both **World Wars**, armed forces recruited specialist movement control staffs, many of whom were civilian transport and supply experts. Spaced along the lines of communication, movement control strands (very often joint Service) reached out from HQs to ports, railway stations, airfields and all manner of depots where movement orders were executed in collaboration with civil agencies. Closer to the front, the operational naval, army and air staffs worked together on beaches, at maintenance centres and airheads directing men, equipment and supplies into logistics channels. Military police played a prominent role manning traffic-control centres and in route direction closer to the front where tactical movement and defensive measures become much more acute and have to be dovetailed into operational plans. Indeed the closer to the front the more likely that movement becomes a controlled activity, geared to time of day, the situation and future plans. For signs of movement can often indicate forthcoming intentions and have to be scheduled astutely.

History provides many examples of the impact of movement control on operations. Examples are provided in the preparations for war (see **Mobilization**). Lack of control by the French during the **Franco-Prussian War** was notoriously disastrous. Failures by the Germans to integrate rail and road movements during the **Austro-Prussian War** lost them opportunities after the Battle of Königgrätz and contributed to their armies' exhaustion at the Battle of the **Marne** during World War I. In both campaigns railway stock stood idle failing effectual provision to off-load them into road vehicles. On the other hand, skilful, high-density rail movements of reinforcements from one place to another during **World War I** were major factors in the stabilization of threatened trench fronts.

The exceedingly widespread **World War II**, with its large theatres of war threatened by **blockade** and shipping shortage from naval and air action, created demands for world-wide control of shipping to minimize waste. Intricate communication networks helped prevent ships being held up in ports which could not accept their cargoes. **Convoy** routeing took account of priorities of movement as well as avoidance of attack. The rapid development of air supply called for special air traffic control compatible with handling arrangements at base and front – the Germans set an example of this during the **Spanish Civil War**. The finest immediate postwar example of the techniques involved is, of course, the **Berlin** airlift, with its precisely integrated systems of deliveries to airfields in the West, rapid loading of aircraft, scheduled flights along **radar** and **radio** controlled corridors, and swift unloading and turn-round at Berlin, where reception was geared to a nonstop service. These practices are repeated with still greater sophistication for most **cold** and **limited war** operations – and are on constant stand-by.

Mukden, Battles of. Mukden controls the Liao corridor and, during the **Russo-Japanese War** of 1904, was the key to southern Manchuria. By mid-February 1905 the weary but victorious Japanese army of 310,000 under General Oyama had chased an almost equal Russian force, under General Kuropatkin, into a 40-mile-long entrenched line defending the city. The Japanese attacked with *élan*, but made only slow progress and always lost momentum owing to inability to maintain the leading troops and the shell supply. After three weeks of virtual deadlock, as in **World War I** 10 years later, Kuropatkin (with his army intact) was forced to withdraw from the city, with heavy loss of material, because of the danger of encirclement. But the Japanese were in no condition to follow as the war drew to a close. About 100,000 Russians died and some 70,000 Japanese.

In the so-called Mukden Incident of 1931, the city was seized on a spurious excuse from the Chinese by the Japanese in September as the latter assumed control of Manchuria. It was overrun again on 20 August 1945 when the Red Army swept through almost unopposed to **Port Arthur** to wipe out a very old score. After the Russians had withdrawn in March 1946, in the hope of the Chinese Communists taking possession with abandoned Japanese weapons, the Nationalists struck quickly and by the 15th, in fierce fighting, had won control. This penultimate phase in the **Chinese Civil War** was short-lived. **Mao Tse-tung** needed Manchuria

as a firm base with its direct link to Russia, and sent General Lin Pao to finish the job in January 1947. Battles raged. General **Chiang Kai-shek** took command in person in January 1948 – and won. But in September the Communist offensive was renewed, the Nationalist army was almost wiped out at the battle of Mukden-Chinchow on 30 October and the city occupied next day.

Museums, Military. For the student of history, museums provide rich sources of information through visual display, archives and libraries. Since the Renaissance, collections of weapons and the like, many of them privately owned, have been made. Not until the 17th and 18th centuries were many public collections formed, usually in capital cities, such as Paris, Rome, St Petersburg and London, where arms and armour were displayed in historic buildings. The Industrial Revolution and the growth of **technology** widened the need for and scope of military museums, which became repositories for machinery, records and illustrations that inventors and manufacturers could study for ideas and methods. At the same time, as a result of improving travel arrangements, an increasing number of people were able to visit the central museums with relative ease for educational purposes, nostalgia and as a leisure activity.

Some military museums try to cover every aspect of specific periods, such as the Imperial War Museum in London which deals with the **World Wars** and subsequent wars only. Others, like the Smithsonian Museum in Washington, include military equipment among other technical exhibits. Most major nations have their own naval, army and air museums, often displaying working examples of ships and machines in **dockyards**, army camps and airfields. On a smaller and simpler scale are the collections of artefacts and uniforms belonging to ships' companies, corps, regiments and squadrons which have found homes in local depots, separated from national collections. Inevitably there is duplication; often a researcher has to hunt far and wide for some information.

Display techniques have evolved over the years from the static kind to the far more imaginative modern, active type. Rows of mute display cases are giving way to exhibitions of working models or the real thing; interrelated moving picture shows with sound effects; and, in some cases, audience participation to arouse a sense of involvement with reality. The military Services often envisage their museums as **propaganda** for enhancement of their public relations and as a spur to **recruiting**. Pacifists sometimes point to them as centres for peace studies. Whatever the assumed purpose, military museums everywhere are visited by a great many people, who often pay an entrance fee and belong to societies of friends of the museum.

Mussolini, Benito (1883–1945). A demagogic Italian socialist who, as a soldier, was wounded in a grenade-training accident in 1917. Involvement with Fascism after **World War I** and the use of violence to advance his struggle for power made him Italy's Chief Minister in 1922 and, in 1925, Dictator. His bullying foreign policy led to the Italo-Ethiopian War (**Ethiopian (Abyssinian) wars**) of 1935, strong involvement on the Nationalist side in the **Spanish Civil War** in 1936 and the occupation of Albania in 1939.

A close association with **Hitler** after 1936 led to founding of the Axis in May 1939 and entry into **World War II** on Germany's side on 10 June 1940, when he felt little fighting was needed for rich pickings. He found his error in successive defeats throughout the **Mediterranean**, in **Greece** and in **East Africa**. It was of no avail when German forces came to his rescue in 1941, despite a glimpse of victory in **Egypt** in 1942. On 25 July 1943, in the aftermath of the loss of North Africa and the impending loss of **Sicily** he was deposed and imprisoned. Rescued by a daring German *coup de main*, he spent the rest of the war as Hitler's lackey until caught and killed by Italian partisans on 28 April 1945.

Nato (North Atlantic Treaty Organization). The organization was brought into being on 4 April 1949 by the North Atlantic Treaty designed for mutual defence against the Russian threat. The signatories were Belgium, Britain, Canada, Denmark, France, Holland, Iceland, Italy, Luxembourg, Norway, Portugal and the USA. Greece and Turkey acceded on 18 February 1952, West Germany on 9 May 1955, Spain in 1982. It is a permanent military alliance with an international council, secretariat and various political and social committees. The military command structure is international and works under a military committee of the Chiefs of Staff of the member nations. It comprises the Supreme Allied Commander Europe (SACEUR), commanding forces on the Continent and in the Mediterranean, the Supreme Allied Commander Atlantic (SACLANT) and C-in-C English Channel Area (CINCHAN), whose headquarters are responsible for defence planning and supervision and exercising of forces, leaving operational functions to regional headquarters.

The Organization has had many political and military vicissitudes, including France's withdrawal from the integrated staffs in 1966 and her insistence that Nato troops moved out – damage gradually repaired after the death of General de Gaulle. Turkey's similar withdrawal in 1974 took place at a time of crisis with Greece. Several nations have expressed concern at domination by the USA at the same time as the USA has pressed for their increased contributions. As a general rule, Nato's solidarity is related to the measure of Russian and **Warsaw Pact** threat. Peace movements and Soviet President Mikhail Gorbachev's disarmament proposals in the 1980s undoubtedly weakened the alliance – and forced it to reconsider its policies in 1990.

Naval organization. The terminology of naval organization has fluctuated with time and fashion. Not until 1907, for example, did the US Navy use the term 'fleet', which had for more than a thousand years been in use by other navies to describe a group of warships or, indeed, a number of unarmed vehicles under one commander. However, for operational and administrative purposes a naval fleet includes more than its vessels; there are also its shore bases, which can comprise headquarters, signalling stations, airfields and **dockyards**. Fleets are usually of a regional nature, sometimes numbered and often named after their operational area, for example, North Sea, Atlantic, Mediterranean, Black Sea, West, East, Asiatic and Pacific. They are subdivided for functional and tactical purposes into squadrons, flotillas, escort and hunting groups or task forces. Thus a fleet, by number or name, could in **World War II** comprise a squadron of **battleships**, supported by a **cruiser** squadron, one or more separate **destroyer** and **submarine** flotillas and attached units of auxiliary supply vessels. At the same time, under control of its C-in-C it might, as for example was common in the battles of the **Pacific**, have self-contained **aircraft-carriers** and an **amphibious** fleet attached.

Like the other services, navies in peacetime can afford only what limited funds are available as they cope with current tasks and plan for war. **Reserve** forces and their utilization in emergencies and on **mobilization** are essential – but can make rather larger use of civil assets than armies and air forces. The Royal Navy, for example, maintains a fleet of auxiliary **logistic** vessels manned by civilians and armed as necessary. These were the mainstay for ammunition and fuel supply, supplemented by vessels called up from trade, of the Task Force sent to the **Falkland Islands** in 1982. As in the distant past, when merchant ships were permanently armed for self-protection against pirates (among other aggressors) and as was done in both **World Wars** when ocean liners were turned into armed cruisers to assist with **convoy** escort and **blockade**, these ships fought in action. It is a relatively simple matter to mount guns and missiles on deck. In **World War II** some merchant ships carried **fighter** aircraft to be catapulted against enemy **bombers**, while many more were converted to escort aircraft-carriers. The carriage of vertical take-off and landing aircraft (VTOL) simply provides a variation on the theme.

Like all cost-effective organizations, fleets are variable in composition, flexible in operation and subject to changing doctrine under the influence of **technology** and techniques. The organization, for example, of the Federal Fleet in the **American Civil War** operating in the Mississipi River was arranged to satisfy close support of land forces by small, steam-powered vessels using fire-power and amphibious techniques. The Austrian Fleet at the Battle of **Lissa** went into battle in a formation intended to make use of the ram, in addition to modern fire-power. Japanese organization during the **Russo-Japanese War** of 1904, mirroring that of the Royal Navy, made best combined use of battleships, cruisers and destroyers to tackle Russian vessels in port, in coastal waters and on the high seas, demonstrating an operational flexibility in grouping greatly assisted by **radio** to implement regrouping at speed. It was the introduction of the **mine**, the submarine and aircraft which demanded the greatest reorganizations. The technology and techniques that had made it necessary for maintenance and training to form specialized **destroyer** and **torpedo-boat** flotillas at the end of the 19th century called for similar organizations for minelaying, mine-sweeping, submarine and anti-submarine forces, air squadrons and anti-aircraft ships and their weapons. These, in turn, made necessary depot support ships and a proliferation of shore establishments to develop the new weapons and train sailors to use them. The trend escalated vastly throughout both World Wars to cater for

advances in signalling techniques and the calls of amphibious warfare. In addition, there was the vital need to integrate the new technology in individual warships and train leaders to make best tactical use of their units in, for example, the highly complex battles between aircraft-carriers and in the escort of convoys. It all amounted to a never-ending process of evolution since 1945.

Naval warfare. With the introduction of steam engines and considerable increases in **artillery** power and **armour** strength in the 1850s, revolutionary changes were imposed upon the **strategy**, **tactics** and **logistics** of naval warfare. The Battle of Sinope demonstrated the demise of the old wooden-built, broadside-firing sailing ship, as did other incidents in the **Crimean War**. The *Merrimack* versus *Monitor* encounter in 1862 and the Battle of **Lissa** in 1866 showed that fights between lines of 'wooden walls' were obsolete and **battleships** like the French *La Gloire* would be 'lions among lambs'.

Central to the future development of strategy from the start of the 20th century were the advances in **communications**, above all **radio** and **electronics**. They speeded the dissemination of **intelligence**, made possible centralized control of fleets and individual vessels and eased supply arrangements both in ports and at sea, once methods to shift stores from one ship to another had been developed. Almost overnight much guesswork was removed from planning and deployment of resources, as became plain in the naval battles of the **Russo-Japanese War**. The Battle of **Tsushima**, in particular, showed clearly the changes which had been wrought by the latest **battleships**, **cruisers** and **destroyers** and indicated the potential of underwater attack by **mines** and the locomotive **torpedo**. It showed, too, from the low ratios of hits to misses that there was much scope for improvements in **gunnery**. Some of these were incorporated in the Dreadnought battleships and **battle-cruisers**, introduced by the British and used against their German counterparts at **Falkland Islands**, **Dogger Bank** and **Jutland**.

Yet, despite improvements to long-range naval gunnery in **World War I**, Jutland announced the start of the battleship's decline. At that battle Admiral **Jellicoe** was as much inhibited by fear of losing too many ships to gunfire, and thus 'losing the war in an afternoon', as by dread of underwater attack. Minefields prevented pursuit of the Germans. **Submarines** played only a small part, but they had already sunk many warships elsewhere and were imposing **blockade** in a desultory fashion which, in 1917, was to be raised by the Germans to the status of a potentially war-winning campaign. Nor did **aircraft** do much at Jutland, largely because what little information they did supply was barely heeded. But their naval potential had already been demonstrated in Europe, in **East Africa** and at **Gallipoli**. And already embryo **aircraft-carriers** were in existence and would be used before the war's end.

It scarcely seemed to occur to many sailors that the intricate, massed fleets, deployed for World War I to bring maximum artillery fire to bear, were outmoded before **World War II**. Jellicoe's resistance to the **convoy** system for merchant shipping in 1917, allied to his reluctance to detach destroyers from the Fleet for escort duties, was symbolic of an unwillingness to recognize change. Change was imposed accidentally by the Washington Naval Treaty, which restricted battleship and cruiser construction, but permitted the building of the next generation's capital ship, the aircraft-carrier, along with the dive- and torpedo-**bombers** which would send battleships to their graves.

Naval warfare in World War II was a global business, conditioned by underwater craft and aircraft, but governed by the principles stated by Admiral **Mahan** that commerce and logistics were key issues and sea power decisive. Unfortunately, however, his notion that Anglo-American sea power would generate peace proved false because Germany paid little attention to it in 1939 and the Japanese, with a high-grade Fleet, gambled on a victory beyond their powers against the world's largest navies. Indeed, although submarines and aircraft did bring the Axis powers immense successes, it was these weapons which also helped crush them in the Battle of the **Atlantic**, the **Mediterranean** and the **Pacific**. In this war only one battleship was sunk by gunfire alone, but the rest of its class was hunted and refused domination of the seas. In the struggle visual encounters between lines of major surface vessels were unusual, but combat between groups of destroyers, **frigates** and submarines was a regular occurrence. Aircraft-carriers dominated the seas but, as at **Taranto**, **Pearl Harbor**, the **Coral Sea**, **Midway**, the **Philippine Sea** and **Leyte Gulf**, rarely saw the targets they were attacking. Yet, in this naval struggle all contenders were aiming, basically, to maintain or stop commerce in battles, fighting to keep convoys moving or impose blockade, and launching **amphibious** operations to seize or deny strategic bases.

In these battles the underlying struggle was **technological**: in the races to produce, for example, superior **radar** and **sonar** (or countermeasures to them) in submarine warfare; and to develop tactical doctrines, enhanced by greatly improved radio, to outmanoeuvre the enemy while baffling him with false information and subterfuge. In World War I knowledge of enemy **codes and ciphers** was of great value. In World War II it was probably more crucial to the result at sea than on land and in the air; the Axis powers were totally outwitted in this department.

Since 1945 sea power has retained its crucial importance since only about 9 per cent of trans-ocean commercial cargoes go by air. Though aircraft-carriers have played (and continue to play) important roles in **cold** and **limited wars**, and are prime targets of hunters, it is the submarine – above all the nuclear-powered type with nuclear-warhead **missiles** – which has assumed the role of capital ship along with that of deterrent (**Deterrence**) and peace-keeper. It too is tracked and hunted by air and surface forces in both peace and war. In peacetime because, in the event of an outbreak of hostilities, it will be of paramount importance to all contenders to sink enemy boats, most no doubt already at sea, as quickly as possible. In the meantime merchant shipping is the prime target and in need of constant protection to ensure food supply and, of immediate importance, the movement of reinforcements and materials for major forces across the oceans. It is at the same time involved in the struggles for possession of vital terrain (such as Northern Norway, Iceland and Greenland) controlling access to open waters. It is no exaggeration to say that the opening bouts of any future war are constantly in progress in peacetime as surveillance forces study maritime movements, track potential predators and watch for threatening signs.

Navigation. The liquid magnetic compass was introduced in 1862 in an effort to damp out the major oscillations of the dry-card compass then in use. Characteristically perhaps, the Royal Navy clung to its Thomson dry-card compass, which admittedly was very good, until 1906.

Navigation is the combination of direction and velocity to arrive at a desired point. In the mid 19th century velocity at sea was still determined by the log – the number of knots in a line paid out over the ship's stern in a given time determining the speed. Measurement of longitude and latitude were similarly well established, using the sextant and accurate chronometers which had been available since the 17th century.

Aircraft required similar navigational aids once they embarked on long-distance flights, though the magnetic compass had to be modified to reduce the effect of abrupt movements in the air. The log was replaced by the pitot tube to measure air speed and the sextant had to be provided with a liquid-bubble artificial horizon. Airmen also had to take into account the effect of wind, calculating their true ground-speed vector as a sum of air and wind-velocity vectors.

On the ground in the 19th century, navigation as such was not a problem the soldier had to face. His movement was generally slow and over ground with recognizable landmarks that could be related to such maps as were available. In unmapped territory reliance had to be placed on local guides and, though it is true that whole armies did lose direction from time to time, no special navigational skills in the maritime sense were needed. However, the motor vehicle gave the soldier a much greater radius of action, free of the limitations imposed by the horse's need for fodder and water supplies. Long-distance operations in featureless terrain became possible and a requirement for more skilled navigation arose. **Desert warfare** in **World War II**, and especially such special forces as the Long-Range Desert Group, the SAS and Popski's Private Army, soon became adept desert navigators; it is no coincidence that the latter adopted the astrolabe as their cap badge. They mastered the theodolite so as to fix their position by the stars and used the sun compass, originally invented by the Light Car Patrols operating against the North African Senussi in 1915 and perfected by Major R. A. Bagnold for his explorations in the Western Desert in the 1930s. The device, mounted on the vehicle where the driver could see it, relied on the shadow cast by a vertical post on to a horizontal plate graduated in 360 degrees. After a careful initial alignment taking into account local time, the compass plate could be offset to a desired bearing and the heading maintained by watching the fall of the shadow as the vehicle drove along. Long distances across the desert were accurately covered in this way and thus the problems of using a magnetic compass in the constantly changing magnetic field of a small vehicle were overcome.

At sea and in the air the time-honoured methods, though refined, were used throughout World War II, as well as the **electronic** aids which began to appear in the 1940s. The Germans introduced their Knickebein directional radio beams to guide **bombers** to their targets, while in the air and at sea Decca developed Gee, a radio navigation system around the coasts of Britain, first used for bombers and then to control shipping during the invasion of Europe in 1944. The Americans devised a similar system for their offshore shipping known as Loran C. A further development since 1945 has been the appearance of inertial navigation systems using measurement of the direction of the force of gravity with the aid of gyroscopes. Linked with a **computer**, information on heading, velocity, position and corrections for earth rotation can be resolved to provide an accurate fix. This approach has particular attractions in long-range **rocket** missile navigation and has been used extensively for **submarines**.

On land it was the predicted effects of full-scale nuclear war, expected to remove known landmarks, which in the 1950s led to work on automatic navigation aids for land vehicles. Various ideas were tried, generally using computers fed by compasses and signals from the road wheels to resolve direction and distance data into grid references. The problems of fixing accurately the start point, plus inherent errors from, for example, wheel slip, have precluded a really successful answer.

The future seems to lie with the navigational satellite, already widely used by ships and aircraft. Coupled with digital computers giving an instantaneous read-out, navigational satellites in fixed orbit around the earth can provide positional data to an accuracy of a few metres.

Netherlands, Battles for the. Unlike the German plan to invade France in 1914, that for 1940 included the occupation of Holland as well as Belgium, a task given to General von **Bock's**

Army Group B, which had Sixth and Eighteenth Armies, plus General **Kesselring's** Second Air Fleet (which included the **airborne** troops), at its disposal. On 10 May air landings were made at the Moerdijk bridge, Doordrecht, Waalhaven airport and The Hague. Most of the initial objectives were taken even though the Dutch had been forewarned, had manned their defences and started inundations. But although their air defences inflicted very heavy losses on the German Air Force (which lost 304 machines that day on all fronts, including many Ju52 transports on the ground), their army of 400,000 was in no state to cope with the combined airborne and land attacks. Within 24 hours the Germans held key airports and communication centres, and the armies advancing through Maastricht, Arnhem and Groningen were on schedule to link up with the airborne forces within the 72 hours stipulated by Kesselring. The arrival of French troops in the vicinity of Breda on the 13th was too late to deflect the German purpose, though General Student, the airborne commander, was under heavy pressure at Rotterdam. His calls for air support on the 14th led to appalling destruction within the city as the Dutch were negotiating an armistice.

The Dutch were the first to start open resistance to the Germans during the occupation, but their efforts to create a secret army were crippled when the Germans penetrated the **Special Operations Executive** at an early stage and, until November 1943, captured all agents landed. They were only of marginal assistance to the Allied armies when the latter crossed the border from Belgium on 17 September 1944 to link up with the Airborne Army between Eindhoven and **Arnhem** in the vain attempt to invade Germany via North-East Holland. This created a pocket south of the River Maas, between Nijmegen and the Scheldt estuary, which had to be cleared in order to secure the port of Antwerp and open it to shipping, necessitating the series of gruelling battles which Second British and First Canadian Armies fought throughout October to reinforce the corridor to Nijmegen against German counter-attacks, capture s'Hertogenbosch on the 26th and Tilburg on the 28th, and clear the islands of South and North Beveland by 29 October at the same time as the Breskens Pocket, south of the **Scheldt**, was being eliminated. Operations culminated in the capture of the flooded island of **Walcheren** by an extraordinary **amphibious** attack on 1 November.

Southern Holland formed the springboard for the final battle of **Germany** which, after preliminary skirmishing along the River Roer in January, erupted into the major thrusts in February from Nijmegen and Maastricht to sweep clean the west bank of the Rhine. This provided assembly areas for the Rhine crossing and presented First Canadian Army with its opportunity to press on as left flank guard of 21st Army Group. It captured Arnhem on 14 April, having advanced to Gröningen on the 13th, thereby cutting off so-called 'Fortress Holland' to the west, an easily defended area the Canadians had no intention of assaulting but whose populace was starving because of German unwillingness to feed it or surrender. The disastrous situation was relieved by an agreement to airdrop supplies by **bomber** while the surrender was negotiated.

New Guinea, Battles for. The arrival of the Japanese in Northern New Guinea in March 1942 completed their initial plan but tempted them to go a stage farther, so thin was the opposition. In May they sent a force by sea to capture Port Moresby, but it was forced to turn back during the Battle of the **Coral Sea**. Instead their Eighteenth Army tried to march there in July via the Kakoda Trail through **jungle**-clad **mountains**. It met stiff Australian and American resistance, and early in September was brought to a halt 30 miles short of its objective after a subsidiary landing in Milne Bay was repulsed. Henceforward the Japanese were in retreat as the Allies developed a counterstroke, which also faded, in November owing to **logistic** collapse and declining **morale**. On orders from General **MacArthur** it was revived and, on 22 January 1943, after a series of battles at Wau and Gona, the last of the Japanese at Buna were wiped out. Each side lost about 8,000 men in battle, but 13,646 Americans alone were victims of disease.

In June MacArthur felt strong enough to reopen the offensive and aim, in conjunction with Admiral **Halsey's** thrust through the **Solomons**, to isolate the vital enemy base at Rabaul. Operations were preceded by a furious struggle for air superiority, which was won by the Allies together with a bonus from a special mission, based on sound **intelligence**, which shot down Admiral **Yamamoto** on 18 April. Sea and air power were crucial in this most difficult theatre where movement on land was tortuous. During the battle of the **Bismarck Sea** (2–4 March), the sinking of a large convoy of Japanese ships with troops and supplies reinforcing Rabaul was not only a triumph for the Allied aircraft, destroyers and torpedo-boats concerned, but a death blow to the Japanese perimeter garrisons in New Guinea. Landing operations were mostly by amphibious but sometimes **airborne** troops, as they side-stepped towards Morotai. These operations induced numerous Japanese withdrawals elsewhere in the realization that destruction of their mobile forces made it impossible to counter the Allied initiative.

In desperation, in 1944, the Japanese staked much on a determined, static defence of their major base at Hollandia, which the Allies could not ignore. On 22 April, after the customary softening-up from the air, two American divisions landed at Hollandia and Aitape. In five days they converged on, encircled, destroyed or chased into the jungle about half what was left of Eighteenth Army. A month later the Americans landed on the island of Biak and took a month hunting down the 10,000 Japanese defending its strategic airfield. The rest of New Guinea could be cleared almost at leisure since Rabaul was neutralized, and MacArthur was set to invade the **Philippines** in October.

Nightingale, Florence (1820–1920). A child of a rich family whose vocation was nursing and who was made famous when she led a team of nurses to Scutari to care for British wounded from the **Crimea**. She did little actual nursing since her self-assumed role, as a brilliant and extremely forceful organizer, was that of training and disciplining her low-grade nurses and bullying and persuading the government, the Army and its doctors into a complete reconstruction of **medical services**. She was largely successful owing to strong public support and her own talents as an administrator. Her *Notes on Matters Affecting the Health, Efficiency and Hospital Administration of the British Army* and *Notes on Nursing* became bibles not only for the British forces but also for health and nursing services world-wide. After the war she worked to exhaustion establishing nursing training colleges and advising health authorities on the design and running of modern hospitals. She was carried to her grave by six sergeants of the British Army.

Night-vision devices. Armies and navies have

rarely in the past been deterred from night operations when attracted by the element of surprise or need for **surveillance**, but the problem has always been how to see and how to retain control. *Star-shell*, *searchlights* and *flares* were widely used in both World Wars, but it was not until the **electronic** age that night-vision devices specifically designed to help the soldier see in the dark began to appear. The American *sniperscope* was an early example; the Germans also produced similar equipment.

This early equipment depended on infra-red (IR) illumination of the target, often using a searchlight with an IR filter over the lens, sometimes called 'black light'. The viewer, a somewhat cumbersome monocular or binocular, worked on the principle of converting the photonic flux of the incoming light – which cannot be amplified – into an electron flux which can. Thus the observer viewed the target on a luminescent screen and not directly through a lens. Such devices, described as 'active' because they depended on an external IR source, suffered from the disadvantage that an enemy observer with an IR viewer could detect the source and take appropriate action. Nevertheless *IR kits* were in wide use on American and Soviet **tanks** by the 1950s, usually incorporating a searchlight coupled with special gunner's and commander's sights; the driver would have IR headlights and his own viewer to use with them. The UK mounted a Dutch Philips system on the Centurion tank and the Chieftain tank incorporated a built-in three million candlepower Xenon arc IR searchlight.

The next-generation equipment was passive, relying on the ambient light, always present even on the darkest night, to illuminate the target, thus making detection harder. On a dull overcast night the unaided eye can see very little; to improve this to even twilight level requires an enhancement of about 10^5. The *image intensifier* was developed to meet this need, working on the broad principle already described for active systems. However, a single-stage tube could not provide sufficient amplification by itself; a 'cascade' tube with at least three stages, each amplifying the output of the one before, was needed. Hence the equipment tended to be bulky and with a large-diameter object lens to gather in as much light as possible. Nevertheless such image-intensification systems have been fitted to a large number of armoured vehicles.

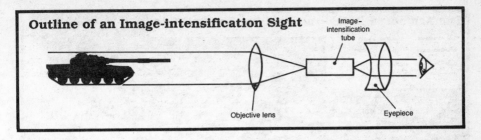

Outline of an Image-intensification Sight

Image-intensification tube

Objective lens

Eyepiece

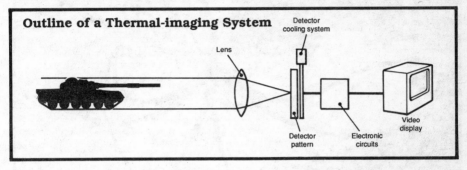

Outline of a Thermal-imaging System

Detector cooling system

Lens

Detector pattern

Electronic circuits

Video display

Attempts to reduce the size of image-intensifiers have produced the 'channel' tube, using the principle of secondary-emission electron multiplication, which can be induced in semi-conductor glass tubes. Channel tubes have obvious applications where small size is vital and they are used, for example, in night-flying goggles for **helicopter** pilots. Similar goggles are in wide use for **infantry** soldiers.

Low-light television (LLTV) represents another approach to the problem. The advantage here is remote viewing and multiple read-out. The disadvantage is LLTV's bulk, its power requirement and its limited performance against moving targets; furthermore the video signal has a tendency to swamping at low light levels.

Yet another technique uses the target's thermal radiation ('black-body radiation'). *Thermal imagers* have been in use for some years, particularly as part of the modern tank's fire-control and surveillance system. The device detects a target as a result of the thermal contrast between one part of it and another, for example the contrast between a tank's hot engine deck and its cooler glacis plate. The lens system of a thermal imager functions much as an optical-lens system, except that the lenses are made of material such as germanium, which will transmit far IR radiation. The output is very similar

to a standard television signal and the display is usually on a television monitor. The British have developed such a system, incorporating it in the fire-control system on Challenger, known as TOGS – Thermal Observation and Gunnery Sight.

All these devices have made theoretically possible the 24-hour battlefield day. It is perhaps wise to remember that in the Yom Kippur War of 1973 both sides used night-vision aids. The strain of operating the equipment was such that the ideal of uninterrupted day and night operations was unattainable; after 36 hours both sides had to call a halt and go to sleep.

Nimitz, Admiral Chester (1885–1966). Nimitz was Chief of Staff to the commander of the US Atlantic submarine force in **World War I**, and thereafter had a fairly diverse career (including being Chief of the Bureau of Navigation in 1939) for one of pronounced character picked for stardom as C-in-C Pacific Fleet on 16 December 1941 after the attack on **Pearl Harbor**. Managing to establish a working relationship with the Chief of Naval Staff, Admiral **King**, he presided over the curbing of Japan's expansion (**Japanese wars of expansion**) in the **Pacific War** and the immensely effective 'island hopping' strategy aimed at the heart of Japan. In his dealings with

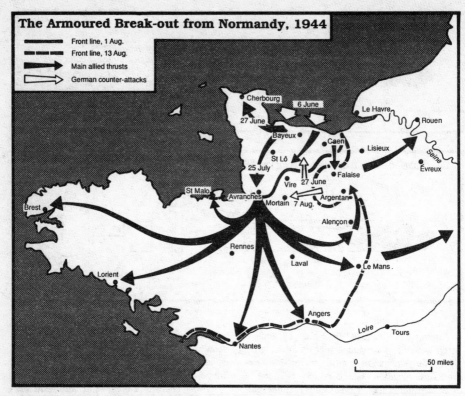

The Armoured Break-out from Normandy, 1944

Front line, 1 Aug.
Front line, 13 Aug.
Main allied thrusts
German counter-attacks

Cherbourg
6 June
Le Havre
Rouen
27 June
Bayeux
Caen
Lisieux
Seine
St Lô
25 July
Vire 27 June
Falaise
Évreux
St Malo
Avranches
Argentan
Mortain 7 Aug.
Brest
Alençon
Rennes
Laval
Le Mans
Lorient
Angers
Loire
Tours
Nantes

0   50 miles

such personalities as General **MacArthur** and Admirals **Halsey**, Spruance and Turner, he steered a steady course with minimal friction, even with King. In operations he judged correctly when the Japanese shifted to the defensive in 1942. In 1944 he knew when to bow to MacArthur in the controversy over invasion of the **Philippines**; but he was also very tense with Halsey when that officer left the St Bernardino Strait unguarded during the Battle of **Leyte Gulf**. He was present at the Japanese surrender. From December 1945 to December 1947 he was Chief of Naval Operations in the difficult post-war years of retrenchment. He published no memoirs.

Nobel, Alfred Bernhard (1833–96). A brilliant and inventive Swedish engineer and chemist who studied **explosives** and in 1867 devised the stable dynamite after experiments with unstable nitroglycerine. He built up a large manufacturing business and invented a wide range of new explosive compounds and devices, such as the jelly-like blasting gelatine, from gun-cotton, in

1876; the smokeless, powerful ballistite (of crucial importance to **ammunition** and the automatic **machine-gun**, as well as **tactics**) in 1885; and sophisticated detonators. Reviled by many for the development and production of so many war materials, he left most of his fortune to the founding of five prizes open to international competition – of which one was for contributions to peace.

Normandy, Battles of. The ancient province of Normandy, though partially occupied by Germans in the **Franco-Prussian War** of 1870–71, was spared a major battle then. Nor in **World War I** was it fought over, seeing nothing of the enemy at all, while in June 1940 the pace at which the Germans chased the defeated French and British forces into Brittany gave no hint of how easily defensible its terrain of small, lush fields was. For the next four years, in fact, its people and the German garrison lived fairly comfortably together, only disturbed occasionally at the coast by small hit-and-run raids and from above by increasing air activity, with very heavy bombing before 6 June 1944 when Allied armies landed in great strength.

Preceded by three **airborne** divisions and a stunning naval and air bombardment, the Allied armies under General **Eisenhower**, commanded in the field by General **Montgomery**, came ashore on a 50-mile front. Against them stood Field Marshal **Rommel**'s Army Group B under C-in-C West, Field Marshal von **Rundstedt**, entrenched behind the Atlantic Wall. Although resistance to the Americans was very effective on one beach (called Omaha) at the base of the Cotentin peninsula, they won a strong foothold – though it took 12 days to fight through to the other side and cut off Cherbourg. Meanwhile the British and Canadians had captured Bayeux and were in sight of **Caen** on the left flank of D-Day, though unable to go further as the Germans sealed off the bridgehead. Fight as well as the Germans did, they were constantly deprived of sufficient strength, partly owing to interdiction by Allied bombing of the lines of communication and also to the unwillingness of **Hitler** and von Rundstedt to transfer troops from the Pas de Calais where the main blow was still expected. As a result, Rommel's attempts to assemble and deliver a decisive counterstroke were repeatedly frustrated.

Throughout June and July, in close country-side ideal for defensive infantry combat, the Germans managed, by the skin of their teeth, to hold on against an opponent who was superior in fire-power and able, despite stormy seas (which destroyed one of the two artificial Mulberry harbours towed from Britain and delayed **logistic** buildup) to more than keep ahead in the reinforcement race. Both sides suffered heavy losses in what was an attritional struggle, one in which Montgomery deliberately used the British and Canadians on the left to attract and smash the German **armoured** forces, leaving the Americans on the right, under General **Bradley**, to take Cherbourg (on 27 June) and assemble a massive force near Saint-Lô to smash through in the direction of Avranches. Caen fell on 13 July. On the 20th the Germans remained pinned to the south of the ruined city by a strong British armoured attack.

On 25 July Bradley opened his attack against thinly held enemy positions and drove south at ever-increasing speed, compelling Hitler to demand a massed armoured counterstroke against the extending American flank. The Americans fended off the blow with relative ease without delaying their advance into Brittany or eastwards towards Le Mans and the German rear (the Germans still held fast at Falaise). Now Hitler's refusal to permit withdrawal or an end to the beaten counterstroke played into Montgomery's hands. As the American threat to Paris began to develop, he also caught the mass of the German Army in a pocket formed by Americans in the south and British and Canadians in the north. The trap finally closed on the 19th with heavy loss to the Germans. After a great many demoralized escapers had raced for the River Seine, attacked all the way from the air, they arrived at the river only to find, in many cases, that they were in yet another pocket with all the bridges destroyed.

Normandy was a difficult battlefield, particularly for the **infantry**, because **artillery**, **mortars** and **machine-guns** held sway and **tanks** found the terrain difficult to penetrate. Once mobility was restored in the final phase the Allied casualty rate fell when armoured forces bullied their way through. Normandy was one of the most costly single Allied battlefields of **World War II**, but it ruined the German Army in the West and made it possible to end the war in 1944 had the subsequent pursuit been conducted in a more rational and concentrated manner, instead of on a wide front as chosen by Eisenhower (see **West Europe campaign**, 1944, and **Arnhem, Battle of**).

North Africa, Battles of, 1940–43. North Africa became a battlefield on 10 June 1940, when Italy declared war on Britain and France, at the same time as the battles of the **Mediterranean Sea** and the siege of **Malta** commenced. Greatly outnumbered as were the British in Egypt (under General **Wavell**), they at once began small-scale **desert** raids against the Italians in Cyrenaica and established a morale superiority, activities which were concurrent with the bombardment of the French Fleet at Oran on 4 July and chasing the Italian Fleet into port, but suspended when the Italian Tenth Army, under Marshal **Graziani**, invaded Egypt on 13 September.

The Italians advanced against light opposition to Sidi-Barrani, where they fortified a number of camps and prepared for the next move. On 9 December, however, the British Western Desert Force of 31,000 men under General Richard O'Connor overwhelmed the camps by surprise

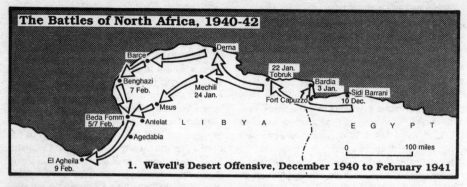

The Battles of North Africa, 1940-42

1. **Wavell's Desert Offensive, December 1940 to February 1941**

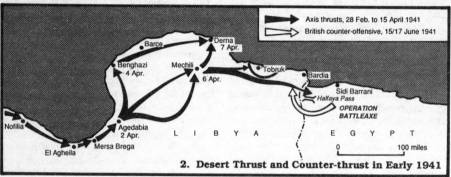

Axis thrusts, 28 Feb. to 15 April 1941
British counter-offensive, 15/17 June 1941

2. **Desert Thrust and Counter-thrust in Early 1941**

and within 48 hours had thrown what was left of Tenth Army out of Egypt, to take refuge in the ports of Bardia and **Tobruk**. Barrani fell on 5 January 1941 and Tobruk on the 22nd, the pursuit brushing aside enemy mobile forces and pressing on to annihilate the Italians at **Beda Fomm** on 5 February, finally raising O'Connor's score in prisoners to 130,000 against his own losses of 500 killed and 1,373 wounded.

Fearing a total Italian collapse, **Hitler** sent a light armoured corps under General **Rommel** to Tripoli. Contrary to orders he probed towards Benghazi, detected frailty among the British forces (which had been weakened by detachments to **Greece** and **Ethiopia**) and plunged eastwards. Stretching beyond the limits of prudence in **desert warfare logistics**, he reached the frontier on 14 April but was prevented by British and Australian troops from capturing Tobruk. By deciding to hold the port, Wavell denied the Axis army vital supplies, and was able himself to mount a limited offensive at the frontier on 14 May, followed on 15 June by a major thrust (making use of new tanks brought by **convoy** through the Mediterranean) to relieve Tobruk.

After three days' fighting this offensive was thrown back by Rommel, whereupon both sides concentrated upon preparing for a race to capture or relieve Tobruk.

On 18 November the British Eighth Army advanced, catching Rommel by surprise and bringing on the Battle of **Sidi Rezegh** in the approaches to Tobruk. Fortunes waxed and waned: Rommel wasting strategic opportunities won by brilliant tactics; the British, under General Auchinleck, persevering until Rommel's logistics collapsed and he was forced, at the year's end, to pull back into Tripolitania. From there he sprang eastwards again on 21 January, once more surprising and demoralizing the British, who were driven back to Gazala, where both sides stopped in exhaustion on 4 February.

Another race began to see who could attack first, won by Rommel on 28 May at the start of the Battle of **Gazala** and the gruelling struggle which led to the fall of Tobruk on 21 June and the pursuit to Mersa Matruh. There Rommel was close to defeat in an attack against a numerically superior British force on 28 June. But the British withdrew in confusion to the shortened, unturn-

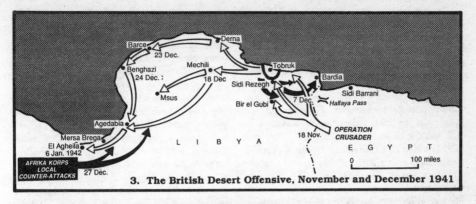

3. The British Desert Offensive, November and December 1941

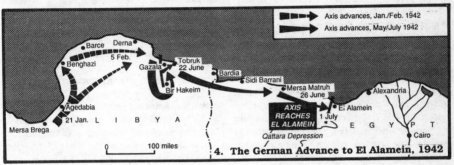

Axis advances, Jan./Feb. 1942
Axis advances, May/July 1942

4. The German Advance to El Alamein, 1942

able line at El **Alamein**, where, in three battles of attrition in July, August and October, Rommel's dream of reaching the Suez Canal was ended.

Starting on 4 November, the routed Axis army retreated with hardly a stop, retiring into Cyrenaica as news came through on the 8th of extensive Anglo-American landings in French North Africa at Casablanca, Oran and Algiers, a surprise stroke which met with only short-lived Vichy French resistance before the whole of Morocco and Algeria was in Allied hands. A British landing at Bône on the 12th posed a terribly menacing threat to Tunisia. To secure Rommel's rear, Field Marshal **Kesselring** rushed German and Italian forces by air and sea into Bizerta and Tunis, narrowly winning the race to prevent those ports falling into Allied hands, thus bringing on the first of the battles of **Tunisia**. Meanwhile Rommel had fallen back to the Tripolitanian frontier and Montgomery's Eighth Army was engaged, until 11 December, in replenishing itself by sea and land, prior to striking at El Agheila and resuming the pursuit. The Axis rearguards barely paused before evacuating Tripoli on 23 January 1943 and motoring to the

temporary safety of the Mareth Line, which the French had once built to keep the Italians out of Tunisia.

At that moment Axis tenure of North Africa, despite the Battle of **Kasserine Pass** and its other spoiling offensives in January and February, was at the mercy of overwhelming Allied naval, land and air power. By 13 May some 275,000 German and Italian prisoners, along with most of their top leaders in Tunisia, were in Allied hands, bringing to a total of about 620,000 the number of Axis troops lost in North Africa since 1940 – approximately three times the Allies' casualties.

North African wars of independence. The partition of Africa and the total seizure or domination of the North by France, Italy, Spain and Britain between 1870 and 1912 was rarely strongly opposed by politically divided and militarily weak nations. Indeed, there was a higher chance of collisions between the European predators than the indigenous peoples, who as often as not were at loggerheads among themselves or in alliance with the colonial rulers as they put down local factions. In Tunisia, for example, between 1865 and 1880, incipient Franco-Italian rivalry was interwoven with raiding by Arabs into Algeria, encouraging the French to occupy the country in 1881. Next came a series of competitive occupations: the Spanish seizure of the Rio de Oro in 1885; the **Italo-Turkish War** which won Italy possession of Tripolitania and Cyrenaica in 1912; the French conquest of the Sahara in small wars between 1900 and 1911; and in 1912 the establishment of a protectorate in Morocco, in the aftermath of the Agadir Incident when Germany, in 1911, tried to infiltrate the region.

Only gradually after **World War I** did nationalism, chiefly Arab-inspired, emerge. It was **World War II**, with the defeats of France and Italy and the overstretching of British strength, which opened the gates to change. Flurries of violent outbreaks produced negotiated settlements in 1952. Unrest in French Morocco in 1947 led to a tribal uprising against the Sultan in 1953, and a civil war of terrorism and raiding which, by 1955, the French could not contain – especially since in 1954 a similar situation in Algeria had erupted into the major **Algerian War of Independence**. To placate the Moroccans, France granted them independence, but also with agreement to keep troops in place to stabilize the situation and cope with frontier incursions from Algeria and Spanish Morocco, where tribal troubles were rife. The whole of North Africa was now in turmoil. Tunisian Arabs, restive since 1952, were helping the Algerian Front de la Libération Nationale (FLN) and acquiring independence in 1955. Egypt, involved in the **Arab–Israeli War** since 1948, was also negotiating, in association with terrorism since 1951, the exodus of the British – and achieving her aim in June 1956, just prior to the **Suez Canal** battle in November. Meanwhile Libya, having been handed independence by the British in 1951 (though retaining a British military presence) refused use of those forces against the Egyptians in 1956.

The departure of the last of the colonial powers in the 1960s left behind pockets of hostility in which factions, often sponsored by Communists orchestrated by Russia, fought the newly created governments. A raiding and skirmishing process continues in parts of Morocco where it borders on Algeria and Mauritania – and wherever Libya, under the military govern-ment of Colonel Gadaffi since 1969 (strongly backed and armed by Russia), chooses to intrude, such as in Chad, with its own Sudan-based civil war, since 1966. In Chad Gadaffi successfully supported Goukouni Oueddi's faction against Hissene Habré's in 1980, only to see Oueddei beaten in 1982 by Habré. The rebuff was avenged when Libyan troops invaded Chad in 1983 before being halted by Habré's Chadians with strong support of French troops. Stalemate followed until 1986 when the Libyans launched air attacks and an invasion of Chad that provoked an alliance of African states, with French logistic support, to take action. In a remarkably well-conducted operation, Habré's Chad army overwhelmed a 4,000-strong Libyan base at Ouadi Doum on 23 March 1987 (capturing 20 jet fighters, helicopters and 200 tanks) to evict the Libyans from Chad.

North Atlantic Treaty Organization. See Nato.

North Sea, Battles of. Domination of the North Sea in both **World Wars** was strategically vital to both Germany and her enemies in the prosecution of **blockade**, securing the safety of important coastal targets and, for Britain, the movement of military material to and from the Continent. The threat of a German invasion in World War I tied down strong British home-defence forces; similarly German troops were diverted to guard the Belgian coast – though only in 1917 did the British seriously plan a coastal operation.

At the start of World War I both sides initiated offensive surface operations, often in conjunction with minelaying, but the Germans were strongly deterred by the Battle of **Heligoland Bight** on 28 August 1914. Thereafter, with the exception of a few major forays into the Sea's central basin, they restricted surface action to night raiding by light forces along the **Flanders** coast and into the **English Channel**. With only 30 **submarines** in commission (against 78 British of which 65 were in home waters), the Germans in 1914 were severely limited in underwater operations, though U9's sinking of three **cruisers** off the River Maas on 22 September, plus another torpedoed on 15 October, and a raid on Scapa Flow on 18 October (which made the Grand Fleet shift to Rosyth while nets were installed) was salutary. Henceforward the **torpedo** and **mine** threats loomed large, requiring vast counter-efforts to safeguard ports and clear

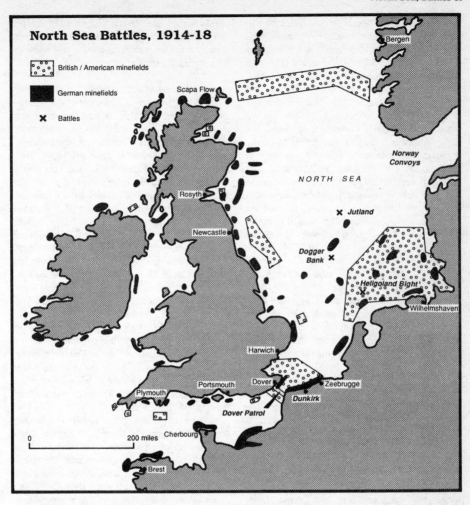

North Sea Battles, 1914-18

- British / American minefields
- German minefields
- ✕ Battles

Bergen

Scapa Flow

Norway Convoys

NORTH SEA

Rosyth

✕ Jutland

Newcastle

Dogger Bank ✕

Heligoland Bight

Wilhelmshaven

Harwich

Portsmouth Dover Zeebrugge

Plymouth Dunkirk

Dover Patrol

Cherbourg

0 200 miles

Brest

the way for commerce and warships when they put to sea.

This was the background to the damaging hit-and-run raids by German **battle-cruisers** and cruisers against British east coast ports on 3 November and 16 December 1914, followed by a third intercepted raid on 24 January which ended with the Battle of **Dogger Bank** and loss of a German cruiser. The German response to this defeat was to institute attacks on 4 February on merchant ships (including neutrals) which made necessary the protection of shipping to and from Holland, Norway, Denmark and Sweden, as well as the introduction of effective **convoys** along the east coast. The Germans realized, however, that this campaign, far from

crippling the Allies, might only lose them neutral sympathy, particularly that of America. They still held hopes of wearing down the Grand Fleet. It was with this in mind that they carried out a hit-and-run cruiser raid against Yarmouth and Lowestoft on 24/25 April 1916, as a preliminary to the sortie of the High Seas Fleet under Vice-Admiral Scheer, which brought on the Battle of **Jutland** on 31 May.

German failure at Jutland, followed by the fiasco of another High Seas Fleet sortie in August (when Scheer withdrew because of a misleading Zeppelin report and Admiral **Jellicoe** did likewise because he feared submarines), persuaded the German High Command that an unlimited submarine campaign against commerce was their

239

main hope of a decision at sea which might win the war. Supplemented by three surface raiders, which broke out in November and December 1916 to cause considerable damage on the high seas, the campaign began on 1 February 1917. Henceforward battles in the North Sea and its approaches were between small forces: the British attempting to prevent U-boats slipping through the English Channel and round the north of Scotland; the Germans trying to hit the submarine hunters at the same time as the British tried by surface raids at Zeebrugge and Ostend in April and May 1918 to block access to the sea. Only occasionally did the High Seas Fleet threaten to put to sea again, but at least every four days the Grand Fleet had to send out a battle squadron to protect convoys to Norway which, in October and December 1917, were ravaged by two fast light cruisers.

In many respects, **World War II**'s North Sea battles started as they had left off in 1918, except that air **bombing** and minelaying were everyday occurrences and much more effective than in the past. The same pattern of convoys and blockade emerged – until the Battle of **Norway** brought both Fleets into action against each other (with heavy losses), and won for Germany an admirable mounting base for the movement of submarines and surface raiders out into the Atlantic and Arctic Oceans. The advantage was vastly augmented when the rest of the West European coastline fell into German hands in 1940, and the Battle of the **Atlantic** became an all-consuming struggle. From June 1940, indeed, the North Sea became a subsidiary starting-point for German raiders setting forth, yet a wide trench against German invasion of Britain and against British hit-and-run **Commando** raids against Norway, Holland and Belgium. In endless coastal fights, bombing substituted for naval bombardment and the most persistent and dangerous surface raiders of each side's convoys were motor **torpedo-boats** stalking by night with minimum fear of air attack.

In 1942, when Germany reverted to the defensive, she viewed the North Sea as a very likely approach for an Allied invasion of Norway. It was therefore in Norwegian waters that much skirmishing took place, though without encounters between major units except when **Arctic convoys** fought their way through. After the reconquest of the French and Belgian Channel ports in October 1944, it was in the mine-infested approaches to the Heligoland Bight and off Holland and Norway that submarine hunters concentrated when seeking the latest U-boats as they emerged from German ports.

Norway, Battles of. From the start of **World War II** the Norwegian government gave tacit permission for German ships to use her territorial waters. The Allies reacted to this by occasionally intercepting German ships in Norwegian waters, notably the *Altmark* on 16 February 1940. **Hitler** then correctly reasoned the British were about to enter Norway and, feeling also that possession of Norwegian bases would assist air and sea attacks against Britain, pre-empted the move. As the Royal Navy began laying mines in Norwegian waters on 8 April they encountered ships of the German invasion force, sank a troopship and damaged others. Next day Germany entered **Denmark** without resistance and in Norway put ashore troops under General Nikolaus von Falkenhorst, at Oslo, Kristiansand, Stavanger, Bergen, Trondheim and Narvik. Mostly they seized their objectives without much trouble and often with the connivance of the Norwegian 'fifth column' under Vidkun Quisling. Indeed, if an officer, in disobedience of a spurious order, had not won time by sinking a German cruiser in Oslo fiord, the King and the government would have been captured.

Norwegian resistance was patchy and mainly concentrated north of Bergen. At Narvik, however, British naval actions on 10 and 13 April sank all 10 German destroyers and the transports prior to landing a small force on the 15th. But it was not until 16 April that the British Army under General Bernard Paget began landing in strength at Namsos and, on the 18th, put a weaker force ashore at Andelsnes, while reinforcing the detachment at Narvik. Meanwhile the Germans had lost two more cruisers but had consolidated in the south and were beginning to advance up-country to link with the garrisons at Trondheim and Narvik. Always they benefited from complete air superiority, which seriously hampered the British, whose **logistic** arrangements were all along in chaos without any extra pressure from the Germans. By 30 April the British at Andelsnes were in dire straits and had to be withdrawn. It was the same at Namsos on 2 May. At Narvik, on the other hand, Norwegian, British and French troops had driven the Germans into the mountains by 28 May,

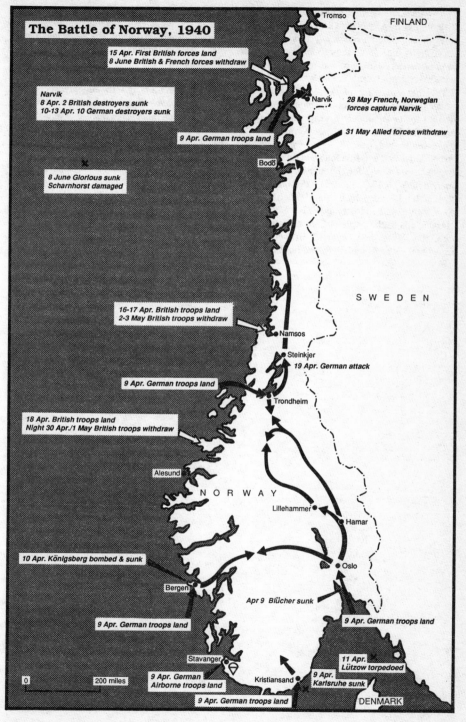

The Battle of Norway, 1940

FINLAND

Tromso

15 Apr. First British forces land
8 June British & French forces withdraw

Narvik
8 Apr. 2 British destroyers sunk
10-13 Apr. 10 German destroyers sunk

Narvik

28 May French, Norwegian
forces capture Narvik

9 Apr. German troops land

31 May Allied forces withdraw

Bodö

8 June Glorious sunk
Scharnhorst damaged

SWEDEN

16-17 Apr. British troops land
2-3 May British troops withdraw

Namsos

Steinkjer

19 Apr. German attack

9 Apr. German troops land

Trondheim

18 Apr. British troops land
Night 30 Apr./1 May British troops withdraw

Alesund

NORWAY

Lillehammer

Hamar

10 Apr. Königsberg bombed & sunk

Bergen

Oslo

Apr 9 Blücher sunk

9 Apr. German troops land

9 Apr. German troops land

Stavanger

11 Apr.
Lützow torpedoed

9 Apr. German
Airborne troops land

Kristiansand

9 Apr.
Karlsruhe sunk

9 Apr. German troops land

DENMARK

0   200 miles

241

but by then the Germans were besieging **Dun-kirk** and a mere foothold in Norway was an irrelevance. Allied evacuation was completed successfully on 8 June, though for the loss of an **aircraft-carrier** and two destroyers in a fight with two German **battle-cruisers**.

For the remainder of the war Norway lay under German occupation, its populace at first divided in its loyalties but gradually swinging against the invaders. As a base for attacks into the Atlantic and, from 1941 onwards, against **Arctic convoys** it was invaluable to the Germans. It was also a target for the first of many **Commando** raids on 4 March 1941 – this one against the Lofoten Islands which caused much damage to shipping and industry but also alerted the Norwegians to the perils of German retribution after the raiders had departed. In fact, it was naval and air raids which, throughout the war, did most damage with numerous attacks on coastal convoys and warships lurking in the fiords – of which that on the **battleship** *Tirpitz*, often damaged and finally sunk on 12 November 1944 by two 12,000lb bombs, was the most notorious. All along it was Hitler's conviction, fed by British hints, that the Allies most certainly would invade Norway which made him retain a very large garrison there instead of in action on other over-stretched fronts. They surrendered peaceably in May 1945.

Nuclear strategy. See **Cold War**, **Deterrence** and **Limited war**.

Nuclear weapons. See **Atom bomb** and **Hydrogen bomb**.

Nuclear winter. See **Deterrence**.

O

Office of Strategic Services (OSS) (see also **CIA**). An American organization which came into being in June 1942 from the founding Coordinator of Information (COI), set up by President **Roosevelt** under Colonel William Donovan in 1941. Initially both organizations were civilian in outlook, focusing on **intelligence, fifth column** and subversive activities, seeing themselves as underground activists. But OSS grew progressively more military in style and operation as it rubbed shoulders with the British **Special Operations Executive** (SOE) and came under direction of the Chiefs of Staff. When working in Britain, this meant virtually coming under SOE control during the mounting and execution of the invasion of France in 1944.

Like SOE, OSS had to endure the typical infighting that went on between the established political, diplomatic and intelligence services. In Europe it delved among the few surviving neutral nations, notably Sweden, Switzerland and Spain (where it indulged in anti-Franco activities); yet not, for State Department policy reasons, in Poland. But it also had a strong combat role, forming Operational Groups (OG), which were somewhat akin to **Commandos**, consisting of parties 34 strong which were inserted from North Africa into Southern France. Members found themselves sent all over the place, some working with local secret armies, others integrated with SOE parties.

OSS was also to be found in Asia, occasionally upsetting the colonial powers because of contacts with nationalist groups in Indo-China, the Dutch East Indies and China. Ostensibly its members fought the Japanese but they were inevitably entangled in the struggles between agents of the colonial powers, the Communists and local nationalist groups, and naturally penetrating the **Philippines** where past American influence had to be restored against the day of liberation. OSS thus acquired contacts in many nations which, post-war, would be involved in their own struggles for independence. When stories of its sensational and potentially embarrassing secret activities became news after **World War II**, the political implications scared the US State Department, which persuaded President Harry Truman to abolish OSS in September 1945.

The exigencies of **cold war**, however, soon reversed that mood. In 1947, by Act of Congress, OSS was restored as the Central Intelligence Agency (**CIA**).

Okinawa, Battles of. This key island in the Ryukyu group (with a garrison of 130,000 under General Mitsuru Ushijima) was the final stepping-stone in Admiral **Nimitz**'s advance across the **Pacific** on Japan. After the customary air and naval bombardments of its three airfields and defences between 14 and 31 March 1945, General Simon Buckner's Tenth US Army, with seven divisions available, landed on 1 April. Already, however, the American and British **aircraft-carriers** had come under sustained attack from **kamikaze** aircraft and, along with 12 other warships, three had suffered damage. The landing was hardly opposed since Ushijima had decided to hold a bastion on the southern peninsula and let the Americans overrun the rest – which they did against moderate resistance by 9 April. Meanwhile on the 6th the Japanese launched an attack by 355 kamikaze and 340 conventional bombers, plus the super-**battleship** *Yamato*, a cruiser and eight destroyers.

Operational Analysis

This valedictory blow sank six American vessels (including two destroyers) and damaged 24 others. But 383 bombers went down and so too did *Yamato* and all but four damaged destroyers, under intense air attacks. Soon the kamikaze attacks resumed, some 3,000 sorties eventually sinking 21 ships and putting 43 out of action, as well as badly damaging 23 others.

On the other island, too, there were heavy losses to both sides. Not until 31 May was the back of the Japanese defence broken, and it was 22 June before the last of 7,400 defenders had been captured after the rest had been killed. US soldiers killed amounted to 7,374 (including General Buckner) plus 32,000 wounded.

Operational analysis. See **Analysis, Operational.**

Opium wars. The introduction of opium into China from Java in the 17th century and its subsequent exploitation by foreign traders in the early 19th (despite prohibition by the Chinese government) led to conflict with European (mainly British) traders in 1839. For three years forces sent by the British East India Company fought to secure the trade in the *First Opium War*, finally capturing Canton, Shanghai and Chingkiang and compelling the Chinese to accept British terms, including a 150 years lease of Hong Kong.

In 1858 the *Second Opium War* began because the Chinese refused to legalize the opium trade and attacked British and French ships. Sporadic actions included Anglo-French bombardments of ports and the Taku Forts, near Tientsin (which were temporarily occupied in May 1858); and another attack on the forts in June 1859 when the British were repulsed with heavy losses, and helped to withdraw by an American squadron. This was followed in August 1860 by seizure of the forts by an Anglo-French force of 18,000 men, which captured Tientsin, defeated 30,000 Chinese in two battles and arrived at Peking, where the Summer Palace was looted and later burned. The Chinese legalized the opium trade and paid substantial reparations.

Optical instruments. In military applications the purpose of optical instruments is generally two-fold: to improve eye performance in the sighting of weapons; and to improve the eye's **surveillance** capability, especially in low-light conditions. Increased magnification helps to make a target more easily identifiable, but the field of view is reduced in proportion and aiming errors are increased; a compromise to meet the requirement is usually necessary.

Throughout the 19th century most weapons were aligned using simple open sights and optical instruments were confined to surveillance. Here the terrestrial telescope had long been in use by field commanders, giving reasonable magnification but usually a very restricted field of view. Towards the close of the century the first binoculars were appearing and the longer weapon ranges, especially of naval guns, were calling for optical equipment to match the improved performance.

World War I created a major demand for optical equipment of all kinds: **range-finders**, sights, clinometers, fire directors, plotters, etc., to improve fire control; for surveillance in trench warfare a particular need for periscopes arose. For the Germans this posed no special problem, they were the acknowledged leaders in optical glass manufacture. The British, however, had become entirely dependent for this on imports from Germany (and some from France); so much so that in 1915 the British government negotiated a deal through the Swiss whereby the Germans supplied 32,000 binoculars to the British Army in return for supplies of rubber, stocks of which had been depleted by the Allied **blockade**. The situation in Britain gradually improved during the war, against an ever-increasing demand for such items as tank periscopes and aircraft sights.

By 1939 the manufacture of optical glass in the UK was well-established and predicted fire from **artillery** of all kinds was entirely dependent on optical instruments, especially the range-finder; however, the monostatic instruments then in use were not entirely satisfactory, errors increasing with the square of the range. The gravest disadvantage of all optical instruments was, of course, their comparative uselessness in poor visibility. The particular long-range demands of naval **gunnery** and of air defence saw range-finding and surveillance by **radar** gradually supplanting optical fire-control systems.

In the field, however, and for aircraft gun- and bomb-sights, the optical instrument still seemed to provide the best answer. A number of British firms working with the Royal Aircraft Establishment combined to produce the equipment needed for British aircraft, while in America Sperry's produced sights for use in their aircraft – simple and robust but, since they assumed steady flight, not of such practical value as the more sophisticated British sights; the latter were subsequently adopted by both countries.

For tanks and direct-fire artillery weapons the simple straight-through telescope was in general use throughout World War II, usually fitted with a graticule (US: reticle), consisting of a series of accurate marks which enable the gunner to apply deflection and range without removing his eye from the instrument. The disadvantage for the tank was that the telescope had to be in generally the same horizontal plane as the gun barrel, which meant that much of the turret had to be exposed above cover to take aim. Later designs adopted the more complicated periscopic sight set in the turret roof, thus reducing exposure. Tactically this was sound, but it resulted in some complex linkages to connect gun to sight. Such sights rely on a combination of prisms and tilting mirrors to provide the required optical path, with modern lens coatings permitting the use of more optical elements than would previously have been possible.

Modern small arms have also called for more elaborate optical sights, especially for night work, and the British Trilux, of prismatic construction similar to half a binocular, is now in service as a typical example.

Though range-finding and long-range surveillance has been largely overtaken by electronics, the need for optical instruments for sighting and surveillance in the combat zone remains.

Oran, Battles of. When France surrendered to Germany in June 1940, Admiral **Darlan**, as Minister of Marine, instructed the Fleet to destroy its ships rather than let them fall intact into enemy hands. Of this the British were unaware, but in any case they could never be sure what circumstances might arise that would allow the Germans to take possession of such formidable units. On 3 July the British took steps to secure French warships in British ports and instructed Vice-Admiral Sir James Somerville to neutralize or destroy two **battleships** and two modern **battle-cruisers** lying at Oran or in the nearby base of Mers el Kebir. Devious negotiations ceased at a point when the French decided to break out and fight. A British battle-cruiser and two battleships opened fire as the French began to move, sinking one battleship and crippling the two battle-cruisers, but letting the rest of the squadron escape to Toulon. More than 1,000 French sailors were killed in a dolorous action.

On 8 November 1942 Oran was the scene of some of the toughest French resistance to the Allied invasion of French North Africa. American landings on either side of the port were unopposed, but a suicidal attempt by two small British ships, under American colours and carrying 400 American soldiers, to seize the port and ships intact was repulsed with heavy loss. This encouraged the French, who fought well for more than two days until an armoured column broke through to the city centre, where surrender was agreed.

P

Pacific Ocean War, 1941–5. As a basis of the long-intended **Japanese war of expansion**, domination of the Pacific was essential, something well understood by the Americans and British when they noted the progressive fortification of islands in Japanese possession and studied the infiltration of China (**Chinese–Japanese wars**), and South-East Asia in the 1930s. It was Japan's tragedy that she fell into the hands of a bellicose military clique, who had the support of their Emperor Hirohito, and that in 1940 the weakening of Britain at the hands of the Germans tempted them to gamble upon winning a decisive naval victory against the Americans. This would have helped them to seize a strategic perimeter defence from the **Aleutian Islands** through Marcus and Wake Islands to **New Guinea** and the Dutch East Indies, extending also into **Malaya** and **Burma**. The gamble was forced upon the Japanese when, in September 1940, President **Roosevelt** tried to deter Japan by placing an embargo on shipments of oil, scrap iron and steel from America, a measure which posed Japan the choice of curbing her ambitions or going to war. On the admission by Admiral **Yamamoto** that he could only guarantee 'playing Hell for eighteen months', they opted for an undeclared war.

On 7 December 1941 they made the surprise attack on **Pearl Harbor** and began their rampage through the **Philippines**, at **Hong Kong**, and into Malaya, the Dutch East Indies and Burma, via Indo-China and Thailand. Destruction of the Allied Fleet off Malaya and in the Battle of the **Java Sea** opened the way to completion of their initial plan by April 1942, during a remarkable period of successes in which the Americans lost their bases on Guam and Wake Islands. How-

ever, with the **aircraft-carriers** that had survived Pearl Harbor the Americans in this period raided Japanese bases in the Gilbert and the Marshall Islands in February, as well as Marcus and Wake Islands, but were repulsed when attempting a raid on Rabaul. In March they struck at Lae and Salamaua before, in April, bombing Tokyo. At this point the Japanese decided to extend their perimeter by capturing the Aleutians, Midway Island and Port Moresby in New Guinea, thus also posing a further threat to Australia, Port Darwin having already been bombed in February. But surprise was lost. This scheme, like most other Japanese plans, was fully revealed to the Allies by decryption of **radio** signals.

At the battles of the **Coral Sea** and **Midway** the Japanese aircraft-carrier fleet was ruined, thus removing the vital, mobile force that alone could secure the static island bases of the perimeter defensive system, and permitting the first tenuous Allied **amphibious** counterstroke at **Guadalcanal** in August. Henceforward the initiative rested with General **MacArthur** in the South-West Pacific area and Admiral **Nimitz** in the central and South Pacific areas. MacArthur developed the counter-offensive in New Guinea which, in conjunction with Nimitz's advance through the **Solomon Islands** in 1943, led to the isolation of Rabaul. Nimitz opened his drive towards Japan in the **Gilbert Islands** in November, followed in February 1944 by the taking of Kwajalein Island and Eniwetok in the Marshalls – the latter operations remarkable for the wiping out of some 10,000 Japanese at a cost of only 771 American dead. Next came the assault on the **Mariana Islands** and Guam and the related naval Battle of the **Philippine Sea** in June, leading to President Roosevelt's decision,

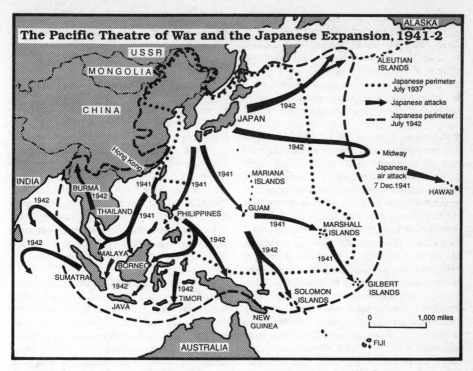

The Pacific Theatre of War and the Japanese Expansion, 1941-2

for political as much as military reasons, to support MacArthur's desire to invade the Philippines instead of, as Nimitz wished, going straight to Formosa or China, before invading Japan. As it was, the **blockade** of Japan by **submarines** (mainly American), which sank 57 per cent of the 8·5 million tonnes of merchant shipping lost in addition to 201 out of 686 warships put down, plus Nimitz's neutralization of Palau Island and the victory of his aircraft in the Battle of **Formosa**, in October, went far to achieving his original aim. For in conjunction with the assault on the Philippines (which brought on the conclusive Battle of **Leyte Gulf**) in October, began the Battle of **Japan**, made possible by American possession of air bases in the Marianas from which long-range B29 bombers could operate. The aerial bombardment multiplied in destruction after the capture of **Iwojima** in March 1945 and, in June, the conclusion of the bloody battle for **Okinawa**. At this point Japan was prostrate. As her forces in the Philippines were broken, Australian troops landed in Borneo to recapture the oilfields she had gone to war for in 1941. The dropping of the **atom bombs** on Hiroshima and Nagasaki in August merely provided a convenient excuse to call off a war she never had much hope of winning.

Paris, Siege of. After the initial German victories of the **Franco-Prussian War**, including **Sedan**, part of the French Army withdrew into Paris, which was besieged on 19 September 1870. Behind two formidable fortress lines, a garrison of 220,000 (of whom only about 50,000 were trained) plus 300,000 untrained *gardes nationales* of revolutionary outlook, came under command of the President, General Louis Trochu. Few preparations had been made for siege. Supplies were short. But General von **Moltke** had neither the desire nor the means to assault when so many of his resources were employed elsewhere and his lines of communication harried by **guerrillas**. Indeed, not until 5 January was it possible to assemble the siege train with sufficient ammunition for a sustained bombardment. Meanwhile a revolt by the *gardes nationales* had been put down by Trochu on 31 October and two ineptly managed sorties by the garrison had collapsed in November and December as starvation and disease loomed.

Von Moltke was under severe political press-

247

ure to finish the job quickly, but wisely depended upon the bombardment and time to do so. Failures by the French armies in the field to defeat the Prussians, and a third disastrous attempt at sortie on 19 January 1871 (when the *gardes nationales* fired on their own side), finally compelled Trochu to conclude an armistice on the 26th. Civil war ensued in the spring.

Patton, General George (1885–1945). An American cavalryman with charisma and flair who ably led a unit of the US Army's Tank Corps in **World War** I but, between the wars, played a rather negative part in the development of **armoured** forces. In North Africa in **World War II** he commanded the assault on Casablanca on 8 November 1942, and took over and revived II Corps in the aftermath of its defeat at **Kasserine**. He led Seventh Army in the Battle of **Sicily** in July 1943, but was afterwards dismissed for the much-publicized slapping of a soldier suffering from **combat fatigue**. Given command of Third Army in 1944, he led it in the break-out from **Normandy** and the pursuit to Germany, in which his intriguing and his selfish cornering of supplies had a controversial affect on Allied strategy. His counterstroke during the Ardennes Offensive in December 1944 was highly effective, as was the dash with which he led Third Army in the Battle of **Germany** in 1945. He was killed in a motor accident in December 1945.

Pearl Harbor raid. As main US base for the US Pacific Fleet, the military installations on Hawaii and the **dockyard** at Pearl Harbor were obvious targets for attack by the Japanese. Moreover, the Americans had precise **intelligence** that such a blow was to be expected on 7 December 1941, but failed to take measures, apart from sending the **aircraft-carriers** to sea, to thwart it. Admiral **Yamamoto**'s plan to sink the entire Pacific Fleet in harbour by air attack was based on the concept of a single crushing blow such as Japan had delivered against the Russians at **Port Arthur** and **Tsushima** in 1904 and 1905 respectively. He gambled upon permanently destroying America's capability to restore her strength in the **Pacific War**.

The well-prepared blows by 200 aircraft in two waves, under command of Vice-Admiral Chuiki Nagumo, sank, crippled or damaged all eight **battleships** present and severely damaged many other vessels, including three **cruisers** and four **destroyers**. Many aircraft were also destroyed and over 2,200 servicemen killed at a cost to the Japanese of 100 men, 29 aircraft and five midget **submarines**, the latter failing in their missions.

The attack gave the Japanese complete freedom of action in the Pacific but was not the decisive victory Yamamoto desired. By failing to locate and sink the aircraft-carriers and, on Nagumo's part, not launching a third strike to wreck the oil-storage tanks and dockyard, these assets survived to help speed American recovery and ruin the Japanese striking force within the next six months at **Coral Sea** and **Midway**. But the shock to the United States was the most telling blow and its iniquity embittered the nation, enforcing its determination to destroy Japan. The subsequent controversy over culpability has kept speculation alive ever since.

Pershing, General John (1860–1948). An American officer who acquired immense experience in the Indian War (**American Indian Wars**) of 1886; in Cuba during the **Spanish–American War**; in minor **Philippines** actions; as an observer of the **Russo-Japanese War**; and as Commander US forces in the **Mexican War** against Pancho Villa in 1916, before being appointed C-in-C US Army in Europe after America entered **World War** I in April 1917. For over a year Pershing had too few troops to play the part of an independent force leader. Unwillingly he was compelled by circumstances to place individual divisions under French or British command in helping to stem the **Hindenburg offensive** in the spring of 1918. Indeed, his Army was largely equipped with Allied heavy weapons, because of America's unreadiness for war, and never became self-sufficient. Only at the battles of **Saint-Mihiel** in September and **Argonne** in October was a degree of independence achieved, in battles which revealed the troops' inexperience offset by courage. After the war, from 1921 until retirement in 1924, he was a conservative Army Chief of Staff.

Persian Gulf wars. Until the discoveries of enormous oil deposits in the Arab states and Persia in the 20th century, and the rapid increase in demand for that mineral, the Persian Gulf area had been Persian-dominated. Meanwhile European nations tried to keep the peace for benefit of trade, and in 1853 Britain took responsibility by treaty for ensuring the outlawing of war at sea in the Gulf. This, of course, allowed her to expand her influence as protector of some Arab states (thus becoming a rival of the Turks in Mesopotamia), and to worry about Russian and German schemes to connect the Gulf to the Mediterranean by **railway**. But apart from minor skirmishes with the Arab states prior to October 1914, when Turkey entered **World War I** on the side of the Central Powers, Britain did maintain peace and a growing prosperity for the Gulf states. Persia, on the other hand, posed problems. Despite British objections, she invaded Afghanistan in 1855 and in consequence found herself, in 1856, invaded by Britain and forced to withdraw from Afghanistan in 1857. Russia continued to be acquisitive and in 1909, at the end of the Persian Revolution which had started in 1905, brutally suppressed a revolt at Tabriz. In 1911 she unsuccessfully attempted to return the deposed Shah to power, prior to occupying North Persia in a move which forced the British to take control of the oilfields in the South West to safeguard them against all comers, including the Turks.

Throughout the **Mesopotamia** campaign, however, only sporadic fighting took place in Western Persia, while the Gulf remained tranquil. Indeed, it largely stayed that way until the outbreak of **World War II**, waxing mightily rich as more and more oilfields were discovered on both sides of the water and as its strategic importance became paramount. In May 1941, however, German stimulation of an Iraqi revolt compelled Britain to take complete control of that country by sending in troops from Palestine and through Basra rapidly to link up with the temporarily besieged inland garrisons as the rebellion collapsed. Likewise in August, Britain and Russia, judging that a significant German presence in Iran (Persia) threatened the vital oilfields and might prevent the establishment of a land route for supplies from the Gulf to Russia, entered the country against minor resistance and secured all the vital places undamaged. By 1943, with massive American aid, an important supply system was working.

Gradual British military withdrawal from Iran and the other Gulf states took place after World War II in company with bellicose Iranian moves to nationalize her oilfields and threats of renewed British occupation. Though on the brink of civil war in 1953, once that crisis was resolved Iran's modernization, including that of her armed forces, steadily drew the nation out of chaos into prominence. Sometimes she interfered in the business of Arab states. As always there was Russian involvement in the affairs of Iran and also, from 1958, in Communist-orientated Iraq. But not until the outbreak of the **Iran–Iraq War** in 1980 was the Gulf infected by general war. Even then, despite the conflicting interests of the major powers and the fanaticism of the Iranians, that bloody struggle was contained before it was stopped in 1988.

On 2 August 1990 Iraq invaded Kuwait for her oil and for control of the head of the Gulf. Organized resistance was quelled in 24 hours. Among United Nations' resolutions, the tenth gave authority to retake Kuwait by force. Saudi Arabia was reinforced by an alliance of forces from nine Arab nations, the USA, Europe (mainly Britain and France) and detachments from several other nations, all under the command of US General Norman Schwarzkopf. **Blockade** was imposed. **Propaganda** and **psychological warfare** were rife. Iraq's Saddam Hussein having refused to withdraw, on 17 January 1991 UN air forces rapidly won supremacy, ruined Iraq's economy and battered her surface forces. During a classic **desert war** of envelopment, which began on 24 February, the Iraqi Army was routed, Kuwait overrun in one hundred hours and Iraq compelled to obey the UN when the USA's President George Bush called a cease fire. Of the 42 Iraq divisions in southern Iraq approximately 75%, including some 4,900 tanks and 2,300 guns, were lost at a price of 150 Allied killed. **Technology's effects**, notably **smart munitions**, had a revolutionary impact both on operations and future **deterrence**. Iraq fell into internal strife.

Pétain, Marshal Philippe (1856–1951). A French officer who, as a Brigade commander at the age of 58 with no active service experience in August 1914, became a Corps commander at **Arras** in May 1915 and, in June, an Army commander. Sent to **Verdun** on 26 February 1916 to stop the rot, he became a hero of France in doing so. Likewise, when made C-in-C in May 1917 at the nadir of the French Army's fortunes, he was able to quell a mutiny and sufficiently restore fighting spirit to withstand the **Hindenburg offensive** in 1918 and bring the war to a successful conclusion. Regarded as having greater military wisdom than perhaps he merited, he tended in various appointments after 1918 to ossify the French Army's development by failing, like many another, to understand the latest effects of **technology**.

When French resistance was broken by the Germans in June 1940, he was called upon to form a government and make peace. By retaining control over the fleet, a small army and the colonies, he was able, from Vichy, to salvage some slight French self-respect and pursue an unrealistic policy aimed at isolating the nation from the war. Senility condemned him to the role of a mere figurehead. Tried after the war for his complicity in post-1940 events, the sentence of death was commuted to life imprisonment.

Petersburg, Siege of. In the aftermath of the costly **Wilderness** battles of the **American Civil War**, General **Grant** crossed the James River on 13 June 1864 and marched on the fortified, but only thinly defended, **railway** junction of Petersburg in an endeavour to encircle Richmond. This most skilful operation caught General **Lee** off balance, but the Federal army fumbled its attempt to rush the city, giving Lee time to reinforce and win a three days battle on 18 June. From then on Grant's side-steps round Petersburg to the south and west were repeatedly countered by the Confederates. On 30 July the explosion of a four-tonne **mine** under a redoubt opened a gap which the Federals casually failed to exploit. Subsequently, as fast as the Federals advanced, admirably supplied from their base on the James River, the Confederates dug new trenches or counter-attacked in a grim battle of attrition which ground to a halt in cold and wet on 28 October. It left the citizens of Petersburg and Richmond to suffer a winter short of supplies, on the verge of defeat. Yet despite Grant's renewed attempts in 1865 to take the town, it held out under severe pressure until 2 April when Lee withdrew on the eve of the war's end.

Philippines, Battles of the. In 1896 an insurrection against the Philippines' Spanish rulers was an overture to the **Spanish–American War** of 1898 and the sale of the islands to America. Next year an insurrection in favour of Filipino independence virtually placed American troops in Manila under siege. This compelled the Americans, under General Arthur MacArthur, to begin counter-**guerrilla** operations with 100,000 troops, in a war which spread throughout the islands and lasted until 1905 at a cost of 4,234 American dead and close on 16,000 Filipinos dead plus another 100,000 dying from starvation.

When the Japanese attacked the islands in December 1941, neither the American Fleet (smashed at **Pearl Harbor**) nor the garrison were able to stand for long at either **Bataan** or **Corregidor**. During the Japanese occupation small nationalist and some Communist resistance groups were formed, although without much American assistance since OSS was mainly excluded by both Admiral **Nimitz** and General Douglas **MacArthur**, prior to the invasion of October 1944. As a prelude to the landing on 20 October by Sixth Army (General Walter Kreuger), the US Navy had won a series of great victories during June in the Battle of the **Philippine Sea** and off **Formosa** (13–16 October) – and in direct support of the operation finally would crush the Japanese Fleet in the Battle of **Leyte Gulf**.

But that made little difference to 350,000 Japanese under General Tomoyuki Yamashita who, making no effort to oppose landings on the beaches, decided to concentrate his forces on Leyte for a decisive struggle for the Philippines. For nearly two months he fed in reinforcements until about 70,000 men had been consumed against 15,500 American casualties, and to no lasting avail since Kreuger had the strength to tackle the other islands: Samar in October, Mindoro starting on 15 December, and commencement of the invasion of Luzon with a major landing on 9 January 1945 at Lingayen Gulf. This became the base for an overland advance of a month's duration to Manila, supported by furious naval and air bombardments of the Japanese, who, for a few days until they ran out of aircraft, made **kamikaze** attacks which sank an escort **aircraft-carrier** and, among several ships, damaged a **battleship** and four **cruisers**. The arrival of General Robert Eichelberger's Eighth Army on 30 January, however, brought overbearing strength against Yamashita whose forces became split up as they withdrew into **jungle** and **mountainous** terrain in the north-east of Luzon. There 50,000 of them held out until the war's end against the Americans, local guerrillas run by 13 agents of the OSS, and the reformed Philippine Army.

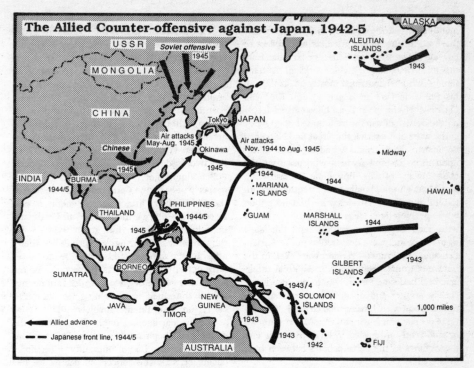

The Allied Counter-offensive against Japan, 1942-5

In July 1946 the Philippines Republic was formed, permitting US forces to remain. At once a Communist-inspired guerrilla war, the Hukbalahap rebellion, broke out on Luzon and continued until 1954 when the last of its leaders was captured. Since then, however, Communist, racial and religious groups have violently opposed the government.

Philippine Sea, Battle of the. The American invasion of the **Mariana Islands** in June 1944 and the landing on Saipan on the 15th impelled the Japanese to risk Admiral Jisaburo Ozawa's Fleet in a major battle against Admiral Raymond Spruance's Fifth Fleet. Ozawa, with five **battleships**, 11 heavy and two light **cruisers**, 28 **destroyers** and nine **aircraft-carriers**, with 473 aircraft, pitted his force on 19 June against Spruance's seven battleships, 21 cruisers, 69 destroyers and 15 carriers, with 956 aircraft. Ozawa launched four successive carrier air strikes on the heels of attacks by land-based machines. But in training and technology his airmen were outclassed in what became known as 'The Great Marianas Turkey Shoot'. They scored only two bomb hits on battleships and

shot down only 14 American fighters and one bomber. They lost 301 machines that day, plus another 145, two carriers and numerous other ships after Spruance's bombers countered on the 20th. A decisive American victory marred by the loss of 80 aircraft which landed in the sea when they ran out of fuel trying to find their carriers in the dark.

Philosophers, Military. Among philosophers, those who specialize in the military sphere may possibly be at greatest risk of error since war is so amorphous as to be an art – not, as sometimes suggested, a science. The imponderables of so diverse an art, which are subject to the full blast of human eccentricity, are immense and incalculable. As a breed therefore, military philosophers, notably those of the 19th and 20th centuries who were at the mercy of rapidly changing technological effects (**Technology, Effects of**) and interpretations of history, tend to be renowned for the frequency with which they have been wide of the mark and the manner in which, rather like gunners, they count their hits and forget their misses.

In this entry only the celebrities who have

won notoriety by originality of thought will be mentioned, bearing in mind that for every star there are innumerable satellites who reflect or develop the latest perceptions. For example, from the mid 19th century the works of Antoine Jomini (who concentrated mostly on strategy in his *Précis de l'art de la guerre*) and Karl von Clausewitz (who in *On War* philosophized deeply on the nature of war) were founded upon study of the wars of Frederick the Great and Napoleon Bonaparte. Their treatises had profound effects upon those serving soldiers who practised the changing art of war. But while General H. K. von **Moltke** undoubtedly paid attention to both Jomini and von Clausewitz, he had no option but to develop fresh ideas and doctrine to utilize with such success the **railway** and the latest weapons of increased destruction in the **Austro-Prussian** and **Franco-Prussian wars**. Yet, in the nature of human behaviour, these great thinkers, who had taken such care to produce large, closely argued and authoritative works, were understood (or misunderstood) by only a handful of people; and fewer still were those equipped or sufficiently interested to level criticisms and reveal flaws in the fierce debates between high intellectuals.

The compulsion towards total war waged offensively by the nation in arms was not only expounded by Jomini and von Clausewitz but swallowed whole as inevitable by national and military leaders – a philosophy which merged with the radical thoughts of Karl Marx and Friedrich Engels as they developed the concept of the revolutionary state. It therefore conditioned the conduct of **World War I** and the **Russian revolutionary wars**, but without prophesying that the offensive would be stifled by the latest technology and techniques, which lent significant bias to the power of defence. Such massive misguidance revealed serious flaws in military philosophers' methods. None of them had possession of all the relevant facts, all were deficient in scientific or technical education, and none were trained in **operational analysis**, which was an unknown science. They tended also to misinterpret history and could sometimes be accused of making unfounded assumptions amounting to guesswork. Significantly, however, the somewhat academic, but technically aware American Admiral **Mahan** arrived very close to practical truth concerning **naval warfare**.

Still reeling from the shock waves of World War I, the philosophers of the 1920s and 1930s had a feast propounding new ways of waging war economically with the latest weapon systems of high destruction. But advocates of **air warfare**'s effects, above all General **Douhet**, General **Mitchell** and General Sir Hugh **Trenchard**, postulated the dominance of independent air power without pointing out that the state of the art made it impractical, and therefore inadmissible when **World War II** broke out in 1937. Of the two leading British philosophers, General **Fuller** almost got it right (but was taken up properly only by the Germans) when he backed the philosophy of attack against enemy morale by complementary **armoured** and **air forces**; and Captain Basil **Liddell Hart** got it wrong – for though until 1935 he agreed with Fuller, thereafter, by the fudging of history, allied to ignorance of technology's effects, he propounded the superiority of the defence in order to influence British statesmen to abstain, quite unrealistically, from a Continental involvement.

The nuclear age has naturally generated the greatest philosophical disputation of all time concerning the very fate of humanity, a beneficial debate because the concept of **deterrence** has prevailed. Many indeed are the propositions linked to deterrence with its associated national policies and strategies. But no longer do the opinions of only a few seers dominate the ensuing private and public debates, as in the past. The monopoly of a handful of enthusiasts and pedants has been broken by a very large school of well-educated experts and sceptics who criticize and challenge effectively. Committees, study groups and operational analysis organizations now submerge the individual. Air Marshal **Slessor** may well have been the last of the great military philosophers when, in the 1950s and with a wealth of experience at his disposal, he propounded with simple clarity the theory of ultimate deterrence which, so far, has prevented global nuclear war.

Photography. The impact of photography on war may be said to have started with the work of Roger Fenton in the **Crimea** in 1855 and with the remarkable pictures obtained by Brady, Gardner and O'Sullivan during the **American Civil War**. However, these pioneers were merely recording events, not assisting commanders in making combat decisions. Nevertheless, the implications were clear, especially when in 1858 Gaston Tournachon was able to take aerial photographs of Paris from a balloon. The first use of aerial photography in war was during the **Italian War of Independence** in 1859.

Reconnaissance was, by 1914, clearly seen as a role for **aircraft** and the development of the portable roll-film camera by Kodak in 1888 made photography from the air a practical possibility. It was in 1914 that the British had, in one day, photographed from an aircraft the whole of the Isle of Wight and the Solent fortifications, developing the negatives in the air ready for printing on landing.

No army could afford to ignore this new spy in the sky. As **World War I** progressed techniques improved so that it was not long before a complete mosaic of the defences along the Western Front had been produced for the commanders to study. An elaborate programme of reconnaissance flights ensured that the picture was regularly updated and changes noted.

The 1930s saw the military emphasis concentrating on aerial photography, as it has continued to do. It was during this period that the development or adaptation of aircraft specifically for the photo reconnaissance task began, a typical example being the German Dornier Do17, fitted with the latest high-definition cameras and capable of speeds over 250mph. It was during this inter-war period too that photo-reconnaissance developed beyond merely observing and recording the enemy's defences. In the conquest of **Abyssinia** in 1935 the Italians successfully used aerial survey to plan their advances into otherwise unmapped terrain.

It was, however, during **World War II** that photo reconnaissance really came into its own. By the 1940s the hand-held cameras of 1914 had long been supplanted by properly fitted equipment, usually mounted in the floor of the aircraft and pointing straight down. It was important to ensure that each exposure overlapped the next so that a complete mosaic of the area could be built up. This required straight and accurate flying, often coupled with a shutterless technique whereby the film ran continuously past a slit at a rate matched exactly to the image movement in the camera's focal plane as the aircraft flew along (known as image-motion compensation).

Improvements in equipment meant that the menace of the reconnaissance aircraft was even more evident, together with the need to destroy such aircraft before they could regain their own lines. The only defence was speed and so, to reduce weight, reconnaissance aircraft were stripped of all non-essentials, including armament. Flying reconnaissance missions required no little personal courage and, as the bombing offensive over Europe developed, the need for ever deeper photographic penetration into enemy territory arose; to be met by the British with the development of the De Havilland Mosquito, specifically designed for this role (though subsequently used for many others).

The task was not, of course, confined to taking pictures. An essential phase, having got the film safely back to base, was the timely interpretation of what the camera had revealed. This was highly skilled, sometimes intuitive, work and special photo-interpretation units were formed. Their job was often made easier by stereoscopic photographs, produced by twin cameras mounted with lenses 2·5in apart to simulate the view seen by the left and right eye respectively. The picture had to be looked at through special stereoscopic viewers to get the three-dimensional effect, but otherwise flat pictures could be seen in sharp relief in this way, revealing much more information.

Developments since 1945 have revealed the need for two levels of photoreconnaissance. In the combat zone low-level photoreconnaissance is provided by drones or **remotely piloted vehicles** (RPV), flown over enemy lines. They are most useful for such spot tasks as discovering whether a bridge is intact or not; strip searches on a straight flight path can also be carried out, but the reaction time will be governed by the time taken to interpret the film when it has been processed. **Cold War** requirements were for high-level deep penetration of the opposition's territory, and for this the Americans produced such aircraft as the U2, flying so high as to be virtually out of sight from the ground. However, it is the reconnaissance satellite which, with the latest camera techniques, has provided the real breakthrough. It is now possible to obtain detailed imagery of almost any part of the earth's surface from suitably positioned satellites. The pictures, though taken from several hundred miles up, reveal intimate details of ground activity and are an essential tool in providing accurate and timely information of a potential opponent's intentions.

Finally, while the main emphasis has been on aerial reconnaissance, it should not be forgotten that photography has had a considerable indirect influence on the development of military equipment; in particular, high-speed cameras are used extensively in weapon trials in order to observe the behaviour of projectiles in flight. There are numerous other examples in weapons development.

Pilsudski, Marshal Józef (1867–1935). A Polish revolutionary bent on freeing his country from Russian rule who, in 1908, formed a secret military cell in Lvóv as the cadre of a future Polish Army. He foresaw a war between the Central Powers and Russia in which the latter would be defeated and give Poland her liberty. After the outbreak of **World War I** he commanded 1 Polish Brigade in the Polish Legion which was formed by Austria–Hungary. In 1916, after Poland was cleared of Russians, he was made Chief of the Military Department in the Polish Council of State set up by the Central Powers, but was imprisoned in July 1917 for refusing to swear loyalty to the German and Austrian armed forces. With Germany defeated in November 1918, he returned home, where he was acclaimed as a hero and made Head of State. He led the Army and saved his country in the subsequent **Russo-Polish War**, remaining at the helm until his resignation in May 1923, but returning to office in 1926 to become, until his death, Minister of Defence and *de facto* controller of foreign affairs.

Plate, Battle of the River. At the outbreak of **World War II** the German armoured **cruiser** *Graf von Spee* was in the South Atlantic and Indian Ocean raiding Allied commerce. Eleven ships had fallen to her by 13 December 1939 when she made contact with three Royal Navy cruisers off the mouth of the River Plate. The German's six 11in guns outranged the batteries of British 8in and 6in guns and put one cruiser out of action. But the others closed the range and did sufficient damage to force *Graf von Spee* to shelter for repairs in Montevideo. Bluffed into thinking a superior enemy force was waiting outside, the German Captain Hans Langsdorff was ordered to scuttle his ship in the river mouth.

Polish campaigns. Traditionally in conflict with Germany and Russia, Poland's brief spell of total independence between the **World Wars** was won by Marshal **Pilsudski** in the **Russo-Polish War** of 1919 to 1921. German resurgence under **Hitler**, and the signing of the non-aggression pact between Germany and Russia in August 1939, doomed the country. The Polish forces, strong in numbers but weak in equipment, delayed **mobilization** for political purposes. They could offer only fierce but hopeless resistance on 1 September when the Germans advanced from the west on three axes and on a fourth southwards from East Prussia. The Polish Corridor was at once cut, the southern half of the country overrun and **Warsaw** attacked by tanks on the 8th. A Polish counterstroke on the Bzura River was soon snuffed out. Immobilized armies everywhere were surrounded and forced to surrender including the heavily bombarded Warsaw garrison, which surrendered on the 27th. All resistance ended on 5 October. By then the Red Army had driven into eastern Poland, where it remained until annihilated at the start of the **Russo-German War** in June 1941.

During both German and Russian occupations, Polish resistance and sabotage arose, some fostered by **SOE** and the emigrant government in the West, some by Communist cells. Secret armies were formed. On 19 April 1943 the remaining Jews of the Warsaw Ghetto took up arms for three weeks until killed or removed to German extermination camps. On 17 July 1944 the Red Army, with Polish formations under command, crossed the River Bug and entered Poland in pursuit of a smashed German Army Group Centre. The Russians also had problems, chiefly those of supply in a devastated country, yet kept going for about 300 miles before forming a bridgehead across the Vistula River on 29 July and coming within sight of Warsaw on the 31st. Next day the Polish Home Army rose up, but the Red Army (on Josef **Stalin**'s cynical instructions) stopped dead and the penultimate, bizarre siege of **Warsaw** began.

Not until 17 January 1945 was Marshal **Zhukov** ready to attack again in Poland, though this time the conquest of the remainder of the country was completed quickly against General **Guderian**'s hopelessly outnumbered forces. Warsaw fell on the 17th when the Russian spearheads already were well on their way to overrunning East Prussia and crossing the West German frontier on 23 January. Once more Poland was under Russian rule.

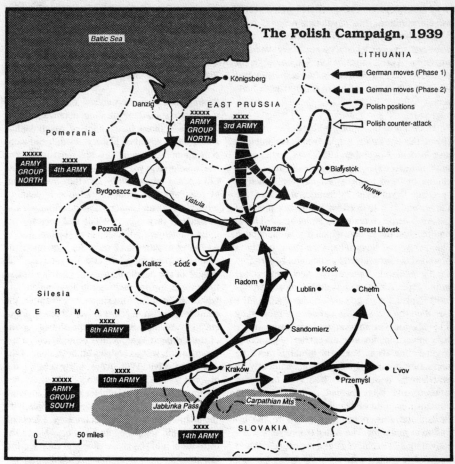

The Polish Campaign, 1939

LITHUANIA

← German moves (Phase 1)
◄■■■ German moves (Phase 2)
Polish positions
Polish counter-attack

Baltic Sea

Königsberg

Danzig

EAST PRUSSIA

XXXXX
ARMY
GROUP
NORTH

XXXX
3rd ARMY

Pomerania

XXXXX
ARMY
GROUP
NORTH

XXXX
4th ARMY

Białystok

Narew

Bydgoszcz

Vistula

Poznań

Warsaw

Brest Litovsk

Kalisz   Łódź

Radom

Kock

Lublin

Chełm

Silesia

GERMANY

XXXX
8th ARMY

Sandomierz

XXXX
10th ARMY

Kraków

L'vov

XXXXX
ARMY
GROUP
SOUTH

Przemyśl

Jablunka Pass

Carpathian Mts

0   50 miles

XXXX
14th ARMY

SLOVAKIA

Port Arthur, Sieges of. This ice-free port fell into Japanese hands on 19 November 1894 during the **Chinese–Japanese War** when 10,000 Chinese put up timid resistance to the Japanese assault under General Maresuke Nogi. But the fruits of victory, to Japanese rage, were snatched away by Russia in a diplomatic manoeuvre.

Thus Port Arthur was a prime Japanese objective at the start of the **Russo-Japanese War** on 8 February 1904 when the Fleet within was attacked without warning by **torpedo-boats** prior to a very damaging bombardment of ships and forts by the Japanese Fleet. By no means prepared for war, let alone the siege General Nogi had again been ordered to impose, the garrison of 40,000 under General Anatoli Stössel prepared for battle as the Russian Fleet was defeated at sea and driven back into port. Stössel's modern forts

(**Fortifications**), which were put in order before Nogi launched his first attack on 25 May, were well protected by barbed wire, searchlights, **artillery** and **machine-guns** with ample ammunition and supplies enough for six months for the garrison plus 18,000 civilians.

Anxious to seize the port before the fleet put to sea, Nogi attacked without the help of a siege train and was bloodily repulsed. It took two months to bring in heavy guns, yet progress was still slow and casualties enormous after they had arrived. Moreover, gun barrels began to wear out as ammunition supply was depleted, and as the Japanese were weakened by disease. Not until 5 December, after a prolonged battle, did they capture the key 203 Metre Hill dominating the harbour, enabling the emplacement of artillery to destroy the ships at anchor and apply

255

irresistible pressure on Stössel. Still well supplied by ammunition, his casualties amounted to 31,000, leaving few survivors fit for duty who were not ravaged by scurvy and starvation. He surrendered on 2 January 1905 to an opponent who had suffered 59,000 battle casualties and whose 34,000 sick included 21,000 with beri-beri.

Port Said, Battle of. Among the battles for the **Suez Canal**, the one by an Anglo-French **amphibious** task force in November 1956 was perhaps the most ponderous and yet significant. It was the climax to three months' preparation aimed at coercing **Egypt** over international use of the Canal, and it coincided with another phase of the **Arab–Israeli wars** when Israel invaded Sinai and reached the Canal, which had already been blocked by the Egyptians. Five days' bombing preceded the amphibious attack and neutralized the Egyptian air force as the fleet approached from North Africa and Malta. Airborne troops from Cyprus seized ground on either side of the Canal on the 6th and were at once reinforced by 415 **Marine Commando** soldiers flown in by **helicopter** from an **aircraft-carrier** – a tactical trend-setting event. Seaborne landings met little opposition because the Egyptians had nearly all withdrawn. Within a few hours an armoured column had been formed and was rushing Southwards, but heavy political pressure on the British and French brought a halt to the invasion at midnight. The Allied troops were withdrawn by 22 December after a misconceived and bungled operation which taught many lessons, not least the desirability for swift military intervention if political events demanded it.

Pound, Admiral Sir Dudley (1877–1943). An officer who won a reputation on Admiral Lord Fisher's Staff before **World War I**, he commanded a **battleship** at **Jutland** and was Director of Naval Operations 1917–18. He was C-in-C Mediterranean Fleet at the time of the **Spanish Civil War** and the Italian invasion of **Albania** in April 1939, prior to becoming First Sea Lord and Chief of Naval Staff. He therefore bore the brunt of the Royal Navy's transition to **World War II** and guided it through adversity until fortunes improved in 1942 and the Battle of the **Atlantic** was won in May 1943. In this period he suffered strong criticism for over-centralization and errors during the Convoy PQ17 affair. As a

member of the Joint and Combined Chiefs of Staff Committees he knew no respite. He died on 21 October shortly after resigning following a stroke.

Prisoners of war. See **Geneva Conventions.**

Propaganda is the organized use of publicity material to spread information, doctrine or practices. As a main instrument of **psychological warfare** it is as old as history, though the word only came into use in 1662 by derivation from the missionary work of the Roman Catholic Church's Congregation for the Propagation of the Faith. In modern parlance it deals in white (truth) and black (lies) information and embraces every possible civil and military activity – offensive and defensive – before, during and after a war. Its efficacy depends upon the means of dissemination and the literacy and insight of the people addressed, plus the skill of the propagandists in judging how, when and where to direct their messages. For example, the educated British electorate was readily influenced by William Russell's impassioned reports of the **Crimean War**, which brought down the government, just as peoples on both sides of the **American Civil War** were fairly easily and quickly reached and influenced via the latest **communications** through leaflets and journalism. Modern propaganda, indeed, emerged with the technological effects (**Technology, Effects of**) of **telegraph**, **telephone** and **radio**, allied to the introduction of the typewriter and rotary printing machines, and of mass-circulation newspapers after the 1860s.

World War I first indicated how decisive and more easily distributed propaganda had become. On the Allied side in 1914 a Campaign of Hate against Germany was generated by the newspapers and supported by official Belgian and British committees investigating alleged atrocities, very few of which were fully substantiated as breaches of the existing **laws of war**. Along with the propaganda generated in 1915 from public indignation at the execution of nurse Edith Cavell for organizing the escape of English soldiers from Belgium, public opinion was steered into supporting a total, 'just' war, which stimulated **recruiting** and the introduction of **conscription** in Britain and elsewhere. Germany's rebuttals of these accusations were not always well conceived, especially in neutral countries and, above all, the USA (where both sides conducted a war of words to win public support for their cause), where it induced resentment and was often countered.

More difficult was the introduction of propaganda among the enemy, by techniques which the British and French developed most successfully from 1915 onwards in association with blockade. Through interception of enemy mail, for example, sensitive subjects were detected and attacked by special propaganda organizations. Leaflets and other printed material, which improved in sophistication with experience based on evidence of impact, were introduced through neutral countries, dropped from the air among the Central Powers, or fired by mortars into the front line. They refuted anti-Allied propaganda and spread rumours which eventually convinced the people on the home front, as well as the fighting men, that the War was lost. The process was also adroitly used by the Germans in helping start the Russian Revolution (Russian revolutionary wars) in 1917.

Between the World Wars, propaganda techniques were mightily enhanced by the introduction of public radio broadcasting systems which could reach even the illiterate in every part of the world, a facility grasped most ruthlessly by the Communists when indoctrinating the masses to spread the Revolution, and by the Fascist powers as they also planned expansion. The German Propaganda Ministry directed by Josef Göbbels won enormous successes by the manner in which Hitler's chosen victims and their allies were undermined and sometimes taken over without a shot being fired. Göbbels' principle, that an oft-repeated lie eventually would be believed, became standard practice in dictatorships. He employed every vestige of the propagandist's art to mislead the German people into an unshakeable, apathetic resistance against hopeless odds – as well as to assist the armed forces win victories over opponents baffled by a barrage of misleading information.

In guerrilla and cold wars it has been commonplace, in the struggles for public support of causes, to emphasize indoctrination and terror by propaganda. Every political and diplomatic initiative is supported and every advantage taken of opposition weaknesses. Many military attacks are designed and executed specifically for propaganda purposes. The separation of truth from fiction has become so difficult that, quite frequently, there is rejection of both in an atmosphere of confused cynicism. The suggestion is that, as the people's insights are improved by education, they find it easier to recognize the real issues through the subterfuge sometimes called 'disinformation'.

Prussian wars. See Austro-Prussian War, Denmark, Invasions of and Franco-Prussian War.

Psychological warfare. Attack upon and defence of the minds and behaviour of leaders and followers of armed forces and the populace always have been natural and essential activities in time of peace and war. Although in some people's minds synonymous with propaganda warfare, its ramifications and execution go well beyond that single though important indoctrinating function. In the assault upon morale and resolution, intimidation by demonstrations of overwhelming power through displays of strength and deafening noise has frequently decided an issue by crucially undermining or cowing resistance. The well-timed and coordinated application of terror against unprepared forces through the use of concentrated artillery and rocket fire, bombing, chemicals, flame, tanks and, indeed, any kind of unusual weapons system, have had strong psychological effects by encouragement and discouragement. An element of psychological warfare is also found in the propagation of threats of secret weapons and stimulated dread of the unknown.

Wise commanders seek psychological advantages and guard against their opponents' ploys to obtain surprise by subtle, indirect methods. Few finer examples of this art were displayed than those by commanders during the American Civil War, such as Generals Lee, Grant and Sherman, when they endeavoured to strike unexpectedly against sensitive objectives; or by Admiral Togo when he imposed a crushing impression of Japanese superiority over the Russian naval commanders from the outset of the Russo-Japanese War. These were attributes which many European commanders lost sight of in World War I when leaders tended to attempt to impose, head-on, a physical superiority, instead of attacking the minds and resolves of the enemy. There was nothing psychologically unusual in the fact that many defeated German leaders afterwards conceded the decisive effects of the Allied blockade, of propaganda, tanks and the higher quality of their *matériel*. They tried, as they planned for World War II, not to be caught out in those ways again.

A feature of both Fascist and Communist Staff organizations, post-World War I, was the appointment of specialist officers in headquarters to advise on and implement psychological measures. In fact they were usually involved mainly with propaganda in its various defensive and offensive aspects, but their mere presence was significant, as many charismatic leaders, such as Admiral Halsey and Generals Guderian, MacArthur, Montgomery and Rommel, realized when they copied politicians by employing propagandists to publicize their talents and, in Rommel's case, actually win him the admiration of the enemy.

Psychological warfare is of the essence of guerrilla and cold wars. In such special circumstances related to emotive causes, the vital necessity to attack the morale of outnumbered but dedicated partisans has long been recognized, just as the best partisan leaders, such as Giuseppé Garibaldi and Mao Tse-tung, have held their followers together by persuasive measures and sound propaganda. Few antiguerrilla campaigns have been waged with such skill as by the British during the Malayan War of Independence. The Communists antagonized their supporters by cruelty, while General Templer shrewdly won what he termed 'the battle of hearts and minds' by demonstrating the cause of democratic freedom through minimum force, a psychological strategy which, if applied in Vietnam by the French, might have saved much bloodshed.

Public relations, Military. There has always been a special need for sound relationships between the armed forces and the rest of society, if only because these somewhat disparate, yet dependent, communities have to live alongside each other. Military service, particularly the conscripted (Conscription) kind, is rarely popular with the majority and the serviceman's outlook is often misunderstood by civilians, to the detriment of recruiting and good neighbourliness – and vice versa. From the distant past there has been a need to reconcile the differences for the common good – notably in times of emergency – by demonstrating the advantages and virtues of military life. Although the term 'public relations' did not come into use until after World War I,

the techniques of advertising and persuasion by professional publicity people had long been established. Poster and newspaper advertisements were used in the 19th century to attract recruits, together with naval reviews, army tattoos and parades and, in the 20th century, air displays.

The combination of heightening political tensions and proliferating technology of the 20th century, culminating in World War I's immense use of mechanization and electronic (Electronics) communications, changed the approach in military public relations. While sail, animal and foot power sufficed, the demand for mechanically trained artisans in the Services was slight and the need for publicity minimal. The coming of the petrol engine and electronics compelled the armed forces to widen their contacts with technical colleges and industry, not only in the hunt for officers and men of technical bent but also by the need to explain military requirements to those establishments. The process in due course, and most strongly in the present day, operated in reverse when colleges and industry began looking increasingly to the armed forces to provide them with ready-trained experts, particularly those who have graduated from military colleges and schools of technology. In effect this created exchanges in personnel and cross-fertilization of ideas.

Until World War II public relations were studied and organized by the armed forces only in a haphazard way, for political reasons if no other, to explain how the servicemen were being cared for and employed. This process, in those democracies like Britain and the USA which retained conscription in peacetime for the first time, produced a call to employ specialist public relations officers at headquarters. Here they advised on and implemented schemes fostering understanding with civilian organizations and, vitally important, the information media of press, radio and television, a function which naturally overlapped into the field of psychological warfare and propaganda in certain operational circumstances.

Pusan Perimeter, Battle of. The final objective of the North Korean Army in its invasion of the south during the Korean War of 1950 was the industrial port of Pusan through which nearly all United Nations forces were arriving. Already in some logistic difficulty, on 5 August the North

Koreans ran into a 150-mile-long, prepared Eighth Army line running northwards from Tsushima Strait, then along the Naktong River to Taegu and eastwards to Pohang. Constantly bombed from the air, they were unable at once to mount a co-ordinated assault. Instead they frittered away resources in local assaults which were fairly easily contained by the over-stretched, mobile, mainly American defenders. Not until 26 August was a strong attack launched to make a 20-mile penetration near Taegu. This offensive, too, lost momentum and was brought to a halt on 15 September. This was just as the landing at **Inchon** was taking place and 24 hours before the Perimeter garrison began its planned break-out, an operation which took five days in overcoming stiff North Korean opposition, which only collapsed in rout when it became clear that envelopment from the north was imminent.

Q

Q-ships. As an anti-**submarine** measure in **World War** I, the British in 1915 began employing merchant ships with concealed armament as decoys. They sailed alone to lure the submarine into surfacing to use its gun in order to save torpedoes. Some crew members would simulate a panic abandonment of ship while the others waited until their attacker closed the range before disclosing their guns and opening fire. Increased caution by U-boat commanders gradually reduced their effectiveness, which was never immense. By the war's end only 11 U-boats had been sunk for the loss of 27 Q-ships, most of which went down after introduction of the **convoy** system in May 1917. In **World War II** the Japanese also used them in desperation, but to little effect.

Race to the Sea. When the German retreat from the **Marne** came to an entrenched halt at the Battle of the **Aisne** on 18 September 1914, both Germans and Allies continued in their attempts to outflank each other by a succession of north-wards side-steps, manoeuvres which were commensurate with the ability to transport by road, railway and, on the British part, by sea sufficient men and resources for offensive action at selected places. From the outset possession of the Channel ports was acknowledged by both sides as crucial, though inevitably each shuffle ended in yet another collision and an extension of the wired-in trench barrier. On 23 September a French thrust from Roye threatened the vital German railhead at Saint-Quentin but was brought to a halt and thrown on the defensive next day as German pressure there and also north of the Somme was asserted – encounters which tested the French severely between Albert and Bapaume on the 29th. Yet it was a drawn battle of similar consequence to the struggle brought on by the well-prepared assault by Sixth German Army at **Arras** on 2 October, which so nearly encircled that strategic centre but also ended in stalemate.

Meanwhile the Belgian Army, under siege in Antwerp (which fell on 9 October), was with British help clinging to **Flanders** and its ports as two German cavalry corps thrust towards Haze-brouk, a breakthrough which was checked only by the timely arrival in strength of the British Expeditionary Force (BEF) and thrown back east of Ypres, thus ending on 15 October the so-called Race to the Sea. For that day the Belgians secured Nieuport on the left by the coast, the French covered the Yser Canal and the BEF had filled the gap by joining hands with the French on the La Bassée Canal on the eve of the First Battle of Ypres (see map page 262).

Radar. A system which measures the following electronically: *range*, by timing the passage of **electromagnetic** waves to and from a target; *direction*, by using a suitable antenna to project the waves in a narrow beam, antenna direction indicating target direction; *velocity* or *target movement*, by the Doppler effect, that is, the difference between the transmitted frequency and the reflected frequency from a moving target.

The German scientist Heinrich Hertz in 1885 was the first to demonstrate in his laboratory the reflection of radio waves from a metallic object. It was experiments in ways to improve long-range radio signals which led to the discovery in the 1920s of the ionosphere. This in turn led to studies of the application of very-high-frequency microwaves and, with the development of the cathode-ray oscilloscope, provided the essentials for a practical radar system.

The Germans were still in the lead when, in 1933 and secretly, their Navy's signal research division was able using radar to detect a ship in Kiel harbour; soon afterwards the French in-stalled radar in the liner *Normandie* as an aid to iceberg detection.

In 1934 the British took a major step into the field when Robert Watson-Watt of the National Physical Laboratory showed that an aircraft could be detected by 'floodlighting' using a 50m-wavelength beam. The aircraft could be indicated on a cathode-ray oscilloscope in such a way that position, altitude and course could be plotted. By fitting friendly aircraft with a pulse repeater the ground operator could distinguish friend from foe; intercepting aircraft could thus

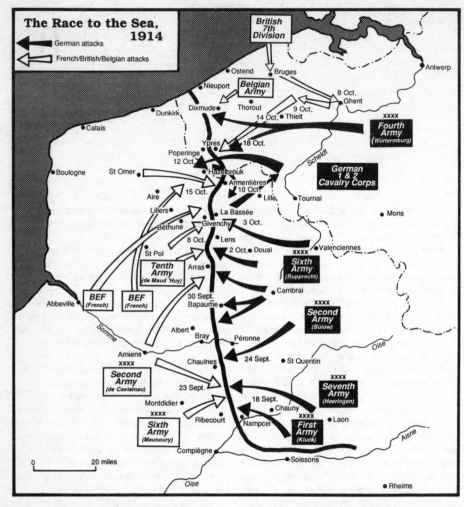

The Race to the Sea, 1914

German attacks
French/British/Belgian attacks

Antwerp

British 7th Division

Ostend • Bruges
Nieuport
Belgian Army
8 Oct. Ghent
Dixmude • Thorout 9 Oct.
Dunkirk 14 Oct. • Thielt
Calais

xxxx
Fourth Army (Würtermburg)

Ypres • 18 Oct.
Poperinge
12 Oct.
Boulogne St Omer Hazelbrouk
Armentières
10 Oct.
Aire 15 Oct. Lille • Tournai
Lillers • La Bassée
Béthune Givenchy 3 Oct.
8 Oct. • Lens
St Pol 2 Oct. • Douai
Tenth Army (de Maud 'Huy) Arras •

German 1 & 2 Cavalry Corps

Scheldt

Mons

xxxx
Sixth Army (Rupprecht)

Valenciennes

Cambrai
Abbeville • BEF (French) BEF (French)
30 Sept.
Bapaume

xxxx
Second Army (Bülow)

Somme
Albert • Bray Péronne
Amiens Oise
xxxx
Second Army (de Castelnau) Chaulnes 24 Sept. • St Quentin
23 Sept.
Montdidier • 18 Sept. • Chauny
xxxx
Sixth Army (Maunoury) Ribecourt Nampcel • Laon

xxxx
Seventh Army (Heeringen)

xxxx
First Army (Kluck)

Compiègne • Aisne
0   20 miles
• Soissons
Oise
• Rheims

be directed to a tactically advantageous position from which to attack the enemy bombers. A historic experiment was carried out at Daventry in 1935 which confirmed Watson-Watt's findings and led to the Chain Home system of radar stations which, by the time war came in 1939, stretched from Netherbutton in the Orkneys to Ventnor in the Isle of Wight.

Effective though the Chain Home system was (60 per cent reliability out to 70 miles at 20,000ft) it was but a first step; further developments soon opened up the possibility of dramatic improvements in the world of **surveillance, range-finding** and target acquisition. To start with, however, both German and British radar

followed broadly similar lines. Chain Home operated on 8–13m wavelength while early British 'beam' sets (Chain Home Low) used 1·5m. The German Freya worked on 2·4m, usually in conjunction with Würzburg providing direction for **anti-aircraft** guns and searchlights. The German Seetakt ship-watching and ranging set operated on a wavelength of 80cm.

There were other developments under way. By 1937 the British had developed a first airborne radar which enabled a **fighter** aircraft to detect and fly to within visual distance of a bomber at night. A 6m GL radar for anti-aircraft guns was capable, by 1941, of reducing the kill rate from 20,000 rounds per aircraft in 1940 to 4,000 rounds per aircraft.

However, a further major step was in the offing, described by Watson-Watt as 'the centimetric revolution'. It had long been realized that a narrow-beam radar of say, 10cm wavelength, would be a fundamental advance, providing an accurate measurement of bearing angles and able to avoid both the clutter of random echoes and most enemy jamming. The problem lay in generating adequate power; the valves then available were only really satisfactory for wavelengths of about 1·5m. The breakthrough came with the resonant-cavity magnetron valve developed by Professor Oliphant and his team at Birmingham University. In 1940 a trial device produced hundreds of watts and a production version later that year gave 10kW at 10cm, thus providing the essential element for centimetric radar.

A number of developments flowed from this during the remainder of **World War II**: improved fire control and range-finding for air defence; H2S, an airborne centimetric radar which, combined with the Plan Position Indicator developed from the cathode-ray oscilloscope, created a radar map helping a bomber crew to find their objective; and the Type 271 ship-borne radar, developed for spotting surfaced U-boats, but equally successful in detecting other surface objects – the commanding officer of HMS *Orchis*, the trials ship, was quoted as saying, 'after being in a ship fitted with Type 271, night navigation in one without will seem a perilous business'.

Radar was initially seen as an aid to detection of aircraft and ships. The clutter from objects on the ground at first made it an unlikely tool for the soldier. However, since 1945 great strides have been made in refining radar capabilities. Small radars for close-range ground surveillance, for range-finding and for missile tracking are in general use in many armies.

Radar is of course an active system and is thus susceptible to jamming. However, jamming is not always successful and other ways to avoid detection have been sought. One such is the development of the 'stealth' aircraft such as the recently introduced American B2 bomber, which has the radar signature of a much smaller aircraft. Radar reflectivity is best from flat metal objects, worst from non-conducting materials with rounded surfaces. B2 is therefore con-structed with as few flat surfaces as possible and maximizes the use of plastics and other non-conducting materials; the engines, for instance, are buried within the non-conducting wings. Similar 'stealth' materials have been used to coat the outer surfaces of combat vehicles in an effort to reduce their radar signature.

In summary, radar can be used on land, sea and in the air, for the detection and location of aircraft, ships, moving targets on the battlefield and of rockets and artillery shells. In addition radar has a good range-finding capability. However, the equipment can be a massive static installation with large rotating antennas; on the other hand, radars may be mounted on ships or aircraft, on vehicles or even be hand-held. While radar is little affected by climatic conditions and is effective at night, it is often bulky, the antenna may be prominent – even the most modern phased-array versions with no rotating parts – and it is an active system open to countermeasures.

Radiation. Devastating though the blast and thermal effects of nuclear weapons are, it is the unseen radiations resulting from a nuclear explosion which terrify many people most. These radiation effects are not necessarily the most lethal; it is immediate radiation, occurring within 60 seconds of a burst, which releases alpha, beta, gamma and neutron particles, which is. The last two can cause serious casualties to exposed troops since they travel several thousand metres. Residual radiation, consisting of beta and gamma particles, which can kill, is found in the ground after a fireball has touched it and in the fall-out from the dust sucked up into the atmosphere – a hazard to vehicles trying to cross the area and to personnel downwind of the target.

Radio. The principles of radio communication had been postulated in the mid 19th century by the British scientists Maxwell and Faraday: that electromechanical energy could be transmitted through space at the speed of light and without the need for a connecting cable. And it was another Briton, Sir William Preece who, in 1892, managed to transmit a radio signal over a distance of 364m. But it is to the Italian Guglielmo Marconi, working in Britain in 1895, that we owe the first demonstrations of radio's potential. His transmitter and receiver were founded upon an induction coil, an untuned spark gap and a simple antenna, the signal being activated by telegraph key. Marconi's equipment was able to transmit over a distance of 1·6 km and only two years later he was transmitting Morse code from the Isle of Wight to a tug at sea. Progress was swift and by 1901 Marconi was able to send messages routinely to ships at sea and even across the Atlantic – some 4,800km.

As in so much to do with electronics, technological improvements followed hot on the heels of each other and in 1904 the heterodyne principle was first used, a significant refinement; the vacuum diode valve was introduced by the Briton John Fleming, who coined the word **electronics**; there were rapid improvements in the reliability and miniaturization (though still bulky by modern standards) of equipment; and trials with radio direction-finding had taken place, with military thinkers already appreciating that the location of a radio transmitter could provide valuable intelligence of enemy deployment.

Despite the traditional military resistance to innovation, the possibilities that radio opened up both for land and sea operations were rapidly appreciated, the Germans in particular being quick to grasp the potential. By the start of **World War I** horse-drawn mobile radio detachments were in service with the German Army, operating over about 200km; static sets at GHQ having a range of about 1,100km. However, the Chief of Signals had not been informed of the operational plan in 1914 and this lack of coordination meant that his equipment was not deployed to best advantage when the German Army advanced into enemy territory.

Right from the start of active operations the problem of security arose, in that radio transmissions could be picked up by friend and foe alike. Both sides in World War I set up monitoring stations to intercept the enemy's radio traffic and to break the codes which each used to conceal their intentions. Thus it was seen that radio could be a two-edged weapon.

At sea, communications over long distances had been well established by 1914. Since the **Russo-Japanese War** of 1904 **Admiralties** ashore were able to control navies afloat in a way which foreshadowed the direct governmental influence over far-away military operations so evident in the **Falklands** War. Evidence, perhaps paradoxical, of the power of radio in naval operations at that time is that during the Battle of **Jutland** the radio silence imposed on ships of the Royal Navy was a significant contribution to Admiral **Jellicoe**'s success.

On the German side there was particular interest in radio control of their **submarine** fleet, limited by the fact that the boats could only communicate when on the surface. Radio was used to guide U-boats to their quarry, though with little success as the British were able to intercept the signals and take appropriate action.

Aircraft were not generally large enough at this stage to carry unwieldy radio equipment, though it had been used from a balloon in 1915, during the Dardanelles campaign. What the aircraft pilot needed was voice radio, pioneered in 1904 by Valdemar Poulsen but not seriously developed until the 1920s. The use of ever higher frequencies and the continued reduction in equipment size and weight meant that soon aircraft could communicate directly with their controllers on the ground and with other aircraft.

The smaller, more robust, sets now appearing meant that vehicles could also be equipped, giving the army true mobile communications. It was quickly appreciated that voice radio was the only realistic way to control large numbers of tanks and 1931 saw the first practical demonstration of this in Britain with a complete tank brigade, all vehicles fitted with crystal-frequency-controlled radio, deploying to the direct radio orders of their commander, Brigadier Charles Broad.

This was the way ahead and by **World War II** the vehicle-borne radio was in wide use, with the ubiquitous and reliable (though needing skill to operate) No. 19 high frequency (HF) set, available to the British Army by 1940; and in service world-wide for many years thereafter. The Germans, however, used very high frequency (VHF) sets in tanks, similar to those used for voice control of fighter aircraft during the Battle of **Britain**, in which radio communications played a vital role.

The military environment continued to call for ever smaller, simpler to operate, more robust, interference-free and longer-range equipment. The unceasing electronic developments of the late 20th century have made possible improvements to military radio that were inconceivable in 1945. No single system provides all the user's needs and on the battlefield one can expect to find radios operating in the HF and VHF bands for communications between units and back to brigades. The equipment may be vehicle-borne, manpack or hand-held; the different types may have varied capabilities, but all will be compatible with each other in use.

For communication between higher formations, brigade–division–corps, radio relay (first used in World War II by the Germans and later between General **Montgomery**'s headquarters in Normandy and London) has found British favour, using VHF, ultra high or super high frequencies. The system is generally line of sight, which can impose location problems, but it does provide secure telephone-type conversations. An arrangement of interlocking nodal stations ensures that if one station is destroyed the network is not disrupted. The nodes of such a system, static when operating but able to close down and move without affecting the rest of the network, could be distributed, for example, over a corps area of operations, forming a lattice into which mobile users can connect at any point. A system of computerized switching routes messages automatically through the most convenient nodes.

Finally, satellites increasingly play their part also, via communications satellites in geostationary orbits at about 36,000km above the earth. Within its 'footprint' the satellite is continuously available to the user and the lack of screening means that the higher radio bands can be used, providing high-capacity good-quality communications. Initially such links could only be provided between static ground stations and ships at sea, chiefly on account of the large antenna dishes required to capture the signal. However, the increasing power of satellites means that antennas small enough for vehicle-mounted, manpack or even hand-held stations can be produced. Tactical satellite communications such as these are the likely ways forward in the future, aided by the revolution in microelectronics.

Raeder, Admiral Erich (1876–1960). A man of diminutive stature who was Admiral von **Hipper**'s Chief of Staff at the Battle of **Jutland** and became professional Chief of the German Navy in 1928. He thus was responsible for its recovery from the cuts imposed by the Versailles Treaty and the building programme prior to **World War II**. He gave priority to **battleships** and other surface vessels over **submarines** and **aircraft-carriers**. As a brilliant strategist, Raeder disapproved of **Hitler**'s premature entry into war, but once embarked on that course aggressively promoted the invasion of **Norway** and the Battle of the **Atlantic** in 1940. At the same time he did little to encourage invasions of **Britain** or Russia (**Russo-German wars**), arguing instead in favour of strangling Britain through a **blockade** imposed by occupation of **North Africa**, domination of the Atlantic and closure of the **Mediterranean Sea**. Hitler only half-embraced this strategy, largely because he failed fully to grasp the meaning and importance of maritime warfare. Yet Raeder did not put all his weight behind the vital submarine campaign and resigned as Navy C-in-C in January 1943 when Hitler ordered demobilization of surface ships as surface raiders. In 1946 he was sentenced at Nürnberg to life imprisonment for **war crimes**, but released in 1955.

Raiders, US. See **Commandos**.

Railways. It is perhaps worth noting, when considering military railways, that the Duke of Wellington, victor of Waterloo, was the principal guest on the world's first passenger train, running from Liverpool to Manchester in September 1832. The potential impact on operations of the leap in mobility which the railway conferred was not lost on European military planners and, as early as 1848, the Prussians were able to move by rail to Cracow a complete corps of 12,000 men, together with their horses, guns and impedimenta.

Indeed it was the Germans, placed as they were across the middle of Europe and with their enduring dread of having to fight a war on two fronts, who were probably the first fully to appreciate the implications of this new form of transport. It was in the 1840s and 50s that the railway age really got into its stride and the Germans made sure that, as the railway tracks spread across their country, they would be laid out to serve military as well as civil purposes. A glance at a railway map of Germany up to 1939 clearly shows that the main trunk routes are on an East/West axis. This foresight served Germany well in the **Austro-Prussian War** of 1866; in the **Franco-Prussian War** of 1870, when she was able to mobilize and move her armies to the frontier well before the French; then again in both World Wars when the war on two fronts became a grim reality. In **World War II** especially, Germany was able to switch personnel and stores to and fro by rail almost at will, despite Allied bombing, and almost to the very end of hostilities.

However, for the first great war of the railway era we must turn to the **American Civil War** of 1861–5. Both North and South had extensive railway networks, though the latter was much fragmented. This ability to transport large numbers of men and quantities of stores over long distances in a short time gave strategy a new dimension and was an important factor in making cities such as **Atlanta** – a key junction in the Southern network – a worthwhile objective. The war also revealed very clearly the limitations of the railway in any conditions of mobile warfare. The line was vulnerable, tying down large forces to guard it, and there still remained the problem of transporting to the troops in the front line the stores the railway carried; the horse and cart was still the only means of doing that.

It was perhaps during **World War I** in Europe that the military railway really came into its own, in the conditions of static trench warfare that prevailed. The strategic advantage held by the Germans has already been described; though not so conveniently laid out, the French railways too were an essential link in the Allied logistic chain, with convenient spurs laid from the main lines to assembly areas and stores depots immediately behind the front. For instance, the problem of moving tanks from factories in the UK to the combat zone, in the total absence of the road transporter so familiar in a modern army, was really no problem at all; almost every factory had its private railway spur and, apart from the Channel crossing, the vehicles were delivered to the troops in the assembly areas entirely by rail.

For the transport of supplies forward from the railheads, tramways were built, often running right into the front line, sometimes on wooden rails which could be relaid in a new direction with comparative ease. The motive power for these light railways came from small motor tractors, though John Glubb, writing in his diary in 1916, tells us: 'In front of High Wood, in view of the enemy, the trucks are pushed by hand . . . easier . . . than to carry the load on one's back.'

Railways were also of significance elsewhere: one was laid to accompany General **Allenby's** troops advancing across the **Sinai** from **Egypt** into Palestine; and the railway from Damascus to Medina in the Hejaz – a Turkish lifeline – was a frequent target for T. E. **Lawrence's** Arab raiders. A 50-mile section of that same railway was torn up by Australian engineers in **World War II** and relaid from Ma'an to Ras al Neqb to provide a railhead for stores flooding in through the port of Aqaba in southern Jordan, on their way to Russia via the Iran supply route.

By 1939 the flexibility of motor transport meant that railways, except for the strategic movement of stores and men, did not have so great an impact on logistics as in previous wars. They did, however, have one curious, perhaps unexpected, impact. It had been decreed that all British **tanks** should be able to travel anywhere on the British railway network. This requirement automatically limited a tank's width, thereby limiting the turret-ring diameter, which in turn limited the size of gun that could be mounted in the turret, a factor which dogged British tank design throughout World War II.

Post-1945 extensive rail movement of military equipment and personnel appears to have been largely confined to the Warsaw Pact countries, where distances are so much greater than in the West. In Nato **logistic** planning railways, though still playing their part, are no longer a significant priority.

Ramsay, Admiral Sir Bertram (1883–1945). Ramsay made a name for himself serving in the famous **destroyer** HMS *Broke* in the Dover Patrol from 1915 to 1918 and, after a sound career until 1938, was recalled from retirement in 1939 as Flag Officer, Dover, with the task of defending the English Channel at its narrowest. In May 1940 he brilliantly managed the evacuation from **Dunkirk** and made preparations to repel the expected invasion of Britain. In this sector until the summer of 1942, when he was appointed Commander of an Allied naval force preparing to invade France that year, he fended off German motor **torpedo-boats**, struck at German coastal convoys, collaborated with small hit-and-run **Commando** raids against the enemy coast, directed an unavailing attempt to prevent the passage of two German **battle-cruisers** and a **cruiser** in February 1942, and kept watch and ward. In 1943 he commanded the Eastern Naval

Task Force for the invasion of **Sicily**, prior to appointment as Commander of the Allied Naval Forces for the invasion of **Normandy** in June 1944. He was killed in an air crash on 2 January 1945.

Range-finders. In the mid 19th century the only way to determine the range to a target was by *visual estimation*, a highly inaccurate method still in use for tank guns till well after **World War II**. However, as effective ranges and the intrinsic accuracy of direct-fire weapons improved, the need for an accurate range-finder became overwhelming; and nowhere more so than in the naval sphere with the introduction of capital ships like *Dreadnought* and the new fast **battle-cruisers**, operating at high speed and at much greater distances from the enemy.

Optical solutions were the *coincidence range-finder*, first produced by Barr and Stroud in Britain in 1880, and a more accurate device, the stereoscopic range-finder, being pioneered by German firms at about the same time. These instruments were incorporated in the new fire-control equipment being developed by both countries for their respective warships and were in service in time for **World War I**. The weakness of the British equipment, which normally required the mean of several readings to produce a reasonably accurate range, was revealed all too clearly at **Jutland** in 1916 where, as the official history says, there was 'totally insufficient time ... in some cases for a single range to be obtained' as fleeting targets appeared briefly through the haze. The German *stereoscopic range-finders*, inherently more accurate and quicker to use, coupled with their electrical fire-control equipment, enabled the guns to be brought to bear more rapidly. For a much smaller expenditure of **ammunition** the Germans destroyed three British battle-cruisers in short order.

Both types of optical range-finder depend for their accuracy on the base length between the lenses, anything less than one metre being of very little use; indeed some of those developed for anti-aircraft guns in World War II had a base length of up to 5·5m. Since 1945 optical range-finders have appeared on **tanks** also, limited in effectiveness by cross-turret dimensions. The latest development for tanks is the **laser** *range-finder*, accurate to within 5m at 10,000m range. The technique relies on the

time taken for light pulses to be reflected from a target to give a measure of range. Measurement by **radar** works on a broadly similar principle using radio-wave pulses, such systems being more suitable for air defence and an aircraft environment.

Rangoon, Battles of. As the main port of entry into **Burma**, Rangoon was the principal strategic target for Japanese bombers before their army began to invade on 12 January 1942. British and American fighters shot down 27 enemy for the loss of six on 23 and 25 December 1941 (when 5,000 people were killed in the city) plus a further 50 between 23 and 29 January, and another 37 out of 170 on 25 February. But by then the Japanese Army had won the Battle of the **Sittang River** and was closing in on Rangoon, which was abandoned without a fight on 7 March, thus depriving the Allied air defence of the **radar** early warning system which had made possible its victories over the Japanese Army Air Force.

Henceforward Rangoon was the main Japanese supply base for Burma and therefore, from 1943, not only the target of Allied **strategic bombing** but, far more effectively in terms of **blockade**, for sea **mines** laid in the port's approaches. Indeed, Japanese **logistics** were already severely impaired when General **Slim**'s land forces, advancing from Meiktila, were just beaten to the recapture of the city by the arrival of an **amphibious** force on 3 May 1945 – though an RAF pilot already had landed on the 1st to find that the enemy had departed that day.

Reconnaissance aircraft. Virtually all aircraft are capable of reconnaissance of some sort, even if not specially equipped for the task. From the beginning this was regarded by many sea and land commanders as the most important role in **air warfare**, although there was instinctive mistrust of **intelligence** won by this method until confidence grew and certain types of machine were equipped for air **photography**; and poor results until they were grouped in specialized reconnaissance organizations. For it was soon realized that the most valuable information came from pilots and observers already familiar with surface operations, and also that the best results were achieved from aircraft which were good observation platforms and flew at speeds and altitudes that were compatible with survival. Airships, for example, were useless since, like all slow and low-flying machines seeking detailed information, they were extremely vulnerable to ground fire. Gradually, methods for requesting and astutely launching reconnaissance missions, and then rapidly interpreting and delivering the results, were evolved. By World War II, a differentiation between short-range tactical missions and long-range strategic ones had emerged. Even so, the aircraft mostly used were long-range fighters stripped of armament and fitted with cameras – perhaps the most famous being the very fast, high-altitude British Spitfire and the Mosquito.

Jet engines naturally made possible even higher flights with less risk of interception while the latest photographic and electronic surveillance technology produced ever clearer information about minute objects and sources of energy. Simultaneously, aircraft specially designed for the work appeared, notably the subsonic American U2, a jet-powered sailplane, with its altitude of 90,000ft, and the Lockheed SR71 with an altitude in excess of 90,000ft and a speed of Mach 3·5. They filled the gap between slow-flying helicopters, searching for tactical information when flying nap-of-the-earth, remotely piloted vehicles and reconnaissance satellite vehicles orbiting in space (see Space vehicles). All have been flying vital operational missions in peace and war.

Recruiting. The recruitment of suitable officers and men prepared to face the dangers and hardships of service in armed forces is among the most difficult of fundamental military activities. There are very rarely enough naturally dedicated candidates with the required qualifications, even when called upon to serve patriotically in a popular, just war, such as World War I temporarily was. Through history inducements of high rewards and glory have been essential, particularly to obtain leaders and technologists in short supply. Conscription in one form or another was found unavoidable and became common from the 18th century to fill the ranks of nations in arms. But a cadre of long-service volunteers remained essential. Also, as frequently demonstrated, small groups of well-trained volunteers were often superior in battle to an impressed mass.

The rules and inducements of recruiting are mostly established at national level and imple-

mented either centrally or regionally by the armed services involved. Territorial and community groups, colleges, universities and technical institutes have usually been recruiting grounds, with particular emphasis on the latter as the quality of person demanded by technology's effects rose. Moreover, as higher educational standards improved sophisticated insights in the 20th century, no longer was the right person attracted without reasonable offers of good standards of living, care and training, along with pay comparable with civil rates. As a general rule, successful recruiting has been the result of carefully considered campaigns, with a strong public relations bias, aimed at people who are looking for a special life-style of adventure and comradeship, and with sound training which civil life does not always supply.

Red Cross Society. After the Battle of Solferino in 1859, Henri Dunant wrote A Souvenir of Solferino which aroused public indignation at treatment of the wounded. As a result, what became the International Committee of the Red Cross was formed in 1863 in Geneva by 14 nations; the Committee wrote the first Red Cross Convention. Over the years it also undertook responsibilities for prisoners of war and grew, along with the Muslim Red Crescent Society and the Iranian Red Lion and Sun Society, into a formally recognized, international organization dedicated to the welfare of both the military and civilians in peacetime as well as war. It is related to the Geneva Conventions, at the heart of the laws of war and usually allowed to function effectively, even by the most inhumane nations and combatants, because the odium of not doing so has so often prompted punitive diplomatic, criminal and economic proceedings.

Regimental system. A regiment is an Army (and sometimes Air Force) Organization of both operational and administrative purpose. The word regiment itself has several different meanings, dating from the 16th century. Usually it means a single unit of cavalry and sometimes of infantry, too; though more often than not a regiment of the latter has consisted, on both sides of the Atlantic, of two or more units (battalions). In the British Army, and some armies derived from it, the Corps of Artillery is still known as the Royal Regiment of Artillery, though it comprises, like the Royal Tank Regiment, a varying quantity of numbered units.

Many regiments trace their ancestry to founding commanders and/or territorial connections, and cherish their historic traditions and battle honours as the basis of efficiency and **morale**. They also draw immense strength from the sense of family in them, which reflects the quality and common sense of commanding officers and the senior warrant and non-commissioned officers. For administrative purposes, regiments require a home depot where its affairs are ordered, **recruiting** arranged, veterans' welfare cared for and, with some, **training** carried out. Occasionally the system is criticized by cost-conscious accountants and politicians as an expensive luxury. But the American Army, which once dispensed with it, has repented and revived it as a vital element of combat spirit.

Remotely piloted vehicles (RPV). The first proposals or examples of unmanned **aircraft** as rocket-propelled mail carriers or as targets for **anti-aircraft** practice began to appear in the 1920s. A British example was the Queen Bee **radio**-controlled DH Tiger Moth machine which at once was visualized as a remotely controlled flying bomb – the sort of **rocket and guided missile** with which the Germans took the lead in **World War II** and which since has been developed in numerous forms.

This entry concentrates upon the RPVs designed for **reconnaissance** and **electronic** warfare (EW). As developed since the 1950s they have been either jet-propelled or driven by an airscrew; fly at supersonic, but usually at subsonic, speeds; weigh between 200lb and 10,000lb; and, because of their relatively small size, are difficult targets to detect and hit. Most types are of the winged variety, although **helicopter** types and hovering platforms have been made. They have the advantages of being cheap and easily handled from small, mobile ground stations which service, launch and recover them. To accomplish their tasks, which include visual and electronic surveillance of tactical activity, target acquisition, radio relay, electronic jamming and the suppression or decoying of missiles, they carry **photographic** or **television** cameras and/or various kinds of electronic sensors which, in order to save time and possible loss of information, can transmit their discoveries in flight. Guidance can be manual/optical by radio from a ground or air control post, through on-board television or by pre-flight programming.

Considerable use was made of RPVs in **Vietnam**, where the Americans flew 3,435 missions between 1964 and 1975. They were used extensively by the Israelis in the Yom Kippur War of 1973 and in **Lebanon** in the 1980s to jam **radar**. They clearly have great potential in naval warfare as inexpensive vehicles for long-term patrols which otherwise call for much more complicated and more vulnerable aeroplanes manned by several experts. It is, indeed, a major attraction of the RPV that it economizes not only in material resources but also in the use of and risk to skilled personnel – and carries out its task without possibility of deflection by the human urge of self-preservation.

Research and development (R&D), Military. Generally seen as a modern development in the procurement of military equipment but, in British service at least, weapons research can be traced to antiquity in work carried out by the Ordnance Board and there are records of formal trials going back to the 18th century. Probably the oldest R&D establishment, as the term R&D is understood today, is the experimental department of HMS *Excellent* – latterly a shore-based gunnery training establishment, but originally a seagoing vessel carrying out gunnery equipment trials in the 1830s. HMS *Vernon* is a similar establishment concerned with underwater weapons. For the British Army most research continued to be carried out under the general control of the Ordnance Board until well into the 20th century, as in the area of weapons safety it still is, through the Board's various special committees.

Aircraft introduced a new dimension, for which there was no historical precedent. Fundamental research into the principles of flight began in France, with both scientists and the military involved, but it was the British who led the way in state-controlled research into aeronautics with an advisory committee set up in 1908 under Lord Rayleigh. It included, perhaps most significantly, the Director of Artillery, representing the Balloon Factory at Farnborough. Most significant because it was at the Royal Aircraft Establishment, as it became after **World War I** and as the Royal Aerospace Establishment (RAE) as it now is, that so much research into military aircraft has been done.

When war came in 1914, R&D was nevertheless still in its infancy in relation to the wide requirements of modern war, and World War I revealed to both warring sides the inadequacies of their research programmes. Committees and establishments to meet various needs proliferated in France and Britain. Coming into the war late, the United States was able to benefit to some extent from others' mistakes, with the formation in 1916 of a National Research Council. Russia, though possessing talented scientists such as Vladimir Ipatieff, was heavily dependent on Western technological aid and did little research of her own. Italy had a Department for Invention and Research under Vito Volterra, but was also dependent on others for technological support. In Germany the situation was rather different, with industrial research already very well established. There seemed little need for the independent groups of scientific advisers found necessary amongst the Allies. Nevertheless individual scientists were recruited to help with particular projects such as new weapons for trench warfare and **radio** for **aircraft** and **submarine** communication. One establishment that did play a part was the Kaiser Wilhelm Institute for Physics and Electrochemistry, which became involved in chemical warfare research.

Following the Armistice in 1918 the attitude to military R&D varied from country to country. In Germany, industrially based research departments, including the Kaiser Wilhelm Institute, reverted to peaceful projects without interference from the victorious Allies, thus remaining available to the military when the need arose. The exception was the German Navy's signal research division, which remained in being and enabled Germany to enter the **radar** field in 1933. In France the scientists soon lost interest in defence matters and in America the dream of an independent body to co-ordinate military scientific research was never realized.

Only in Britain – where admittedly many scientists were equally disenchanted with military work – were a significant number of R&D establishments kept alive: for example the Admiralty Research Laboratory at Teddington, the Explosives Research Department at Woolwich (looking at armour-piercing ammunition and flashless propellant), the nearby Wireless Experimental Establishment (considering vehicle-borne radio) and, of course, RAE Farnborough.

Thus the experience of World War I set the scene for what was to come, the increasingly complex equipment requirements of **World War II** calling for equally elaborate R&D programmes, not only to ensure that the equipment reaching the soldier was fit for its task, but also that it should be cost-effective, though the military and Treasury view of what constituted cost-effectiveness frequently differed.

There can be no doubt that the various R&D establishments that were set up in Britain during World War II played a crucial role in eventual victory. The two most prominent to emerge for land-service equipment were the Fighting Vehicles and Armament Research and Development Establishments, achieving an international reputation in their field in the post-1945 military world. Increasingly, however, financial restraints have limited their, and other establishments' activities, several of them having been grouped under the general umbrella of the Royal Armament Research and Development Establishment, with many of their functions being turned over to civilian contractors or transferred to the armaments firms themselves. The concept of the semi-independent scientific advisory service is thus being eroded, with a situation not unlike that obtaining before 1914 gradually returning.

Reserve forces (sometimes called **militia**). Military forces and formations without reserves do not last long in war. Reserves of trained personnel have to be established firmly and in sufficient quantity in peacetime (which is what this entry is chiefly about), and handled with strategic and tactical wisdom in war and combat. But whereas a prudent commander conserves his reserves by committing them sparingly to battle and re-creating them whenever possible from disengaged units as well as drawing on a supply of reinforcements, he is liable to be in difficulty if that supply runs out or if it is of inferior quality. It is for governments to ensure that does not happen.

While the terms of enlistment for recruits and conscripts (see **Recruiting** and **Conscription**) are at the statutory heart of armed forces, their numbers have to be related to the state of a nation's population and its economic and industrial resources, along with the dimensions of tasks envisaged in times of emergency when **mobilization** is proclaimed. Usually reserve forces are cheaper to maintain than permanent ones, although less likely to be so well trained or readily available. A balance has to be struck between how much training of reservists can be carried out in peacetime, to what extent that disrupts the permanent forces' efficiency as it prepares for immediate action in an emergency, and the degree of disruption to the civil economy and people's lives that is politically acceptable. Since the 1850s, militarily sophisticated nations which created massed forces have employed different systems to form complementary categories of reservists to suit various circumstances – and yet meet the approval of the populace.

For example, prior to **World War I** the German Army maintained a sizeable standing force containing a strong, long-serving professional cadre which trained and administered the annual intake of conscripts in permanent units and formations. The **infantry** soldier served for two years, the **cavalry** or **artillery** three. On discharge he transferred to the Reserve and was liable for one month's training a year, probably as a member of a Reserve unit or formation designated for action within a few weeks of war's outbreak, but perhaps as a replacement in a permanent unit. At the age of 27 he would be transferred to the *Landwehr*, whose units were formed in time of war and had trained very little, and finally aged 39 into the *Landsturm*, whose task was home defence, but also was a source of reservists.

The voluntary system favoured by the British, on the other hand, depended upon the call-up of reservists who had completed their term of permanent service but were still liable for recall from the Reserve as part of their original contract. In addition, the British formed the all-volunteer Territorial Army (TA), staffed by a few regulars, which was based on the **regimental system** and organized to produce formed Reserve units and formations when called out in time of war. Chaos ensued, however, when Field Marshal Lord **Kitchener** rejected the TA in favour of an entirely new volunteer force with little or no military training and even fewer items of equipment.

World War I, with its unprecedented call on personnel for both the armed forces and the **home front** and industry, taught the need for careful manpower planning such as was applied by most nations in **World War II**. Although on mobilization most members of Reserve forces were absorbed into the Services, some among them could be held back to use their skills in a vital war job on the home front. Such people were sometimes categorized as belonging to reserved occupations. Indeed, the handling of Reserve forces in World War II was fairly cautious in the realization that Reserve units thrust semi-trained into combat were doubly disadvantaged. Ships' companies often comprised a mixture of trained regulars, rejoined reservists and complete newcomers. Although complete Reserve army formations existed, precautions were taken to delay their introduction to combat and to lace them with a sizeable regular element. As for the forming of new Air Force units, these often waited upon training and equipment since there was rarely a shortage of volunteers. Time to retrain reservists is always critical, but in many cases, owing to the initially slow development of the war, it was available.

From the 1950s on, when threats of **cold** and **limited war** appeared quickly with little warning, and the menace of nuclear war, with the possibility of enormous casualties, loomed large, the feasibility of employing sufficient reserves for immense tasks, operating the latest highly complicated equipment, often appeared impractical. The result was that only the major powers – America, Russia and China – felt they could afford both large permanent and reserve forces in peacetime for any kind of foreseeable task. Smaller nations like Britain chose to abandon the concept of Reserve formations for prolonged total war. They concentrated on higher-quality Reserve units and special categories of **logistic** personnel to support the regulars, provide replacements and perform home defence – and hoped for shorter, limited emergencies.

Rhineland, Battle of the. When the German Ardennes counter-offensive collapsed in January 1945 and **Hitler** issued a characteristic standfast order to his forces west of the River Rhine, the remnants of the German Army were doomed. As its salient contracted under strong pressure from unshaken Allied forces, British and American attacks on the 15th near Roermond and along the upper River Roer threatened the **Siegfried Line**. These were preparatory moves that, together with the clearing of the Colmar pocket between 20 January and 9 February, set the scene for the series of major offensives aimed at driving the Germans back to and over the Rhine to win the Battle of **Germany** and end **World War II** in the West.

On 8 February Field Marshal **Montgomery's** 21st Army Group attacked from Nijmegen, up

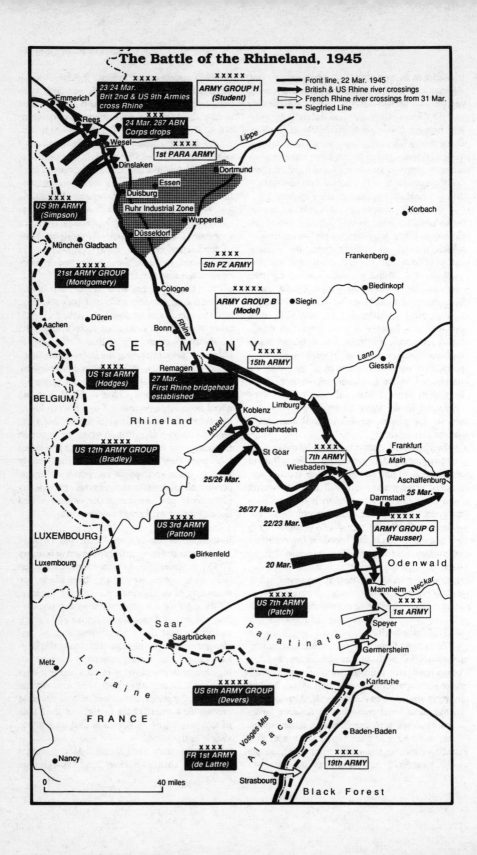

The Battle of the Rhineland, 1945

Legend:
— Front line, 22 Mar. 1945
➤ British & US Rhine river crossings
▷ French Rhine river crossings from 31 Mar.
- - - Siegfried Line

XXXX 23/24 Mar. Brit 2nd & US 9th Armies cross Rhine

XXXXX ARMY GROUP H (Student)

XXX 24 Mar. 287 ABN Corps drops

XXXX 1st PARA ARMY

XXXX US 9th ARMY (Simpson)

XXXXX 21st ARMY GROUP (Montgomery)

XXXX 5th PZ ARMY

XXXXX ARMY GROUP B (Model)

XXXX 15th ARMY

XXXX US 1st ARMY (Hodges)

27 Mar. First Rhine bridgehead established

XXXXX US 12th ARMY GROUP (Bradley)

25/26 Mar.

XXXX 7th ARMY

26/27 Mar.

22/23 Mar.

XXXX US 3rd ARMY (Patton)

XXXXX ARMY GROUP G (Hausser)

20 Mar.

25 Mar.

XXXX US 7th ARMY (Patch)

XXXX 1st ARMY

XXXXX US 6th ARMY GROUP (Devers)

XXXX FR 1st ARMY (de Lattre)

XXXX 19th ARMY

GERMANY

BELGIUM

LUXEMBOURG

FRANCE

Rhineland

Saar

Palatinate

Lorraine

Alsace

Odenwald

Black Forest

Emmerich, Rees, Wesel, Dinslaken, Dortmund, Essen, Duisburg, Ruhr Industrial Zone, Wuppertal, Düsseldorf, München Gladbach, Korbach, Frankenberg, Cologne, Biedinkopf, Siegin, Aachen, Düren, Bonn, Remagen, Lann, Giessin, Koblenz, Limburg, Oberlahnstein, St Goar, Mosel, Wiesbaden, Frankfurt, Main, Aschaffenburg, Darmstadt, Birkenfeld, Mannheim, Neckar, Luxembourg, Speyer, Germersheim, Saarbrücken, Metz, Karlsruhe, Baden-Baden, Nancy, Vosges Mts, Strasbourg, Lippe, Rhine

0 —— 40 miles

the Rhine towards Wesel. It suffered from bad weather and sodden ground, but made slow progress also because, owing to inundations by the Germans of the Roer valley, the American contribution with a southern pincer claw was delayed, thus enabling the Germans to spare troops fiercely to resist the British. But this made it all the easier for the Americans to break out on the 23rd when conditions improved. The pincers met on 3 March with catastrophic effect on the Germans. Meanwhile General **Bradley**'s 12th Army Group had pushed forward from Düren in the direction of Cologne, Bonn and Koblenz, reaching the Rhine on the 5th and, by a celebrated *coup de main*, seizing intact on the 7th the railway bridge at Remagen to establish a bridgehead. The move gave space and opportunity, too, for a broad-fronted advance across the River Moselle which, against crumbling resistance and in conjunction with General Jacob Devers's 6th Army Group, cleared the remainder of the west bank of the Rhine by 25 March, a sweep crowned by an opportunist crossing of the river near Oppenheim by General **Patton**'s Third Army on 22 March.

At this moment the German Army east of the river was in disarray. The massive crossings of the Rhine between Rees and Dinslaken by 21st Army Group on the 23rd, and the exploitation, at a stunning pace, by 12th Army Group of its bridgeheads in the south, were operations against what was only patchy, though in many places unyielding, resistance that could only lead to the overrunning of a Germany long ago defeated.

Richthofen, Captain Baron Manfred von (1892–1918). A cavalry officer who learned to fly in 1915 and piloted **reconnaissance aircraft** until transferring to **fighters** in September 1916. He began at once rapidly to shoot down many enemy aircraft, very properly concentrating on reconnaissance machines investigating the secret Hindenburg (Siegfried) Line, but also demonstrating great courage and skill in fighter combat. He commanded a fighter group in June 1917 and led it brilliantly until shot down and killed on 21 April 1918, at which moment he was credited with 80 victories as the top-scoring ace of World War I.

Ridgway, General Matthew Bunker (b. 1895). A parachute leader (see **Airborne forces**) who par-

ticipated in the scattered landing in **Sicily** in July 1943, but successfully commanded an airborne division on 6 June 1944 in Normandy. At **Arnhem** in September he commanded XVIII Airborne Corps, but with only partial success, owing to failure to seize the Nijmegen bridge on the 17th. In December 1950 he took command of Eighth Army at the nadir of its fortunes in **Korea** and completely revived it to smash the Communist offensives of 1951. After taking over as C-in-C United Nations forces from General **MacArthur** in April, he stabilized the front along the 38th Parallel. From 1952 to 1953 he was Supreme Commander Allied Forces in Europe and from 1953 until retirement in 1955, Chief of Staff US Army.

Rifles. By 1840 a rifled muzzle-loading musket began to replace the old smooth-bores and during the **Crimean War** 15 years later the French Minié rifle in the hands of British and French troops wreaked havoc amongst the dense masses of Russian infantry, at short range the bullets passing through several bodies. In fact, it was the increased range and accuracy offered by the rifle that was its chief attraction, with the cutting of grooves in the barrel being the main obstacle to mass production. The early weapons were virtually handmade, rarely even to a standard calibre, but as industry gradually overcame these problems the end of the smooth-bore musket as the soldier's personal weapon was inevitable.

Previously in the hands of private firms, in 1853 the British began the transition to official designs with the introduction of the first Enfield muzzle-loading rifle (and unwittingly helping to precipitate the **Indian Mutiny** by the use of cartridges smeared with animal fat, repugnant to Muslim and Hindu alike). The Prussian needle-gun of 1848, on the other hand, was already a breech-loader and later some Enfield rifles were converted to this Snider design. It was the introduction of the solid-drawn brass cartridge which really opened the way for the modern breech-loaders, the Martini-Henry, Lee-Metford and Lee-Enfield soon appearing. Once the problem of breech-loading had been overcome the designers' attention then turned to loading methods using automatic or semi-automatic means; the Winchester repeating rifle from America is a successful early example. However, this complicated weapon, of perhaps questionable reliability in the hands of the ordinary soldier and with a short barrel implying limited range and accuracy, did not appeal to most armies except as a cavalry carbine. The infantry soldier generally retained the longer-barrelled single-shot rifle of simple robust construction or, towards the end of the 19th century, the five- or ten-round magazine rifle such as the 7·7mm (·303in) Lee-Enfield. Versions of this weapon were to see the British infantryman through the **Boer War** and two **World Wars**; it was capable of accurate rapid fire out to several hundred metres and, equipped with telescopic sights and in the hands of a trained sniper, was deadly.

After World War II it was realized that most infantry rifle fire was used suppressively and at comparatively short ranges; there was not the need for the long-range very accurate weapon, heavy to carry and cumbersome to handle in a largely vehicle-orientated army. Standardization with allies was also important, leading in the 1950s to the adoption by the British of the Belgian 7·62mm FN self-loading rifle, modified for Britain to fire single shot only, following a long-held belief in the value of restrained single-round aimed fire.

Perhaps the best-known and probably most widely used post-1945 rifle is the Russian 7·62mm automatic AK47, now being replaced by the AKM; simple, robust and reasonably accurate out to 300m. British experience against forces equipped with the AK47 has led to a change in attitude reflected in the recent introduction into British service of the 5·56mm SA80, a radical new design of fully automatic individual weapon, combining the roles of both rifle and sub-machine-gun. SA80 is considered to be sufficiently lethal, with sufficient range (300–400m) and accuracy for normal rifle-combat ranges. Being very much lighter and with less jump (like the American M16 it is 'straight through', i.e. the barrel is in line with the shoulder rather than the eye), weapon training is easier for the recruit. A far cry in appearance from the rifle of World War II, weapons like SA80 are the likely pattern for the future.

Riga, Battles of. Before **World War I** the port of Riga was the third most important industrialized Russian city and, by the autumn of 1915 as the Germans approached, it had been stripped of its assets. It remained in Russian hands however until, as a possible first step of an advance on Petrograd, the Germans attacked on 1 September 1917. Their aim was further to shake the morale of post-Revolution Russia and eliminate its unreliable Twelfth Army protecting the city. The attack by General Oscar von Hutier's Eighth Army was notable as the first, and not entirely successful, use of the new infiltration **tactics** supported by a surprise intense bombardment – and benefited from cover by early morning mist. Although forewarned, the Russians were unable to take adequate precautions and, for the most part, decamped or surrendered.

Riga was also the scene of confused fighting when it fell to Bolshevik Russian troops on 4 January 1919, was retaken by German and Latvian forces in March and finally, after a year's turmoil in which the German Freikorps was brutally active, resumed its ancient function as capital of an independent Latvia, only to be reoccupied by the Germans on 24 June 1941 after a stiff fight against surrounded Russians at the outset of the advance on **Leningrad** via **Lithuania**.

Once more in August 1944 it had the misfortune to be threatened with yet another siege. In the wake of the collapse of German Army Group Centre, Army Group North withdrew on the city as the Russians overran Estonia and swept into Lithuania. A corridor through Lithuania to East Prussia was held open for a few weeks in desperate fighting while **Hitler** refused to permit withdrawal from the city and the Courland peninsula. On 28 September the Russians struck again, closing the corridor and reaching the outskirts of Riga on 10 October. For five days bitter street fighting took place. Far too late, Hitler allowed the survivors to withdraw into Courland, where they remained to the war's end.

Riot control. Before modern police forces (armed in most instances though unarmed in Britain) were formed in the mid 19th century, it was customary for outbreaks of rioting to be quelled by military forces. This implied the use of arms rather than minimal strength and persuasion, such as civil police controlled by popular governments are trained to employ. Yet generally the use of deadly force to deal with rioting, particularly of the armed political kind, has been deemed a military matter once the police admit, owing to the size of a problem or the inadequacies of their equipment and training, that matters have gone beyond their control. Even so, wise civil authorities only call on the military for riot control as a last resort if they desire to avoid provoking more serious violence, such as rebellion and **guerrilla warfare**.

Popular governments in the 20th century have learnt gradually the hard way how to contain riots by subtle methods and have come to appreciate the political value of moderation. It was discovered that suppressing riots without care for life did not necessarily stamp out resistance. Probably the merciless quelling of unpopular, anarchic riots during the Siege of **Paris** in 1871 was unavoidable under the threat of civil war, but the pitiless crushing of political gatherings in Russia, which admittedly bordered on insurrection from 1906 to 1914, indicated panic on the part of rulers. Their insensitive use of brute force in the manner accustomed exacerbated a resentment and mistrust which in 1917 proved fatal as revolution broke out. Similarly, as the British discovered in the aftermath of political protest in India in 1919, the use of excessive force of arms by soldiers can be counter-productive if exploited by shrewd **propagandists**. It was one of the ironies of the **Amritsar Massacre** that General Dyer's military overreaction to moderate Indian protests against aspects of British rule probably shortened the British regime by many years.

Yet Amritsar produced another ironic and beneficial effect since it forced the British to recognize the political ineptitude of uninhibited force for riot control and made them adopt the restrictive rules for applying minimum force which have stood the test of time and much practice. Henceforward the military would be used in support of the civil power only when formally requested. Thereupon the military commander was not only in complete charge but also had to complete the task of restoring order by the use of prescribed minimum force. Firearms were not to be used except in self-defence, or by single shots aimed to kill identified trouble-makers after due warning. The system proved reasonably effective and was copied by most nations which had proper regard for humanity and public opinion. Furthermore, the rules could include use of such incapacitating weapons as high-pressure water hoses, non-toxic gas and baton rounds (rubber or plastic bullets) to help disperse unruly crowds. That was better, it was discovered, than the bullying

use of **tanks**, which were not only the antithesis of efficient minimum force but sometimes highly provocative and a useful propaganda weapon in hostile hands.

But nations (mostly the dictatorial kind) with scant regard for and a deep fear of public opinion have many times flagrantly used maximum force to cause excessive loss of life. Fascist Italian and German forces of law and order had little regard for minimum force as they came to power in the 1920s and 1930s. Communist Russia in East Germany, Hungary, Czechoslovakia and her own provinces since 1945 has used everything from tanks downwards to crush riots, methods copied by the Chinese in 1989 in their own country. But unlike lesser dictators clinging to power by their finger-nails, the leaders of the superpowers who rule by outright suppression of public opinion have a better chance of surviving isolated riots, even though they risk damaging their nations' economic and political standing.

Roberts, Field Marshal (Lord) Frederick, VC (1832–1914). A Gunner in the Bengal Army of the East India Company who distinguished himself during the **Indian Mutiny**, in Abyssinia in 1868, and in the Second Afghan War (**Afghanistan, Battles of**) in 1878–80 when, at Kandahar, he routed the Afghan Army to become a household name as 'Bobs' in Britain. In 1885 he became C-in-C the Indian Army and was responsible for considerable improvements in its condition. Sent to South Africa to lead recovery in the aftermath of the initial set-backs of the **Boer War**, he revitalized the British Army and led it to the capture of Pretoria. He was then recalled to England to become C-in-C of the British Army in 1901, a post to which he was not suited but which terminated with the very necessary Army reorganization and the abolition of his job in 1904. An ardent supporter of **conscription**, he did what he could in semi-retirement to prepare Britain for the forthcoming **World War I**.

Robertson, Field Marshal Sir William (1860–1933). A Trooper who joined 16 Lancers in 1877, was commissioned in 1888 and became an expert in **intelligence** matters. In 1897 he was the first ranker to graduate at the Staff College of which, in 1910 (having served in Intelligence during the **Boer War**), he became

Commandant. In charge of the British Expeditionary Force's logistics in France in 1914, in January 1915 he became its Chief of Staff until appointed Chief of the Imperial General Staff in December. Soon he found himself fighting hard against the politicians who wished to win the war in some other theatre of war than France. The quarrel led to a rupture with the Prime Minister, David Lloyd George, against whom, with his gruff Scottish speech, he was no match in debate. He was posted to a home command in February 1918.

Rockets and guided missiles. Rockets were used in war as early as the 10th century, but had dropped out of favour by the 15th and remained forgotten for about 300 years. The British Army having been subjected to Indian rocket fire during the siege of Seringapatam in 1799, Colonel William Congreve was asked to develop a system for use by the Royal Artillery. His successful design of a warhead attached to a long stick for stability in flight had a range of several thousand metres.

Rocket systems continued to be developed during the 19th century with William Hale producing a spin-stabilized version which was 100 years ahead of its time. Both Congreve and Hale rockets were used during the **American Civil War** with a variety of payloads – solid shot, grenades, musket balls, incendiaries – but without marked success. Rocketry then languished until **World War I** when there was a somewhat abortive British attempt to develop rockets for the attack of balloons. However, interest revived again in the 1930s during the general fear of massed air attack, with an idea for rocket barrages against aircraft. The project got to the trial stage, with firings taking place in Jamaica to preserve secrecy.

Despite these stillborn attempts, Congreve's dictum of a century before – 'the facility of firing a great number of rounds in a short time, or even instantaneously, with small means' – was still attractive and in Germany and Russia, and later in America, interest in multiple-launched rocket systems reawakened during **World War II**. Rockets were not accurate, but the ability to saturate a whole area with high explosive at short notice could provide very effective support for hard-pressed infantry. Specially equipped landing-craft, for example, supported the Normandy landings in 1944 in this way; but large-scale firings were mainly confined to the fighting in Russia and the lead was in German hands under Doctor Werner von **Braun**.

Aircraft rockets were also under development in Britain as early as 1940, with the first airborne trials conducted over Chichester Harbour in 1941. The aircraft rocket was seen primarily as an **anti-tank** weapon, though armour-piercing warheads as originally fitted were found to be ineffective; surprisingly, high explosive proved to be better, the steep attack angle tending to dislodge the tank turret or even blow it off altogether. All this activity, culminating in the German V2, led to the development of the long-range *free-flight rocket* (FFR) of the postwar era.

FFR accuracy has improved markedly over the years, but it still cannot compete with the gun for close-support tasks, mainly because of its long minimum range; the French 145mm Rafale, for instance, even with the use of air brakes, cannot engage a target closer than 10km. In addition, though many rounds can be fired simultaneously or very quickly from a multiple launcher, reload time compares unfavourably with that of a gun. However, large rockets can carry a variety of payloads, including a nuclear warhead (see **Atom bomb** and **Hydrogen bomb**), suitable for attacking an area target. They are perhaps best suited as carriers for terminally guided sub-munitions, designed for top attack of armoured vehicle concentrations, typically at ranges of about 30km.

In response to the wide range of Soviet FFR systems, America has introduced the Multiple-Launch Rocket System (MLRS), built by the Vought Corporation and a good example of the concept. MLRS has two pods, each of six rockets, mounted on a tracked launcher. The 12 227mm rockets, each weighing about 270kg, can be ripple-fired in about one minute, with a comparatively short reload time. A pre-surveyed site is not needed and redeployment is therefore rapid.

The guided missile, as the term implies, is a rocket which can be guided all the way to the target. Guided missiles are usually classified as: *surface-to-surface* (SSM), of which the *anti-tank guided weapon* (ATGW) is a special case; **surface-to-air** (SAM) for air defence; *air-to-surface* (ASM) for aircraft ground attack and *air-to-air* (AAM) for aerial combat.

Before the end of World War II Germany was

already working on an ATGW system called X-7 which, though it never came into service, foreshadowed most types in use today, all steered to the target by signals transmitted by the operator via a fine wire paid out by the missile as it flies. Later developments have allowed for semi-automatic guidance, relieving the operator of the worst aspects of tracking; the future for ATGW probably lies in some form of heat-seeking 'fire and forget' system where the missile homes automatically on to the target after launch.

SSMs, excluding ATGW, vary from tactical systems in the 200–2,000km bracket, where the FFR would be hopelessly inaccurate, to the very-long-range *Intercontinental ballistic missile* (ICBM). Most such systems use some form of inertial guidance, the cruise missile coupling this with a terrain-following system providing continuous course monitoring. SSMs have proved particularly attractive for ship-versus-ship engagements and have largely supplanted the long-range naval gun. Strategic SSMs are often submarine-launched to protect the launch platform.

SAM systems range from low-level missiles such as the American Stinger, to the very advanced Safeguard system designed to protect the USA from ICBM attack. In the medium range Britain has Rapier, effective out to 7km at 3,000m, the nearest Soviet equivalent being SA8 (12km at 5,000m).

ASMs are comparatively short-range, though they can attack over-the-horizon targets; systems are usually radar- or, in some cases, television-guided. AAMs, in forms such as the American Sidewinder, used successfully in **Korea** in the 1950s, and now the more recent Firestreak, have supplanted the machine-gun and cannon for aerial combat (see also **smart munitions**).

Romania, Battles of. Romania, which became an independent kingdom in 1878, had long been the prey of powerful neighbours and, with the production of oil on a large scale in 1854, of great strategic importance. Her troops played a role in the **Russo-Turkish War** of 1877–8. In the Second **Balkan War** of 1913 her Army advanced almost unopposed into Bulgaria to help bring a quick political settlement.

On 27 August 1916, however, she unwisely allowed herself to be persuaded by the Allies and the continuing success of Russia's **Brusilov**

Offensive to attack the Central Powers. The Romanian broad-fronted offensives into the Transylvania Alps and Bulgaria were soon brought to a halt by well-co-ordinated resistance. In September her forces were flung back at the Vulkan and Red Tower Passes by the German Ninth Army, under General von **Falkenhayn**, and in the Dobruja by combined German-Bulgarian forces under Field Marshal August von Mackensen. The advancing Central Powers rapidly developed a pincer movement against Romanian armies whose plans for a counterstroke were captured. This led to a heavy defeat at the Arges River on 4 December and the closing of the pincers on Bucharest on the 6th. Some 350,000 Romanians were casualties with most of their weapons as the Germans pursued them towards the Ploeşti oilfields and the Russian frontier. But already the oilfields and their stocks, along with other installations, were in flames as the result of extremely effective sabotage arranged by Major John Norton-Griffith, a British engineer. The economic effects of this on the Central Powers were enormous since it was many months before production was restored. Meanwhile the broken Romanian Army was in dire peril once the Russian Revolution (**Russian revolutionary wars**) began in February 1917. In August von Mackensen's offensive finally brought it to surrender after a prolonged stand at Maraşti – though an armistice was delayed until 6 December when Russia withdrew from the war.

Post-1918, a reconstituted Romania had little desire for involvement in **World War II** and offered no immediate resistance to German occupation in 1940 on the eve of the invasions of the Balkans and Russia, although in January 1941 there was a serious uprising which was crushed by Romanians and Germans. Yet she willingly sent troops to fight at the German side in Russia in June and found herself at war with Britain and America that same year. In 1942 and 1943 the heavily defended oilfields were attacked by American **strategic bombers** but with little success and at high cost. However, the loss of many troops at **Stalingrad** in 1943 was a shock which, a year later, influenced a secret group to join the Allies against Germany. The plot was activated by a *coup d'état* led by King Michael on 23 August as Russian troops began flooding in after smashing German Army Group South Ukraine on the River Pruth. German attempts to evict King Michael's government were stopped by loyal Romanians and their bombing of Bucharest on the 25th merely hastened a declaration of war. The city fell on the 31st, 24 hours after Ploeşti's oilfields had been captured. German attempts to make a stand in the Transylvanian Alps came to nothing as the Russians pressed on into Hungary and Yugoslavia. By 6 September almost the entire country had been cleared – but only as a prelude to the imposition of a Communist regime under Russian domination.

Rommel, Field Marshal Erwin (1891–1944). A German **infantry** officer of immense tactical skill who won the Ordre pour le Mérite in 1917 but was rejected for General Staff training after **World War I**. In the 1930s he was adopted as a **propaganda** hero by Josef Göbbels and recommended to **Hitler** who appointed him commander of his bodyguard in 1939. As commander of an **armoured** division in France in 1940 he won applause; and from 1941 to 1943 in **North Africa** as, successively, commander of Afrika Korps and Panzer Army Afrika, acquired great renown for his flair. But as a logistician and strategist he was flawed, as his conduct of the advance to El **Alamein** and subsequent retreat demonstrated. Still in Hitler's favour, he was made commander, temporarily, of an Army Group in Southern Europe before given command of Army Group B in North-West Europe. He pinned the defence of the Atlantic Wall on the hope of defeating invasion on the beaches, but in **Normandy** was overwhelmed by superior Allied forces and personally wounded on 17 July 1944. By then he was implicated in the attempt to assassinate Hitler and in October was forced to commit suicide to spare Hitler the embarrassment of condemning to death a hero of the Nazi Party.

Roosevelt, Franklin D. (1882–1945). A Democrat of immense political charisma and astuteness who became Assistant Secretary of the US Navy in 1913 and a keen student of naval affairs. As President of the USA in 1933, when faced with the task of reviving the nation's economy, a programme of rearmament to stimulate industry was among his measures. As C-in-C the armed forces he was compelled at the outbreak of **World War II** in 1937 to prepare for hostilities with Japan and, in 1939, the danger posed by war in Europe. After the fall of France in 1940 he accelerated the expansion of the armed forces, placed an embargo on the export of oil and iron products to Japan and, in line with a belief that war with Germany was likely, steered the nation to support of those powers, Britain first, who fought the Axis.

After **Pearl Harbor** he concentrated upon collaboration with Britain, Russia and China in the formulation of a strategy which gave priority to the defeat of Germany before Japan. With Winston **Churchill** he had sound relations but found Josef **Stalin** and **Chiang Kai-shek** more difficult to deal with. In his Army Chief of Staff, General **Marshall**, he found a kindred spirit, but the prickly, less than brilliant Chief of Naval Staff, Admiral **King**, often caused him problems. His strategic decisions, influenced by the Allied Combined Chiefs of Staff organization set up in 1942, usually reflected political as much as military factors. He had an innovative mind and readily supported **guerrilla warfare** and the making of the **atom bomb** with secret funding, but in his shaping of the post-war world a belief that he could 'handle' Stalin proved illusory – as he may have come to realize, shortly before his death on 12 April 1945, when Stalin's intransigence and expansionist activities already were producing what became the **Cold War**.

Rumania. See **Romania**.

Rundstedt, Field Marshal Gerd von (1875–1953). An **infantryman** and Chief of Staff of a corps in **World War I** who rose to be commander of Army Group A, which in 1939 executed the decisive strokes of the **Polish campaign** in September and the Battle of **France** in 1940. However, he was instrumental in allowing the British to escape at **Dunkirk** and in December 1941 was relieved of command by **Hitler** after confessing defeat in Russia, yet reinstated as C-in-C West next year. In July 1944 he was again relieved of command on the eve of disaster in **Normandy** for telling the High Command to make peace, but reinstated yet again, to his last job, the figurehead command of the Ardennes offensive in December.

Russian revolutionary wars. Discontent with the Tsarist regime came to a head in the riots and insurrection of 1906 following the disastrous **Russo-Japanese War**. It simmered until **World War I** in 1914, went off the boil and then hotted up in 1916 with news of the **Brusilov Offensive's** failure. In March 1917 (February by the Russian calendar) it erupted into the riots, demonstrations and military mutiny of the Revolution which deposed the Tsar and brought two feuding governments into being: one of professional leaders; the other a Bolshevik Soviet claiming to represent the people. The sending by the Germans of the Marxist leader, Vladimir Lenin, from Switzerland to Petrograd in a sealed train in April vitalized the Bolsheviks. After failure of the military to overthrow the Workers' Soviet and continue the war against Germany, the Bolsheviks seized power in October and set the scene for the struggle to come.

This entry concentrates upon military operations after Lenin had taken Russia out of the war in December. Revolts by Cossacks against the Bolsheviks began at once in the south, and sparked insurrections elsewhere along with major foreign interventions in 1918, which created a seething cauldron throughout the land. In the west the Germans, Austrians and Turks, in breach of the Peace Treaty, moved against unco-ordinated Bolshevik opposition in the Baltic states, White Russia, Ukraine and Armenia; while Persian-based British troops took Baku and the Japanese and Americans occupied Vladivostok in the Far East. But when the Central Powers began to weaken as the World War drew to a close, numerous factional **guerrilla** groups appeared to stir the brew in company with the intervention of major anti-Bolshevik forces (which were sent in 1918 by the Allies to distract Germany from her **Hindenburg offensive** in the west), plus foreign armies such as the Poles and the Czechoslovaks. These self-interested groups fought either alongside or logistically supported so-called White Russian forces of Tsarist inclinations who pitted themselves against the Bolsheviks (renamed Communists in March 1918). By August 1918 civil war was in full swing as the Communist government proclaimed a state of emergency and a campaign of 'Red Terror' to retain power by dictatorial brutality (see map page 280).

In June 1918 the Czech Legion of 100,000 ex-prisoners of war armed themselves from the Communists, took control of the Trans-Siberian railway and moved west in conjunction with a Siberian-based White Army under Admiral Alexander Kolchak. But Kolchak was defeated in 1919 and the Czechs sent to Vladivostok

where they were evacuated by the Americans. Meanwhile (see map), the White armies and small Allied contingents were applying strong pressure against the Communists, whose ruthlessness lost them much support. Instead of the international revolution Lenin called for under Russian leadership, the country was riven by factions as the Poles invaded the Ukraine and reached **Kiev**; and as the Ukrainians, the Balts and the Finns struggled for independence (see **Russo-Polish**, **Warsaw**, **Kharkov** and **Lithuania** battles).

Yet it was this dictatorial ruthlessness, applied with fanaticism and astute **propaganda** by the Communists, which gradually tilted the scales against the far less unified Whites and their half-hearted foreign supporters. Exhaustion brought an end to the Russian attempt to spread the Revolution to Germany, via Poland, as support for the equally exhausted Whites and their Allies collapsed. By 1921, at a price of some 13 million dead from combat and famine and a ruined economy, the internal position was secured but Communist ambitions thwarted.

Russo-German wars. *1914–18*. Originally the Germans had rejected the concept of attacking on the Eastern Front at the commencement of **World War I** because they wished first to defeat France in the west. They gave way before the urging of General **Conrad von Hötzendorf**, who demanded an immediate attack by the Austrian armies before the Russians could complete their **mobilization** (see **Austria's east-front campaigns, 1914–17**). In any case the Russian advance, ordered by Grand Duke Nicholas into East Prussia and which began on 17 August 1914, absorbed the German Eighth Army in the frontier Battles of Stalluponen (where the Russian First Army was badly mauled) and at Gumbinnen, on the 20th, which was a draw followed by the German commander's loss of nerve (and his sacking) and a further German retirement. At this moment Generals von **Hindenburg** and **Ludendorff** arrived and, by the 31st, had won the Battle of **Tannenberg**, to achieve a lasting superiority over the large but ill-equipped and poorly led Russian Army.

Henceforward, as the Austrians also fell into decline after defeat in Galicia and the Battle of Rava Ruska on 11 September, the Germans played the leading role in the east, first saving the Austrians from further defeat at the two

Russian Revolutionary Wars, 1917-20

BARENTS SEA

Entente Fleet

Murmansk

British
French
Canadians
Italians
Serbs

NORWAY

WHITE
SEA

Canadians
Americans
Archangel

Finns

British
French

S W E D E N

FINLAND

Helsinki

Kronstadt

Petrograd (Leningrad)

B O L S H E V I K

Perm

British
Fleet

Yudenich
1918-20

Kornilov 1917

R U S S I A

BALTIC
SEA

Letts
Riga

Pskov

Nizhniy-Novgorod

Kazan

Kolchak
1918-19

LATVIA

Germans

Moscow

Czechs

LITHUANIA

GERMANY

Smolensk

Kaluga

Tula

Samara

Minsk

Mogilev

Warsaw

Tambov

Penza

Orenburg

P O L A N D

Poles

Gomel

Orel

Saratov

Zhitomir

Voronezh

CZECHOSLOVAKIA

Kiev

Denikin 1919

Kharkov

HUNGARY

Tsaritsyn
(Stalingrad)

Romanians

Rostov-
on-Don

Novocherkassk

R O M A N I A

Odessa

Astrakhan

French

Simferopol

French

Novorossiysk

B U L G A R I A

British

BLACK SEA

CASPIAN

Entente
Fleet

British

SEA

Batum

Baku

Krasnovodsk

Kars

British
1918-19

Boundary of the Russian Empire 1914

Eastern front, Mar. 1917

Area controlled by the Bolsheviks, Aug. 1918

White Russian Army

Non-Russian anti-Bolshevik forces

0   500 miles

battles of **Warsaw** in October and November, after Hindenburg had taken over on 1 November as C-in-C Austro-German Eastern Front, then, in conjunction with the Austrians, crushing the Russians in Galicia at the Battle of Łódź on 25 November. The Russians never recovered from these blows as, throughout the winter of 1914/15, Hindenburg applied pressure in the battles of the Masurian Lakes and the Austrians, stiffened by German troops, held firm in the Carpathian mountains. These struggles were overtures to the **Gorlice offensive** in 1915, when the initial German attacks broke the Russians and the Central Powers rolled them back along the length of the front.

Again in 1916, when the Germans were hard pressed on the Western Front, they had to spare troops to prop up the Austrians as the **Brusilov offensive** threatened a débâcle. Yet this was a turning-point. The Russian Revolution (**Russian revolutionary wars**) in March 1917 removed any further threat to the Central Powers in the east. After containing the ill-founded Russian Kerensky Offensive on 1 July (which collapsed in 16 days of chaos after the Austrians had also shown signs of breaking), it was a relatively simple matter for the Germans (with Austrian assistance) to pursue into Ukraine the broken 'revolutionaries' whose **logistic** system, not for the first time, fell apart. When an armistice was concluded at Brest-Litovsk on 15 December, it became of little moral account, after a political wrangle with the Russian Bolshevik government provoked the Germans, in February 1918, to occupy Ukraine in an almost unopposed advance against thoroughly demoralized troops.

This occupation might well have wrecked the Russian Revolution had not the Germans been defeated that year in the West and the Allies insisted upon withdrawal of the forces of the Central Powers within their own boundaries. They thereby ensured the future of the Communist Soviet Russia which Adolf **Hitler**, long before 1941, had chosen as his main objective for destruction in **World War II**.

1941–5. In July 1940, having won the Battle of **France** and seeming to be on the verge of conquering **Britain**, Hitler instructed his commanders to prepare an invasion of Russia, an operation which some, in hindsight, said was terrifying in prospect but which, to many at the time, looked promising of victory. For the German C-in-C, Field Marshal von **Brauchitsch**, like Hitler was deluded by **intelligence** which was correct as to some Russian military weakness, but misleading about the large number of formations that might reinforce the West if, as occurred, the Japanese declined to attack Russia in the Far East. He was also ill-served by the General Staff, which miscalculated the **logistic** situation. For they sent the Wehrmacht into a vast campaign with resources enough for only a short war, which it was thought would be concluded before the onset of winter. Nor had they allowed for subtractions of force following increasing involvements, early in 1941, in the **Mediterranean**, the **Balkans** and **North Africa**.

There was prolonged debate between Hitler and his High Command over initial thrust lines and objectives. Nevertheless, when the invasion was launched on 22 June 1941, the main objectives, for both political and military reasons, were **Leningrad**, **Smolensk**, **Kiev** and Ukraine; followed by pursuit of the, assumed, broken enemy to **Moscow**. Try as hard as the Germans would to conceal their intentions, they were not to know that the Russians were being supplied with copious warnings. Nor was it to be hoped that complete surprise would be achieved because, for political reasons, Josef **Stalin** was unprepared to take heed and place his forces on alert; nor that the equipment, **training** and **logistic** states of the Red Army and Red Air Force would reduce them almost to impotence in places. Yet, although the triumphant advances to the initial objectives made these things plain by mid-September, the subsequent pursuit to Moscow demonstrated the fallibility of the original German concept. For many Russians, spurred on by **propaganda** which spoke of German cruelty and called for a patriotic war, fought hard – and with good effect under General **Zhukov**, who created most Russian victories including the winter offensive which saved Moscow. Yet although the hard-pressed Germans defeated the winter offensive of 1941/2, before lunging into the Caucasus in June to capture oil – and arrived at **Stalingrad** for a prestigious battle of attrition – the task was already beyond them.

The catastrophe at Stalingrad in February 1943 was merely the prelude to a long, rarely checked withdrawal from the Caucasus into Ukraine, a retreat offset by such local victories as the **Kharkov** counterstroke in March and the abortive **Kursk** offensive in July. Further

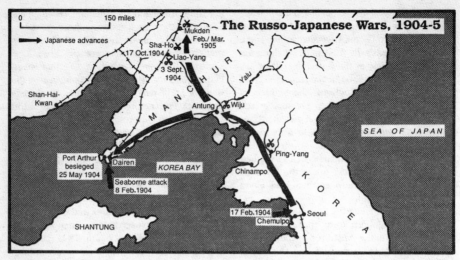

The Russo-Japanese Wars, 1904-5

0   150 miles

→ Japanese advances

Mukden Feb./ Mar. 1905
Sha-Ho 17 Oct.1904
Liao-Yang
3 Sept. 1904
M A N C H U R I A
Yalu
Shan-Hai-Kwan
Antung Wiju
SEA OF JAPAN
Port Arthur besieged 25 May 1904
Dairen
KOREA BAY
Chinampo
Ping-Yang
Seaborne attack 8 Feb.1904
K O R E A
17 Feb.1904 Seoul
Chemulpo
SHANTUNG

withdrawals followed inevitably, grudgingly made in the face of Hitler's insistence upon unyielding defence, until the Germans crossed the 1941 start line and continued backwards into Germany in 1944 as their resources dwindled to desperately low levels on West, South and East Fronts. Yet now too the whole process of Russian advance in the most savage and brutal fighting revolved around their ability to overcome logistic difficulties in a countryside with devastated lines of communication. Indeed, but for the provision by America of 376,211 trucks, 51,503 jeeps, 1,964 locomotives (plus 11,075 items of rolling-stock), and vast quantities of signalling equipment, Russian participation in the final Battle of **Germany** in January 1945 and of **Berlin** in April and May might not have taken place.

Russo-Japanese wars. After being diplomatically humiliated when compelled to yield **Port Arthur** to Russia after capturing it in the **Chinese–Japanese War** of 1894, the Japanese were bent on vengeance. Signs of Russian political confusion, their failure to reinforce Manchurian forces and the near completion of the Trans-Siberian railway persuaded the Japanese to strike without declaration of war on 8 February 1904. That night **torpedo-boats** entered Port Arthur harbour, sank several ships and withdrew under cover of a bombardment by Admiral **Togo's** fleet. Meanwhile a Japanese invasion fleet on its way to Chemulpo (where the army landed on the 17th) fought off Russian warships to complete domina-

tion at sea as the main Russian fleet remained in Port Arthur.

Outnumbered 10 to 1 on land, and in **logistic** chaos, the Russians went on the defensive while they began transferring forces from the west, the gap in the railway at Lake Baikal making this difficult. Meanwhile Admiral Stepan Makarov took command of the fleet and began harassing Togo, a strategy brought to an end when Makarov was drowned on 13 April after his flagship struck a **mine**. Meanwhile the Japanese Army was approaching Port Arthur, defeating the Russians under General Zasulich at the **Yalu River** on 1 May, and landing on the Laiotung Peninsula on the 5th before commencing the siege on the 25th. By this time the Japanese Army under Marshal Iwao Oyama was starting to concentrate for the invasion of Manchuria. On 14 June a Russian attempt to relieve Port Arthur was broken at the Battle of Telissu and on the 23rd a sortie by the fleet, now under Admiral Vilgelm Vitgeft, came to nothing.

In mid-July the Japanese began to advance into Manchuria, winning the Battle of Moteinlung on the 31st and compelling the Russians under General Alexei Kuropatkin to withdraw, provoking the Russian warships at Port Arthur to break out to join the rest of the fleet at Vladivostok. But at the Battle of the **Yellow Sea** on 10 August, Togo won a crushing victory – and thereby set in motion the Russian plan to send their Baltic Fleet to the Far East where it too met its doom at the Battle of **Tsushima** on 27 May 1905.

Meanwhile Oyama defeated the well-entrenched and reinforced Russians at Liaoyang on 3 September, at a cost to his army of 23,000 men and to the Russians of 19,000. Following up the Russian retreat with 170,000 men, he again defeated Kuropatkin's 200,000 at Sha-Ho on 17 October with respective losses of 20,000 and 40,000. These were engagements which showed only too impressively the immense killing power of modern weapons, how very difficult it was to exploit local successes and the problems of keeping a modern army's **logistics** working adequately. At Sandepu on 27 January 1905, Oyama was fortunate in a snowstorm to avoid defeat by Kuropatkin when the Russians failed to recognize their opportunities in a counterstroke. The stalemate persuaded the Russians to withdraw to **Mukden** and fight the culminating land battle of a war which ended in mutual, utter exhaustion, but with Japan's accomplishment of her war aims.

Twice more the two nations fought in Manchuria as further instalments of the continuing **Japanese wars of expansion**. These were the series of incidents on the Mongolian frontier in 1938, culminating in the Japanese rebuff at the Battle of **Khalkin** Gol in 1939, and the Russian invasion of 9 August 1945 when their experienced mechanized armies overran a weak Kwantung Army of about 600,000 in six days, and swept on into North Korea at the close of **World War II**.

Russo-Polish wars. The Polish state's extinction (by Russia, Prussia and Austria in the 19th century) and re-emergence (in 1917 at the beginning of the **Russian revolutionary wars**) took place at times of insurrection or war. **World War I**, as General **Piłsudski** visualized it, gave the Poles a chance to rid themselves of the hated Russians. In 1916 Poland was re-established by the Central Powers as a buffer state with an army (from the Polish Legion formed in 1914), which gave vital substance against predatory neighbours. Indeed, no sooner had World War I come to an end in November 1918 than Poland was threatened by Germans retreating from Russia and Ukrainians setting up a state of their own in Galicia. The Germans, with Allied help, were expelled, as were the Ukrainians, in stiff fighting. Taking advantage of Russian weakness in 1920, Piłsudski then pushed eastwards to **Kiev** and the River Beresina in White Russia

with a view to re-establishing the frontiers of 1772. At the same time, however, the Communist Russians appreciated that the best chance of stabilizing the Revolution against the Whites and their Allied supporters, was to spread the Revolution by the invasion of Germany.

On 15 May 1920, the Red Army under Marshals Mikhail Tukhachevsky and Semen Budenny began a double envelopment of Polish forces at Kiev. They chased them back to Lvov and, seemingly irresistible, began the Battle of **Warsaw** at the end of July. Between 16 and 25 August, however, Piłsudski launched a counterstroke against a **logistically** overstretched opponent whose collapse brought an end to a war which had never been officially declared.

One point both Germans and Russians agreed upon, and enshrined in their treaty of August 1939, was the extermination of Poland and the Poles. The German invasion of Poland on 1 September had that in mind and was related to the secret clause agreeing occupation of the eastern half of the country by the Russians. The move, which started on the 17th against scanty defence, put an end to Poland as a nation. Suspended animation lasted in purgatory with irrepressible resistance until the Red Army, driven out by the Germans in June 1941, returned in August 1944 to re-create the state. The Poles had to endure redrawn frontiers under Russian dominance, and an inferior standard of living, as the lesser of two evils. But they are beginning to change this (see map page 284).

Russo-Turkish wars. Since the 17th century and the commencement of Russian expansion under Peter the Great, the declining Turkish Ottoman Empire suffered from Russian and other nations' depredations. The war which broke out between them on 4 October 1853, to trigger the **Crimean War**, was but the eighth since the 1676–81 war and was distinguished by sturdy Turkish resistance on land at the Battle of Oltenitza, in Romania on 4 November, and the destruction of the Turkish naval squadron at Sinope on the 30th which prompted the British and French to come to Turkey's aid.

The War of 1877–8 had its origins in the so-called Eastern Question, in events in the **Balkans** and in chronic Turkish weakening. Turkish repression in Herzegovina–Bosnia provided Russia with an excuse to mobilize (**Mobilization**) and declare war with a view to invading Romania in

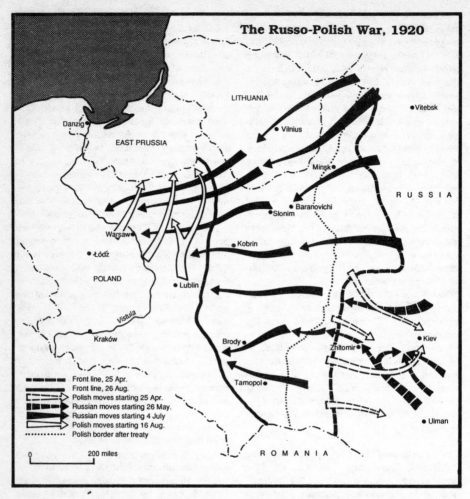

The Russo-Polish War, 1920

LITHUANIA

•Vitebsk

Danzig•

• Vilnius

EAST PRUSSIA

Minsk•

R U S S I A

•Baranovichi
•Slonim

Warsaw•

• Kobrin

• Łódź

POLAND

• Lublin

Vistula

Kraków

Brody •

Zhitomir•

• Kiev

Tarnopol •

• Ulman

- – – – – Front line, 25 Apr.
- ━━━━━ Front line, 26 Aug.
- Polish moves starting 25 Apr.
- Russian moves starting 26 May.
- Russian moves starting 4 July
- Polish moves starting 16 Aug.
- ··········· Polish border after treaty

0   200 miles

R O M A N I A

May *en route* via Bulgaria to Adrianople and Constantinople. While minor operations were carried out in the Caucasus in April, culminating in the siege and capture of Kars by the Russians on 18 November, the focus was on Grand Duke Nicholas's army of 275,000 well-armed and supported men. They crossed the Danube in May to push back half that number of Turks under Abdul Kerim. By mid-July Russian advanced guards had penetrated to within 90 miles of Adrianople, which lay open to capture by a concentrated Russian follow-up. But the Russians were distracted by the threat of a Turkish force strongly fortifying Plevna, which they besieged and repeatedly assaulted instead of driving hard for Adrianople. The siege lasted from

19 July until 10 December, when the garrison under Osman Pasha attempted a valedictory sortie and then surrendered. Meanwhile the Russians, who were bogged down in Bulgaria by indecision and ineffectual Turkish counter-strokes, stirred themselves. Early in January they outmanoeuvred the outnumbered Turks to the south of the Skipka Pass, encircled them at Senova on the 8th and captured 36,000 men. Twelve days later Adrianople fell and the Russians pressed on to within striking distance of Constantinople before an armistice was signed on the 31st.

The War of 1914–18. Turkey's entry into **World War I** on the side of the Central Powers on 29 October 1914 was a severe blow to the

Russians because it closed the Dardanelles to supplies from the Allies – and thus prompted the battles of **Gallipoli** in 1915. In so far as fighting between the two countries was concerned, however, this took place mainly in the Black Sea and the Caucasus. The Turkish Fleet, significantly reinforced by a German **battle-cruiser** and a **cruiser** which had escaped from the Mediterranean in August, bombarded Russian bases at Odessa, Sevastopol and Theodosia and generally managed to hold the seas. But a Turkish attempt to capture Kars and invade the Caucasus was prevented in appalling winter conditions at the Battle of Sarikamish on 3 January 1915 when 100,000 Russians overcame 95,000 Turks (with the loss of nearly 80,000) and hurled them back on Erzerum. A typical attritional struggle broke out in July near Lake Van in the Armenian mountains to coincide with the **Gorlice offensive** but led only to heavy casualties and minor territorial adjustments.

In January 1916, however, the Russians under General Nikolai Yudenich launched a major offensive from Kars with the aim of capturing Erzerum and Trebizond. Again the Turks suffered grievously from the cold as they fell back to yield Erzerum on 16 February and Trebizond on 18 April. But neither then, nor in July when the Turks attempted a counter-offensive with disastrous results, was anything conclusive achieved. Indeed the only Turkish successes were at Mus and Bitlis in mid-August when General **Kemal** scored local victories to bolster a reputation which, at that moment, was under a cloud. But the failure of the **Brusilov offensive**, followed by the outbreak of the Russian Revolution (**Russian revolutionary wars**) in March 1917, effectively ended serious combat in the Caucasus. Nevertheless, Turkey in February 1918, taking advantage of Russian collapse along with the other Central Powers, seized the opportunity to recover territory and win rich pickings. With German complicity, she thrust into Armenia, recapturing Kars on 27 April and moving on Baku where, in September, she ejected the small British force which had seized the oil installations, gains which she forfeited in 1919 after World War I had come to an end.

S

SACEUR. The Supreme Allied Commander Europe was first appointed by the Nato Defence Council in December 1950 as its senior military member and commander of forces on the Continent and in the Mediterranean, in addition to being C-in-C Europe (CINCEUR). General **Eisenhower** was the first SACEUR, a post always filled by an American soldier or airman. The appointment, which naturally has strong political implications, is principally concerned with the formulation of **strategy** and the co-ordination and control of the disparate national armed forces, a task requiring as much diplomatic as military skill.

Saigon, Battles of. In 1859 at a time of anti-Christian troubles in Cochin-China, King Tu Duc besieged a Franco-Spanish garrison of 1,000 from March 1860 to February 1861, when a French relieving force won the Battle of Chi-hoa and forced Tu Doc to cede Cochin-China to France. Under French rule the city and port flourished. In **World War II** it was the main Japanese headquarters in South-East Asia and a hotbed of intrigue by nationalists and the French.

During the **Vietnam wars**, it was, from 1946, a centre of French resistance to numerous Vietminh attacks against the extensive **logistic** and communications facilities of the city. Its population was swelled by refugees, and Vietminh guerrillas, from about one million to well over two million at the height of the war. Following French withdrawal and the division of the country in 1954 it became the capital of South Vietnam and, after 1959, a major US base. It thus became it a major target for North Vietnam subversion and attacks until the débâcle of April

1975 when the city fell amid scenes of terror and chaos.

Saint-Mihiel, Battle of. At the conclusion of the **Hindenburg offensives** in July 1919 a salient 15 miles deep and 20 wide at its base remained to the south-east of Verdun. Marshal **Foch** decided to eliminate it and, after a dispute with General **Pershing**, agreed it should be the US Army's first major operation of **World War I**. On 8 September General **Ludendorff** ordered evacuation of a so obviously vulnerable and superfluous position. This was by no means complete when First US Army attacked on the 12th behind a heavy bombardment from 3,000 guns (nearly all French), supported by 332 tanks (232 French) and 1,500 aircraft (only 609 piloted by Americans). The Germans withdrew at once, although the fast-moving Americans (who suffered 7,000 casualties) eventually captured 15,000 men and 250 guns. But on the 13th chaotic traffic conditions prevented petrol reaching the tanks, which thus were unable to exploit opportunities. The battle was called off on the 16th.

Saint-Nazaire raid. In **World War II** the port of Saint-Nazaire assumed great importance as a base for German **submarines** and, with its huge dock, for **battleships**. On the night of 28 March 1942, a British force of motor boats supporting the **destroyer** *Campbeltown* entered the port. *Campbeltown* embedded herself in the dock gates and the **Commando** she carried landed to wreck port installations. Withdrawal took place under heavy fire with considerable losses. But next morning a very large explosive charge in her bows was detonated by time fuse and the gates destroyed. Not only was the dock put out of action for the rest of the war, the Germans were persuaded to accelerate work, at immense cost and with only marginal benefit, on the port defences of the Atlantic Wall.

Salerno, Battle of. On 9 September 1943, six days after the **Italian campaign** began in Calabria and timed to coincide with the announcement of an armistice between Italy and the Allies, Fifth US Army under General **Clark** began landing in the Bay of Salerno. Neither Field Marshal **Kesselring** nor the German Tenth Army Commander, General Heinrich von Vietinghoff, were entirely surprised, but their concentration of troops at Salerno was conditioned by the major distraction of disarming the Italian Army. The invaders were met by alert defenders and by nightfall had established only four small, unconnected bridgeheads. Meanwhile German air attacks against shipping (scoring 85 hits and sinking four transports, a **cruiser** and seven **landing-craft**) were part of a race to mount a decisive counter-attack before the Allies were strong enough to break out. The Germans nearly won the race on the 12th and 13th when their six divisions made headway, but were finally checked by the dropping of an American parachute brigade, intense naval and army **artillery** fire and air attacks.

By the 15th a stalemate had been reached, to be broken when General **Montgomery**'s Eighth Army, approaching from the south, made contact on the 16th. Only then did Kesselring order a withdrawal.

Salonika campaign. Salonika fell into Greek hands in November 1912 at the conclusion of the First **Balkan War**. In November 1914 it became a base for supply of Allied munitions to Serbia in the **Serbo-Austrian battles**, and was secured, at Greek request, by Allied troops in October 1915 under threat of attack following the Serbian defeat. In November an Allied force under General Maurice Sarrail was repelled when it advanced up the Vardar Valley into Bulgaria. Henceforward the Salonika Front became a very expensive Allied side-show in which casualties from sickness and disease were almost as debilitating as from combat.

By August 1916 the Anglo-French-Serbian forces amounted to 368,000. But their offensive designs were disrupted at the Battle of Florina

on the 27th by a well-conducted Bulgarian–German pre-emptive offensive. The ensuing Allied stroke towards Monastir, lasting from 10 September to 19 November, made only limited and costly headway, ending a year's wastage with a price of 50,000 men against their opponents' 60,000. Sarrail, with only 100,000 men fit out of a force of 600,000, could do little more in 1917 than mount minor local attacks for fighting's sake. The stalemate remained unchanged after Greece entered the war on 27 June, despite reinforcements. General Guillaumat took over in December to reorganize the Allied armies, but not until he handed over to General Franchet d'Esperey in July 1918 was another strong move made.

On 15 September, as the Central Powers reeled back in defeat on all other fronts, 200,000 Allied troops out of 600,000 attacked 400,000 Bulgars (bereft of German troops). In this Battle of the Vardar, a deep penetration by the Serbs opened a gap which was exploited by the French and, on the 18th, by a British diversionary attack. All at once the Bulgarians broke under air attack and a pursuit which gathered such momentum in a fluid situation that French **cavalry** were actually able to make a contribution. And although the Bulgars were granted an armistice on the 29th, d'Esperey kept thrusting to cross the Danube on 10 November, poised to overrun Hungary when the war came to an end next day.

SALT. See **Strategic Arms Limitation Treaties.**

SBS (Special Boat Squadron). See **Special forces.**

Scheldt River, Battles of. When Antwerp fell to the British on 4 September 1944 its port became the only undamaged or unoccupied one in Allied hands and the key to their **logistic** problems as they strove to win the Battle of **Germany** that year. But instead of ordering the immediate clearance of the approaches to the port along the West Scheldt, Field Marshal **Montgomery** concentrated on the Battle of **Arnhem** and the clearance of the lesser Channel ports of Le Havre, Boulogne and **Calais**, leaving **Hitler** time to reinforce General Gustav von Zangen's Fifteenth Army, which garrisoned the Breskens Pocket and the islands of Walcheren and South and North Beveland. Not until the 27th was General

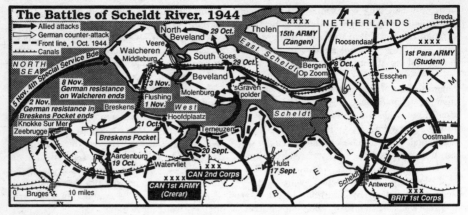

The Battles of Scheldt River, 1944

Henry Crerar's First Canadian Army ordered to win access to the port.

The attack from Antwerp to South Beveland on 2 October and into the Breskens Pocket on 19 October developed, like all the subsequent struggles for the Scheldt, into an infantry grapple in lowlands much of which was inundated. On 3 October the sea dikes of Walcheren had been breached by bombing, but without forcing the Germans to withdraw before the floods. Not until the 21st, against fierce resistance, was the Pocket cleared and the South Beveland isthmus penetrated on the 26th. Then, on the 28th, an **amphibious** assault was made on the south shore of South Beveland, to link next day with Canadians advancing down the isthmus and complete the overrunning of that island. Walcheren was invaded on 1 November by British **Marines, Commandos** and infantry who, in many instances, reached their inland objectives in amphibious craft. Minesweeping began on the 4th but the port was not open until the 27th.

Schlieffen, General Count Alfred von (1833–1913). A particularly dedicated member of the Great German General Staff who was at the Battle of Königgrätz and took part in the **Franco-Prussian War**. He is best known as the Chief of the General Staff who, between 1891 and 1905 in the belief that a European war was inevitable, drew up the famous Plan which gave priority to knocking out France before crushing Russia. The Plan, with modifications, was put into operation at the beginning of **World War I**, and was revealed as defective because it underestimated the **logistic** problems as well as French and British determination and combat skill. In-

stead of winning a short war, it brought defeat at the Battle of the **Marne**, to ensure a losing long war of disastrous long-term political effects such as he was incapable of visualizing.

SEATO (South-East Asia Treaty Organization). A collective defence treaty signed on 8 September 1954 by Australia, France, New Zealand, Pakistan, the Philippines, Thailand, Britain and America to resist Communist expansion in South-East Asia. Although Vietnam was not a member its defence by SEATO powers was included. The headquarters was in Bangkok. Strategy was based on mobile forces in and around the region. Neither Britain nor France was a fervent participant and Pakistan withdrew in 1971 after the **Indo-Pakistani War**. In 1975, after the **Vietnam War**, the organization phased itself out of existence.

Secret services. Secret organizations to provide **intelligence** of enemy activities and to run counter-espionage as part of a nation's defences are as ancient as conflict. Without prior knowledge of hostile intentions and lacking defences against enemy prying, the best-laid military plans can be ruined. Stories about Secret Service work are numerous because of their mystery and the insights they offer about the inner workings of government and war-making. But they are rarely historically complete and usually inaccurate, if only because records usually remain, of necessity, eternally secret. A remarkable exception, though itself leaving much unsaid, including the vital budgeting, is the five-volume British official history of intelligence (see Bibliography) in the Second World War which, among many revelations, categorically demolished a host of legends and journalistic myths.

Secret Service work is not restricted to purely military matters. For example, the American Secret Service was set up in 1865 to combat counterfeiting of the new paper currency and only subsequently acquired other duties, including protection of the President in 1901, investigation of fraud and, in **World War I**, of violations of neutrality. Tsarist Russia, with its traditional passion for concealment and conspiracy, ran numerous agencies, many of them tasked to quell subversion, such as the Cheka, the GPU and the OGPU, which changed names and colour but greatly expanded their activities during and after the Revolution to become the NKVD, NKGB and KGB with tentacles of espionage and subversion reaching throughout the world. Germany, too, had its Prussian police force for internal security and, in due course, the agencies of Nazism including the RSHA and the Gestapo. Britain formed its Secret Service in 1909 under the Foreign Office, in response to the deterioration of international relationships, to 'be a screen between the Service departments and foreign spies; to act as an intermediary between the Service departments and British agents abroad; to take charge of counterespionage'.

The ramifications during **World War I** of Secret Service work linked to diplomacy and **propaganda**, military operations and subversion, security and **code and cipher** breaking, taught vital lessons for prolific use in **World War II** and the subsequent **Cold War**. Never in a tranquil environment, they performed their duties in anonymity, furtiveness and an atmosphere of intrigue, mistrust and interdepartmental feuding which frequently made people wonder whose side they were on. There were traditional rivalries between the different Service intelligence branches and problems of co-ordination. Ever more vital **technological effects** required closer monitoring as well as providing improved methods of **electronic** surveillance. The advent in Britain in 1940 of the overlapping **Special Operations Executive** (SOE) and in the USA in 1942 of the **Office of Strategic Services** (OSS) produced much friction. Later, in the USA, there were overlappings and jealousies among the Federal Bureau of Investigation, the Secret Service and the CIA (Central Intelligence Agency).

The presentation of Secret Service matters to the public is usually either guarded or sensational, and often deliberately misleading or provocative as part of the struggle between agencies. Not infrequently one adversary denigrates or tricks another into an indiscretion. The pressures applied by politicians of one persuasion to undermine the opposition by disclosures and scandals concerning secret activities are simply part of the game. Bland requests, on democratic grounds, for increased freedom of access to Secret Service work are not always what they seem – and certainly the antithesis of the essence of what intelligence gathering and security work is about. But woe betide any organization, civil or military, which drops the guard that secret information from reliable sources provides.

Sedan, Battles of. The ancient town of Metz, guarding the River Meuse at one of the gateways to France, has experienced many wars but few battles more crucial to the history of France and Europe than those of 1870 and 1940.

1870. During the **Franco-Prussian War**, after the French Army of Marshal **Bazaine** had retired into **Metz**, the Army of Châlons under Marshal **MacMahon** with Napoleon III in company, moved to its relief. But on its approach, on 29 August, the French collided with the Germans at Beaumont and retreated in disorder on Sedan where MacMahon intended to reorganize. Seizing the opportunity, General Helmuth von **Moltke** ordered the Third and Meuse Armies to encircle the city from two directions, a brilliant manoeuvre completed on the 31st before the French could escape. Next day at first light, when short of ammunition and supplies, the French (with MacMahon among the wounded) awaited their fate in positions largely overlooked by the Germans. Watched by the Kaiser, Chancellor von Bismarck and von Moltke, the Germans held the line of the Meuse and attacked the French flank and rear where the defences were frailest. Fight with desperation as the French did, their case was hopeless. At 1100hrs, 2 September, Napoleon surrendered with MacMahon's entire army amounting to 104,000 men and 419 guns. German casualties were about 9,000 in a complete victory which decided the war.

1940. At the start of the Battle of **France** on 12 May, the advanced guard of General **Guderian**'s XIX Corps reached the outskirts of Sedan in three days after brushing aside French covering forces in the Ardennes. Next afternoon, in preparation for a pre-planned assault across the River Meuse on either side of the town, the French artillery positions were neutralized by prolonged bombing while high-velocity anti-aircraft guns fired directly into the embrasures of French pillboxes on the south bank. Under cover of this fire, German infantry crossed to secure bridgeheads with relative ease and expand them during the night while rafts and bridges were constructed to carry **tanks** and other heavy equipment. French counter-attacks did not materialize owing to command inertia and a corrosive panic which seized their soldiers. On the evening of the 14th Guderian appreciated that the 12-mile gap which had opened in the French defences allowed his corps to pass through to the west in the drive towards the English Channel. That day, too, French counter-attacks began to develop at Stonne on his southern flank. These, along with air attacks on the bridges (which incurred extremely heavy losses to the **bombers**), caused some concern and continued for several days to come – but never in sufficient strength to restore the situation.

Seeckt, General Hans von (1866–1936). An officer who served on the Staff throughout **World War I** and won acclaim as General August von Mackensen's Chief of Staff in the **Gorlice** and Serbian offensives of 1915 and the **Romanian** campaign of 1916–17; and as Chief of Staff to the Turkish Army in 1917 and 1918. After the war he commanded Frontier Force North in the approaches to East Prussia in a difficult political/military situation which he managed with consummate skill.

In 1919 he became head of the *Truppenamt* which, following the Versailles Treaty, did duty in place of the proscribed General Staff. In 1920 he was made Commander of the Army (*Reichswehr*). In these appointments he saved Germany from successive uprisings (*putsch*), disbanded the swashbuckling anti-Communist *Freikorps* and took the Army out of politics while having it support the government in power. At the same time he remodelled the Army in the light of the lessons of World War I and the constraints of Versailles; established secret industrial arrangements to develop the latest **technology** and weapons with countries such as Sweden, Argentina and, above all, Russia; and encour-

aged the brilliant members of the *Truppenamt* such as von **Bock**, von **Rundstedt**, Walter Wever, **Kesselring** and Kurt Student to update doctrine, introduce the latest organizations and methods and create, in secret, an **air force, tank** force and **airborne force**. Political indiscretions in 1926 lost him the job. But he entered politics as a member of the *Reichstag*, from 1930 until 1932, and in 1934 and 1935 headed a mission to help **Chiang Kai-shek** reorganize the Chinese Army and fight a **guerrilla war**.

Sensors. The battlefield commander has always needed to know what was happening beyond his limits of vision, '. . . what lay on the other side of the hill' (Wellington). The term 'sensor', however, has come to mean the development since **World War II** of **electronic surveillance** devices which will detect enemy movement and pass the information to the waiting watcher. In a much more primitive form, such devices were used during **World War I**, where microphones were placed to pick up the noise of enemy sappers digging below the listener's lines.

In the late 20th century electronic and electro-optic techniques have allowed the development of a variety of devices to give the modern army almost continuous 24-hour all-weather surveillance. Most such devices are ground-based, with the tethered platform perhaps the most unusual. A rotor-powered platform, flown at about 300m altitude, carries a variety of sensors: **radar, television**, infra-red etc. Information is transmitted to the ground via the tethering cable and, in one case at least, fuel is pumped up to the platform engine via the same cable.

In more general use, however, is the *remote ground sensor*, such as the US Remotely Monitored Battlefield Sensor System (REMBASS) which, like most of its kind, has three basic elements: the sensor itself, which may be one of three types of acoustic/seismic sensor; the repeater, which passes on radio signals from the sensor to the monitor; the monitor, where the data is processed. The system can differentiate between wheeled and tracked vehicles out to 500m and men at 50m; data can be displayed electronically on the monitor or hard copies can be printed. Sensors may be hand-emplaced, fired from artillery or dropped from the air.

Such systems place the commander's eyes and ears well behind the enemy's lines, without the risk to costly foot patrols.

Senussi wars. The nomadic, desert tribes of Cyrenaica, who were generally left to their own devices by the Turks, naturally sided against the Italians in the **Italo-Turkish War** of 1911, though without much profit. But after the Turks made peace in October 1912, the Senussi, with slight Turkish support, went on fighting the Italians in a sporadic **guerrilla war**. The struggle persisted until the Italians entered **World War I** on the Allied side in 1915, whereupon the Central Powers encouraged the Senussi to greater belligerence and shipped in arms by **submarine**. The capture of the crew of the British ship *Tara* in November 1915, and a Senussi invasion of Egypt, compelled the British to send a force, including armoured cars and **aircraft**, into Cyrenaica. There ensued a **desert warfare** campaign of encounters (called 'affairs') in which the Senussi, who fought well, were driven back and gradually hunted down. The war was virtually brought to an end on 24 February 1916 near Sidi Barrani when a British cavalry charge put to flight a large Senussi column. And on 17 March armoured cars rescued the sailors from their prison at Bir Hakeim after a 120-mile, cross-desert raid.

Seoul, Battles of. As capital of South Korea and a route centre, the city was a prime objective of the North Koreans at the outbreak of the **Korean War** on 25 June 1950. Within five days their twin-pronged advance had smashed the poorly trained and equipped South's forces and seized bridges intact over the Han River. But the North was ejected with equal speed and minimal resistance when, on 26 September following the **Inchon** counterstroke, it was reoccupied against only scattered resistance from an army which was disintegrating.

China's intervention across the **Yalu** in November and the subsequent, precipitate UN retreat to the 38th Parallel brought Seoul under the enemy's heel once more when a renewed Chinese offensive on 1 January made headway. This time resistance along the Han and in the vicinity of the city was fiercer than previously, with more damage inflicted. But the occupation was of quite short duration because the UN counterstroke on 25 January, aimed at the North's **logistic** base at Chunchon, had leverage and caused a grudging withdrawal by the North to the Han. On 14 March one object of General **Ridgway's** offensive was achieved as Kimpo air-

port was brought back into UN use and the enemy evacuated Seoul for the last time.

Serbo-Austrian battles, 1914–16. Although Austria's hatred of the Serbs was a prime cause of the outbreak of **World War I** on 28 July 1914, her invasion of Serbia with 200,000 men under General Oskar Potiorek on 12 August was, owing to Russia's involvement, an improvisation against an efficiently mobilized (see **Mobilization**) opponent, under Marshal Radomir Putnik, defending mountainous terrain with practised skill. Chiefly it was ammunition shortage which, after their victory at the Battle of Jadar (12–21 August), forced the Serbs to withdraw before the reinforced Austrians after the Battle of the Drina (8–13 September) and evacuate Belgrade on 2 December. But ammunition had arrived from France, to be used most effectively at the Battle of Kolubra (3–9 December). There the Austrian Army, weakened by defeats in Galicia against the Russians, collapsed and was forced to evacuate Serbia with the loss of 227,000 out of 450,000 men against 170,000 out of 400,000 Serbs (see map page 292).

The need to improve communications with Turkey eventually prompted the Germans to push Bulgaria into the war on 11 October 1915, four days after two strong German–Austrian armies launched an invasion under Field Marshal August von Mackensen. The Serbian army, ridden by typhoid and overstretched on the northern frontier against the excellent German divisions attacking on either side of Belgrade, left its southern flank facing Bulgaria almost undefended. Yet the Serbs at first gave the Germans (who suffered dire **logistic** problems) much trouble and delayed their advance. But when the well-trained Bulgarian Army advanced towards the Vardar and threatened to envelop the Serbs, von Mackensen's strategy paid off. Not in the slightest deterred by the threat to their left flank from the fumbled thrust of an Anglo-French army up the Vardar Valley from **Salonika**, the Bulgars kept moving, forcing the Serbians to accelerate their retreat in mid-November as the German–Bulgarian pincers began to close. By the 29th the country was almost engulfed, with withdrawal to the sea, in appalling winter conditions through the mountains of Montenegro and Albania, the only option. Nearly 400,000 Serbs were casualties or prisoners, the survivors escaping by ship, eventually to join the Allies in Salonika.

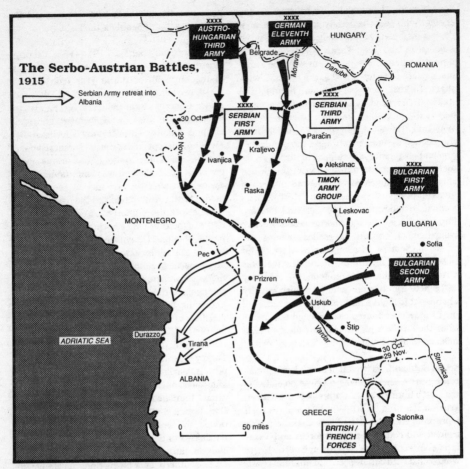

The Serbo-Austrian Battles, 1915

→ Serbian Army retreat into Albania

Serbo-Bulgarian War. In 1885 the proposed union of Bulgaria with Eastern Rumelia provoked Serbia, with Austrian support, into a preventive war. Any hope of achieving surprise by a lightning attack was forfeited by political shilly-shally, so that when Serbia declared war on 13 November the campaigning season was well advanced and the Bulgars ready. At the Battle of Slivnitza on the 19th the Serbs under King Milan were defeated by the Bulgars under Prince Alexander, who then invaded Serbia and, on the 26th and 27th, outfought the Serbs – and might have overrun the country had not the Austrians intervened.

Sevastopol, Sieges of. The naval base of Sevastopol was the prime Anglo-French objective of the misconceived **Crimean War** in 1854 – and

by no means ready for the siege which began on 8 October. Indeed, it might well have fallen but for the incompetence of the Allies and the efforts of Colonel Frants Todleben in rapidly putting right the fortifications and stocking the magazines. In fact, although the Allied Fleet **blockaded** the place, which came under bombardment on the 17th, it was never entirely isolated. And such were the effects of Russian counter-battery fire, the explosion of the main French magazine and a storm at sea, which wrecked ships, that an assault was postponed until 7 June, when the outer defences were at last seized. But attacks on the key Malakoff and Redan fortresses 10 days later were abject failures, with 4–5,000 men lost to both sides. Not until 7 September, in a most carefully prepared assault, timed for surprise by synchronized watches, did the French capture the Malakoff, from where they dominated the Redan, which the British had again failed to take. That night the Russians completed demolitions and withdrew from the city and port.

In October 1941 the German Army invested the city, although the siege was not complete until General von **Manstein**'s Eleventh Army had cleared the Crimea in May. His four-week-long assault, with a pulverizing **artillery** and **air** bombardment of the strong fortifications and meticulous preparation, was notable for relatively low German casualties, nothing like the some 120,000 Russian losses, of whom 90,000 were prisoners along with vast booty.

On 9 October 1943, after a brilliantly conducted withdrawal by General Ewald von Kleist from the Kuban across the wide Kerch Strait, the Russians were poised to recover the Crimea and Sevastopol. But von Kleist had punished the Russians severely and managed to remove 256,000 men, 73,000 horses with their 28,000 wagons, 21,000 motor vehicles and 1,815 guns, and was not followed up. When in April 1944 the Russians re-entered the Crimea, **Hitler** for once permitted a yielding defence of this prestigious bastion. The final Russian assault on Sevastopol on 7 May was merely checked for two days to allow most of the garrison to be evacuated by sea.

Seven Days Battle, The. The first prolonged struggle of the **American Civil War**, which decided the fate of the Federal invasion of the Yorktown Peninsula in 1862. After the landing in March, General George **McClellan**, with 90,000 men, advanced without undue haste towards Richmond against 15,000 Confederates, coming within sight of the city on 25 May – by which time the Confederates numbered 60,000. On the 1st the drawn battle of Fair Oaks was fought, stopping dead the Federal advance. The same day General **Lee** took command of the Confederates and on the 25th began a series of manoeuvres which pushed McClellan back at Oak Grove, Mechanicsville, Gaines Mill, Savage's Station, Frayser's Farm and Malvern Hill. Only at Gaines Mill did Lee win the fight while, at Malvern Hill on 1 July, the Federals won a resounding victory, which McClellan failed to recognize when persuaded to abandon offensive operations and retire to a beach-head at Harrison's Landing, whence the Army was

evacuated. The Federals suffered some 10,000 casualties, the Confederates 21,000, figures which spoke for themselves in terms of generalship.

Shenandoah Valley campaigns. Throughout the **American Civil War** this 20-mile-wide, 120-mile-long fertile valley with its good communications dominated the fighting in the approaches to Washington and Richmond and conferred more advantages on the Confederate than the Federal side. First **Bull Run** on 21 July 1861 was the outcome of Confederate forces debouching through Winchester and Ashby's Gap to reinforce the army facing the Federal advance from Washington. The so-called Valley Campaign of 1862 with its continuous fighting, including General Thomas Jackson's superb manoeuvres and victories at McDowell (18 May), Winchester (25 May) and Port Republic (9 June), was the essential distraction from the Federal threat to Richmond, via the Yorktown Peninsula, prior to General **Lee**'s victory in the **Seven Days Battle** on 1 July. Second **Bull Run**, on 30 August, again made use of the Valley and its gaps, in a victory which prepared the way for Lee's invasion of the North on 4 September (based on the Valley). This reached its climax at the Battle of Antietam on the 17th when Lee's 50,000 men defeated General George McClellan's 90,000, yet gave President **Lincoln** the strategic success he needed to help deter the European powers from supporting the Confederates.

Lee used the Valley as base and bowling alley for distractions and offensives. The Federal defeat at Fredericksburg on 13 December was the result of his emergence from the Valley to strike General Ambrose Burnside's army in flank. Following the Battle of Chancellorsville on 6 May 1863 (where Jackson's death offset Lee's victory), it was from the Valley that the Confederates reappeared, having won the Battle of Brandy Station on 9 June and Second Winchester on the 14th, to execute the invasion of the North which recoiled at **Gettysburg** on 3 July.

Once more, on 2 July 1864, while General **Grant** was fighting within sight of Richmond at Petersburg, 13,000 Confederate troops under General Jubal Early created a distraction by erupting into Maryland from the Valley, winning the Battle of Monocracy on the 9th and terrorizing Washington at its outskirts. Grant's reaction was more than enough to chase Early off on the 12th, until again, on the 30th after winning local successes at Kernstown and Winchester on 24th July, he was back. At that Grant decided to stamp out the threat for good. He sent an army of 48,000 under General Philip Sheridan up the Valley from Harper's Ferry to lay it waste and destroy Early. At Third Winchester on 19 September, Fisher's Hill on the 22nd and Cedar Creek on 19 September – all of them fiercely contested battles which cost the Federals dear but merely prolonged the war – the Valley's economy was destroyed and Early's force run down. On 2 March 1865, at Waynesboro, he had but 1,000 men to oppose General George Custer's cavalry and was routed.

Sherman, General William (1820–91). A West Point graduate who fought in the **Mexican War** in 1846 but left the Army in 1853. He rejoined on the Federal side for the **American Civil War** and served as a colonel at First **Bull Run**. At the Battle of **Shiloh** on 6/7 April 1862 he won the lasting confidence of General **Grant** and thereafter played leading parts in the Mississippi River campaigns, the Battle of **Vicksburg** and, as Commander of the Army of the Tennessee, the Battles of **Chattanooga** in 1863. But it is for the thrust to **Atlanta** in 1864 and the **March to the Sea** across Georgia for which he is most renowned (and by some Confederates reviled) as he struck northwards to wreck the South's war potential.

After the war he was sent west to deal with the Indians and settle the country while the transcontinental **railways** were under construction. In 1869 President Grant recalled him to be Commanding General of the Army, a post he held until 1883 with as little political involvement as possible and the distinction of forming a main Army Training Centre at Fort Leavenworth.

Shiloh, Battle of. In February 1862 General **Grant** seized Forts Henry and Donelson, thus putting himself astride the vital Tennessee and Cumberland rivers and forming the base from which to move upstream and cut the equally important Charleston to Memphis railway. The Confederates concentrated 40,000 men under General Albert Johnston at Corinth and surprised Grant's 62,000 at Shiloh on 6 April. Few were experienced. The first shock, at breakfast time, was borne by General **Sherman**'s troops, who fell back. For two days, as both sides fed in reserves, the **infantry** and **artillery** slogged it out by firepower with minimal manoeuvre. Johnston was killed among 11,000 Confederate casualties. Grant lost 14,000 and was in no state to pursue the Confederates decisively. But he had won Lincoln's trust; and the war in the west turned irrevocably in the Federal favour.

Sicily, Battles of. Sicily in 1860 was the arena for **Garibaldi**'s most sensational campaign when, on 11 May, he landed at Marsala with his Thousand Redshirts to lead the revolt against the Kingdom of Naples as part of the **Italian wars of independence**. Gathering support from a people who had little liking for Naples, Garibaldi met and defeated a small Neapolitan force at Catalafimi on the 15th, reached Palermo on the 27th and finally overwhelmed the Neapolitans at Milazzo on 20 July, prior to crossing the Strait of Messina (with help from the Royal Navy) on 22 August as one more step towards the unification of Italy.

In **World War II** Sicily was the main base for Axis air attacks against **Malta** and convoys making the passage of the Mediterranean. But with the capture by the Allies of North Africa in May 1943 and of the island of Pantelleria on 11 June, the Italian garrison had little spirit of resistance against the expected invasion. German troops provided the core of defence while bombing of airfields and military installations intensified. The assault by Eighth (British) Army (General **Montgomery**) and Seventh (US) Army (General **Patton**) on 11 July was hampered by bad weather – the **airborne** troops being badly scattered with many coming down in the sea. But firm bridgeheads were quickly seized. Only at Gela on the 10th was a counter-attack against the landing made. Mostly the Italians surrendered as the Americans cleared Western Sicily. But in the North-East corner and on the slopes of Mount Etna, the Germans established a bridgehead which held up the British in heavy fighting. This was outflanked in the north by **amphibious** landings at the same time as Field Marshal **Kesselring** was pleading with **Hitler** to be allowed to evacuate the Axis garrison to the mainland. The Italians were already leaving on 3 August: but not until the 11th did the Germans, covered by intense **anti-aircraft** fire, begin to cross from

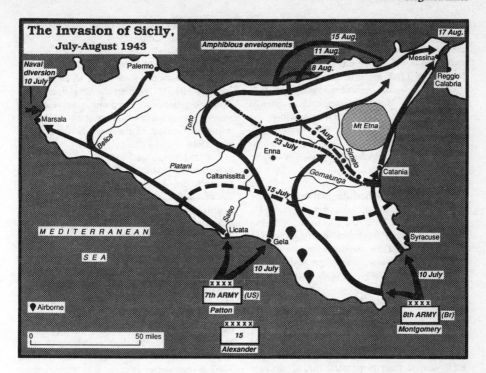

The Invasion of Sicily,
July-August 1943

Amphibious envelopments

15 Aug.

11 Aug.

17 Aug.

8 Aug.

Messina

Reggio
Calabria

Naval
diversion
10 July

Palermo

Marsala

Torto

Belice

2 Aug

Mt Etna

Simeto

23 July

Platani

Enna

Caltanissitta

Gornalunga

Catania

15 July

M E D I T E R R A N E A N

Salso

S E A

Licata

Gela

Syracuse

10 July

10 July

● Airborne

0   50 miles

XXXX
7th ARMY (US)
Patton

XXXX
8th ARMY (Br)
Montgomery

XXXXX
15
Alexander

Messina. Remarkably, by the 16th they had saved 100,000 men, 50 tanks and 9,800 vehicles. Nevertheless, against 16,500 Allied casualties had to be scored 164,000 from the Axis of whom 32,000 were Germans.

Sidi Rezegh, Battle of. In **North Africa** on 18 November 1941 the British Eighth Army (under General Alan Cunningham) advanced from the Egyptian frontier to the relief of **Tobruk**. Amid much confusion its armoured brigades, with about 700 **tanks**, clashed with General **Rommel's** Italian–German force with some 410 tanks. By the evening of the 23rd Rommel had won the fight for the vital ridge of Sidi Rezegh, a tactical advantage he attempted to convert into a strategic one by driving round the British flank into their rear. But General Auchinleck, who had taken over from Cunningham, held firm at the frontier and took advantage of the enemy's absence to reinforce his forces at Sidi Rezegh, thus creating a serious threat to Rommel's rear and compelling him to return at a disadvantage. Now, as the garrison of Tobruk broke out, Rommel ran short of tanks and fuel, compelling him to withdraw towards Benghazi.

Siegfried Lines. Two of the strongest and most extensive **fortifications** ever built by the Germans were named after the legendary and usually triumphant Teutonic hero Siegfried.

In **World War I**, in 1916/17, they constructed a triple-lined entrenched position, with dense barbed wire and a few pillboxes, extending from Arras to Soissons; and withdrew into it in March 1917. Known to the Allies as the Hindenburg Line, it was partially turned by the British at **Arras** in April, and breached in two hours on 20 November during the tank Battle of **Cambrai**. Following the collapse of the **Hindenburg offensive** and the Battle of **Amiens** in August 1918, the Germans withdrew once more into the Line. Again, at the end of August, it was penetrated at Arras during a general Allied advance which finally broke through the Line near Cambrai in mid-October as the Germans continued their well-conducted withdrawal.

In 1937, in readiness for **World War II**, **Hitler** ordered construction of another Siegfried Line of concrete and steel emplacements from the Swiss frontier to Luxembourg, with lesser works extending along the Belgian and Dutch frontiers. This was not tested until September 1944 when

Allied troops reached the vicinity of Aachen. There, from mid-November to mid-December, attempts in adverse weather to break into **Germany** made only marginal progress and were brought to a halt when the Germans launched an offensive in the Ardennes. Between 8 February and 10 March, however, the Line was outflanked by the Canadians and British in the north, and then penetrated with relative ease between Roermond and Trier by American thrusts which outflanked the strong southern sector.

Sikh Insurrection. After the final defeat by the British of the martial Sikh nation in 1849, the bulk of the population was incorporated in the province of Punjab and many joined the Indian Army. Their support for the British during the **Indian Mutiny** was significant, as was their courageous part in both **World Wars**. With declaration of Indian independence in August 1947, about 10 per cent of the Sikh population found itself under Pakistani rule while the rest lived in India.

In 1969 a movement appeared, largely based on religious grounds, for a separate Sikh state: Khalistan. It then burgeoned into a struggle between moderates and the fanatical Akali Dal, who demanded separation from India, something the Indian government could not allow since it might cause the disintegration of modern India. In the wake of minor protests there emerged in 1978 a campaign of religious infighting, sabotage, demonstrations, assassination of moderate leaders and the hijacking of airliners. In 1983 the self-styled National Council of Khalistan declared Amritsar a holy city. This prompted government countermeasures, which led to civil war between Hindus and Sikhs. When the situation worsened in 1984 the Indian Army entered the sacred Golden Temple in Amritsar to rout out the heavily armed extremists. The Punjab came under virtual military control. The Sikh Regiment exhibited signs of disaffection, which were exacerbated following the reaction when the Prime Minister, Mrs Indira Gandhi, was assassinated by two Sikh members of her bodyguard.

Looting and heavy fighting with high casualties among the populace followed. Terrorism persisted, not only in the Punjab but elsewhere, with the blowing-up of an Indian airliner over the Atlantic and serious international inci-dents to emphasize separatist determination. The struggle continues.

Sinai, Battles for. In **World War I** British troops advancing from the **Suez Canal** to **Gaza** via El Arish in 1916/17 crossed the Sinai desert only lightly opposed. The Egyptian Army took the same route as it advanced unopposed into Palestine at the start of the **Arab–Israeli wars** in May 1948.

But on 29 October 1956 when, with Anglo-French connivance, the Israelis under General **Dayan** attacked four Egyptian divisions between Kuntilla and Nitzana, the Egyptians were routed within hours, once their forward positions had fallen, a débâcle followed by a link-up on the 30th with an Israeli **airborne** drop at the Mitla Pass, pursuit to Bir Gafgafa and a point within 30 miles of the Canal where the Israelis halted on 1 November. Next day mobile forces headed down the coastal road from Eilat and from the Mitla Pass, via Ras el Sudr, to Sharm el Sheik, which fell on the 5th to complete conquest of the entire peninsula. Under diplomatic pressure, however, the Israelis then withdrew to their start lines, not to attack again until 5 June 1967 in the Six-Day War.

This time, in what was a pre-emptive offensive against a very large Russian-equipped Egyptian force concentrated between Kuntilla and Rafah, a fourth axis of advance, from Gaza towards El Arish, was added to those of 1956. The Israelis also were well-equipped, far better trained, and benefited, too, from a masterly air-strike against the enemy bases which achieved air superiority at once. For the first 48 hours there was heavy fighting across the northern sectors, but once penetrations had been made to El Arish, Abu Ageila and Nakhle, demoralization afflicted the Arabs, who either surrendered or bolted for the Canal, suffering further defeats to their reserves at Romani, Jebel Libni and Bir Gafgafa. The way was thereby opened to the reconquest of the remainder of the peninsula before a cease-fire was called on the 10th.

On 7 October 1973 the Yom Kippur War began in the Sinai when the Egyptian Army, under General Saad Shazli, carried out a brilliant crossing of the Suez Canal, captured most of the Israeli **fortifications** (the Bar Lev Line) and defeated an anticipated counter-attack on the 8th. Yet Shazli resisted until the 13th all suggestions for exploitation aimed at the Mitla and

Gidi Passes – and thereby sealed the fate of his armour when it ran headlong into Israeli tanks on the 14th. That day 2,000 tanks clashed, with over 200 Egyptian tanks and only 10 Israeli tanks lost. This Israeli tactical victory prepared the way for General Sharon's preplanned crossing of the Suez Canal into Egypt early on the 16th, a crossing preceded on the 15th by another furious battle to the east of the Canal near Chinese Farm when the Israelis lost over 70 out of 280 tanks and the Egyptians 150 in a fight which ensured Sharon's success next day as the Yom Kippur War reached its climax.

Singapore, Battle of. The Japanese advance under General Yamashita through **Malaya** to reach Singapore island on 31 January 1942 unhinged a defensive system which had not anticipated attack from the mainland. Furthermore, loss of men up-country, along with defeat at sea and in the air, made General A. E. Percival's task almost hopeless. For the British, Indian and Australian reinforcements which had recently arrived were unacclimatized and unready for immediate combat. Bombing of the city and its defences caused severe casualties and further demoralization. Yamashita launched his main assault into the island's north-west corner on the night of 8 February. By dawn on the 9th a bridgehead had been secured against the Australians and two divisions were across. Almost as a formality the advance reached the city outskirts on the 14th as resistance crumbled. Percival surrendered next day. The battle had cost the Japanese 9,284 casualties; 130,000 British were prisoners, 9,000 were killed or wounded.

Sittang River, Battle of. In **Burma** on 31 January 1942, General Thomas Hutton's Burma Army was in retreat from Moulmein towards **Rangoon** with General Shojira Iida's Fifteenth Army in hot pursuit across the River Salween. Hutton gave ground unwillingly and declined to permit a quick move behind the River Sittang. On 21 February the rearguard (17th Indian Division) were crossing when Japanese troops, who had infiltrated upstream, tried to rush the bridge. The garrison held firm until dawn the next day when enemy pressure became intolerable. The divisional commander permitted demolition – leaving much heavy equipment in enemy hands, though most of the men managed to swim to

safety without their weapons. It was a crippling set-back for Burma Army.

Slessor, Air Marshal Sir John (1897–1979). An airman with much operational experience in **World War I**, the 1920s and 1930s who, as a Staff officer, contributed significantly to Royal Air Force policy in **World War II**. In 1943 he commanded Coastal Command at the height of the Battle of the **Atlantic** and in 1944 was Deputy Air C-in-C Allied Forces in the Mediterranean. He retired in 1952 when Chief of the Air Staff and was responsible for formulating and publicizing a rational strategy of ultimate **deterrence** based on nuclear weapons.

Slim, Field Marshal (Viscount) William (1891–1970). An infantryman who saw service at **Gallipoli** and in **Mesopotamia, France** and Belgium in **World War I** and subsequently in India. In **World War II** he commanded a brigade in Eritrea and a division in Iraq and Iran before taking command of I Burma Corps in 1942 during the retreat to India. In October 1943 he took command of Fourteenth Army in time to cope with the Japanese offensives in the **Arakan**, at **Imphal** and **Kohima**. Those victories he exploited brilliantly with resources that were rarely more than adequate – though he did benefit from substantial tactical air and transport support in the drive past Mandalay to **Rangoon** in May 1945.

For a short period in 1948 he left the Army to become Deputy Chairman of British Railways, but was recalled as Chief of the Imperial General Staff in November when he found himself poised for instant resignation owing to a clash with the government. None the less, he survived in the post until 1952 when, as a Field Marshal, he was appointed Governor-General of Australia.

Smart munitions. The problem of destroying pinpoint targets, either from the air or by using long-range artillery, has long exercised the ingenuity of the weapon designer. The bridge, always an important military objective, provides the classic target. Dive-bombers, air-to-surface rockets, conventional bombs – all have been tried, with limited success; while attempting to knock out a bridge using long-range indirect artillery fire inevitably uses up an immense amount of ammunition.

It was not until the 1960s that a worthwhile answer seemed to have been found, in the so-

called 'smart' (i.e. clever) bomb. An early example was the 498kg *Walleye gliding bomb*,
deployed in the Vietnam War in 1967 by the
United States. Controlled from the parent aircraft
via a television camera in the nose of the bomb,
which had movable fins, the device could be
steered to its target with some accuracy.

Far more deadly was the next generation,
which included the 908kg *electro-optical guided
bomb* (EOGB) and the 1362kg *laser-guided
bomb* (LGB). The first was a development of
Walleye, enabling the controller to locate the
target on his television screen and designate it
to the bomb; then leaving the bomb, after release, to find its own way to the target. For the
LGB the target is illuminated from the launch
aircraft with a **laser**, a **sensor** in the bomb detecting the illumination and using the reflection
from it to guide the bomb on its way to a strike.
The success rate against isolated targets in Vietnam was remarkable, with no fewer than 106
bridges being destroyed during a single three-
month period in 1972. The virtues of such
'fire and forget' weapons were demonstrated
in the 1991 **Persian Gulf War** when targets were
attacked with significant precision and minimal
risk to innocent civilians.

The concept of smart munitions has an artillery application also, in the need to attack
armour at long range with indirect fire, with the
particular aim of breaking up a concentration
before an attack can develop. The problem has
been that large-calibre low-velocity shells fired
over long distances inevitably have a wide dis-
persion at the target. Accuracy can be achieved
if some form of guidance can be provided in the
shell itself, perhaps reacting to laser target marking operated by a forward observation officer.
Such a weapon is known as a *cannon-launched
guided projectile*. Future developments using
micro-electronics and millimetric wave radar
may well allow the projectile to seek out the
target for itself.

Smoke in warfare. Firearms introduced a special
dimension to the battlefield when the simultaneous discharge of large numbers of cannon and
muskets blanketed the area in dense clouds of
smoke, to the extent that troops were often
firing blind into the murk; smoke also exposed
otherwise concealed positions. Hence the search,
in the latter part of the 19th century, for smokeless powder to be used as a propellant.

Once smokeless propellants were available it
became obvious, if it had not been appreciated
before, that while 'the fog of war' was a hin-
drance to good shooting, it could be the soldier's
friend in concealing his own tactical movement.
Paradoxically, therefore, the need arose during
World War I for screening smoke. The task was
not as easy as it might appear. Though there are
a number of chemical substances which, when
ignited or exposed to the atmosphere, will give
off clouds of smoke, the problem lies in building
up a screen of sufficient density quickly enough.
There are two main substances used: white phos-
phorus (WP) and hexachlorethane (HCE).

WP has the advantage that it produces a
cloud of very dense white smoke almost instantaneously; ideal for a short-term local screen.
However, it dissipates quickly, pillaring into
the air; furthermore WP has unpleasant anti-
personnel burning effects which can affect
friendly forces. HCE, which is not harmful, tends
to cling to the ground, can be built up into a
long-lasting screen, but takes time to develop. It
is usually contained in several small canisters
carried in artillery shell, bursting on impact.

One of the original ideas for smoke shell was a
filling of 'noxious gases' (see **Chemical warfare**),
intended to make an enemy position untenable.
The need to deal with the armoured personnel
carrier (see **Armoured fighting vehicles**) has
resurrected this idea, since conventional anti-
armour rounds may well immobilize the vehicle
but leave the infantry section within comparatively unscathed. A round has been designed
which will penetrate the crew compartment
and, once within, release a smoke agent, forcing the crew to dismount where they can be
neutralized by small-arms fire.

In the war at sea the introduction of the coal-
fired steam engine immediately produced concealment problems for ships otherwise hidden
below the horizon. Careful trimming of the
furnaces helped to conceal the tell-tale smoke
and some ships were provided with 'smoke
boxes', to which exhaust smoke could be
diverted for short periods, then released to atmosphere later. At other times exhaust smoke from
the funnels could be deliberately increased to
provide tactical concealment. In a modern
diesel-engined ship the order 'make smoke' can
be met by passing unburnt diesel fuel over the
hot exhaust, a similar device for armoured
vehicles having been pioneered by Russia and

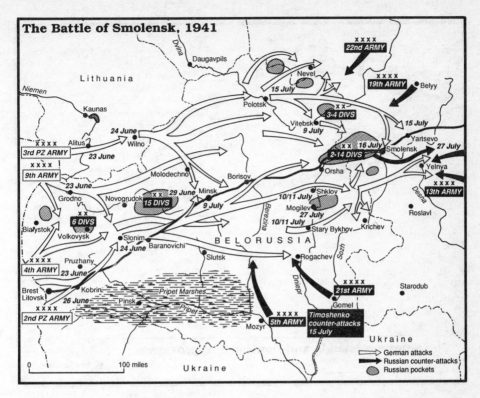

The Battle of Smolensk, 1941

more recently copied in the West; wasteful of fuel, but producing rapid, effective concealment.

Smoke can thus be a friend or enemy on the battlefield, but in either case always subject to the vagaries of wind and weather.

Smolensk, Battles of. The primary objective of Field Marshal von **Bock**'s Army Group Centre at the start of the **Russo-German War** on 22 June 1941 was the route centre of Smolensk. His two **infantry** armies and two **tank** Groups clashed with General D. G. Pavlov's numerically superior West Front, the majority of whose tanks were either unroadworthy or short of fuel and ammunition. By leaps and bounds von Bock overran enemy formations at Minsk on the 29th, though the infantry were finding it difficult to keep up and deal with the bypassed enemy. On 16 July General **Guderian**'s tanks reached Smolensk, bypassing between 12 and 14 enemy divisions. Difficulties of co-ordination, supply shortages and enemy counterstrokes permitted many Russians to escape before the pocket, yielding 100,000 prisoners, 2,000 tanks and 1,900 guns, was cleared on 5 August, opening the way for the advance on **Moscow**.

Smuts, Field Marshal Jan (1870–1950). A great South African statesman who worked for Anglo-Boer understanding but during the **Boer War** led a **Commando** against the British. Before **World War I** he was Minister of Defence and helped General Louis Botha eject the Germans from South-West Africa in 1915. In 1916 he was C-in-C in **East Africa**, but in March 1917 joined the War Cabinet in London to play a strong role in creating the Royal Air Force, among other valuable services. From 1919 to 1924 he was Prime Minister of South Africa and, as Deputy Prime Minister in 1939, defeated the anti-British Prime Minister, J. B. Hertzog, over South Africa's neutrality. Then, as Prime Minister and C-in-C the Armed Forces, he carried the divided nation into **World War II**, in which capacities he travelled the war zones and contributed notably to British and Allied War Councils.

SOE. See **Special Operations Executive**.

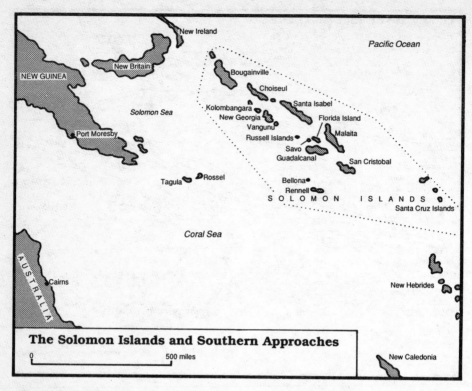

The Solomon Islands and Southern Approaches

0   500 miles

Solomon Sea, Battles of the. The Japanese presence on **Guadalcanal** island and throughout the Solomons in May 1942, along with the Battle of the **Coral Sea**, denoted a turning-point in the **Pacific Ocean War**. Within two months the Allied counter-offensive had opened on Guadalcanal, forcing the Japanese to commit major forces to support their expanded empire's perimeter. In and around the 'Slot' – the central **channel** among the islands – intense naval and air battles took place to sustain the fight for Guadalcanal. Admiral **Fletcher**'s decision on 7 August to withdraw the **aircraft-carriers**, for fear of loss, gave the Japanese an advantage which was enhanced on the 9th at the Battle of Savo Island when four out of eight Allied **cruisers** (one of them Australian) and a **destroyer** were sunk; only one Japanese cruiser went down. This forced the **amphibious** ships to retire from Guadalcanal. Yet the Japanese missed this opportunity to reinforce Guadalcanal until 22 August, by which time Fletcher's three carriers had returned to engage three Japanese carriers under Admiral Nobutake Kondo. At the subsequent Battle of the Eastern Solomons, one American carrier was damaged. But although the Japanese lost a light carrier, a destroyer and 90 aircraft, and had a seaplane carrier damaged, they again failed to press home their attack with **battleships** and cruisers.

On 31 August the Americans had another carrier damaged by a submarine and, on 15 September, lost the carrier *Wasp*, depriving them again of carrier support off Guadalcanal and also that of the battleship *North Carolina*, which was badly damaged by a submarine's torpedoes. Yet from 11 to 13 October at the Battle of Cape Esperanto, both sides simultaneously reinforced Guadalcanal in a remarkable series of events in which the Japanese lost or had damaged, in a night action, three cruisers and three destroyers. They still managed, under Admiral Raizo Tanaka, to take control of the Slot on the 13th and 15th and, with two battleships supported by cruisers and destroyers, bombard Henderson Field on Guadalcanal.

On 18 October Admiral **Halsey** took command in the area and Admiral Thomas Kincaid, now with two carriers, relieved Fletcher. This change almost coincided with an attempt by Admiral **Yamamoto** to have Kondo win a decisive victory against the weakened Americans. At the Battle of Santa Cruz Islands on 26/27 October Kondo almost succeeded, sinking one and damaging the other American carrier, though suffering damage to two of his four carriers from simultaneous attacks by the Americans. But Kondo also lost 100 aircraft and withdrew instead of finishing off the remaining American carrier, as well he might.

On 12 November the struggle reached a climax of almost continuous encounters in three days' fighting as the Japanese strove desperately to reinforce Guadalcanal. With only five cruisers and eight destroyers, Rear-Admiral Daniel Callaghan tried to head off Kondo's two battleships, two cruisers and 14 destroyers in a tumultuous night battle at short range. Kondo lost a battleship and two cruisers (with all other ships damaged) and Callaghan (who was killed) two cruisers and four destroyers, plus all but one of the rest damaged. Day and night the slaughter continued as Kondo forced through his convoy with the loss of seven transports. But when Kincaid sent in two battleships (one of which was instantly put out of action), the *Washington*, using **radar**, fought 14 ships, left one battleship and a destroyer sinking – and conclusively secured American dominance of the Slot. For although the Japanese charged again on 30 November (when they sank an American cruiser off Tassafaronga), on 29 January they declined battle off Rennell's Island, 10 days before successfully evacuating Guadalcanal.

Somme, Battle of the. To take pressure off the French Army at **Verdun**, the British Army, with French support, launched an offensive against the Germans on 24 June 1916 on either side of the River Somme. Like so many attacks in **World War I**, this one by General **Haig** was bent on attrition with no strategic objective. After seven days' bombardment by **artillery**, which lacked sufficient medium and heavy guns and whose **ammunition** was 25 per cent defective, the assault went in on 1 July on a 20-mile front. It made little progress and cost the British alone 60,000 casualties. It continued until 13 November, crawling forward only eight miles and costing the British 420,000 casualties, the French 195,000 and the Germans 650,000.

But though, once more, artillery and infantry failed to open a gap for the **cavalry**, the surprise use of 32 **tanks** on 15 September offered hope for the future.

The battle did succeed in making the Germans desist at Verdun, and it also compelled them to revert to the defensive on all fronts when Generals **Hindenburg** and **Ludendorff** recognized that their Army was demoralized and had lost the cream of its combat leaders. At the same time the British painfully learnt lessons which they applied in subsequent battles.

Sonar. An acronym derived from *sound navigation* and *ranging*, a piezo-electric system using ultrasonic, electromagnetic waves to detect underwater objects, particularly **submarines**. Invented by the British and French in 1918, it directs short pulses towards an object (and, of course, the sea-bed) which are reflected and then detected, the lapse of time being measured to give distance to the object. It was not ready for use in **World War I**, however.

Developed during the 1920s and 1930s and called ASDIC (after the Anti-Submarine Detection Investigation Committee) by the British, it was assumed (in insufficiently exhaustive trials which, even so, produced only 50 per cent detections) to provide the answer to the submarine menace. This complacency deflected attention from submarine warfare and **anti-submarine weapon** systems, until experience by British **destroyers** hunting submarines during the **Spanish Civil War** discovered that all was not well. The troubles were multifarious. Sometimes the pulse would reflect from debris or a shoal of fish, placing demands upon the interpretative skill of the operator – or a submarine might escape detection from the pulse altogether by diving below different temperature levels. This meant that, even after a firm contact had been made, an astute submarine commander could evade the enemy by skilful manoeuvres. On the other hand, the click heard by submarine crews when the pulse made contact on the hull could have a demoralizing and deterrent effect, especially when followed by the crash of nearby depth charges.

As **World War II** progressed, improved Sonar equipment was produced and integrated with more effective weapon systems and improved tracking techniques to deal with deeper-diving submarines: in April 1943 the British developed an Asdic which could, in some circumstances, maintain contact with a deeply submerged boat; and Asdic Type 147B could measure a submarine's depth – a capability which made it worth fitting Sonar in submarines. Then in February 1945 a British boat, using passive Sonar, detected and plotted an enemy boat and struck it with a straight-running torpedo (noting that when a submarine uses active Sonar to detect its prey, it also advertises its own presence).

Since World War II intensive efforts have been undertaken by the major naval powers to improve Sonar in the crucial fight against deep-diving, quiet-running submarines. More powerful and sensitive sets are not enough. It has been found expedient to use **aircraft** far more: for example, by dropping patterns of Sonar buoys to detect, fix and transmit to the aircraft or a ship sufficient data to give the exact location of a boat which happens to be beyond the range of ship-borne instruments; or by employing hovering **helicopters** with a 'dipping Sonar', a device which is winched below the temperature layers to improve the chances of a contact and send back sufficient information, via **computers**, upon which to base an accurate attack. Sonar is not infallible; just another important aid among the many weapon systems of anti-submarine forces in a never-ending contest of technologies and techniques.

South African wars. To the age-long struggles between indigenous South African Black peoples was added, in the mid 19th century, the contests between Boers and the British as they expanded northwards from Cape Colony. From 1850 to 1878 there were the **Kaffir Wars**, involving all three racial elements as the Boer Republic was formed in 1852 and established itself in Transvaal. Then, in the Orange Free State, the displaced Basuto tribe under King Mosheshu fought the Boers from 1858 to 1868 until Britain annexed Basutoland to curb Boer ambitions. This period was enlivened from 1862 to 1864 by rival Boer groups fighting each other in the Transvaal Civil War; and then in 1877 by the British, urged on by local, anti-Boer traders, seizing the Transvaal. In 1879 there was the **Zulu War** in which, at **Isandhlwana**, the British suffered a bad, temporary set-back.

But then came the Transvaal Revolt, sometimes known the *First Boer War*, when in January 1881 Petrus Joubert led 2,000 Boers into Natal and defeated 1,400 British at Laing's

Nek on the 28th. This was followed by the Battle of Majuba on 27 February when 550 Boers, using superior **rifle** fire and fieldcraft, again beat the British, to regain the independence of Transvaal under Boer government. Henceforward, as the British put down a Zulu rebellion in 1887 and, in 1893, crushed the Matabele tribe when it tried to conquer the Mashona, the British and Boers were spoiling for a fight. A raid by 500 British under Dr L. Starr Jameson on 29 December 1895 (intended by Cecil Rhodes to stimulate an uprising by British residents in Transvaal to advance his dream of a unified South Africa under British control) was rounded up by Boer **Commandos** at Krugersdorp on 2 January 1896.

Tension mounted, however, as Britain concluded a non-intervention agreement with Germany in 1898 and prepared for the *Second Boer War*, which broke out on 11 October 1899 on the expiry of an ultimatum from the Boers demanding cancellation of British **mobilization**, announced on 22 September. The ensuing battles were between the highly mobile marksmen of the Boer Commandos and the better-disciplined but, at first, over-confident and not so well-led British Army. But although the Boers were able to invade British territory and besiege Mafeking, Ladysmith and Kimberley in the first few days, and also win certain dramatic encounters, they were neither well-enough organized and armed nor **logistically** prepared for war against a major power, armed with **machine-guns** and the latest equipment which, by **blockade** and political pressure, excluded all outside assistance. Nevertheless, in the approaches to Ladysmith in October, the British were forced back, and at Modder River on 28 November, when advancing to the relief of Kimberley, made to retire in exhaustion after losing a fire-fight. Meanwhile at Stormberg, on 10 December, a raiding Commando ambushed a British force at the same time as, at Magersfontein, another British force was on the verge of being repulsed with 1,000 casualties by 8,000 Boers entrenched on a hill.

Next the British Corps, sent from England, advanced under General Sir Redvers **Buller** to the relief of Ladysmith and was successively beaten by General Louis Botha at Colenso on 15 December, at Spion Kop on 23 January 1900 and at Vaal Kranz on 5 February. But the arrival of Field Marshal Lord **Roberts** as C-in-C, and a reorganization of the Army by his Chief of Staff,

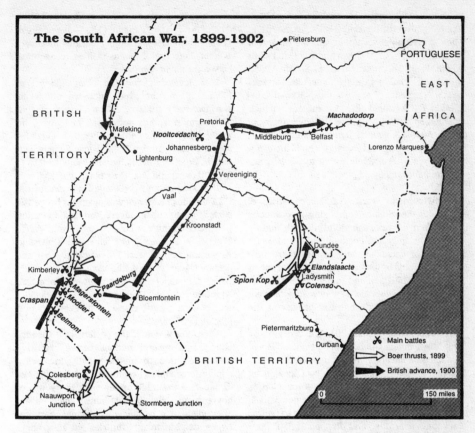

The South African War, 1899-1902

Pietersburg

PORTUGUESE

EAST

AFRICA

BRITISH

Mafeking

Nooitcedacht✗

Johannesberg

Lightenburg

Pretoria

Machadodorp

Middleburg   Belfast

Lorenzo Marques

TERRITORY

Vereeniging

Vaal

Kroonstadt

Dundee

Kimberley

Paardeburg

Magerstontein

Modder R.

Elandslaacte

Ladysmith

Spion Kop ✗   ✗ Colenso

Craspan

Belmont

Bloemfontein

Pietermaritzburg

Durban

BRITISH TERRITORY

Colesberg

Naauwport
Junction

Stormberg Junction

✗ Main battles

⟹ Boer thrusts, 1899

⟹ British advance, 1900

0   150 miles

General **Kitchener** (which did as much harm as good), paved the way for the advance under General **French** which relieved Kimberley on 15 February. And although Kitchener's incompetence at Paardeberg on the 18th led to a local defeat by the main Boer force under General Piet Cronjé, it was only a matter of time (extended owing to both sides' chaotic logistic arrangements) before Cronjé was forced to surrender at Paardeberg on 27 February. Ladysmith was relieved on the 28th by Buller; the Orange Free State and Transvaal were invaded; Mafeking relieved on 18 May; and Pretoria taken on 13 June as the routed Boers were pursued into Portuguese East Africa. The subsequent **guerrilla war** continued until May 1902 with terrible hardships on the Boer side, but the end was inevitable in a war costing nearly 29,000 British and an unknown number of Boer casualties, including those who died of disease in **concentration camps**.

Yet in April 1915 it was Generals **Smuts** and Botha who took the British side to lead South African columns against Germany's South-West Africa colony, which they had acquired in 1884. In this campaign 9,000 German troops, under General von Heyerdebreck, withdrew into the interior, rapidly pursued by up to 50,000 well-supplied opponents until surrendering on 9 July, after a battle fought on territory thereafter called Namibia where, since 1975 in the aftermath of the Portuguese Revolution, there has been a frontier guerrilla war associated with the fighting in Angola (see **West African wars**).

This struggle has threatened South Africa, as have those going on along her North-East frontiers, the extension of the guerrilla war between White and Black nationalists within Southern Rhodesia, which came to an end with a Black victory in 1979 and the establishment of modern Zimbabwe. A similar struggle since 1964 in Portuguese East Africa produced an

303

independent Marxist Mozambique in 1975, where fighting still continues between the ruling Marxist Frelimo government and the insurgent Renamo which, in 1979, withdrew into South Africa. From there, on behalf of South Africa, the latter has conducted guerrilla attacks against elements of the African National Congress (ANC), based in Mozambique, which operates sporadically against the government of South Africa. A government that, in defence of White supremacy and *apartheid*, has ruled in a state of semi-siege, while trying to weaken her Black neighbours by all possible means.

South American wars. The 13 countries of this huge continent, comprising populations drawn from all over the world, though mainly from Spain, Italy and Portugal, have endured a fair share of wars. Until very recently these have been conducted by forces armed by the European powers and the USA; and sometimes with great ferocity on a large scale. Few new lessons were learnt. This entry concentrates briefly on the major wars.

The López War (1864–70). The struggle by Argentina, Banda Oriental (Uruguay) and Brazil to overcome Paraguay under her predatory dictator, Francisco López. Attacks by López on all three nations persuaded them to form a Triple Alliance, which took six years, six major battles, heavy losses and a **guerrilla** campaign to reduce Paraguay to ruins, and its population from 1,400,000 to 221,000.

The Peruvian–Spanish War (1864–6). Spain's attempts to settle its differences with Peru by force prompted Chile, Bolivia and Ecuador to form defensive alliances with Peru and fight back. This was mainly a minor naval war, which operated to Spain's political disadvantage before she called it off and accepted mediation by the USA.

The Pacific War (1879–84). A mainly **amphibious** war for control of mineral resources in which Chile fought Peru and Boliva when the latter combine oppressed Chilean prospecting companies. In the war the newly formed Chilean Navy won control of the sea to **blockade** Peru and then invade coastal regions with forces up to 20,000 strong. The campaign eventually won vital Peruvian and Bolivian territory for Chile.

In **World War I** only Brazil declared war, for political advantage, against Germany in October 1918. And until the 1930s the continent was stirred only by revolutions in Colombia (1900–3), in Peru (1914), Ecuador (1924–5) and Brazil (1924), plus random border clashes involving Bolivia, Peru and Chile, as well as competition between Bolivia and Paraguay.

This developed into the *Gran Chaco War (1932–5)*, a fight which included minor **air warfare**, for control of a large border region. The German-trained Bolivian Army proved no match for a vastly expanded, 60,000-strong Paraguayan Army, under Colonel José Estigarribia, which crushed the Bolivians (who lost over 30,000 men) and won their political objectives.

The political and economic influence of the USA on South America was never far below the surface in the 20th century and had a bearing on these countries' behaviour during **World War II**. By January 1942, all except Chile and Argentina (which were Fascist-orientated) had declared war against the Axis, though only Brazil sent troops to fight in Italy. Chile and Argentina did not feel constrained to declare war however, until, respectively, February and March 1945.

After World War II the pattern of bellicosity changed as several nations began extensive industrialization to match rapidly increasing populations; and as Communist intrigue further destabilized the traditionally volatile systems of government. Revolutions and *coups d'état* abounded. In a period when formal wars between neighbouring countries fell into abeyance, insurrection and guerrilla warfare was spread across frontiers in the aftermath of Fidel **Castro**'s seizure of power in Cuba in 1959. His widespread Marxist movement, strongly supported by Russia, met the resistance of right-wing, militarist dictatorships in many a violent struggle for power; notably in Paraguay, Bolivia, Brazil and Argentina. Yet South America, so involved with its own troubles, rarely looked outwards except to trade. The major exception was Argentina's adventure in 1982 which caused the disastrous, undeclared **Falklands** War against Britain.

South-East Asia campaigns. As a political entity, the European-dominated area consisting of Burma, French Indo-China (Vietnam), Malaya, Borneo and the Dutch East Indies (Indonesia) did not achieve recognition until **World War II** when **Japanese expansion** loomed large from the north. But starting in December 1941 it suffered from many great encounters (see **Burma, Malaya, Singapore, Sumatra and Java Battles**) and was on the fringe of the **Pacific Ocean War** and the **Philippines** battles prior to Japan's final defeat in 1945. Thereupon it was afflicted by the **Indonesian, Malayan** and **Vietnam wars of independence** and the **Cambodia** battles, struggles which took place against a background of concern about Communist Chinese and Russian intervention. The latter prompted the creation of **SEATO**, a treaty whose signatories by their variable contributions guaranteed, by military and political means, the state of reasonable stability achieved in the 1980s.

Space vehicles. The development, under German leadership during **World War II** of **rockets and guided missiles** ensured the advent of space travel, in special vehicles. When in 1957 the Russians put a 184lb sphere called Sputnik I into an orbit around the earth of between 143 and 584 miles, they initiated fierce competition between the superpowers and a new sort of military contest. Indeed, the vast majority of the innumerable vehicles sent into space since have been of military use. They fall into three categories: those orbiting the earth at altitudes below 22,300 miles; those which are in geostationary orbit at that height; and those which escape the earth's gravity and fly into deep space. It is the first two with which this entry is mainly concerned.

Military space vehicles have many functions: **communications, surveillance,** weather forecasting, **navigation** and use as missile platforms. From the start **radio** signals linked vehicles to earth for monitoring and control. It was only a matter of time, therefore, before messages and, in 1961, **television** pictures, would be relayed from one part of the earth to another via a satellite vehicle. The technique was rapidly enhanced by **electronic** discoveries and **computers** which enabled solar-powered, geostationary vehicles to provide continuous, multi-channel communications world-wide, or to eavesdrop on electronic communications not normally receivable by any other method. Cameras (see **Photography**) were also set up at an early stage to bring back or transmit pictures of the earth's surface – with significant **reconnaissance** and **charts and maps** potential. Not only was it possible for orbiting satellites to obtain detailed pictures for **intelligence** purposes, far more accurate

charts and maps also could be drawn which made possible precise navigation as well as pinpoint delivery of missiles to their targets. The process is amplified by the use of **sensors** to detect electronic radiations from an almost unlimited range of sources. This facility made concealment and *electronic countermeasures* (ECM) more vital and difficult than ever.

American space vehicles began to be used in combat situations for weather forecasting in 1965 during the **Vietnam War.** In the 1973 Yom Kippur War (**Arab–Israeli wars**) Russian surveillance satellites kept the Egyptians informed of the extent of the Israeli penetration across the Suez Canal. In 1982, America diverted orbiting satellites to assist the British during the **Falklands** War. There have been other occasions when these vehicles have been of immense use in providing intelligence to a client, but they are of far greater **deterrence** value since they help reduce the possibility of military surprise by such secretive nations as Russia, which has traditionally forbidden foreign access to its lands – not just sensitive localities. Equipped with cameras and sensors satellites are constantly on watch for signs of unusual and threatening activity.

To help achieve maximum effect from missiles it might be desirable to destroy space vehicles that can detect their launch. Anti-satellite vehicles and weapon systems thus have a part to play and are being developed – and might also have to deal with weapon systems aboard orbiting space vehicles. It would also be desirable to eliminate or disrupt enemy communications and surveillance systems. Such attacks could not be performed in isolation, they would break treaties and constitute acts of war, with the same consequences as violations in international waters or land invasion. (See also **Strategic Arms Limitation Treaties, Strategic Defence Initiative** (SDI) and **Technology, Effects of.**)

Spanish–American War. American involvement in the **Cuban War** with Spain in 1895, the shrill anti-Spanish **propaganda** of the Hearst and Pulitzer Press and the blowing-up in Havana harbour of the US **battleship** *Maine* (probably owing to accidental detonation of its magazine) quite unexpectedly landed the USA at war with Spain on 25 April 1898. Neither side was ready, least of all the American Army, whose **mobilization** was a farce and **logistics** in chaos from administrative inadequacies and dire shortages. It was hard-pressed to raise the existing force of 28,000 to 68,000 in time to invade Cuba on 22 June. The US Navy, however, was ready. On 1 May Commodore George Dewey's five **cruisers** and two gunboats steamed into Manila Harbour in the **Philippines** and, for only eight wounded, sank a technically outclassed Spanish squadron of four cruisers and six other vessels, and subdued the local forts. Yet not until 30 June did 10,000 soldiers arrive from America and, with the help of Filipino **guerrillas**, at last capture blockaded Manila on 13 August.

Meanwhile the Spanish Fleet, with four cruisers and three destroyers, had evaded Rear-Admiral William Sampson's fleet of five battleships and two cruisers and, on 19 May, entered Santiago harbour in Cuba. There it was at once **blockaded** and, like the Spanish Army of 200,000 under General Arsénio Linares, remained passive when an American army of 17,000 under General William Shafter disembarked near Santiago. There were no horses or mules for six regiments of US Cavalry or their transport; and the wagons and ambulances provided were quite unsuitable for the rough tracks and terrain. Moreover, malaria and yellow fever, which were rife at the landing-place, at once infected the entire invading force.

Yet at the Battles of San Juan and El Caney on 1 July, the Americans defeated a Spanish force of 35,000 and penned 13,000 of them in Santiago, compelling the Spanish Fleet to make a dash for the sea – straight into the guns of the US Fleet in Santiago Bay where they were wiped out at a cost to the Americans of one killed and one wounded. On shore, however, the American Army was wasting away from disease: it only required Santiago's garrison commander to hold on and they would have departed. As it was he supinely surrendered on 17 July, allowing the Americans to ship home their men for quarantine on Long Island.

On 4 August, 5,000 Americans landed in Puerto Rico and, in a sensibly organized campaign, had almost mopped up the demoralized Spaniards before hostilities were brought to an end on 13 August. Nevertheless, this revelation of the American Army's shortcomings paid a dividend in modernization as it entered the 20th century.

Spanish Civil War. The fall of the Spanish Monarchy in 1930 and the divisions between the Left and Right political groups, plus various provincial demands for autonomy which frequently lapsed into violence, by the summer of 1936 had made Spain almost ungovernable. On 13 July an army mutiny, under General **Franco** in Morocco, provided the spark for a civil war throughout the mainland. The contest rapidly resolved itself into a fight between Franco's Nationalist Fascist forces (supported by Germany and Italy) and the Communist-inspired government forces (supported by Russia and Mexico and left-wing enthusiasts).

From its initial power bases in the south and north-west (less the Basque province in the north), the Nationalists developed a strategy aimed at seizing **Madrid** and clearing the country from west to east. With the cream of the Army on his side and the so-called **fifth column** working underground in **guerrilla warfare**, Franco was able in August to make rapid progress. The Nationalists seized Badajoz (to link up their western holdings) and advanced to within striking distance of Madrid, which was besieged in November. Soon, too, the Basques were driven into Bilbao, which was besieged on 1 April 1937, and chased out of Guernica after a heavy tactical bombing attack on the 25th in support of ground forces, which Russian **propaganda** brilliantly exploited as an example of typical Fascist bestiality. By then the international character of the war was plain. Attempts by the League of Nations to contain the war went on against a background of manpower and logistic assistance by the Fascist and Communist powers. Both sides attempted **blockade** to cut off the import of equipment and supplies, but neither had naval or air forces capable of the task, nor could they sink or stop and search neutral shipping with impunity for fear of the international ructions that would result. Even so, there were many incidents involving British, French and American warships (of the International Patrol) which were trying to protect neutral merchant ships (many of which were sunk or damaged) against Spanish, German and Italian aircraft and warships, including **submarines**.

By 1937 the Germans and Italians had substantial ground and air forces involved (including the **Condor Legion**). By then too the government had also been reinforced by modern Russian equipment and sympathetic inter-

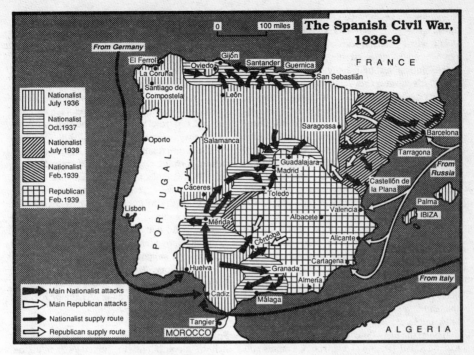

The Spanish Civil War, 1936-9

0   100 miles

From Germany

El Ferrol · Oviedo · Gijón · Santander · Guernica · San Sebastián · FRANCE
La Coruña
Santiago de Compostela · León
Oporto · Salamanca · Saragossa · Barcelona
Tarragona
Guadalajara · Madrid · *From Russia*
PORTUGAL · Cáceres · Toledo · Castellón de la Plana
Lisbon · Mérida · Albacete · Valencia · Palma
Córdoba · Alicante · IBIZA
Huelva · Granada · Cartagena · Almería · *From Italy*
Cadiz · Málaga
Tangier · ALGERIA
MOROCCO

Nationalist July 1936
Nationalist Oct.1937
Nationalist July 1938
Nationalist Feb.1939
Republican Feb.1939

Main Nationalist attacks
Main Republican attacks
Nationalist supply route
Republican supply route

national volunteers for the fight against Fascism, and that year Nationalist expansion was largely contained. Two Italian divisions made a very poor showing in the Battle of Guadalajara in March. Madrid held out, although Bilbao fell in June and the government offensives with Russian **tanks** and **aircraft** near Madrid in July, and in Aragón in August and September, merely prolonged a stalemate. The situation partially loosened after the Nationalists checked a government attack at Teruel early in 1938 and, starting in February, drove the enemy back towards Tarragona and Barcelona. The victory was denied conclusive rewards when the government counter-attacked along the River Ebro at the end of July to stabilize the front.

But the government forces were suffering from the same innumerable differences of opinion within their ranks that had made them vulnerable in 1936. When the Nationalists attacked again towards Tarragona and Barcelona on 23 December, this vital front began to disintegrate along with government **morale** everywhere. Barcelona fell on 26 January 1939. Next day Britain and France recognized Franco's government as Russian support began to dwindle. When Madrid fell on 28 March it

was the signal for the government to lay down its arms next day.

Various estimates put total losses from battle, air raids and political executions at close on one million. The country was ruined in what, for the military of the major Fascist and Communist powers, was treated as a trial for some of their latest equipments, though by no means all their techniques. For example **armoured** forces were not properly employed in the deep penetration role, and **strategic bombing** was not deliberately practised. In the main, these 'new' arms used embellished **World War I** tactics, without revealing their true potential or flaws.

Special forces. The history of war is littered with élite units formed to carry out specialist roles requiring outstanding prowess and a high standard of training. More often than not they have been recruited from volunteers of high intelligence and strong physique. In this entry only uniformed units are considered, although even these have been known to operate in plain clothes on the fringes of the **laws of war**. The action by Major John Norton-Griffiths and his batman in organizing the destruction, with civilian assistance, of the Romanian oilfields in

307

November 1916 may be considered a special-forces epic – just. Such acts were rare in **World War I**, when **guerrilla warfare** was unusual, but not infrequent between the wars and, for example, during the **Spanish Civil War** by members of the **fifth column** and Communist groups.

In its modern sense the term may be said to originate with the use by the German military intelligence service (*Abwehr*) of the **Brandenburg Regiment** for raiding and counter-guerrilla tasks. But the Germans were never enthusiastic raiders, leaving it to the British with their formation in July 1940 of the **Commandos** to develop hit-and-run attacks against the enemy coast. From their ranks emerged, within a few weeks, **airborne forces** and a Special Boat Section to operate from folding canoes. The latter would expand into Special Boat Squadrons (each known as SBS) which, like Commandos, still are part of the Royal Marines; Combined Operations Pilotage Parties (COPP), whose role in canoes or other small craft was beach reconnaissance and the guidance of **amphibious** forces to their landing-places; and such canoe demolition parties as the Royal Marine Boom Patrol Detachment (RMBPD) and 14 (Arctic) Commando which, like the SBS, also were experts at attaching limpet mines to enemy ships. Also derived from the Commandos was the Special Air Service (SAS), along with units like Popski's Private Army, which began life in **North Africa** in 1941 for desert raiding alongside the Long-Range Desert Group (LRDG), whose primary role was reconnaissance behind the enemy lines in the desert but who readily adapted to other environments. The latter were both disbanded after **World War II**, along with Army Commandos, but the SAS was re-formed as a very special, discreet raiding élite in **cold** and **limited war** operations, as well as for stay-behind parties and, in many celebrated incidents, armed aid to the civil power when a terrorist situation got beyond police capability.

There have been many imitators. In World War II the Americans formed Marine Raider and Army Ranger units which copied and, to begin with, were trained by the British Commandos. Within the **Office of Strategic Services** (OSS) they also formed uniformed operational groups which helped organize guerrilla parties behind the enemy lines in Europe under British **Special Operations Executive** (SOE) directions. Many governments have raised SAS-type units

for counter-terrorist actions that require extremely sophisticated weapons and techniques.

In 1952 the Americans formed Army Special Forces on Operational Group lines to work with guerrillas behind the enemy lines. In 1957 they were introduced into Vietnam to organize civilian groups against North Vietnamese infiltration into the South. They developed and expanded this role throughout the war until, at peak, they were controlling 42,000 members of Civilian Irregular Defence Groups (CIDG), besides forming South Vietnam's special forces. In 1961 President John Kennedy authorized them to wear a green beret, an honour they were to justify in many other areas of conflict besides Vietnam.

Russia and her allies also field special forces, generally known as Spetsnaz, whose role is raiding and the support of subversive elements in enemy territory. They were used for counter-insurgency work in **Afghanistan** and are fully expected to be in the lead of any major Russian operation of the future.

Special Operations Executive (SOE). When Britain stood alone in July 1940, Winston **Churchill**'s government decided that the only immediate ways of striking back at the Axis were through **strategic bombing** plus subversion and **guerrilla warfare**. To execute the latter and 'set Europe ablaze' they formed SOE, under a junior Minister, Hugh Dalton, within the Ministry of Economic Warfare (MEW). Its initial membership consisted of certain Army officers already involved with these practices and a handful of city bankers and the like who recruited the remainder of what was an amateur organization that learnt as it went. Inevitably its existence was resented by other Ministries, particularly the Foreign Office and its **Secret Service**, and there were always problems of co-ordination when it overlapped into the territories of **intelligence**, the three Service ministries and the Combined Operations Directorate (which some thought should be merged with SOE for hit-and-run raiding).

SOE formed specialist departments, including one for each enemy-occupied country of Europe, where it began sending agents to create the cells and communication systems needed to receive weapons and supplies for sabotage groups and secret armies. It also set up branches in the other theatres of war: North Africa and

South-East Asia. Progress was slow; resistance to the sowing of civil strife and sabotage was strong and universal. Political rivalries and divisions were pronounced as SOE groups found themselves not only fighting skilful enemy counter-subversion agencies but also involved in 'friendly' national politics. There were many set-backs and disasters due to inevitable errors and the incompetence of inadequately trained agents and from flawed systems. Attempts to abolish or restrict SOE were common. Not until 1943 did it begin to show results from its many cells throughout Europe (less those in Holland which were penetrated early by the Germans and never developed their potential), armed from air drops and improved by training. Wherever Allied troops advanced into Axis-held countries the way would be prepared to some extent by SOE-run groups of saboteurs who also provided invaluable intelligence. But, to the end, most of the larger secret armies waited until 'the time was ripe' – meaning when the enemy had almost departed. For the perils and penalties of resistance were terrifying from ruthless enemy measures which created from the outset many martyrs.

SOE was disbanded quickly after the war. To what extent it contributed to final victory is impossible to evaluate, if only because subversion and sabotage are unquantifiable and the story, riddled by legend, untruths and exaggerations, can never be wholly told. But it can be said that, because of the collaboration with the **Office of Strategic Services** (OSS) and various other national groups, the Axis was somewhat diverted and that many post-war political conditions were, for better or worse, formed.

SS (*Schutzstaffel*). Adolf **Hitler**'s bodyguard; formed in 1922, it became known as Protection Squads in 1925 and SS again in 1932 when Hitler came to power. Under Heinrich Himmler it conspired to expand and enter almost every sphere of Germany, from government downwards through the judiciary and police forces, industry and the armed forces to become a state within the state. It recruited hard, unscrupulous people, many of criminal tendencies, who were dedicated to the service of Hitler. It operated secret police, ran the **concentration camps** and racial extermination campaigns and, in 1934, formed a military wing known as the *Waffen* (Armed) SS. This was formed into *Standarten*

(regiments) which, in the years to come, would be grouped into SS brigades, divisions, corps and armies that recruited the cream of available men (including foreigners), and benefited from larger establishments and better equipment than ordinary Army organizations. It is likely that, without the SS, Hitler's regime would have been brought down long before Germany suffered the final ravages of **World War II**, so tight was its grip on the nation from 1942 onwards.

Staffs, Military. Composed of the officers who assist commanders to organize, control, train and supply military units and formations in peace and war. Trained in staff colleges, they are an élite which plans and also advises the commander while directing the supporting services. In modern organizations they work in headquarters divided into five branches (which often are known by letters, such as G or S, and numbers) co-ordinated by a Chief of Staff or the senior Operations Staff Officer. For example:

G1 deals with personnel, disciplinary matters, awards and ceremonial.

G2 with **intelligence**.

G3 co-ordinates and deals with operations.

G4 deals with **logistics**.

G5 with civil affairs.

Branches are staffed by officers classified by grades: the 3rd grade is often a captain who deals with routine, day-to-day matters; the 2nd a major who deals with policy, planning and future events; and the 1st a lieutenant-colonel who co-ordinates in close consultation with the commander, while thinking further ahead.

Commanders, who have always required staffs, needed them even more when formal organizations became commoner in the 17th century. Their functions have widened and numbers increased as much in proportion to additional units and formations as to enlarged **logistic** requirements and to **technological effects**. The need thus arose for war academies (like the one set up in Holland in 1617 by John of Nassau) and the specialist staff colleges (like universities) which were developed as the result of experience during the Napoleonic wars in the early 19th century (see **Education, Military**). These were followed by the setting-up by General Helmuth von **Moltke** of the Great Prussian General Staff, composed of most carefully selected staff officers of outstanding character, intellect, initiative and high moral tone. Its officers were trained to express themselves fearlessly and control subordinate formations and units through the issue of general directives rather than detailed orders. The system which called for precise procedures linked to carefully studied doctrine, became the model for all staffs to follow. It applied not only to Armies but also to Navies (the US Naval War College was the first, in 1884) and, in due course, to Air Forces.

The increasing complexity of technology and logistics, after 1850, naturally imposed far heavier demands on staffs. To begin with they tended to be slow in adapting to advances in science, which required them either to become themselves strongly aware technically, or to welcome specialist technical staff officers within their cult. For example, the German General Staff, for all its reputation, did not come fully to grips with the characteristics of the latest **communications** systems and **mechanization**. As a result, Germany lost the Battle of the **Marne** in 1914. Nor did the opening of Technical Staff Colleges prior to **World War II** close the divide between General Staff officers and the technical officers whom they disdained, although commanders and staff officers such as Field Marshal **Kesselring**, General **Guderian** and Air Marshal **Dowding** were notable exceptions.

World War II also underlined the need, already realized, for joint and combined staffs. The more it became necessary for sea, land and air forces, as well as allies, to work together under one commander, the more he required harmonized staffs, regardless of service, arm or nationality. The supreme example of this was the Allied Expeditionary Force which, under General **Eisenhower**, invaded Europe in 1944, controlled by an integrated, international staff. It was this organization which began to develop the standard operating procedures that Nato's international staff system employs today, largely using English for its highly diverse communication system.

Stalin, Josef (1879–1953). A Georgian who came to note as agitator, **propagandist** and guerrilla leader in the Russian Revolution of 1905 and as a prominent politico-military leader during the **Russian revolutionary wars**. In 1917 Vladimir Lenin made him People's Commissar with a seat on the Military Council under Leon Trotsky, who used him as an Inspector of the Army in a trouble-shooting role which included organizing

the defence of Tsaritsyn (**Stalingrad**) in 1918, Petrograd (**Leningrad**) in 1919, and in 1920 the **Polish Campaign** and the defeat of General Petr Wrangel's White Army. In 1924 he succeeded Lenin to become dictator and generalissimo of Soviet Russia, a position he used to reorganize and modernize the armed forces, with emphasis on the Army and Air arm.

An utterly ruthless person, he purged the nation and armed forces so thoroughly of their best leaders in the 1930s that, when the threat of war with Japan and Germany became unmistakable, all were in a deplorable state of fear, inefficiency and demoralization. The fumbled **Finland Campaign** of 1939/40 exposed deficiencies which could not be rectified in time for the German invasion of June 1941. This was one reason for Stalin's desperate attempts to appease **Hitler**, his refusal to adopt defence measures until the last moment, and thus a cause of the Russian débâcle. During the **Russo-German War** he overcentralized command, although gradually growing to trust and delegate more authority to selected generals, above all **Zhukov**.

Politically, Stalin won immense post-war gains for Russia in the 'liberated' territories, a traditionally Russian expansionist policy he pursued with vigour to bring about the **Cold War** and such incidents as the **Berlin** siege in 1948–9 that stiffened Western resistance.

Stalingrad, Battle of. Under its name of Tsaritsyn, this city on the River Volga was an important objective for the White armies during the **Russian Revolutionary War**. From June to November 1918 it was a Bolshevik bastion. In 1919 it became the objective of General Petr Wrangel's White Army during General Anton **Denikin**'s abortive attempt to link up with Admiral Kolchak's Army. But again it held out until 17 June, by which time the Whites were crumbling to destruction.

In the summer of 1942 it became the objective of General Friederich von Paulus's Sixth Army – the flank guard and subsidiary operation of Hitler's thrust to seize the Caucasian oilfields until Hitler became obsessed by the urge to capture a place named after Josef **Stalin** who, for a month in 1918, had ruled it. The ensuing battle of attrition in the streets was more to the Russian than the German advantage, since it weakened and then starved the thrust into the Caucasus. By October Hitler had committed the

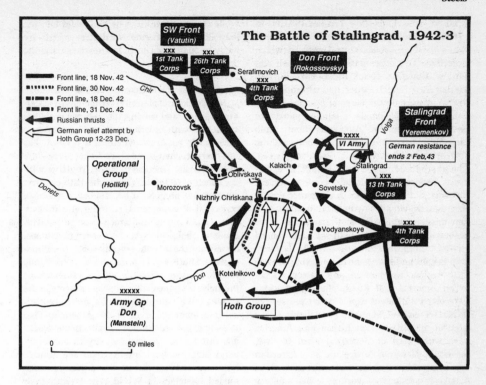

The Battle of Stalingrad, 1942-3

SW Front (Vatutin)

xxx 1st Tank Corps

xxx 26th Tank Corps

Serafimovich

Don Front (Rokossovsky)

xxx 4th Tank Corps

Chir

Front line, 18 Nov. 42
Front line, 30 Nov. 42
Front line, 18 Dec. 42
Front line, 31 Dec. 42
Russian thrusts
German relief attempt by Hoth Group 12-23 Dec.

Volga

Stalingrad Front (Yeremenkov)

xxxx VI Army

German resistance ends 2 Feb. 43

Operational Group (Hollidt)

Donets

Morozovsk

Oblivskaya

Kalach

Stalingrad

Sovetsky

xxx 13 th Tank Corps

Nizhniy Chriskana

Vodyanskoye

xxx 4th Tank Corps

Don

Kotelnikovo

xxxxx Army Gp Don (Manstein)

Hoth Group

0   50 miles

mobile Fourth Panzer Army to Stalingrad and closed down other fronts. But on 19 November greatly reinforced Russian forces under General **Zhukov** were launched against the thinly held flanks of the German salient. Within five days he had trapped the Germans, whom Hitler refused to let break out but, instead, put on inadequate air supply in worsening weather, having instructed Field Marshal von **Manstein** to relieve them.

In appalling conditions, from 12 to 23 December, von Manstein battled to within 35 miles of the garrison, but then was struck by a heavy counter-attack which threw his exhausted Army back to **Kharkov**. Von Paulus's men were left to their fate against Russian attacks which consumed them on 31 January 1943.

The city is now called Volgograd.

Steels. It was Henry Bessemer's 1856 process for making mild steel by decarbonizing molten pig-iron with an air blast that provided the first cheap method of mass production. The military applications were almost endless and the improvements to equipment immediate, especially in **artillery** where barrels and projectiles made of

steel were able to withstand greater pressures, resulting in more powerful, less bulky weapons with greater range and destructive power.

Early armoured warships used wrought iron, which tended to shatter when struck. Steel was more resilient and, when special alloys began to appear in the 1880s, many developed by Robert Hadfield, steel armour proved its worth, not only for warships but, later in **World Wars I** and II, for **tanks**. Armour was further improved in the 1930s by the development of nickel–chromium–molybdenum steels, and rolled homogeneous armour has generally been used on tanks ever since, with various improvements in quality and as a basis for special armour arrangements combined with other materials. At the same time steel is the essential basis of armour-piercing shot designed to penetrate armour protection.

Tank tracks too, at first notoriously short-lived, have benefited from the development of manganese steel, to the extent that nowadays tracks rarely need replacement.

Steel has become as essential an ingredient of military equipment as it is in most aspects of civilian life.

Strategic Arms Limitation Treaties (SALT). In 1968 the nuclear powers, less France and China, signed the Non-Proliferation Treaty to which more than 100 other nations added their signatures. However, Israel, India, Pakistan and South Africa, which either had aspirations to possess or were on the verge of possessing nuclear weapons, abstained – a familiar pattern in **disarmament** matters. After this damp squib came talks from 1969 to 1979 between the nuclear powers, but chiefly America and Russia, which produced the SALT 1 and 2 agreements designed to limit and control nuclear weapons. But by then a fresh arms race was in progress involving deployment of the latest Russian missiles, which led to fresh suspicions of insincerity on the part of both sides and refusal by the Americans to ratify SALT 2. Since then Britain and France have refused to include their nuclear weapons in any agreement between America and Russia and negotiations have taken a different aspect under pressure of Russia's President Mikhail Gorbachev's skilful political initiatives. Both Russia and America have withdrawn or destroyed most of their newest missiles from Europe and have agreed to the witnessing of those removals as well as limited inspections of various other military weapon systems, including the chemical kind. But though, in political terms, progress seems to have been made (along with troop withdrawals), the number of weapons remaining is almost as large as ever and rather more daunting in an atmosphere of dubious bonhomie.

Strategic bombing. See **Bombing, Strategic.**

Strategic Defence Initiative (SDI). Sometimes known as Star Wars, this $30 billion project, announced by President Ronald Reagan in March 1983, was said to be aimed at a very sophisticated, complex ground and space **surveillance** system, designed to provide protection for the USA, probably by missiles, X-rays and **lasers**, against missile attack. To those sceptics who doubted its technical feasibility and feared the cost, had to be added people, the Russians to the fore, who claimed it destabilized the current nuclear balance by acquiring a new technology for the West which Russia could neither afford nor, perhaps, acquire – even though Reagan offered to share the **technology.** SDI remains a weight in the politico-strategic balance and a factor in **Strategic Arms Limitation** talks. Mean-

while research continues by both sides into the feasibility of all manner of devices which are likely to add significantly to knowledge and the **deterrence** equation.

Strategy. In simple terms of the art of war, strategy is the technique of planning campaigns by selecting the aims and solving the **logistics** problems connected with moving men and resources to their battle positions, where, if a decision has not been reached through diplomacy, they are used tactically (**Tactics**) in battle. Together with the effects of **technology** since the 18th century, strategy has progressed beyond being seen as a collection of stratagems, cunning and trickery into a more intellectual process connected with evolving political systems, **communications**, society and the influence of philosophy (see **Philosophers, Military**). The principles of **war** continue to rule every progression but the ramifications multiply: from the rather guileless naïvety of the **Crimean War**; through the far more sophisticated strategic conduct of the **American Civil War**, with the Federal side's application of **blockade** through sea power, mobility through **railways** and the land attack upon the South's economy and **logistics**; to the distraught, misguided strategies of **World War I** (with their initial belief in short wars) and the evolution, prior to **World War II**, of grand strategy. This is the discipline which embraces the entire apparatus of state politics, economics, logistics and **propaganda** alongside the threat or application of military force. It appeared piecemeal during the **Russian revolutionary wars** and the associated long wars to spread Communism world-wide.

Without perhaps fully realizing it, Adolf **Hitler** developed grand strategy in the 1930s and, by so doing, baffled his opponents by bluff before they came to understand and create an adequate **deterrent** to his attacks. And yet his military strategy, such as it was once the bluff was called, fell far short of being grand, arguably, indeed, being opportunist and thus lacking the foresighted thread of anticipation which is of the essence of sound military strategy. For no matter the age or the circumstances, a workable strategy is not to be conjured up at a moment's notice: aims have to be identified and selected with a view to their desirability; then exposed to critical examination of feasibility and the likely enemy strategy and reactions. Once a course or courses have been decided upon, sufficient time is required to plan and then position men and resources – which in global war can be a long-drawn-out process not easily amenable to the sudden switches of aim or execution Hitler often indulged in. Like **mobilization**, which is closely related to strategy, large-scale projects are not always reversible at short notice.

With the coming of **nuclear weapons** and of **aircraft** and **rockets and guided missiles** to deliver them from long range, the associated strategy of the **deterrent** has appeared, thus broadening the scope of strategy itself. For, as was soon discerned, there is a considerable difference between the somewhat ponderous preparation of a knock-out blow by World War II means and the feasibility of achieving that aim by pressing a few buttons to deliver that blow. The realization concentrated minds upon the, at times, abstract calculations and postulations concerned with striking so-called credible nuclear balances to ensure that one side could not steal a telling advantage over the other. This balancing of power created, by default as well as deceit, the vast stocks of superfluous warheads neither side wanted to use but which were expanded in the name of insurance, plus vast and intricate preparations to fight a major war without weapons of mass destruction in case nobody risked using them.

But while as an essential, integral part of the implementation of deterrence, profound public intellectual debate proceeded, conventional **limited wars** of long duration were fought under the shield of the nuclear deterrent. The **Arab–Israeli**, **Korean**, **Vietnam**, **Indo-Pakistani**, **Iran–Iraq** and **Afghanistan** wars were simply the most long-standing among many smaller ones which rarely reached a conclusion because the strategy of prolonged resistance by dedicated minorities using modern techniques of armed resistance and subversion is so difficult to counter. In the days of formal wars, strategic thought was based, for the most part, upon achieving results quickly and at the least cost. Since the Russian Revolution, the world has been afflicted by philosophers and leaders whose strategies are messianic in their fervent beliefs and perseverance in reaching for objectives, regardless of how long it takes or how much it costs. There is no saying, in a setting of almost perpetual war in which rival superpowers are inextricably involved, where that sort of Third World War will lead.

Submarines. The first attempt to use a submer-sible boat at war was by Sergeant Ezra Lee in David Bushnell's screw-propelled *Turtle* against a British warship on 6 September 1776. It failed because Lee could not attach the explosive charge to the ship's bottom. Numerous projects went on being experimented with, but not until the **American Civil War**, on 5 October 1863, was there a successful attack by a submarine on shipping, when the semi-submersible, steam-propelled *David* severely damaged a Federal iron-clad with a spar **torpedo** – shortly before practical locomotive torpedoes became available.

Not until electric and oil fuel motors were available in the 1880s did a practical mechanically driven, fully submersible boat become feasible. In 1886 Lieutenant Isaac Peral of Spain built an electrically powered boat. The following year a Russian electric boat with four torpedoes appeared at the same time as the periscope was introduced elsewhere. The next major step forward came in 1895 with *Plunger*, the streamlined boat of John Holland of America, propelled by electricity when submerged and by a steam engine on the surface, which also charged the batteries. He vastly improved upon the system in his boat of 1900, which substituted a petrol engine for steam; and it was further developed in Maxim Laubeuf's *Aigret* in 1904 with its safer, oil-fuelled diesel engine. By 1910 surface speeds of 10 knots and of eight when submerged were normal; Holland's earlier methods of depth control by variable water ballasting and tilting elevators further advanced; and double-skinned hulls provided other advantages, including deeper diving capability.

By **World War I** in 1914, indeed, there were submarines in service with surface speeds up to 16 knots and 10 submerged, displacements of 700 tonnes, and crews of 35, armed with a gun as well as four torpedo-tubes that could be reloaded from reserves when submerged. They made the submarine into what Admiral Lord **Fisher** had recognized in 1910 as a revolutionary weapon system for offensive effect. How right he was became apparent during the **English Channel** and **North Sea battles** when submarines, used for reconnaissance and ambush, had a major **tactical** impact on fleet operations, quite apart from their **strategic** effect through their reviled employment by the Germans, from 1915 onwards, as an instrument of **blockade**, with unrestricted attacks against merchant shipping from February 1917. The introduction of **convoys** and, in due course, **sonar** tended to inhibit submarine design developments between the wars. But in Germany Karl **Dönitz** was demonstrating by trials the feasibility of controlling U-boat 'packs' by **radio** to detect and then concentrate them against convoys; and also the tactical advantage of attacking by night on the surface. But if at first neither his boats nor those of the French and British made much impact in **World War II**, it was apparent by 1940 that sonar did not sound the submarine's death knell.

Dönitz's submarines and methods were offered a wonderful chance after June 1940 in the Battle of the **Atlantic**. Given greater resources and more assistance at the outset he might have won. As it was, in the interests of quantity production, he condoned delay in the introduction of significantly faster boats and could not keep pace with the cumulative effects of Allied countermeasures which forced changes of tactics upon him. Deliveries of supply boats to keep operational U-boats longer at sea were slow and too late; improved counter-**electronic** devices were retarded; faster and deeper-diving boats, plus the snorkel tube which enabled a boat to breathe while running its diesel engine and charging its batteries submerged (thus saving it from being exposed to surprise air attack when surfaced), were not ready until 1944. As it was, the introduction of faster boats produced a crisis that might have been catastrophic for the Allies if the war had not ended in May 1945. The catastrophe would have equalled that suffered by the Japanese in the **Pacific Ocean War** where, because they had neglected **anti-submarine weapons**, their warships and merchant vessels suffered such enormous losses that, in 1945, the blockade of Japan was complete, with disastrous consequences.

Since World War II the submarine has become a capital ship of dominating strategic importance. The introduction by the Americans in 1955 of a nuclear-powered boat with an environmental regeneration plant and high performance **communications** and **navigation** systems made feasible underwater voyages restrained in time only by the endurance of their crews and the food stored aboard. The true submarines that followed were developed by the Americans, the Russians, the British and the French into boats displacing 25,000 tonnes with a reputed speed of 40 knots and a depth-holding capability of between 2,000 and 3,000ft. These characteristics made them extremely difficult to detect, track and attack. Such vessels could carry, in addition to torpedoes, guided missiles (see **Rockets and guided missiles**) such as *Polaris*, with a nuclear warhead that could be launched from beneath the surface to strike targets that, in the present day, can be 3,000 miles inland, making the nuclear-weapon-armed boats a most effective, elusive arm of the **deterrent**.

Sudan campaigns. In the latter half of the 19th century the Sudan was invaded in stages by **Egypt** in small wars which involved the British and impinged upon the **Ethiopian wars**. After the Battle of Tel el Kebir in 1882, Britain dominated Egypt and therefore had an interest when, in that year, the Mahdi Mohammed Ahmed turned religious ferment into the incorrectly named 'dervish' uprising, and won a few skirmishes against the Egyptians. But when at El Obeid on 3 November 1883 his fanatics wiped out 10,000 Egyptian troops and followed up on 4 February 1884 with another victory at El Teb, Egypt was driven out of Sudan. Meanwhile General Charles Gordon, who in January had been sent by the British to evacuate Khartoum, was himself besieged until, a year later, he and the garrison were massacred – just two days before a fumbled British expedition fought its way through.

Mahdist control became absolute after the Mahdi died in 1885 and was succeeded by King Abdullah, who was challenged in 1896 when the British and Egyptians, provoked by unwelcome French initiatives, decided to reconquer the Sudan. It took General **Kitchener**, with an Anglo-Egyptian Army, over two years to advance up the River Nile to win battles at Dongola (21 September 1896), Abu Hamed (7 August 1897) and Atbara River (8 April 1898) before the *coup de grâce* was administered at Omdurman on 2 September when his far better armed 26,000 (for 500 casualties) destroyed Abdullah's 40,000.

Sudan then came under Anglo-Egyptian control and a target in 1940 for two minor Italian incursions, which were soon driven back. In 1956, responding to strong nationalist sentiment and occasional violence in the past, the British and Egyptians withdrew from what became the Republic of Sudan, which was soon torn by *coups d'état* and a rebellion in 1963 that destabilized the country and produced the hostilities between north and south which sporadically continue, along with cross-frontier incidents associated with the **Ethiopian** civil war.

Suez Canal, Battles of the. When the 100 miles long, 100 feet wide canal linking Port Said to Suez was opened in 1869, providing a short cut for ships from Europe to the Far East, it also brought into existence a waterway of the utmost strategic importance: what the Germans called 'the jugular vein of the British Empire'. Therefore when **World War I** broke out and Turkey joined

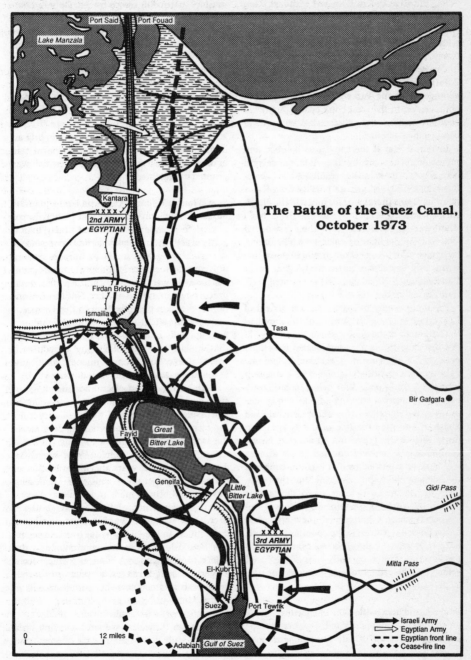

The Battle of the Suez Canal, October 1973

the Central Powers, the Germans eagerly pressed for an attack upon it. In mid-January 1915 a Turkish corps of 20,000 men with nine batteries of artillery, under General Djemal Pasha, set off across the Sinai Desert. It arrived within striking distance of a strong British and Egyptian garrison on 2 February and next day attacked, without benefit of surprise, in four places between El Qantara and El Shallufah. Coming under heavy fire, which eventually cost some 2,000 casualties, and failing to co-ordinate their arrangements, the Turks got only a few men in pontoons on to the west bank before they were counter-attacked and wiped out. A withdrawal began almost at once.

In World War II the canal was bombed and mined from the air by the Axis on several occasions without lasting results. As an objective which deserved greater priority than Hitler allowed, it was threatened for much of the North Africa battles, particularly during those of El Alamein in 1942. But not until the Arab–Israeli War of 1956 did fighting again take place along its banks, when Anglo-French amphibious, airborne and helicopter-borne troops landed at Port Said on 5 November and penetrated to El Qantara before the war was called off.

Far more deadly to Egypt was the arrival of Israeli troops along the length of the canal in the aftermath of the Six Days War in June 1967. For this time the Israelis established a fortified position, forcing closure of the canal. Sporadic fighting went on until 6 October 1973, erupting into the Yom Kippur War when a brilliantly executed, surprise crossing of the canal was made by the Egyptian Army under General Saad Shazli. It smashed the line of the Israelis and drove them back, provoking an abortive Israeli counter-attack on land and heavy air attacks which were punished by the Russian-equipped air defences along the west bank. But the tables were turned on 16 October when the Israelis carried out their long-planned crossing at Deversoir. Forming a bridgehead, their armoured forces fanned out to seize the canal as far south as Suez, to wipe out the air defences and envelop the Egyptian armies on both sides of the canal before a final cease-fire was arranged on the 24th.

Sumatra and Java battles. On 14 February 1942, on the eve of Singapore's fall, Japanese troops landed at Banka as 700 airborne troops dropped to seize the oilfields of Palembang. The weak, local Dutch defences crumbled at the start of an inevitable Allied deterioration throughout the East Indies as the Japanese, with complete air mastery, poured in troops by sea. Only in Lombok Strait on the 18th/19th did the Japanese lose one transport ship prior to a landing on Bali; and on the 20th on Timor, which was captured with parachutists' assistance, thus isolating Java. For already the Allied naval squadron upon which defence of the East Indies rested was being whittled away in the Java Sea Battle that ended in total defeat on 29 February. Next day the Japanese made widespread landings along the north coast of Java, prompting an immediate decision by the Dutch to evacuate and, on the 8th, a call for a cease-fire which was granted on the 9th.

Surveillance, Military. At sea, on land and in the air the observation of enemy and friendly forces is vital to provide sufficient and timely intelligence of activity and deployments. It makes use of seeing, hearing and smelling, human sensory procedures which, until the appearance of optical instruments, were unassisted and depended upon practice and ingrained abilities. Until the invention of the man-lifting balloon in the 18th century and aircraft in the 20th, scouting techniques were specially practised to obtain close observation, making use of photography as soon as it was available. But the employment of small craft at sea and patrols on land were and are vital.

With the arrival of electronics the range of surveillance techniques was at once widened and exploited. Sonar had a surveillance role. Intercepted radio transmissions made possible the location through direction finding (DF) of a transmitter's position, helping draw useful deductions. Over the years the interpretation of patterns of electronic emissions, including navigational beams, made it possible to discern enemy deployments and intentions without necessarily reading a word of what was being transmitted. In the 1930s, radar began to supersede sound locators to add enormously to the ability to detect aircraft (and also ships) from longer and longer ranges, a system of surveillance with a remoteness that permitted radical changes in scouting and patrolling methods – but yet another source of emissions for intelligence.

When gas (Chemical warfare) was first used in 1915, only the human sense of smell and

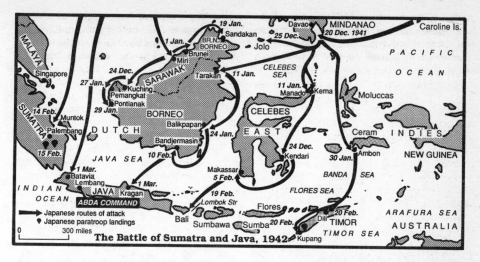

The Battle of Sumatra and Java, 1942

respiratory discomfort gave clear warning. But in due course sensors were used for detection, and subsequently developed extensively to monitor, through heat, sound and 'sniffing', the presence of targets of interest to the special organizations created to control and co-ordinate a mass of information, gleaned from the meanest person with binoculars to the loftiest space vehicle with sensors and cameras, which is central to C³I.

Syrian battles. Until modern Syria, under French mandate, came into being in 1920 (partly as a result of the **Arab Revolt**), it had been stamped upon by many powers, Turkey being the most recent. France, in practice, treated Syria as a colony.

On 8 June 1941, having helped the Germans foster an anti-British movement in Iraq, her Vichy-controlled government, with 35,000 troops, resisted an invasion by 20,000 British and Free French troops under General Sir Henry Wilson. Wilson sent in four separate columns from Palestine and Iraq with Beirut, Damascus and Palmyra as the main objectives. The principal opposition was along the Litani River and took two days to break. But gradually the French, including the **Foreign Legion**, gave way, although inflicting heavy casualties. Damascus fell on the 21st, Beirut on 15 July, the day the French surrendered. Many of their men subsequently transferred to the Free French forces.

Complete independence followed in 1946

when, as a founder member of the Arab League, Syria became involved in Palestinian affairs and the **Arab–Israeli wars**. But her operations at Safed in May 1948 were defeated and she signed a truce with Israel in July 1949, having made but slight military impact. Neither did she play an active part in the war of 1956, nor a leading role in that of 1967, although the ground and air raids she mounted against Israel were overtures to the Six-Day War. For by then the Russian-armed Syrian Army was a force to be reckoned with, bent on a major role against the Israelis. When Israel opened her pre-emptive war on 5 June, therefore, Syrian airfields were struck heavily. And no sooner were the battles against Egypt and Jordan won than, on the 9th, the Israelis assaulted the Golan Heights to rout the Syrians within 36 hours and gain possession of this vital, strategic territory. This ground was the initial objective of the Syrians when, heavily rearmed by Russia, they attacked towards the River Jordan on 7 October at the start of the Yom Kippur War.

With benefit of surprise against a mere handful of Israeli brigades, three Syrian infantry and two armoured divisions plunged into the attack advancing to within five miles of the river. Desperately the Israelis fed in troops as they were mobilized, first to check and then, on the 10th, hurl back the Syrians in a counterstroke which not only routed them but also the Iraqi and Jordanian forces which arrived in support. Had not the situation on the southern front against Egypt been critical, the Israelis would have been virtually free to pursue to Damascus. At the cease-fire on the 22nd, Syria had lost 1,150 tanks (867 intact) and some 4,000 troops; and the Iraqis and Jordanians another 150 between them.

But Russia rearmed Syria which remained as intransigent as ever, declining to join Egypt in peace with Israel and becoming inextricably and deviously involved in the continuing **Lebanon** battles.

T

Tactics. The art of fighting a battle at sea, on land and in the air but subordinate to **strategy**. For example, no matter how skilfully the German commanders in **World War II** won numerous tactical victories, they could not compensate for **Hitler's** inept strategic insights. Tactical applications in wars and battles are to be found in many entries in this Encyclopedia and also under **Air, Amphibious, Chemical, Desert** and **Flame warfare, Fortifications, Guerrilla, Jungle, Mountain, Naval** and **Psychological warfare.** It will be seen that the best tacticians searched for the enemy's weak spots in flank, rear or by overhead approach, while at the same time guarding against surprise and enemy countermeasures. They made good use of the principles of war (see **War, Principles of**) to achieve mobility, fire-power, protection and cunning in pursuit of their aims in attack, defence and withdrawal, and often were those who understood best how to harness **technology's effects.** The most important of these were **aircraft, aircraft-carriers, armour, armoured fighting vehicles,** signal **communications, electronics, engineering, gas, gunnery, logistics, machine-guns, mechanization, mines, nuclear weapons, rockets** and **guided missiles, submarines, surveillance** instruments and **torpedoes.**

War's multiplicity demands the formulation of doctrines to guide tacticians in the heat of battle. Tactical doctrine is a touchstone for leaders under pressure and is central to **training, drills** and Standard Operating Procedures (SOP). But doctrine is neither immutable nor sacrosanct. Among the greatest modern tacticians are to be found innovators such as Admirals Lord **Fisher, Yamamoto** and **Dönitz;** and Generals **Sherman,** von **Moltke** (the Elder),

Fuller, Hobart, Guderian, Zhukov, Douhet and **Mitchell,** in addition to guerrilla leaders like **Lawrence** and **Mao Tse-tung,** who were not hidebound by orthodoxy.

Taiwan. See **Formosa.**

Tal, General Israel (b. 1924). An NCO in the British Army in **World War II** who fought in Italy (**Italian campaign, 1943–5**) and then joined in the **Israeli fight for independence.** As commander of Israel's Armoured Corps he procured modern British and American **tanks** and, as he trained this **armoured** force, concentrated most on the need for excellence in **gunnery.** In June 1965 he commanded an armoured division in the Six Days War and made the decisive breakthrough from Gaza to El Arish. During the Yom Kippur War he was Deputy Chief of Staff. Afterwards he became adviser to the Minister of Defence on development and organization, with a leading part in designing and developing the innovative, now battle-proven Merkava tank.

Tanks. See **Armoured fighting vehicles.**

Tannenberg, Battle of. At the start of **World War I** the Germans, while they attacked France, intended their Eighth Army (under General Max von Prittwitz) to stand on the defensive in East Prussia against the anticipated Russian offensive. The Russian First Army (General Pavel Rennenkampf) advanced towards Königsberg, fought the inconclusive Battles of Stallupönen (17 August) and Gumbinnen (20 August) but failed to follow up when the Germans withdrew. Meanwhile Second Army (General Alexander Samsonov) advanced northwards to cut the railway between Allenstein and Deutsch-Eylau, and thus take Prittwitz in flank and rear. Prittwitz lost his nerve, ordered the abandonment of East Prussia – and was at once replaced by Generals **Hindenburg** and **Ludendorff**. When they arrived it was to learn, through **radio** intercept, that Rennenkampf was almost stationary. They were presented with a plan to screen Rennenkampf with a single cavalry division while safely concentrating the entire Eighth Army against Samsonov. This was achieved by the 25th – and almost undetected by the Russians, who dispensed with **cavalry** reconnaissance.

Already on the 24th, Second (Russian) Army's centre had been checked at Orlau, but this minor set-back did not stop the wings advancing on a 50-mile front between Soldau and Ortelsburg to Bischofsburg. On the 26th the Germans closed in upon both Russian flanks finally to complete an encirclement on the 30th which netted 125,000 men and 500 guns – a defeat that forced First Russian Army to withdraw eastwards, pursued by the Germans. The Russians never fully recovered from this defeat. But the victory reinforced German self-confidence besides giving them, for better or worse, the redoubtable Hindenburg–Ludendorff duo.

Technology, Effects of. Towards the middle of the 19th century the study of science and engineering, which had been accelerating and intensifying since the Industrial Revolution in the 18th century, spread widely to affect dramatically the military profession, as it did the rest of society. From numerous entries in this Encyclopedia can be gleaned the impact of: improved **communications** (those of signals, **railways**, roads and air); new materials, such as **aluminium** and **steel**, and various kinds of **explosive** (including **nuclear**); and new weapons and weapon systems. These inventions and developments had a radical effect on thinking, organizations and methods. This effect ushered in a period of such rapid and all-embracing change that leaders in government, administration, commerce and the military services (the vast majority of whom had not enjoyed a scientific and technical education) were unable to assimilate (let alone benefit from) what was on offer.

The underlying theme of war since 1850 is that of the struggle between old and new concepts, interwoven with social, educational and institutional changes that have created wide divisions between classically and technically orientated groups. In addition to these changes, which continue to be resisted strongly by those who fear for their occupations and peace of mind, it can be seen that although weight of numbers in war still has a significant bearing, it can be overborne by more skilful use of new technologies, like the original **mechanized** forces on sea, land and in the air which demonstrated that, even when few in number, they could rout larger, technically inferior numbers. On the other hand, the sheer weight of technological effect sometimes produces a self-defeating result. The unbridled search for new knowledge through extravagant **research and development** (R&D) can produce confusion and also obscure the identification of essentials, in addition to wasting energy, time and money. This aspect of technology has led to much heart-searching and numerous endeavours at control which are often related to the cry for **disarmament**. Setting aside the possibility of mutual destruction through loss of control of technology, it is not to be expected that the progressive urge will be abandoned. This makes it all the more essential that military people should at least be technically aware and never dismissive of new ideas.

Telegraph and teleprinters. Mechanical telegraph systems had been used successfully during the Napoleonic wars in the early 19th century and a British version, invented by the Reverend John Gamble and used by the British Army in the Peninsular War, was still in service in an improved form for ship-to-shore signalling in the 1940s. However, it was the invention of the electric telegraph, transmitting electrical impulses along a wire, which by the mid 19th century had transformed communications generally. The invention by Samuel Morse in 1850 of his code, together with the 'sounding' key which enabled a skilled operator to write down messages directly as they were received, meant that traffic volume could be increased and transmissions accelerated.

The first military use of the electric telegraph was during the **Crimean War** (1854). A submarine cable 547km long was laid from the British base at Varna in Bulgaria to the Crimean peninsula. This link, connected by land cable to Paris and London, enabled Napoleon III to harass his commanders with unhelpful suggestions and the British War Office to do the same with theirs.

These problems were not helped by depredations on the cables laid overland by soldiers removing the insulation for pipe stems and by the local inhabitants, who found the copper wire irresistible. The telegraph did not really have a significant effect on operations in the Crimea, unlike the Indian Mutiny of 1857 where, since the system was controlled by the British, it proved to be a decisive factor.

The telegraph really came into prominence during the American Civil War (1861), when troop and supply movements were effectively controlled by the rapid and accurate passing of information. However, this war also exposed the vulnerability of line communications, the cutting and large-scale removal of which was a frequent objective of enemy raiding cavalry. It was during this war too that real efforts were made to speed up the laying of line near the combat area, the North equipping special telegraph wagon trains with insulated cable and lightweight poles (an example soon followed by the European armies). By linking such lines with the permanent civilian telegraph system messages could be transmitted from, for example, the government in Washington to commanders in the field.

Meanwhile, technological improvements were growing apace, with Gintl's duplex circuits appearing in 1853, whereby two messages in opposite directions could be sent simultaneously on the same line, followed in 1874 by Thomas Edison's quadruplex system allowing four simultaneous messages to be sent. Meanwhile Baudot's 1872 time-division multiplex system had appeared, still used in some teletype machines.

The invention of the typewriter and its development the teleprinter, linked to the telegraph system, added a further dimension to communications. Consisting of a typewriter keyboard and a printer, the key strokes generated electrical impulses which were translated into the printed word at the receiving end, the system being secure as long as land line was used. Radio teleprinter (US: teletype) systems introduced in the 1920s had to use encoded signals. Teleprinter circuits were used extensively throughout World War II, notably in the forward areas by the Germans in Russia, using the latest multi-channel carrier frequency systems: sending along bare wires simultaneously electronically separated modulations in enormous quantity.

In the post-World War II period teleprinter facilities linked by radio to all formation headquarters were a commonplace.

Although during World War I telephone and in later years voice radio to some extent supplanted the telegraph, the use of microwave radio and space satellites carrying as many as 1,800 channels on a single circuit, combined with teleprinter terminals capable of printing 1,000 lines per minute, means that telegraph systems still have a significant part to play in military communications.

Telephone. Alexander Graham Bell, a speech therapist, invented the telephone in 1876 and by 1880 it was in general use. The basic principles of operation are that air-pressure changes induced by the human voice cause a diaphragm to vibrate, the vibrations in turn creating changes in electrical current through a variable resistor. At the receiver an electromagnet translates the fluctuations in current once more into vibrations on a diaphragm, which the listener hears as human speech. The only fundamental change to Bell's invention, though there have been many refinements of it, has been the modern use of digital transmission in the form of pulses, rather than the earlier analogue system of current changes. This makes for greater clarity and an ability for lines to carry more simultaneous conversations.

The telephone was used by the US Army during the Spanish–American War at the end of the 19th century, during the Boer War and during the Russo-Japanese War of 1904; but in none of these did the device play a significant part, the equipment being insufficiently robust for the rigours of field conditions. It was World War I which really gave the telephone its chance, especially under the comparatively static conditions of the Western Front. The German, French and British all had well-developed signal services by 1914. It has been said that Russian Army communications, on the other hand, were approximately at the level of the Americans' at the time of their Civil War some 50 years before; the Russian defeat at Tannenberg was in large measure a result of this.

On the Western Front telephone lines spread everywhere in a vast network, both behind the combat area and right into the front lines, so that it was not long before virtually every platoon had direct telephone contact with its company headquarters and so on up the chain of command. Literally thousands of miles of cable were laid, much of it underground, though often strung along the sides of trenches. The effect on operations was significant, in that far larger forces than before could be effectively controlled from the rear; the voice and hence the personality of a commander could be heard and felt at a lower level; massed **artillery** fire could be controlled directly by a forward observer in the trenches, or in a tethered balloon. A more mixed blessing was the political control that could now be exercised over the generals by governments in London, Paris and Berlin.

The chief problem lay in the maintenance of the miles of cable, constantly disrupted by shellfire, and the threat to security from the enemy tapping in to lines and listening to conversations. So bad did this become that there are records of new battalions moving into the line and being greeted by their regimental march played by the Germans opposite. In an effort to combat phone tapping the British introduced the Fullerphone. By setting up an impedance coil and two condensers, Major Fuller, the inventor, was able to control the rise and fall of current waves up and down the line. A commutator prevented the current surging back into the line, it being momentarily stored in the condenser. Morse signals could thus be sent securely down the line, though normal voice conversation was not protected. This combination of telephone and telegraphy was not new, a device having been produced by van Rysselburgh in 1902, but the military application had not previously been developed.

The Fullerphone was virtually handmade and hence expensive; there were never enough. But by mid-1916 it was in general use, some 10,000 being supplied to the British Army and 5,000 to the Americans. The equipment remained in service as a field telephone throughout most of **World War II**.

The weakness of the telephone emerged once mobile operations became more general – as the Germans had already found during their invasion of France and Belgium in 1914. Nevertheless, the telephone remained an important part of the field army equipment throughout World War II, special vehicles being able to lay line at up to 160km per day. The instruments became more robust and the use of multi-core cable and more sophisticated portable exchanges meant that telephone communication could be relied upon under even the most adverse conditions.

It is only now in the late 20th century that, following improvements in **radio**, for forward units the telephone is no longer essential in combat communications.

Television. The conversion of a scene in motion, plus its attendant sound, into an electronic signal transmitted to a receiving antenna and converted to a visible picture on a cathode-ray tube. The idea had first been proposed, in essence as it finally evolved, in 1908 by the British inventor A. A. Campbell Swinton; translated into the practical transmission of pictures in 1926 (though by mechanical means); but set on its true course in 1923 when the Russian–American Vladimir Zworykin patented the iconoscope cathode-ray camera tube on which television would ultimately depend. The system as we know it today relies on the bombardment by electrons of a fluorescent-coated screen in a scanning motion to create the picture. Work to achieve success was going on in a number of countries in the 1930s, the leading British engineer in the field being J. Logie Baird.

There were a number of military applications, once commercial television became a reality, of which **radar** was the first to bear fruit. To use television pictures for direct military **surveillance**, an obvious use, was, however, another matter; the early receivers were both bulky and fragile and television cameras totally unsuited for use in the field. This application was not seriously pursued during **World War II**, but towards the end of that conflict the Germans had already proved the feasibility of television guidance for missiles, though nothing had been put into service.

Bulk and fragility of the equipment remained the problems, not really overcome until miniaturization of **electronic** components became a reality with the development of the transistor in the 1950s, and later the electronic chip. Thereafter developments were rapid and the American television-guided 453kg *Walleye gliding bomb* was used successfully in 1967 during the **Vietnam War**, particularly for attacks on bridges, always difficult to hit from the air. Walleye had a television camera in its nose, transmitting pictures back to the parent aircraft, standing off at a distance to allow the controller to guide the bomb to its target comparatively unhindered.

There are now a number of such guidance systems available to both the Warsaw Pact and Nato forces. Further developments include the so-called **smart** bombs, typically the 906kg *electro-optical guided bomb*, which enables its controller to locate the target on his television screen, designate it to the bomb which then, after release, finds it own way to the target.

Television for **surveillance** has had some success and has been used in action by the Israelis. The most likely application is to have a camera mounted on a **remotely piloted vehicle** (RPV), either for general 'over the hill' surveillance or to provide the necessary reference picture for a laser target designator. The problem chiefly lies in the wide bandwidth required for television channels, plus the extra communication links needed to guide the RPV and point the television camera in the required direction, channels always at a premium in the forefront of the battle. An RPV-mounted television surveillance system needs a not inconsiderable control organization to take full advantage of the facility and this must be seen against the added hazard of electronic countermeasures, to which television is always susceptible. Nevertheless, a number of countries have developed, or are developing, television surveillance systems for use in the field.

Tet Offensive. Tet is a national holiday in Vietnam and was chosen by General **Giap** as the time for a decisive offensive against South Vietnam by the North Vietnamese Army (NVA) and the Vietcong (VC) guerrillas. As a diversion, on 21 January 1968, the US bastion at Khe Sanh was attacked. Then, on the 30th, Saigon, Hué and most other important centres were struck. Fighting was fierce. The US and the South's forces had been expecting something of the sort and inflicted heavy losses. Hoping to strangle the enemy's **logistics**, Giap had neither allowed for a massive supply operation by **aircraft, helicopters** and **armoured fighting vehicles** being able to maintain every base intact, nor for South Vietnamese unwillingness to rise up on his side. After about two weeks he admitted defeat, though the siege of Khe Sanh lasted into April.

Yet Giap and Ho Chi Minh had timed the offensive well to coincide with the American public's belief that the war was almost won and over. For the extensive **television** coverage and

false news media **propaganda**, which implied that the US and South Vietnam had been surprised and defeated, actually handed a strategic victory to the North, which in fact had been beaten comprehensively. Indeed, so severe were Vietcong losses that never again was it the same. Nor was the NVA fit for a major offensive for two or more years. But the USA suffered from a self-inflicted wound when its government, lacking public support as well as faith in victory, sought ways of escape from a long war which still continued.

Tito, Marshal (Josip Broz) (1892–1980). A Croatian who was captured by the Russians in **World War I**, joined the Yugoslav Communist Party in 1920 and by 1937 had become its secretary-general and a leading subversive. Not until the Germans invaded Russia in June 1941 **(Russo-German wars)** did he take up arms against them in his own country (which they had conquered in April). But thereafter his leadership of the Communist Partisans (so called to distinguish them from the Royalist Chetniks) in **Yugoslavia**'s battles was inspiring and most resourceful. And all the more so since, until June 1943, he carried on almost unaided by the Allies. As C-in-C he suffered hardships along with his followers and had several narrow escapes from the Germans and Italians, who put a large price on his head. When victory was won he made himself Marshal and was elected Prime Minister. His greatest skills lay in unifying a divided nation, and escaping, by political manoeuvring, the embraces of Russian Communism.

Tobruk, Sieges of. As one of the few ports midway between the Egyptian frontier and Benghazi, Tobruk was **logistically** important in Cyrenaica during the **North African campaigns** of World War II. After the defeat of the Italian Tenth Army in Egypt in December 1940 and the fall of Bardia on 6 January 1941, it was surrounded by the British Western Desert Force who captured it on the 22nd, together with 25,000 prisoners, 200 guns and 125 tanks, after a short, sharp assault that carried all before it.

But after the Axis army under General **Rommel** had defeated the British south of Benghazi in April, and arrived outside Tobruk on the 7th, it was the British turn to undergo siege, most successfully. From within the old, but improved, Italian **fortifications** they repulsed several attacks in April and May, yet failed to achieve relief from a counterstroke in June. From then on reinforcements and supplies came in perilously by sea until, on 18 November, a major British offensive from Egypt pre-empted a renewed assault by Rommel, leading to the hectic **Sidi Rezegh** battle which finally broke the siege as the Axis were driven back. Yet within a few weeks the Axis had riposted, though to be held at bay at Gazala a few miles west of the port's perimeter defences.

The **Gazala** battle of May/June was started by **Rommel** with Tobruk as its main objective. Because the British were defeated in the mobile battle, Tobruk once more came under siege on 18 June, although for political reasons only. For, initially, General Sir Claude Auchinleck had no intention of garrisoning the place as his Eighth Army retired into Egypt. Rommel, readapting his original plan (and finding dumped ammunition still where he had left it in November) immediately attacked a demoralized British garrison on the 20th and instantly broke in. The following evening the Axis had full possession of the port, some 33,000 prisoners and immense quantities of guns, vehicles, fuel, ammunition and supplies. There was enough to convince Rommel that, rather than stop to concentrate on the taking of **Malta** (as required by Field Marshal **Kesselring**), this was an opportunity to drive east and conquer **Egypt**.

Togo, Admiral (Count) Heihachiro (1848–1934). On 25 July 1894, when commanding the Japanese **cruiser** *Naniwa*, Captain Togo fired the first shots in what, on 18 July, became the declared **Chinese–Japanese War**. He won glory at the Battle of the **Yalu River** and later played a leading role in preparing the Fleet for the **Russo-Japanese War** of 1904. When, as Commander of the Combined Fleet, he directed the initial naval attack on **Port Arthur** on 8 February. His leadership in the ensuing campaign, including the Battle of the **Yellow Sea**, was brilliant and decisive in what were the first modern naval battles, a prowess he underlined by his skilled conservation of ships in his conduct of the **blockade** of Port Arthur and the annihilation of the Russian Baltic Fleet at the Battle of **Tsushima**. It was Togo's innovative and disciplined spirit which inspired the Japanese Navy throughout the campaigns of **World War II**.

Torpedo. Named after an electric-ray fish, the torpedo originally was a moored sea **mine** invented in 1805 by Robert Fulton. This entry, however, deals only with locomotive torpedoes, the combined invention of Robert Whitehead and an Austrian naval officer, Giovanni Lupis. In 1866 Whitehead demonstrated a 14ft-long underwater missile with 18lb of **explosive** in the nose, driven by a compressed-air motor at six knots to a range of 700 yards. It was launched from tubes, controlled in depth by a hydrostatic valve operating elevators called hydroplanes and, to begin with, ran straight. Within 10 years specialized fast **torpedo-boats** were being built to mount it and before 1900 it was recognized as the **submarine**'s natural and principal weapon.

By extending the scope of underwater attack, the torpedo revolutionized **naval warfare**. First used successfully in action with indeterminate results in 1877 during the **Russo-Turkish War**, it helped win major victories for the Japanese at **Wei-Hai-Wei** in 1895 and in the surprise attack on **Port Arthur** on 8 February 1904. By this time an Austrian, Ludwig Obry, had adapted the gyroscope to give directional control, which considerably improved tactical flexibility. In addition, warheads were increased in diameter to 18in, along with improved motors driven by burning fuel with compressed air to give speeds up to 30 knots, plus extended range. Torpedoes such as these began to hold sway in **World War I**. The mere suspicion of approaching torpedo tracks had tactical influence by inducing manoeuvres which, by evading hits, affected the outcome of major engagements such as **Jutland**. In the submarine campaigns against commerce they became increasingly important once boats were compelled to attack while submerged, instead of surfacing to engage more economically with gunfire. At the same time the practice of dropping torpedoes from **aircraft**, first done by an Italian, Capitano Guidoni in 1911, announced yet another new era in naval warfare.

Between the World Wars extensive **Research and development** raised the performance of torpedoes, although without always improving results. Although the introduction of electric motors enhanced tactical versatility by almost eliminating the tell-tale track, there were numerous malfunctions, notably from the temperamental, magnetic-effect exploders intended to replace contact pistols. Indeed, only Japan produced a fully reliable torpedo for **Word War II**: the 24in Long Lance with a speed, powered by a liquid-oxygen motor, of 36 knots for 22 miles, or 49 knots for 11 miles. This was a battle-winning weapon introduced with deadly effect at the Battle of the **Java Sea** in February 1942. Indeed torpedoes were the vital weapon, without which naval victories, from the sinking of Italian warships at Taranto in November 1940 to the Battles of the **Atlantic, Pearl Harbor** and **Pacific Ocean**, would have been very different if not impossible.

During World War II further advances in design and performance were made. The Germans took a lead with torpedoes which ran zigzag or figure-of-eight courses, but most promisingly introduced the acoustic kind which 'homed' on to their target's noise: systems which called for equally sophisticated, yet quite simple countermeasures. Since then the search has been on, in general terms, for torpedoes which can outpace, outdive and follow to impact the fast, deep-diving submarine; or can skim and submerge at higher speeds, **rocket**-assisted, to targets far over the horizon. They are fuelled by ever-improving compounds, incorporate **sonar** and **electronic** technology with miniaturized components and are fitted with all manner of devices to provide immunity from countermeasures. For example, the wire-guided type (based on *anti-tank guided weapon* (ATGW) systems) have security attractions and can be controlled from hovering **helicopters** which, by no means incidentally, are ideal carriers of torpedoes, including special, small-sized versions.

Torpedo-boats. The concept of a boat to specialize in **torpedo** attack followed swiftly upon the proving of the Whitehead weapon. In 1876 the British built the 19-knot *Lightning* with a swivelling tube in the bow, and the next year the French produced a 14-knot boat with two underwater, axial tubes. Design philosophy complied with a tactical doctrine that said speed gave adequate protection while **armour**, owing to its weight, bulk and cost, could not be justified. The result by the mid-1880s was big flotillas for mass attacks by cheap, lightly armed or unarmed, unarmoured boats of about 40 tonnes, usually with fixed tubes. These tactics were employed by the Japanese, by night, at **Wei-Hai-Wei** in 1895 and at **Port Arthur** on 8 February 1904. The threat this posed compelled the construction

of torpedo-boat **destroyers**, which also carried torpedoes and were enhanced by batteries of tubes.

The concept of the light boat nevertheless survived, in spite of high losses of such vessels when exposed to fire from destroyers, the secondary armament of larger ships and from **coast defences**. In **World War I** they were maids of all work, particularly in narrow waters such as the **English Channel**. Elusiveness was vital there, plus shallow draught, as it was for the British *coastal motor-boats* (CMB) or *motor launches* (ML), craft powered by petrol engines with speeds over 35 knots, and the Italian MAS (*motor anti-submarine*) boats. Built in large numbers, they were used against **submarines** and all kinds of surface vessel, as well as for **convoy** escorts and for raids such as that against Zeebrugge. They were, in fact, the forerunners, of the hard-chine boats that were developed in the mid-1930s as *motor torpedo-boats* (MTB), with fixed, forward-axial tubes. The British developed these extensively and introduced them to the USA as PT (*patrol torpedo*) boats; unlike the German *Schnellboote*, they were made of wood, not metal. The German 105-tonne S boats (known by the Allies as E (for Enemy) boats) were fine examples of the genre with two tubes, 20mm and 37mm guns, a speed of 42 knots and good sea-keeping ability. First built in 1929 they, like their Italian counterparts, spent **World War II** fighting the British off the shores of Europe in countless engagements, mainly by night.

Similar boats are still in service, armed with **rocket missiles**. Russian- and French-designed types have been used in the **Arab–Israeli wars** with great effect. The Danish and Norwegian navies see a vital role for them among fiords and islands. They are attractive to small maritime nations intent on low-cost defence, or in the fight against smugglers and gun-runners; operations, in other words, where speed is vital and the faster hydrofoil boat comes into its own.

Training is at the root of military prowess and **morale**. When reading this entry reference to **Drill, Education, Military** and **Staffs, Military** might well be useful along with reflection on entries elsewhere giving insight into what effect training, together with **technology**'s effects, has had upon military history over the generations. They underline the vital need for systematic and enlightened teaching practices to prepare and, to some extent, condition all ranks for the performance of their tasks. These duties are in certain respects unique, but in others simply a variation of current civilian practices: but they also indicate how current trends, doctrine and social behaviour impinge upon training policy, its content, methods of instruction and application of technical aids in a comprehensive, cost-effective manner.

Before the invention of mechanical printing and the ready availability of written military instructional manuals, teaching was in the hands of the educated minority, who had access only to a few master works, such as Sun Tzu's *Art of War*. Most information was passed down by word of mouth and much lost in the process. Owing to lack of systematic analysis of recorded experience, therefore, only limited progress was made. The setting-up in the 17th century of military colleges, with their own libraries and archives, lay at the heart of profoundly studied doctrines and the establishment of training directorates. From them the staff disseminated syllabuses in writing and implemented them through the training programmes of the colleges, schools and established units, whose commanders were personally responsible for their subordinates' training.

Training reflects weapons' characteristics and their effect on **tactics**. In 1850 instruction was largely repetitive and drilled, without much call on initiative and usually unit-based, with extremely rare dependence upon very few central schools of instruction. Thereafter, the introduction of more complicated weapons, requiring attendant skills and supporting organizations, called for teaching methods beyond commanding officers' capabilities. Experts to operate steam engines, **railways**, breech-loading **artillery**, **machine-guns**, **telegraph**, **telephones**, **radio** and **aircraft** had to be taught in special schools and supervised within the complex systems devised within the training directorates of the Service Ministries. Over the years there evolved training programmes for recruits, who would be given basic instruction in military behaviour and weapons before progressing to higher proficiency as part of a group, probably learning a specialist trade on the way and, desirably, how to teach, lead and command others.

Sooner or later the recruit would join a ship's crew, as part of a team trained in some special-ized function on board; or become a member of an army or air force unit. He would take part in group exercises which increased in scale and complexity as a ship 'worked up' to full efficiency; or in a year's training programme progressed by stages to major, formation exercises. Training should be a never-ending process, one in which there is always something new to learn as well as old to revise and improve upon. Innovation should evolve alongside repetition to raise standards of performance to an excellence in which the individual learns to do many different tasks and officers to function two or three levels above their present rank.

With the increase in numbers of weapons of high technology and the rising intensification of military activity since the 1920s, realistic training has become extremely difficult to arrange economically. In a more crowded and environmentally sensitive world, space for exercises is harder to come by. At the same time practice with operational ships, army equipment, aircraft and their weapons is extremely expensive in wear and tear as well as fuel and ammunition expenditure. Since the 1920s increasing use has been made of classroom simulators, to teach tank crews, for example, how to drive and aim their weapons before working on and, perhaps, damaging the real thing. In the 1960s economics and the **electronic** revolution, apart from common-sense teaching practice, demanded extensive use of realistic simulators. A strong lead came from **air forces** and civil airlines in the training of air crew. Soon the armies were acquiring improved driving and **gunnery** simulators, while the navies developed systems for teaching tactics without going to sea. **Computers** and **television** contributed vitally to the development of complex war-gaming facilities. They were not inexpensive, but cheaper and almost as realistic as the real thing, besides having the advantage of 'playback' to help rub in lessons prior to repetition of the exercise.

Transport aircraft. Long after the symbolic air supply of besieged Kut al Amara in **Mesopotamia** in 1916, the design of transport aircraft lagged behind combat types. Air trooping, notably by the British in the 1920s, was usually carried out in converted **bombers** from **World War I**. But with civil transports for nascent air lines, the German all-metal tri-motor Junkers Ju52 of 1932 being noteworthy, came a new dimension.

As multi-engined **aircraft** with greater capacity, longer range, higher speeds and improved reliability came into service, the military seized upon the advantages of mobility offered. The movement by air of General **Franco**'s Moroccan troops at the start of the **Spanish Civil War** was as significant as the adaptation of airliners for parachute and other **airborne** operations throughout **World War II**. In parallel with air transport's demonstrations of flexibility and capacity for **logistic** and operational purposes, its mobility was augmented by the essential construction, world-wide, of the airfields and maintenance facilities its own **logistics** demanded.

In the course of the air supply of **Tunisia** and **Stalingrad** in 1942, and in support of the **Pacific Ocean War** and the **Burma** battles, military air transport laid the foundations of present-day civil air networks. The process was reinforced by the **Berlin airlift** in 1948–9 and the reinforcement of Korea (**Korean wars**) in 1950, and given its most significant boost by the introduction into service in 1950 and 1952 of, respectively, the British Viscount turbo-jet and the Comet jet airliners. The vast power of the jet engine made feasible more reliable transports of such economy that, by the 1960s, air transports had outmoded troop-ships by a substantial margin of cost-effectiveness and had spurred the construction of cargo aircraft, such as the Lockheed Galaxy with its 117 tonnes lift, which could solve emergency logistic problems as by no other means. In the 1980s vast air-transport fleets revolutionized **strategic** mobility to an extent undreamed of, and also with immense impact on national military policies and budgets, including the practice of reinforcing theatres of war by flying in troops to operate pre-positioned heavy equipment.

Trenchard, Marshal of the Royal Air Force (Viscount) Hugh (1873–1956). A soldier of dominating personality who fought in the **Boer War** but learnt to fly in 1913, ready to take a leading part in **World War I**. In August 1915 he took command of the Royal Flying Corps in France as it was fast expanding. He developed a **tactical** doctrine based on offensive action over the enemy lines and thus greatly helped the ground forces. But it was very expensive in air crews. In January 1918 he became Britain's first Chief of the Air Staff, to play a vital role in the creation of the Royal Air Force (RAF) on 1 April. In June he took command of the Independent Air Force, tasked (at his suggestion) to carry out **strategic bombing** of industrial targets in Germany. This proved a costly and by no means very effective strategy, yet it convinced Trenchard that air forces were capable of winning by independent action, an article of faith similar to those of General **Douhet**, and one he imposed on the RAF when again made Chief of the Air Staff and began a fight, from 1919 until 1929, to save the RAF from extinction.

Trenchard was a modern administrator with technological awareness. To his credit stand the RAF's cadet, staff and apprentice colleges upon which its excellence and spirit were founded, a system he tried, controversially between 1931 and 1935, to impose when reforming the Metropolitan Police. But when offered the job of Minister of Defence by Winston **Churchill** at the nadir of Britain's fortunes in May 1940, he declined in doubt of the task's practicability. It was his pride, however, to savour the RAF's saving of Britain that year.

Truman, President Harry (1884–1972). A bank clerk who became Vice-President of the USA and succeeded President **Roosevelt** when the latter died on 12 April 1945. A man of strong resolution, it was his destiny to take military decisions of world-shaking importance as **World War II** drew to a close. He gave the order to drop the **atom bomb** on Japan at the same time as the Potsdam conference was indicating the brewing troubles of the war's aftermath. Recognizing the Russian Communist threat to Europe, he pronounced in 1947 the so-called Truman Doctrine pledging the USA's support for free people resisting armed minorities, and leading, at the start of the **Cold War**, to the Marshall Plan to restore European prosperity; the setting-up of Nato in the shadow of the **Berlin** siege; and taking the lead in **United Nations** intervention in the **Korean War**. Lacking military training, Truman nevertheless had a Commander-in-Chief's attribute in his ability to analyse factors and convert them into positive decisions. His sacking of General **MacArthur** in 1951 was by no means the least courageous act of this great President, whose domestic politics were set in a low key.

Tsushima, Battle of. After the elimination of the Russian Far East Fleet at the Battle of the **Yellow**

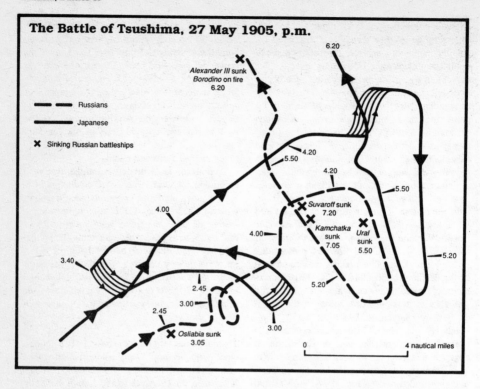

The Battle of Tsushima, 27 May 1905, p.m.

6.20

Alexander III sunk
Borodino on fire
6.20

- – – Russians
- —— Japanese
- ✖ Sinking Russian battleships

4.20
5.50

4.20

5.50

4.00

✖ Suvaroff sunk
7.20
✖
Kamchatka
sunk
7.05

✖ Ural
sunk
5.50

4.00

5.20

3.40

2.45
3.00
5.20

2.45

3.00

✖ Osliabia sunk
3.05

0   4 nautical miles

Sea on 10 August 1904, and with **Port Arthur** tightly besieged, the Russians decided in desperation to send their Baltic Fleet, under Admiral Zinovy Rozhdestvensky, to Vladivostok in hope of restoring the situation. Neither its 12 **battleships**, nine **cruisers** and nine **destroyers**, nor their crews, were fit for battle. This was especially so at the end of the 20,000 miles voyage, during which mechanical defects were chronic and **logistics**, particularly coaling arrangements by all manner of devious means, a nightmare. Passing through the North Sea they fired in panic on British trawlers, imagining them Japanese **torpedo-boats**. A few went through the **Suez Canal**, the main body round the Cape of Good Hope. Morale declined from the day of sailing on 10 October to the evening of 26 May 1905 when, with the **Russo-Japanese** War already won by Japan, they neared Tsushima Straits.

Here cruised Admiral **Togo** with 10 battleships, 18 cruisers, 21 destroyers and 60 torpedo-boats. Fully repaired, faster by two to three knots, battle hardened and well informed of the Russian strength and course by **radio** intercepts and scouting cruisers, the Combined Fleet was superior in all respects. From first contact on the 27th, Togo and his captains outmanoeuvred Rozhdestvensky, whose formation lapsed into confusion under cruiser fire before Togo's battleships got within range at 1405hrs. With precision Togo repeated the classic 'crossing of the T' to bring concentrated fire against the outclassed Russian battleships. One by one they were sunk or chased into the gloom where they scattered and were hunted through the night and into the following day. Statistics speak for themselves. The Japanese lost only three torpedo-boats and 117 killed. Only three Russian ships reached Vladivostok; all their battleships were sunk, captured or interned in neutral ports; and 4,830 men were killed and 5,917 captured. Of 100 Japanese torpedoes fired only seven hit, but they accounted for two battleships and two cruisers.

Tunisia, Battles of. The Franco-Italian rivalry, which led to France seizing Tunisia in 1881, always rankled with the Italians who, after the French defeat in 1940, stationed an Armistice Commission in the country, and as the **Mediter-**

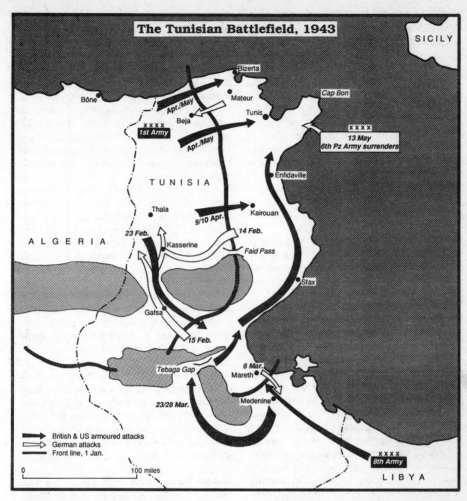

The Tunisian Battlefield, 1943

SICILY

Bizerta

Bône

Mateur

Cap Bon

Beja

Tunis

XXXX
1st Army

XXXX
13 May
6th Pz Army surrenders

TUNISIA

Enfidaville

Thala

Kairouan

9/10 Apr.

Apr./May

23 Feb.

14 Feb.

ALGERIA

Kasserine

Faid Pass

Sfax

Gafsa

15 Feb.

Tebaga Gap

6 Mar.
Mareth

23/28 Mar.

Medenine

➡ British & US armoured attacks
▷ German attacks
— Front line, 1 Jan.

0   100 miles

XXXX
8th Army

LIBYA

ranean battles intensified, regularly sailed convoys in Tunisian waters to beat the British blockade of Libya and Cyrenaica. Tunisia, therefore, was a prime Anglo-American objective of the invasion of the French **North African** colonies in November 1942, and the principal destination of German and Italian troops sent under Field Marshal **Kesselring** to secure the rear of Axis troops retreating towards Benghazi and Tripoli in the aftermath of defeat at El **Alamein**.

British **airborne** troops landed at Bône on 12 November to spearhead the thrust by General Kenneth Anderson's First (British) Army for the vital ports of Tunis and Bizerta. The British, reinforced later by American troops, got to within 20 miles of Tunis on 28 November before being pushed back to Medjez el Bab by an enemy with shorter lines of communication who won the reinforcement race. Eighth (British) Army was approaching Tripoli, but would not reach the old French Mareth Line in southern Tunisia until mid-February 1943. Meanwhile General Jürgen von Arnim took command of Axis forces in the north to launch an attack which gained possession of the passes through the mountains of the Eastern Dorsale, as springboards for spoiling attacks against the gathering Allied might. This purely delaying offensive culminated in the American débâcles of the **Kasserine Pass** battles and the ultimate defeat of Field Marshal **Rommel** when he tried to exploit northwards to cut off the Allied armies in Tunisia. The attempt never

329

had much hope of success in the light of the steadily worsening Axis supply state, von Arnim's preference for a direct attack in the north and his unwillingness to co-operate with Rommel, and the ever-increasing Allied strength.

On 6 March Rommel was repulsed in the south at Medenine. Fourteen days later Eighth Army attacked the Mareth Line as II (US) Corps moved towards Gabes. Now under General **Alexander**, the Allies tried to envelop the First Italian–German Army in the south, but failed to stop its pell-mell dash for the mountain strongholds of the north. The Axis troops fought well, but blockade starved them until a combined Allied offensive inevitably broke through to Tunis and Bizerta on 3 May.

Turbines. Any of various devices that convert the energy in a stream of fluid (water, steam, gas) into mechanical energy by passing the stream through a system of fixed and moving fan blades, causing the latter to rotate.

As the 19th century ended Britain, builder of 80 per cent of the world's ships, could fairly claim to be the leader in marine technology. In 1889 Sir Charles Parsons had taken the design of existing turbine engines a step further by fitting several stages of blades to a main shaft in order to improve efficiency and increase the power delivered. In 1897 one of his engines was installed in a 44-tonne boat called *Turbinia* and displayed before an astonished world as it sped at 34 knots amongst the British Fleet, assembled at Spithead for Queen Victoria's Diamond Jubilee Review. *Turbinia* was followed in 1899 by HMS *Viper*, a 550-tonne torpedo-boat, similarly powered and capable of 30 knots. The scene was set for the widespread introduction of marine turbine engines, infinitely more flexible and reliable than the reciprocating engines they replaced.

The impact of the turbine on the military scene was not confined to ships, dramatic though that was. In the decade preceding **World War II** there was a revived interest (following experimental work in France and Switzerland prior to 1914) in the gas turbine as a means of powering aircraft. The Germans took the lead initially with their jet-powered Heinkel HE178, which first flew in 1939. Their subsequent Messerschmitt ME262, though achieving operational service in 1944, was never satisfactory.

In Britain the name of Frank Whittle will always be associated with the development of jet power. Improvements in turbine-blade design, withstanding temperatures in excess of 3,000°C and the centrifugal effects of rotations at 30,000rpm or more, allowed Whittle to design an engine which linked an internal combustion turbine with a jet nozzle, the main components comprising a single-stage centrifugal compressor, a single-stage turbine, and a single combustion chamber into which liquid fuel was injected and burnt. Part of the exhaust gases thus generated drove the turbine, the remainder expanding through the jet nozzle. This simple design had the success it deserved when the first Meteor jet aircraft, based on Whittle's design, took to the air operationally in 1944, deployed against the V1 flying-bomb attacks. Subsequent refinements yielding improved performance, better fuel economy and quietness in operation have led to jet power being used for most of the world's military and civilian aircraft.

The gas turbine has also found an application as a power source for land vehicles. The American M1 Abrams main battle **tank** and its variants use a Lycoming 1500bhp gas-turbine engine which can produce more power for a given size than can a diesel; but the much higher fuel consumption requires much larger fuel tanks for an equivalent radius of action. Thus, while the vehicle has an impressive performance, little space or weight has been saved in the overall size of the power pack and its ancillaries. Nevertheless a trend has been set which other designs are likely to follow.

Turkish wars. The Ottoman Empire's decline, dating from the 16th century and caused, among other things, by endemic wars, the corruption of the élite military janissaries and harem influence, entered its final phase with the Battle of Sinope on 30 November 1853 in the opening phase of the **Crimean War**. It was of little account that the Turks had defeated the Russians at Oltenitza on 4 November and would hold their own (with British help) in the Caucasus at the siege of Kars, until forced by starvation and disease to surrender on 26 November 1855; Turkey was regarded as the 'sick man of Europe' and legitimate prey by predators.

After the **Russo-Turkish War** of 1877–8 she paid a large indemnity and gave up Montenegro, Serbia, Romania and Bulgaria along with places in Asia. She held her own in the incompetently managed **Greek–Turkish War** of 1897 but suffered defeat in the **Italo-Turkish War** of 1911–12 to lose Libya, Rhodes and the Dodecanese islands. This, however, was due not to military defeat by the Italians but to the onset of the **Balkan Wars** in 1912, in which defeat cost her Crete and the remainder of her European possessions, less Gallipoli and the province of Edirne.

Her decision, prompted by a political party favouring war, to join the Central Powers in **World War I** was fatal. Immediately under attack in the Caucasus, **Mesopotamia** and at **Gallipoli**, her failure to cut the **Suez Canal** in 1915 was her only significant attempt at a major **strategic** blow. Admirable as was her defence of Gallipoli and fortunate for her the British incompetence which brought them disaster in Mesopotamia in 1916, Turkey spent most of the war in retreat, propped up by barely adequate German aid and advice. The onset of the **Arab revolt**, and successive defeats in 1917 and 1918 in Palestine and Mesopotamia, wore her down, although, in the aftermath of stricken Russia's withdrawal from the war in 1917, she managed to seize territory there.

When exhaustion brought inevitable collapse of the Ottoman Empire in 1918 it was the shrewd leadership of General **Kemal Atatürk** which saved something from the wreck. His victories in the **Greek–Turkish War** of 1920–22 bought time for the modernization which was far too long overdue. Since then, aside from long-standing friction with Greece and armed involvement in the **Cyprus imbroglio**, she has managed the longest spell of peace in her history.

U

United Nations (UN) Forces. Under Chapter VII of the United Nations Charter of 1945 it was envisaged that, by decision of the Security Council, economic and diplomatic measures and action by sea, land and air forces could be taken against threats to peace or aggression. Although separate UN forces were once envisaged, practice demanded the assembly of military groups drawn from member nations for so-called police actions. The first, still the largest ever use of UN force, began in June 1950 when the Security Council passed a resolution for an end to hostilities in the **Korean War** and asked member nations to assist – a move which avoided an inevitable veto since Russia was currently boycotting the Council. Many Western nations complied on the South's side while the Communist states supported the North. Since then there have been many uses of international UN forces (including Communist and non-Communist troops together). Principally these have been the **Arab–Israeli Wars**, starting in 1956 after the Anglo-French attack on **Suez** and subsequently to the present day in **Lebanon**; in the Belgian Congo (Zaire) civil war in 1960 with 20,000 men; in **Cyprus** to restrain Greek and Turk animosity; in Namibia to settle differences between Angola and **South Africa**; in Iran in 1988 to police the settlement of the **Iran–Iraq War**; in **Central America**; and in **India** and **Pakistan**.

The choice of troops for joint groups is often made delicate by diplomatic sensitivity. Nations with a pronounced political bias are either excluded or balanced by troops from other interested parties. Certain nations with clear neutral detachment have frequently contributed – especially Canada. UN forces were awarded a Nobel Peace Prize in 1988. The troops involved wear their own uniforms except for a light blue beret. Many casualties have been suffered performing what, very often, are thankless tasks.

V1. The 'flying bomb', as it was popularly known, was launched by the Germans against targets in Britain and Belgium from June 1944 until March 1945. It may fairly be described as the world's first cruise missile, powered as it was by a pulse jet engine (patented in 1907 by the Frenchman Victor de Karavodine) and flying comparatively slowly (580kph) and at low altitude (600–900m) to its target. With a payload of 900kg and a range of 240km, V1 was guided by a gyroscopic automatic pilot monitored by magnetic compass, its dive on to the target at a measured distance being determined by the number of revolutions of a small propeller.

With its simple guidance system (though at least proof against electronic countermeasures), V1 was essentially inaccurate and mostly launched from simple ramps against the general target of London. It could be launched from aircraft, a few northern cities becoming targets to V1s launched from over the North Sea.

Some 10,492 V1s were launched against Britain, of which 3,531 penetrated the defences. Nearly 4,000 were downed by a combination of balloon cables, fighter aircraft and guns using the new radar proximity fuse. The remainder failed either on launch or in flight.

V2. The development of the German V2 stemmed from work by Dr von **Braun** in 1936 on the German rocket A4. Powered by liquid fuel (hydrogen peroxide and liquid oxygen), the rocket motor developed 27,180kg of thrust, propelling the missile with its 906kg warhead to an altitude of 97km and giving it a range of 350km. Though V2's autopilot was a wonder of technology, the electric torque motor driving the gyros being the smallest of its kind yet made, it was no more accurate than V1, largely because of launch inaccuracies and motor shut-off variations (arising from current supply frequency variations) and poor pick-up from the pitch gyros to the control-surface servos.

V2, like V1, was unaffected by electronic countermeasures and, additionally, could not be intercepted by the defences once it had been launched. Effort was therefore concentrated on attacking the launch sites, once Paris had been attacked on 6 September 1944, soon followed by the launch of 3,195 missiles against Britain and Belgium, attacks ending in March 1945.

Though V2's effectiveness was modest (under two killed per missile, though with some morale effect since there was no attack warning), its significance as a forerunner of modern ballistic missiles cannot be denied.

Verdun, Battles of. This fortress city on the River Meuse guards a traditional gateway into France. In the **Franco-Prussian War** it withstood siege for nearly two months. Afterwards, with the new German frontier only 30 miles distant, it was provided with some very modern **fortifications** which held firm at the start of **World War I**.

In 1916 General von **Falkenhayn** decided on an experiment in attritional warfare at Verdun by limited German **infantry** attacks supported by unlimited **artillery** fire designed to 'bleed the French Army white' in a 'mincing machine'. Correctly he reasoned that the fall of Verdun would deal a shattering blow to French **morale** and, perhaps, win the war. Unbeknown to him the French no longer had faith in forts and had not only largely disarmed them but also permit-

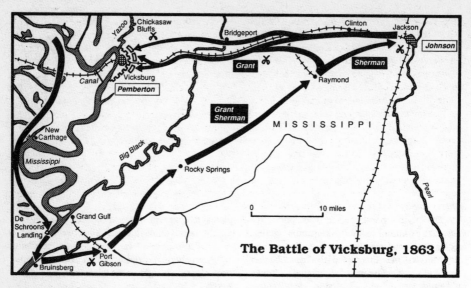

The Battle of Vicksburg, 1863

ted the entrenchments to fall into decay. Incorrectly he had not allowed for such fierce enemy resistance that his own Infantry would also be bled white. The offensive started on 21 February on an eight-mile front with support from over 1,200 guns well supplied with ammunition. The vital, but undefended, Fort Douaumont fell on the 25th to cause an almost fatal crisis of confidence. Next day General **Pétain** was placed in command by Marshal **Joffre**, told to hold out and, fortuitously, was given time to repair the defences before the Germans renewed their main assault.

The key to Pétain's success was supply by motor vehicles along the only main road leading into Verdun, the **railway** being out of action from shell-fire. The next German mistake was to change their tactics and expose their infantry to as much attrition as the French; followed by Falkenhayn's decision, for political and prestige reasons, to continue the assault long after it was recognized as counter-productive. It ground on into July with appalling losses until the British offensive on the **Somme** gave Falkenhayn an excuse to call it off. But the French, now under General Robert Nivelle, counter-attacked, recapturing Douaumont on 24 October and Fort Vaux, which had been lost on 9 June, on 2 November. By then Falkenhayn had been replaced by **Hindenburg**; and the casualty bill, amounting to 542,000 French and 434,000 Germans, had almost ruined the **morale** of both sides.

Vicksburg, Battle of. The essentially decisive moves of the **American Civil War** were made in April 1862 after the **Shiloh** campaign and the capture of New Orleans (by Commodore David Farragut's squadron) gave the Federals dominance over the Mississippi River. Destruction of Confederate gunboats at New Orleans let Farragut steam up-river against the key city of Vicksburg, with the aim of cutting the Confederacy in half and ruining its war economy. But in June he withdrew after suffering heavy damage against its forts and failing to prevent the ironclad *Arkansas* breaking through to the city, which the Confederates, under General John Pemberton, now fortified extensively.

In July command of weakened Federal armies in the West passed to General **Grant**, who nevertheless won defensive victories at the Battles of Iuka (19/20 September) and Corinth (3/4 October). By November, however, he felt strong enough to move against Vicksburg, sending an **amphibious** force of 40,000 under General **Sherman** and Admiral David Porter down-river from Memphis (which had fallen in June); and in December himself advancing towards Grand Junction. But he stalled owing to loss of his supplies at Holly Springs to a Confederate raid on the 20th; and Sherman's attempt to storm Vicksburg via Chickasaw Bluffs was repulsed with heavy loss on the 29th.

From January to April 1863, Grant manoeuvred Sherman, Porter and Farragut round

Vicksburg via the west bank, dominating the river and progressively shifting the army southwards to cross the Mississippi at Hard Times and strike eastwards towards Jackson. On 1 May Grant cast off from his communications, drove back the thoroughly confused Confederates at Port Gibson, forced General Joseph Johnston out of Jackson on the 14th and then turned west to defeat Pemberton at Champion's Hill on the 16th. Meanwhile Sherman protected Grant's rear at Jackson, prior to using the only available pontoon bridge to cross the Big Black River and complete Vicksburg's encirclement from the north. Two costly assaults on the 19th and 22nd finally convinced Grant that bombardment and raw starvation were the best way to capture the city, leaving Sherman to prevent Johnston interfering from the east. On 4 July Pemberton surrendered with his emaciated force.

Vietnam War. So far as the government of North Vietnam was concerned, the end of the **Indo-China War of Independence** in 1954 was but a pause in the war. In January 1959 they decided to initiate an 'armed struggle' against South Vietnam; in May started construction of the Ho Chi Minh Trail; and in April 1960 imposed military conscription and began the infiltration of the North Vietnamese Army (NVA) cadres into the south to support the indigenous Vietcong (VC) guerrillas. Also in April 1959 President **Eisenhower** announced that the USA would support the South and began increasing the number of advisers in place – of whom two were killed by the VC in July.

As the USA intensified its efforts to train, equip and expand the South Vietnamese Armed Forces (SVNAF), General **Giap** increased pressure with widespread attacks. Only slowly did the Americans and SVNAF come to realize they were faced with a well-supplied NVA effort behind the VC's guerrilla warfare. Not until mid-1961, when several Army **helicopter** troop-lift squadrons were brought in, were Americans permitted to fire 'in self-defence' – escalations in force and intent which were but a hint of what would come. For at the end of 1961 there were only 3,205 Americans present, but at the end of 1962 11,300 were engaged in a big shooting war, though attacks by land or air upon the North and the Ho Chi Minh Trail were still forbidden and always would be hampered by rules of engagement.

In January 1963 the VC inflicted a severe defeat on the Army of the Republic of Vietnam (ARVN) (the old SVNAF) at Ap Bac. Simultaneously their shrewd **propaganda** began to undermine resistance within a divided government. Not until June 1964 did the USA really grasp the nettle by appointing General **Westmoreland** to command and permitting a less inhibited war, including **blockade** of the North's coastline and **bombing** of the North in retaliation for an attack on a US destroyer in August. In successive years the intensity of fighting grew at sea, on land and on both sides of the frontier in the air. Hamstrung by politics the frustrated forces of the South fought with one hand behind their backs while Giap, the NVA and VC exploited every opportunity.

One escalatory milestone followed another; 1965 saw air attacks, opposed by **fighters** and **rocket missiles**, against **logistics** targets in the North and the arrival of Australian, New Zealand, and South Korean troops. As the first American **armoured** forces began to deploy, it began to dawn that this was something more than a guerrilla war and the peace movements sounded louder in the USA. In 1966 the Battles of **Hanoi** began in earnest, there was defoliation by herbicides of the jungle to destroy enemy cover, and Filipino troops joined in, bringing so-called Free World Military Forces in the South to 385,000 Americans, 736,000 ARVN and 52,500 others. The year 1967, when a report showing how easily armoured forces could operate in the South brought an overdue change in tactics, was also a time for the anti-war movement in the USA to make a significant impact; and a year when total US casualties for the war reached 16,000 and the ARVN 60,500. All this was on the eve of the climactic siege of Khe Sanh and the **Tet Offensive** in January 1968, with the comprehensive defeat of Giap which was rooted very much in the use of **transport aircraft** and **helicopters**. The latter sometimes flew in flocks of 200 or more machines to break sieges and strike the enemy rear by so-called sky-cavalry tactics. Yet the USA lost strategically from her self-inflicted wound of virulent anti-war propaganda, which government failed to withstand in what was an election year.

From then until 1973 successive US governments sought ways out of their dilemma while the fighting went on. The North might have been beaten if General Westmoreland had been

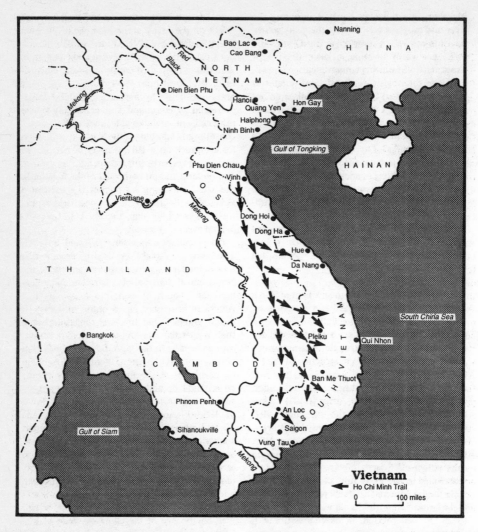

Vietnam
◄── Ho Chi Minh Trail
0   100 miles

allowed to invade Laos and cut the Ho Chi Minh Trail in the same manner as the raids into **Cambodia** in 1970 eliminated a major NVA base and produced a stinging victory which only had to be followed up. For use of massed fire-power and the latest **technology**, including solid-state **electronics**, **surveillance**, sea-**mines** and **smart** weapons, was bringing the North's economy and logistics to the verge of collapse. And defeat of its spring offensive in 1972 seriously undermined the North's confidence as well as Giap's credibility. But as usual a politically scared US government dithered – until, in December 1972 (after a Presidential election

had been won), it finally lost patience with the North's procrastination over peace negotiations and ordered unrestricted bombing of all targets connected with the enemy's war effort. This **strategic bombing** brought a cease-fire in January 1973, followed by the progressive withdrawal of US troops down to a total of 50 on 31 December 1974. Never before had the USA lost a war. Moreover Giap's successor, General **Dung**, had already topped up the Ho Chi Minh Trail supply line and, on 13 December 1974, launched the attack which swept aside a demoralized ARVN with such rapidity that **Saigon** was captured with hardly a fight on 30 April 1975 to end the war.

Villers-Bretonneux, Battles of. On 24 November 1870, at a nadir in France's history in the **Franco-Prussian War**, 17,000 soldiers under General Bourbaki gave as good as they got against a superior Prussian force on the ground overlooking this small village, 12 miles to the east of **Amiens** – which fell, notwithstanding. On 24 April 1917, after the first battle of the **Hindenburg Offensive** had stopped short on the same ground on the 4th, British and Australian troops, with three heavy Mark IV and seven light Whippet **tanks**, fought five German divisions, with fifteen heavy A7V tanks, in the first tank-versus-tank battle.

General Georg von der Marwitz's limited aim was to seize the high ground to obtain direct observation of Amiens and then 'act according to the situation'. In foggy conditions, made denser by gas (**Chemical warfare**) and smoke, the German tanks entered the village ahead of the **infantry** they were supporting and drove towards the woods and the village of Cachy beyond. Here they encountered the three Mark IV tanks, damaging and driving off two, being shot up by the third, which knocked out one A7V as the German assault lost momentum. To the south of this skirmish the attack made less progress towards Cachy because initially the A7Vs lost direction. They too were unsupported since, in the midst of this fight, the seven British Whippets arrived and scattered the infantry. The attack faded, even though an A7V, unseen by the Whippets, had set fire to one, damaged another and driven off the rest. The demoralized German infantry, however, had suffered enough and declined to go on.

Vimy Ridge, Battles of. This long, northwards-facing, steep escarpment dominating the Plain of Douai and shielding **Arras**, fell into German hands in August 1914 at the start of **World War I**. In October it was a start line during the **Race to the Sea** to encircle Arras, a struggle which failed to reach its prime objective but neverthe-less left the adjacent St Lorette spur also in German hands. There in May, June and September 1915 the French strove with fanatical courage to recapture this vital ground, attacking with little hope of cheap success since they were deficient of adequate heavy **artillery** and **ammunition** to overcome the already very strong enemy **fortifications**. St Lorette fell but not one inch of Vimy Ridge.

In March 1916 the British took over this sector and at once entered into a vicious underground struggle with the Germans, who had tunnelled deeply into the chalk substrata. Mining and counter-mining went on to the accompaniment of raids on the surface, a battle the British won before the Canadian Corps, under General **Currie**, took over in October. In the British offensive at Arras on 9 April 1917, it was Currie's task to secure the left flank by seizing the Ridge with his four divisions on a 7,000 yards frontage. The subjugation of the German defences was carried out by over 1,000 guns (including 400 heavies) which fired 80,000 tonnes of ammunition in three weeks further to pulverize a quagmire. But the infantry, who had reached their assault positions in the safety of tunnels dug far back behind the lines, went over the top with confidence in a meticulous, well-rehearsed plan. Nearly all objectives were taken – the remainder falling on the 10th and 12th.

For the rest of the war the Ridge remained firmly in Allied hands, easily withstanding a major German assault on 28 March 1918 as part of the **Hindenburg Offensive** and acting as a springboard for the British and Canadian attack which, on 25 August, pushed the Germans to final defeat.

But in **World War II** the Germans were back again, seizing the Ridge on 24 May 1940 in the aftermath of a stiff fight for Arras and the slopes of the St Lorette spur – a symbolic act of the Battle of **France** – only to lose it again without a fight to British troops on 31 August 1944.

W

Walcheren Island, Battle of. In October 1944, when contemplating how to end the **Scheldt River** battles by capturing Walcheren, General Guy Simmonds, commander II (Canadian) Corps, proposed **bombing** breaches in the dikes to let in the sea and thus maroon the 8,000-strong German garrison in its **fortifications**. The breaching was carried out on the 3rd. By the 20th two-thirds of this below-sea-level island was inundated. Meanwhile **amphibious** forces had been preparing to make landings in Buffalo Amtracs near Westkappelle and Flushing, following an assault across the causeway from South Beveland on the 31st. On the 1st this lodgement was eliminated, but Allied **Commandos**, supported by heavy air attacks, land and naval bombardment, and by swimming and minesweeping tanks, sailed into Flushing harbour and through the gap in the dikes at Westkappelle. The surprised and stranded Germans could only fight where they stood while the Commandos advanced along the dikes and manoeuvred in Amtracs, systematically capturing batteries which continued to dominate the Scheldt until the 4th, when minesweeping began. Resistance ended when Middelburg fell to swimming Buffaloes on the 6th.

War crimes. See Crimes, War.

War, Laws of. See Laws of war.

War, Principles of. The statement of succinct principles of war as a foundation for the conduct of **strategy** and **tactics** is a 20th-century phenomenon. Prior to 1921, when ten principles were first presented in the British **training** manual *Field Service Regulations (FSR)* by Colonel **Fuller**, military wisdom had been contained in the often voluminous works of **philosophers** and the maxims of great commanders, works which were often discursive and aimed at a small élite. Fuller wanted an easier way to understanding by the mass of average students, and has been copied by many nations, including those of the **Nato** powers. He argued also in his *Lectures on FSR III* that, regardless of circumstances and new **technology**, strategy and tactics always have been governed, consciously or unconsciously, by his principles of war. They are:

1. *Selection and Maintenance of the Aim*, which speaks for itself and may well be the product of a commander's original assessment of the situation or simply an adaptation of somebody else's stated *aim*. But it does govern plans, orders and their execution, most of which are affected by the other nine principles.

2. *Maintenance of Morale*. Without sound **morale**, failure is likely no matter how good the plan. The wise commander never ignores its importance and works diligently to enhance it.

3. *Surprise*. An enemy who is left undisturbed and psychologically composed is all the more able to counter the best-conceived plan. The catastrophic consequences of acting without surprise were commonplace in **World War I**, until the advent of the **tank** and unregistered **artillery** fire at the Battle of **Cambrai** in November 1917 reintroduced the feasibility of attacking without need of prolonged preparations.

4. *Economy of Effort*, designed to make the best use of all resources in time and space, and in order to create and maintain a **reserve**.

5. *Concentration of Force*. The fairly obvious need to apply maximum effort against the enemy, preferably where he is known or thought to be weakest. In other words, to be stronger

than the enemy, without necessarily committing larger numbers.

6. *Security*. Meaning the necessity to guard against enemy threats and actions. A principle which calls for first-class **intelligence** and counter-intelligence work. As an element of **C³I** in the **electronics** era this becomes vital.

7. *Offensive Action*, which demands a posture or adoption of attack to win the initiative and throw an enemy off balance. To fail in this aspect through supine inactivity is to court disaster, particularly when faced by resourceful opponents.

8. *Flexibility* is the retention of a capability to react to changing circumstances, especially by mobility, the rapid switching of fire-power and arrangement of sufficient **logistic** resources.

9. *Co-operation* is the need to work closely and amicably with all friendly forces, particularly allies. Keys to this are **communications** and the establishment of secure links, as well as sound relationships between commanders, **staffs** and subordinates. This is a never-ending business, best based on long-established personal associations.

10. *Administration*, focusing attention on the vital necessity of foresight in planning and smoothly functioning **communications** and transport which keep **logistics** working efficiently.

All principles, notably the briefly expressed kind, are open to debate. There is a tendency to value some among the ten higher than others. For example, after the *aim*, *surprise* and *flexibility* are occasionally rated the most important. Less frequently *administration* is placed high, yet, as entries in this Encyclopedia often indicate, in the final analysis operations hinge upon this basic principle.

Warsaw, Battles of. In World War I, during the autumn of 1914 after the Russian defeat at **Tannenberg** and Austro-Hungary's defeat in Galicia, the East Front battles began to centre on Warsaw. By 17 September the German Ninth Army, under General **Hindenburg**, had concentrated between Łódź and Cracow to begin an advance on Warsaw with a view to relieving pressure on the Austrians. But in this, the *First Battle*, the Russians under Grand Duke Nicholas reacted swiftly, blocking 18 German divisions with 60 of their own to the south of the city, and throwing them back to their start line.

The *Second Battle* followed on 11 November when Ninth Army (now under General August von Mackensen), advanced towards Łódź from Strzelno with its left flank on the Vistula River directed on Warsaw. This pre-empted a new Russian offensive but led to heavy fighting at Łódź where. again, the Germans were beaten and forced to fall back, after inflicting heavy losses on the Russians. Eventually Warsaw fell without a fight to the Germans on 7 August 1915 as the Russians conducted their front-wide withdrawal following the **Gorlice offensive**.

Warsaw was not a major objective again until August 1920 when, as capital of the newly formed Polish state under General **Piłsudski**, it stood in the way of the advancing Communist Russian Red Army under Marshal Mikhail Tukhachevsky. This thrust by 200,000 Russians towards Germany in pursuit of the Polish Army (see **Russo-Polish War**) reached the outskirts of the city on 14 August. But the Russians were at the end of their **logistic** tether, whereas Piłsudski, with 180,000 none-too-well-supplied troops, held the city and was content to let the enemy bypass to the northward while he prepared a classic counterstroke. On the 16th the Poles struck the thin, surprised Russian left flank to the north of Lublin. They drove deep into the enemy rear at the same time as another thrust hit the Russian spearhead to the west. The Russians collapsed, either surrendering or dashing into internment in East Prussia. In all they lost 150,000 men and all their equipment, the Poles suffering 50,000 casualties to raise the siege of Warsaw and win the war.

World War II brought Warsaw's worst ordeal when the German Army came in sight on 7 September. An attempt with tanks to brush aside the defences was stopped with heavy loss. But **Hitler** had already decided the Poles were to be annihilated, and ordered the city's immediate subjugation by **bombing** and **artillery**. The Poles, their position hopeless, resisted until the 27th when their mayor surrendered.

From 1939 to 1944 the people of Warsaw were treated as slaves, particularly the Jews, who were incarcerated in their ghetto. On 19 April 1943 those few Jews who had not already been transported for extermination, rose up in desperation and fought the Germans for three weeks before themselves being destroyed. Hope of liberation in Warsaw rose again on 1 August

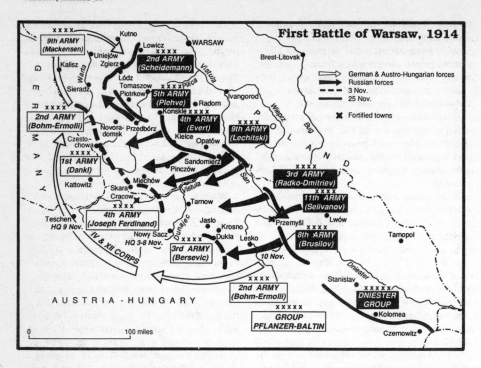

First Battle of Warsaw, 1914

9th ARMY (Mackensen)

Kutno
Lowicz
WARSAW
Brest-Litovsk
Uniejów
Zgierz
2nd ARMY (Scheidemann)
Kalisz
Sieradz
Lódz
Tomaszow
Piotrkow
5th ARMY (Plehve)
Pilica
Ivangorod
Radom
Novoradomsk
Przedbórz
4th ARMY (Evert)
Konskie
2nd ARMY (Bohm-Ermolli)
Czesto-chowa
1st ARMY (Dankl)
Kielce
Opatów
9th ARMY (Lechitski)
Kattowitz
Skara
Miechów
Pinczów
Sandomierz
3rd ARMY (Radko-Dmitriev)
11th ARMY (Selivanov)
Cracow
Vistula
San
Tarnow
Przemyśl
Lwów
Teschen HQ 9 Nov.
4th ARMY (Joseph Ferdinand)
Jaslo
Krosno
Dukla
8th ARMY (Brusilov)
Tarnopol
Nowy Sacz HQ 3-8 Nov.
Dunajec
Lesko
3rd ARMY (Bersevic)
10 Nov.
Dniester
IV & XII CORPS
Stanislav
DNIESTER GROUP
AUSTRIA - HUNGARY
2nd ARMY (Bohm-Ermolli)
Kolomea
GROUP PFLANZER-BALTIN
Czernowitz

German & Austro-Hungarian forces
Russian forces
3 Nov.
25 Nov.
Fortified towns

0   100 miles

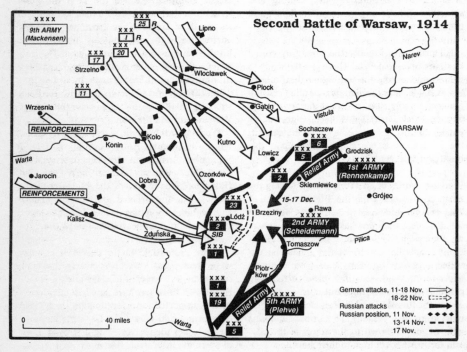

Second Battle of Warsaw, 1914

9th ARMY (Mackensen)
25 R
1 R
20
17
Strzelno
11
Wrzesnia
REINFORCEMENTS
Konin
Kolo
Kutno
Jarocin
Dobra
Ozorków
REINFORCEMENTS
Kalisz
Zduńska
23
2 SIB
Lódz
1
1
19
5th ARMY (Plehve)
Lipno
Wloclawek
Plock
Gabin
Vistula
Narev
Bug
Sochaczew
6
5
2
Relief Army
WARSAW
Grodzisk
1st ARMY (Rennenkampf)
Skierniewice
Grójec
15-17 Dec.
Brzeziny
Rawa
2nd ARMY (Scheidemann)
Tomaszow
Pilica
Piotr-ków
Relief Army
Warta

German attacks, 11-18 Nov.
18-22 Nov.
Russian attacks
Russian position, 11 Nov.
13-14 Nov.
17 Nov.

0   40 miles

1944 when the so-called Home Army (partly supported by the Polish government and the **Special Operations Executive** in London) took up their hidden arms under General Tadeusz Bór-Komorowski. The Russians arrived outside Praga on the other side of the river a few days later but, according to Josef **Stalin**, were in no condition to help the Home Army, even if it was politically desirable to try. So the Poles, supported only by supplies dropped by Allied aircraft flying from Italy, were left to their doom as the Germans tore the city to pieces before all resistance ended on 2 October. An estimated 100,000 Poles died, exacerbating the traditional Polish hatred of Russians and Germans and marking, in some opinions, the start of the **Cold War**. Eventually the Russians occupied the evacuated city on 17 January 1945.

Warsaw Pact. This 20-year mutual-defence pact was signed between Russia, Albania, Bulgaria, Czechoslovakia, East Germany, Hungary, Poland and Romania on 14 May 1955 as a counter to the recently announced admission of West Germany into **Nato**. Mainly it aimed at unified military command under Russian control and legal justification for the location of their troops in Eastern Europe. Like Nato it has suffered over the years from recurring outbreaks of anti-Russian nationalism, peaking in Hungary in 1956, Czechoslovakia in 1968 and since 1980 in a widespread manner. But it still controls formidable forces which outnumber Nato despite **disarmament** proposals by Mikhail Gorbachev and the revolutions in Eastern Europe in 1989. In 1991 as an arm of Soviet power it is virtually extinct.

Wavell, Field Marshal (Viscount) Archibald (1883–1950). A British infantryman with a diverse record in **World War I** who played a leading part in educating the British Army between the World Wars. In July 1939 he was made C-in-C of the new Middle East Command with wide responsibilities and meagre forces to protect vital Allied resources and lines of communication. After the Italians declared war in June 1940 he fought, until June 1941, the Battles of **North Africa**, **Abyssinia**, **Greece**, **Crete**, Iraq and **Syria**: one of the most testing year's campaigning any general has had to bear and yet finish with position intact. No sooner had he taken command in India than the Japanese

attacked. In December 1941 he was made Supreme Commander South-West Pacific, again with inadequate forces to fight a strong opponent who won in **Malaya**, **Singapore**, the Dutch East Indies and **Burma**. A highly respected, erudite but rather taciturn man, in June 1943 he was made the penultimate Viceroy of India and endured a difficult period until retirement in February 1947.

Wei-Hai-Wei, Battle of. During the **Chinese–Japanese War**, on 19 January 1895, a Japanese army under Marshal Iwao Oyama landed within 20 miles of the naval base of Wei-Hai-Wei with the intention of eliminating the Chinese Fleet. Supported by the Fleet under Admiral Yuko Ito, Oyama laid siege to the town and its fortifications on the 30th, bringing fire to bear on the two **battleships**, four **cruisers** and 15 **torpedo-boats** in the harbour. Simultaneously, Ito began a series of night **torpedo** attacks, culminating in the sinking of a battleship on 5 February, followed by an attempted escape in which only two Chinese torpedo-boats got away. On 12 February the port was captured and the few surviving naval vessels surrendered. Only two Japanese torpedo-boats were lost, with 15 killed and 31 wounded.

West African wars. The traditional pattern of tribal wars in this vast region was radically altered in the latter half of the 19th century when the European powers forced their way in. The French occupation of Senegal and the upper Niger coincided with the Tuculor people's own civil war into the 1890s, while British traders in the Gold Coast (now Ghana) provoked wars with the Ashantis in 1873/4, and from 1893 and 1896. The wars prompted the British also to complete seizure of Nigeria between 1897 and 1903 and as a counter to the French. Meanwhile the Germans had taken over Togoland and the Cameroons in 1884; the Spanish acquired Rio de Oro and a slice of Guinea in 1885; and the Belgians assumed sovereignty over the Congo. Each conquest or 'pacification' had its own small wars and uprisings, fought in undeveloped countries where rivers were strategically vital. The struggles, which persisted in the 20th century, included uprisings in Portuguese Angola in 1902 and German South-West Africa in 1903 which were put down.

At the start of **World War I**, Germany's Togoland and the Cameroons, with their naval bases and **radio** stations, were prime Allied objectives. Campaigns between small forces went on into 1916 as the Germans, cut off from help, were driven inland. But though soon overrun in Togoland, the Germans resisted in Cameroon against overstretched, outnumbered Allied forces (24,500 to 19,500), until overcome in mid-1915 by converging British and Franco-Belgian columns. But not until March 1916 did the last pocket surrender.

The West African coast was also of vital strategic importance in **World War II**, and the objective of British and Free French forces seeking to take over Vichy-held territory and prevent a German presence. Failure at **Dakar** in September 1940 was offset by Free French acquisition of the Congo prior to moving towards Chad and North Africa.

Like the rest of Africa's states, those in the west struggled for and won independence after World War II. It started with the peaceful creation of Ghana in 1957 and the negotiated grants of independence in 1960 to all French colonies, but deteriorated into the complete breakdown of order in the Belgian Congo (now Zaire) in 1960 when an explosive mixture of anti-colonialism, tribalism and Communism started a civil war which lasted until 1969 and featured the temporary secession of Katanga, with much destruction and bloodshed. The imbroglio was as bad as that which broke out in Angola in 1961; it forced the Portuguese to grant independence to a Marxist government in 1974, whereupon anti-Marxist Unita forces, supported by South Africa, began a **guerrilla** war which, in 1976, was intensified by the arrival of Fidel **Castro**'s Cuban troops. The struggle continued into 1989 as pressure for the removal of the Cubans coincided with a United Nations peace formula which also could free neighbouring Namibia from involvement both in **South African** and West African wars.

Meanwhile in Nigeria, which achieved independence in 1960, there was much internal instability and, in 1967, the secession of its eastern region, Biafra. After initial military success, the Biafrans were driven back and, over three years of bitter fighting, starved into surrender.

A rebellion in Liberia which broke out in 1990 against the government of President Samuel Doe, ended in victory for the rebels of the National Patriotic Front after heavy fighting. But civil war continues.

West Europe campaigns. From the start of **World War II** West Europe was in the front line, although only in 1940 and 1944/5 were major campaigns fought on land, the remaining periods being occupied by **naval**, **air** and hit-and-run **amphibious warfare**.

1940. The German invasions of **Denmark** and **Norway** started on 9 April and were followed by the invasion of **Holland** and Belgium on 10 May as the immediate prelude to the Battle of **France**. These campaigns might have won the war for **Hitler** had he not let the British escape from **Dunkirk**. Or if he had been more foresighted and determined in trying to win the Battle of **Britain** before turning against Russia. As it was he gave Britain breathing space to rebuild her forces and mount the **strategic bombing** offensive and the **Commando** raids, neither of which, between 1940 and the **Normandy** landing in 1944, brought Germany to her knees, although each contributed strongly to wearing her down and diverting considerable effort from other fronts. Indeed, Commando raids against Norway helped persuade Hitler that the Allies would invade there, while those at **Saint-Nazaire** and **Dieppe** deeply influenced the 1944 invasion of France since they focused German attention on the vital importance of ports to an invader, causing immense diversion of capital expenditure on static defences. The **fortifications** were hardly tested, because the Allies managed to supply their armies over the beaches and through the prefabricated Mulberry harbour.

1944. The massive air offensive and the defeat of the U-boats in the Battle of the **Atlantic**, along with excellent deception measures and extremely well prepared amphibious and **airborne** warfare techniques and **technology**, ensured the success of the landing in Normandy on 6 June. Thereafter it was mainly a question of who won the reinforcement race between the invaders from the sea and the Germans trying to keep their rail and road links open against air attack and sabotage from **Special Operations Executive**-sponsored **guerrillas**. Because the Germans lost this race and also because Hitler insisted upon unyielding defence of Normandy, the destruction of his forces during the break-out was all the more complete in mid-August. But the war might have ended sooner if Generals **Eisenhower** and **Montgomery** had co-ordinated their plans better and taken more care over **logistics**. For whoever of them was right in the argument over whether a narrow or broad-fronted advance into Germany was best, Eisenhower was at fault (against advice) in setting up his HQ on the west side of the Cotentin peninsula, where its signal **communications** with the rapidly advancing armies were totally inadequate – thus preventing him controlling events. And Montgomery erred, despite warnings from Admiral **Ramsay**, by his failure to concentrate on the capture and opening up of Antwerp, with inevitably serious supply shortages. As a result the advancing armies were neither properly commanded nor controlled by the Supreme Commander and the bold attempts to win either at **Arnhem** or by breaking through the **Siegfried Line** came to naught with everybody waiting for the deferred **Scheldt River** battles to be concluded.

This provided Hitler with the opportunity to launch his valedictory and self-consuming **Ardennes offensive** in December before the **Rhineland** battles in February and March 1945 announced the closing stages of the Battle of Germany.

Westmoreland, General William (b. 1914). An American Gunner who, in **World War II**, fought in **North Africa**, **Sicily** and North-West Europe, and as an **airborne** regiment commander in **Korea**. On 20 June 1964 he took command of the US Military Assistance Command Vietnam (MACV). On 2 August North Vietnamese **torpedo-boats** attacked an American **destroyer** in the Tonkin Gulf. Almost at once, **bombing** of North Vietnam was authorized by Washington and Westmoreland was appointed commander of US forces in Vietnam as the enemy stepped up his offensive, producing an escalation of the **Vietnam War**. Until made Army Chief of Staff in the summer of 1968 he did what was **tactically** necessary, frequently hampered by **strategic** restrictions imposed in election years from Washington and elsewhere (compare with **Grant**'s experience in the **Wilderness** campaign, below). He was forbidden to attack the vital **Ho Chi Minh Trail** upon which the enemy's **logistics** depended and was conscious of the anti-war feeling in the USA which managed to convert his victory in the **Tet Offensive** of 1968 into a defeat. He remains a politically controversial figure in the aftermath of an out-of-court settlement in 1984 when he sued the Columbia Broad-

casting System for libel over its implication of suppression or alteration of intelligence data relating to the Tet Offensive.

Wilderness, Battles of the. In March 1864 General **Grant** was made General in Chief of the Federal Army and, in an election year despite a strong vocal anti-war lobby, given a free hand by President **Lincoln** to win the **American Civil War**. (Compare with General **Westmoreland**'s experience, above.) Grant aimed to destroy the Confederate forces defending Richmond while General **Sherman** carried out the **March to the Sea** from **Chattanooga** via **Atlanta**. On 4 May his 105,000 men crossed the River Rapidan and next day encountered General **Lee's** 60,000 troops in an area of thickets 14 miles long and 10 miles wide known as the Wilderness. Two days later, after intense combat amid brush fires, he emerged on the other side with 16,000 fewer men against 12,000 fewer Confederates, but ready to begin the series of flanking and counter-flanking manoeuvres against Lee which enabled progress towards Richmond – an objective Lee had to defend. At Spotsylvania on the 8th the armies fought again, with Lee hanging on tenaciously, repelling one attack after another until forced to retire on the 18th with losses of 12,000 against Grant's 14,000. In this period a Federal **cavalry** raid under General Philip Sheridan routed Lee's cavalry under General J. E. B. Stuart (who was killed) at the Battle of Yellow Tavern to deprive Lee of a vital reconnaissance force.

Grant continued southwards, trying to get between Lee and Richmond until again brought to battle on the 23rd at the North Anna River. Once more Lee thwarted Grant's manoeuvres and inflicted a **tactical** defeat at the expense of **strategic** advantage in this attritional struggle. But while Grant was being reinforced by well-equipped men, Lee had to weaken his other fronts to hold on. At the Battle of Cold Harbor, between 3 and 12 June, Lee inflicted 13,000 casualties on Grant against 3,000 of his own; no fewer than 7,000 Federal losses, against 1,500 Confederates, occurred in the space of an hour's head-on struggle at the start. Yet remorselessly Grant pursued his aim: he dealt firmly with a Confederate raid from the **Shenandoah Valley** against Washington; and deceived Lee with the impression of reverting to the defensive though, in fact, preparing a highly imaginative swing with the bulk of his army, round Lee's

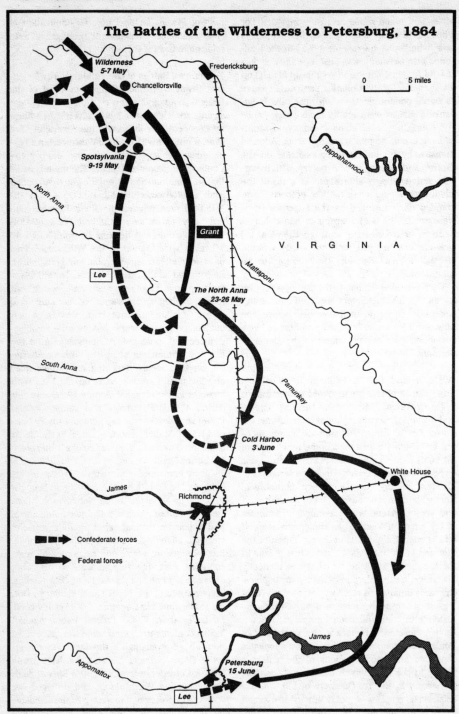

The Battles of the Wilderness to Petersburg, 1864

0 ___ 5 miles

Wilderness 5-7 May

Fredericksburg

Chancellorsville

Spotsylvania 9-19 May

North Anna

Grant

Lee

V I R G I N I A

Mattaponi

The North Anna 23-26 May

South Anna

Pamunkey

Cold Harbor 3 June

James

White House

Richmond

Confederate forces

Federal forces

James

Appomattox

Petersburg 15 June

Lee

Rappahannock

right flank. Unopposed, he crossed the Chick-ahominy and James rivers, using specially made pontoon bridges (constructed by **engineers** in eight hours), to appear before **Petersburg** on the 15th. Lee, deprived of his cavalry's 'eyes', was totally surprised and, for once, slow to react. If things had gone better for Grant at Petersburg, Richmond might have fallen with decisive consequences.

Women's military forces. There are few periods in military history when women have been totally excluded from military service or completely denied a combat role. Since 1854 and Florence **Nightingale**'s reforming zeal in the **Crimean War**, they have been closely involved with **medical services**. Before and during the **American Civil War**, Harriet Tubman ran a very secure 'Underground Railroad' for escaping slaves, spied for the Federals and took part in raids against the Confederates. Espionage has long been a woman's activity and so too has combat. The 6ft 2in Mary Denis was an officer in the Minnesota Regiment and Loretta Velasquez disguised herself as a man to fight for the Confederates at First **Bull Run**; later captured as a spy she escaped, and then joined the **infantry** to take part in **guerrilla warfare**, when she was wounded and her sex at last revealed. But 2,500 women members (all wives of the king) of Dahomey's Amazon Army fought the French in **West Africa** in 1892.

Not until **World War I** were women recruited in large numbers into the armed forces, mainly by the British and French but not at all by the Germans, while the US Navy, plagued with doubts about legality, recruited 13,000 as signals yeomen. In Britain, units of volunteer ambulance drivers saw service in the theatres of war. As in France, the aim later was to free men for front-line service by putting women into uniform as members of women's military units doing a variety of non-combat tasks. It was the Communists in the full flush of egalitarianism during the **Russian Revolutionary War** who welcomed women into combat alongside the men – a tradition they preserved in the struggles of the proletariat in other countries. Indeed, women showed quite as much courage and stamina as men (to the surprise of many among the latter) and were particularly effective in subversive **guerrilla warfare** as communicators as well as combatants. Many fought in the **Spanish Civil War** and in **Mao Tse-tung**'s campaigns in China.

Yet prior to **World War II** they were still largely excluded from the German forces and kept to administrative work in other nations, except in Russia. But as the war intensified they found extensive employment in partisan groups, operating in plain clothes throughout the Axis-occupied territories. The story of all Communist partisans, notably those of **Yugoslavia** and Russia, is packed with women's deeds in every sphere, like the exploits of women agents sent in by the **Special Operations Executive** (SOE) to help found and control resistance bands in **West Europe**. Only a minority anywhere fought in the front line or as air crew, though they often made **propaganda** headlines. The Russian Lydia Livak was killed in 1943 after becoming an **ace** with 12 victories and the Russians also had an all-women **fighter** unit with 38 enemy aircraft to its credit, as well as **bomber** units. Prominence was also given to women snipers with large scores of Germans shot.

Most nations' armed services have retained women's units – naval, army and air force – and gradually, for equality of rights, have widened and integrated their roles with those of men. As technicians, operational pilots and qualified combat soldiers they have achieved higher command. Only on the question of sheer physical strength (as with men) can there be any bar to their combat military service in the future.

World Wars. The next two entries purport to give an overview only of these cataclysmic events of the 20th century. Naturally, many historians consider that these two major wars were the result of the wild expansionist policies of the foregoing 70 or more years; that they followed each other as an almost logical consequence; and that the subsequent violence of the first total wars was the inevitable outcome of the sudden and accelerating disruption of society along with the institutional changes they initiated. These struggles were accompanied by wholesale destruction and slaughter, in company with genocide, and, through the lowering of moral standards, threaten civilization to the roots to the present day.

World War I. The causes of this war, starting 28 July 1914, were many and varied, ranging through nationalist vengeance to pay off old scores, trade rivalries and the almost uncontrolled militarism which, under bellicose General

The First World War in Europe, 1914-18

Central Powers
Allies
Russian

Staffs, influenced weak royal autocracies and their ineffectual democratic governments. **Propaganda** helped make this a popular war – to begin with. Some states were well prepared for it – notably, on land Germany and France, and at sea Britain and Japan – unlike Austro-Hungary, Russia and Serbia, who were in decline from previous wars and unfit for intense armed conflict. As for Italy, Romania, Portugal and America, who joined later, they became caught up in something they could not easily avoid. The nations that began the war did so in the belief that offensive action would make it a short one and that it would be 'over by Christmas'. But insufficient understanding of **technology's effects** and **logistics** put paid to that gross misconception.

The failure by both the Germans and the French and British to reach a conclusion in 1914 during the operations connected with the Battle of the **Marne** and the subsequent **Race to the Sea**, was their inability to overcome modern defensive systems and solve the logistic equation. As was also the case in the Serbo-Austrian battles and, on the east front, the Battles of

Austria and Germany versus the Russians. The Russians lost at **Tannenberg** but won twice before **Warsaw** as stalemate set in. **Artillery** and **machine-guns** forced **infantry** underground, behind barbed wire, and doomed **cavalry** so that reconnaissance became increasingly the function of **air forces**. Likewise at sea the threat of **mines** and **torpedoes** denied admirals the decisive battles they had envisaged. **Blockade** and warfare against commerce predominated; **submarines** and aircraft played an ever larger part. Nothing had gone to plan. Nobody could think of a way out of the impasse through diplomacy, because each country was led to believe in victory. And the military leaders, faced by a sort of siege warfare against unturnable **fortifications**, were barren of ways to win without vast expenditure of lives and material – thus fostering the philosophy of attritional warfare. Indeed, at this stage, only Japan profited by siding with the Allies. For a mere 1,207 casualties, she drove the Germans out of Tsing-tao in 1914 and in due course acquired ex-German islands to strengthen her position in the Pacific Ocean.

Only the **Gorlice Offensive**, in 1915, had a decisive look as the Russians fell back in disorder and demoralization. Elsewhere that year, and also in 1916 and much of 1917, stalemate predominated: on **Vimy Ridge**, in Champagne, at **Verdun** and on the **Somme**, as well as in Italy, the **Balkans**, at **Gallipoli**, in **Egypt**, Palestine, **Mesopotamia** and, to some extent, in East and West Africa. Neither the defeats of Serbia in 1915, nor of **Romania** and the **Brusilov Offensive** in 1916, were conclusive. And the sea Battles of **Dogger Bank** and **Jutland** did little more than consolidate the Royal Navy's obvious supremacy yet without making it possible to enter the Baltic and help Russia or land armies behind the German lines. Indeed the paucity and ineptitude of **amphibious** operations were as remarkable as the exaggerations of **strategic bombing**'s effects.

Not until 1917 did attrition break the impasse when blockade began to hurt both sides. The Russian Revolution, Germany's unlimited submarine campaign against commerce, America's entry into the war and the mutiny of the French Army in the aftermath of the Battle of Chemin des Dames, conjointly disturbed the military balance. Initially it went Germany's way in **Flanders** and at **Caporetto** in October. But the Battle of **Cambrai**, with the first use of massed **tanks** and unregistered artillery fire to restore the principle of surprise (see **War, Principles of**) to land battles, hinted at radical military change, one that became doctrine after the **Hindenburg Offensive** in 1918 had been snuffed out by successive surprise counter-attacks which preceded the definitive tank counterstroke Battle of **Amiens** on 8 August. This all-arms battle cracked the German morale and broke her leaders' resolve as Allied armies everywhere else overran the disastrously weakened Central Powers: in Palestine, the Balkans and Italy. The unexpected collapse washed away monarchies and governments in waves of revolution by the masses, who were stimulated by hopes of a new dawn in Russia, clouded by the **Russian revolutionary wars**. As it reshaped the post-war world, the Versailles Peace Treaty took note of these events in Russia, but other than extract the Central Powers' forces from their midst, did little to curb them.

The total cost in lives from combat has been estimated at a little over eight million, and there were also, very approximately, $6\frac{1}{2}$ million civilian deaths attributable to a war which some were deluded into thinking would end war.

World War II. This war, though caused by some reasons similar to those that caused its predecessor, was affected by two other important aspects. Nobody was ready for it and it was unpopular. Arguably the initiation of the **Chinese–Japanese War** on 7 July 1937, which was the next stage of **Japan's wars of expansion**, started World War II. The Japanese flaunted a policy of greed and aggrandisement, stimulated by a belief that the Occidental powers might bend to their bellicosity. The sins were like those that corrupted the criminally minded minions of Adolf **Hitler** and Benito **Mussolini** as, in the guise of revolution, they imposed Fascist rule on Germany and Italy.

Militarily, too, this war was different from World War I since Hitler, as the motivating aggressive force in Europe, was a political opportunist whose shrewd grand **strategy**, which unopposed conquered Austria and Czechoslovakia, was not complemented by a properly thought-out military strategy. The invasion of Poland (**Polish campaigns**) on 1 September 1939 was a gamble with a Wehrmacht that was ready only for a short war. The decision to attack **France**, via **Holland** and Belgium in May 1940 was as unexpected and unprepared a notion as the subsequent spur-of-the-moment decision to precede it by the invasions of **Denmark** and **Norway** in April. Hitler got away with all three by a combination of surprise, the Wehrmacht's prowess, the introduction of sophisticated **tactics** and **propaganda**, and the latest **technology**, plus the inescapable fact that none of his opponents (like his ally Italy when she joined forces in June 1940 in the hope of easy pickings after the Battle of **France**), was ready for modern war.

Hitler's superficial understanding of military strategy was revealed the moment he failed to concentrate on winning the Battle of **Britain** with an immediate (and feasible) invasion. He suicidally overstretched Axis capability by preparing not only for the gigantic **Russo-German War** in 1941 but also, simultaneously, being drawn into Italy's **North Africa battles**, the invasions of **Yugoslavia**, **Greece** and **Crete** and peripheral adventures in **Syria** and Iraq – besides an attempt to bring Britain to her knees by night **bombing** and in the Battle of the **Atlantic**. It was another

The Second World War
in Europe :
Axis Expansion, 1939-42
━━━━ Limit of Axis expansion 1942

symptom of Axis capriciousness that as Japan (deprived by American embargoes of vital war materials) indicated a clear intention to spread the war into the Pacific Ocean and South-East Asia, no joint strategic plan and little political co-ordination was arranged. Indeed, Hitler did not share his plan to invade Russia with Japan and was kept in the dark about the timing of the attack on **Pearl Harbor** on 7 December and Japan's subsequent plans.

Yet despite these defects and the extraordinary over-confidence of the Axis in challenging the rest of the world, it is remarkable that it came so close to winning in 1941 and 1942. Undeniably this was more a manifestation of Allied un-readiness and outmoded thinking than of moral

or material Axis superiority – claim the opposite as Axis leaders would. Pre-war sins of omission lay at the heart of defeats which rolled the Russians back to the Caucasus and **Stalingrad** in August 1942, drove the British into Egypt, and forfeited to the Axis China's entire coastline (including **Hong Kong**), the **Philippines**, **Malaya**, the Dutch East Indies, **Burma** and many key islands in the **Pacific Ocean War**. So too did the unwillingness of the Allied leaders to recognize the horror of the threat and create firm policies with modern military forces as a **deterrent** to Axis ambitions.

It was the Allied tragedy that, having allowed the enemy to seize such vast territories at such relatively low cost in less than three years, it

The Second World War in Europe:
Allied Advances, 1942-5
Limit of Axis expansion

would take more than three years at very high cost, starting with the Battle of **Midway** on 5 June 1942, to win them back. But the length of time needed to raise, train, equip and supply the Allied counter-offensives might have been a lot longer had they not, by use of superior **communications** and assisted by a great willingness to co-operate among themselves, devised a coherent, joint, aggressive strategy in January 1942. This was the most vital achievement of Winston **Churchill** and President **Roosevelt** when they pooled their ideas and resources for offensives which would concentrate more against Germany than Japan, yet providing strength enough to throw the latter on the defensive.

The unveiling of this strategy was slow and controlled by **logistic** restraints. It was also conditioned by political factors such as the thorny problems of collaboration with Russia and China, to keep them in the war, and plans to reshape the world when peace returned. It was accompanied by disagreements over priorities related to prestige and practicalities, for example, the merits of **strategic bombing** as a war-winning concept as well as insurance of the survival of independent air forces, and the American readiness, ·for prestige and politics, to risk disaster with an invasion of France in 1942 which gave way to the prudence of British peripheral attacks upon southern Europe via Algeria and **Tunisia** and into **Sicily** and Italy (**Italian campaign, 1943–5**) in 1943, thus postponing the invasion of France until 1944. Or the high-level American debate between those like Admiral **Nimitz**, who wanted to head more directly against Japan, and General **MacArthur**, who persuaded Roosevelt of the political and military advantages of tackling the Philippines first in 1944. And so many other crucial decisions like the deliberate introduction of the cult of **guerrilla warfare** into politically sensitive lands (with untold post-war consequences); and the development of the **atom bomb** to pre-empt any possibility of the enemy building one; and dropping them on Hiroshima and Nagasaki to present Japan with a face-saving excuse to admit defeat and save an entire nation from hara-kiri.

Whatever the short-term consequences on the Axis powers in terms of destruction and on the world in loss of life from the controversial and unpremeditated announcement of the policy of unconditional surrender in January 1943, no Versailles peace treaty was needed to reshape the old order this time. It was reshaped instead by *force majeure* of the victorious powers and, shortly, by instinctive nationalist reactions to correct the depredations of the colonial expansions of the past and restore racial and religious independence, by protracted wars if necessary. To attain that state of freedom, the roughly estimated price in military dead was some 15 million, plus attributable civilian deaths anything between 26 and 34 million.

Yalu River, Battles of the. On 17 September 1894, during the **Chinese–Japanese War** a Japanese squadron of four heavy and four light, plus two obsolete **cruisers**, encountered two slower Chinese ironclad **battleships**, four light cruisers and six **torpedo boats** between the Yalu River and Haiyang Island. This therefore pitted, respectively, three 12·6in guns and 62 quick-firing 6in and 4·7in guns against eight old 12in pieces and others of lesser calibre; the Chinese under Admiral Ting, having only 14 rounds per gun. Admiral Yuko Ito completely outmanoeuvred and then overwhelmed the Chinese with fire, though the Chinese fought back well, severely damaging the lightly armoured Japanese. The Chinese lost five ships from superior Japanese gunnery, both battleships surviving however. Five torpedoes were fired but none hit. The Chinese retired into **Wei-Hai-Wei** and the Japanese crossed the Yalu unopposed into Manchuria on 25 October.

There was another battle of the Yalu, on land, on 30 April 1904 during the **Russo-Japanese War**, when a Japanese army of 40,000, advancing from Korea, was unwisely engaged by a mere 7,000 Russians who suffered 2,500 casualties and were bundled back into Manchuria.

Yamamoto, Admiral Isoruku (1884–1943). As a young officer Yamamoto was seriously wounded at the Battle of **Tsushima**, but survived to become a **gunnery** specialist prior to taking a lead in the development of **aircraft-carrier** operations and, in the Aeronautics Department, direction of its **technology**. From being Navy vice-minister in 1936 he was given command of the Japanese Combined Fleet in 1940. With personal knowledge of the USA and Britain he was better aware than most Japanese of the danger of war against them. But he was also a gambler who, though warning of the considerable risks of war, staked all upon the **Pearl Harbor** raid to win a decisive victory. It was his misfortune to be served by leading subordinates who did not thoroughly understand his concepts. As a result neither at Pearl Harbor nor with any of the ensuing aircraft-carrier raids were comprehensive results achieved. Defeat at **Midway** in June 1942 marked the start of a decline which he recognized prior to being intercepted, shot down and killed by American fighters on 18 April 1943.

Yellow Sea, Battle of the. By the beginning of August 1904 **Port Arthur**'s siege was complete and the Tsar ordered Admiral Vilgelm Vitgeft, with six **battleships**, five **cruisers** and eight **destroyers** to break out and make for Vladivostok. Admiral Togo, with four battleships, 19 cruisers and eight destroyers, intercepted as the Russians emerged on the 10th. A running fight ensued until, within 30 minutes of dusk, the Russians looked almost safe. But then a hit from a 12in shell killed Vitgeft. This threw the fleet into a confusion made worse when, at last, Admiral Prince Ukhtomski discovered he was in command and led a panicky retreat for Port Arthur. Some ships made for Vladivostok but became scattered and either were sunk or found internment in various neutral ports – one as far distant as Saigon. The rest re-entered Port Arthur to await their ultimate doom under the Japanese Army's guns.

Yemen, Battles of the. Before, during and after the

Arab Revolt and the removal of Turkish hegemony in **World War I**, the Yemen suffered from traditional tribal turbulence, although the British Protectorate in Southern Yemen, based on Aden, gave a measure of law and order. With the erosion of British power and after joining the Arab League Security Pact in 1950, Imam Ahmed of Yemen promoted tribal raids across the South Yemeni border in 1954. These aggressions increased in frequency and menace after he joined Egypt and Saudi Arabia in the Jidda Pact of 1956, federated with the United Arab Republic (UAR) in 1958 and accepted Communist assistance. When Ahmed died in 1962 his successor was deposed in a revolution which proclaimed the Yemen Arab Republic. Civil war broke out. The rebel pro-Communist government, supported by the UAR and some 35,000 Egyptian troops, fought the anti-Communist royalists, who were helped by Saudi Arabia. Meanwhile Britain resisted Yemeni attempts to penetrate South Yemen. A truce in the civil war was called in August 1965, but it was only temporary. Pressure against South Yemen increased and there was extensive fighting in the Radfan along with violence in Aden while diplomacy was applied.

Egyptian troops withdrew from Yemen in October 1967 and the British from Aden and South Yemen as the latter became an independent republic in November. But no sooner had the Yemeni civil war come to an end in 1969 than elements of the Popular Front for the Liberation of Oman and the Arabian Gulf (PFLOAG) began entering Oman from South Yemen via the mountainous area of Dhofar. The Sultan of Oman's Armed Forces (SAF) with discreet British assistance, gradually dominated this area to prevent PFLOAG camel trains getting through with supplies for the insurgents. SAF employed a combination of mobile land/air operations, based on lines of field **fortifications**, to clear the Dhofar of insurgents. It largely managed to do so by December 1975, thus enabling the Sultan to pacify the Dhofar by a policy of modernization. But South Yemen, with its strong Communist support and presence in Aden, remains a potent source of dissidence in Arabia and **East Africa**.

Ypres. See Flanders, Battles of.

Yugoslavia, Battles of. This largely mountainous state with its indented coastline of many islands was brought into being in 1919 by the amalgamation of the often incompatible Serb, Croat and Slovene peoples, whose machinations were increasingly bedevilled by the Communist Party's animosity to the royalists. This bubbling pot of dissent was invaded by the Germans on 6 April 1941 to eradicate the rebellion which, on 25 March, had overturned the government after it had joined the Anti-Comintern Pact with the Axis powers. Belgrade was heavily bombed as German and Hungarian troops converged on the city (which fell on the 12th), as Italians advanced through Dalmatia to Dubrovnik by the 17th, and the Germans moved in from Bulgaria to Skopje on the 7th, at the same time as they invaded **Greece** to reach Salonika on the 9th. The Yugoslav forces were caught off balance and barely **mobilized** but some took up arms and retired into the mountains to continue resistance.

Two ethnically and politically disparate **guerrilla** groups were formed: (a) in Serbia, under the royalist Colonel Dragoljub Mihailović, the so-called Chetniks; (b) in Croatia, the Communist partisans of **Tito** which became active after Germany had invaded Russia in June. Not only did they overspill into each other's territory, as well as Dalmatia and Montenegro, they also, as time went by, fought each other – the Chetniks sometimes allying themselves with the Italians and the puppet Serbian Fascist regime of General Mila Nedić to do so. In a mire of treachery and pitiless **guerrilla warfare**, the contestants struggled for political power almost as much as they fought the Fascists. At first the Chetniks prospered because they had the support of their exiled government in London and the **Special Operations Executive** (SOE) based in Cairo. But gradually SOE agents discovered that the Chetniks were not making best use against the Axis of the resources being delivered to them, and that the partisans (because they were Communists and had a policy stating they fought for the unification of Yugoslavia) were hurting the Germans.

In the summer of 1943 SOE began giving help to the partisans without withdrawing liaison from the Chetniks who, henceforward, began to atrophy. Partisan attacks became even more effective after they had helped themselves to some of the arms belonging to surrendering Italians in September 1943. But they drew upon

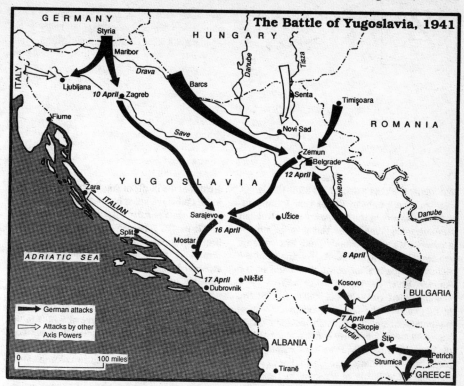

The Battle of Yugoslavia, 1941

themselves the fiercest of the German/Italian/Ustaši (pro-Fascist Serbs) series of seven offensives, which the Axis called counter-guerrilla operations. Number Seven in May 1944 was nearly successful in its attempt by the German **Brandenburg Regiment**, SS and Army troops to capture Tito, his staff and the Allied missions in one swoop – which cost 6,000 partisan casualties. It failed as the Allies poured in supplies and their **Commandos** began raiding and later occupying islands for bases along the coast. Early in September the Russians arrived in Bulgaria (which changed sides) and the German army passed through in retreat from Greece, brushing partisans aside when they attempted to intervene but eventually evacuating Belgrade for a triumphant liberation by partisans in October and the start of Tito's unifying regime.

Z

Zhukov, Marshal Georgi (1896–1974). A peasant who fought in **World War I** and commanded **Cavalry** in the Red Army in the **Russian Revolutionary War**. After the war he studied armoured warfare (**Armour**) and, in Germany, science. He first won fame in command of the victorious Russian forces at the Battle of the **Khalkin River** in August 1939 and in 1941 was appointed Army Chief of Staff by Josef **Stalin**. In that capacity he failed to convince Stalin of the imminence of the German invasion on 22 June 1941. But for nearly every major battle of the **Russo-German War** he was employed to plan and/or command at the front. For example, he fought the Battle of **Moscow** in December 1941, and planned the victories of **Stalingrad** in 1942 and **Kursk** in 1943. He dominated the re-entry into White Russia and Poland in 1944, and personally commanded the capture of Berlin in 1945.

In 1946 he was welcomed home as a hero and almost immediately exiled to the provinces by the ever-paranoiac Stalin. But he was brought back after Stalin's death in 1953 as First Deputy Minister of Defence, becoming Minister of Defence in 1955 and, shortly after, a member of the Praesidium of the Communist Party Central Committee. He was dismissed in 1957 and not returned to favour until 1966.

Zulu wars. The Zulu nation had developed by 1850 into a sophisticated military autocracy whose king controlled a well-trained infantry army, mainly armed with **edged weapons**. Inevitably it was embroiled in the **South African wars** in addition to its own internal feuding, such as the civil war of 1856 between the factions of rival sons for the succession. The struggle was decided at the Battle of Tugela River in December when Cetewayo killed his brother and most supporters, thus ensuring the throne for himself in 1872. In 1877 he came into dispute with the British over border demarcations after they took control of the Transvaal. When the British attempted to reach a settlement on conditions aimed at undermining the Zulu military system with its 40,000 soldiers, Cetewayo refused to give way.

On 11 January 1879 a force of 5,000 British and 8,200 native troops under General Lord Chelmsford invaded Zululand in three widely dispersed columns. The centre column, about 4,100 strong, was surprised and annihilated in the open at **Isandhlwana** on the 22nd. Next day a regiment of Zulus struck at a detachment of 80 British (some 35 of them sick) at Rorke's Drift. From within a small perimeter, with 27 killed or wounded, six attacks were beaten off. About 350 Zulus were killed. Shortly after a second British column was surrounded at Eshowe and held out until April after Chelmsford's relief force had defeated the Zulus at Gingindlovu. Meanwhile the third column, under Colonel Evelyn Wood, evaded 20,000 Zulus until brought to battle at Kambula on 29 March. In four hours Wood lost about 100 out of 400 British troops, but killed 1,000 Zulus to turn the campaign in British favour.

By June, Chelmsford had been reinforced from England. This time he advanced with artillery in support of his 4,200 British and 100 native troops. On 4 July he met 10,000 Zulus at Ulundi, formed square as in days gone by and broke the charging Zulus with devastating fire-power before unleashing 300 **cavalry** to finish the business. British casualties were about 100, but the

Zulus lost about 1,500 and were forced to accept British dominion, though without annexation, a policy which let the Zulus indulge in another civil war, in 1883/4, when Cetewayo was beaten by Zibelu. He in turn was ousted by Dinizulu, who revolted unsuccessfully in 1887 after the British had annexed Zululand.

Chronology

Important Wars, New Technology and Weapons

Year	War	Technology/Weapons
Pre-1850		Rocket missile. Parachute. Manually-propelled submarine. Isolation of aluminium. Steamships. Steam railway. Canned food. Telegraph. Breech-loading rifle. Anaesthetics. Sea-mines. Rodman powder. Boydell footed-wheel tractor. All-metal cartridges.
1850–64	Taiping Rebellion	
1852		Repeater rifle.
1854–6	Crimea	
1855		Cowen's armoured fighting vehicle. Refrigeration.
1856–60	Second Opium	
1856		Bessemer steel.
1857–8	Indian Mutiny	
1858		Heliograph. Aerial photography.
1859	Austro-Piedmontese	*La Gloire* armoured ship. Breech-loading artillery. Hand-rotated machine-gun. First successful oil well.
1860		Magazine rifle.
1861–5	American Civil	Turreted ironclad warship.

Year	War	Technology/Weapons
1861–7	Franco-Mexican	Pasteurized food.
1864	Danish-Prussian	
1865		Antiseptics.
1866	**Austro-Prussian** **Austro-Italian**	Locomotive **torpedo**.
1867		Typewriter.
1870–71	**Franco-Prussian**	
1874		Barbed wire.
1876		**Telephone**. Four-stroke petrol engine. **Torpedo-boat**.
1877–8	**Russo-Turkish**	
1878–80	Second **Afghan**	Dynamo.
1880–81	First **Boer**	
1882		Armoured **steel**.
1883–5	Chinese–French	
1884		**Destroyer**.
1885		Four-wheel motor carriage. Smokeless powder. Semi-automatic **machine-gun**.
1886		Electric-powered **submarine**.
1887		Steerable non-rigid airship.
1888		Portable roll-film camera.
1892		First detected **radio** signal.
1894–5	**Chinese–Japanese**	
1895		First transmission and reception of **radio**. Gyroscope.
1898		Steam-driven turbine engine.
1898	**Spanish–American**	

Year	War	Technology/Weapons
1899–1901	Second **Boer**	Armoured car.
1900–1901	**Boxer Rebellion**	
1900		Petrol-electric **submarine**. Rigid airship.
1901		Transatlantic **radio** link.
1902		Thermionic diode valve.
1903		Powered, heavier-than-air flying machine.
1904–5	**Russo-Japanese**	**Radio** direction-finding (DF).
1905		Dreadnought **battleship**.
1906		**Radio** crystal detector.
1909		Duralumin.
1910		Aerial **bombing**. Armed **aircraft**. Shipborne **aircraft**.
1911–50	**Chinese Civil**	
1911–12	**Italo-Turkish**	**Seaplane**. Airborne **torpedo**.
1912–13	**Balkan**	**Aircraft** catapult.
1914–18	**World War I**	
1915		Poison gas. **Flame-thrower**.
1916		Tank.
1917		**Aircraft-carrier**. Sonar
1918–22	**Russian Revolutionary**	
1919	**Third Afghan**	
1920	**Russo-Polish**	

Year	War	Technology/Weapons
1920–22	**Greek–Turkish**	
1921		Teleprinter.
1923		Autogiro. Cathode-ray tube.
1925		Short-wave, crystal-controlled **radio**.
1926		*Enigma* encoding machine.
1927		**Radio**-beacon **navigation**. Parachute troops.
1933		**Radar**.
1935–6	Italo-Ethiopian	
1936–9	**Spanish Civil**	Helicopter.
1937		Radio-beam **navigation**.
1937–45	**Chinese–Japanese World War II**	
1939	**German–Polish Russo-Japanese**	**Jet aircraft**. Electromechanical **computer**.
1942		Nerve gas.
1943		Infra-red **night-vision** viewer. Guided **rocket missile**.
1944		Programmable electronic digital **computer**. Cruise **rocket missile**.
1945–	**Cold War**	Atom bomb.
1945–9	**Indonesian War of Independence**	
1945–54	French **Indo-China**	
1946–9	**Greek Civil**	
1948–	**Arab–Israeli**	
1948–60	**Malayan War of Independence**	
1949		Transistor.

Year	War	Technology/Weapons
1950–53	**Korean**	
1953		**Hydrogen bomb. Ground-effect machine.**
1954–	African wars of independence	Inertial **navigation.**
1955		Nuclear-powered **submarine.**
1956	Suez	
1957		**Space satellite vehicle.**
1959–74	**Vietnam**	
1960		**Laser. Microchip.**
1965	**Indo-Pakistani**	
1967	Six Days **Arab–Israeli**	
1971	**Indo-Pakistani** (Bangladesh)	
1973	Yom Kippur	
1979–88	**Iran–Iraq**	
1979–89	Russia-Afghanistan	
1982	**Falkland Islands**	

Bibliography

In the interests of simplicity this Bibliography of general reference literature is composed of as few works as possible consistent with providing maximum coverage of key subjects. The titles listed direct attention towards additional bibliographies and reading matter intended to assist in further studies across the vast field of military history and literature.

Aircraft and Air Warfare

Brown, D., Shores, C., and Macksey, K., *The Guinness History of Air Warfare*, Guinness, 1976

Jane's All the World Aircraft, Jane's Publishing

Robinson, D., *The Zeppelin in Combat*, Foulis, 1961

Armour and Artillery

Crow, D., and Icks, R., *Encyclopedia of Tanks*, Barrie & Jenkins, 1975

Jane's Armour and Artillery, Jane's Publishing

Macksey, K., *The Guinness Book of Tank Facts and Feats*, Guinness, 1980

Ogorkiewicz, R., *Armour*, Stephens, 1960

Bibliographies

Albion, D., *Naval and Maritime History. An Annotated Bibliography*, Manson Institute, 1972

Ensor, A. G., *Subject Bibliography of the Second World War*, Deutsch, 1977

Ensor, A. G., *Subject Bibliography of the First World War*, Deutsch, 1979

Higham, R., *Official Histories*, Kansas State University, 1970

Higham, R., *A Guide to the Sources of British Military History*, California University Press, 1971

Higham, R., *A Guide to the Sources of US Military History*, Archon, 1975

Keegan, J., and Wheatcroft, A., *Who's Who in Military History*, Hutchinson, 1976

Lewis, J. R., *Uncertain Judgements. A Bibliography of War Crimes Trials*, Clio, 1970

Tunney, C., *Biographical Dictionary of World War I*, Dent, 1972

Communications and Code Systems

Baker, W. J., *A History of the Marconi Company*, Methuen, 1970

Jane's Military Communications, Jane's Publishing

Kahn, D., *The Code-Breakers*, Weidenfeld & Nicolson

Encyclopedias and Works of General Interest

Clarke, I. F., *Voices Prophesying War*, Oxford University Press, 1966

Colliers Encyclopedia, P. F. Collier

Collins, *Modern Thought*, Collins, 1988

Dupuy, R. E., and T. N., *The Encyclopedia of Military History*, Macdonald, 1970

Earle, E. M., *Makers of Modern Strategy*, Princeton University Press, 1952

Encyclopaedia Britannica, Benton

Fuller, J. F. C., *The Decisive Battles of the Western World* (3 vols.), Eyre & Spottiswoode, 1956

Bibliography

Ladd, J., *Commandos and Rangers*, Macdonald, 1970

Ruffner, F. G., and Thomas, R. C., *Code Name Dictionary* (includes military slang), Gale, 1963

United States Government, *Soviet Military Power*, 1981–

Intelligence (see also Wars)

Hinsley, F. H., *et al.*, *British Military Intelligence in the Second World War* (5 vols.), HMSO, 1979–88

Lewin, R., *The Other Ultra*, Hutchinson, 1982

Logistics

Jane's Combat Support, Jane's Publishing

Macksey, K., *For Want of a Nail*, Brassey's, 1989

Quotations

Heinl, R. D., *The Dictionary of Military and Naval Quotations*, US Naval Institute, 1966

Ships and Naval Warfare

Dyer, G. C., *The Amphibians Came to Conquer* (2 vols.), US Government, 1969

Frere Cook, G., and Macksey, K., *Guinness History of Naval Warfare*, Guinness, 1975

Jane's Fighting Ships, Jane's Publishing

Space

Pebbels, C., *Battle for Space*, Beaufort, 1983

Technology (Military)

Macksey, K., *Technology in War*, Arms & Armour, 1987

Wars (listed chronologically)

Baring Pemberton, W., *The Battles of the Crimean War*, 1962

Catton, B., *A Centennial History of the [US] Civil War* (2 vols.), 1965

Bonnal, H., *Sadowa*, 1907

Howard, M., *The Franco-Prussian War*, Hart-Davis, 1962

O'Toole, G. J. A., *The Spanish War 1898*, Norton, 1982

Farwell, B., *The Great Anglo-Boer War*, Harper & Row, 1976

Anon., *British Official History of the Russo-Japanese War* (5 vols.), HMSO, 1909

Pitt, B. (ed.), *Purnell's History of the First World War* (8 vols.), BPC, 1969

Pitt, B. (ed.), *Purnell's History of the Second World War* (8 vols), BPC, 1966

Herzog, C., *The Arab–Israeli Wars*, Arms & Armour, 1982

Short, A., *The Communist Insurrection in Malaya 1948–60*, Muller, 1975

Summers, H. G., *Vietnam War Almanac*, Fact on File, 1985

Barzilay, D., *The British Army in Ulster* (5 vols.), Century

Brown, D., *The Royal Navy and the Falklands War*, Cooper, 1987

Weapons

Jane's Infantry Weapons, Jane's Publishing

Jane's Weapon Systems, Jane's Publishing

Index